DAVID GOLDBLATT

THE GAMES

A GLOBAL HISTORY OF THE OLYMPICS

PAN BOOKS

First published 2016 by Macmillan

This paperback edition first published with a new chapter 2018 by Pan Books
an imprint of Pan Macmillan
20 New Wharf Road, London N1 9RR
Associated companies throughout the world
www.panmacmillan.com

ISBN 978-1-4472-9887-8

Typeset by Ellipsis, Glasgow
Printed and bound by CPI Group (UK) Ltd, Croydon, CR0 4YY

THE GAMES

David Goldblatt was born in 1965 and inherited, for his sins, Tottenham Hotspur from his father. He has published three highly acclaimed books on football: *The Ball is Round* (2006), an astonishingly ambitious global history of the game, *Futebol Nation* (2014), a footballing history of Brazil, and *The Game of Our Lives* (2014), about the meaning and making of English football. He has also edited *The World Football Yearbook*, made sporting documentaries for BBC Radio, reported for the *Guardian* and the *New York Times* and teaches at De Montfort University, Leicester and Pitzer College, Los Angeles.

Also by David Goldblatt

THE BALL IS ROUND

THE FOOTBALL BOOK

THE GAME OF OUR LIVES

FUTEBOL NATION

Contents

List of Illustrations

Coming on Strong, Amsterdam 1928, London 1948.
— Lina Radke wins the only women's 800m at the games before the 1960s.
— Fanny Blankers-Koen wins the 200m.

From Ephebes to Abstraction: Olympic posters, 1912 to 1964.

The Empire Strikes Back, Rome 1960: the Ethiopian Abebe Bikila wins the marathon beneath the Arch of Constantine.

The Science Fiction Olympics, Tokyo 1964: Tange Kenzo's Yoyogi National Gymnasium.

The Image Remains, Mexico 1968.
— Tommie Smith (centre) and John Carlos give the black power salute supported by Australian Peter Norman.
— Bob Beamon jumps 8.9m and off the scale.

Spectacle vs Anti-Spectacle, Munich 1972, Los Angeles 1984.
— Armed police, live on German television, drop onto the roof above the apartments where the Israeli Olympic team are being held hostage.
— Lionel Richie takes fiesta to the closing ceremony.

Perfection, Montreal 1976: Rumanian teenager Nadia Comăneci on the beam – the first ever performance to be awarded a perfect score of 10.

For Love of Brand and Country, Barcelona 1992.
— The Dream Team, (left to right) Larry Bird, Scottie Pippin, Michael Jordan, Clyde Drexler, Karl Malone, receive their gold medals.
— The view from the Montjuic Aquatics Complex.

Welcome Home, Athens 2004.
— The Hellinikon Olympic canoe and kayak centre, ten years after the games.
— The Olympic Swimming Complex remains unused to this day.

The Anti-Olympics, Vancouver 2010 and Rio 2016.
— A man protests near the newly opened Olympic tent village in downtown Vancouver.
— Another family home in Villa Autodromo is demolished, under guard, to make way for the Olympic Park.

Introduction

O Sport, pleasure of the Gods, essence of life!
You appeared suddenly in the midst of the grey clearing which
    writhes with the drudgery of modern existence.
Like the radiant messenger of a past age, when mankind still
    smiled.
And the glimmer of dawn lit up the mountain tops
And flecks of light dotted the ground in the gloomy forests.

Georges Hohrod and M. Eschbach
Gold Medal Winner, 1912 Olympic Arts Competition

Baron de Coubertin had long believed that sport was not antithetical to the arts, but a distinct and important component of a society's cultural life. It therefore seemed natural to him, though not to many athletes and artists of the time, that the Olympic Games should also stage artistic, literary and musical competitions on the theme of sport. In the run up to the 1912 Stockholm Olympics, he made repeated attempts to persuade the Swedish hosts to stage such an event, but after consulting their own artistic community and finding them either baffled or antipathetic to the notion, they politely declined the offer. Unperturbed, the baron announced independently that there would be a competitive artistic strand to the 1912 games and sent out a call for entries to be posted to his own address, where, as far as one can tell, he alone served as the judging panel.

In the poetry section, the prize went to Hohrod and Eschbach's florid 'Ode to Sport'. It certainly would have appealed to the baron's own rather peculiar religiosity and overdramatic understanding of ancient and modern sporting history. Yet, in some important ways, they were absolutely right. The ancient world had its games, but the modern world played sport. Starting in the mid-eighteenth century through to the early twentieth century, in Northern Europe and the

United States, the majority of the sports we now play were codified from older games and recent experiments, or – like basketball and handball – invented completely anew. Unlike almost all pre-modern games, they were separated out from religious or local calendars, rituals and purposes, acquiring their own internal meanings and pleasures. Unlike the intense parochialism of the pre-modern world, these sports were given stable written form that allowed them to spread nationally and then globally, secured by the creation of modern rational bureaucracies to administer them. All of which meant that, at precisely the moment that the rise of industrial capitalism and militarism was making the world a harsher, more miserable, more instrumental place, they also fostered an alternative – the organized play of modern sport.

Hohrod and Eschbach, as well as prolix poets, were names taken from two villages (Hohrodberg and Eschbach-au-Val, to be precise) close to the birthplace of Coubertin's wife, and were thus, in addition, his rather obvious pseudonym. Having set up his own competition to which he submitted his own poem, which he then adjudged the winner, I think we must assume he rather liked it, but a century later time has not been kind to Coubertin's words. Submitted in French and German, these versions of the poem have some tiny scraps of rhythm, form and rhyme, but the English translations read with the same ponderous pomposity as a school sermon. Given the sanctimonious tone of the words, this is perhaps its natural genre. For the most part, it is just an excruciatingly bad exegesis on the model of amateur gentlemanly sport, pioneered in the elite educational and military institutions of the West in the nineteenth century, where sport built the character and moral framework required to rule empires and their unwashed masses. It was this and only this group of athletes, and this kind of sport, that was getting the mountain tops of modernity glimmering.

Thus not much can be salvaged of Coubertin's ideological legacy, either from this poem or the world of gentlemanly sport from which it arose. Amateurism and its elite codes have been abandoned by the Olympics, and Coubertin's deeply held belief that the games were primarily a spiritual affair and form of modern religion has been quietly forgotten in the Olympics' transition from a gentleman's club and neo-Hellenic athletic cult to a global bureaucracy that stages a secular commercialized celebration of a universal humanity. To my ear, just two stanzas of 'Ode to Sport' seem to still speak to us. First, in a quite uncharacteristic celebration of sport's capacity to level social differences, to make talent and ability transparent in an otherwise unjust world, the baron intoned:

> O sport you are justice!
> The perfect equity that men strive for in vain in their social institutions rises around you of its own accord.

Then, in a language that carries traces of sexual excitement and drug-induced states of ecstasy and alternative consciousness, he praises sport's visceral and intellectual pleasures:

> O sport you are joy!
> At your behest flesh dances and eyes smile;
> Blood runs abundantly through the arteries.
> Thoughts stretch out on a brighter clearer horizon.

It was not quite Coubertin's intention to create a global stage on which battles for equality and inclusion along the line of class, ethnicity, gender, disability and sexuality might be fought out. Nor, even in his most ebullient moments, did he imagine the Olympic movement and its games as a place for collective delirium, reflection or laughter, but despite everything the Olympics continues to offer both. This book is primarily about how Baron de Coubertin and his peculiar vision of the sporting spectacle became the global norm and a global bureaucracy, but along the way it is the story of the athletes who strove for perfect equity and who made our flesh dance, ours eyes smile and our thinking expand.

1

THIS GRANDIOSE AND SALUTARY TASK:
THE REINVENTION OF THE OLYMPIC GAMES

ATHENS 1896

Where are all your theatres and marble statues?
Where are your Olympic Games?

Panagiotis Soutsos, 1833

It is clear that the telegraph, railways, the telephone, the passionate research in science, congresses and exhibitions have done more for peace than any treaty or diplomatic convention. Well, I hope that athletics will do even more . . .

Let us export rowers, runners and fencers: there is the free trade of the future, and on the day it is introduced within the walls of old Europe the cause of peace will have received a new and mighty stay.

This is enough to encourage your servant to dream now . . . to continue and complete, on a basis suited to the conditions of modern life, this grandiose and salutary task, namely the restoration of the Olympic Games

Baron de Coubertin, 1892

ONE

Baron de Coubertin's 1892 speech may have been the most significant public call for the creation of a modern Olympic Games, but it was hardly the first. More than half a century beforehand, in his poem 'Dialogues of the Dead', the Greek nationalist publisher and ideologue, Panagiotis Soutsos, imagined the ghost of Plato speaking to the newly independent but devastated Greek nation. Now, finally free of Ottoman suzerainty, what was modern Greece? Where were its great spectacles, arts and athletics?[1] He was sufficiently fired by the thought to write to the Greek minister of the interior proposing that the Greek state should revive the ancient Olympics, rotating the games every four years around a distinctly modern nationalist circuit of locations: Athens, the new capital city; Tripoli, in the heart of the Peloponnese; Messolonghi, a stronghold of Greek resistance during the war; and the island of Hyrda, which had provided key naval forces to fight the Turks.[2] Olympia itself, but for a few walls and columns, remained encased in silt.

On this occasion, the meaning of the ancient games was bound to a Greek nationalist project, but for over 300 years, fed by the rediscovery and reanimation of the lost literature of antiquity, all kinds of Europeans had been reinterpreting the ancient Olympics, drawing on its imagery and language, even staging their own Olympian festivals that tied the Greek games, however anachronistically, to causes as diverse as the politics of pleasure in the English Counter-Reformation and the popular celebration of the French Revolution.

In the sixty years between Soutsos' poem and Coubertin's address, there would be dozens more Olympic events, recreations and spectacles, now shaped by the emergence and globalization of modern sports and the actual excavation of Olympia itself. Soutsos was the first to call for a revival of the games, Coubertin was the first to bind that notion to some form of internationalism and make it happen, but both ideas emerged from a long and bizarre encounter between

European modernity and an ancient religious festival – already a millennium past when Columbus landed in the Americas – about which they and we know only fragments.

Conventional Olympic histories have it that Roman Emperor Theodosius I banned the games by edict in 392 CE, and that over the next 200 years the sanctuary of Olympia was destroyed by a combination of neglect and fire. Earthquakes and river flooding in the fifth and sixth centuries left most of the site broken and then buried deep in alluvial silt. What structures remained were scavenged for stone and the metal braces and dowels that held the great columns together. The real target of Theodosius' edict, however, was pagan practices, in particular those of the old polytheistic state religion of Rome: temples, oracles and sanctuaries, and the practices of devotional offering and sacrifice to the old gods. The policing of the Theodosian code was hardly comprehensive, with the emperor's military forces busy fighting both a civil war within the empire and a border war with the Goths. Rather than a sudden death, it is more likely that the games limped on in some reduced capacity, squeezed by a climate increasingly hostile to its central religious practices and associations. The Byzantine historian Lucian reported that 'The Olympic Games existed for a long time until Theodosius the younger, who was the son of Arcadius', suggesting that the Olympics finally expired under Theodosius II, around 436 CE.[3]

By then, the heart of the games had been ripped out. According to George Kedrenos, the eleventh-century Byzantine chronicler, the gigantic gold and ivory statue of Zeus that sat in his temple at Olympia had been transferred to the palace of Lausas and finally perished around 475 CE in one of the huge urban fires that periodically swept Constantinople, but his Olympian cult was already dead. Lucian wrote, 'After the temple of Olympian Zeus had been burnt down, the festival of the Eleans and Olympic contest were abandoned.'[4] Earthquakes and huge river floods in the middle of the sixth century finished the job.*[5] Once lost to the silt, the successive overlords of

---

* Recent analysis of the sediments at Olympia suggests that they are far too thick to have been produced just by the Kladeos river that runs past the sanctuary. In fact, the composition of the sediment, which includes abundant remains of marine micro-organisms, suggests that Olympia was subject to catastrophic flooding caused by tsunamis – seabed earthquakes that sent huge waves of water up river and on to the sanctuary.

the Peloponnese – Byzantines, Franks, Ottomans and Venetians – paid the site no heed.

For over a millennium, all that really survived of the Olympic Games were words, and they would await the Renaissance humanist scholars who rediscovered and compiled the work of antiquity. As the availability of books increased in the sixteenth century, in the original Greek, Latin and vernacular translation, key individual works with significant material on the games became easily available to the small but growing reading public. In England, for example, in the last quarter of the century alone there were translations of Plutarch's *Lives of the Noble Greeks and Romans,* Herodotus' *Histories* and Homer's *Iliad.* From the latter, and its account of Patroclus' funeral games at the wall of Troy, interested readers would have known that athletics could be a sacred rite. From Plutarch they would have become familiar with Alexander the Great's Olympic career, and from Herodotus they knew that Olympia offered glory – in its many varied and transferable forms – but not cash prizes.* Later readers would benefit, above all, from the brilliant, detailed first-hand accounts of Olympia and the games in *Description of Greece* by the second-century itinerant geographer Pausanias.[6] Modern Europe might still not have established quite why the Greeks played games or why they venerated them, but having read Pausanias, they could be in no doubt as to their importance: 'Many are the sights to be seen in Greece, and many are the wonders to be heard; but on nothing does Heaven bestow more care than on the Eleusinian rites and the Olympic games.'

Writers were certainly tuning in. Composed in the early 1590s, Shakespeare's *Henry VI, Part 3* has Prince George attempting to rally his Yorkist troops:

> And, if we thrive, promise them such rewards
> As victors wear at the Olympian games.

A decade later, in *Troilus and Cressida*, the elderly Greek Prince Nestor describes his Trojan adversary, Hector, in battle:

> And I have seen thee pause, and take thy breath,
> When that a ring of Greeks have hemm'd thee in,
> Like an Olympian wrestling

---

* This fact left Herodotus' Persians aghast: 'Mardonius, what kind of men are these that you have pitted us against? It is not for money they contend but for glory of achievement!'

In 1633, Michael Drayton hailed Robert Dover as the 'great inventor and champion of the English olimpicks.'[7] Drayton, a noted poet of the era, was just one of thirty-three contributors to *Anallia Dubrensia*, a collection celebrating Robert Dover's Cotswold Games.

Held since 1612 in the natural amphitheatre formed by Dover Hill in Chipping Camden, in the west of England, the Cotswold Games mixed pageantry and patronage, offered feasting, dancing, games, gambling and cash prizes for sports and contests. A mock castle was erected on the hill, and a large crowd gathered to watch hare coursing and horse racing, wrestling and shin kicking, stick fighting and hammer throwing. Dover was born in Norfolk in 1582, into the Catholic gentry in Elizabeth's increasingly Protestant England. Educated at Cambridge, he practised law at Gray's Inn in London before retreating to his small estate in the country. By all accounts a charismatic and charming man, a lover of festivities and mirth, he established and gave his name to the Cotswold Games as an act of both local patronage and national politics. Rural contests and fairs were widespread in Stuart England, local patrons quietly supporting them, but Dover took centre stage at his own games, made them considerably larger than other events and introduced proceedings dressed in the cast-offs of King James I. This was a very deliberate celebration of the king's rule and his attitudes to popular pleasures and pastimes, which, given the steady rise of more militant, ascetic and puritanical forms of Protestantism in seventeenth-century England, was a matter of pressing political importance. By the 1630s, puritan landlords and gentry were banning such activities on their land and closing down rural fairs. The outbreak of civil war in 1642 and the defeat of the royalist cause in 1645 brought a halt to proceedings. Dover died in 1652 under Cromwell's sternly ascetic Protectorate, and the games disappeared. There were a series of revivals after the restoration of the monarchy in 1660, but the olympick moniker was lost and Dover's games, though always popular and boisterous, became 'just another country drunken festival.'[8]

The Cotswold Games may have lost their Olympic connection, but Olympia retained a place in Europe's literary imagination and its popular cultures. Writing in the late seventeenth century, John Milton, in *Paradise Lost*, described the flight of Satan's hordes as:

> Part on the plain, or in the air sublime,
> Upon the wing, or in swift race contend,
> As at th' Olympian games or Pythian fields

More winsomely, Voltaire, during his short stay in England in the early eighteenth century, wrote that, on arriving at a sporting festival on the banks of the Thames, 'I fancied that I had been transported to the Olympic games.'[9] Friedrich Schiller, one of Germany's enlightenment polymaths, took the ancient games as an example of 'play as an element of the beautiful' in his *Aesthetic Essays*. From the sublime to the ridiculous: we find, in 1786, the London press reporting a 'burlesque imitation' of the Olympic Games in which the female contestants were 'placed on a platform, with horses' collars to exhibit through.' Over their heads were painted the words 'The ugliest grinner shall be the winner' and they were awarded a prize of a 'gold-laced hat'. In 1794, *The Times* described a chariot race staged at Newmarket between Nanny Hodges and Lady Lads for the then indescribably large sum of 500 guineas as, 'something like a revival of the Olympic Games to supply the turf gentry and the rapid decay of horse-racing'.*[10]

For another half century, popular – if not elite – knowledge of the Olympics was more likely to be garnered at the circus than in the library. As late as the 1850s, Olympic spectaculars and recreations on horseback could be seen in New York at Franconni's Hippodrome, across Britain with Pablo Fanque's travelling Circus Royal, and in Edinburgh at Madam Macarte's Magic Ring and Grand Equestrian Establishment. Pablo Fanque, Britain's first black circus master, and his 'unrivalled equestrian troupe' offered 'new and novel features in the Olympian Games.' Madame Macarte's posters promised that, 'the Extraordinary Evolutions of the Gymnastic Professors will forcibly

---

* It is hard to imagine anything less like a revival of the ancient Olympic Games than the showdown at Newmarket; though gambling was not unknown at the ancient games, women and money prizes were entirely absent, and one staged the games in honour of Zeus rather than to promote the health of the horse-racing fraternity. The best of the eighteenth-century accounts of the games – like the English poet Gilbert West's 1749 *Dissertation on the Olympick Games* and Jean-Jacques Barthélemy's 1778 picaresque novel *Travels of Anacharsis the younger in Greece* – were based on a more systemic and scholarly reading of the ancient written sources than hitherto, and would have made at least this much clear. But why let details get in the way of a good show?

recall to the Classical mind the old Olympian Games.' The most ambitious but least successful revivalist was the fabulously named Colonel Charles Random, a man of uncertain social origins and even more uncertain military career, who purchased the considerable grounds of Cremorne House in Chelsea, west London, and, in 1831, created 'the stadium' – or, to give it its full title, 'The British National Arena for Manly and Defensive Exercises, Equestrian, Chivalric, and Aquatic Games, and Skilful Amusing Pastimes.' In 1832, and again in 1838 to celebrate the coronation of Queen Victoria, he proposed staging his own Olympic Games. Sadly, it seems these efforts came to naught and the stadium's main business for the next few decades was the fetes, fairs and spectaculars normal for a slightly risqué Victorian pleasure garden.

For Europe to acquire a more rounded knowledge of the ancient games, and for their influence on the continent's imagination to crystallize, something more than words was required. Someone needed to actually go to Olympia and take a look.

TWO

Scholars, antiquarians, tomb raiders and treasure hunters had been poking around in the ruins of European antiquity since the fifteenth century. From the late seventeenth century onwards, they actually began to dig some sites up. Pompeii and Herculaneum were uncovered in the mid-eighteenth century. Napoleon's military adventures in Egypt were accompanied by a vast scientific mission that, amongst other things, unearthed the Rosetta Stone. A growing band of antique collectors and serious Hellenic scholars had begun to wonder whether Olympia might be found and what it might yield. The French Benedictine monk and voracious antiquarian, Bernard de Montfaucon, wrote in 1723 to the Bishop of Corfu, whose diocese included the site of Olympia: 'What wealth of treasures are thus buried underground. The strange thing is that I believe, nobody has ever thought of excavating on that site.' Johann Joachim Winkelmann, the singularly most important classicist of the eighteenth century and the central interpreter of Greco-Roman art and architecture, was profoundly moved by the homoeroticism of the era's sculpture and the culture of the gymnasium and the games. He made repeated calls to his patrons in the Vatican to explore Olympia, but to no avail. In any case, before digging could begin, someone from outside the western Peloponnese actually had to go to Olympia and şee if anything was there at all. The task fell to Richard Chandler, the English antiquarian, who was charged by the Society of Dilettanti – a London club of aristocratic collectors and Greco-Roman art lovers – to travel through Greece acquiring objects, copying inscriptions and making illustrations of antique remains. In addition to buying a few fragments of the Parthenon in Athens, Chandler made his way to Olympia in 1766, where he was furiously bitten by insects and burnt by the sun. His sense of anticlimax on arrival was palpable: 'We commenced our survey of the spot before us with a degree of expectation from which our disappointment on finding it almost naked received a considerable addition.' There were merely 'scattered remnants of brick buildings, and the vestiges of stone walls.'[1]

Disappointing as this was, the Hellenists of western Europe at least knew how to get to Olympia and, in 1787, Louis Favel, commissioned by the French ambassador to Constantinople, made the first topographical sketches of the site.* In 1828, a significant French expeditionary force had landed in the Peloponnese to support the Greek rebels in their war of independence with the Ottoman Empire. Like Napoleon's great Egyptian expedition, though on a smaller scale, the military were accompanied by the *Mission Scientifique de Morée* – a collection of archaeologists, geographers, botanists and artists. Six weeks of work in 1829 allowed them to unearth a significant part of the ruins of the Temple of Zeus, including a number of metopes. These carved marble tablets that formed part of the exterior of the building – illustrating the twelve tasks of Hercules – were whisked off to the Louvre in Paris, where they remain. Still, the five metres of silt that encased the temple, not to mention the clearly vast extent of the site, demanded something more systematic.[2]

It took six years to finally excavate the temple but nearly twenty-five years for the German classicist, Professor Ernst Curtius, to make it happen. Two decades of complex diplomacy between Greece and Germany saw a deal finally agreed in 1874 in which the Germans would pay and dig, and the Greek government would keep the finds. Six years of work revealed not only the Temple of Zeus, but most of the buildings mentioned by Pausanias and the other key sources, like the Temple of Hera, the Echo colonnade and the Macedonian royal family's very own temple of statuary – the Philippeion. The excavation of the entire site took another century, completed only in the 1970s when heavy-duty machinery was used to uncover all of the stadium and hippodrome. The physical record has been supplemented by a century of scholarly work, situating the Olympic Games in a much broader understanding of the Hellenic world and its body and athletics cultures. Considerable disputes remain in interpretation,

---

* Colonel William Leake, an experienced military cartographer, was sent by the British government to survey the coasts of Albania and the Peloponnese as part of their shadow war against the French in the region. He found himself in Olympia in 1805 and conducted a full and accurate survey of the site, though it wasn't until 1830 that it was published in his *Travels in the Morea*.

but what follows is a condensed account of our generation's understanding of the ancient games.[3]

The Greeks themselves – conventionally, if very unreliably – dated the first ancient Olympiad to 776 BCE, but more than two centuries before this, the sanctuary of Olympia had been a place of religious worship and ritual. Indeed, there is some evidence of sacrificial rites from the Mycenaean age, half a millennium before. It seems more likely that the local games, initially organized under the aegis of the city state, Ellis, and possibly of funereal origins, were played in the eighth century BCE, and acquired a Panhellenic audience and meaning in the seventh century BCE. This shift can be tracked by examining the geographical origin of Olympic champions. First they came from just the western Peloponnese, then from Athens and Sparta, and, from the sixth century BCE onwards, from Thessaly in northern Greece and the colonies of Sicily and Southern Italy. Olympia was then joined in a quadrennial circuit of athletic festivals by the Pythian, Nemean and Isthmian games, which confirmed the central place of athletic competition in Greek religion, culture and politics.

Always polytheistic, many gods were celebrated there, but from the early fifth century BCE, the Olympics became synonymous with the cult of Zeus – king of the gods – and the Olympian Games became the first amongst equals on the circuit. The building of the Temple of Zeus, the largest and grandest in the inner sacred zone of Olympia, known as the Altis, was begun around 490 BCE. However, the building itself was entirely eclipsed around 430 BCE by the installation of Pheidias' great Statue of Zeus. Considered by Herodotus to be one of the seven wonders of the ancient world, it was a huge and imposing figure of marble, gold and ivory on a throne, a human-size Nike – the goddess of victory – held in one of Zeus' hands. At the same time, the athletics stadium at Olympia, first laid down in the sixth century BCE, was shifted south and enlarged and joined by an enormous gravel-tracked hippodrome; both were surrounded by earthen banks that allowed them to accommodate at least 45,000 spectators.

It is worth dwelling for a moment on the numbers involved at the games, for they consisted a significant percentage of the free-born men of the entire Greek world – perhaps 5 per cent – who would not only have had to travel considerable distances but would have to endure considerable hardships in the harsh sun of a Greek August. For the very elite, there were villas and hostels. The Romans, as ever, added impressive infrastructure, including new hotels, Emperor Nero's own personal villa, the great baths of Kladeos and the civic miracle of fresh running water. This was delivered by aqueduct to the great nymphaeum – a monumental multi-storey marble water-feature, built by the richest man in second-century Greece, Herodes Atticus. But, for the most part, there was hardship in the temporary tent cities that would spring up in the meadows around the sanctuary. Epictetus, as one might expect of a Stoic, thought it worth toughing things out: 'Are you not scorched with heat? Are you not cramped for room? Is not washing difficult? Do you not get your fill of noise and clamour and other annoyances? Yet I fancy that when you set against all these hardships the magnificence of the spectacle you will bear them.'

What drew such extraordinary crowds to the games was a complex mixture of motives drawn from the wider body cultures of the Hellenic and Roman worlds. For over 1,000 years, the gymnasium – the place where one goes nude – was the centre of civic and recreational life for the elite of free-born men, released from most practical activities by wealth, patriarchal families and slave labour. The precise ways in which civic responsibilities interacted with the athletic and physical work of the gymnasium varied. In some city states, athletics was a preparation for war, as all citizens were required to take up arms if required. In others, the relationship between physical health, mental health and civic virtue was emphasized, and everywhere the cult of athletic male beauty meant that many Greeks thought that to look good was also to be good.

Athletes and spectators alike were called to Olympia some months in advance by heralds that crossed the Hellenic world to announce the games. Indeed, the games continued throughout the bitter fighting of the fifth-century Peloponnesian wars.

A five-day programme of events at Olympia was settled in the fifth century and remained unchanged until the second century, when the Romans conquered Greece. They rebranded Zeus as Jupiter, made it a six-day affair, and kept it that way until the games' demise nearly six hundred years later. On the opening day, judges and officials – the Hellanodikai – the athletes, their trainers and their relatives were all required to gather at the Temple of Zeus and swear an oath, 'that they would be guilty of no foul play and that they would be fair and not accept bribes.'[4] However, as the Zanes – a series of bronze figures that lined the route to Olympia's stadiums – attest, there was plenty of cheating and plenty of bribery. These statues of Zeus were paid for by the fines levied on rule breakers, and served as an example to future athletes. There were also competitions amongst the trumpeters and heralds – the *salpinktes* and the *keryx* respectively – the winners of which would announce the athletes for the rest of the week and hail their accomplishments.

The second day began with blood sacrifices at the many altars and temples around the site, then the crowd would move on to the hippodrome to watch chariot races (two- and four-horse variants) and simple horse-and-rider contests. Despite the perilous quality of these events, the prizes for the winners were awarded to the wealthy owners of the horses rather than their riders. Day three was reserved for the pentathlon, in which competitors ran, threw the discus and javelin, and jumped with weights in a manner no one was quite able to accurately capture. If no winner had emerged by this point (though on what basis that was determined remains unclear), there would be wrestling to decide the victor. Day four was given over to the festival of Pelops, the slaughter of a hundred oxen, and the boys' athletic contests, accompanied by a great deal of feasting.

On day five, it was back to the stadium for running and fighting. There were three races, with heats and finals of around twenty athletes each: the *stade* was a sprint down a single length of the stadium; the *diaulos* was the *stade* and back again; and the *dolichos* – literally the 'long one' – was run over twenty-four circuits of the arena, around 5,000 metres. Wrestling came in two forms: *kato pale* was a grasping, roiling-in-the-sand-pit version and *orthos pale* was a more formal, standing, grip-and-trip-based struggle. Boxing, recognizable to modern eyes, was conducted without gloves, though the Romans, bloodthirsty as ever, encouraged the introduction of knuckledusters. Finally came the *pankration* – literally, the 'all power' – a no-holds-barred fight that prohibited only biting and gouging of the eyes. The final day was given over to celebration: first, a parade of athletes, in which they were showered with twigs, cuttings and flowers; then the award of olive wreaths to the victors, cut from the groves of the Altis in the Temple of Zeus; and finally a sacred feast for the judges and the champions alone.

Much of this was known in Coubertin's time, and much of his interpretation of the spiritual celebration of athleticism and the body, the glory of competition and the honour of endeavour and participation, was successfully melded with his take on the Anglo-Saxon sports-and-education ethic. There was, of course, an enormous gulf between the two, but Coubertin's attempt to bridge them was, if achingly conservative, unscholarly, romantic and patriarchal, at least plausible.

What will not stand is his reading of the ancient games' relationship to amateurism and to politics. In the case of the former, the prohibition on professional participation in the modern games, and the incredibly strict definitions applied to the notion of amateurism, were justified and morally burnished for more than half a century by appeals to an imagined past. Avery Brundage, IOC president in the 1960s, could still argue, 'The amateur code coming to us from antiquity embraces the highest moral laws.'[5]

In fact, although there were no cash prizes at Olympia, the games were set within an often highly professionalized and commercialized sporting culture. Beyond Olympia, there was a widespread circuit of athletic and sporting competitions all over the eastern Mediterranean, with prizes in cash and other goods. Participation in those races didn't debar athletes from Olympia. Ambitious politicians, like the sixth-century Athenian, Solon, were known to offer rewards to champions on their return home. Five hundred years later, Mark Antony noted that Olympian laurels were regularly transmuted into exemptions from military service, tracts of land, pensions and tax breaks. Pausanias reported that a Cretan, Sotades, a champion in the long race at Olympia, appeared and won it the next time as an Ephesian, for the city had paid handsomely for his allegiance.

Coubertin's attempt to find classical precedents for his internationalist and pacific modern Olympics also meant evoking a sporting culture that thought itself divorced from political power and political concerns. This is not how it appeared to the ancients. Herodotus thought that the Athenian Kylon, emboldened by his victory in the *diaulos* in 640 BCE, went on to launch a coup d'état at home. While Cimon, an Athenian aristocrat, exiled by the city's ruler, Pisistratus, 'happened to take the Olympic prize in the four-horse chariot . . . At the next Olympic games he won with the same horses, but permitted Pisistratus to be proclaimed victor, and by resigning the victory to him he came back from exile to his own property under truce.'[6] Other Greek tyrants that appear on the victory rolls of Olympia include Kypselis of Corinth and the Orthagorides of Sikyon.

Perhaps more tellingly, as Coubertin would find out himself when he actually began to stage sporting spectaculars and rituals, Olympia was a space for politicians to be seen in. We see this in Plutarch's account of the arrival of Themistocles – a fifth-century-BCE populist Athenian general – at the games: 'the audience neglected the contestants all day long to gaze on him, and pointed him out with admiring applause to visiting strangers, so that he too was delighted, and confessed to his friends that he was now reaping in full measure the harvest of his toils in behalf of Hellas.'[7] Olympia was always a place in which political capital could be generated and traded. As Coubertin was to find out, it would be no different in the modern world; indeed, these features of the games would be amplified and magnified many times over.

THREE

Europe's classicists and scholars had preserved and interpreted the written record of the ancient games. Europe's archaeologists and antiquarians had surveyed and excavated Olympia. Literature, the press and the circus had kept the idea of the Olympics in popular circulation. Yet none of them were actually playing games or connecting the culture of ancient athletics to the new sports, gymnastics and physical education movements that were beginning to emerge in Europe; in fact, no 'Olympic' sporting festivals had been staged since the demise of Robert Dover's Cotswold Games in the mid-seventeenth century. These connections were first re-established in the late eighteenth and early nineteenth century in Germany, France and Sweden, but the most successful and influential Olympic revival movements, and the ones that would actively shape Coubertin's revivalism, emerged in the mid-nineteenth century in Britain and Greece, where the idea of the Olympic Games was bound to more powerful social forces: the emergence of the games ethic and the moral virtues of modern sport in the former, nationalism in the latter.

The games had also acquired a new life, though one with a very different political meaning, in France, where their revival was proposed by Charles Gilbert Romme, a leading figure in the politics of the French Revolution. A member of the legislative assembly and a supporter of Robespierre, Romme's key work was the creation of a new rationalized republican calendar, designed to excise royalist and religious references, and to embrace the decimalization of time and space that the new metric system was introducing. Five extra days were added to align with the solar year, and every fourth year there would be a leap day. Romme thought that the leap day might be a good occasion for staging public festivities and games: 'we suggest calling it the French Olympiad and the final year the Olympics Year.'[1] It was a notion that found considerable support amongst republicans of all shades. Pierre Daunou argued, 'let France adopt as her own these brilliant solemnities. It is time to revive these salutary inventions: assemble there the exercises of all games, music, dancing, running, wrestling.' In 1793, Georges Danton, then president of the Committee of Public Safety, spoke to the National Convention: 'bearing in mind the Olympic Games, I request that the Convention give over the Champ de Mars to national games.' Danton would soon lose his post and then his head, but the idea of games on the Champs de Mars would endure. In 1796, Paris staged a popular festival of sports and races, referred to as the Republican Olympiad, attracting crowds in the hundreds of thousands. Le Monitor reported that 'they resembled those young Spartans who, gathered in the theatre for the Olympic Games, offered the assembled Greek population a shining example of the morals of the nation.' They played 'games, races, exercises full of movement and magnificence.' Heralds dressed in republican red, white and blue announced competitions; military bands accompanied the races. A Parisian butcher won the wrestling, the long-distance race went to a sergeant major. Winners were wreathed in laurels, rewarded with French-manufactured goods – pistols, sabres, vases and watches – and paraded before the crowd. Two more Olympian festivals were staged, and there were even calls in 1798 to extend them, like the Revolution, to foreign neighbours. But by 1799 Napoleon was in charge and there was no more time for games until Coubertin's intervention almost a century later to really ignite a serious and sustainable Olympic revival movement.

As the dominant power of the era, the inventor and diffuser of innumerable modern sports and the crucible of the modern games ethic that saw sport as central to the emotional, moral and intellectual development of its elites, Victorian Britain might seem an obvious catalyst for reviving the games. However, it was not the public schools or Oxford and Cambridge universities, thick with aristocratic sportsmen and classicists, that took on the Olympic idea, but Dr William Penny Brookes, a doctor and Justice of the Peace from the small Shropshire market town of Much Wenlock.[2] In 1850, as a subsection of the Much Wenlock Agricultural Reading Society, he established the Wenlock Olympian Class, the purpose of which the inaugural minutes make clear: 'the promotion of the moral, physical and intellectual improvement of the inhabitants of the town . . . by the encouragement of outdoor recreations and by the award of prizes annually at public meetings for skill in athletic exercises and industrial attainments.'

Later that year, the first Much Wenlock Olympian Games were held (and, but for two world wars, have continued ever since). Eclectic in every way, the games were part rural fair, part school sports day. They featured professionals and amateurs, men and women, locals and outsiders, and created events for the old and the very young. There was cricket, football, archery, hurdling and running, with very considerable cash prizes in the professional version of the events. Simultaneously, there were blindfold, wheelbarrow and sack races, donkey riding, blind man's buff and, most popular of all, faux-medieval tilting at the ring. As the games grew more popular, Brookes added processions and pageantry, poetry competitions, shooting, cycling and an ever-changing and eclectic pentathlon. The odd classical reference like this aside, Much Wenlock's Olympian credentials were always rather thin, the name a mere gilding on what was a typical Victorian social enterprise that combined civic pride and patronage, rational recreation and entertainment, and Brookes' genuine concern for the well being of the rural poor and the urban working classes. In 1860, Brookes wrote to the mayors of five local towns proposing that they combine forces to stage a Shropshire Olympian Games. These were held over the next four years, the biggest attracting 15,000 spectators, until torrential rain washed out the 1864 games in Shrewsbury and a lack of civic enthusiasm closed them down.

Civic enthusiasm was not in short supply at the Liverpool Athletic Club, founded in 1862 with the express purpose of nurturing amateur sports and the gentlemanly ethics of fair play, and instructing both the lower orders and the sedentary sceptics of the middle classes of the value of physical education.[3] The club's moving forces were Charles Melly and John Hully. Melly, educated at Rugby College, a stronghold of the games ethic, was a busy philanthropist who endowed the city with drinking fountains, new parks and green spaces, and built outdoor gymnasiums. John Hully was a flamboyant, self-styled 'gymnasiarch', much given to eccentric costumes, who displayed immense enthusiasm for the moral and physical benefits of exercise. Both subscribed to Juvenal's now familiar motto, *mens sana in corpore sano* – a healthy mind in a healthy body – and, in June 1862, they placed it at the head of an advertisement in the *Liverpool Daily Post* for their 'Grand Olympic Festival'. Unlike Much Wenlock, the organizers did not offer cash prizes and places

for professionals, but silver and bronze medals for 'gentlemen amateurs' and ticket prices in the stands to match. The upmarket clientele
was promised a steeplechase, gymnastics, fencing (sabres and broad-
swords), wrestling and boxing, running, jumping and throwing the
cricket ball; 'no effort will be spared by the committee . . . to render
the festival worthy of its immortal title.' The Liverpool Grand Olympic Festival proved disorganized but immensely popular. Despite
hapless scheduling and crowds that overflowed onto the playing
fields, three annual festivals were staged, 12,000 spectators attending the second one in 1863. The *Liverpool Post* wrote with glee, 'If
ever a name was fairly transferred from an ancient to a modern
institution it is the case of those Olympic allusions by which the great
athletic festivals of our day distinguish themselves from mere sordid
sporting contests.' The 1864 festival, held at the Zoological Gardens,
proved less savoury, with the arrival of many professional athletes
who were all refused permission to participate. Undeterred, they
ran in an impromptu fringe of athletic races sponsored by local book-
makers.

The last energies of these English proto-Olympians coalesced in
1865 when a meeting was called in London with a view to forming
a National Olympian Association (NOA), attended by, amongst
others, John Hulley and other representatives from Liverpool, Dr
Brookes, and Ernst Ravenstein of the London-based German Gymnastic Society. The NOA was envisaged as an organization that could
'bring into focus the many physical, athletic and gymnastic clubs
that were spreading all over the country', and stage national games
open to 'all comers' – a category that did not include women or
professionals, but on the matter of class origins, at least, it was neutral. London was the natural choice as the venue for the inaugural
NOA games in 1866. The city, aside from its huge population and
potential audience, held most of the nation's key sporting organizations – like the MCC and the newly formed FA – as well as serving
as home to many of the leading aristocratic sportsmen. Neither
responded well to the formation of the NOA or the call to attend its
games. The idea that this collection of provincial nonentities and a
German gymnast could establish organizational and symbolic control over sport was simply unthinkable. An alternative organization,
the Amateur Athletics Club (AAC), was quickly established, although
it was noted that its 'prospectus, published in February 1866, bears

signs of having been cobbled together over Christmas with no more purpose than to thwart the National Olympian Association.'[4] To make their opposition clear, the new sporting elite held their own national championships in the elegant gardens of Beaufort House in west London, charged the astronomical price of a guinea for entrance and ruled that anyone who had participated in an open competition or the NOA games would be ineligible to compete at theirs. The National Olympian Games proved more demotic, with 10,000 spectators watching the athletics at Crystal Palace in 1866 and similar numbers going to watch the swimming, racing and gymnastics in Birmingham in 1867.

This was the high water mark of the British Olympic revival movement. Disconnected from and at times actively opposed by the sporting elites of London and the universities, this alliance of provincial enthusiasts and philanthropists had neither the money nor the political capital to forge an enduring and successful sporting spectacle or movement. In 1868, unable to get any significant sporting club in one of the major cities to act as hosts, the games shrank back to a more Wenlockian affair held in the Shropshire town of Wellington. Two further Shropshire games were held in 1874 and 1875, but they could no longer be considered national in any sense. At the same time, the AAC consolidated its hold over national athletic events and turned itself into the Amateur Athletics Association (AAA), which came to run the sport nationally. The final NOA games, held in 1883 in the tiny village of Hadley, north of Much Wenlock, were microscopic. Dr Brookes and the Much Wenlock games themselves endured, and Brookes continued to campaign for the British government to support popular physical education, and to correspond with the Greek authorities and others about the possibility of staging a revived Olympic Games, but for a long time his reach and influence was nugatory. In Britain, the presence of the Olympics shrank back to just the small north-eastern town of Morpeth, where, from 1870 through to the beginning of the First World War, the Morpeth Olympic Games were staged – a more urban, drunken, raucous and commercial version of the Much Wenlock games, without the faux-classical pageantry or even a modicum of its Hellenic pretensions.

Hellenic pretensions carried a lot more weight in modern Greece. As we have seen, the first call for the revival of the games came from the poet Panagiotis Soutsos in 1835, just a few years after Greece had won its independence from the Ottoman Empire. Soutsos' most important convert to the cause was the fabulously wealthy shipping magnate Evangelos Zappas.[5] In 1856, seeking a nationalist legacy for his fortune, Zappas wrote to King Otto proposing a revived Olympic Games to be held in a renovated Panathenaic Stadium in central Athens (built in around 300 BC but long ruined), with prizes for the winners, all paid for by a very considerable financial bequest. Foreign minister Alexander Rangavis, who thought this interest in sport incomprehensible, replied that money might be better spent on a permanent building that could house a quadrennial exhibition of Greek agricultural, industrial and educational advances, with a single day reserved in the programme for athletic games and amusements. A deal was agreed in 1858, and in 1859 the first 'Zappas Olympic Games', as they were locally known, were held. They were, however, just a small component of Rangavis' month-long programme of agriculture exhibitions, displays of manufacturing innovations, and art and drama competitions.

Held in a cobbled city square in Athens over three Sundays, there was running, horse and chariot races, discus and javelin competitions modelled on the ancient sources, as well as the climbing of a greasy pole. The games were opened by the king and queen, medals bearing the words 'First Olympic Crown' were issued and prizes were plentiful. The crowds appear to have been large, and athletes came from across the Greek-speaking world to attend, but the organization was poor. Few spectators could actually see much of the events and, when the crowd pushed towards the front, the local press reported that one policeman 'who was supposed to keep order showed so much incompetence that his horse ran every which way and hit men and women.'[6] A more contemptuous columnist thought 'there never was a more ridiculous affair than the comedy that took place in the Plateia Loudovikou; and one would truly err if we were to term it Olympic Games.'[7]

In 1865, Zappas died, leaving much of his huge fortune to the continuing task of reviving the games. King Otto was now in exile; he had been replaced in 1862 by George I, a teenage Danish prince who was the choice of the Concert of Europe and the Greek elite. An enthusiast for sports, and conscious of his limited Hellenic credentials, King George readily backed the staging of a second games in

1870, once again as part of a bigger agro-industrial festival. Using just a portion of the Zappas bequest, the Panathenaic Stadium was rebuilt, if not yet clad in marble, a small grandstand was erected, and considerable travel expenses and prizes were offered to athletes travelling from all over the Greek-speaking world. There was also more symbolic borrowing from antiquity, with competitors asked to take a formal oath and announcements by heralds. The games began with the singing of an Olympic hymn, and champions received laurel wreaths. They were deemed by most Greeks a great success and attracted a crowd of 30,000, but some, like Philip Ioannou, an aristocratic classicist and a member of the organizing committee, were appalled by the presence of athletes from working-class backgrounds – like Troungas, the pole-climbing champion and stone cutter – and despaired at the absence of 'well educated youth'. At the next games, in 1875, the organizer and gentleman gymnast Ioannis Phokianos ensured that only athletes from the 'higher social orders' would be allowed to compete. Potential athletes would have to attend Phokianos' own gym for two months, having applied through their university. This ensured the games were full of 'young men from the cultured class . . . instead of the working class men who had come to the first two Olympiads.' Despite the glee in the press that the games would be 'much more respectable', they were a disaster. The stadium was entirely unfit for competition, the spectators had to pull up thorn bushes and move rocks to find space to sit, and the mood of the crowd, already restless due to the hapless organization of events, was made worse by long and unintelligible speeches by Phokianos.

Not surprisingly, the Zappas Olympic committee kept a rather low profile for the next decade, spending its time and nearly all of Zappas' money on building the magnificent Zappeion: the long-promised neoclassical exhibition-hall-cum-temple, completed in 1888. They proposed a fourth Zappas games, but the committee never really had its heart in it. Revivalism survived in the form of the newly formed Panhellenic Gymnastic Society – the centre of aristocratic sport in Athens – which held its own small Panhellenic games in 1891 and 1893, and attracted both King George and Crown Prince Constantine as spectators and patrons, and, in 1890, Constantine had gone so far as to sign a royal decree announcing that a four-yearly cycle of Greek Olympics would begin again in 1892. But if the Greek monarchy and its allies wanted to revive the games, they were going to need support from somewhere else.

FOUR

Pierre de Coubertin's body lies in Lausanne, his heart was buried at Olympia, but he was born in France and definitively shaped by the travails of its Third Republic. Born in Paris in 1863 as Baron Charles Pierre Fredy de Coubertin, he was the fourth child of a long-established French aristocratic family. Coubertin would have taken his first communion in 1870, the year of the disaster of Sedan, when the Prussians captured the Emperor and put the French army to flight in the early stages of the short-lived Franco-Prussian War. After the fall of Paris in 1871, the victorious armies of the now-united German Empire imposed a peace treaty, withdrew and took Alsace-Lorraine and almost every last vestige of French national confidence with them. With the Emperor in exile and the old order utterly discredited, the French Third Republic was established. Coubertin's parents marked him out for a career in the priesthood and, in 1874, sent him to the Jesuit college Saint Ignace. With very few concessions to the nineteenth century, the packed curriculum concentrated on monastic ritual and pious devotion, intensive study of Greek and Latin, and special classes in rhetoric. 'From Latin one went to law; from rhetoric to drawing-room conversation; to speech making in the general council to political life.'[1] All of this was animated by creating an atmosphere of competitiveness amongst the students: stimulating rivalries by publishing and comparing results; offering prizes to the best and, in conscious emulation of the classical balance of mind and body, encouraging fencing, riding, boxing and rowing, in all of which Coubertin was an active participant.

Draconian as a Jesuitical education might have been, it could hardly compete with the huge economic, social and technological changes sweeping through the Third Republic in the shaping of its students. Paris was the great cosmopolitan laboratory of the belle époque, the most important node in the European and global networks of art, philosophy, literature, music and design, and home to a whole series of great universal exhibitions and world fairs. By the time Coubertin had left school, the outwardly conformist schoolboy had decisively broken with the key beliefs of his parents and much of his social class, rejecting a career in the priesthood and politically becoming *un rallie* – an aristocratic supporter of the Republic. Coubertin enrolled at the Ecole Libre – an elite school of the new social sciences and public administration, and home for internationalists, pacifists and progressives of all sorts – where he took a whole variety of classes as they pleased him. It was an intellectual atmosphere of experimentation and iconoclasm that suited him well. But, useful as studying was, Coubertin clearly yearned for something more in keeping with his status as an aristocrat, a man of standing in the world.

Perhaps the best insight into Coubertin's state of mind in the early 1880s can be found in his *Roman d'un Rallie*, a very thinly disguised semi-autobiographical novel in which an unbearably syrupy love story and picaresque travelogue provided the framework for Coubertin's memoirs and his social and moral commentary.[2] The central character, Etienne, is a young aristocratic man struggling to find his place and purpose in the world: 'Etienne was sick from being pushed towards action and not being able to act. Action, he saw it everywhere, in the most varied and attractive forms. What he subconsciously sought in his private studies were motives for action.'[3]

For most of the 1880s, Coubertin was a man in search of both a role in the world, but also a grander and higher mission and purpose. Self-education was part of the solution, but the key for Coubertin was travel – the privilege and expectation of any aristocrat with scholarly pretensions – and it was his time in Britain and the United States that allowed him to focus his interests in sport, educational reform and national development.

Coubertin stood in a long tradition of French travellers and writers who had visited Britain. He was both anglophile and anglophobe, a division that often turned on the author's attitude to the nation's aristocracy: was it a bastion of monarchism and worthy traditions or an increasing anachronism? Coubertin was no monarchist, nor did he wish to become an anachronism, as he scornfully described some of his class, 'imprisoned in the ruins of a dead past.' But an alternative position was available. Amongst the most well-read travelogues of the era, one Coubertin was very familiar with, was Hippolyte Taine's *Notes on England*.[4] His account of the British aristocracy thought the 'nobility . . . as citizens are the most enlightened, the most independent and most useful of the whole nation.'

What made them this way? In 1883, he swept through Oxford, Cambridge, Eton, Harrow and Rugby. By 1887, he had Christ's Hospital, Charterhouse, Marlborough, Wellington, Westminster and Winchester under his belt. On this question, Coubertin's most important literary guide was an English-language copy of Thomas Hughes' *Tom Brown's School Days*. He claimed to have carried it 'on all my peregrinations through the public schools of England the better to help me bring them to life again, in order to understand it.'[5] Indeed, his times in England, and the book that followed in 1888, L'Education Angleterre, are best understood as a series of glorious confirmations of his own reading of *Tom Brown*, rather than as a critical or reflective examination of what was in front of him. Amongst the bestselling books of the nineteenth century, *Tom Brown* was an amalgam of sententious memoirs and wishful thinking on the part of its author – Thomas Hughes, a pupil at Rugby in the 1840s – which came to define the meaning of the public-school experience of the games' ethic for generations. On close reading, its ponderous didacticism, moral pomposity and cloying sentimentality is occasionally shot through with more subversive meanings – a barely concealed homoeroticism, flashes of real human warmth and a disdain for the cruel and violent excesses of these appalling institutions – but Coubertin was never a man for close reading. Coubertin argued that the 'supreme goal of the English masters is to make men to lead them.' As to how they managed this, the answer was simple: 'All who I questioned on the subject were unanimous in their answers; they have only to rejoice in the state of school morality, and they loudly declare that sport is the cause of it.' Coubertin fervently believed that all of this was the work of Thomas Arnold the reforming headmaster of Rugby school from the 1820s, which was inevitably the site of his own famous epiphany: 'In the twilight, alone in the great gothic chapel of Rugby, my eyes fixed on the great funeral slab on which, without epitaph, the great name of Thomas Arnold was inscribed, I dreamed that I saw before me the cornerstone of the British Empire.'[6]

Whether this account of Arnold's influence and Coubertin's own time at Rugby is 'consciously created myth'[7] or a form of 'deep and multiple determined wish fulfilment', as his biographers have argued, it was certainly inaccurate.[8] In actual fact, Arnold was almost entirely indifferent to sport; at best, he was reported watching games from the sidelines, but he was neither a participant nor an advocate. Rather than games, his educational revolution began with the inculcation of religiosity as the precondition of creating Christian gentlemen. While this was accomplished, in part, by paying a little more attention to the moral and emotional well being of students than had been the norm hitherto, discipline and order were equally paramount. Arnold was, at the time, obsessed with the innate sinfulness of boys. His regime made liberal use of corporal punishment, as was the norm in England, and the well-known abuses of the fagging system continued through the century.

Coubertin managed to airbrush most of this from his account. In fact, the sporting traditions of both Rugby and other public schools were the creation of a younger generation of schoolmasters, who, though they took their lead from Arnold, found games were by far the most effective mechanism for controlling their charges and moulding their moral outlook and behaviour. Team sports, above all, offered an arena for the cultivation of a manly physique and gentlemanly disposition. Competitive but not cut-throat, they inculcated respect for authority and the rule of law without crushing individuals. The wider athletic culture aspired to the Hellenic virtues of a balance between mental and physical health. Above all, it reserved a place for glory and honour, bravery and valour.

Coubertin's distillation of the public-school games ethic, moulded by this generation of teachers and the muscular Christians of the second half of the nineteenth century, like Charles Kingsley, would in time form a core component of his syncretic notion of Olympism. In the late 1880s, he deployed it to argue for the profound reform of French education, and not just for the elites, but for the masses too. He certainly thought that the English model and its focus on team sports and ball games was preferable to the regimented gymnastics of the German Turnen tradition. Many in France had looked to Prussia, its traditions of nationalist gymnastics, drill and military success, and called for the transformation of French physical education and the armed forces on German lines. Coubertin, by contrast, argued, 'It is citizens more than soldiers that France needs. It is not militarism that our education needs, but freedom.'[9]

Coubertin had his cause, but now he sought action; in 1888, he helped form and run the General Committee for the Propagation of

Physical Exercise in Education, fronted by the ex-prime minister and, by then, an elderly republican statesman, Jules Simon. The organization was an educational policy campaign, a tribune for the virtues of amateur sports and a bureaucratic organization putting on athletics, football and rugby tournaments. In 1890, it fused with a smaller competitor to create the USFSA (Union des Societies Françaises de Sports Athletiques). Too anglophile for more extreme nationalist tastes, opponents, like socialist and science-fiction writer, Paschal Grousset, created the Ligue Nationale de L'Education Physique, and railed against the importation of English games and manners. Grousset even called for the creation of a national French version of the ancient Olympic Games. Amazingly, just three years before he would launch his own brand of revivalism, Coubertin was dismissive of the notion, even a little contemptuous. 'Grousset's ligue makes a great fuss. It sets out at war, it has reminiscences of the Olympic Games and visions of ceremonies at the foot of the Eiffel Tower where the head of state will crown the young athletes with laurel. And then at the very time they talk about military defence, they declare they do not want to exert political action . . . This is all a lot: it is even too much.'[10] Yet this is precisely what Coubertin would go on to create, and the revival of the Olympic Games would become, for him, the cause of all causes, combining innumerable personal and political, sporting and intellectual strands in his life.

In his own fantastically unreliable memoir, published in 1908, Coubertin was vague about when and how he came up with the idea of reviving the ancient games. Certainly this early episode of scepticism was edited out of the story. Indeed, the baron went on to rewrite his own intellectual biography to make himself appear a lifelong dreamy Hellenophile. 'When and how the need associated itself in my mind with the idea of reestablishing the Olympic Games I couldn't say . . . I was familiar with the term. Nothing in ancient history had made me more of a dreamer than Olympia. This City of dream . . . raised its colonnades and porticos unceasingly before my adolescent mind. Long before I thought of drawing from its ruins a principle of revival, I would rebuild it in my mind, to make the shape of its silhouette live again.'[11] While there is no doubt that Coubertin's Jesuit education would have ensured that he was familiar with some of the classical texts on the games, and he was probably aware of some of the information emerging from the German excavations at

Olympia too, there is little sign in his records, bookshelves or notes that he took an abiding interest in the subject, or that he had made any significant connection between the ancient games and his educational-reform work, or his increasingly internationalist frame of mind. In fact, the most likely explanation for his volte-face, at the very least the catalyst for change in Coubertin's mind, was his encounter with Dr Brookes and the Much Wenlock Olympics.

In early 1889, Coubertin had put out a call through the columns of English newspapers for correspondents who would care to communicate on the matter of physical education. Dr Penny Brookes was one of his respondents, sending a steady stream of Olympic-related letters, cuttings and reports to Coubertin. The baron clearly took note and, later that year, in a speech at the International Congress on Physical Exercise – his contribution to the Exposition Universelle, held in Paris in 1889 – he praised Brookes' ideas and initiatives, directly quoting a speech he had made at the 1866 National Olympian Festival in London: 'How can one not agree with the words uttered by a perspicacious speaker at an athletic contest which took place some twenty years ago at Crystal Palace?'[12] Interestingly, Coubertin made no direct reference to the Olympian aspect of the event. In his later correspondence with Brookes, which deals in some depth with the virtues and promise of integrating physical education into the nation's curriculum and resulted in an agreement to attend the Much Wenlock games in October 1890, the issue of the ancient Olympics did not arise. On the eve of his arrival, Brookes thought the purpose of the exercise was merely 'to enlighten Baron Pierre de Coubertin who desires to introduce athletics more largely among his own countrymen.' The town had already held the games, as usual, in May that year, but this was a special performance. The sport really wasn't much to write home about, but Brookes went big on pageantry. Competitors arrived in elaborate costume and processed through a stage-set triumphal arch bearing the words, 'Welcome to Baron Pierre de Coubertin and Prosperity to France.' The baron was asked to plant an oak tree, and they bathed the sapling in champagne. The field was decorated with banners in ancient Greek, quoting the classics. The games themselves were short: eclectic track-and-field events were followed by tilting at the ring and an elaborate faux-medieval prize giving, then on to a grand dinner. Brookes made Coubertin an honorary member of the Wenlock Olympian Society;

Coubertin made his host an honorary member of the USFSA. They also had some time alone, the doctor introducing the baron to his scrapbooks, his Olympic-revival archive and correspondence, and his personal library – and, in the course of this, the history of both his National Olympian Association, the various Zappas revivals and his own subsequent exchanges with the Greeks.

Something must have clicked. On his return to France, Coubertin wrote an article entitled '*Les Jeux Olympiques à Much Wenlock – Une Page de L'Histoire de Athlétisme*'. 'What characterizes it is the veil of poetry that envelops it and the scent of antiquity which comes from it. Dr Brookes, more keenly than any other has sensed the mysterious influence that Greek civilization, across the ages, still exerts on humanity.'[13] Coubertin made it plain, as he would never do again: 'If the Olympic games which modern Greece could not bring back to life are revised today, the credit is due not to a Greek but to Dr Brookes.'

FIVE

It seems indisputable that it was only in the months after his visit to Much Wenlock, that Coubertin became an Olympic revivalist. In the process, he would draw widely on the ideas and experiments of his predecessors, though he rarely ever acknowledged them, but he was no mere jackdaw. In the eighteen months between the publication of his Much Wenlock article and his 1892 speech at the Sorbonne, where he first proposed an Olympic revival, he forged a unique version of the modern games. Moreover, unlike his predecessors, he would be able to create an international social and political coalition that could make it happen. Perhaps Coubertin's greatest advantage was his capacity to think big. In the 1790s, the French revolutionaries had called for the new European republic to join them at their Olympiad. In the 1860s, the NAO had asked for, though not received, applications from overseas athletes to join them. The Much Wenlock games were irredeemably provincial, the Zappas games were played for just a Greek audience and tied to a Greek cause, and though both were able to draw upon the nascent sports cultures and clubs of their time, neither was able to tap into the aristocratic networks of athletic prestige, cultural capital and political influence.

Coubertin, by contrast, fused his Olympic revivalism with the most universal call of all – internationalism – envisaging the games not as a recreation or country fair, but as a grand, if restrained, urban cosmopolitan spectacular, and he had the personal connections and ideological appeal that could tie the revival of the Olympic Games to the gentlemen athletes of the industrialized world.

Although he had rejected a career in diplomacy, one of the few avenues open to him, Coubertin's social rank and connections made him a natural part of the world of international affairs. Since the establishment of the Concert of Europe at the end of the Napoleonic wars, the crowned heads of Europe had been increasingly in the habit of calling conferences amongst themselves and meeting face to face.[1] Only semi-institutionalized as a system of international diplomacy, it was never entirely clear who amongst European royalty was entitled to call a conference, or on what subject, and over the course of the nineteenth century, the practice spread to both obscure monarchs and even to more junior members of the European aristocracy, concerned with everything from the global protection of intellectual property to the rules of war and the building of the Suez Canal. Not only did Coubertin have access to these kinds of networks, but he was, through his travels and his growing body of correspondents, connected to some of the key sports associations, universities and elite athletics clubs in Europe and North America.

As we shall see, the most effective way of mobilizing these forces was on the question of amateurism in sport and then the common task of international congresses – to discuss, propose and try to set international norms in their field of expertise. However, as is clear from the new language and arguments of the baron after 1892, amateurism was not an animating force for him, but a mere means to an end. More important was the cause of internationalism, pacifism and peace amongst nations, ideas he first encountered at the Ecole Libre and which were part of the heady intellectual mix of Parisian society. It is notable that the honorary supporters of the 1894 congress to revive the games, which Coubertin would go on to hold, included, alongside a collection of cosmopolitan royalty, all the leading figures of the nascent international peace movement, centred on Paris.[2] This world of international associations and conferences intersected with the key nodes in the global networks of cultural exchange in the belle époque – the world fairs that had begun with the 1851 Great Exhibition in London and had recently peaked in scale and influence with the 1889 Paris Exposition Universelle, at which Coubertin had spoken. The lectures and small displays of Swedish Ling gymnastics that Coubertin helped arrange at the fair brought international sport to the periphery of these new global spectaculars and their grand interpretations of modernity.

In 1891, the imperialist agitator John Astley Cooper made the next leap. Writing in *Great Britain: The Imperial and Asiatic Quarterly*, he proposed an international sporting spectacular that could stand on its own: 'A Pan-Britannic-Pan-Anglican Contest and Festival every four years as a means of increasing goodwill and good understanding of the British Empire', uniting the motherland, the white dominions and the colonies. Coubertin followed the same line of thought, but with more cosmopolitan intentions.[3]

There was a final component to the mix. Coubertin had, of course, made pragmatic arguments for playing sport and introducing it into schools – like the creation of gentlemen, the national benefits of a healthy population, and the moral and political arguments for playing them internationally – but these ideas would have only made the case for the staging of secular international sporting festivities, like the Pan-Britannic games. To revive the ancient games, even under modern conditions, was to enter the realm of the sacred. Fond of quoting Pindar, who thought that 'The gods are the friends of the games', Coubertin recognized and was greatly attracted to the indelibly religious character of the ancient Olympics. Indeed, he thought the ancients, on observing modern sports, 'would be astonished to find no expression or suggestion of the religious idea of purification and sanctified action.'[4] However, in actual fact, 'like the athletics of antiquity, modern athletics is a religion, a cult, an impassioned soaring which is capable of going from play to heroism.'[5] The Catholic aristocrat, searching for glory and heroes, marooned in an increasingly demotic and secular world, had found his vocation, his gods and a stage on which to venerate them.

SIX

In November 1892, less than two years after his time in Much Wenlock, Coubertin assembled a trio of speakers at the Sorbonne, at a conference held to celebrate the fifth anniversary of the foundation of the USFSA. Georges Bourdon, the theatre critic and one of the founders of Racing Club de Paris, the French capital's leading sports club, spoke on ancient sport; the diplomat and writer Jules Jusserand covered chivalry and medieval sports; and then Coubertin was billed to speak on modern sports. 'International competitions' was his theme:

> It is clear that the telegraph, railways, the telephone, the passionate research in science, congresses and exhibitions have done more for peace than any treaty or diplomatic convention. Well, I hope that athletics will do even more . . . Let us export rowers, runners and fencers: there is the free trade of the future, and on the day it is introduced within the walls of old Europe the cause of peace will have received a new and mighty stay. This is enough to encourage your servant to dream now . . . to continue and complete, on a basis suited to the conditions of modern life, this grandiose and salutary task, namely the restoration of the Olympic Games.

Initial responses were not good. Coubertin recalled, 'Naturally I had foreseen every eventuality except what actually happened. Opposition? Objections? Irony? Or even indifference. Not at all. Everyone applauded . . . but no one had really understood.'[1] Some in the audience, thinking the whole thing an elaborate pageant, joked as to whether the athletes would be naked.

Undeterred, Coubertin looked for other opportunities to make his pitch and, in 1893, Adolphe de Pallisaux, an amateur walking champion and the treasurer of Racing Club, offered him one. Pallisaux suggested the USFSA host an international conference on the principles and problems of amateurism in the sporting world – an issue perplexing elite and aristocratic athletes all across the industrialized world as they attempted to keep the new industrial classes out of their games and clubs, simultaneously preserving the social exclusivity and moral purity of their version of sport.

Coubertin seized on the opportunity, actively supporting the proposal and suggesting that his Olympic idea might also form a small element of the discussions. In a letter sent out in January 1894, Coubertin invited the sporting world to the International Congress of Amateurs. The first seven items on the proposed agenda concerned the definition of amateurism, issues of broken-time payments, payment of gate money and methods of disqualification. Sneaking in at number eight was 'The possibility of re-establishing the Olympic Games. Under what conditions would it be feasible?' In the covering letter, Coubertin elaborated a little further, suggesting that, 'the establishment of the Olympic Games on a basis and in the conditions in keeping with the needs of modern life would bring together, every four years, representatives of the nations of the world face to face, and one is permitted to think that these peaceful, courteous contests constitute the best form of internationalism.'

Initial interest was thin. Trips to the USA and to Britain in late 1893 failed to drum up any public support or interest, but, through the spring of 1894, the baron assembled the other essential components of the congress. Baron de Courcel, a French state senator and former ambassador to Berlin, was persuaded to act as a grand figurehead. Racing Club agreed to host a grand dinner and sporting fete for the guests. The letterhead of the congress was gilded by an enormous list of Coubertin's correspondents: the King of Belgium, the Prince of Wales, the Crown Princes of Greece and Sweden, and the Russian Grand Duke Vladimir. Coubertin also knew how to cover his back, and invited the British imperialist commentator John Astley Cooper to be an honorary member of the congress.

On the final set of invitations, sent out in a flurry in May 1894, the meeting was now known as the International Athletic Congress rather than the International Amateur Congress and the Olympic component was creeping up the agenda. It now comprised three items out of ten. Coubertin had also been working the Greek back-channels and, in the months before the meeting in Paris, secured two key allies. First, through the agency of Charles Waldstein, the archaeologist and director of the American School in Athens, Greek Prince Constantine agreed to be an honorary member. The details of their conversations remain unknown, but it seems more than likely, given Constantine's and the whole royal house's enthusiasm for the Zappas games, and their own failed efforts to stage an Olympic festival in 1892, that they would have also been enthusiastic about hosting this version of the revival. Second, Coubertin acquired a Greek delegate to the congress who would be able to make the case for him that Athens should do so: the elderly Greek writer Dimitrios Vikelas, whose patriotic adventure story, *Loukis Lara*, set during the Greek war of independence, proved a bestseller at home and then a pan-European hit. Coubertin asked him to chair the committee that would deal with the revival of the Olympic Games.

Coubertin's congress, now retitled for the third time, was described in the official programme as the Paris International Congress for the Re-establishment of the Olympic Games. It had attracted seventy-eight delegates from sports clubs and organizational bodies, drawn mainly from France and predominantly from Europe (including Austria, Belgium, Britain, Bohemia, Greece, Italy, Russia, Spain and Sweden), with an unofficial German presence (still opposed by many prickly French patriots), a sprinkling of Americans and a single New Zealander. Proceedings opened in the great amphitheatre of the Sorbonne, where 2,000 members of the audience heard the recently discovered and translated 'Hymn to Apollo', a classical ode set to music by the composer Gabriel Fauré. Coubertin thought they listened 'with religious silence to the divine melody which lived again to salute the Olympic revival across the dimension the ages', and that 'Hellenism infiltrated the whole hall.'[2] For most of those attending, the week was a round of social engagements and festivities: bicycle races and tennis competitions, grand dinner receptions with Parisian dignitaries and an evening fete at the grounds of Racing Club de Paris that combined athletic races, a high-society party and tremendous celebratory fireworks.

Back at the Sorbonne, the two committees got down to work. At the opening session of the Olympic committee, there was a strong case made for London as the inaugural host, rather than Athens, but with his consummate committee skills, Coubertin persuaded the meeting to leave the question open until the end of the week, by which time support for a London games would have melted away and, emboldened by a congratulatory telegram from the Greek king, Coubertin would have mobilized all his supporters. At the decisive moment in the final plenary discussions, Vikelas spoke to the congress, advocating an Athens games; 'a Greek institution was being revived for which a Greek city was an appropriate host.' Much to his surprise, Vikelas' suggestions were warmly received and graciously accepted.

The congress went on to confirm that the first games should be held in Athens in 1896, the next in Paris in 1900. Under the strict terms established by the congress' other committee, they would be open only to amateurs, with the exception of fencing masters. The initial list of proposed sports was long, including athletics, aquatics, gymnastics, cycling, wrestling, equestrian sports, boxing, polo and shooting. In a splendidly offbeat note, Coubertin also insisted on a special prize being awarded for the most interesting mountaineering achievement accomplished since the last games.

A permanent committee was established with Vikelas as its titular president and Coubertin as the general secretary. The rest of the members, effectively hand-picked by Coubertin, included middle-class educational reformers – like the Hungarian Ference Kemeney, the Czech Jiri Guth-Jarkovsky, and the Argentine Dr Jose Zubiau – but also senior military officers – like the Swede Major Victor Balck, and the Russian General Boutowsky – who were not only sportsmen, but active in integrating athletic training in their own armed forces. The British and Americans were well represented by Coubertin's long-term confidant, Princeton professor of history, William Sloane, a patron of collegiate athletics; Baron Ampthill, later viceroy of India, who was a leading light in the Henley Regatta and Oxbridge rowing scenes; Charles Herbert, honorary secretary of Britain's Amateur Athletic Association (AAA); and Leonard Cuff, captain of the New Zealand national cricket team.

Coubertin later wrote that he formed the International Olympic Committee along the lines of the Henley Regatta, 'composed of three concentric circles: a small core of earnest and hard-working members; a nursery of willing members ready to be taught; finally a facade of more or less useful people whose presence satisfied national pretensions at the same time as it gave prestige to the committee as a whole'; thus the first IOC was rounded out with a smattering of Italian and Belgian aristocrats and a little more glitter.[3]

The congress may have finished on a high, but the award of the games was not received well by the Greek government. On his return to Athens, Vikelas met Prime Minster Tricoupis, who, he reported, 'would have much preferred that the question of the Olympic Games had never arisen.' His encounters with Dragoumis and the Zappas foundation were little short of disastrous, with their deciding to have no part in the games. The baron arrived in November and was met by a letter from Dragoumis which argued that there was no way, given the economic situation, that Greece could host the games, that in any case athletic sports were insufficiently developed in Greece and that he should start the ball rolling in Paris in 1900 instead. Greek prime minister, Tricoupis, paid him a visit in his hotel rooms and made the same arguments. Coubertin countered by arguing that a very small budget would be sufficient, perhaps as little as 250,000 drachmas. Then he went to work, gaining the full support of Prince Constantine, relentlessly handing out his business card, and speaking, cajoling and meeting with Athenian high society. Invited by supporters of the games to address the Parnassos Literary Society, he appealed to Greek patriotism: 'Gentlemen, did your fathers carefully weigh their chances of victory before rising up against the Turks? If they had, you would not be here, free men this very moment.' Sensing that there might be some concern, given the limited development of modern sports in Greece, that they would not fare well, he implored, 'When we had begun to play football matches against the English, we expected to lose. But the seventh time we played them, we beat them . . . Dishonour here would not consist of being beaten; it would consist of not contending.'[4]

Despite official opposition, Coubertin was able to convene a meeting at the Zappion to discuss plans for the games. Dragoumis opened the meeting but departed immediately, refusing to have anything to do with the conversation. Coubertin had a few allies amongst the assembled Greek gentlemen, but most were active supporters of Prime Minister Tricoupis. Coubertin announced that Prince Constantine had agreed to act as honorary president, that the bill for the games really wouldn't be as much as they imagined, chose four vice-presidents and declared them the organizing committee of the 1896 Athens games. He then left for Paris by way of Olympia: 'We arrived there late in the evening. I had to wait for dawn to see the outline of the sacred place of which I had so often dreamed. All

morning long I wandered amongst its ruins.'[5] The lifelong Hellenophile stayed just a morning before heading home. It was the first of
only two visits to the site in his lifetime; the second would be in the
1920s and was hardly any more considered. His fleeting stays and
rather hazy memoir suggest that Coubertin had already extracted
what he needed and wanted from the ancient games, and no amount
of archaeological science or close textual study of the sources was
about to deflect him from the inspiration he had acquired or the
vision he had established.

SEVEN

One wonders quite how long Coubertin's Olympian reverie lasted. It would not have been long after his return to France that the post would have brought news of the chaos in Athens. The committee that he had left behind, some of whom were not merely sceptics about the games but opponents, convened, examined the proposed budgets and, in despair at ever making it happen, collectively resigned. In parliament, the opposition took up the cause of the games, calling on Prime Minister Tricoupis to support them as a matter of national honour, but with little effect. As one MP put it: 'Today the whole world thinks that the games will take place in Greece; while the eyes of the entire civilized world, with inquisitiveness and interest, are turned on us – the descendants of those who first founded the Olympic Games – the government of the place works against it, the Olympic committee loses all courage, and the organizing committee is ready to commit suicide.'[1]

Into this vacuum stepped the royal house and, in particular, Crown Prince Constantine. He established and steered a new organizing committee, mobilized the monarchy's own networks of supporters, traded favours and began preparations. An initial series of public donations were supplemented by a huge gift from George Averoff, a rich Greek businessman living in Alexandria and already responsible for funding a series of public projects and national monuments in Athens. Almost a million drachmas enabled the ancient Panathenaic Stadium, part renovated for the Zappas games of previous years, to be completely rebuilt and re-clad in marble. Averoff got a statue of himself outside for his troubles. The fall of the Tricoupis government in 1895 saw the new and more Olympic-friendly administration make extensive loans to the committee, large enough to fund the construction of a new velodrome and a shooting range, secured against ticket sales and an issue of special commemorative postage stamps.

The final months of preparation offered many of the tropes that still structure Olympic coverage a century later. Rumours persisted that the stadium and other facilities would not be ready on time, leading to a furious exchange of letters in *The Times*. Foreign journalists, like this *New York Times* correspondent, came to dig for dirt: 'There were plenty of old tin cans and rubbish scattered where once the silver Ulysses sparkled to the sea: the grove of Academe reminded me of picturesque bits in shanty town.'[2] The enthusiasts and the boosters talked things up, like Coubertin's breezy *Letter from Athens*, published just before the games: 'Everywhere people are shining up the marble, applying new plaster and fresh paint; they are paving, cleaning, decorating . . . Every evening at about five o'clock the citizens come here to cast an admiring eye upon the work being done at the stadium.' First-hand accounts suggest that Athens was buzzing. The games were scheduled to start, as Panagiotis Soutsos had argued for over half a century beforehand, on Greek Independence Day. The city hummed with visitors whose 'polyglottic confusion of tongues amounted almost to a babel', while crowds scrambled for tickets to the opening ceremony; estimates vary between 50,000 and 70,000 in attendance. The writer Anninos recalled the moment: 'The various outfits of the ladies, their varied coiffures, the movement of their fans amid the black mass of several thousand spectators, the brilliant uniforms and the plumes of the officers, the striking colours of the floating flags, the lively semicircle of spectators who, without tickets, occupied the tops of the hills surrounding the stadium, that made a most curious and imposing ensemble.'[3]

The arrival of the royal entourage signalled the start of formal proceedings. The crown prince welcomed the king. The king opened the games and the band struck up the Olympic hymn. 'The silence which followed the impressive performance was of intense expectancy; the Olympian Games were about to be reprised after the lapse of hundreds of years. Suddenly the clear startling notes of a bugle were heard, and from the ancient tunnel . . . the contestants for the first event appeared.'[4]

Over the next two weeks, 241 athletes competed in forty-three events in nine different sports: a small but illuminating cross-section of the urban elites of the industrializing world and their sporting cultures. They were, needless to say, all men, and, but for the clean-cut American college boys, nearly all men with the signature waxed moustache of the young scions of the haute bourgeois and aristocracy, aped by the aspirant middle classes. They were also all white Europeans, or North Americans of European descent. The Chilean national Olympic committee continues to insist that Luis Subercaseaux Errázuriz, then at school in France and later ambassador to the Vatican and a peripatetic diplomat, competed in the heats of the 100 metres, 800 metres and 1,500 metres, but no one else, including the IOC, agrees. The Greek team was drawn from across the diaspora on the basis of ethnicity rather than citizenship, with athletes from Egypt, Ottoman Anatolia and Cyprus – then part of the British Empire. The Bulgarians have tried to claim the shooter Charles Champaud as one of their own, but he was unquestionably a Swiss teacher. Despite a few athletes drawn from more modest Greek family backgrounds, the majority were not. Amongst the shooting medallists were Pantelis Karasevdas and Ioannis Frangoudis, then junior officers who both rose to very senior positions in the Greek army. Charilaos Vasilakos, a law student and marathon runner, ascended to the very apex of the Greek civil service, while fencers Ioannis Georgiadis and Periklis Pierrakos-Mavromichalis finished their careers as the nation's leading professor of toxicology and the minister of the interior respectively. The Americans who went to Athens were equally blue blooded, the majority being students at Harvard, Princeton or the upmarket Boston Athletic Club. The Hungarians, Austrians and Germans were overwhelmingly upper-middle-class men, with a strong professional and Jewish presence, like the Hungarian swimming champion and architect Alfred Hajos, or the Austrian swimmers, the lawyer Otto Herschmann, and the doctor Paul Neumann. The Germans, especially the gymnasts, came in defiance of the ultra-nationalist *Deutsche Turnenbund*, the institutional guardian of the Germanic version of the modern sport, which considered the games so dangerously un-German and cosmopolitan that they forbade participation by any of their members under threat of expulsion.

The British contingent was small – just six – a consequence of the lofty indifference of the sporting establishment to Coubertin's venture and what G. S. Robertson, a recently graduated Oxford Classicist and hammer-thrower, splenetically described the organizers' 'suicidal policy of devoting the greater share of attention to continental athletes.'[5] In the absence of the core of Britain's elite sporting culture

– the public-schoolboys of Oxford and Cambridge, the armed forces and the clubs of London – the British presence had a more imperial feel, the competitors drawn from the colonies or colonial backgrounds. Charles Gmelin, the Oxford sprinter, was born in Bengal to Christian missionaries. His university contemporary, John Boland, the son of an Irish businessman, and later an Irish nationalist MP at Westminster, came and won the tennis competition. Launceston Elliot, who tried his hand at weightlifting and wrestling, was born in India and came from a Scottish aristocratic family which had held many imperial offices. Lower down the social scale, Edwin Flack, the middle-distance runner, was working for his father's solid accountancy firm in Australia. On the lowest rung of all were Britain's cyclists, Edward Battell and Frederick Keeping, Irish and English respectively, both on the domestic staff of the British Embassy in Athens, an occupation considered so dangerously close to professionalism that, at one point, the organizing committee toyed with their exclusion from the games.

Italy's Carlo Airoldi actually was excluded. A well-known and successful long-distance runner in Italy and France, he had won the enormously long and prestigious Milano–Barcellona race in 1895. Without personal wealth, Airoldi planned to fund a trip to Athens by jogging most of the way there, supported by the Italian sports paper, *La Bicicletta*. Airoldi made it to Dubrovnik, took a boat to Patras and, after another gruelling week of walking along the railway tracks, arrived in Athens. He attempted to register for the marathon, but his sponsored walk and the prize money he had won the previous year deemed him a professional and thus ineligible. This left Giuseppe Rivabella, an engineer and rifleman, then living in Samos, as the nation's sole representative at the games.

In this world of gentlemen amateurs, without the kind of high-pressure specialization that characterizes rationalized and commercial sport, many athletes could compete not just in multiple events, but multiple sports. The Austrian fencer Adolf Schmal won the twelve-hour cycle race; the German Carl Schumann won both the gymnastics and the wrestling. The Dane Viggo Jensen had a crack at weightlifting, shooting, gymnastics and the shot put. There was, for the right of kind of gentleman, who happened to be in town, the chance to join in, whatever their sporting experience. John Boland, the tennis player, had been invited to Athens by a Greek colleague at

Oxford and only joined the games on arrival. The shooting competitions could accommodate Greek university students entirely new to the discipline, and – it seems, on a whim – both Coubertin's American academic confidant, Charles Waldstein, and Anastasios Metaxas, the Greek architect who had supervised the rebuilding of the Panathenaic Stadium, were also able to sign up.

What the games could not accommodate were the hugely popular but now increasingly professional and commercialized sports of the industrial world: football and cricket, boxing and horse racing, American baseball – all were absent. Cycling, which had become tremendously popular in France and the Low Countries, was represented at the games by track racing at the new velodrome, as well as long-distance road-races, but the Olympic tournament was already in the shadow of its professional counterparts. None of the leading riders was present in Athens, all of whom competed later that year in the first classic professional road race – the Pairs Roubaix.

Much more characteristic of Athens 1896 were fencing and shooting – competitions offering the most reassuringly elite of demeanours. The latter were held at the newly built range in the genteel suburb of Kalithea, and were ceremonially opened and blessed by the Bishop of Cephalonia, after which Queen Olga fired a rifle bedecked with flowers. The fencing was held in the Zappeion – the first time that Zappas' grand building had actually staged a sporting event – assiduously attended by the Greek royal family and their other royal guests. The competition also featured the only permitted professionals at the games – for the fencing masters, without whom Europe's aristocracy and militaries could not learn this martial art, were considered to be gentlemen.

The participants at the 1896 games may have nearly all been part of a transnational class of bourgeois athletes, but, as the staging of many of the events demonstrated, there were few fixed international standards, and considerable differences of opinion between different nations and their sporting cultures as to what constituted the rules and formats of different sports, and how they should be judged. In the athletics, for example, the track was a most unorthodox 330 yards, with peculiarly tight ends that made comparison with any other conditions impossible. Most athletics meets ran their races anticlockwise; the 1896 games were run clockwise. As to the issue of technique, there was a gigantic gulf between American hurdlers, who could jump and run without breaking step, and the neophyte Greek athletes, who had to jump, stop and start again; similarly, the American sprinters began races with a crouching start, the rest stood inefficiently erect. The swimming was particularly haphazard. As Athens had no indoor pool, it was staged between two buoys in the Bay of Piraeus, at some considerable distance from the jetties and the small crowd that gathered to watch. The water proved bitingly cold, the performances heroic but, in terms of times, utterly dismal. The winner – Hungarian, Alfred Hajos – found it so freezing that, 'My will to live completely overcame my desire to win.' The wrestling, conducted under hastily constructed rules that tried to bridge the differences between different countries' styles of fighting, produced a bout that went on so long that it had to be stopped for fading light and concluded the next day. The weightlifting proved controversial when the Briton, Launceston Elliot, and the Dane, Jensen Viggo, tied for weight in the one-armed lift, requiring Prince George, as the chair of the judges, to decide the competition on 'style'. When it came to gymnastics, style was in the eye of the beholder. The games featured an unambiguously German version of the sport, but from a British perspective, G. S. Robertson was unconvinced that gymnastics was a sport at all, certainly not one that should receive the same kind of accolades reserved for the sports of the Anglo-Saxon world. 'An Olympic wreath is far too precious a thing to be squandered on good form in hopping over a horse or swarming up a rope.'[6]

In one area, Athens innovated: the marathon. The race was the invention of Michel Bréal, a French philologist and acolyte of Coubertin's, who drew on Herodotus' account of the Battle of Marathon, c. 490 BCE. In this version of the tale, the Athenian army, having defeated the Persian invaders and forced them into their ships, realized that the enemy could now attack an undefended Athens from the sea, forcing them to return home at speed. Bréal proposed a race from the battlefield to Athens, staged on the coastal route and finishing in the Panathenaic Stadium – a distance of around twenty-five miles.

It proved to be the most important event of the games, generating the kind of modern mythological hero and collective stadium spectacle that raised the 1896 Olympics above the level of a country-house games weekend or a mere historical recreation. A crowd of at least 80,000 people spent a long and increasingly tense afternoon at the stadium, waiting for the runners, periodically being updated by messengers on bike or horseback. First, the French pacesetter, Lermusiaux, cracked in the heat, forcing him to return to Athens in a horse-drawn cart. Then the Australian, Flack, took the lead, but, after a series of runners collapsed, the man who entered the stadium first was the Greek, Spyridon Louis. The crowd went wild. The king and the crown prince descended to the track to run alongside him and, when he had finished the race, members of the royal entourage and the organizing committee embraced and kissed him. Coubertin was simply amazed: 'Egad! The excitement and the enthusiasm were simply indescribable. One of the most extraordinary sights that I can remember. Its imprint stays with me.'[7] Louis was instantly cast as a national hero, his admittedly modest past rewritten to imagine him as a raw earthen peasant, the foundation of the nation. Stories abounded of offers of marriage, lands and honours bestowed. Even Greek satirist, Georgios Souris, rarely complimentary of anyone, was reduced to simple nationalist praise: 'May Louis hear today the hymns of Pindar. Long live the race, the people and the crown.'[8]

The closing ceremony, delayed a day by foul weather, managed to combine something of the unruly school fete with a real reverence of ancient traditions, albeit newly invented ancient traditions. G. S. Robertson, with the breathtaking chutzpah and self-importance that came from being a member of the British ruling class at the very pinnacle of its power, inserted himself into the proceedings, and read a Pindaric victory ode to the games themselves, which he had composed in ancient Greek. The athletes were called individually by a herald, and the king handed out the prizes: silver medals and laurels of olive branches cut from the sacred groves of Olympia to the winners of competitions; a bronze medal and laurel of bay for the runners-up. For Spyridon Louis, there was his very own marathon cup, donated by Bréal, and an ancient Greek painted vase, then diplomas for everybody else. The dress code was strictly black tie and top hat, except for Louis, who was dressed in the nationalist panto-mime costume of the Greek peasantry: the fustanella. When he appeared, according to one observer, 'A rumble as of thunder burst from every side.' The champions took a circuit of the stadium, received the applause of the crowd, and then the king declared the 'First International Olympic Games' ended.

They were international games, but they were also understood as a peculiarly Greek triumph. American observer Rufus B. Richardson was condescending, if generous: 'it is a small and poor kingdom but, like ancient Hellas, great in qualities of soul.' Spyridon Lambros, the Greek nationalist historian, comparing the state of the nation during the games to the era of political upheaval and social backwardness when the current royal house was installed, stated that 'the Greece of 1896 has far outdistanced the Greece of 1862.' Indeed, the monarchy was so emboldened by the success of the Olympics that, at a huge banquet held during the games for all the athletes and foreign dignitaries in town, the king wondered whether they might 'appoint our land as a peaceful meeting place of the nations, as a continuous and permanent site of the Olympic Games.' Coubertin, in a deliciously acid memoir, said, 'I decided to play the simpleton, the man who did not understand. I decided to ignore the King's speech.'[9] He was equally piqued by the failure of the royal house or the post-stadium crowd to acknowledge his role in inviting and animating the games, writing: 'I don't care what the Greek newspapers say about me. When it comes to ingratitude, Greece easily wins first prize . . . You all got your branches – so did even Mr Robertson – in a full stadium from the hands of the King. I am the only one whose name, if ever mentioned, was spoken only in secret.'[10]

The international audience was hugely impressed. Most thought the games had captured something of what they perceived to be the glories of antiquity. G. S. Robertson thought their success lay in 'the triumph of sentiment, of association, of distinction, of unique splendour.' Rufus B. Richardson was 'almost persuaded that old times had come around again when there was nothing more serious to do than outrun, outlaw and outwrestle.' The 1896 Olympic high-jump champion, Ellery Clark, with the chance to compare Athens to other games he would later attend, wrote that, 'nothing could equal this first revival. The flavour of the Athenian soil, the indefinable poetic charm of knowing one's self thus linked with the past, a successor to the great heroic figures of olden times – the splendid sportsmanship of the whole affair.' Charles Waldstein declared the games, 'A stupendous success', as one might expect of a long-term supporter of the project, but the measure of the games' impact, at least on those who were present, is better measured by a former sceptic, like G. S. Robertson, who counselled, 'To those that followed closely the preliminaries to the revival of the Olympic Meeting, it appeared certain that the games would be a disastrous failure. This was not the case, though the nature of the success obtained can scarcely have corresponded with the expectations of the promoters.'[11] As with almost every project, however miraculous its inception, the real challenge would be to do it again.

2

ALL THE FUN OF THE FAIR: THE OLYMPICS AT THE END OF THE BELLE ÉPOQUE

PARIS 1900 • ST LOUIS 1904 • ATHENS 1906 • LONDON 1908

STOCKHOLM 1912 • BERLIN 1916

It is a particular attraction of world fairs that they form a momentary centre of world civilization, assembling the products of the entire world . . . as if in a single picture.

Georg Simmel

We should be careful never to allow the Games to become dependent upon or be taken over by a big fair where their philosophical value vanishes into thin air and their educational merit becomes nil . . . It was not until 1912 that the break was finally completed in Sweden . . . Olympism would no longer be reduced to the role of humiliated vassal.

Baron de Coubertin

ONE

Viewed from the wreckage of interwar Europe, the French looked back to the three or four decades before the First World War and pronounced them *La Belle Époque*. Americans remembered it as the Gilded Era, Britain as the high point of Victorian and imperial power. Europe and America had experienced almost four decades of break-neck industrial growth and profound social change, alongside the introduction of epochal technological innovations, from electricity to powered flight to the automobile. In a world more connected than ever before, there was imperial expansion abroad, yet peace between the major powers, and the greatest celebrations and condensations of these extraordinary changes were the world fairs. Georg Simmel, the German sociologist, thought them the 'momentary centres of world civilization', for they surely constituted the most concentrated set of cultural exchanges and interactions of the era.[1] Six million people, nearly a quarter of England's population, visited the Crystal Palace in 1851; the same fraction of Americans, twenty-eight million in total, bought a ticket to the Chicago Columbian Exposition in 1893. Fifteen million went to Paris in 1867, twenty-three million in 1889 and fifty million in 1900, more than the entire population of France.[2] Of course, they were overwhelmingly national visitors, but the fairs also attracted a significant number of tourists; dozens of foreign governments and companies sponsored pavilions, and an increasingly large and global press corps reported on them. However, their bid to encapsulate the world in a single narrative theme or in a fairground of pavilions was always undercut by the fractured nature of globalization in the late nineteenth century. If there was a world civilization, then it was a massively asymmetric one, split by global imperial rivalries and deeply troubled by military shadow-boxing and rising nationalisms.

Coubertin was never a man for complex truths, describing the relationship of the early Olympics to the world fairs as one of 'humiliating vassalage.' It was certainly a relationship in which he lost a lot of control over where the games were staged, and they were not always sufficiently aligned with the baron's neo-Hellenic athletic cult and its syncretic mixture of muscularity and internationalism. Coubertin's personal pique aside, he was right to argue that the Olympic Games of the belle époque were overshadowed in the popular consciousness and press by the wider festivities in which they were embedded; but then, for most of the public elite, male sport was a marginal interest compared to technological wonder, cornucopias of consumer fantasy and theme-park orientalist exotica. Moreover, in the absence of other sponsors, the fairs also provided the material setting and financial context in which some kind of games could take place, and in which the global status of sport in general and the Olympics in particular could be entrenched. The modern Olympics has inherited the grandiose universalism of the world fairs, as well as their complex relationship with commerce and business. To this legacy we can add the games' increasingly significant impact on the fabric of their host cities and their capacity for narrower and more parochial agendas.

What did the crowds come to see? As the original's full title – 'The Great Exhibition of the Works of Industry of all Nations' – suggests, they came to see, in object form, the machines and the products that were making the new global industrial economy: the capital goods, the sources of power and the new sinews of electronic communications and mechanized transport that, from the mid-nineteenth century to the beginning of the First World War, were creating a historically unprecedented level of international trade, investment and cultural exchange. In Philadelphia in 1876, the crowd flocked to see the telephone; later expositions would introduce or popularize the typewriter, electric light, escalators, sound recording, cinema and X-ray machines. It was in this era of emerging mass consumption that many now globally ubiquitous products – candyfloss, hot dogs, the zipper – and brands – Heinz Ketchup and Dr Pepper – began their popular ascent.

Yet, for all their brash commercialism, the world fairs always aspired to be something more than an exercise in product development and marketing. Alongside industry, they showcased the leading edge of ideas and inventions in agriculture, urban management, military technology, medicine and hygiene, the fine arts and music.

Their layouts and catalogues revealed all manner of systems for classifying and studying this increasingly complex world, combining the logics of the museum and the antiquarian, the encyclopaedia and library catalogue. Attracting attention and visitors from all over the world, they provided the perfect environment in which to host international cultural conferences of every kind. The 1893 Chicago Fair was the venue for the World Parliament of Religion, the World's Congress of Representative Women and the International Congress of Mathematicians. In 1904, the St Louis International Congress of the Arts and Sciences gathered thousands of scholars from across the Western world, and set itself the doomed encyclopaedic task of reviewing the state of learning and progress in hundreds of academic and intellectual subdisciplines, quixotically asking whether it might all be seen as one great unifiable system of universal reason.

The form of the world fairs was sufficiently pliable that it could be adapted to any number of imperial or national cultural projects. The Great Exhibition was, of course, a statement of British economic modernity and dominance, when the workshop of the world produced 50 per cent of all manufactured goods, but also noted the increasing global reach and importance of the British Empire. Other European powers, from Spain to Germany, countered with their own spectaculars. The Austro-Hungarian Empire, unable to compete as an industrial centre, made the 1873 Vienna world fair a celebration of education and culture. The Belgians chose the automobile and their new Congolese empire as the stars of their show. The grandest statements of all came from America and France. The 1876 Philadelphia Centennial Exhibition viewed the modern world through the lens of a century of American independence. Chicago, in 1893, dated modernity, a year late, from the Colombian 'discovery' four hundred years beforehand. The French Third Republic tied their Exposition Universelle in 1900 to the new century to come.

Like the modern Olympic Games, the world fairs were urban as well as national or global events, known by their host city rather than their nation state. Although much of the infrastructure of the exhibitions was temporary, pop-up architecture, they all left their mark on the shape and the built fabric of their cities, as well as the urban imagination. The Eiffel Tower, built for the 1889 *Exposition Universelle*, and not envisaged as a permanent structure, is perhaps the best known and now enduring piece of iconic architecture to emerge from the world fairs of the belle époque, but, at the time, the global public thrilled to Joseph Paxton's extraordinary Crystal Palace – the wrought-iron industrial mutant version of the genteel greenhouse – the Rotunda in Vienna and the White City of Chicago. Inevitably, with such enormous numbers attending the world fairs, more commercial and opportunistic spectacles grew up alongside them in an informal fringe, like Buffalo Bill's hugely popular Wild West Show in Paris, in 1889.

Where, then, within this great moving cabinet of curiosities, could one find sport? Initially, it occupied just a small corner: the North Transept Gallery of the Great Exhibition, to be precise, where, as part of the 'Miscellaneous Manufactures and Small Wares' display, the Victorian sporting enthusiast could choose from real tennis rackets, golf balls from Scotland, fishing rods, billiards tables and the first recorded croquet set with the rules included. There was a range of cricket equipment, experimental bats and, 'in the absence of a first-rate bowler', a leather catapult. Gilbert's supplied 'footballs of leather, expressly dressed for the purpose', archers could choose from 'English long bows for ladies and gentlemen, composed of different rare woods.'[3] In 1867, at the Second French Empire's *Exposition Universelle*, a small section of the main grounds were reserved for sport and physical exercise, including a mock-up of a 'Saxon' gymnasium and displays of the new bicycles.

Given that sport was so marginal at these events, it is remarkable how often the exhibitions themselves were compared to the ancient Olympics, with Panhellenic athletic competition amongst the Greek city-states replaced by global economic competition amongst modern nations. The *Spectator* described the Great Exhibition as 'This Olympic Games of industry, this tournament of commerce.' In Philadelphia, in 1876, Americans made the same connection: 'What the Olympic Games were to all the tribes of the Greeks, that are in the spirit of modern times the universal exhibitions to all tribes, all nations of the civilized world.'

While metaphorically useful, sport remained a minor element of the mix until the closing years of the century, a reflection of the still limited levels of participation in organized sport in even the most developed urban cultures of western Europe and the United States. A measure, then, of the increasing popularity and status of sport was its elevated presence at the *Exposition Universelle*, held in Paris in 1889, at which Coubertin and the USFSA helped organize a Congress of Physical Exercises and put on school games, athletics, rowing and swimming tournaments, a demonstration of Swedish Ling gymnastics and a wildly popular Scottish Highland games. At the Chicago World's Fair, the anthropologist, Stuart Cullin, curated a fabulous 'Games of the World' exhibition that displayed card, board and dice games from many cultures, while ample space was allocated to the products of the burgeoning sport-goods industry. The Stock Pavilion, a 15,000-seat arena, alternated between livestock shows and sporting entertainments, including mass demonstrations of Turnen gymnastics by German-Americans and Sokol gymnastics by Czech-Americans, a game of lacrosse played between two Native American teams, games of Gaelic and Association football, and five American football matches, one of which was an early and experimental night game under lights. Three months after opening and beset by money worries, the organizers started putting on more gimmicky spectaculars. In particular, swimming and boat races were staged between teams of Zulus, South Americans, Native Americans, Dahomeans and Turks, recruited from the various concessions and entertainments of the Midway Plaisance. The *Chicago Tribune* reported, 'the races were notable for the lack of clothing worn by the contestants and the serious way in which they went at the task of winning five-dollar gold pieces.'[4]

Thus, at the turn of the century, sport had become a more regular item on the world fairs' menu of events, in its wholesome educational and pedagogic form, as a commercial enterprise and as a curio or theatrical spectacle. All three elements would shape the Olympic Games of 1900, 1904 and 1908, which were held alongside the *Exposition Universelle* in Paris, the Louisiana Purchase Centennial Exposition in St Louis and the Franco-British Imperial Exhibition in London, respectively.

Coubertin had always known that his plan to hold the 1900 games in Paris would coincide with the *Exposition Universelle*, itself in the making since 1892. Assuming that the organizers would welcome the Olympics as the jewel in its sporting and athletic programme, the baron formed a committee and compiled an ambitious plan for Alfred Picard, the stern commissioner in charge of the entire affair. His suggestions were not taken terribly seriously. Picard thought the whole project absurd, and in any case the organizers had long planned to include a very substantial programme of sporting

activities – known as the *Concours internationaux d'exercices physiques et de sports* – to be run by Daniel Mérillon, the head of the
French shooting association. It is sometimes argued that the IOC
ceded control of the 1900 games, but in actual fact they were merely
allowed to label some of the exposition's own programme as Olympic. Coubertin fussed around the edges but had almost no influence
on any aspect of the games.

Things were little better in 1904. Coubertin's travels in the
United States, and the obvious strengths of its amateur and collegiate
sporting cultures, made the country the natural choice for the third
games. He quietly encouraged his contacts in Chicago to bid, and, in
the summer of 1900, a committee was formed by William Harper,
president of the University of Chicago, and a leading city lawyer,
Henry J. Furber, which attracted considerable support from the city's
upmarket athletics clubs and investors. Despite a late bid by St Louis,
the games were awarded to Chicago in 1901; thousands of students
at the university celebrated by raising a huge bonfire on Marshall
Field. In early 1901, a share issue raised money, plans for a new
lakeside stadium with an early version of a retractable roof were
published and, with Alfred J. Spading, the sports-equipment magnate, now on the committee, the idea of a vast Olympic athletics-goods
expo was floated. However, in May 1902, the Louisiana Purchase
Centennial Exhibition, a world fair planned initially for 1903 in
St Louis, was put back a year to 1904. A clash with the Chicago
Olympics was now inevitable and the exhibition organizers, with
millions of dollars sunk into their still incomplete fairground, immediately put it around that they would be holding alternative athletic
entertainments. The St Louis machine ratcheted up the pressure,
seeking the support of the American Athletic Union and making two
ominous visits to Chicago. Alfred Burnham, a shareholder in the
Chicago games, wrote that, 'the St Louis people are "making love" to
the AAU', and that they were 'pulling every string' to make the city
give up the games.[5] The threat of a St Louis sporting alternative to a
Chicago Olympics, and the collapse of the stadium proposals due to
planning regulations, saw Henry J. Furber tell the *Chicago Tribune,*
'We've given up.' He sent a telegram to Coubertin to let him know
that there would have to be change. Coubertin accepted, though he
would pointedly fail to attend the games themselves.

Coubertin would have preferred, one suspects, for the 1906

Athens Olympics not to have happened at all. His memoir on the games was blunt: 'Completely lacking in attraction.' Once again, this was more a judgement on the politics of the occasion than on the quality of the ritual and sporting spectacle. Since King George's appeal, made midway through the 1896 games, to make Greece the permanent home of the modern Olympics, the royal house and its supporters had been busy. A bill enshrining Greece's hosting rights and presenting a quadrennial cycle of Greek Olympics, beginning in 1898, was drafted and passed by parliament. However, the Greek uprising in Ottoman Crete in 1897 that turned into a short Greco-Turkish war distracted everyone from doing anything in 1898. At the same time, advocates for the Greeks on the IOC were also at work. Coubertin continued to dismiss the Greek proposals, allowing them at best to be Panhellenic games, but certainly not official Olympic Games; but, in 1901, the German members of the IOC put the Greek proposal to a vote – that they should stage their own intercalated games in between the IOC's other Olympiads, the first in 1906 – and the Greeks won. Despite the withering disinterest of Coubertin himself, many members of the IOC ware enthusiastic supporters and attended the 1906 games in considerable numbers. The baron sulked in Paris at a congress of his own making on the arts and sport. He was saved from this irksome intrusion into his plans by the political instability of the late Ottoman Empire. Greek government committees were formed to organize further Olympiads in 1910 and 1914, but on both occasions they were stymied and then sidelined by the country's bitter entanglements in Macedonia in 1907 and 1908, and in the Balkan Wars of 1912 and 1913.

Coubertin had long favoured Rome as the site of the 1908 games, rather floridly justifying his choice because, 'there alone, after its excursions to utilitarian America, would Olympus be able to don the sumptuous toga, woven with skill and much thought, in which I had wanted to clothe it from the beginning.'[6] An organizing committee was formed, but never managed to set a budget, raise funds, or make peace with athletic and financial interests in the north of the country. On the verge of returning the games to the IOC, the Italians were offered an honourable way out when Vesuvius erupted. Arguing that scarce funds were required to help with the disaster, the Italians stepped down, leaving the way clear for London and the British aristocratic sporting establishment to finally pick up the Olympic baton.

The 1908 London Olympics was organized by the kind of gentlemen athletes that Coubertin preferred, like the chair of the British Olympic Association, Lord Desborough, an Edwardian politician and sporting polymath, both a big-game hunter and mountaineer, with a flair for fencing, cricket and rowing. Even then, the entire event hinged on the support of Imre Kiralfy, a Hungarian Jew and theatrical impresario, whose Franco-British Imperial Exhibition would provide the stadium and the setting for the games.

Finally, in 1912, Coubertin got what he had been looking for. He had by now regained control over the IOC, removing or neutralizing a number of opponents, and recruiting new blood that would ensure his legacy, like Kanō Jigorō, the Japanese educational reformer and inventor of judo, who was the committee's first Asian member, and the Belgian Count Henri de Baillet-Latour who would in time become Coubertin's successor. Having fended off a bid from Berlin and promised the 1916 games to the Germans, Coubertin and the IOC delivered the 1912 games to Stockholm and the safe hands of Sweden's royal family, army and its eminently gentlemanly sporting establishment, asking that 'the Games must be kept more purely athletic; they must be more dignified, more discreet; more in accordance with classic and artistic requirements; more intimate'.[7] Above all, this was to be the first Olympics since 1896 under the IOC's direction, entirely free of the world-fair and exhibition circuit, but now graced with the ritual and demeanour Coubertin thought appropriate to the gravitas of his project. Despite a few breaches here and there, and its dangerous brush with the commercial populism of the world fairs, the IOC's Olympics at the end of the belle époque remained a gilded world of gentlemanly, European amateur sport. A few working-class professionals did slip in through the back, but they were curtly shown the door. Women swimmers, archers, tennis players and golfers would at least end the exclusive male cadre of Athens 1896, but much of the games and many of its sports remained an entirely masculine preserve. In its own terms, Stockholm 1912 was a considerable success, domestically and internationally, and entrenched the place of the Olympic movement in both global culture and global sport. It was a connection strong enough for the institution and its dalliance with pacifism to survive the trauma of the First World War, then less than two years away. The same could not be said of the dozens of Olympians who would serve in the war and be slaughtered.

TWO

Planned in 1892, lavishly funded by successive French governments, and headed by Alfred Picard, the Paris *Exposition Universelle* of 1900 was the largest and best attended of all the world fairs of the belle époque. It was ideologically ambitious, but ambivalent. On the one hand, it was to serve as, 'a summation of the philosophy of the nineteenth century'; on the other hand, it was intended as a future-orientated exposition of what the new century might look like. Sport was going to be part of that, but in quite what form, it remained to be seen. The efforts of the exhibition organizers to locate sport within its encyclopaedic systems of classification were, on occasion, bizarre. In the official catalogue, skating and fencing were considered subsections of the cutlery industry, rowing was filed under life saving, and track-and-field clubs were listed amongst providential societies.

However, their grasp of the importance of sport was not in doubt. When Coubertin and his committee presented their programme for a 1900 Olympic Games, not dissimilar to that seen at Athens in 1896, Picard was contemptuous, describing them as 'Cheap and unfit to represent the nation', neither grand nor popular nor democratic enough for the French Third Republic.[1] Nor did he have any truck with Coubertin's neo-Hellenism and his strange Olympic spiritualism, which he considered 'absurd anachronisms'.

Thus, the 1900 Olympic Games took place roughly from mid-May to late October, but with no opening ceremony and no closing ceremony, no medals or victory laurels, hymns or choirs, and not a hint of Olympic iconography in the official or publicity material. Officially, they were the *Concours internationaux d'exercices physiques et de sports*, but the press got confused as to what to call any of the events, referring to them, almost at random, as the 'festival games', the 'Olympian festival' and the 'international games'. To this day, it remains a matter of some dispute as to precisely which events were Olympic and which were not, and it is only the IOC's retrospective gaze that makes them so. At the time, almost no one – crowd, competitors or press – thought there was an Olympic Games going on at all.

The sports on show included all of those present at the 1896 games, but for boxing, weightlifting and wrestling. In addition, Paris featured many of the team sports absent from Athens, like football, rugby and cricket, as well as pelota, *jeu de paume*, golf, bowling and croquet. Even further from the Olympic roster of sports, the Paris games included a huge motorsports programme, balloon and motor-boat racing, competitions in the most demotic of pastimes, like fishing and pigeon racing, high-society get-togethers at the golf and the polo, and mass participation events of up to 8,000 gymnasts and 5,000 archers, which dwarfed the smaller international competitions held alongside them. There were also national competitions in military preparedness and life saving, national school games and a prestigious academic congress on hygiene and physiology. Though the athletes were predominately amateurs, there was no ban on professionals, with special competitions set aside for them in lawn tennis, pelota, shooting and cycling.

Stanley Rowley, the Australian sprinter, was not impressed: 'To treat these events as world's championships would be really an insult to the important events they are supposed to be. They are treated by most of the competitors as A HUGE JOKE'.[2] The cricket was reduced to a single match amongst Britons – the touring Devon Wanderers and a team made up of expatriates living in Paris. Football was a three-way affair between English amateurs Upton Park, a French XI pulled together by the USFSA and a bunch of Belgian university students. Mosley Wanderers, the English entrants in a similarly minuscule rugby competition, arrived, played and left on the same day, without knowing that they were at the Olympics. The swimming competition, held in the dirty waters of the Seine, bordered on the comical, featuring an obstacle race that required competitors to climb over a pole, slip under the hull of one boat and then clamber over a second. In croquet, according to the official report, 'M. André Despres, civil engineer by profession and the legislator of croquet, lavished the most enlightened and devoted care on the tournament. Baron Gourgaud provided him with a sand court built specially for the occasion, not without expense, in a pretty corner of the Cercle de Bois de Boulogne.' It was hardly worth it. 'Spectators were not at all numerous; although I must mention an English lover of the game who made the journey from Nice to Paris . . . unless I am very much mistaken, however, this gentleman was the only paying spectator.'[3]

Yet, not everyone was as disappointed as Coubertin. The popular sports newspaper, *L'Auto-Vélo*, went as far as to argue that 'since the time when every four years Olympic Games aroused in Greece and throughout the ancient world extreme emotion, never before has sport been so honoured than this year, never has it gathered such a crowd . . . Sport has definitely become a new religion.'[4]

Four years later the show had gone west and grown even larger: the Louisiana Purchase Centennial Exposition of 1904 was vast in its physical scale. The grounds were built in the same Beaux Arts pop-up style of the 1893 Chicago World's Fair, but they were twice the size, boasting 1,500 buildings, fifty miles of walkways, pavilions from sixty-two nations and forty-three of the then forty-five states of the USA. In its promotional materials it promised not only to turn a buck for the investors putting up nearly twenty million dollars, but to host the by now obligatory 'exhibition of human progress . . . the newest and noblest achievements, its triumph of skills and science, its most approved solutions of social problems.'[5]

The sporting programme ran for over six months, from May to November. Constructed by James Sullivan, also head of the exhibition's Department of Physical Culture and president of the American Athletic Union, it reflected a strain of thinking in America in which sport was not merely a gentlemanly pursuit, but part of what President Theodore Roosevelt had called 'the strenuous life.' With the American frontier now closed, where would the next generation learn the manly virtues and acquire the physical strength that created the nation? Sport, love of the outdoors, scouting and physical recreations, not just for the elite, but for the whole nation were what was required. With the application of new scientific and medical knowledge, and its rational modern forms of training and administration, America could create a nation of healthy sportsmen.

Sullivan's sporting programme, much to Coubertin's chagrin, reflected all these different elements. It included state athletic championships for Missouri schoolboys, intercollegiate basketball and baseball tournaments, the YMCA national athletics championships, days devoted to Gaelic sports and exhibitions of Turnen and Sokol gymnastics, as well as golf, archery, croquet, swimming, lacrosse and fencing competitions.

When it came to the Olympic Games, as understood by the IOC, most of it took place in late August and early September, though it was hard for anyone other than the organizers to get any real sense of the different status of these occasions. Nearly all of the events were hidden away in the small and unadorned Francis Field stadium and gymnasium, which was part of the campus of the University of Washington, tucked into a small corner of the fairground behind the wildly popular aeronautical concourse. Aquatic events had to make do with the artificial lake created by the Palace of Agriculture.

The whole affair began with a virtually non-existent opening ceremony at the Olympic interscholastic meet in May. The chair of the exposition's organizing committee, David Francis, and Secretary of State John Milton Hay walked from the field to their box in the grandstands, 'The Star-Spangled Banner' was played and the races began. It wasn't any grander in August for the beginning of the Olympic programme proper. On this occasion, Francis and James Sullivan took a cursory stroll down a double file of athletes before the band started playing, indicating it was time for everyone to disperse and warm up.

Just 687 athletes came to St Louis, and, of those, 526 were Americans and 56 were from Canada. Amongst the hundred or so from outside of North America, there were small contingents from the British Empire, Cuba, Germany, Austria, Greece, Hungary and Switzerland, but no French, Italian or Scandinavian presence, let alone Asians or Africans. It concluded, not surprisingly, as an overwhelming victory for the Americans, who won seventy of the ninety-four gold medals. In track and field, they won twenty-one out of twenty-two events and took forty-two out of forty-four second and third places.[6] The boxing, the tug of war, cycling, tennis and roque (a short-lived urban American craze for croquet on concrete) were entirely American affairs. Football and lacrosse were North American-only world championships, played between local athletic clubs and Canadian teams. There were some furious encounters between the Americans and the Germans. In the water polo, the Americans deemed that a partially inflated volleyball was suitable for use and that a goal was scored by holding the ball in the net, rather than throwing it into the net. The Germans dubbed this 'soft water polo' and refused to compete. In the diving, the Germans brought their own board, complete with special coconut matting, and insisted that scoring should be on the basis on acrobatic movements alone, rather than the quality of entry into the water. The Americans disagreed. Thus, an incandescent Alfred Braunschweiger refused to compete in a bronze-medal play-off with an American he felt he had already beaten. The German commissioner to the St Louis World's Fair, Dr Theodore Lewald, later a member of the IOC, had donated a bronze statue for the winning diver, but he was so incensed at the outcome that he refused to award it. These spats aside, the American press were reduced to recasting the competition as a domestic duel between the old east-coast establishment and the new universities and athletes of the Pacific west.

The crowd at nearly all the sports was thin, national press coverage was poor and international coverage almost non-existent. What attracted more attention than the official IOC-endorsed Olympic programme at the time was the sporting programme at the Department of Anthropology's model Indian School, designed to show off a sanitized version of the traditional way of life and to demonstrate the power of education as an instrument of assimilation and control.[7] At the Indian School, students boxed, played baseball, ran track-and-field and, as part of the wider sports programme, hosted the first all-Native American college football match. It was played between two Indian schools, Carlisle and Haskill, in front of a standing-room-only crowd, 12,000 strong – bigger than any Olympic crowd in 1904. Most notable of all, and the element of the 1904 games that has had the longest resonance, were the athletic competitions of the Anthropology Days.[8]

Strange as it may seem in the twenty-first century, the presence of a Department of Anthropology and of mock tribal villages and colonial exhibits was to be expected. The presence of indigenous peoples and colonial subjects at the world fairs rose sharply towards the end of the nineteenth century as the tentacles of empire reached ever further around the globe. In the 1880s, for example, the French empire expanded, acquiring new protectorates in Tunisia, Indo-China and Madagascar, as well as increasing its influence in the Pacific, while almost the entirety of Africa was carved up amongst competing European powers. By 1900, the importance of empire was such that, at that year's Paris *Exposition Universelle*, an enormous zone was devoted to the French colonial empire, featuring ten different villages, from French India and the Caribbean to the Pacific and North Africa, and an entire section reserved for the colonial exhibits of other powers. Within the main fairground of the Louisiana Purchase Exposition, in addition to the extensive Indian villages and the presence of the Japanese Ainu and the South American Patagonians, the spoils of the new American empire were on display in the large Philippine village. Under the auspices of the US Department of War, 1,200 Filipinos were assembled to perform in a giant 'reservation'.

Sport and anthropology, science and spectacular came together on the Anthropology Days, dubbed 'the tribal games' by the local press. They were the creation of James Sullivan and William J. McGee, head of the exhibition's Department of Anthropology. McGee, referred to sometimes as 'the overlord of the savages', held to a variant of the scientific racism that located all human beings in a biologically determined hierarchy of races that began with backward black primitivism and ascended to civilized white progress. He was, as far as one can see in his other writings, a pretty conventional European supremacist, but at the fair, taking the opportunity to needle Sullivan and the scientific rationalists of the Department of Physical Culture, he was promoting a romantic athletic primitivism. The press were full of his claims that these more natural, if backward, peoples would prove superior athletes. Between the official fairground and the labour force of the Pike, McGee thought that St Louis had 'a more complete assembly of the peoples of the world than has ever been brought together before.'[9] It was an extraordinary opportunity, therefore, to examine many of the assumptions of anthropology.

To test the theories, two days of games were held, consisting of different 'native' and 'civilized' sports, the results of which could then be compared to those of Caucasian and Olympian athletes. They were, of course, a farce. The participants, many of whom had not the faintest idea of what they were being asked to join in with, were totally unaware of the rules and techniques of Olympic sports. Until just a few days beforehand, McGee was still planning swimming and water-polo events for people who could not swim. Faced with the weight-throwing competition, many of them simply refused to do something so silly. On the first day, they were organized, on a very ad hoc basis, into 'racial teams' – Filipinos, Patagonians, Native Americans, Syrians and Africans – and took part in sprint relay races, the high jump, tug of war, shot-putting, javelin and baseball throwing. Towards the end of the second day, many of the participants organized their own amusements, including pole climbing, mud fighting and archery. The official report of the games concluded, 'The representatives of the savage and uncivilized tribes proved themselves inferior athletes, greatly overrated.'[10] One African had run the hundred-yard dash in a time 'that can be beaten by any twelve-year-old American schoolboy.' It concluded, with some self-satisfaction, 'The savage is not the natural athlete we have been led to believe.' Romantic athleticism in sport might be dead, but pseudoscience that undergirded a hierarchy of race, both athletic and intellectual, was alive and well.

If the St Louis games and its athletes really were the pinnacle of civilization, then the marathon brings to mind Gandhi's quip, when asked what he thought of Western civilization: 'I think it would be a good idea.' Thirty-two runners started the race, but only fourteen finished. The temperatures were in the high nineties (over thirty-five degrees Celsius), the atmosphere was humid and muggy, and all had to contend with great volumes of dust thrown up from the rocky, uneven surfaces of Missouri's hopeless roads. There was no fresh water available to the runners until twelve miles into the race, at which point the American, William Grace, drank so much that he suffered a near fatal haemorrhage of the stomach just four miles further on. Others, erroneously believing that fluid intake during the race would be injurious, subsisted on wet sponges and brandy-drenched flannels. Félix Carvajal, a postman who had made his own way to the games from Cuba, lost his travel money in a dice game in New Orleans, arrived penniless in St Louis, and then ran the race in heavy shoes and cut-down trousers. Despite stopping to eat and to chat to spectators, he finished fourth. Two Africans then working on the Boer War concession, Len Tau and Jan Mashiani, were amongst the few that did finish – for novices, a very creditable ninth and twelfth – and that after Tau had had to run an additional mile to get away from an aggressive dog.

The American Fred Lorz was the first athlete to enter the stadium and 'pandemonium reigned for a few moments', until it became clear that he had made at least part of the way there on the back of a truck and was disqualified. Thomas Hicks, then in second and slowed to a walk, managed to get himself over the line. It transpired that his coach, Charles Lucas, had refused him water during the race, but administered a mad concoction of strychnine, alcohol and egg whites, then perfectly legal. He was lucky; two of the winning American water-polo team were dead six months later, almost certainly having contracted typhoid from the exhibition's lagoon, a sump for the animal and vegetable waste from other exhibits, and a festering pool of bacteria and disease by August.

THREE

In terms of his own direct influence, the 1906 Athens games were the nadir of Coubertin's fortunes. Having been forced to give way by the rest of the IOC over their staging and status, he did his very best to completely ignore them. He printed the games' programme in his *Revue Olympique*, but failed to actually mention the dates of the event. In a later edition, previewing the Athens Olympics, he managed fourteen pages of text inviting the reader to explore the meaning of Greek art and history, but referenced the games themselves just once; amazingly, his recommended tour of Athens failed to include the Olympic stadium on its itinerary.[1] While many members of the IOC did attend the games, Coubertin remained in Paris at a conference on the 'Arts, Letters and Sport' at the Comedie Française; he was lucky that a potential coup, which hatched in Athens in his absence and would have made the Crown Prince of Greece the new president of the IOC, fizzled out. A generation later, an IOC commission chaired by Avery Brundage, the baron's sycophantic American acolyte, would refuse to recognize Athens 1906 as an Olympic Games.

Yet, paradoxically, this was the Olympics that came closest to Coubertin's vision. It was well organized by the right class of people, offered a streamlined but diverse programme of sports in a short, compressed timetable, focused upon a singular and magnificent ancient stadium and was entirely shorn of the ideological clutter and the vulgar, commercial hurly-burly of the world fairs. It attracted more athletes than Athens 1896 and St Louis 1904 combined, and they were, for the most part, of impeccably gentlemanly origins. More than that, the opening ceremony gave the occasion the gravitas and ritual that Coubertin had found so lacking in the previous two games. Both the Greek and the British royal families were in attendance and, for the first time, a parade of nations was conducted in which the 900 participants marched behind name plates and flags, into and around the stadium.

If the course of Greece's international affairs would kill off this threat to Coubertin's Olympics, it remained to be seen whether London 1908, tied like its two predecessors to a huge exhibition, could rescue the experiment from the marginality and insignificance of Paris and St Louis. It did so for four interconnected reasons. First, the character of the Franco-British Imperial Exhibition of 1908 was markedly less ideological and overbearing than the *Exposition Universelle* and the Louisiana Purchase Centennial, animated as they were by the triumphal march of progress and science, and gilded by innumerable academic conferences. London 1908 had neither great intellectual gatherings nor such grand and universalistic aspirations; it was an altogether more comfortable and saccharine celebration of what had practically been achieved. Consequently, the Franco-British exhibition, culturally and spatially, gave a lot more room to the games. Second, issues of racist anthropology aside, the games of 1900 and 1904 did not become entwined with the wider political and cultural messages of their time or their respective world fairs. The games of 1908, by contrast, exposed British imperial anxieties, dramatized most acutely by the conflict between the British and the American athletics teams – an avatar of the wider economic and political conflict between the ruling empire and the rising power. Third, the London games – both in terms of the parade of nations at the opening ceremony and the way in which the games were followed – entrenched the national dimension of these notionally international games; though, what was a nation, and who made up that nation were unresolved questions. Finally, as in 1896, the marathon would deliver a sporting spectacular of sufficient narrative power that the games would become fixed in the wider popular consciousness.

The single most important person in making the London 1908 games happen was not Coubertin, or the chairman of the organizing committee, Lord Desborough, but Imre Kiralfy. Born in Budapest in 1845 as Imre Königsbaum, he and his brother took to the road with a wildly popular Magyar folk-dancing act; they graduated to arranging fetes and fairs in Brussels before heading for America and vaudeville, where their shows acquired a reputation for flamboyance and long lines of chorus girls. In 1887, Imre went into partnership with the circus impresario Phineas Barnum, and took his extravaganzas to a new level with stage versions of *Around the World in*

Eighty Days, *The Fall of Babylon* and *Nero: The Burning of Rome*. He then moved to London, where he was put in charge of the Earls Court exhibition ground in west London, which, though large, was never capacious enough to match Kiralfy's ambitions. He got the opportunity to fulfil them in 1904, when the French and British governments came to a complex series of agreements over colonial spheres of influence, and opened a new era of diplomatic and military cooperation, known colloquially as the *Entente Cordiale*. In this context, there was considerable enthusiasm from the French Chambers of Commerce and others to put on some kind of joint exhibition, and Kiralfy was the man to put it all together.

He acquired royal and governmental support, leased a huge area of old industrial scrubland on the west side of London, near Shepherd's Bush, raised significant investment from the Rothschilds and started putting up the set and building new train links and stations at the site in early 1907. Approached by Lord Desborough and the British Olympic association, who had taken on the games without any real sense of where they would actually stage them, Kiralfy offered them a deal: the exhibition would build them a stadium worthy of the occasion, but take three-quarters of the gate and programme money. He even threw in an advance, desperately needed by the aristocratic but still penurious committee. They, of course, said yes.

Over the nearly six months it was open, 8.4 million people came to see the Franco-British Imperial Exhibition, but everyone knew it as the White City. Inspired by its namesake at the 1893 Chicago World's Fair, it was more architecturally eclectic and light-hearted than its predecessor. Intricate and ornate, the balance of pleasure garden and industrial exhibit was tipped firmly in favour of the former, with its skyline of domes and pinnacles, rotundas and turrets, spires and bell towers. In a single building, one could find features derived from Arabic, Gothic and Far Eastern architecture. Doric columns paralleled Arabian minarets, Siamese balconies hung over shallow ponds, a great network of shaded arcades and sculpted paths led one, in just a short stroll, through Oxbridge colleges and Haussmann's Paris, past the Taj Mahal and the Gare du Nord. But the heart of the White City was its popular pleasures: night-time promenading, lit by a thousand soft electric bulbs; swan boats gliding on the lagoon in the Court of Honour; and the long snaking queue for the Flip-Flap, a fairground ride whose huge cantilevered steel-lattice arms carried thrill seekers high above the exhibition with a chance to view the vastness of imperial London. The ostensible theme of the show, the British and French empires, was consigned to the northern edge of the White City, where visitors could choose from a cluster of colonial palaces: French Tunisia and Algeria, India, Ceylon, Australia and Canada, and, largest of all, a great mock Irish village – Bally-maclinton – where fresh-faced Coleens churned butter and spun wool, in an Ireland cleansed of conflict and republicanism.

The largest structure of all, though, was the stadium. Originally intended to be built with the same wildly extravagant details as the rest of the White City, it was never completed and much of it consisted of exposed scaffolding, temporary fences and very basic benches. But what it lacked in finish, it made up for in scale. The exhibition's advertising, perhaps unaware of the Greek origins of the games, claimed the stadium was 'as broad as the Circus Maximus of ancient Rome and longer than the Coliseum.' One thousand feet long at its greatest extent, it could fit the entire Panathenaic Stadium of 1896 into just the playing field, set within its running track. Rather more impressive, in terms of facilities and finish, was the Imperial Sports Club, built by the exhibition at the south end of the stadium as a base for the organizing committee and the natural home of London society when at the games; for most of the 1,900 aristocrats and diplomats that signed up, from the Duke of Westminster to the Russian ambassador, Shepherd's Bush had been hitherto terra incognita. Another white palace topped by a dome, it was a pop-up Edwardian gentlemen's club, complete with wood-panelled dining and smoking rooms. Membership ensured car parking for the newly motorized, a private entrance to the stadium and the best seats in the house.

Amongst the great wave of commentary that appeared in the British press as to the meaning and purpose of the games, three different currents of thought can be discerned. First, although it was a remarkably quiet voice, one could hear a straightforward, optimistic, international Olympism. Lord Desborough, speaking to the *Daily News* on the eve of the games, argued: 'The underlying hope is that the youth, and especially the athletic youth, of the different nations represented, by meeting each other in friendly rivalry, will get to know each other better and appreciate each other more. Perhaps, indeed, through these Olympic Games good feeling between nation and nation – the good feeling which helps to prevent the outbreak of war – may be at least as well promoted as by diplomatists sitting round a board.'[2]

The *Evening Standard*, however, thought the geopolitical potential of the games was not the possibility of building peace, but the symbolic establishment of Britain's rightful place as the global hegemon, the creator of universal rules, including sporting rules, that were naturally accepted by the rest of the world. The paper also argued that it was not a matter of how many medals the empire won, but the scale of the show and the zeal for leadership that attendance at the games would indicate:

> England has led the way in manly sports. The games which her sons first played, or reduced to order by rules and regulations, have been adopted by many nations. She lays down the law in full assurance that it will be obeyed without assistance from Dreadnoughts and Maxims. Holding the position she does in the world of sport, she will suffer lasting disgrace if the games of 1908 are not only equal in extent and interest to those which preceded them, but so far superior as to develop a vast increase of zeal for those international gatherings.[3]

The *Bystander*, although tongue in cheek, satirized a third attitude to the games: the anxiety that Britain's imperial domination was no longer secure and that the physical and sporting conduct of the nation was both cause and consequence of this decline. It was only a few years since the British army, at the height of the Anglo-South African war, had found that the vast majority of its working-class recruits were in such poor health that they could not be accepted for active service. It wasn't going to be just a matter of showing up and applauding the winners, but being the winners.

> Oh British Empire, great and free.
> Attend! The moment's psychic:
> Rome fell, and so it seems shall we
> Unless we win the high kick.
> Our fame, once great, will wholly go
> To pot – a thought that curdles –
> If in the sprints we make no show
> And fail across the hurdles.[4]

In retrospect, though, this was the twilight of European empires. Ten years later, at the end of the First World War, the German, Russian, Austro-Hungarian and Ottoman empires would be in ruins. Another quarter of a century and a Second World War would dismantle the British, French, Dutch and Belgian versions. The future would be made by nations and nation states. Taking Athens 1906 as its model, the opening ceremony of the 1908 games paid homage to this with a huge parade of nations before King Edward VII and a cluster of European monarchs and crown princes. During the games, the press reported that, 'it was not the names of the individual athletes that leapt to their countrymen's lips but that of their nation, just as the names of Sparta and Athens must have resounded over the plains of Olympia.'[5]

The Americans, in particular, worried about how the overall Olympic athletic championships between nations would be decided, and how many points should be awarded to each nation for a first, second or third place. James Sullivan, head of the US team in London, devised his own system. The *San Francisco Chronicle* went as far as to claim that the British were dreaming up some dastardly counting scheme that would privilege their athletes and ensure the championship. In fact, there was no such system – certainly not one that was ever officially endorsed; the entire conceit was an invention of the press, with the active support of the athletic establishment.

However, as Theodore Cook mused in the 1908 official report, the British were more perplexed by a question of 'no small difficulty': never mind how many points a country accumulated, what actually was a 'country'? The organizers were working with the IOC definition first laid down in 1906, which made a country or a nation, 'any territory having separate representation on the International Olympic Committee; or where no such representation exists, any territory under one sovereign jurisdiction.'[6] The latter half of the rule worked just fine for unambiguously independent nation states, but the first half left room for manoeuvre for territories, nations and identities that had not acquired national independence and, crucially, had a friend on the IOC.

Thus, in both 1906 and 1908, a Bohemian team marched in the parade of nations, though Bohemia was merely a majority Czech-speaking province of the Austro-Hungarian Empire, albeit one with a long-defunct monarchy and a semi-autonomous diet. However, in the IOC's universe, the presence of Jiří Guth-Jarkovský on the committee made it an admissible and separate territory. At the same time, the empire itself was split, in Olympic terms, into an Austrian and Hungarian team, reflecting the uneasy constitutional compromise of 1867, in which the two crowns were given equal standing under a single, centralized imperial state.

The representation of the British Empire, in 1908, proved equally complex, with separate teams and flags for South Africa, Canada, Australasia and Great Britain. Yet South Africa, at the time, was just a geographical expression that politically encompassed four separate colonies and had to be allocated a temporary and quickly invented flag – a red ensign with a springbok. Canada, a confederation of colonies, had the semblance of a nation state at home, but externally it was a mere dominion, its foreign policy and military controlled from London. Australasia was Australia plus New Zealand, the former only coming into existence as a federation of previously separate colonies in 1901, the latter acquiring dominion status in 1907. Great Britain itself might have been considered a nation, but, as the United Kingdom of Great Britain and Ireland, it contained within it a very considerable population who marched under its flag with the greatest of reluctance. In 1904, Tom Kieley won the decathlon, and is listed officially as a member of the British team, but, as a committed Irish nationalist, he disdained the notion and considered himself an independent or Irish competitor. In Athens, in 1906, Peter O'Connor won the gold medal in the hop, step and jump, and silver in the long jump. He had been sent under the aegis of the Gaelic Athletic Association, but the organizers refused to recognize it as a national Olympic committee and he and another two Irish athletes were transferred to the British team. In protest, O'Connor celebrated his victory by scaling a flagpole in the stadium and hoisting an Irish tricolour, guarded by his colleague, Con Leahy.

Flags proved problematic at the 1908 games. For the opening ceremony, the stadium had been bedecked with all the competitors' flags, except that the organizers failed to put up either an American or a Swedish one; to make matters worse, they had managed to hoist a Chinese and a Japanese flag, neither of whom were attending. More politically problematic was the status of the Finnish flag. Part of Sweden until 1809, it was then incorporated in the Russian Empire as the semi-autonomous Duchy of Finland, a status that proved increasingly irksome to the Finnish population, who would eventually declare independence in 1917. The team had arrived late in London due to boiler troubles on their liner, but they made it and, having brought their own flag with them, asked the organizers if they could parade behind it. The Russians, whose team of just six athletes was actually absent from the opening ceremony, flatly refused to countenance this, but accepted the compromise of a Finnish team with nameplate but no flag, marching out of alphabetical order. The same diplomatic solution was used in Stockholm, in 1912, when the Finns again paraded with a nameplate but no flag. The Swedish audience, more knowledgeable of and sympathetic to the Finns' struggle for independence, roundly applauded them, while the band struck up 'The March of the Finnish Cavalry', an old and popular Swedish military march commemorating the Finns' role in the Thirty Years War, given a nationalist edge in 1872 by the lyrics of Finnish composer Zacharias Topelius.

Almost everywhere in the world, the nation was a male nation, with citizenship, the franchise and armed service reserved for men. The Olympic sporting nations proved little different: 1896 was an entirely male affair; 1900, at least as it has been reconstructed in the records, featured twenty-two women playing tennis, golf and croquet. St Louis and Athens 1906 had just six women competitors each: archers in America and tennis players in Greece. The London games managed thirty-seven women, but this was out of a total of 2,008 athletes and restricted to just figure skating and archery, though a group of Danish women gymnasts, performing in non-competitive displays at the games, attracted a lot of attention with the 'graceful proportions of their nether limbs'.

The male gaze was as active as ever in 1912, when forty-seven women competed in Stockholm. Commenting on the parade of nations, the local press noted that, 'whenever the women appeared there was tremendous applause, for the Austrian gymnasts, for the Australian swimmers in their long green coats which had a certain similarity to bath robes, and the Danish female gymnasts.' Male or female, these were, to all intents and purposes, white nations.

Only two athletes of colour competed at the 1908 games: the African-American runner John Taylor, who won a gold medal as part of a relay team, and Tom Longboat, an Onondaga Indian, running in the marathon for Canada. They had few predecessors. At the 1900 games, Constantin Henriquez, a black Haitian medical student at the University of Paris, was a member of the victorious French rugby and tug-of-war teams. In 1904, in addition to the two South Africans who ran their first marathon, there was George Poage, the African-American hurdler and double bronze-medal winner.

The 1908 parade of nations was splendid, and the games themselves featured the largest number of athletes yet to attend a games, but the crowds were desperately disappointing. There were perhaps just 30,000 people present, and they were lost in the vast bowl of the White City stadium, which was easily capable of taking 80,000 or more. The question of attendance at the games was a pressing issue, even before the opening ceremony. The early summer had seen a whole series of Olympic events put on in London – shooting, real and lawn tennis, *jeu de paume*, racquets and polo – but, despite the impeccably elite and aristocratic pedigree of these sports, they failed to disturb the standard beats of the London summer season.

This would perhaps have been less worrying if the ticket prices for the games had been pitched at a wider audience, but cheaper seats were few in number. Even at two shillings they were a stretch for many, and they were uncovered, subject to awful showers and located at a very considerable distance from the action. As *Tatler* acidly put it, 'The general public, who I suppose are the principal patronizers of these affairs, objected, and most rightly too, to be placed for their modest one shilling or two shillings, somewhere in the altitude of the flip-flap and refused to be comforted with the information that the greatest athletic meeting in the world was taking place somewhere far away in the distance.'[7] Crowds were even thinner, and the weather even more dismal, during the opening week, so much so that the *Daily Mail* declared it a matter of national importance, for the foreign press would 'go to their homes with the news that the British race is showing signs of deterioration and that we are decadent alike in sporting instinct and physical endowments.'[8] A second wave of advertising, the blessing of better weather and some sharp reductions in ticket prices brought an upturn in crowds in the second week, which saved the nation's blushes, but hardly filled the stands to the rafters.

For those that did attend, the most compelling narrative thread was the contests and conflicts between Britain and America. The 1908 games were just one small set of sporting conflicts in a much bigger, more complex relationship in which the close linguistic, ethnic and imperial ties of the seventeenth and eighteenth centuries – the War of Independence not withstanding – were being modulated by new Americans with new anti-British grievances. German- and Dutch-Americans had been amongst the biggest critics of the Anglo-South African war. The long and increasingly bitter struggle for Irish home rule and Irish independence resonated throughout the diaspora, but, above all, amongst Irish-Americans, who were enthusiastic and successful athletes. Both the mainstream and the Irish-republican press in America took every opportunity in their coverage of the games to stir these pots.

Even before the Olympics had started, the *World* reported that, 'the arrangements which have been provided for the American Olympic team here in London are unsatisfactory.'[9] The abrasive James Sullivan, appalled by the dismal accommodation available in London, had moved the entire team to Brighton. In the days before the opening ceremony, the Americans clashed with the organizers over the rules of the pole vault and the results of their draw for the heats of the 1,500 metres. The Americans allowed vaulters to dig a small hole in which to strike the pole before jumping, and let them land on a bed of sand. The British allowed neither. The draw for the 1,500 metres, held in secret, had placed four of America's best prospects against each other, with the opportunity for just one to advance. James Sullivan's comments to the American press were part of a rising cacophony of suspicion, hyperbole and nationalist rancour: 'It is either extraordinary bad luck or the manner in which the drawings have been made that has resulted in such unfavourable conditions for the Americans.'[10]

Matters were taken to a higher pitch in the press, reporting on the opening ceremony, which observed that the American team's flag alone was not lowered when presented to King Edward. Ralph Rose, the flag carrier, is supposed to have said, 'This flag dips to no earthly king.' Whether he did or not, that's how the American sporting nation saw and still remembers this very post-colonial act of republican defiance.

Confirmation of British mendacity came in the tug of war and the 400 metres. The Americans, with a scratch team made up of field athletes and wrestlers, were drawn against a team from the Liverpool police force. Observing what they believed to be the regulations, the

Americans wore track shoes. The police wore their standard-issue boots with steel-rimmed heels and demolished the Americans, who claimed immediately that their footwear was inadmissible. The British, while denying that the rules had been broken, and pointing to the importance of technique and teamwork, offered a second round without boots. The furious Americans declined and walked out, and their management, in protest, refused to attend the grand dinner thrown by Lord Desborough that evening. In the retelling of the story, the British team's footwear grew ever larger. The *New York Evening Post* claimed, 'They had inch-thick soles and were heavier than those worn in the English navy and the headman had spikes fastened to his shoes.' The *New York Evening World* thought them 'as big as North River ferryboats.'[11]

The 400-metre final pitted the American favourite, John Carpenter, against a British army lieutenant, Wyndham Halswelle. In the final hundred metres of the race, with Carpenter leading, Halswelle attempted to pass him on the outside, but, in the words of Dr Roscoe Badger, one of the many judges policing this event, 'the further they went, the wider Carpenter went out from the verge, keeping his right shoulder sufficiently in front of Mr Halswelle to prevent his passing.' Carpenter was immediately disqualified, but, after a series of apoplectic encounters between the American and the organizers, a rerun was offered with stringed lanes. Carpenter declined, the rest of the Americans in the race followed, and Halswelle was left to run a second final alone. The US coach, Mike Murphy, commented that 'highway robbery is pretty strong language but there are no other words for it.' The Irish-republican press began calling for the breaking of diplomatic relations and the mainstream weren't far behind.

Yet, for all this, the athletics proved to be an unambiguous American triumph. Great Britain may have won the most medals overall in 1908, but in track and field, which had become the main theatre of opposition, the Americans won thirteen gold medals to Britain's paltry five. The team returned to a New York ticker-tape parade and a personal audience with the very fountainhead of the 'strenuous life' and commander-in-chief of rising progressive America, President Theodore Roosevelt. As *Vanity Fair*, then a London-based magazine, put it: 'The Americans have beaten us decisively. Ask any boy at Eton or Harrow what events he would like to win in the sports and he will tell you . . . the races or one of the jumps.' One had to concede that the American way not only worked, but was the model of the future. *Vanity Fair* went on to say, 'Of course there is a great deal to be said for the British way of taking matters comfortably, and yet doing pretty well thank you', but individual pluck alone would no longer do. British sport, like British society, needed to modernize. 'The individual does not see his little fault: perhaps indeed he cherishes it, but the trainer won't have it; gets it corrected and the man's time improves. Our teams must put themselves under trainers if they would win the next Olympic games.'[12]

While all of this made for tremendous scuttlebutt and sold a lot of papers, it wasn't a truly popular or compelling set of sporting contests; as with both Athens in 1900 and St Louis in 1904, it was the marathon that provided this in 1908. Indeed, the *New York Times*, in hyperbolic mode, reported that, 'It was a spectacle the like of which none living had ever seen and none who saw it expect it to be repeated.'[13] The race was run from the royal castle at Windsor, with the railway station serving as the athletes' dressing room. The course went through the Metroland of north-west London and the growing suburban villages of Uxbridge, Ickenham and Ruislip, before turning south through Harrow and Willesden. By the twenty-mile mark, and despite the provision of hot and cold Oxo, rice pudding and raisins, eau de cologne, brandy and strychnine, fifty-five runners had been whittled down to just twenty-nine, with three out in front: the South African, Charles Heffron; the Italian, Dorando Pietri, a confectioner from Capri; and the Irish-American, Johnny Hayes. With less than two miles to go, Heffron was in the lead and, when offered a glass of champagne by a roadside admirer, he downed it to loud cheers. Half a mile later, on Old Oak Lane, he disintegrated as alcohol-induced cramps set in; a glazed-eyed Pietri took the lead. The *New York Evening Post* described the scene at the stadium: 'Outside the crowd were pressing around the gates, while the police pushed them back, shouting time and time again that there were no more tickets to be had.' Arthur Conan Doyle was on the edge of his seat: 'We are waiting, eighty thousand of us, for the man to appear, waiting anxiously, eagerly, with long, turbulent swayings and heavings, which mark the impatience of the multitude.'[14]

When Pietri entered the stadium, the band started playing 'See, the Conquering Hero Comes', but this conquering hero, clearly utterly exhausted and disorientated, turned the wrong way and started to run away from the finishing line, until herded back in the right direction. 'He staggered along the cinder path like a man in a dream, his gait being neither a walk nor a run, but simply a flounder, with arms shaking and legs tottering.' A strange and unruly semicircle of officials gathered around this Chaplinesque figure, with his odd gait, small moustache and tied handkerchief on his head, desperate to assist but attempting not to. The *New York Evening Post* had the crowd crying, 'Let him alone! Don't kill him! That's not sport!' He fell three times and was caught by helping hands; on the bend of the final straight, he was held up and massaged.

At this point, the American, Johnny Hayes, entered the stadium at a steady lope, with Pietri just yards from the line but on the ground. The *Daily Mail* reported, 'Carried away by the excitement of the moment, two officials raised Dorando to his feet and supported him while he covered ten feeble yards.' Some British officials wanted to deny this, but after incandescent protest from the Americans, the message from the Imperial Sports Club was that Pietri had been disqualified and Hayes made the winner.

At a banquet just a few hours later, Lord Desborough reported that 'Her Majesty [Queen Alexandra] felt so keenly that the Italians should have some honour for the success of their champion that she had decided to present Dorando Pietri with a special cup at her own expense.'[15] At the closing ceremony, she presented cups to both Pietri and to Hayes. The Italian press made the most of the contrast, claiming that Pietri took a glorious lap of honour while the crowd cheered, 'Long Live Italy!' Hayes was carried on a kitchen table by his team mates and *L'Illustrazione Italiana* reported that, 'the applause lacked the warmth and spontaneity of that which an instant earlier had acclaimed the Italian champion. Here and there in the crowd there were boos.'[16] In the following weeks, there would be offers of music-hall stardom, public subscriptions and lavish gifts for the Italian. At the apex of its power, Britain would revel in glorious failure rather than measure itself by the simple steady American metrics of success.

FOUR

Unlike any of its predecessors, Stockholm 1912 was crisis free. There was no funding gap and no last-minute changes of plan or location. Coubertin was more firmly in charge of the IOC, and the IOC more firmly in charge of their own games than ever before. They were able to insist that the Swedes radically expand the rather minimalist programme of games they initially proposed, and introduce Coubertin's own personal sporting hobby-horse – a modern pentathlon for military officers.

The Swedish organizers, for their part, were formed from a powerful cluster of conservative social forces: the royal family, the aristocracy, the military, and industrial capital were all represented. They brought more than a decade's experience of organizing their own winter-sport Nordic games, were allied to a centralized sports federation that mobilized all the different elements of the country's sporting culture, and received the support of the national government, who were quietly funding them via public lotteries, without having to face any scrutiny or debate in the Riksdag – Sweden's parliament.

The IOC did not get things all its own way. The Swedes insisted that they could not tolerate boxing at their games, and Coubertin's persistent request for them to hold an arts Olympiad and competition alongside the sports was turned down; the committee consultations with the Swedish art world resulted in the widespread ridicule of the idea. What they did put on was precisely the kind of ceremonially dignified, gentlemanly festival of sport that Coubertin had always wanted, free of the ideological clutter and commercial vulgarity of the world fairs, but at the same time with a glimpse of the modern – global in its reach, rational in its organization and technologically adept.

Just over 2,400 athletes from twenty-eight countries attended, including, for the first time, teams from Egypt, Serbia, Ottoman

Turkey (with a contingent of Armenians), Japan and Chile, all of which made Stockholm the first games with competitors from every continent. It was also the last games at which athletes could register to compete as a private individual, like the British army officer Arnold Jackson, who, though rejected by the national team, went on to win the gold medal in the 1,500 metres; everyone else came via invitations from their national Olympic committees. The Swedes also rationalized the timetable of the games, setting out a compressed schedule in which nearly all of the events occurred within an extended Olympic week in mid-July.

The sporting programme was also pruned. Experiments with motorsports and ballooning were over. Obviously minority pastimes, like *jeu de paume*, racquets and pelota were abandoned. Cricket, already deemed insufficiently global by the organizers of the 1908 games, was not revived. There was still space for the unusual – Stockholm featured demonstrations of Icelandic wrestling – but not on the main programme. There would, unfortunately, be no repeat of the live-pigeon shooting at Paris 1900, or the magnificent bike-polo tournament held in London, in which two teams of seven cyclists on road bikes charged up and down a football pitch, waving their polo mallets. Electronic timing devices, triggered by the starting gun, were introduced to supplement hand-held stopwatches, and cameras that determined photo finishes were used for the first time. Mindful of the problems over the neutrality of judges at the 1908 games, the Swedes worked hard to raise the technical level of referees and to establish international rules and standards. Both foreign journalists and potential tourists were courted more assiduously than hitherto, and an official film of the games was commissioned.

The needs of the spectators were more closely catered to, with the creation of special noticeboards to display results, and the use of buglers and heralds with megaphones – speaking in Swedish and English – to announce events. Visitors to the aquatic events would find competitors' swim hats coloured by nationality and individually numbered as well. In the realm of ritual, the Swedes kept things very simple: the opening ceremony was a disciplined parade of nations, followed by a hymn, a Swedish prayer, heralds and a short speech from the king. Even then, one American reporter thought it, 'By far the most memorable international event ever.'[1]

The *New York Times* might have been entranced by the ascetic simplicity of the opening ceremony, but, in popular Swedish memory, the games were something much more bountiful – the Sunshine Olympics. Athens 1896 had been blighted by cold unseasonable rains so awful that they had delayed the closing ceremony. Paris, stretched over six months, saw all kinds of weather and little of it good. London 1908 was beset by the vagaries and miseries of a rainy English summer – drizzle, showers and fog – but, in 1912, at last, the Olympics was blessed by warm continuous sunshine: 'The sun burns with an intense July glow down at the Olympic Stadium, and the spectators on its unroofed stands suffer as in a sauna. The ladies have dressed in their thinnest and most see-through blouses and keep their fans in constant motion, while the gentlemen ignore Swedish conventions, take off their jackets and sometimes also their waistcoats, and loosen their starched collars a bit.'[2]

Stockholm was loosening up in the heat, and once stiff and in-different sceptics to the games were melting, even becoming enthralled by the spectacle and – according to the labour movement's newspaper, *Aftonbladet* – acquiring an unhealthy nationalist lust for victory: 'How many human beings in this city have up to now taken an interest in putting the shot? Or in wrestling? This has been roughly on a par with a flea circus in ordinary people's eyes, some-thing extremely vulgar . . . But at this moment director generals and assistant secretaries are on their knees, asking higher powers for victory in wrestling, so as to increases our points score.'[3]

The Paris games, scattered across the city, were overwhelmed by the *Exposition Universelle* and left no trace. In St Louis, the games were penned into the gigantic Exhibition Park, which stood at one remove from the rest of the city and would, and in short order, be entirely demolished. In London, the sheer scale of the main stadium, and the considerably greater status accorded to the games by its British hosts, allowed the Olympics to be architecturally visible within the fantastical White City of the Franco-British exhibition, but its presence in the wider urban environment was limited to the route of the marathon and a fleeting stay at the elite sports clubs, where many of the smaller events – like real tennis and polo – were staged. Athens was a small enough city in 1896 and 1906 for the games to have a real impact, but, even then, only the opening and closing ceremonies and the marathon attracted large crowds.

The combination of fabulous weather and Olympic fever sent

Stockholm and the games outside and into the streets, creating a relationship between the host city and the Olympics that had hitherto eluded it. The newly built main stadium, a romantic brick castle of small rounded towers and turrets, was right in the centre of the city. Attendance at nearly all the events, rowing excepted, was good. Ticket prices were, for the most part, expensive enough to exclude the poor, but the presence of standing spaces in the main stadium ensured a social mix. Above all, on a meadow owned by the army, close to the stadium, a temporary pleasure garden – Olympia – was erected, and attracted a bigger paying crowd than all of the Olympic sports put together.

The Stockholm games were also the first to feature really ecstatic, voluble crowds. A report from the tennis tournament – in Sweden, the most genteel of sports – found that, 'Thunderous applause has over and over again echoed through the pavilion, the spectators have shouted their bravos a hundred times.' It was a crowd engrossed in the minutiae and the drama of the match: 'The game on the court was followed with intense interest, people stamped, tapped their sticks, feet and umbrellas on the floor when a difficult ball was taken, and sighed worse than the players when a ball was missed or went out.'[4] As the photographic evidence of games suggests, there was a very significant female component to the crowd, even more so at elite events, like the tennis, fencing and equestrian competitions, where Stockholm's high society put on the best and biggest hats and dressed up for the occasion.

It was not to everyone's taste. The columnist Else Kleen wrote, 'It is alarming to see pearled silk at two o'clock in the afternoon at a sports competition!' Maria Rieck-Müller, writing in *Idun* magazine, found their engagement even more surprising. 'Who would have imagined thousands of well-mannered Swedish women taking part in ovations with body and soul, the like of which we have hitherto known only through description from exotic galas.'[5]

The crowds also sang, for Stockholm was the most musical of Olympic Games. Athens and London had featured the Olympic hymn and national anthems in their ceremonies, mobilized military bands and large singing choruses, but Stockholm did all of that and boasted at least one band at almost every venue of the games. Not only did they fill in time between events, but, on occasion, also commented upon them. During the parade of nations, the arrival of the Finnish team was met with an impromptu rendition of 'The March of the Finnish Cavalry'. After the final of the 400-metre breaststroke, won by the German, Walter Bathe, ahead of a Swede and a Briton, the band successively struck up the German, Swedish and British national anthems.

Alongside the games, Stockholm was hosting a national song festival, which had attracted 4,000 singers to the capital. An 8,000-seat temporary auditorium had been erected for the musical events, and the festival culminated with 6,000 people performing in the Olympic stadium itself. In this context, and in greater numbers and at higher volumes than ever before, the crowd would break into the old song '*Du gamla, Du fria*', which, without any official endorsement, was emerging as the national anthem. When the Swedish king arrived to see his team play England in the football, the English in the crowd struck up 'For He's a Jolly Good Fellow' and received a royal wave. On one extraordinary occasion, the crowd called for music. Awaiting news of the marathon, 'It seemed as if the huge Olympic Stadium had gone to sleep. Then some strange rhythmic cries were heard from the northern stand . . . Someone found the situation boring and was shouting for music . . . just before the information about the marathon race arrived, a playful waltz was executed, and the northern stand was calm again.'[6]

The crowds were as boisterous, if not more so, at the football, as a Danish report on the Sweden–Holland game makes clear: 'The large stand at the end of the Olympic Stadium was boiling with life, people were waving their hats and flags, they were waving their sticks, they were shouting and the shouts grew to dreadful roars that shook the earth.'[7] Swedes themselves were a little disconcerted by how nationalist fervour could grip their own crowds: 'It is feverish with enthusiasm and boils with resentment, thousands of clenched fists are raised to the skies, in a death blow for the defeated, in salute to the favourites.' In the absence of a Swedish team or athlete, allegiances could be transferred, as they were to the Danes in their football game against England. 'But then the Danes score, and there's an eruption, people applaud, cheer, stamp, shout, rise up, move their hats, wave small Danish flags – just imagine a shy Stockholmer . . . waving a Danish miniature flagpole.'[8] Significantly, the Stockholm games were the first major public event at which the Swedish flag

– still thought of by many Swedes as an aristocratic curiosity – was flown as the emblem of the whole nation.

These kinds of emotion did, on occasion, boil over: enraged by perceived bias in the refereeing of the Sweden–England water-polo match, one Swede stood up and led hundreds of furious members of the audience out in protest; at the conclusion of the Denmark–England match, there was a 'disgraceful episode' of cushion-throwing from the grandstand and onto the pitch. Their own crowds aside, the Swedish press were particularly taken by the American ra-ra-ra collegiate tradition of rooting, with its repetitions and its rhymes and its individualized chants: 'The 200-metres run was electrified by the American cheering team. The name Craig was chanted in an absolutely ear-splitting way.'[9] The Americans certainly felt more at home than they had in London: 'There, cheering and flag waving was frowned upon as bad form and American spectators were criticized for outbursts of enthusiasm and college yells. Here flags and badges are thicker than leaves on trees. Today's proceedings were as tumultuous as a college football game.'[10]

Amongst the most excited of spectators was the baron himself. As he had gleefully announced in his *Revue Olympique*, 'The Holy Ghost of sport illuminated my colleagues and they accepted a competition to which I attach great importance', and now, in Stockholm, the modern pentathlon would make its debut.[11] The idea that there should be a contemporary variant on the classical five-event competition at Olympia had been around in elite sporting circles for some time, particularly the idea that such an event could be a test, even a recruiting ground, for the all-round or complete athlete. For military enthusiasts like the Swede, Victor Balck, a combination of martial disciplines (fencing and riding) with endurance racing was the perfect test of a military officer's capabilities. For aristocratic generalists like Coubertin, struggling with an era of increasing professionalization and specialization, the sporting and intellectual polymath was preferred to the narrow technocrat and the monomaniacal athlete. It was a current of thinking so strong that the French newspaper *Le Matin* could report on its romantic appeal: 'Who do you want to marry? The young modern girl answers: a complete athlete! The complete athlete is fashionable.' The creation of the modern pentathlon was the outcome of considerable debate and committee work, shaped, in part, by questions of practicality and facilities, but, in the official account of the games, Coubertin gave it some legendary flourish: 'The choice of the five diverse and unrelated sports which make up the Modern Pentathlon arose out of the romantic, rough adventures of a liaison officer whose horse is brought down in enemy territory; having defended himself with his pistol and sword he swims across a raging river and delivers the message on foot.' At an earlier stage in the discussion, Coubertin had, somewhat quixotically, imagined a modern pentathlon open to all, with the organizers supplying horses to athletes to ensure this. Even more surprisingly, a fifteen-year-old young woman from Britain, Helen Preece, attempted to register for the competition, only to be rejected by the Swedish Olympic organizers. Consequently, all but three of the competitors held a commission, a young major, George Patton, came sixth for the United States, and all three medallists were lieutenants in the Swedish army.

One might imagine, then, that our Parisian belle would have sought out the gold-medal winner in the modern pentathlon, Gösta Åsbrink, but at Stockholm there no was competition. Apocryphally, the King of Sweden hailed Jim Thorpe, gold medallist in both the pentathlon and the decathlon: 'You, sir, are the greatest athlete in the world,' to which Thorpe apparently replied, 'Thanks, King.' It is a quote that only appeared three decades after the games, in a magazine interview, but its blend of shyness and self-assuredness rings true. Jim Thorpe was born to parents of mixed Native American and European heritage in Oklahoma's Indian Territory. Orphaned, he spent his youth – in between bouts of truancy, backwoods hunting and farm work – as a boarder at the federal government's Carlisle Indian Industrial School in Pennsylvania. Here, he excelled at every sport he turned his hand to – athletics, football, baseball, lacrosse – and won the intercollegiate ballroom-dancing championships in 1912. Thorpe only began training for the decathlon in the spring of that year, and was so unfamiliar with the javelin that, at the US Olympic trials, he threw it from a standing start, unaware that a run-up was permitted. He still came second. His performance in Stockholm remains, for all the complexities of cross-generational comparison, at the very apex of Olympic achievements. Not only did he win the pentathlon and decathlon, but he won them with times and distances that would have brought him another great handful of gold medals in the individual disciplines, and he established records in the decathlon that would, in some cases, last sixty years. On the second day of the event, he had lost his shoes and managed these kinds of performances wearing an odd pair that had been found for him, and thick socks to make them fit.

A year later, stories in the press began to circulate that Thorpe had been paid to play baseball in Rocky Mount, North Carolina, in 1909 and 1910. He had been paid a pittance for his troubles and, despite the fact that the complaint came after the thirty-day statute of limitation laid out in the Olympic rule book, the IOC retrospectively stripped him of his medals and expunged him from the record. In an act of breathtaking meanness, although the IOC gave his family souvenir medals in 1982, they left their records unaltered.

Here, truly, was a cabinet of curiosities: a celebration of human athleticism that excluded, self-evidently, the greatest all-rounder of the era; a festival of peace and pacifism that catered to the cult of the warrior; the apogee of the internationalism of the belle époque, ever more closely aligned with nationalist sentiment, display and power. In Stockholm, the sun had shone on the sporting nations, but even then, in the midst of the most apparently benign patriotism, there were shadows. The Swedes had, at one point, worried that the coming European conflagration would take place during their games. It didn't, but to one rare and prescient German observer, writing in 1913, it was obviously mere prelude. 'The Olympic Games are a war, a real war. You can be sure that many participants are willing to offer – without hesitation – several years of their life for a victory of the fatherlands . . . The Olympic idea of the modern era has given us a symbol of world war which does not show its military character very openly, but – for those who can read sports statistics – it gives us enough insight into world ranking.'[12] In August 1914, they would be put to the test.

3

NOT THE ONLY GAME IN TOWN: THE OLYMPICS AND ITS CHALLENGERS IN THE 1920S

ANTWERP 1920 • PARIS 1924 • AMSTERDAM 1928

CHAMONIX 1924 • ST MORITZ 1928

In whose honour do you now assemble?
What Anchises dead or what Patroclus do you celebrate in
    your funeral games?
Upon that word she ceased,
for on the night a distant murmur stole
that echoed like a torrent in the hills,
the thousand-footed tramp of marching men.

Nearer they came and nearer, till the host
seemed passing the arena; one there was
he who stayed and stood within the lessening arc
of moonlight near us.
Helmeted he came but weaponless.
'We are the dead!' he cried, 'whom you commemorate.
From those warrior hills, whose streams have bled with battle
    we have marched,
from ruined towns and blasted pasturage,
from barren trenches pitted with the steel
of hideous hailstorms, rusted with the rain
of careless blood . . .'

> *Sir Theodore Cook*
> *Pindaric ode, submitted to the Antwerp 1920*
> *Olympics arts competition*

ONE

When the Olympic Games reconvened in Antwerp, in 1920, the stench of death was in the air. Sir Theodore Cook – Oxbridge classicist, Olympic fencer and editor of the *Field* – spoke for many of his class in his Pindaric ode to the games. The goddess Atlanta asks, 'In whose honour do you now assemble? What Anchises dead or what Patroclus do you celebrate in your funeral games?' The dead in the trenches, in Ypres, answer, 'We are the dead . . . we have marched, from ruined towns and blasted pasturage, from barren trenches pitted with the steel of hideous hailstorms'.[1] On the triumphal arch that served as the ceremonial entrance to the hastily reconstructed Olympic stadium, where one might have expected a classical discus thrower, a sculpture of a Belgian soldier lobbing a hand grenade had been placed. Aileen Riggin, the young American diver and gold medallist at the games, took a day off to go sightseeing on the recently evacuated battlefields of Belgium and found the legacy of the war more visceral: 'There were German helmets lying on the field, and we brought some home with us. I picked up a boot and dropped it very hurriedly when I saw that it still had the remains of a human foot inside.'[2] Even the Panglossian Coubertin, reflecting on the opening ceremony of the games, observed, 'here and there could be noticed a person whose gait was less elastic than usual, whose face looked older; but the power of endurance remained great.'[3]

The ceremony itself had begun in Notre Dame Cathedral, where Cardinal Mercier, Prelate of Belgium, addressed athletes, the IOC and international military representatives, saying of sports that, 'Before 1914, they were used as a preparation for war . . . today, they are a preparation for peace . . . and for the dreadful eventualities which have not yet disappeared over the horizon.' In a thinly veiled reference to the Germans, he argued, 'Athletes are not simply a violent and arrogant interpretation of Nietzsche's outlook on life . . . We are not, thank God, savages, and we pride ourselves on civilizing those who still are.'[4]

The idea that Europe and its high sporting tribune – Olympism – was going to be civilizing anyone soon, given the ease and enthusiasm with which sport went to war in August 1914, seemed almost absurd. The Yorkshire cricket captain, A. W. White, had walked off the field of play during a match with Lancashire to join his regiment. The nationalist gymnasts of Germany, France and central Europe did much the same. British rugby closed down and signed up, the nation's football stadiums served as the most important recruiting ground of the nation's armed forces. Henri Desgrange, creator of the Tour de France, raged in the pages of his sports newspaper, *L'Auto*: 'The Prussians are a bunch of bastards . . . dirty square heads . . . You've got to get them this time . . . this is the big match that you have to play and you must use every trick that you have learnt in sport'.[5] Even Baron de Coubertin heard the call and re-joined the French army. He resigned his presidency of the IOC for the duration of the war, arguing, 'I do not think it is right that our committee should be led by a soldier.'

Coubertin, already sixty-one years old, never made it to the front, but amongst the millions of officers and men of every army, younger Olympians could inevitably be found. Thus, the notion of sport as an international peacemaker was amongst the earliest casualties of the war. There were more to come. More than two dozen cyclists from the Tour de France perished, as did over a hundred Olympic athletes. In Britain alone, thirty-four first-class cricketers, twenty-seven England rugby internationals, hundreds of professional footballers and over forty Olympians fell victim to the conflict. A drop in the ocean of blood, a fraction of the nearly 890,000 British war dead, the 1.3 million French, the 1.7 million Germans or the 15 million that perished globally, but they are representative in their way.

Thus, in early 1919, when the IOC first reconvened after the war, its central internationalist political claims looked threadbare and its core athletic constituency – the privileged sporting young men of Europe and Northern America – had been decimated. The British army had lost 13 per cent of its recruits and 20 per cent of its officers, while 28 per cent of the military's Oxbridge graduates from 1910 to 1914 – the spine of British Olympism – perished. The IOC and Coubertin were able to announce, with some trepidation, that the games would be re-established and held in Antwerp in 1920, but it was already clear that the world in which the IOC operated had changed forever, and that the monopoly it once held on international sporting festivals was going to be broken. For the next decade, the Olympic movement would be under attack both ideologically and institutionally.

If, on one hand, the war itself had seriously weakened the Olympic movement, on the other, the political and cultural fallout of the conflict generated new and more powerful alternatives and opponents. First and foremost, the political and cultural landscape of the industrialized world was transformed by the Russian Revolution and the faltering emergence of universal suffrage. Everywhere, the traditional political and social hierarchies were cracking. Labour challenged the rule of capital; women challenged the rule of men. Mass cultures and the new communications technologies threatened the high arts. Each had a sporting dimension. In Europe, the workers' sports movement grew rapidly in size and ambition, and, in the 1920s, was able to host its own Workers' Olympics on a scale that exceeded anything the IOC had managed. Women and the deaf, long excluded on medical and ideological grounds from mainstream sporting organizations, began to organize their own international federations and competitions, and, in the case of women's sport, extract some concessions from the otherwise unbendingly conservative IOC. Progressive politics and excluded minorities, though, had no monopoly over this politicization of sport. The 1920s also saw the steady growth of religious sporting organizations, both Catholic and Protestant, and the reinvention of pre-war hyper-nationalist sport in its fascist guise, first its Italian variant, then German.

If these social movements challenged the IOC on its own territory, aping its ceremonies and sharing its suspicion of commercialism, the booming professional sports of the era challenged the Olympics on entirely different grounds. In the interwar era, American baseball and English football led the way in creating popular, commercial sporting spectaculars. Individual stars and their agents found all kinds of new ways – exhibitions, endorsements, biographies – to turn their athletic skills into a living. The IOC continued to resist the advance of professionals and, when necessary, excluded leading athletes from the games. Finally, the IOC's Eurocentric world, and all the underlying imperial theories of racial superiority that white athletic excellence had underwritten, began to be challenged by a new generation of athletes from the peripheries and the colonies. In the 1920s, China, the Philippines and Japan would send their first Olympians to the games and Japan would win its first medals. Egypt, finally free of direct colonial control, would make its Olympic debut. India, where the forces of nationalism and self-rule were rising, would be allowed a distinct identity at the games, and, in the form of its hockey team, would offer a sharp rebuke to the colonial metropole. Latin-American football would dazzle the world at the games, and the Uruguayans, above all, would offer models of sport and masculinity quite at odds with the starchy formalities and repressed sexualities of the English public school or the European officers' mess.

Despite such a multifaceted set of ideological and political challenges, the Olympic Games remained the pre-eminent global sporting spectacle. Given that the Olympic movement would never be able to match the extraordinary energy of the popular crowds or the saturation coverage of the new celebrities of professional sport, it invested instead in devising new rituals and symbols, traditions, ceremonies and architectural statements that gave the games gravitas, if not stardust. The IOC also proved surprisingly lithe, its philosophy of Olympism just flexible enough to adapt to the changing times: winter sports and women's athletics were incorporated into the games on the IOC's terms. Though still a minute network, it had the institutional stability to manage a transition of leadership from Coubertin, who stepped down in 1924 to be replaced by the Belgian, Count Henri de Baillet-Latour. The IOC was also able to assert its rule over the burgeoning world of international sports federations, and secure its own future with the award of the 1932 and 1936 games to Los Angeles and Berlin. But, before it could step into the future, the Olympics needed to deal with the immediate past.

TWO

What appeared to be the first challenge to the Olympic movement came in June 1919, when the Inter-Allied Games were held in Paris. They were the creation of Elwood Stanley Brown, the chief physical-education officer of the AEF – the American Expeditionary Force – stationed in Europe. Brown had cut his sporting teeth in the YMCA, first as a basketball coach in the United States, and then as a sporting and Protestant evangelical missionary in the Philippines. Once there, he had introduced basketball to America's new colony, where it became the country's most popular sport.[1] Connecting up with the rapidly growing networks of YMCAs across East Asia, Brown was instrumental in staging the Far Eastern games of 1913 – the region's first international multi-sports competition. He was then recruited by the US Army and, together with the YMCA, they provided extensive sporting facilities and recreation opportunities to allied soldiers through the network of Foyers du Soldat sports clubs – over 1,500 of them by the time of the armistice – established behind the front lines.[2]

But just as Brown was using sport to help prosecute the war, he was already beginning to think about how it might help secure the peace. Writing in 1917, he argued, 'Two million men are now engaged in the strenuous game of beating the Hun. When this is suddenly taken away, no mental, moral or social programme, however extensive, will meet the need. Physical action will be the call: games and informal competitive play will be the answer.'[3] Alongside recreational games and regimental competition, Brown called for 'Interallied athletic contests – open only to soldiers of the Allied Armies – a great set of military Olympic Games.' His idea was met with enthusiasm by the army's commander-in-chief in Europe, General Pershing, and a date was set for mid-1919. In an act of imperial largesse, the Americans would actually build a new stadium in the suburbs east of Paris to stage the games, the YMCA would pay, and then they would hand it over to their French hosts.

The British declined an invitation, but teams from sixteen armies and over 1,400 athletes did put in an appearance. Coubertin, alert to the value of the Olympic brand, was alarmed by the newspapers' description of the proposed games as 'the American Olympiad' or the 'Inter-Allied Olympics'. Having secured the agreement of the organizers not to use the term, he felt that, on balance, the games would help revive the sporting world and show, 'that the muscular value and the sporting outburst were not in decline.'[4] Coubertin did not attend, but the people of Paris, starved of this kind of peaceful spectacular, were enthusiastic. What appears as hyperbole in the official report is confirmed as accurate by photographic evidence: 'the games were played before crowds so immense that the number of spectators could not have been increased except by the use of aeroplanes or observation balloons.'[5] Had he attended, the baron might have been less sanguine in his judgement, for the games, held between 22 June and 6 July 1919, were marked by discord and bitter disputations.

In the first place, the games had an unapologetically American slant. Basketball and volleyball, invented by the YMCA in the 1890s and seen as the cutting edge of the new American sporting empire, featured heavily in the programme and would spread across Europe over the next two decades. Baseball was given pride of place at the closing ceremony. American rules for boxing were preferred to the more conventional British rules, while European gymnastics and its regimented hyper-nationalism was explicitly excluded from the schedule. Second, when the Americans were in competition with the French, the atmosphere became volatile – borderline riotous, on occasion – especially at the boxing and water-polo competitions. Even the official report admitted, 'As soon as "La Guerre" was "fini" another "Guerre" started, France against America.'[6] It was a situation not dissimilar to that in the negotiating rooms of the Palace of Versailles, where French and American delegates were bitterly divided over the shape of the new Europe, the form of the emerging peace treaty to be signed and the extent to which Germany would be punished. The French got their way at the treaty table, but the Americans won the games. Better fed, better organized, prepared and funded than the exhausted Europeans, the Americans won almost everything; the *New York Times* delighted in noting how

American performances would have broken French athletic records. The local press considered the games 'an admirable means of propaganda for the United States.' The YMCA was more gung-ho: 'The American Army proved to the world that "all work and no play" is not for the general good of a soldier. The American system of play has made its mark on the world at large.'[7]

In some ways, given the closeness of the IOC to many of the world's militaries, these games were a complementary force rather than a challenge. Even so, they suggested that the Olympics was going to have to adapt to the sporting imperialism of the United States and, more pressingly, to the rising tide of nationalism in sporting competitions.

In fact, the crude oppositions and conflicts of the 1919 games would be repeated many times over in both press coverage of the Olympics and the behaviour of many of its crowds, which constantly challenged and undercut its claims to internationalism and peacemaking. Belgian nationalism, hardly the most rabid or vociferous, erupted at the Antwerp games in 1920 when perceived refereeing injustices cost the hosts a water-polo game and ignited a near riot. *The Times*, appalled by the rancorous nationalism on display at the Paris games in 1924, wrote, 'Miscellaneous turbulence, shameful disorder, storms of abuse, free fights and the drowning of national anthems of friendly nations by shouting and booing are not conducive to an atmosphere of Olympic calm.'[8] Despite repeated attempts by the IOC to ban medal counts and to refuse the idea that anyone could 'win the Olympics', the American press proved relentless and creative in tabulating this. Wherever they came in the table, the press and the public of the new states of Europe – like Finland, Ireland, the Baltic States and Poland – saw their Olympic debuts as vital components in securing and defining the nation. The French Foreign Office, once indifferent to the games, now thought them 'an affair of state', and, prior to the 1920 Antwerp games, thought it, 'absolutely vital that France does not lose in the eyes of the world of athletics, which is predominant in numerous countries such as America, Britain and the Scandinavian countries, the prestige which had been bestowed upon it by that supreme sport: war.'[9] Just two years after the greatest military cataclysm in history, one sustained by the most virulent of nationalism, had come to an end, Justice Weeks, an American member of the IOC, who had pledged to represent the

Olympic movement rather than his home nation, sought the team to the Antwerp games with the thought that 'our fine young men and women are going to carry our flag of victory over there on the battlefield of peace, just as they carried our flag to victory on the battlefields of war.'[10]

THREE

Antwerp's Olympics certainly hadn't been planned as a funeral games, but that is what they became. Left in suspended animation by the war, the decision to hold the 1920 games was reconfirmed in April 1919, but both the IOC and the Belgian organizers knew it was a fraught task, logistically and politically. Coubertin asked that, 'fortune smile on Belgium for its brave and magnificent gesture', and must have been relieved that the thorny question of who would and who would not be invited to the games was shifted from the IOC to the local organizers. The defeated central imperial powers, now reduced to mere nation states – Germany, Turkey, Hungary and Austria – were not invited, nor, consumed by its civil war, was Russia. Indeed, feelings against the Germans ran so high that, in the figure-skating competition, the Swede, Magda Julin, was prevented from performing to Johann Strauss' 'Blue Danube' on the grounds that it was too Teutonic.[1]

The Olympic Games had been awarded to Antwerp in 1913 in a different world.[2] At the IOC Paris congress, the city had outflanked Rome, Budapest and Amsterdam to host the games, the bid backed by a confident coalition of Antwerp's bourgeois sportsmen and the financial and political circles within which they moved. The expensively prepared and sumptuously illustrated guide to the city, which served as the bid's main form of advertising, imagined the games as a celebration of the fine arts, sport and commerce. Antwerp's elite also thought it would be a useful instrument in drumming up business for this port city and centre of the global diamond trade. Sport was at the centre of bourgeois social life in Antwerp, much of it based at the Beerschot Club in the well-heeled suburb of Kiel – the proposed site of the future Olympic stadium. The club itself had been founded by the archetypal sporting dandy of the belle époque in Antwerp – Alfred Grisar. Scion of a wealthy merchant family, he was an accomplished footballer, athlete and polo player, and is reputed to have practised clay-pigeon shooting by asking the Beerschot foot-ball players to practise high punts into the air, which he blew away. When the club steward complained that he was shooting up every last ball in the place, he replied, 'Have no fear; put it all on my bill.'

Given that the organizers had just over a year to put on the games, and given that finances were stretched after four grinding years of war and occupation, the Antwerp Olympics was a little patchy and a little ad hoc. Housing the 2,600 competitors and their coaches was a logistical nightmare. The Red Cross and the Belgian army, who were to have supplied furniture, beds and other equip-ment, were busy dealing with the continent's gigantic refugee crisis, forcing the committee to go and buy their own stuff. The Dutch team ended up on a cramped boat in the harbour, most of the shooters were placed in military barracks, cheap hotels were commandeered for athletes, while the grandees of the national Olympic committees took the best accommodation on offer. The final regulations and schedule of events were sent out late, and the stadium was com-pleted with just days to spare. Yet, on 14 August 1920, to the sound of 200 military bugles, King Albert of the Belgians joined Baron de Coubertin in the now rechristened Olympic stadium. Alongside the usual anthems, cannons and choruses, the Olympic flag, with its five interlocking rings, made its first public appearance. The Olympic oath was sworn for the first time – on this occasion, by the irrepress-ible and flamboyant Belgian fencer Victor Boin.

Reporting on the day, *De Standaard* wrote, 'The grandstand is full but the terraces are predominantly empty.' *Les Sports* made the same point: 'All this is quite nice . . . but it certainly lacks people.' The same problem had been evident a few months earlier at the Belgian Olym-pic trials: 'that stadium was almost completely empty. Athletics thus missed a unique opportunity to gain higher esteem among the "common people".'[3] In part, this was a consequence of hopeless advertising. A report on the opening night of the ice-hockey compe-tition began, 'Friday evening at nine o'clock, the Olympic Games were supposed to begin. How many Antwerp citizens were aware of this? Due to the paper shortage, only a very little advertising has appeared on our walls.' Ticket prices were also beyond the reach of many of Antwerp's poorer citizens; 5,000 francs was the touts' asking price for a ticket to the figure skating. Track cycling, which had a real following amongst workers, was ignored. 'When the cycling races took place, the entrance price to the stadium was much too high for the working class . . . there wasn't a living soul . . . An hour ago a handful of spectators filed out of the velodrome, and the Olympic track races were over.'⁴ The road races were equally poorly attended, a fact that stood in sharp contrast to the gigantic popular celebrations that received Philippe Thys, Belgian winner of that year's Tour de France, in Anderlecht, just a few weeks after the conclusion of the Antwerp games. Even when, a week into the games, the organizers made tickets free to war invalids and school children, and then to everyone else, the people still did not come.

The weather wasn't so great, either. In fact, it was relentlessly bad through most of the games. The official report claimed, 'the track remained in excellent condition, in spite of the extremely wet weather', but British Olympian, Philip Noel-Baker, thought it in a 'precarious condition' and equipped with 'mediocre faculties'. De Standaard was morose: 'the pitiless rain has already spoiled all festivities in Antwerp for four days and is beginning to hamper our Olympiad badly.'

In actual fact, there were two separate Antwerp Olympic Games going on: the francophone bourgeois Olympics, centred on the Beerschot stadium, and a popular fringe, held elsewhere, centred on boxing and football. Belgium was a society deeply divided by class, religion and language. This was true of both sport and politics. Gymnastics, the oldest organized sport in the country, had three separate federations: a francophone bourgeois organization, a workers' federation and a Catholic federation. The fact that they managed to simultaneously perform at an exhibition event at the Olympic stadium was considered politically remarkable. On the right, Flemish nationalists organized opposition to the economic, linguistic and political dominance of Francophone Walloons by establishing their own sports clubs too. This was no mere undercurrent to the games. Just a month before the start of the Olympics, Antwerp's police had shot dead Herman van de Reeck at a Flemish nationalist parade in the city; weeks of protest and demonstrations followed.

Those that did go to the Olympic stadiums saw the athletics and the aquatics dominated by the Americans. Coubertin thought the newly built Stade Nautique 'the best the Olympics had managed so far', Sport Revue described it as 'truly the most beautiful open-air swimming pool in the world', but the Americans – whose dissatisfaction with European facilities and food was a constant refrain of the Olympics of the 1920s – were appalled, describing it as 'a ditch with an embankment, filled with black cold water.' They resorted to the use of woollens and mufflers, hot-water bottles and massage to keep warm. In the long-distance running races, the Finns emerged as a real athletic power. Hans Kolehmainen won the marathon, while the steely eyed twenty-three-year-old Paavo Nurmi won the 10,000-metre and 8,000-metre cross-country races, a gold in the team cross-country, and a silver in the 5,000 metres. Tennis was played at the Beerschot Tennis Club, an exclusive social and sporting milieu in which the local middle classes courted and cavorted. Fencing, an almost exclusively aristocratic sport in Belgium, was originally scheduled to take place in the gardens of the grand Egmont Palace in Brussels, but was moved into a colonial exhibition hall in Antwerp's Middelheim Park. Either way, the locale made sense. The star was the incomparable Italian, Nedo Nadi, who won five medals. Ostend hosted the polo tournament, in which the US and British teams were composed entirely of military officers, the Spanish were, to a man, titled aristocrats, and the Belgians were drawn from the ranks of their haute bourgeois. A similar social mix could be found in the equestrian events, the modern pentathlon and the shooting.

In class terms, rowing at the 1920 games was a liminal zone. The sport itself was divided between the gentlemen amateurs of elite universities and private rowing clubs, and a working-class tradition of racing boatmen and ferryman, big money prizes, riverside spectaculars and wild gambling. It was a conflict underlined by the contest for the single sculls. This pitched the American bricklayer John B. Kelly against Britain's Jack Beresford, son of a factory owner and commissioned army officer. Earlier in the season, the social gap between the two leading contenders for the gold medal was made clear when Kelly was excluded from the prestigious Henley rowing regatta because the rules of the British Amateur Rowing Association banned manual workers from participating – not a regulation that applied to Beresford. This time around, the contest between them would not be by the tree-lined banks and mown riverside lawns of the Thames, but in the Willebroek Maritime Canal, near Brussels. It was a dank strip of industrial water that offered views of reservoirs, oil tanks and dirty factory walls. Coubertin thought it 'a place so hideous that no attempts have been made to try and hide its ugliness.' Kelly took the gold and then went out and won another in the double sculls. America also triumphed in the coxed eights – the most prestigious event of all, normally reserved for Oxbridge and Ivy-League crews – with a team of well-drilled marines and a serious back-up crew of reserve rowers, doctors, cooks and masseurs. Beresford thought their methods 'an eye opener . . . they were magnificent men.'[5] The age of the gentleman amateur was under assault from both the lower orders and the ruthless rationalism of a state bureaucracy.

Without any sense of irony, the official report on the games stated that, 'The large zoology hall is particularly suitable for boxing and wrestling.' They were certainly the sports most likely to attract a rough local crowd. At one point, the demand for tickets was so large that the zoo's management and the massed ranks of its animal keepers had to be deployed to keep the crowds back. As a port town, with its own rough neighbourhoods, Antwerp had a long tradition of tough men and local champions in both sports, but with the best taken by the professional circuit, the remaining locals put up a desperately poor show. *Sport Revue* argued, 'we have only recently got back white bread and coals, and all other things required to strengthen our physical constitution.' One member of the Finnish delegation was remarkably blunt: 'your races, mutilated by the war and by alcohol, are far away from ours. They lack stamina, they dress too warmly even though they live in a moderately warm country.'[6]

There was, however, some success, especially for Flemish Antwerp, in two other popular sports – archery and weightlifting. Hubert Van Innis won four golds and two silvers in the archery competition, including the local eccentricity, popinjay shooting. Rather than hitting distant targets, archers fired upwards at feathered popinjays held on a high tower. In the weightlifting, Frans De Haes won a gold medal in the featherweight competition and was declared, 'This true child of Antwerp, this unbastardized *seijnoor*.' A member of the right-wing nationalist Frontpartij, De Haes' triumph was made into a public and political celebration of Flemish separatist culture.[7]

None of these sports, though, could compare to the popularity of football. Although originally a game of the Belgian elite, learnt from their peers in England or from visiting students, it had quickly spread to the urban working classes. Played in Antwerp, Ghent and Brussels, the football tournament drew more spectators than all of the other events combined. On the day of the final, between Belgium and Czechoslovakia, the Olympic stadium was actually full and local youths dug a tunnel – known colloquially as the 'Olympic trench' – to gain access to the stands. Jean Langenus, a Belgian referee, recalled, 'The Olympic trench had grown into an enormous gate via which thousands poured in. All around the stadium, fans were hanging like bunches of grapes from the colonnades and trees.'[8] Belgium took a two-goal lead early in the first half, while the Czechs resorted to some brutal play. When, just before half time, the referee sent off the Czech defender Karel Steiner for a violent tackle, the whole team joined him, walking off the pitch and forfeiting the game. Belgium were champions and the crowd invaded the pitch, tore down a Czech flag and carried the players on their shoulders.

The official report was fulsome in its own praise: 'in spite of political, economic and even meteorological conditions . . . the VIIth Olympiad took place with mastery, perfection and dignity.' Almost everyone else thought otherwise. The local press, unusually united across the linguistic divide, concluded that the games had happened in their own bourgeois bubble: 'there has been very little interest shown from larger circles . . . moreover, the whole Olympiad seems to have no connection with local life.' *Ons Volk* was tarter: 'The Olympiad of Antwerp seems to have been successful with regard to the participation of the contestants. They failed with regard to the public interest.'[9] They certainly worked with regard to certain private interests. The Beerschot Club had their newly rebuilt stadium; the Grisar family, who owned much of the land around the Beerschot stadium, had seen their property values climb; and, when at last it was revealed that the games were running a substantial deficit, the tab fell to the beleaguered Belgian Olympic Committee and was then quietly picked up by the government and the Belgian taxpayer. Antwerp may have looked desperately antiquated, with one foot still in the belle époque, but, in this regard, at least, it was a hint of the future.

FOUR

Women's participation in sport in Europe and North America had been growing through the late nineteenth century, though invariably within the paternalistic parameters of physical education rather than sporting competition. The coming of the First World War changed that, and Britain, the United States and France were at the leading edge of that shift. Mass conscription of young men meant that large numbers of women were required to fill their places in the industrial labour market. Transport, munitions, factory work – all off limits to women before the war and generally considered far too physical for these frail creatures – now employed them in their tens of thousands. Empowered and emboldened, this generation of women also had access to the previously restricted world of male leisure and recreation – like works and commercial sports clubs and government playing fields. In Britain, women fought their way into athletics, swimming and gymnastics, but it was football that really boomed. Factory teams were formed all across the north of England in the closing years of the First World War, the most famous of them – Dick, Kerr's Ladies – based in a munitions factory in Preston. Playing both competitive fixtures and big charity and fundraising games, women's football proved enormously popular, with crowds as large as 50,000. The shameful decision of the Football Association in 1921 to exclude women from all FA affiliated clubs and fields, a decision copied by other European football associations, brought this era of female football mania to an end. In France, the same energies saw women taking up cycling, football, rugby and track-and-field sports with enthusiasm, and forming the first women-only sports clubs after the First World War.

The Olympic movement was slow, even resistant, in responding to these changes. Coubertin himself thought women's sport 'the most unaesthetic sight human eyes could contemplate', and, in 1912, argued, 'The Olympic Games must be reserved for men . . . We must continue to try to achieve the following definition: the solemn and periodic exaltation of male athleticism, with internationalism as a base, loyalty as a means, art for its setting, and female applause as its reward.[1]' Consequently, there were just sixty-five women competing at Antwerp in 1920, out of 2,561 athletes. This was marginally better than the forty-eight that made it to Stockholm in 1912, but barely. Equestrianism and sailing were open to both genders, though both were overwhelmingly male. The IOC had already decided that only women's fencing would be added to the programme of the 1924 games, while athletics and gymnastics were considered beyond the pale of female participation. Women's competitions were restricted to tennis, swimming and diving. Given the opportunity, this is where the first generation of great women Olympians made their mark.

Women's swimming, which debuted at the 1912 Olympic Games, had come to function as an important subculture in North America and Europe. Swimming became a mark of modernity and self-reliance, a new kind of urban femininity, particularly marked amongst Jewish women in the United States and central Europe. It was a rare zone in which women's competitive sport was encouraged and participants were permitted to dress in a relatively revealing fashion – a fact that ensured the sport would get more photographic coverage in the newspapers than any other women's sport of the era, and that swimmers were constantly being cast as naiads, nymphs or mermaids. Swimming associations everywhere worried about what was permissible, whether athletes should have to wear a robe when not actually in the pool, and issued obsessively detailed dress regulations. By the 1920s, two American women would become the sport's first stars. Gertrude Ederle, daughter of a New York butcher, won a pair of bronze medals at the Paris games, and a gold as part of the freestyle relay team. For the pre-Olympic favourite it was a disappointing haul, but good enough to earn her a place in the returning team's New York ticker-tape parade. However, the pinnacle of her sporting career came in 1926, a year after turning professional, when, at the second attempt, she became the first woman to swim the English Channel, and in a time faster than any of the men who had come before her. The American press thought its social and political meanings to be obvious: 'a battle won for feminism.' She returned to New York to her very own ticker-tape reception on Broadway. For a few years, stage and screen beckoned. President Coolidge came and said hello, Hollywood cast Ederle as herself in *Swim Girl, Swim*, but then injury and illness led her back to obscurity. Sybil Bauer, from Chicago, smashed the men's world record in the 440-yard backstroke prior to the Paris games, and across America there were calls for her to take on the men at the Olympics. It didn't happen, but she took the gold medal and broke the Olympic sprint record. Yet, despite this breathtaking athletic feat, the press coverage was almost desperate to point out her dependence on her male coach, and to feminize her: 'Miss Bauer wears her hair cut short, as so many girl swimmers do, for comfort as well as becomingness. She is not spoiled by her success, and enjoys life very much.'[2]

While swimming could grab the occasional headline and reshape perceptions of women and sport, the influence of tennis – the favoured game of upper-class women – and its two great stars of the 1920s was far wider reaching. The Frenchwoman Suzanne Lenglen, who won the gold in the singles and mixed doubles at Antwerp, and Helen Wills, an American, who did the same at Paris in 1924, were the first women athletes who achieved enduring international celebrity status. Lenglen had a global following and won Wimbledon – then, as now, a greater sporting accolade than the Olympic title – four times between 1919 and 1925. Wills went on an unbroken run of Wimbledon victories from 1927 to 1933 and was the first person to appear on the front cover of *Time* magazine twice. Wills remained an amateur all through her career, but Lenglen was able to carve out a professional life in tennis, and one that was not dependent on poorly paid coaching. A global round of hugely popular exhibition games was combined with a consultancy at the London department store, Selfridges, where she regally held tennis salons, advising ladies on the choice of rackets and suitable dress for the court. Shortly before her untimely death, in 1939, a movie career beckoned when she starred in her first film, the 1935 light drama, *Things are Looking Up*. Wills and Lenglen only played a single, if much anticipated, match against each other, in France, in 1925, narrowly won by Lenglen. In their different ways, both came to define a new kind of athletic femininity, charged with a sexuality and seriousness not encountered before.

Lenglen was noted for her style, the quickness of her movements, the innovative nature of her play and her mastery of a wide range of shots. She struck a slightly louche figure, enjoying sips of brandy between games and a cigarette after the match. Her clothes drew as many comments. Relaxed, appropriate, stylish, she sported daringly sleeveless blouses and dresses, accessorized with silk wraps and brightly coloured headscarves, wore short skirts and gauzy fabric so thin that the silhouette of her lithe, slim body could be clearly discerned. Helen Wills offered less glamour, but her upbringing in southern California, and her looks, gave the American press the endless narrative of the all-American girl made good: a safe middle-class figure in the hitherto supremely haute bourgeois world of the tennis and country club. Her style was altogether tougher than Len-glen's, the press noting how she married 'man-like stokes with feminine grace.' Her signature outfit was the knee-length pleated skirt and the plastic sun-visor, suggesting that she was, on the court, all business – a demeanour characteristic of many sports champions, but one that the male press found difficult to deal with in a woman athlete, describing her as having 'all the warmth and animation of a deceased codfish', or being a 'heartless crusher of lesser talents.'[3]

These complex sporting changes and social currents found their political expression in the shape of Alice Milliat.[4] Born in Nantes in 1884, Milliat had been a rower in her youth and in the early days of her short-lived marriage. Widowed after just four years, and child-less, she found her way into the administration of the emerging women's sports movement in France, first as president of Femina, the country's first women's sports club, then as treasurer of the newly created FSFSF (Federation of French Women's Sports Clubs), and, in 1919, she took on the presidency. In this capacity, she was engaged in both organizing sporting events and influencing public policy – in France, but internationally too. In late 1919, Milliat wrote directly to the IOC requesting that they take on a proper programme of women's sports for the 1920 Antwerp games, only to meet 'A solid wall of refusal.' In response, she and the FSFSF staged the 1921 Inter-national Women's Games in Monte Carlo, with athletes from five nations: France, Britain, Italy, Norway and Sweden. The races were accompanied by displays of the new gymnastic dance methods of the Parisian choreographer Irene Popar, and her students – an attempt to fuse exercise, gymnastics and dance, without resort to the ugly angularity and regimentation of the mainstream masculine gym-nastic traditions. The games were successful enough for a congress to be called in Paris later that year, where, alongside a Franco-

British women's athletics meet, European delegates created a global women's sports organization – the Federation Sportive Feminine Internationale (FSFI) – and made Milliat the president.

They were all back the following year, at Paris' Pershing stadium, where 20,000 spectators gathered to watch the first Women's Olympics – a term still freely available, as the IOC, still blissfully unaware of the laws of intellectual property, singularly failed to copyright or trademark its name or its symbols. Over a single day, seventy-seven athletes from five nations competed in a full track-and-field programme. Although a strikingly radical move for the time, it was not clear that Milliat or the FSFI were bent on a separatist strategy. In their own campaigning work, Milliat would often make a moderate case for the importance of women's sport, or moderate enough to chime with the obsessive natalism of post-war France. Sport nurtured 'an abdominal vigour, a healthy force, a nervous resistance to better address the role of women: motherhood.' In this vein, the FSFI continued to campaign to get women's sport properly represented at the Olympic Games, and for its own work and status to be incorporated into the emerging network of global sport federations.

Initially, the IOC and its allies continued to hold fast to their positions, but it had been rattled. This was the first political test for Count Henri de Baillet-Latour, the new president of the IOC, who had taken over the post from de Coubertin in 1925. A Belgian aristocrat and occasional diplomat, he had been at the centre of the Belgian bourgeois sporting nation for a quarter of a century – organizing its Olympic teams, helping stage the Antwerp games, serving on government bodies and the IOC itself. He brought a modicum of institutional order to the IOC, regularizing its bureaucracy, actually ensuring its decisions were followed up, and working to improve the technical standards of the games' staging and judging. However, in his attitude to amateurism and women in sport, he was as conservative as his predecessor. Conscious of the IOCs brand, he bemoaned the use of the term 'Olympics' by the upstart women. Indeed, he would have preferred no compromise at all with them, writing, 'I can only hope for one thing: to soon see the day when women are completely free from the tutelage of men so that they can organize their own worldwide women's games, because this would allow us to exclude them completely from the Olympic games'.[5] But with the women's sports movement refusing to go away, and the FSFI staging a second Women's Olympics in Gothenburg in 1926, the pressure was on.

Sigfrid Edström, the Swedish president of the newly formed International Amateur Athletic Federation (IAAF), was aware of the threat. Without consulting the FSFI, he made the suggestion to the IOC that the 1928 games should include a limited women's athletic programme and that his new organization should, in some way or another, take control of these threatening independents. Milliat responded vigorously to the limited Olympic offer, arguing, 'Women's participation in the Olympic Games can only make sense if it is total, since women's athletics has proved itself and does not want to serve as an experiment for the Olympic committee.' But she could not get a better deal.[6] At the same time, the FSFI, after much internal discussion, agreed to be regulated by the IAAF, trading its independence for inclusion in the ruling order and the recognition of its own records as official women's world records. It wasn't much, but there was very little more that the FSFI could do. It continued to hold women's international games, in Prague in 1930 and London in 1934, and agreed to drop the term 'Olympics', but its perennial financial problems became terminal when the French government rescinded its subsidy in 1936. Milliat, now exhausted and ill, retired from public life and the FSFI went with her.

She did, however, make it to the Amsterdam games in 1928 as a technical official, and was joined by 290 women from twenty-five countries, almost four times the number in Antwerp just eight years beforehand. Moreover, in addition to the traditional 'feminine' Olympic sports, women were now also competing in gymnastics and in five athletics events. Of these, it was the 800 metres that made the biggest impact. The race was won by the German, Linda Radke; the silver went to the Japanese, Kinuye Hitomi; both, like all 800-metre athletes after a sprint finish, were exhausted. It was all too much for the male athletic establishment. *De Maasbode* wrote, 'It was a pitiful spectacle: to see there girls tumble down after the finish like dead sparrows. This distance is far too strenuous for women.' The *Daily Telegraph*'s correspondent agreed: 'The final of the 800 m for women was a demonstration of what girls may do to suffer and win renown as athletes and made a deep impression on me. But it left me firmly convinced that it would have been better if it had not been done.'[7]

On this kind of evidence, pretty much alone, no more women's races of longer than 200 metres were run at the Olympic Games until 1968.

FIVE

Antwerp had three rivals for the 1920 games; for the next Olympics, Paris had eight. Nine cities, four from North America and five from Europe, bid to host the 1924 games – the most ever, and an indicator of the rising global standing of the Olympics amongst urban elites. If it was a competition, Paris certainly had the advantage, for Coubertin had long planned for the games to return to the French capital, giving his homeland the opportunity to improve on the disastrous organization of the 1900 games and providing a suitable swan song for his retirement as president of the IOC. A quarter of a century since the games had been lost amongst the ballyhoo of the *Exposition Universelle*, and consigned to obscure spaces in the Bois de Boulogne, the place of sport in French high culture had decisively shifted. No longer scorned by the academy, it was increasingly seen as a serious subject of both intellectual engagement and public policy – a point underlined by the Ministry of War taking control of the nation's physical education.[1] French intellectuals, hostile or indifferent to the 1900 games, filled the judging panels of the 1924 Olympic art competition. The French Academy of Fine Arts was enlisted to help, and leading figures from across Europe were recruited, including composers Igor Stravinsky, Béla Bartók and Maurice Ravel, and the then literary giants, Italian proto-fascist polymath, Gabriele D'Annunzio, and the Swedish and Belgian Nobel laureates, Selma Lagerlöf and Maurice Maeterlinck. The musicians on the judging panel took the event so seriously that they felt they could not award a single medal to the entrants. In the literature competition, the French poet, Géo-Charles – the pen name of Charles Guyot, editor of the prestigious *Montparnasse Review* – won the gold medal with his composition, *Jeux Olympiques* – a stage play that combined sport, dance, poetry and music. Jack Butler Yeats – the younger brother of the poet, W. B. Yeats – took a silver medal in the painting competition, and was hailed in the Irish press with the nationalistic fervour others were reserving for their athletes.[2]

Consequently, there was real political support for the games in France. The French Foreign Office took direct control of much of the organization, secured a budget of twenty million francs and built a new Olympic stadium – Stade de Colombes – and a fabulous art-nouveaux swimming complex. As became increasingly commonplace, international politics and domestic economic problems appeared to threaten the hosts on the eve of the games. The international crisis that followed the French occupation of the Ruhr in 1923, and the terrible flooding of Paris that followed that winter, were certainly bad enough for Coubertin to make discreet enquiries to Los Angeles, to see if these prospective hosts might be able to step in, if all else failed. There was, in the end, no need, and the IOC could turn to putting its own house in order.

In an attempt to avert the kind of ugly conflict over biased judging and conflicting regulations that had plagued Antwerp, the IOC began a process of rationalization in the organization of the games. Henceforth, the rules and the Olympic programmes of each sport were to be set by the international federations that governed them, not the IOC. Those sports without such a federation, like archery, would henceforth be excluded from the games. The IOC also took the opportunity to try and trim some of the more unconventional competitions from the games – like the tug of war, golf and the fifty-six-pounds weight-throwing competitions – while those with the most limited geographical reach – like polo, tennis and rugby union – would follow them out of the door after the games concluded.

The games began much as they had in Antwerp, and deployed the same icons and rituals, heralds and trumpets; the basic formula of the athletes' parade, mercifully short speeches, the Olympic flag, hymn, oath and the doves of peace was now in place. Only the addition of the new Olympic motto – *Citius, Altius, Fortius*; Faster, Higher, Stronger – was new. At first sight, the composition of the VIP stands suggested the Olympics was as elite an affair as ever. Alongside Gaston Doumerguè, the president of France, and the usual suspects from the IOC, one would have found the kings of Sweden and Romania; Haile Selassie, the regent of Abyssinia; Britain's heir to the throne, the Prince of Wales; and the American commander-in-chief in France during the war, General Pershing. The opening ceremony, although conducted in torrid summer heat rather than Antwerp's dismal drizzle, was barely altered. However, close inspection suggests three important changes.

First, while the parade of nations still had no Soviet or German presence, the old imperial powers now reappeared as the shrunken nation states, Austria, Hungary, Turkey and Bulgaria. Alongside them, many of the new post-imperial nations of Europe made their debut, including Estonia, Lithuania, Ireland, Poland and Yugoslavia. From Asia, China sent its first team, albeit just two of them, as did the Philippines; from the western hemisphere, Ecuador, Haiti and Uruguay sent theirs. Second, in stark contrast to Antwerp, the Stade de Colombes was full that day and would be full on most of the days that competitions took place. Indeed, all over the city, crowds were large, mixed and ebullient. Paris 1924 was easily the best-attended games so far. There was, of course, an elite and middle-class component to the crowds, but they had a markedly more demotic character than hitherto. While Antwerp had put on trade and art exhibitions, alongside the games, in bourgeois palaces, Paris had an international sporting exposition at the fabulously lowbrow Magic City – the town's most popular amusement park and ballroom. While Antwerp hid boxing and its proletarian crowd away at the Zoo, Paris put it on at the Winter Velodrome, the city centre's liveliest sporting venue, and one that had a predominantly working-class audience for the grand cycling races it staged. Third, the gentlemen of the press, and they were gentlemen, were a bigger contingent than any single national team; almost a thousand journalists were accredited to the games. Moreover, newsreel cameramen were present at almost every event – though, much to the annoyance of the foreign press, all image rights were reserved for French media companies – and, for the first time, competitions were broadcast live on the radio.

Thus, beneath the apparently tranquil water of the IOC's vision of Olympism, this combination of sporting nationalism, popular crowds and a popular sporting press meant that the narrative of the games took a different turn. Indeed, in their immediate aftermath, *The Times* argued that the nationalism on display constituted something close to an international crisis: 'The peace of the world is too precious to justify any risk – however wild the case might seem – of its being sacrificed on the altar of international sport.'[3] The French and US press were considerably less alarmed, but were amongst the most vociferous in publishing national medal tables and attempting to calculate who – despite the opposition of the IOC and its attempt to ban medal tables – might have won the overall Olympic crown.

Although many varieties of nationalism were in play at Paris 1924, none was louder or more evocatively articulated than American nationalism: young, brash and gung-ho. The United States, now more engaged in international politics and clearly challenging for global influence like never before, also had the world's most inventive and garrulous sports press to script the games in heroic terms. On the departure of the American sprinters across the Atlantic, Grantland Rice thought them, 'The greatest sprinting squad ever gathered under one flag since Greece decided . . . that athletic games were the foundation of national fiber.' Some were more prosaic, describing them as, 'America's army of athletes, coaches, trainers, rubbers and managers', but Rice also threw in some myth: 'Modern Jasons who . . . sailed for the golden fleece of Olympic flame.' The French were no less prepared for the symbolic battle. The IOC member, the Marquis de Polignac, speaking in Paris, replied, 'If . . . the United States loves a fighter, they will simply worship France after the Olympic Games.'[4]

The rugby competition, held some months in advance of the main show, certainly set the tone for the rest of the games. Trouble began at customs, where a six-hour wait for French officials to process the team's paperwork saw the US forwards form up as a scrum and force their way off the boat. The local press branded them 'street fighters and saloon brawlers.' In their first game against Romania, the Americans were hissed by the French crowd and afterwards the squad found itself jostled in the streets by irate Parisians. The final against the hosts, played in front of 50,000 people and a very large contingent of police, was far worse. The crowd, hostile from the start, cheered when one American, John O'Neil, left the field with internal stomach injuries. One paper reported that, 'women in the bleachers shrieked instructions at the American players as to what anatomical portions of the visitors they wished destroyed.' But, despite relentless on-field fighting and off-field screaming, the Americans finished 17–3 ahead. The raising of the Stars and Stripes was met by 'cold silence, broken only by cat calls and boos.' One American recalled the medal ceremony taking place in front of people 'who wanted to rip us to shreds.' Another recalled them 'throwing bottles and rocks and clawing at us through the fence.'

Matters continued in a similar vein that summer. The women's diving competition, in which the Americans were dominant, had moments of rancour. Clearly biased national judging roused the crowd, sections of which threatened to throw the judges in the pool, and required the intervention of the gendarmerie in the stands. Johnny Weissmuller, America's leading male swimmer, was repeatedly booed as he powered his way to three freestyle gold medals. Contempt could be returned. In the tennis competition, America's clean sweep of all five gold medals produced the headline, 'America first, the rest nowhere.' The press was full of complaints about the condition of the courts, the sourness of the atmosphere and even the claim, never substantiated, that the local builders had deliberately left peepholes in the women's changing room.

The boxing had the rowdiest crowds of all. In a welterweight bout, the Italian, Giuseppe Oldani, was disqualified by the English referee, T. H. Walker, for continually holding his Canadian opponent. Oldani threw himself to the canvas, imploring the officials to change their mind, bursting theatrically into tears. The crowd, taking his side, bombarded the ring with litter, coins, walking-cane knobs and abuse. Over an hour passed before a guard of American, South African and British boxers could escort the referee from the ring.* Less public, equally furious and more bloody were the duals that resulted from the fencing competition. It was clear in the final round

---

* In the final of the same competition, Jean Delarge of Belgium scored a points victory over the Argentine, Héctor Méndez. This produced a similar response from the Argentinians in the audience. Matters were made substantially worse by a Belgian member of the crowd, who charged into their midst, unfurling a Belgian flag. In the middleweight division, the Englishman Harry Mallin was defeated on points by the Frenchman Roger Brousse. Despite obvious teeth marks on Mallin's chest, the referee had refused to stop the bout. However, the marks had been seen by a Swedish ringside official, who filed a protest. An inquiry was held and determined that Mallin had clearly been bitten. Brousse's only defence was the claim that his jaw would snap involuntarily when punching. He was disqualified and the decision was announced at the next night's boxing competition. Brousse, who was present at the velodrome, was distraught. He was lifted onto the shoulders of his supporters and carried around the arena while fury rose to riot proportions, the crowd heading for the ring and the officials that were present. A large cohort of gendarmes was required to impose some sort of order.

of the sabre competition that Italian fencers were going easy on the team favourite, Oreste Puliti, so as to ease his path to the final. The tactic was denounced by the French judge, Lajoux, and the Hungarian judge, Kovacs. Puliti made threatening remarks to both men and was disqualified. The following evening, Puliti and Kovacs met at the Parisian cabaret, the Folies Bergères. The exchange turned violent and satisfaction was demanded. That November, the two met on the Yugoslav–Italian border and duelled for over an hour, and both men were seriously injured before the contest was stopped.[5]

The Puliti affair alone suggested that, boxing notwithstanding, the games remained an enclave of European upper-class masculinity, structured by nineteenth-century militaristic and hierarchical codes of honour. Here, again, Paris 1924 gave a glimpse of a different kind of athlete staking his claim. Harold Osborn, whose gold medals in the high jump and decathlon made him the athlete of the games, came from a humble farming family in rural Illinois. American swimmer, Johnny Weissmuller, born in Romania, grew up poor, in the coal-mining districts of the east and in the slums of Chicago, before swimming and then the movie industry took him to Beverly Hills. Most unconventional of all, William DeHart Hubbard's gold medal in the long jump was the first to be won by an African American. Shamefully, it was only reported in the black press at home. The British runners, Harold Abrahams and Eric Liddell, won the 100 metres and 400 metres respectively and, in their own ways, broke the model of British aristocratic athletics. Abrahams, despite a very privileged middle-class background, including the army and Oxbridge, was Jewish and thus remained at one remove from the overwhelmingly Anglican and quietly anti-Semitic circles of British Olympian culture. Liddell, who refused to compete in his favoured event (the 100 metres) because its heats were held on a Sunday, was from more lowly clerical stock, whose hard-line Protestant sabbatarianism made him an odd-man-out too.

These athletes were celebrated by their home nations, but none received the global accolades and coverage accorded the Finnish runner, Paavo Nurmi, and the Uruguayan football team. They make an odd couple, the ascetic metronomic Finn and the flamboyant bohemian Latino footballers. But, for all their differences, they brought to the Olympics for the first time a sense of star quality and celebrity that was internationally appealing. Nurmi was simply extraordinary. In the midst of a torrid Parisian heatwave, and on occasion racing through city air polluted by poisonous gases from local factories, Nurmi ran seven races in six days, including the finals of the 5,000 metres and the 1,500 metres within ninety minutes of each other. He won these, as well as the individual cross-country, the team cross-country and the 3,000-metre team race. He would have won the 10,000 metres, if the Finnish team had let him race. Furious at this, he went home and smashed the 10,000-metre record. *Miroir des Sports* was ecstatic: 'Paavo Nurmi goes beyond the limits of humanity.' The *Guardian* memorably captured his intensity:

> He reduced the 1924 Olympic Games in Paris to a farce, a series of exhibition races. In race after race Nurmi would reel off lap after lap, never varying his pace or stride by a fraction, drawing inexorably farther and farther away. He would win by the length of a street, and a blue and white flag would go fluttering up the flagstaff and everybody would stand to attention while the band played the Finnish national anthem. Everybody, that is to say, except Nurmi, for Nurmi would not be there. He did not stop when he had broken the tape; he ran straight to where his clothes were lying on the grass, picked them up, and ran on into the dressing room. And that was the last we saw of him until the next massacre was due to take place.[6]

The Uruguayans offered something very different. Almost totally ignored before their first game against Yugoslavia, who they slaughtered 7–0, they immediately won a huge following amongst the international press and the French public. *Gazzetta dello Sport* wrote of their 'musical phrasing' and 'stylistic perfection.' The Spaniard Enrique Carcellach wrote, 'I did not suspect that football could be brought to this degree of virtuosity. They were playing chess with their feet.' Forty-five thousand then watched them dispatch the hosts 5–1. The final was a complete sell-out, leaving 10,000 ticketless fans outside. Gabriel Hanot was dazzled. Writing after they had beaten Switzerland in the final, 3–0: 'The Uruguayans are supple disciples of the spirit of fitness rather than geometry. They have pushed towards perfection the art of the feint and swerve and the dodge, but they also know how to play quick and direct. They created a beautiful football . . . Before these fine athletes, who are to the English professionals like Arab thoroughbreds next to farm horses, the Swiss were disconcerted.[7]

While the team as a whole was celebrated by the football connoisseurs, it was the Afro-Uruguayan defender José Andrade who captured the public imagination and the newspaper headlines. He was reported slipping out of the team hotel, rubbing shoulders with the elite in tea rooms and brasseries, and taking to the floor to dance to the sounds of Argentinian orchestras. In the press, Andrade's blackness was presented with the same exotic hyper-sexuality accorded to Josephine Baker – the African-American singer who would be a star of the Parisian cabaret circuit for much of the decade. His encounter with the outré author Colette, published in *Le Matin*, captures something of this obsession: 'Uruguayans are a strange combination of civilization and barbarism. Dancing "le tango" they are wonderful, sublime, better than the best gigolo. But they also dance African cannibal dances that make you shiver.'[8]

If the 1924 Paris games had a more demotic atmosphere than the Olympics hitherto, and gave more exposure to women's sport and athletes of colour, its universalism did not extend to the disabled. But, just as French republican traditions and sporting organizations had given a decisive push to women's sport, so they would also help nurture a vision of sport that could encompass bodies whose form and functioning were radically different from the norm. Thus, the first International Deaf Olympics was held in Paris, just weeks after the IOC's games had closed and in many of the same venues, still bathed in Olympian kudos.[9] It is not surprising that this breakthrough should have happened in France, for the development of a distinct and politically organized deaf community here was in advance of any other nation. The work of the Abbé Charles-Michel de l'Épée in the late eighteenth century had established a network of educational institutions for the deaf that incorporated their sign language and made it central to the educational process rather than repressing it. Shaped by the febrile political culture of the revolution and the early republics, and their diamond-hard insistence on equality and universalism, the educated deaf community began to articulate a collective identity and insist on their equal inclusion in the public sphere; as early as 1834, a committee for the defence of French sign language had been established, and with it the deaf community's tradition of mixing sociability, political networking and lavish banqueting.

The political networks and ideas established in the early nine-teenth century were reinvigorated by the decisions of the Milan Conference – shorthand for the infamous Second International Con-gress on Education of the Deaf – held in 1880. This carefully curated selection of reactionary deaf educators – only one of the 164 dele-gates was actually deaf – was brought together with the express intention of making oral language the singular medium of deaf education and either banning sign languages or relegating them to a shameful margin. The French deaf community was amongst the most active and organized in opposing these ideas. It was in this milieu that the first sports club for the deaf emerged. The community caught the same cycling bug that gripped the rest of France and, in Paris, in 1899, Le Club Cycliste des Sourds-Muets was founded. Unlike its hearing counterparts, the club was explicitly open to women. A decade later, two more clubs emerged from leading schools for the deaf: Asnières, for the working classes, and Saint-Jacques, for the bourgeois. By 1921, there were nine. The pull of sports clubs was not merely athletic; indeed, according to this partic-ipant, issues of language and sociability came first: 'We have the same communication problems, the same rejection of sign language. Our need to come together to share our experiences becomes palp-able when we meet. When I finished school I quite naturally gravitated to homes for the deaf and specialist sports associations.'[10]

The key figure in the French deaf sports movement was Eugène Rubens-Alcais, a metal worker, obsessive cyclist and deaf political activist, who, in 1914, founded and edited the journal *Sportsman Silencieux*. It was both a journal of sporting record and an instrument of political action. There remained, in the hearing world, a deep suspicion and prejudice towards the deaf. The argument that sport was somehow more risky or dangerous for the deaf persisted, while the inaccessibility of sign language to the hearing allowed them to perceive the deaf as clannish and untrustworthy. In late 1917 and early 1918, the pages of *Sportsman Silencieux* chronicled a series of furious arguments with the French football authorities. Deaf foot-ballers claimed that they were systematically disadvantaged by officials and had points unfairly docked from their total. *Sportsman Silencieux* was advocating independence: 'The hearing have inter-national federations of cycling, football, athletics, etc. The working classes have the Fédération sportive du travail [Athletic Federation of Workers]. Why then shouldn't there be a specific federation for deaf mutes?' In July 1918, they formed the world's first deaf athletic federation, the FSSMF (Federation Sportive des Sourds-Muets de France – the French Athletic Federation of Deaf Mutes). They also acquired a powerful political patron, Henri Pate, the high commissioner for sports at the Ministry of War, who forced the national sports federations to accept the FSSMF as a legitimate partner. Emboldened by these successes, *Sportsman Silencieux* made the case for an international federation of deaf sports organizations and then, inevitably, for staging a Deaf Olympics. 'It is France that rekindled the true Olympic spirit and now, thirty years later, the games are once again to be held in Paris after a tour of the world. It is France which opened the first school for deaf mutes . . . thus it is to France that the privilege of hosting the first Deaf Olympics should devolve.'

The games took their ceremonial cue from the Olympics, opening at the Pershing stadium with a parade of the 140 athletes that attended from nine European countries, though no Germans were allowed; teams wore national uniforms, the Belgians in red, the French in blue; a representative of the Ministry of War watched the Olympic oath sworn in international sign language. There was a week of athletics, swimming, football, tennis, shooting and cycling, and the French won almost everything, but there is no record of competitive medal counts or official disputations. In fact, the main reports are of a fantastically good banquet. Two hundred and fifty guests gathered – foreign delegations, Parisian politicians, representatives of the French government and the entire deaf intelligentsia – to trade toasts, speeches and congratulations. The party made it through to six o'clock in the morning, closing with cheers – signed and spoken – of '*Vivent les Sports!*' and '*Vive a Jamais l'Entente Cordiale!*'

SIX

If the IOC and its Olympic Games were challenged by the sports movements of the marginalized, and forced to cede some ground, the 1920s saw it open up new territory: winter sports. Prior to 1924, figure skating had made an appearance at the London and Antwerp games, and the Belgians had hosted a small ice-hockey tournament as well, but both the IOC and the Nordic sports movement had resisted the incorporation of the most popular and widespread sports: skiing, skating, sledging. The Scandinavians, particularly the Swede, Colonel Victor Balck – a member of the IOC and a key figure in the creation of the Nordic Games, the region's own winter-sports festival – were keen to preserve their exclusive cultural control over these sports.[1] The IOC, and primarily Coubertin, were generally indifferent and on occasion scornful of winter sports. He found the alliance of Swiss hoteliers and English eccentrics that created the new Alpine version of skiing particularly odious: 'The number of those participating has greatly increased . . . but the quality has fallen . . . The fault . . . lies with . . . the hoteliers who outbid each other [from] solely pecuniary interest, and hence the new clientele they have thus produced . . . Noisy and intrusive . . . idlers . . . sports humbugs . . . poseurs with leggings and jerseys.'[2]

However, the organizing committee of the 1924 Paris games, ably supported by their own Alpine tourist industry and both central and provincial governments, insisted on holding a winter sports festival in Chamonix in 1924.[3] As an advert for the French tourist industry, it was mixed. The influx of athletes, coaches and spectators resulted in an accommodation crisis; private homes were mobilized and opulent ballrooms and billiard halls converted into dormitories. Nonetheless, over 250 athletes from sixteen nations put on a show with enough show business to overload the region's transport system with the curious, and enough gravitas that, on hearing of the death of former US president, Woodrow Wilson, the ice-hockey final between Canada and the United States featured a special rendition of 'The Star-Spangled Banner', tributes to the deceased, and flags hung at half mast. At the closing ceremony, Coubertin struck an odd note when he awarded a special Olympic prize to mountaineering in general – for its supposed Olympian purity. Never ones to miss an opportunity, though, Coubertin and the IOC could see that the winter games worked, and retrospectively announced the festival was now the first Olympic winter games. Over the next two years, they steadily ground down their Scandinavian opponents, who acquiesced to the holding of the Winter Olympic Games every four years, the next to be held in St Moritz in 1928. The Nordic Games continued, but they dwindled in size and resonance. Winter sports were now brought within the IOC's sporting empire.

Nordic skiing, and its complex relationship to national identities in Scandinavia, especially Norway, was just one of the IOC's new protectorates. The Chamonix games also featured distance skating, curling and ice hockey, and, although all of these sports had begun to acquire a cosmopolitan appeal, they were also closely tied to the emergent national identities and cultures of the Netherlands, Scotland and Canada respectively. Sledging, bobsleigh and the emerging disciplines of Alpine skiing brought a different constituency to the winter games, and one that would be most important in shaping them over the next century: winter-sports resort owners, ambitious local governments and eccentric sports pioneers and adrenalin junkies, from the inventors of downhill and slalom skiing before the Second World War, to the creators of snowboarding, mogulling and freestyling in the late twentieth century.

Skiing, although widespread across Eurasia as a mode of transport, emerged in its modern sporting form in Norway in the third quarter of the nineteenth century. It had survived as a mode of transport and recreation in rural Norway, returning to the capital, Christiania – later, Oslo – via civil servants and military officers who had served in the provinces, and visiting university students from all over the country. The fascination with skiing was part of a wider revival of Norwegian folklore that served as the ideological ingredient of a nascent Norwegian nationalism. Prior to 1814, Norway had been ruled by Denmark, but was ceded to Sweden, which had ruled the country as a dual monarchy. From the mid-century, a Norwegian nationalist and then independence movement emerged. By the time the first organized skiing race was held in 1866, the local press was reporting that the arena was 'Seething with ladies and gentlemen who wanted to be spectators at this lively, attractive and genuinely Norwegian spectacle.'[4] Other reports claimed that 'skiing, that true national sport which, having once been practised . . . all over the country, then . . . was falling into disuse . . . has now re-emerged . . . as one of the best exercises.' New ski designs and sticks had made long cross-country races much easier, and new bindings and ramps allowed ski jumping to develop.

What turned skiing into a national obsession and a cultic representation of the new Norway was Fridtjof Nansen's 1888 ski-trek across Greenland. A scientific rather than a sporting expedition, Nansen was not actually a devotee of modern sport and competitive forms of skiing; indeed, he disapproved. Yet, despite the moralizing of his much-read journals, the relationship between Norway, skiing and sport was sealed by his celebrity. The Swedes embraced skiing in the late nineteenth century, and its sporting elites, like Colonel Balck, saw the sport as a way of defining and showcasing both Swedish and more widely Nordic values and identities. Every year but one between 1901 and 1926, the Swedes staged an annual week of Nordic games in Stockholm, combining skating, skiing, ice hockey, bandy and dog-sled racing with picaresque displays of peasant costumes and handicrafts, in an eclectic mix of winter sports, Scandinavian romanticism, royalism and nationalism.

Skating on blades honed from the shank bones and the ribs of large mammals is, according to an archaeological record that stretches from China to Finland, at least 3,000 years old. However, modern skating, using metal blades and sharpened edges, which allow far greater speeds and manoeuvrability, begins in the Netherlands in the fifteenth and sixteenth centuries. The technology spread to Britain and across northern Europe over the next hundred years. During the eighteenth and nineteenth centuries, skating took two divergent paths. Amongst aristocratic and bourgeois circles, in particular, figure skating came to be the dominant practice. In Louis XVI's France, it was a pastime of the court alone; in Germany, for many years, women were excluded. In the late nineteenth and early twentieth century, it was codified as a competitive sport in Britain, but its stiff, formal choreography was challenged by the technical wizardry of continental Europeans, like the Swede, Ulrich Salchow, and by the balletic and dance-influenced skating of Americans, like Jackson Haines.[5]

However, in the Netherlands and the fenlands of eastern England, skating remained a popular cross-class activity, with a preference for racing. Both landscapes were criss-crossed with ditches, rivers, canals and lakes. Both were blessed by winters that were cold enough to properly freeze these natural racing rinks, but mild enough that they were not constantly covered in snow or swept by winds so fierce that no recreation was possible. In this context, landlord and tavern owners were enthusiastic promoters of races, offering prizes for the winners and selling drinks at the rest stops. Audiences for the events were huge and cut across class, gender and region. Alongside this, a small amateur skating movement emerged, upper class in origin and, through its amateurism rules, determined to exclude the professionals and provincials – a move that made the popular nationalism of the Dutch skate-scene even more intense.

The people of northern Europe have been hurling flat-bottomed objects across the ice since the Romans left town. In the sixteenth-century paintings of Pieter Bruegel, the Dutch appear to be rolling stones across a frozen pond at a target. A Bavarian and Austrian version of the game – *Eisstockschießen* – appears in medieval chronicles. However, the version that emerged as the international standard in the nineteenth and twentieth centuries was the Scottish game, curling. The game featured in the novels of Walter Scott, was a favourite topic of the most literate members of the Scottish Kirk and appeared in the work of three key members of the Scots poetic canon: Allan Ramsay, James Hogg and Robert Burns. In 'Tam Samson's Elegy', Burns evocatively captures the place of curling in the Scottish winter:

> When winter muffles up his cloak:
> And Binds the mire like a rock;
> When to the loughs the curlers flock,
> Wi' Gleesome speed

By the nineteenth century, the sport was often referred to as 'Scotland's ain game.' Over time, the Scots introduced rounded and polished stones, for smoothness of movement, an iron handle on the stone, to allow sophisticated spin and control, and they abandoned contests over distance while developing the modern form of curling as bowls on ice. Curling organizations formed in Edinburgh in the eighteenth century, while, in the early nineteenth, the Royal Caledonian Curling Club became the custodian of the sport and its rules. From here, diasporic Scots carried the game to continental Europe, western Canada and the northern United States, where it proved phenomenally popular.[6]

Canada may have had the largest number of curlers in the world, but the office of national sport had been unambiguously claimed by ice hockey. The game emerged out of multiple experiments with a variety of ball-and-stick games on the ice parks and lakes of colonial nineteenth-century Canada. English field hockey, shinty and bandy all combined to produce a game first codified by the elite students of McGill University in Montreal, in 1879, who, for the first time, played with a wooden puck rather than a ball. Within twenty years there would be a club in every village and town in Canada; Montreal itself would have over one hundred; in this, it was truly rare – a popular cultural phenomenon, equally at home in francophone and anglophone Canada. By the turn of the century, the game would have spread across the arboreal Midwest and eastern seaboard of the United States. Not merely a popular craze, it had gone professional in a variety of new leagues, and acquired its ultimate trophy, the Stanley Cup, from a retiring governor general of Canada. By the time the Canadians won their gold medals at Chamonix in 1924, and St Moritz, 1928, they were the unquestioned masters of the game, winning the tournament without conceding a single goal.

The Canadians swept that opposition aside on a rink built by the exclusive Kulm Hotel in St Moritz. The alliance of the games with Alpine hoteliers established in Chamonix took a leap forward in this most upmarket of Alpine resorts. For many years, the town had survived as a site of pilgrimage and as a spa, but in the late nineteenth century it got a massive boost from a new kind of health tourism. Beginning in Davos, but spreading across the Swiss Alps, sufferers from tuberculosis came to take the mountain air and recover, and the English were amongst the most enthusiastic. While some took to their beds or merely walked briskly, an eccentric selection of English travellers, bon viveurs and daredevils took to sledding and tobogganing. Indeed, the craze got so out of hand that Caspar Badrutt, owner of the Kulm Hotel, built the first dedicated half-pipe run for sledging, to keep them off the streets and in his expensive suites. It worked.

In 1885, British military officers formed the St Moritz Tobogganing Club and went one stage further than Badrutt, creating the first purpose-built toboggan course, the Cresta Run. A second track was added in 1902, for bobsleigh, which apocryphally had begun life when an Englishman, Wilson Smith, strapped two sleds together and took them for a ride. In 1928, the Cresta Run hosted the bobsleigh competition at the St Moritz Winter Olympics and gave birth to the skeleton – tobogganing head-first down the Cresta Run. Hitherto, the Olympics had failed to capture the speed and adrenalin mania of the new motorsports that were proving so popular in Europe: here at least, at the end of the roaring twenties, it had a response.

SEVEN

At their most sententious, early twentieth-century socialist intellectuals simply despised physical culture in general and sport in particular. Lenin's colleague, Nikolay Valentinov, recalled one such comrade: 'There were things in my room that made him turn away with unconcealed disgust: heavy dumb-bells and weights. He was unable to understand how a man calling himself a Social Democrat, or simply any intelligent man, could take any interest in athletics, in such rough "circus" business as weight-lifting.'[1] However, by the 1920s, Fritz Wildung, a German social democrat and a key figure in building the workers' sports movement in Europe, could make the quite contrary argument: 'The sport of the proletariat must be placed in the service of socialism. It should become a powerful lever of the new culture, whose bearer will be the proletariat. Sport is a chain breaker . . . a liberator from physical and spiritual slavery.'[2] By the late 1920s, even the most ascetic Bolshevik had come round to the role of sports in the global class struggle. For a brief moment, the workers' sports movement offered a real ideological challenge to Olympism, its Workers' Olympics a real alternative cosmopolitan spectacle.

This shift was driven by the early and enthusiastic embrace of sport by the German working class. In the early 1890s, Bismarck's anti-socialist laws were revoked. Workers' organizations of all kinds, previously illegal, were now permitted, and amongst the fastest growing of these were sports clubs. Drawing on a tradition of radical democratic gymnastic clubs, born of the 1848 revolutions, and the example of political purpose in sport given by the ultra-nationalist Turnen gymnastic clubs, German workers were quick to form their own sporting clubs and national associations, or break from bourgeois organizations. By 1914, these clubs could boast almost 200,000 members, including a free sailing association, a national network of workers' chess clubs and the immensely popular Di Natur Freunde, a workers' hiking and nature-walking movement. As late as 1908, one German socialist legislator still worried that, if workers joined cycling clubs, 'when will they get the free time for trade union and party work?' But this kind of criticism was soon lost beneath a wave of new arguments for worker sport: it was a practical political tool; the personal health and well-being of workers was itself of political import; and sport could nurture the alternative cultural values of a socialist society.[3]

Worker cyclists were amongst the most militant in Germany, like young men and women across the continent, invigorated and liberated by access to this cheap and life-changing form of transport. 'When we consider the party and the trade union in this class war as the main block of the army which is marching forward like the infantry and the artillery, then we worker cyclists are the red hussars, the cavalry of the class war. We can reach territory which is inaccessible for the main forces . . . and we can directly use bicycles for the class struggle.' Drawing on the biological and medical arguments normally reserved for nationalists and eugenists, some German socialists began to argue that, 'Sport is an instrument of class hygiene . . . It is a means of the upbreeding of the class.' Sport was also seen as a way of keeping workers away from alcohol and its attendant social problems. A more individualistic and liberatory conception of physical exercise was offered in this pamphlet:[4]

Workers and Physical Culturalists!

Ever more workers are realizing that free physical culture is part of your socialist education.

You do not have liberty over your own body, as your work, as your living conditions are hindering you from being yourself.

Liberate yourself from these coercions. Liberate yourself from prejudices even toward your nude body!

The workers' front must stand together in the liberation of the body.

All agreed that the ultimate point of sport was that it 'strengthens the chances of the proletarian class to be physically prepared for the class war.' At the same time, worker sports offered an intellectual critique of the alternatives. Olympian elitism was challenged: 'Bourgeois sport is without exception geared to individual top performance. Records! Records! Records! That is the magic word that defines everything.'[5] Commercialized sports were castigated at the same time: 'people who go in for professional sport, their bodies become merchandise, they are bought and sold and cast aside when they are useless.' By contrast, workers' sports would be open – especially welcoming to women – and alongside a reasonable level of competition, it would also make space for mass participation and socialist pageants. In this world, working-class youths could be shielded from bourgeois and nationalist values; physical culture would serve as the international language of peace and solidarity.

Following the German example, workers' sports clubs began to emerge around the turn of the century in Switzerland and the Czech lands of the Austro-Hungarian Empire, as well as in the imperial cities of Vienna and Budapest. A decade later, they were followed by their Scandinavian, British, French and Belgian peers, and the first informal international competitions between worker athletes were held in 1913 in France, Germany and Belgium.

Internationalism and anti-militarism had always been a component of the early workers'-sport movement, but, in the wake of the First World War, it became, perhaps, its central concern. As early as 1919, the Socialist International had approved the creation of an international socialist sports movement. At the Lucerne Congress, held in September 1920, the Socialist Workers' Sports International (SWSI) was launched, promising, 'The cultivation of physical exercise, sport, gymnastics and hiking within the working classes and especially among the youth of both sexes.' Above all, with the intention that, 'in our sporting events we must face each other eye to eye and get to know that none of us is the enemy.'[6]

By 1930, the SWSI could boast a membership of over four million people, making it, by some way, the largest working-class cultural movement of the era. Germany remained the heartland, with over one and a half million members. Elsewhere, its strongholds were in Switzerland, Austria and the newly independent Czechoslovakia, Poland and Finland. As with the wider politics of the era, the Czechs and the Poles were fragmented by language and ethnicity. In Poland alone, there were four separate workers' sports organizations, for Poles, Ukrainians, Germans and Jews. In Austria, Red Vienna was the redoubt of socialism. Its sports movement boasted a quarter of a million members, and, after acquiring a renovated aerodrome, it possessed the largest gym hall in the world. Members could also be found outside Europe, as a small worker-sport movement developed in the US and Canada, while, in Palestine, the leftist Hapoel movement separated from the Maccabi sports clubs and joined the SWSI. French and British contributions, though, were small: the French, hampered by viscous internal discord, the British by the almost complete indifference of the Labour party and the trade-union movement to the project.[7]

Always planned as an alternative to the IOC games, from which the Germans were still excluded, the SWSI held its first Workers' Olympics in Frankfurt, in 1925. With financial backing from both the national government and Frankfurt's liberal Jewish mayor, Ludwig Landmann, 75,000 Reichsmarks was spent putting on the show. Schools, municipal buildings and the city's athletic stadium were draped in bunting and flags; temporary tent cities were thrown up to accommodate the tens of thousands of visitors. The whole event was on a scale that far exceeded anything put on at the IOC's games. One hundred and fifty thousand people watched the opening ceremony, during which a vast parade of 8,000 gymnasts marched into the stadium. The local socialist press eulogized: 'Like a powerful battalion of the proletariat behind a sea of red flags, living lines and diagonals, well trained harmonic bodies, only dressed with short black trousers, stood stiff like stone pillars or waved in the cadence of the music. It was an unforgettable sight of health, life and strength and in sync united tanned bodies . . . the female gymnasts were another fabulous sight, the bodies of future mothers bending in the sunlight.'[8]

A choir of 1,200 sang 'The Internationale' beneath the slogan 'no more war'. It was noted how well the French, in particular, were received by their erstwhile foes. Alongside a huge programme of athletic events and mass gymnastic displays, there were musical marches, children's parades and a performance by 60,000 people of the piece, 'Workers' Struggle for the Earth', in which the Choir of the Powerful and the Choir of Diplomats served as chorus to the fight between finance capital and the youth of the world. The local liberal press concluded, 'One might politically stand to these activities as one wishes but the first 1925 Workers' Olympics has been such a generous event. Nobody should underestimate the strength of working class sports organisations'.[9]

The 1925 games certainly gave the impression of a strong and unified workers' sports movement, but, as with every aspect of the politics of the left in the interwar era, its potential was undermined by the fundamental split between communists that emerged after the Russian Revolution – between the socialists and social democrats. The first communist gymnastic clubs emerged in Berlin in 1920, where athletes had cut their political teeth fighting alongside the Spartacus movement in the city's notorious political street battles. Small communist sports clubs were also founded in France, Sweden, Finland, Italy and Hungary, and, in 1921, the Comintern – the Soviet committee responsible for controlling foreign communist movements – called for the creation of its own sports organization, the Red Sports International (RSI). Under the Russian, Nikolai Podvosky, a man with no sporting experience of any kind, the RSI's main achievements were to ratchet up the level of class-war rhetoric, spend a great deal of time decrying the comprises of the SWSI, and organize demonstrations at a variety of international events, calling for the inclusion of the Soviet Union. While their entryism in national sports movements was tolerated in the name of unity by many social democrats, the Germans eventually lost patience and expelled them.

The communist movement's practical riposte to the 1925 games was the Workers' Winter Olympics and the Moscow Spartakiad, both held in 1928. The winter games, never emulated by the SWSI, were held in Oslo and Moscow and featured hockey, ski jumping, skating and separate cross-country skiing races for postal workers, rural dwellers and border guards. The Spartakiad was a much grander affair. Over 6,000 athletes competed, 600 of them from a dozen other countries, in a sports programme that was more wide-reaching than that of the contemporaneous Amsterdam Olympic Games. It opened with a water festival on the Moscow River, which was accompanied by a mass stroll of 30,000 through the Lenin Hills, motorcycle and automobile rallies, folk music and poetry readings, and a mock battle between the 'workers of the world' and the 'international bourgeoisie.' The presiding official introducing the games explained, 'We take the word "*Spartakiad*" from Spartacus – the hero of the ancient world and leader of the insurgent slaves . . . Both the Comintern Congress and the Spartakiad unite working people fighting for socialism and communism. They are inseparable in their common struggle for revolution – classical physical culture and the revolutionary militant culture of Marxism–Leninism', and then dedicated the occasion to the Soviet Union's first five-year plan.[10]

While the Soviet Union would continue to hold its own domestic Spartakiads, the chaos of the Terror, the famines and forced industrialization of the 1930s put paid to any more of these international communist spectaculars. Soviet foreign policy had switched from fermenting international revolution to securing socialism in one country. The last hurrah for this era of workers' sport, before fascism and war would destroy it, was the 1931 Workers' Olympiad in Vienna. Strong and well organized as it was, Austrian socialism found itself increasingly under siege in the late 1920s and early 1930s, politically and physically threatened by the forces of far-right nationalism. Consequently, the sports movement served as the main recruiting ground for street and neighbourhood security in working-class Vienna. It was no coincidence that Julius Deutsch, who became head of the movement in 1927, had served as armed-forces minister and run the Republican Defence League – the left's street vigilantes and street fighters. In this context, the 1931 games were always intended as a statement of international political support. 'All social democrats are delighted that the next Olympics are to take place in Austria where our comrades are valiantly fighting fascist reaction. They need the solidarity of the international proletariat.'[11] Seventy-seven thousand athletes, more than half from twenty-six other nations, came to Vienna that summer to support them, most of them housed with local working-class families. More than 200,000 spectators watched them in the movement's very own and newly built stadium. Sixty-five thousand watched the final of the football tournament; 12,000 crammed into the velodrome. Ten thousand comrades staged a complex of tableaux in which the great tower of capital was pulled down and destroyed by the coordinated muscular energies of the international proletariat. The truth was, though, that no amount of sports training or collective discipline would help. Just four years later, as Austria succumbed to a right-wing authoritarian government, its workers' sports movement would be dissolved and its leaders would be dead or in exile. A similar fate would await much of the rest of Europe.

EIGHT

Like Antwerp and Paris, the Amsterdam games were the child of the bourgeois sports nation. Sports, games and pastimes had long had a place in popular Dutch culture – from skating on frozen canals to *kolven*, the Dutch forerunner of golf – but, from the late nineteenth century onwards, the Dutch bourgeois, often educated in England and in regular contact with expatriates, took up English sports with enthusiasm. Cricket allowed them the illusion that they were at home in the Edwardian countryside; rowing and football connected them to the manly pluck and vigour of the public schools and military of the world's greatest modern empire. Athletics, fencing and equestrian sports – all the preserve of the wealthy – also caught on. The men who planned and put on the Amsterdam games were drawn from this milieu: Baron van Tuyll, the Dutchman on the IOC; Captain Pieter Scharroo, soldier, fencer and indefatigable organizer; and the chair of the games' organizing committee, Baron Schimmelpenninck van der Oye. The challenges to the Olympics and its sporting and social allies in the 1920s had been, so far, social movements conjured up by modernity. Nation states and nationalism, ever present at the games, appeared to be the new norm, as the old empires began to be dismantled. Capitalism and commercialism drove the challenge of professional sports. The democratizing wave that followed the First World War fired the workers', women's and deaf sports movements. In the Netherlands, the main opposition to the games was, surprisingly, from forces and ideas forged in the distant past – above all, the stern, joyless voice of seventeenth-century Calvinism, still alive in the Protestant-confessional political parties that secured over a third of seats in the Dutch parliament.[1]

In 1925, the organizing committee and the Dutch government had sought permission from parliament to give a million guilders to the games. They were well aware of the depth of the opposition and had already conceded that events would not be held on a Sunday and that a lottery would not be used to fund the games, but it barely drew the sting of religious opposition. In the debate in the lower house, the Protestant religious parties let fly: 'The Olympic Games bear a heathen character in their origin and essence.' Despite protestations and deeply read arguments from the minister of education that the games were totally compatible with the scriptures, Dutch Calvinism was not having it: 'sport increasingly consists of competitions in which passions are stirred in a very dubious way. God's decrees for life would be replaced by play and self-indulgence, causing the moral degeneration of the nation.' Above all, 'women seized by the mania of sport will lose their feeling of modesty and virtue.' A Liberal MP, Staalman, thought he heard 'the voice of the stake and the witch trials', while a Social Democrat, Schaper, said this was 'the language of an afterbirth from the Middle Ages.' To no avail, the vote was lost. There would be no central-government support for the games. Coubertin acidly recorded in his diary that 'they were aiming for a one-off record in the field of idiocy . . . it is the twentieth century after all.'[2]

Three days later, an open letter to the nation was published in every secular newspaper, calling on the Dutch to support the Olympics. The sports world, hitherto lukewarm about the games, was stung into action by the depth of the clerical anti-sports sentiment. From the largest – like the football association, KNVB – to the smallest – like the amateur Alsatian-breeding society, the harness-racing society of Meppel and the wooden-bowls clubs of Houten – money flooded in. Bourgeois Holland rallied; thousands of individual donations were matched by businesses: Heck's lunchrooms made a donation of a cent for every customer they served; the confectioners, Jamin, sold special Olympic chocolate bars for the cause; and the post office issued the first special collection of Olympic stamps (they sold like wildfire). Beyond the Netherlands, significant funds arrived from collections from patriotic colonists in the Dutch East Indies, rich expatriate Dutch businessmen and even William Wrigley, the American chewing-gum magnate. Combined with money from Amsterdam's council, the games were, to the immense pleasure of the sporting nation, now on.

Hitherto, the relationship between host cities and Olympic architecture had been limited. In 1896, the games led to the restoration of a single, albeit extraordinary, ancient building – the Panathenaic

Stadium. The games of 1900, 1904 and 1908 had been held in temporary, invented settings for the great exhibitions and fairs of the
belle époque, which would vanish into thin air. The new or rebuilt
stadiums of Stockholm, Antwerp and Paris, though not without
architectural merit, were singular projects, disconnected from any
public urban plan other than, in the case of Antwerp, raising the land
values in a bourgeois suburb. Amsterdam 1928 was different. The
games themselves would take their most rational compact form, with
all of the events squeezed into a fortnight rather than dragging on
over many months. The new Olympic stadium was conceived as part
of an integrated exercise in urban planning. It would be built on
reclaimed marshland on the southern edge of the city centre – an
area recently chosen as the zone of expansion under the city government's *Plan Zuiid* – and furnished with new infrastructure and
transport links. A small sports arena had been built here at the turn
of the century and would serve as a secondary venue. Above all, the
whole process of design and building would be handed over to a
single architect and their vision.

The commission went to the eclectic Dutch social democrat, Jan
Wils. His work in the 1920s drew on a variety of influences – the
clinical lines of Mies van der Rohe and the international style,
the Amsterdam school of municipal patterned brickwork, the modernist aesthetics, primary colours and grids of the De Stijl design
movement, and a hint of Frank Lloyd Wright's ornamental flourishes
– and though all would feature in his Olympic stadium, none would
win him the job. More likely was his close association with Captain
Scharroo, a key figure on the organizing committee, who had introduced Wils to Coubertin at the Paris games. This piece of strategic
networking turned into collaboration as the two co-authored the first
book on sports architecture in Dutch, to which Coubertin himself
contributed a preface. *Buildings and Grounds for Gymnastics, Sports
and Games* was, on the one hand, a manual of design and specifica-
tion, but it was also the first book to make the case for the place of
sport and sports facilities in the urban landscape.[3]

Wils didn't get things all his own way, and his first grand plan
was sharply cut back by the organizing committee. Rather than the
permanent restaurant–canteen Wils proposed, the committee preferred a tented village; the two sports halls and the swimming pool
he designed were reconfigured as temporary venues to be removed

after the games. There would be no Olympic village, either, as the organizers mobilized private accommodation and hotel boats to house their visitors. The process of building the stadium was not without conflict. Wildcat strikes broke out on the construction sites; Wils' decision to award the main concrete contract to a hometown company was considered flagrant bias by the construction industry. Opposition councillors in the Amsterdam city government railed against the political opaqueness of the games: 'The entire question of the Olympic Games is shrouded in mystery: their management lies in the hands of a small circle who issue meaningless bulletins from time to time.'[4]

Once built, the stadium was supremely functional, aesthetically simple and quietly appealing. Its internal concrete-and-steel structure was clad with two million bricks, and occasionally adorned with horizontal and vertical patterning, especially around its lintels, entrances and staircases. It contained within itself, and arranged in concentric circles, stands for over 30,000, a concrete banked cycle track, a 400-metre athletic track – the first to use the distances and markings that are now the Olympic norm – and an internal grass rectangle that served as a football and korfball pitch, as well as the venue for gymnastics. Beneath the stands, a continuous circular passage made the excellent facilities for the press, the police, VIPs, coaches and doctors easily available and accessible. The complex's main flourish was the marathon tower on the east side of the stadium – a modernist brick chimney, topped with a metal bowl where, for the first time, a symbolic Olympic flame would be lit (and smoke emitted during daylight hours). In contrast to the bombast of future Olympic flames and cauldrons, Amsterdam's fire would come from simply turning on the municipal gas supply and lighting it. The view, though, was magnificent. Just days before the opening ceremony, sports writer, Leo Lauer, climbed to the top of the tower with Wils and relished the moment: 'There at my feet lay the city on the Amstel in the delicious shroud of summer. It was Saturday, the Saturday of free pure sport!'[5]

Olympic cities had dressed themselves before. Flags, bunting, posters and advertising were certainly visible on the streets and in the squares of Antwerp and Paris. Amsterdam did the same, but to this repertoire of nineteenth-century display it added the sparkling modernity of electric light. At night, the Olympic stadium was bathed by soft yellow beams while the city centre was decked in chains of light: the paths and bridges of the Reguliersgracht, the slender spire of the Westerkerk, and a multicoloured fountain flickering in Frederiksplein. Some in the local press were speechless: 'the spectacle is so lovely and so wondrous that it can hardly be captured in words.' The communist daily, *De Tribune*, saw it differently: 'It was beautiful, the canals were illuminated so brilliantly that everyone forgot how smelly they had been during the day.'[6]

The Olympic occupation of Amsterdam did not go uncontested. The communist papers were predictably grumpy and scathing: 'Amsterdam is dominated by the five rings – five noughts signalling the emptiness, the hollowness and rottenness of this "International of nationalities".' Dutch churches, confessional parties and religious newspapers combined to flood the streets and the bookshops with anti-Olympic pamphlets. Amongst the many titles available were, *Israel and the foreigners, or the evil of the Olympiad in the Netherlands*, *The IXth Olympiad or Ancient Heathenism introduced into the Christian nations* and *From Aviary to the Olympiad*. They were implacable: 'The Olympic Games are the feast of Whitsun of the flesh. Total forbearance towards the Olympic Games befits us Christians. What does not stem from the faith, it is a sin! You would sooner tread on my dead body than that I would put one foot in the stadium with you. This you must say to your children if they should be so depraved as to go there.'[7] An alliance of Protestant, Catholic and temperance societies created the Christian Social Coalition, to provide safe accommodation and prayer meetings for the expected deluge of 'loose women' drawn to the febrile atmosphere of the Olympic city, and the local girls who would be led astray by the merriment.

In sporting terms, there was a strange déjà vu about Amsterdam 1928. Three of its undisputed stars had also been champions in Paris 1924. Johnny Weissmuller was once again the reigning swimmer, winning the 100-metre freestyle, though he was now too old to contest the longer events. Paavo Nurmi, who had dominated long-distance running in Paris, won another gold in the 10,000 metres, but had to cede the steeplechase and the 5,000 metres to his younger competitor, Ville Ritola. The Uruguayan football team retained their title, this time beating Argentina in a replayed final that was not merely sold out but oversubscribed many times over. The game between the champions and the Netherlands was so popular that tens of thousands queued for tickets at the Olympic stadium; an impromptu market was established to service them with liver and beef sandwiches, herring, chocolate, beer and playing cards. When, the next morning, most were disappointed, 'the police had to hit out with their sabres . . . it turned out that only those who joined the queue before 9.30 on Sunday had got tickets.'[8]

None of these champions would return to the Olympics. Weiss-muller was offered the part of Tarzan by MGM, the first of a whole series of American Olympian swimmers to head for Hollywood. Nurmi was refused a place at the Los Angeles games in 1932 because his expenses and accounts from the dozens of exhibition runs and appearances so obviously demonstrated his effective professional status. Football, already openly professional in Britain and Austria, would also go pro in France, Spain, Italy and Latin America over the next decade. FIFA, delighted by the enormous popular success of the Amsterdam tournament, but fearful of losing control over the game, finally created their own World Cup – first hosted and won by the Uruguayans. Football would remain at the Olympics, but it would never mean the same thing again.

Boxing, which had proved the most querulous event four years earlier, reached new heights of official incompetence and popular demotic protest. In a bantamweight bout, the South African, Harry Isaacs, was incomprehensibly declared the winner over the Ameri-can, John Daley – after which, Americans in the crowd stormed the jury table. One judge had actually confused the boxers during the match, and the result was overturned. The local press was appalled when the Dutchman, Karel Miljon, lost on points to the German light heavyweight, Ernst Pistulla, but then celebrated the equally improb-able victory of the home boy, Bep van Klaveren, over his Argentinian opponent, Peralata. Supporters of both boxers declared them win-ners and carried them around the arena while the crowd howled. Worst of all, the incomparable Czech middleweight, Jan Heřmánek, demolished the Italian, Carlo Orlandi, only to lose the fight because the jury had been watching an entirely different bout. The crowd erupted. 'In my thirty-five years of experience in boxing I have never witnessed such turmoil. The police had to intervene to keep the furi-ous Czech supporters away from the jury. There must have been more fighting outside than inside the ring that night. The police came off best.'[9] Towards the end of the tournament, Collard, the Belgian chief judge, found it impossible to get people to be officials.[10]

Compared to Paris, nationalist outbursts and international conflicts were less common, and the Dutch themselves showed a restrained pride and enthusiasm for their own victories. The aristocracy, and its military wing in particular, furnished the gold-medal equestrian team. A teenager, Marie Braun, won the women's 100-metre backstroke. Leene and van Dijk won the tandem competition and received an ovation so long and tumultuous that an exhibition game of korfball in the stadium had to be abandoned to allow them to ride an adequate victory lap.

However, if the Dutch public had a favourite at the games, it was not one of their own, but the British Indian hockey team. The game had been introduced to India by the British army in the late nineteenth century and rapidly diffused to the locals both inside and outside the armed forces. More popular and more socially open than cricket, hockey drew on a huge pool of athletes in India, resulting in a team of exceptional talent being sent to the games. Their reception in the motherland had been frosty at best, racist and dismissive at worst; but, in the Netherlands, they were publicly embraced. At the same time, hockey, unknown to the general public in the Netherlands before the games, became a national craze. The Dutch victory over the Germans, at the first games since 1912, was especially cheered by the stands and the athletes: 'Dutchmen, Spaniards, British Indians and Frenchmen made the changing room resemble a merry-go-round at full speed.' The final against the British Indians was the hottest ticket in town. 'Taxis were nowhere to be had, and the occasional one which became available was stormed immediately. There was only one traffic flow in our great capital, going in the direction of the Olympic stadium . . . all this for a hockey match; hockey, which was virtually unknown to the masses a fortnight ago.'[11] The Indians never looked like anything other than comprehensive victors as they won the first of a streak of six consecutive gold medals in the sport that would make hockey, for a time, the national game of India and an emblem of nationalist politics and the promise of independence.

When the games closed, one editorial looked back on the storm of religious protest and commented, 'Amsterdam has been spared a moral catastrophe. The destruction of Sodom and Gomorrah did not need to be repeated. Close up, the devil, depicted so blackly, is not as bad as anticipated.'[12] The organizers of the Los Angeles games, deeply impressed by the simple functionality of the Amsterdam games, declared it 'a model of the future.' Of course, the Olympics was now going to Hollywood and then Berlin, the heartlands, respectively, of the new consumer capitalism and genocidal fascism. The devil would be back.

4

IT'S SHOWTIME! THE OLYMPICS AS SPECTACLE

LOS ANGELES 1932 • BERLIN 1936 • TOKYO 1940

LAKE PLACID 1932 • GARMISCH-PARTENKIRCHEN 1936

An excited whisper runs like a flash across the stadium.

And then hush.

A voice that fills every corner of the vast bowl breaks forth from the huge electoral announcer.

'Ladies and Gentlemen, the Vice-President of the United States is arriving to officially open the Games.'

The Vice-President arrives at his box and for the first time is clearly identified to the audience. He waves his hand to acknowledge a renewed outburst of cheers.

His gesture brings a hush to the babble of noises.

The time-table on the daily programme is hastily consulted. What comes next?

Official Report of the 1932 Los Angeles Olympics

It is no longer Berlin; it is a film set

Le Jour, *August 1936*

ONE

At the IOC's 1923 congress, prior to the vote that would decide the host of the 1932 games, a central-European delegate asked William Garland, the chair of the Los Angeles bid committee, 'Where is Los Angeles? Is it anywhere near Hollywood?'[1] The city of angels, long elided with its motion-picture industry, would cast the games as a movie, and itself as the set for the cinematic spectacular. The official report deployed the unmistakable grammar of the movie script: stage direction, sound cues and assumed states of mind and feeling. A wide shot of the stadium cuts to a close-up from below the speakers, cuts again to the vice-president entering the box, and then holds that shot for the wave and the cheers. What comes next in the official report is the most extraordinary reconstruction of the opening ceremony as a shooting script:

> From the brass bowl a waft of smoke arises, then a tiny tongue
> of flame rapidly grows into a gregarious golden glaze, symbolic
> of the Olympic spirit. On the field in front of the chorus an
> immense gleaming white Olympic flag with its five intertwined
> rings is flung to the afternoon breeze.[2]

The final shot, taken from a hovering airship, was of the now half empty Coliseum, the audience departing in long lines of traffic heading out all across Los Angeles, the melancholy voice-over musing, 'There lingered in the great amphitheatre a spiritual atmosphere such as must still hover over the ruins of ancient Olympia.' The End. Cut to credits.[3]

At first glance, there could hardly be two Olympiads seemingly more different than Los Angeles 1932 and Berlin 1936: California casual in the golden state versus Germanic formality in the Prussian state. The former was funded on a shoestring, without much help from any level of US government. The California state government permitted a million-dollar bond issue and got its money back. Local businesses raised the money to build the Coliseum – which would serve as the main Olympic stadium – and to take a punt at bidding for the games. The country-club set were on hand to help. The Riviera staged the show jumping and Sunset Fields golf club housed the modern pentathlon. For Berlin, by contrast, the coffers of the German state were opened, and they discharged a torrent of expenditure that even the punctilious bureaucrats of the Reich chancellery could not fully audit. Estimates of forty million Reichsmarks suggest a bigger bill than all the previous games combined. While the 1936 Olympics saw the widespread mobilization of all the powers available to a modern nation state deliberately and systematically framed by a political ideology, the American federal government could barely rouse itself. Republican president Herbert Hoover, besieged in Washington by the Bonus Army protests of mid-1932, refused an invitation to open the games; ex-president Calvin Coolidge also declined the honour. Only the presence of Franklin D. Roosevelt – New York State senator and Democratic presidential contender – at the Lake Placid winter games in early 1932, and his subsequent threat to attend the summer games, brought Vice-President Charles Curtis to the opening ceremony, and then with an entourage of just one. Hitler was a daily presence at the Berlin games, alongside almost the entire Nazi Party elite. While the German diplomatic service was put at the disposal of the Berlin Olympics, its ambassadorial staff serving as athletes' chaperones and press officers, its upper echelons closely concerned themselves with the German presence in international sporting organizations. The US State Department, by contrast, was unwilling, until forced, to waive visas for athletes, lift import taxes on sporting equipment or even send out official invites. As for ideology, the most ideological argument in the American press was Keynesian. *Literary Digest* argued, like many, that the Los Angeles Olympics was 'a depression buster . . . a six million dollar sock on the jaw . . . the sports world's answer to the depression', but, in the face of the most catastrophic economic downturn in American history, it was never more than a post hoc rationalization. Berlin, by contrast, was, despite the constraints of Olympic form and protocol, suffused with ideological content, directed to a greater extent by Joseph Goebbels' Ministry of Propaganda than the local organizing committee.

Thus, on initial reading, the games of the 1930s, or rather their differences, reflect important aspects of the titanic struggles between fascism and democracy, communism and capitalism, and competing global empires, unleashed by the Great Depression and consummated in the Second World War. However, there are two shared aspects of the Los Angeles and Berlin games that make them more similar to each other than any of the preceding Olympics, and point to social forces and changes operating alongside the great conflicts of the era.

First, both were a theatre for the sporting politics of ethnicity and race. When the games had last been held in America, in St Louis, in 1904, the Anthropology Days had seen untrained Africans and Asians asked to compete against leading US athletes or demonstrate 'primitive sports' – but this was a ghastly sideshow rather than integral to the games themselves, and was barely noticed outside by the general public. This time around, in Los Angeles, the presence of African Americans as a part of the American sporting nation was widely discussed in the popular press. At the same time, the perceived Japanese threat to America, both athletic and strategic, was played out in the local coverage of their triumphant athletes and swimmers – first laughably small and foreign, then worrying and inscrutably threatening. In Berlin, the racial theories of the Nazis, which characterized Africans as subhuman and justified the exclusion and persecution of Jews, shadowed every moment of the games' preparations and the meaning of many of its sporting contests.

Second, these narratives of race and ethnicity, alongside the many other stories emerging from the games, were staged with a level of artifice, and broadcast at a scale that simply dwarfed any previous Olympiad. William May Garland, the man who led the campaign to get the games to California and served as the chair of the local organizing committee, had no illusions about the economic rationale for Los Angeles and the real nature of the games: 'the advertising feature would be worth $10,000,000 to this city and vicinity.'[4] Garland was a two-time president of the National Association of Realtors, and made his fortune from the vertiginous property booms that turned Los Angeles from a city of just 100,000 in 1900 to nearly 1.3 million in 1930. He operated at the centre of a network of developers and boosters, realtors, oil companies and movie magnates who, in the early twentieth century, as the region's great historian, Carey McWilliams, put it, 'began to organize Southern California as one of the greatest promotions the world has ever known', selling the Californian good life, the new Mediterranean, paradise on the Pacific.[5] In his letters and interviews with the press, Garland often referred to the athletes as actors and the Olympics as a celebration or a show, the sport itself seemingly ancillary.

It is this driving sensibility, of the Olympic Games as a mediated spectacle, a vehicle for the creation and global distribution of ideas, imagery and messages, that both distinguished the Los Angeles games from its predecessors and made it Berlin's precursor and mentor. Carl Diem, Garland's German equivalent, conducted innumerable interviews and took copious notes and photographs in 1932, which helped shape many aspects of the organization and presentation of the 1936 games. Thus, four years later, as the French newspaper *Le Jour* reported, Berlin had self-evidently been recast as a film set. Its streets were draped in Nazi regalia, its courtyards cleared of washing, its streets cleared of gypsies and criminals. Podiums and platforms had been built for camera crews at strategic points in the city and at the stadiums.

In this, the Los Angeles and Berlin games were the culmination of the Olympic Games' evolution as a media event, a transformation that tracked the explosive growth of the new cultural industries in the decades either side of the First World War, and the increasingly powerful role of commerce and state power in using and shaping them. It hadn't always been like this. In 1896, on the eve of the Athens games, the British press preferred to report on the Oxford and Cambridge boat race rather than Coubertin's Hellenic revivalist fete. Journalists, not normally accorded this level of hospitality by the aristocratic sporting establishment, were invited to the official banquets of the 1896 games as honoured guests, but, even with the promise of a free lunch, few showed up. We do possess the memoirs and warm recollections of participants, like hurdler Thomas Curtis' *High Hurdles and White Gloves*, or the discus-throwing Oxford classicist G. S. Robertson's *An Englishman at the First Modern Olympics*, but they appeared long after the games were over and reached only a narrow, upmarket readership. Getting to the newly literate mass audiences of the world's great industrial cities required newspaper coverage. This was almost absent at the 1900 and 1904 games, but London 1908 got more column inches than any Olympics hitherto. American papers were eager to report the contest with the old empire, and the British tabloids had acquired an appetite for sports photography and its power to sell papers. Thus, by 1912, the Stockholm games could attract 445 journalists, over half of them from overseas, while Paris 1924 and Amsterdam 1928 claimed almost a thousand journalists apiece, drawn not just from Europe, but Latin America and Asia too. Writers and photographers were now joined by the pioneers of the radio industry, which, in the early 1920s, had made the leap from an experimental technology to a commercial operation.[6]

Impressive as the media coverage had been in the 1920s, Los Angeles and Berlin were able to magnify this greatly by adding a global PR operation to the tasks of the organizing committee and by providing unparalleled facilities for the media. Indeed, the very first act of the LA organizing committee was to create a press department that could operate in five languages and was equipped with a global database of over 6,000 periodicals with which to communicate. Olympic facilities were furnished with hundreds of telephones, telegraph and teletype machines. An adapted form of the Dow Jones share-price ticker communicated results, times and records instantaneously. And Los Angeles did not forget the chorus. Unlike other games, the organizers devoted time, money and technology to setting up ticketing offices with phone lines, and selling seats through billboard and newspaper advertising. Prices, for the first time, were deliberately set low, aimed at the widest possible audience. They were rewarded by the largest attendances at an Olympic Games yet. The demotic qualities of American sports culture were also reflected in the language of the American sports press, then blessed with writers of the calibre of Damon Runyon and Paul Gallico, who injected a level of self-conscious drama into the proceedings that no other national sports press could muster. Grantland Rice wrote, 'the world will send fifty rival nations of the world against the United States at Los Angeles', and though the modern world could not match up to Pericles, Socrates or Plato, 'when we compare runners and jumpers, discus and javelin throwers, the betting shows that the Olympic winners of ancient Greece would be left far behind the coming record-breakers of Los Angeles.'[7]

The Germans couldn't offer the same kind of ebullient sporting language, but technologically and organizationally, Berlin outstripped Los Angeles. The Olympic press office produced a monthly magazine, the *Olympic Games News Service*, sending out 24,000 copies of its expensively printed briefings in fourteen different languages. Two hundred thousand Olympic posters were distributed to thirty-five countries. The German railways publicity bureau sent out four million of its own pamphlets. The trio in charge of the games – the secretary and chairman of the organizing committee, Carl Diem and Theodor Lewald, and the Reichssportführer, von Tschammer – were sent on a global tour of sports ministers, officials and journalists. There were forty placard-carrying men at the Oxford and Cambridge boat race, poster displays on the Buenos Aires metro and a Berlin Olympics aeroplane doing stunts above the streets of Chicago. Thus, almost 3,000 journalists, more than the three previous games combined, went to Berlin.[8] LA's ticker-tape machine was matched by Siemens' teletypewriters, run by the Luftwaffe information service, while radio, curiously overlooked by Los Angeles, was superbly catered for: the Berlin Olympic studios made over three thousand transmissions during the games, to forty-three countries. For a few thousand Berliners, the connected and the curious, there were fuzzy images on the first televisions, delivered by fifteen miles of new close-circuit cabling from the Olympic stadium to salons and offices around the city. Television, though, was the future; the technology of the moment was cinema. In this medium, Berlin 1936 not only exceeded Los Angeles, but also redefined the very nature of the Olympic spectacular.

Eighteen ninety-six saw both the first modern Olympic Games and the Lumière Brothers' tour of their revolutionary cinematograph – a machine that allowed them, for the first time, to show a projected moving picture to an audience. Despite early film-makers' interest in sporting occasions, neither the 1900 nor the 1904 games were captured, but the intercalated games of 1906 saw early film companies like Gaumont, Pathé and Warwick, and the celebrated US travel writer, Burton Holmes, send crews to Athens. What survives of their work is overwhelmingly ceremonial, capturing the arrival of King Edward VII of Britain and the grainy ranks of military gymnasts, but no sporting competitions. The 1908 London games were covered by newsreel companies, with more of a taste for the sport itself; the dramatically cut footage of Italian marathon runner, Dorando Pietri, stumbling into the White City stadium and being helped over the finishing line, proved immensely popular. In the 1920s, as cinema became a feature of every modern city and attendances boomed, both the Paris and Amsterdam Olympic Committees commissioned companies to make full-length Olympic films. Bernard Naan's *Les Jeux Olympiques*, shot in Paris, ran in one version to three hours. William Prager's *De Olympische Spielen*, covering the Amsterdam games, lasted over an hour. Both directors began to experiment with the problems of how to shoot competitive sport and how to construct a dramatic narrative out of this. *Les Jeux Olympiques* was distinguished by some remarkable photography of the 1924 Chamonix winter games, including graceful slow-motion sequences of ice skaters, and rapid intercuts that captured something of the mania of bobsleigh and skeleton. Praeger's work, acknowledging the growing status of the leading athletes, had a more systematic focus on individual champions and stars, like Paavo Nurmi and Lord Burghley.[9] Los Angeles cast the entire games as a movie, but, copious newsreels aside, no feature film of the event itself was commissioned: Hollywood preferred to go with the romantic and the screwball comedy instead. In *This Is The Night*, Cary Grant, a javelin thrower, returns unexpectedly early from the LA games to discover that his wife has train tickets for a secret assignation in Venice with her lover. In *Million Dollar Legs*, the curmudgeonly W. C. Fields plays the president of the Republic of Klopstokia, who, for reasons more complex and implausible than anyone need worry about, sends himself and a team to the LA games. It was, as this kind of plot line suggests, 'about as close as Hollywood ever came to the spirit of *Dada*.'[10] The conjoining of a cinematically constructed spectacular with the new alchemy of modernist film-making would await Berlin 1936 and Leni Riefenstahl's *Olympia*.

Olympia broke the mould of Olympic films in many ways. First, Riefenstahl had a degree of active support from the organizers – above all, Goebbels' Ministry of Propaganda – that no other film-maker had acquired.[11] She had total access and total control, and an immeasurably large crew and budget. Second, in terms of technological and cinematic sophistication, there was no comparison. Riefenstahl was able to use aerial cameras in airships, construct rails for tracking shots, dig pits allowing filming from below, use powerful lenses for close-ups and capture the crowds at a level of detail no one had managed before. Third, while earlier films had begun to try and situate the games in a wider social and urban context, combining establishing shots of the Olympic city with parts of the opening ceremony to produce a sense of the spectacle, nothing comes close to Riefenstahl's cut of the 1936 opening ceremony – a bombastic but utterly compelling sequence. Finally, the film was structured by a singular and advanced cinematic aesthetic, honed in Riefenstahl's earlier depiction of the Nazi Party's Nuremberg rallies. *Triumph of the Will* combined her fascination with gargantuan architecture and febrile mass crowds, with dramatic lighting and brilliantly scored music: *Olympia* would draw on all of these. Which *Olympia* one is referring to is a complex matter, for there were a variety of different cuts, including a version for home consumption, more political and openly racist than those sanitized for export. Either way, unlike its predecessors, which disappeared into obscurity, *Olympia* went on international release in 1938 and won the Coppa Mussolini at the Venice film festival in 1939. In the absence of television, which would come to dominate the reporting of the games, *Olympia* came to define the collective popular memory of the Berlin games: not merely a record of the spectacle, but the spectacle itself.

TWO

The Los Angeles and Berlin games not only transformed the ways in which the spectacle could be captured and broadcast, but also changed the very nature of the show. Three theatrical innovations stand out. Two debuted at Los Angeles: the introduction of the now familiar medal ceremony, with national anthems and a three-tiered podium; and the creation of an Olympic village, not just as a practical solution to an accommodation problem, but as a stage for the production of Olympic tableaux and messages. Berlin completed the curious evolution of the modern Olympics' use of mythic fire with the staging of a torch relay from Olympia to the host city.

In 1896, the IOC and the organizers had taken their cue from the little that they knew of prize-giving ceremonies at the ancient games. All the presentations were made at the closing ceremony: winners got olive branches and a silver medal, runners-up got a laurel wreath and a bronze medal. Unlike Olympia, the dress code was strict: a dinner suit and black tie. All the athletes got a diploma for showing up, and the winner of the marathon got an antique vase and a silver cup. There were no ceremonies of any kind at Paris 1900, but there were a lot of medals and a lot of random cups and prizes, many of them only awarded years later. For some – like the fencer Albert Ayet – there was even cash: a 3,000-franc prize to go with his medal in the épée for fencing masters. Only with the London games of 1908 did the now familiar model of official gold, silver and bronze medals, awarded on the day they were won, emerge. Even then, the ceremony lacked drama. There was no podium, no flags, and no music, just the gruff words of IOC grandees and floral bouquets. Flags and music arrived in 1928, but there was still no podium.

It was only after the new IOC president, Count Baillet-Latour, had seen such a device at the 1930 British Empire Games in Hamilton, Ontario, that the IOC began to press for its inclusion. Lake Placid, the winter games in 1932, was, in fact, the first Olympics to use a podium, but Los Angeles went one better, boldly stencilling the numbers 1, 2 and 3 on the different levels and setting the entire ensemble against the photogenic backdrop of the Coliseum's high arches.[1] As ever with rituals, even those that are newly minted, transgression proved to be the most interesting aspect of the ceremony. The Italian runner, Luigi Beccali, the surprise gold-medal winner of the 1,500 metres, was the first athlete to give a fascist salute on an Olympic podium. In Berlin, four years later, Sohn Kee-chung, the Korean marathon champion, would bow his head in shame as the Japanese anthem was played, appalled that he should have run and won under the flag of the colonial oppressor. In time, even bolder and more radical statements would be made from the Olympic podium.

Hitherto, the question of housing at the Olympics had been a practical one, but even at the well-attended Paris and Amsterdam games, the organizers had managed to find enough rooms, hostels and floating boat-hotels to meet demand. Los Angeles, which had no shortage of hotel rooms, could have done the same, but, as a metropolis built on real-estate speculation and the veneration of home ownership, it was bound to think differently. The Los Angeles Olympic village, located amongst the oil derricks and scrubland of the Baldwin Hills, a few miles south-west of downtown, was, in part, an attempt to attract more athletes to the games. It allowed the organizers to offer visitors accommodation, food and transport for just two dollars a day. But there were other agendas, as the official report oozed: 'nations are, after all, only members of one great family – the human family', and this was the family home. The *New York Times*, previewing the village, was a cheerleader for this easy cosmopolitanism: 'Thirty-six flags of thirty-six peoples, created equal in opportunity, will float above the city of Los Angeles in the democratic free-for-all struggle.'[2] The local press would lay it on very thick: the village was 'the talk of several continents because of its model management, almost unbelievable efficiency and charm', and 'its temporary occupants are filled with amazement and delight and are telling the world about the Los Angeles way of doing things.'[3]

The Los Angeles way of doing things included five miles of suburban-style crescent roads and lawns, 550 prefabricated bungalows, a hospital, fire station and post office, souvenir shops and a bank. Security was supplied by hired cowboys and rodeo riders who, on horseback and with lariat in hand, patrolled the wire fence that surrounded the complex. A Spanish colonial-revival building, looking suspiciously like an estate agent's office, functioned as the adminis-tration block at the centre of the village. Two bungalows were furnished but kept empty, serving as show houses for the post-games sell-off to come. Dedicated bus services took competitors to the Olympic park and other venues, movies were shown all day at an open-air amphitheatre, and visitors were encouraged to relax in the spacious lounges decorated with contemporary furniture and Navajo rugs. The tone was all California casual, with participation in the many events, trips and excursions on offer 'in the American manner rather than obligatory'. Arrangements for eating and drinking were minutely prepared for. Prohibition, still in force in 1932, left the French bereft and reduced to drinking sugar-water in an attempt to replace the lost calories of their regular intake of red wine, but, alcohol aside, the hosts were eager to please. The French 'were prom-ised that they would not have to forego their delectable sauces for American gravies', while the Chinese were assured of something as authentic 'as the China coast, rather than the local chop suey restau-rants.'

This was part of a wider strategy, 'making participation in the games less of a penance and more of an old-fashioned American do-as-you-please . . . party.' Informality would underwrite harmony. Once again, the official report was beatific: 'The children of the nations, unsecured by maturity and assumed nationalism, would find in each other brethren of the flesh regardless of colour, race or creed.'[4] Yet, at the same time, the accommodation was actually arranged along imperial lines: the French were housed with members of the Little Etente; the British Empire had a quarter all to itself. Central Europeans, Germans and Scandinavians were thrown together and segregated from the Latins, both European and American. The Brazil-ians were kept separate from both of these groups and Asians were all lumped in one place.

Practical housing issues aside, the village produced a location in which the press could meet the athletes and out of which all kinds of stories and pictures could be manufactured. Malcolm Metcalf, an American javelin thrower, arrived at the village and found that the man carrying his kit to the bungalow was Will Rogers – at the time, one of the biggest stars in Hollywood and light entertainment. The women athletes, housed separately, in accommodation downtown, were the subject of newspaper scuttlebutt and titillation. The headlines read: 'Oo! La! La! Si und Ja: French Girl at the Village' and 'Fair Damsel Crashed Village Gate'. Douglas Fairbanks Junior made a number of well-covered visits, where he was mobbed by Italian and Finnish souvenir hunters. Members of the public gathered at the entrance to the village to catch him and ask for autographs from the rest of the parade, while hawkers sold cigarettes and candy. The press repeatedly reached for a classical comparison, describing Baldwin Hills as 'Mount Olympus', set on the 'Plains of Ellis'. Had they been familiar with the great temporary shack-cities and tented villages that accompanied the ancient games, and the awful hardship of life without running water and toilets in the fierce heat of a Greek August, they might have also drawn comparisons with the hundreds of desperate temporary settlements across the city, housing recent migrants from the Oklahoma dustbowl, African Americans fleeing the strictures and poverty of the South, and tens of thousands of illegal Mexicans.[5]

There is not a shred of evidence that the ancient games saw any torchlight processions. Yes, there was an eternal flame kept alight inside Olympia's Temple of Hera, and there was much burning of offerings to Zeus and the other gods during the games, but there was no specific Olympic fire, cauldron, flame or torch. But why let that get in the way of anything? The Amsterdam games had introduced the Olympic flame, burning municipal gas at the top of the modernist brick marathon tower that overlooked the main stadium, Los Angeles would keep a flame burning in a cauldron inside the Coliseum, but, in Germany, where the 1920s and 1930s had been lit up with torchlight parades of every political colour, something more dramatic appealed.

The idea of a torch relay was the brainchild of Carl Diem, the secretary to the Berlin games organizing committee and its prime intellectual force.[6] Reflecting a long-held strain of German high culture, he imagined that Germany and its sporting traditions were the contemporary incarnation of the Hellenic ideal. Lighting a sacred flame at Olympia and carrying it to Berlin by means of a relay of 3,000 torch-wielding runners would secure the connection. Whether Germany would be connecting with Apollonian Greece – the realm of reason, wisdom and light – or the Dionysian Greece of base desire, unregulated emotion and darkness, remained to be seen.

THREE

Just two days before the opening ceremony of the Los Angeles games, Major George Patton was massing his tanks and cavalry on Pennsylvania Avenue in Washington DC, preparing to disperse by force the marchers of the Bonus Army – desperate First World War veterans and their supporters who had gathered in the capital demanding an early payment of their military pensions. Later on in the evening, they would be chased from their pitiful camps in Hooverville, the slum city on the mud flats south of the White House. The Great Depression, now in its fourth year, had reduced the US government to tear-gassing its own veterans. Yet, undeterred by financial difficulties and prophets of doom, the alliance of developers, boosters, advertisers and media men that made up the organizing committee had brought the Olympic show to town. Now it would blow Hoover, the east coast and the miseries of the Depression off the front pages.

Reporting from downtown on the opening day of the games, the *New York Times* thought it, 'The biggest migration to California since the gold rush.' In actual fact, deterred by distance and depression, less than 1,500 athletes had come to the games, considerably fewer than there had been at Amsterdam; but, what Los Angeles lacked in sheer headcount, it made up for with hyperbole, set-dressing and shows. Pershing Square, at the heart of downtown, was decked out in Olympic bunting and red, white and blue Americana. Hotel and apartment-block lobbies sported Olympic shields. May's department stores on Broadway, anticipating a flood of foreign visitors, hired interpreters to walk their haberdashery and ladies'-wear floors, a flag indicating the interpreter's mother tongue stuck to their back. Everywhere, souvenirs and cheap Olympic memorabilia – matchboxes, key rings, pins and flags – were for sale on the streets. More upmarket shoppers could choose from Olympic-themed Chinese crafts and costume jewellery in Olympic colours. The Biltmore Hotel, the city's most exclusive, was full to overflowing with sports administrators, businessmen and journalists, and would host nine international sporting conferences over the next fortnight. Edward 'Spike' O'Donnell, a notorious Chicago bootlegger and gangster, told the *Los Angeles Times* he was in town 'to attend the Olympic Games and go to church.' Sigfrid Edström, the arch-conservative Swedish president of the International Amateur Athletics Federation and the Swedish General Electric Corporation, mixed Olympic duty with business. The IOC executive met in the high white deco tower of LA's City Hall. Later in the evening, Standard Oil's gigantic neon sign illuminated the Californian night, embellished by the Olympic rings.

Reflecting back on the games, the official report was sanctimonious: 'Not a single note of commercialism was allowed to permeate the consummation of the task.'[1] Presumably none of the report's authors saw the Standard Oil sign or managed to catch the 200 teenagers in white jackets and white gloves handing out Coca-Cola at the Olympic park. Perhaps they were too busy looking at the huge Coca-Cola billboards supporting the games all over the city. Coke was not alone. In fact, Los Angeles was, in conception and execution, the Olympic Games most directly shaped by the forces of commerce and money. It would take the rest of the Olympic movement fifty years to catch up. There were coordinated national advertising campaigns with an Olympic theme for Kellogg's Pep Bran Flakes, Weiss binoculars, and the first generation of supermarkets, like Safeway and Piggly Wiggly. Union 76 Petroleum exhorted its customers to 'Select your gasoline by the Olympic Motto' – a rather convoluted way of saying their gas was higher, faster and stronger. Nisley, the shoe manufacturer, put out a range of 'Olympic winners'. In one of the first examples of guerrilla marketing at the Olympics, Harry Johannes of the Ben-Hur tea company inveigled his way into the village, rounded up the Indian hockey team in their official turbans and took photographs of them holding his tea bags. Amongst local businesses, Helms' Bakery in Culver City was amongst the most enthusiastic, signing up as the official baked-goods supplier to the 1932 games. But Paul Helms, the sharp-eyed owner, had, before the IOC could say, 'Intellectual property', copyrighted the Olympic rings and motto in every state in America. The IOC were powerless to stop him doing whatever he wanted, though all he actually did was brand his aerated industrial bread as Olympic bread and sell it from delivery trucks to the new housewives of suburban, palm-lined Los Angeles.

The planting of palm trees on Los Angeles' newly laid-out avenues had begun in the mid-1920s – a piece of smart real-estate window-dressing – but it had received a massive boost from the Olympics. Over the previous couple of years, the arboreal trim of languid palms that has become one of the city's most notable ciphers was laid down; over 100,000 trees, on 150 miles of boulevard, much of it part of an unemployment relief programme. It was, in part, the promise of a small plot in this littoral paradise that had seen Los Angeles become the fifth-largest city in America – and, within a generation, second only to New York – and the Olympics was an opportunity to embellish that notion. *Game and Gossip,* a glossy monthly which showcased the new Californian affluence of athletic hedonism and glamour, was typical of the boosters. Its Olympic issue hailed the 'Southland' as the world's new playground and touted its latest casual fashions and sportswear.

There was a distinctly Hellenic quality to that vision of California and, for a sheer technicolour rendition, you can't beat the words of the official report: 'The gods smiled on Los Angeles. Into the endless azure vault of the heavens, the sun, a golden ball, pushed slowly and majestically as if the great Zeus himself was riding in his shining chariot from his home on Mount Olympus.'[2] The Coliseum itself was the perfect example of antiquity, Hollywood style. Opened in 1923, it was a thoroughly modern stadium, built out of reinforced concrete. It signalled its Roman namesake with nothing more than a series of high stage-set concrete arches. Rome, Greece, Olympia, whatever; this was now Hellas comes to Hollywood. A caption in the paper on the eve of the games read, 'despite the fact that it contains enough seats for three times the number of mortals that were in the army of Alexander the Great [it] will undoubtedly display the S.R.O (Standing Room Only) signs on July 30th.' *Time* magazine alluded to the Aegean qualities of California, its 'bright landscape, brilliant skies and blue waves', and imagined the inhabitants as twentieth-century Hellenes with 'Spartan pride in physical perfection, Athenian confidence in their own golden age.' Standard Oil had been giving away four-colour copies of the classical statue *Discobolus* as part of its motorists' 'Olympic Vacation.' *Country Life* suggested California had exceeded ancient Greece: 'Are there not mountains in California greater than those in all Hellas, beside which even Olympus itself is but a foothill?'[3]

LA knew how to put on a show, but it threw a good party too. The French consul held a military ball to celebrate the games. The Olympic party put on by British Rear Admiral Sir Reginald Drax in his Beverly Hills base attracted the governor of California, and a small flotilla of European counts, barons and US admirals. The US secretary of the army formally asked Congress for funds to ensure the US military could be present on the cocktail and canapé circuit. In LA itself, Mayor John Porter was a blur of handshaking and name checking. The LA Chamber of Commerce established its own party circuit, peaking with a grand Ball of Nations at the Ambassador Hotel on Wilshire Boulevard. The Hostesses of the Xth Olympic Games was a society affair. Two official hostesses – resident in California, but with their roots in one of the other forty-nine states – were selected and asked to open their wallets and their contact books for parties, receptions, trips and tours for visitors, officials and athletes. Their biggest production was an eclectic theatrical revue, *California Welcomes the World*, held at the Hollywood Bowl and described as 'song, dance and enthralling pictorial impressions.' It combined a history of California with spots that showcased California's idea of other peoples' cultures: Irish jigs, Chinese tiger dances, Swiss yodelling and a human flag made up of Czech émigrés. A similar act of Californian cultural revisionism could be experienced at the ersatz Mexican plaza, Olivera Street, where visitors could soak up a theme-park version of Los Angeles' Latino roots, just a mile or so from some of the biggest illegal Chicano squatter camps.

But the hosts with the most were in Hollywood. The recruitment to the organizing committee of no less than the autocratic populist, Louis B. Mayer, president of MGM, ensured that the movie industry was the games' biggest booster; though Harry Chandler, owner of the *Los Angeles Times* and also a committee member, was no less assiduous in this task. In the run-up to the Olympics, the brightest stars in the firmament were called upon to broadcast to the nation and to Europe, inviting them to Los Angeles; Bela Lugosi, the king of horror schlock; the comic double-act of the age, Laurel and Hardy; Marlene Dietrich, Hollywood's Teutonic femme fatale; and its Mexican princess, Delores del Río. Douglas Fairbanks and Mary Pickford, the industry's power couple of the era, and the comedian Will Rogers starred in 'Come to the Olympics', broadcast by NBC from the Hollywood Bowl, the Olympic village and the Coliseum. During the games, Mayer threw a gigantic party at MGM's studios for 200 Olympic guests, who were treated to lunch with the stars. Will Rogers, then signed to Fox, hosted lunches at their studios for the visiting women athletes. Fairbanks and Pickford were daily attenders at the Coliseum, joined by Bing Crosby, Gary Cooper, Cary Grant and the Marx Brothers. In the evenings, they hosted Olympic parties at their Beverley Hills mansion, Pickfair, and were reported out on the town with the American swimmer, Duke Khanmouko, and the Japanese show jumper and gold medallist, Baron Takeichi Nishi. Will Rogers, his bellboy duties at the Olympic village aside, was a regular feature at the Coliseum and almost every day penned a few words on the Olympics in his hugely popular syndicated telegrams. The gossip columns were in overdrive, reporting that Argentinian Olympians had chased Marlene Dietrich around at a Paramount party, and that Jim Thorpe, the Olympic decathlete, stripped of his medals for professionalism, was snubbed by the organizing committee.

Hollywood mixed business and pleasure. American Olympians had already made the transition from the games to the movies. Nat Pendleton won a silver medal in the wrestling at the 1920 Antwerp games before appearing in over a hundred films, from extravagant biopics like *The Great Ziegfeld* to the Marx Brothers' *At the Circus*. Johnny Weissmuller, the freestyle swimmer who had won five gold medals at two games (1924 and 1928), achieved real, if temporary stardom in the Tarzan movies of the 1930s. A swimmer, Eleanor Holm, recalled, 'I was hardly dry at those Olympics when I was whisked from one studio to another – Warner Brothers, MGM, Paramount – to take screen tests.'[4] Another swimmer, Helene Madison, one of Clarke Gable's dance partners that week, would later star in *The Human Fish* and *The Warrior's Husband*. Buster Crabbe, 400-metre freestyle champion, was spotted by Paramount, where he went on to play another version of Tarzan, romantic leads and the staples of Saturday-morning children's pictures – Flash Gordon and Buck Rogers. Why make a film of the games itself when this was the real story? The athletes were not accorded status because they won a gold medal or excelled at their sport, but doing so gave them the chance to ascend to the realm of real fame and glamour. By night, once the sport was done, the very best parties of all were at the Coconut Grove on Wilshire Boulevard, the nightclub of choice for

Hollywood royalty, like MGM supremo Irving Thalberg, and heart-throb Clark Gable. For two weeks, it was given over to the American athletes who danced with the stars till dawn.[5]

FOUR

Not everyone was reading from the same script. In Chicago, the American Communist Party helped establish the Counter Olympic Committee. Its pamphlets and flyers trained their fire on racism in American sport: 'The Olympics claim they discriminate against no one. This is a rank lie! The National Provisional Counter Olympic Committee states that south of the Mason–Dixon line, Negro athletes are openly Jim-Crowed.' The black press painted a similar picture, decrying the 'lily-white Olympics'. The *Chicago Defender* reported on the fact that the only black employee at the Olympic village was a shoeshine. The *California Eagle* thought the games not 'devoid of the usual and natural difficulties and unpleasant happenings.'[1] More pointedly, it emerged that the black film-star, Clarence Muse, booked to perform at the village, had been told that he could not serve as an official entertainer. The Counter Olympic Committee staged their own small workers' games in Chicago alongside the show in Los Angeles, and attempted to link the games to the long-running campaign to free Tom Mooney – a socialist activist imprisoned for life for the 1916 San Francisco parade bombings in which ten people were killed at the Preparedness Day pro-war march – who had been tried in the atmosphere of a lynch mob. Their flyers noted that 'many of those who are organizing and supporting the Olympics are the same magnates and politicians who helped to grab Tom Mooney.'[2]

But it was always going to be a hard sell. In a sardonic voice, the *Christian Century* could see the dominant arc of the story to come: 'under the inspiration of the southern California climate and the promised presence of practically the entire feminine population of Hollywood, the Americans are expected to clean up.' On the penultimate day of the games, 'Free Tom Mooney' protestors stormed the field of the Coliseum. The *Los Angeles Times* reported that the crowd cheered as the band struck up 'The Star-Spangled Banner' and the police led the protestors from the field.[3]

The *Christian Century* had been right. For two weeks, almost the entirety of the American newspaper and magazine industry hailed US victories: forty-one golds, thirty-two silver medals and twenty bronze. 'Feats that may live as long in human history as their ancient Greek prototypes.' Headline writers thought it a rout: 'Uncle Sam Cleans Up' and 'America Runs Rampant on Olympic Battlefield'. The *Los Angeles Times* asked, 'Who won the Olympics? The answer comes echoing back from the hills like a clap of thunder: the United States.'[4] With the calculus of an emergent superpower, the American press determined that the United States was stronger than any combination of the next four powers. In an atmosphere of unreflective laudatory national celebration – of American college education, science and manly wholesome pluck – the *Los Angeles Times* went so far as to argue that the games were 'unsullied by racial differences'. It was left to Will Rogers to note that the nation being celebrated was neither colour-blind not exclusively masculine: 'Incidentally, the man that brought the first slaves to this country must have had those Olympic Games in mind, for these "Senegambians" have just about run the white man ragged. Every winner is either an American Negro or an American white woman. Wait till we get to golf, bridge and cocktail shaking, then the American white man will come into his own.'[5]

Rogers exaggerated; there was no shortage of clean-cut white college boys on the medal podium for the United States, but now they were joined at the edges of the popular imagination by what the press called 'mermaids', 'Viking women' and 'sable cyclones'.

In some ways, Los Angeles offered little to advance the cause of women's sports. Women made up only 10 per cent of competitors, were housed separately from the men and were still debarred from gymnastics and all of the team sports. They also didn't get much coverage in the mainstream sports press, where the conventional wisdom, prior to the games, was that 'the female of the species may or may not be deadlier than the male, but on the athletic field she isn't graceful.'[6] Beauty, sexual attractiveness and conventional notions of femininity could not be made to fit with the physical form of the female athletic body. At Los Angeles, the men of the American sports press finally worked out what to do with the female Olympians: sexualize the feminine and feminize the masculine. Helene Madison, triple gold medallist, was 'the beautiful New Yorker', while the champion diver Georgia Coleman was always 'Gorgeous Georgia'. The *Chicago Tribune*, like many periodicals, heavily featured photography from the female aquatic competitions, and put it bluntly: 'You get your money's worth at Olympic swim – In Loveliness'. Paul Gallico was certainly getting his, writing of bronze medallist Jane Fauntz that, 'Her marvellous body flowed through the dives with the smoothness of running quicksilver.'[7]

Babe Didrikson didn't fit that mould, but as she was the undisputed athletic star of the games – winning gold in the 80-metre hurdles and javelin, and the silver medal in the high jump – the press and the public had to adapt. She was simply an unbelievable all-round athlete. A white, working-class, wise-cracking Texan, she burst on the scene at the Amateur Athletic Union track-and-field trials, just months before the games. She won five events and booked her place at the Olympics. Many found her physique, demeanour and intensity worryingly masculine, with her 'doorstop jaw and piano-wire muscles', and her 'Viking capacity for baser rage'. But such was her brilliance that the doyens of the sports press went out of their way to reframe her. Grantland Rice, her biggest supporter, now thought that 'A woman doesn't have to look like a weightlifter or a piano mover.' Westbrook Pegler soothed the brow of Main Street, writing of Didrikson, 'the mouth can relax and the eyes smile, and the greatest girl athlete in the world right now, with a special liking for men's games, is as feminine as hairpins.'[8]

American Olympians had never been exclusively white. An African American, George Poage, had won the bronze medal in the 400-metre hurdles at the 1904 games. Jim Thorpe, decathlon champion in Stockholm, was part Native American, and a Hawaiian, Duke Kahanamoku, had won gold in the swimming at Stockholm and Antwerp. In Los Angeles, an African American, Eddie Gordon, would win a gold medal in the broad jump, but it was the sprinters, Eddie Tolan and Ralph Metcalfe, duelling for 100-metre and 200-metre titles, who captured the public imagination and sharply foregrounded the state of racial politics in America. Tolan won the gold in both events, breaking the 100-metre world record and becoming the first black man to receive the soubriquet 'world's fastest human'. The language of the American press went into racialized overdrive, describing the athletes as Negro flashes and dusky thunderbolts; they were 'two black streaks of lighting' or 'two black bolts from the azure of the California sky.' The black press returned the compliment, often referring to the 'white' athletes, but the Southern press was silent. Rather than go through the kinds of contortions that the Northern press went through to explain African-American success – they were natural, gifted, relaxed, simple – they reported the Olympics as if they did not exist.

Explaining Japanese success was an equally problematic task. America's elites were spooked by Japan's invasion of Manchuria in 1931; one tactic before the games was to try and diminish the threat, referring to the Japanese as 'little brown men' and the 'baby entrants' to the games.[9] However, after Chūhei Nambu had won the men's triple jump with a world record leap, Shuhei Nishida the silver in the pole vault, Baron Nishi had won the show jumping and Japan's men's swimming team had taken five of the six available titles, the press had to change tack. The *Christian Century* reported, 'The anti-Japanese Californians who cheered the diminutive Japanese pole vaulter as he went higher and higher could not help but leave with their egos deflated and their appreciation of the talents of other nations enlarged.'[10] The 'flying fish', it was claimed, had webbed feet, or were the physiological result of a culture that had forsworn the use of the chair. Wiser voices pointed to the meticulous nature of Japanese preparations, the use of camera and film technology to analyse athletes' performance and to learn from their competitors, the kind of reverse engineering that was transforming Japanese industry, and a level of government subsidy and corporate support that the American national Olympic committee could only dream of: with significant state funding, Japan sent 180 athletes to the games, second in size only to the US team.

Against this kind of star billing, the rest of the world's nations were reduced to cameos. Argentinian Santiago Lovell won the heavyweight boxing title, while Juan Carlos Zabala took the marathon, and then fainted during the medal ceremony, a move that cemented his popular appeal. Two gold medals for Ireland within an hour – Pat O'Callaghan in the hammer and Bob Tisdall in the 400-metre hurdles – and one for the Indian hockey team, triumphant again, sent quiet anti-imperial messages back home and to Britain. The Brazilians had arrived in a rusty naval cruiser, with nothing from their impecunious government but sacks of coffee beans to pay their way. The water-polo team did make it ashore, and wrote themselves into the plot by concluding their 7–3 defeat by Germany with a polite cheer for their opponents, before massing an attack on the Hungarian referee, whom they perceived as unconscionably biased. The intervention of the LAPD was required.

Will Rogers was a cheerleader, and his telegram signing off from the games spoke for many Angelenos and much of the American press corp. 'You folks all over the United States that thought these Olympic Games was just some real-estate racket of Los Angeles and didn't come, you have been badly fooled. You have missed the greatest show from every angle that was ever held in America.' They hadn't been fooled, it had been a real-estate racket, but it was an unprecedented show. The *Los Angeles Times* saw 'perfection of setting, excellence of management and brilliance of presentation'. IOC president Count Baillet-Latour thought it, 'The crowning glory of the Olympics.' Even the French, normally sparing in their praise for America, declared it, 'a stunning sporting and popular success.'[11] Amsterdam 1928 had been the best attended Olympics hitherto, with 660,000 tickets sold, one third of them for the football matches. Los Angeles sold 1.25 million tickets without any football competition at all; even the Olympic Arts Festival, held close to the Coliseum, attracted 400,000 visitors. Los Angeles also made money; capital costs aside, the box-office takings of over $2 million paid for the show.

Then the props and the stage sets went under the hammer. Hector Dyer, one of America's gold-medal winning 4 x 400-metre relay team, was hired as a salesman at the village. Adverts were run: 'Olympic Cottages, portable, suitable for beach, mountains, auto camps, approved for erection in Los Angeles.' Every single one was sold, some with members of the Australian team still in them, awaiting their ship home. The administration buildings were dismantled for lumber, even the perimeter fence found a buyer. By September, it had all but vanished into thin air.

FIVE

For the small circle of men devoted to German Olympism, it had been a long road to get the games to Berlin. The city had been first awarded the hosting rights to the Olympics at the IOC's Stockholm congress of 1912. However, the 1916 Berlin games never happened. The First World War intervened, and when Europe was finally at peace again, there were no Germans on the IOC and all the defeated central powers were excluded from the Olympics until 1928. Germany's return to the Olympic fold was piloted by Carl Diem and Theodore Lewald, invited onto the IOC in 1924, and, with the support of Coubertin, they launched a bid for the games in 1927. At the IOC's 1931 congress, Berlin, capital of Weimar Germany, was awarded the 1936 games. On 24 January 1933, the local organizing committee of the Berlin Olympics met for the first time; six days later, Adolf Hitler was sworn in as Reich chancellor.

The outlook for the games and its organizers did not look good. Lewald was the son of a Jewish civil servant who had converted to Christianity; Diem, the secretary, had one Jewish grandparent and was himself married to a Jew. Personal considerations aside, the Nazi Party's line on international sport in general, and the Olympics in particular, had been unremittingly hostile. Bruno Malitz, a Nazi ideologue and spokesman, argued, 'All kinds of foreigners have been having a marvellous time at our expense. The sporting promoters have thrown great sums of money about so that the international connections of Germany with her enemies shall be made yet closer.' The Olympics itself was decried as a 'Jewish international enterprise' and 'a plot against the Aryan race by Freemasons and Jews'. The party's newspaper, *Völkischer Beobachter*, had argued that no black athletes should be allowed at the Berlin games. Lewald, in conversation with the IOC president at the 1932 Olympics, assured him the Nazis would be 'absolutely opposed' to the games. In early February 1933, Nazi-supporting students, organized as the Kampfring gegen die Olympischen Spiele – the Fight Against the Olympic Games – demanded that 'the Olympic Games must not be held in Germany', dug up the running track at the Berlin athletics stadium and planted small 'Germanic' oaks in the lanes. In the March elections to the Reichstag, the Nazis and their coalition partners achieved a narrow majority and passed the Enabling Act, which established the legal and political basis of the dictatorship to come.

Called to a meeting with Hitler and Goebbels, his minister of propaganda, a week after the elections, Lewald and Diem expected the worst, only to find that there had been a change of mind. Hitler made it clear that the games would go ahead with his blessing. As Hitler would put it to Goebbels later in the year, 'Germany is in a very bad and difficult situation internationally. It should therefore try to impress world public opinion by cultural means. In this context it is fortunate that the Olympic Games will be held in Germany . . . one has to show the world what the new Germany can do culturally.'[1]

The best guide to what the new Germany could do culturally would have been a close examination of how German sports were being organized. The old sports ministry was dissolved and a senior Nazi installed as the head of the new organization. In this case, the Reichssportführer, Hans von Tschammer und Osten – whose closest encounter with sport hitherto had been wearing highly polished riding boots as part of his party costume – took charge. In keeping with the wider policy of party control over all civil organizations, he was also appointed the head of the German national Olympic committee and the local organizing committee. In the sporting nation, opponents and alternatives were harassed, closed down and eventually dissolved. Workers' sports clubs were liquidated and those sports clubs that remained were subject to ever stricter and harsher control – above all, the exclusion of Jews from membership and use of sport facilities – though many clubs anticipated these regulations and excluded their Jewish members before they were required to do so. Jews were successfully excluded from public facilities like swimming pools, banned from riding horses and confined to ghettoized Jewish sports clubs; after Kristallnacht, in 1938, they would be obliterated. Even the desperately conservative and patriotic Deutsche Turnenschaft – the bastion of Germanic nationalist gymnastics – was dissolved and taken under direct party control in 1936.

In total possession of the sporting infrastructure of the nation, the Nazi regime increasingly deployed sport as an instrument of foreign and domestic policy. As Germany began to challenge and then dismantle the network of restrictions that had been placed upon it since the signing of the Versailles treaty in 1919, the regime used international sport to ingratiate itself with the wider world, and to demonstrate the normality of Nazi Germany. Later, it would be used to signal Germany's increasing power and confidence. Goebbels over-ruled the Hitler Youth and Nazi student organizations that had refused to attend dangerously cosmopolitan international gatherings. The Nazi press was encouraged to take a greater interest in suitably patriotic sports stories. The Foreign Office and its diplomatic corps were deputized to chaperone German athletes abroad, now seen as warriors for Germany and representatives of the German race. At home, sport and exercise was increasingly cast as a patriotic duty, part of a wider campaign to purify and perfect German genetic stock.

If a close examination of Nazi Germany's sporting policy made the brutal totalitarianism and unbending anti-Semitism of the regime clear, the preparations for the Berlin games revealed the scale of its ambitions. Reviewing the early architectural plans for the games, Hitler stated that 'German sport needs something gigantic.' It was the same sensibility that would see him commission Albert Speer to redesign all of Berlin as *Germania*, the capital of the European, even global empire that the Third Reich was destined to become. When, at one point during the construction of the Olympic stadium, it was pointed out that the design and markings of the athletic field were not in concordance with then international standards, Hitler remarked that it made no difference, as all the future Olympic Games would be held in Berlin. Alongside a much bigger and grander sta-dium than the organizing committee had first imagined, and one clad in imperial stone rather than the flimsy glass and steel of Weimar modernism, Hitler and Goebbels called for the plan to include a gigantic assembly field – big enough to accommodate half a million people – and a classically inspired open-air amphitheatre that could take 200,000. They didn't quite get their half million, but the Reichssportfeld was the largest sporting complex in history, and set the precedent for Olympic parks to come.

Almost every subsequent park has required a new metro station and designated Olympic roads and routes. In 1936, one arrived at the Reichssportfeld either from the south, at the newly built S-Bahn station, or by road, on the series of interconnected avenues and boule-vards – labelled the Via Triumphalis. This Olympic highway ran from Unter den Linden in the city centre to the Olympic plaza at the east-ern end of the complex. At the centre of the Reichssportfeld was the Olympic stadium, accommodating 110,000 people, its great oval banking pierced at each end by a monumental gate. In addition, the immaculate landscaped grounds included an elegant streamlined swimming complex that could hold 17,000, a hockey stadium, an equestrian arena, tennis facilities, a large sports-administration and educational complex, and an amphitheatre modelled on the theatre of Epidaurus, a booming Peloponnese city state of the fourth century BCE, with space for a mere 25,000. The biggest element of all was the Maifeld, the huge sunken assembly ground, nearly 400 metres by 300 metres, and easily large enough to accommodate 180,000 people. Engineered for the mass ecstasy of Führer worship, the space was ringed by new and superbly engineered loudspeakers, while one's gaze was directed towards the grandstand and single speaker's podium on the western side of the field. There, a tower rose fifty metres above the stands, topped by an enormous bell. The pet proj-ect of Theodore Lewald, the bell was cast from sixteen and a half tons of steel and embossed with a Gothic German eagle above the five Olympic rings. Manufactured in the Ruhr, it went on a two-month journey through small-town northern Germany, welcomed by ranks of Hitler Youth and SS brigades, whipping up Olympic fever. The motto around the bottom of the bell read, '*Ich rufe die Jugend der Welt*' – 'I call on the youth of the world'. When Lewald had first designed the bell, he was taking his cue from the eighteenth-century enlightenment polymath, Friedrich Schiller, and his poem '*Das Lied von der Glocke*' – 'The Song of the Bell' – whose epigraph ran, 'I call the living, I mourn the dead.' However, the Olympic bell, which received extensive global coverage, was nearly always depicted alongside a portrait of Hitler: a very different Germany to Schiller's and Lewald's was calling.[2]

Nazi Germany's embrace of the games was both a relief for the IOC and a source of continuing anxiety. In mid-1933, President Baillet-Latour, perturbed by both the overenthusiastic involvement of the German state and the shrill racism and xenophobia of Nazi ideology, wrote to the new organizing committee, reminding them that, 'the games are conferred to a city not a country . . . and that they should have no political, racial, national or confessional character.'[3] Less euphemistically, in private, the IOC pressed for assurances that Jews would be allowed to attend, participate and compete for spots on the German team. This pressure forced a formal concession from the Nazis, who announced that 'all the laws regulating the Olympic Games shall be observed', and that 'as a principle, German Jews shall not be excluded from German teams at the Olympiad.'

For the next two years, this was more than enough reassurance for the IOC. Indeed, Baillet-Latour, who had confided that he was 'not personally fond of Jews and of the Jewish influence', was happy to collude in the illusion that the absence of Jews from German sport was primarily a function of their poor athletic genes and, in any case, was a 'minor unimportant detail'. He was not alone. This kind of casual anti-Semitism was the unreflective view of many of his IOC colleagues and his class. Sigfrid Edström thought Jews 'intelligent and unscrupulous. Many of my friends are Jews, so you must not think that I am against them, but they must be kept within certain limits.'[4] The Chicago businessman and American sports administrator, Avery Brundage, another IOC member, boasted to the Germans that his own Chicago sports clubs excluded Jews.

The IOC may have been satisfied, but in Europe, and, above all, in the United States, there was significant organized opposition to the games. The gauntlet was laid down in late 1933 by the AAU (American Athletic Union), who voted to boycott the Berlin Olympics if Jewish participation was not guaranteed 'in fact as well as in theory.' Other boycott movements sprung up in Scandinavia and Britain, only to fizzle out, but in the United States a powerful coalition emerged. Alongside sporting organizations like the AAU, there was immense pressure from Jewish groups, Catholic and Protestant activists appalled by the treatment of Jews and their own churches in Nazi Germany, and the labour movement as well. The leading opponent to the boycott movement, marshalling all the most conservative forces in American sport, was the chair of the American Olympic Committee, Avery Brundage. In an effort to head off the boycott movement, which by 1934 was nationwide and capable of mobilizing tens of thousands of supporters at mass rallies, Brundage sent himself on a fact-finding mission to Germany. There, entertained and ensconced by the Nazi elite and allowed to interview Gestapo-chaperoned representatives of the Jewish community, he concluded that there was no discrimination in German sport and no case for a boycott.[5]

Matters came to a head in 1935 with Hitler's declaration of the Nuremberg Laws, which systematically codified the persecution of Jews and their exclusion from every aspect of public and private life in Germany, and foreshadowed their destruction. In American Olympic circles, securing US participation and defeating the boycott movement hinged on getting the Germans to include at least one athlete of Jewish descent, and pressure was applied through formal and informal channels. The German compromise was to invite two 'half Jews' living outside of Germany to compete at the games: the fencer Helene Mayer, long resident in California, and ice-hockey player Rudi Ball, who had emigrated to Italy. Both accepted the offer. The German compromise was enough. Despite a final rally in Madison Square Gardens in late 1935, and a petition of half a million signatures, Brundage won the decisive votes at the American Athletic Union and the American Olympic Committee. He also took the chance to exclude his opponents from both bodies and install himself and his cronies, confident in Germany's commitment to fair play for the Jews. The following June, Gretel Bergman, the German Jewish high jumper, was allowed to try out for the German Olympic team; she equalled the national record, beat all the other trialists and was still excluded.

Berlin was the main feature, but the 1936 Winter Olympics, held in the dual Bavarian Alpine villages of Garmisch-Partenkirchen, was an intriguing prelude. For the Nazi machine, it was part dress-rehearsal, an exercise in what not to do on opening night. Despite the efforts taken to tone down the now pervasive and vulgar anti-Semitism of everyday life, Count Baillet-Latour and visiting journalists still found appalling posters – 'No Animals, No Jews' – and copies of the most virulently anti-Semitic press around the Olympics site. *Der Stürmer*, a weekly rag whose venom and violence was unparalleled in the Nazi Press, ran an Olympic special edition, which included a cartoon depicting a degenerate Jew looking enviously up at a glowing Aryan champion, with the caption, 'The Jews are our Misfortune'. Baillet-Latour insisted that the posters come down, which they did, and they would also be absent from the streets of Berlin for two weeks in August.

Significantly bigger and better catered for than the previously tiny winter games, the Germans actually built a new slope between the villages, designed to bring the skiers to the enormously expanded press corps at the bottom of the run. Seventy-five thousand spectators and whole regiments of SS guards, storm troopers and Nazi dignitaries shuttled between the mountains and Munich, where they could drink beer with the Reichssportführer, Von Tschammer, at his own Olympic beer garden, or watch the ballet, *The Olympic Rings*, with music by Richard Strauss. The star of the games was, by some way, the Norwegian ice-skater, Sonja Heine, winning her third consecutive Olympic gold medal; she was seen out and about with Hitler himself before departing for a career in Hollywood ice-dance spectaculars, much to the disapproval of the Norwegian nation, which considered her a quisling.

Just weeks after the closing ceremony of the winter games, Hitler sent German troops, against the advice of his general staff and in direct contravention of the Treaty of Versailles, into the demilitarized Rhineland. He did so in full knowledge that even the slightest military resistance from the French and their allies would be enough to stop the occupation in its tracks; yet the countermove never came. The last restraints on the aggression and opportunism of Hitler and his close circle – from cautious Prussian generals to the threat of outside intervention – were gone. Goebbels held a mock election to celebrate, in which Hitler received 98.97 per cent of the vote. Germany no longer required sport to ingratiate itself with the world: it was time to impress and conquer. A month before the Berlin games began, Max Schmeling, the great German heavyweight boxer, took on the African-American sensation Joe Louis in a fight in New York that acquired immense symbolic, racial and geopolitical meaning. Schmeling knocked Louis out. Goebbels recorded the event in his diary: 'Schmeling fought for Germany and won. The white man over the black . . . The whole family is in ecstasy.' Seventy thousand met him on his return home in an orgy of national celebration.[6]

With the Americans now fully committed to attending the games, the final flicker of resistance came from Spain, where, in March 1936, a new republican government had been elected. In June 1936, the International Committee for the Defence of Olympic Ideals met in Paris. Its delegates, mainly drawn from the European workers' sports movements, called for a boycott of Berlin and the creation of an alternative People's Olympiad in July.[7] The Spanish Popular Front government, at its strongest in Barcelona, was eager to attract international support, and invites were hastily despatched. In a fore-shadowing of the great wave of popular support for the republican cause amongst the leftist youth of Europe, thousands of athletes headed for Catalonia. The large French contingent were actually subsidized by the newly installed Popular Front government in Paris. Worker sports clubs sent delegations from Britain, Scandinavia, Czechoslovakia and the Low Countries. Italian and German exiles formed teams, Catalonia and the Basque Country, never present at the IOC's games, were separately represented, and athletes came too from French Algeria, Palestine and the United States. They arrived to find Spain descending into civil war. Two days before the games were due to begin, a coterie of rightist generals made their *pronunciamiento*: a declaration of opposition which triggered fighting in cities across Spain between rebel army units and the motley collection of forces loyal to the Popular Front government. The Olympiad was abandoned, and athletes, now trapped in Barcelona, found themselves sheltering from gunfire, building barricades and even joining the new republican militias, like the British cyclists from the socialist Clarion club, and Clara Thlalmann, a Swiss communist swimmer, who stayed and joined the anarchist Durutti Column.

Now, the capital city of the Reich had to put on its show face. Goebbels called on the cast to perform, stating, 'the future of the Reich will depend upon the impression that is left upon our guests.' Cheap trains and boats had been laid on for visitors from across Europe. Reports in the French and Dutch press found the Germans' relentless and obsequious desire to please comic. In Berlin itself, guests received preferential exchange rates and hotel rates, and jumped every housing queue. *Der Angriff* – 'The Attack' – the paper of the Berlin Nazi Party, which was normally stoking up the fires of xenophobic ultra-nationalism, now implored the city: 'We must be more charming than Parisians, more easygoing then the Viennese, more vivacious than the Romans, more cosmopolitan than London, and more practical than New York.' The German Labour Front, a Nazi ersatz trade union, was sufficiently unconfident that it officially declared a week of mirth and happiness: 'The coming eight days will be days of jollity and cheerfulness. Berliners should . . . with merry hearts and friendly expressions on their faces, receive their Olympic guests.' It only remained for 1 August, the opening day of the games, to dawn. It was showtime.[8]

SIX

For all the sifting of evidence and the scholarly re-examination of documents, we still see the Berlin Olympics through the lens of Leni Riefenstahl and the imagery of *Olympia*. Nowhere is that more obvious than in the historical memory of the torch relay and the opening ceremony. In reality, a group of German technicians, using a specially engineered optical lens, and the great and good of Greek politics gathered at Olympia to light the first torch in the relay. In the film, the setting is infinitely less prosaic, as the camera tracks through ethereal misty ruins, populated by scantily clad female priestesses conjuring mystic Olympian fire, and naked male athletes throwing javelins. Then, to the sound of Herbert Windt's triumphal martial score, the torch makes its way across Europe in a montage of maps, aerial shots of cities, and foggy silhouettes of cityscapes, from Olympia to Sofia, Belgrade, Budapest, Vienna, Prague and finally Berlin.

It is hard not to read these images in hindsight as the viewpoint of Luftwaffe pilots descending through the clouds on bombing raids, and the route itself, in reverse, the same as the one the Wehrmacht would be taking, five years hence, on their conquest of eastern and southern Europe. The torches themselves were made by Krupp, the nation's largest arms manufacturer, and the entire event was freighted with the most intense political meaning. As the torch left Olympia, the German ambassador to Greece announced that it was a gift across the ages, 'To my Führer, Adolf Hitler, and his entire German people.' German organizers encouraged local notaries along the route to give speeches that heralded the gift from the 'new Hellas' to the 'new Germany'. The arrival of the torch in Austria, particularly Vienna, provided the scene of wild demonstrations by local Nazis in support of the much-anticipated Anschluss with Germany. In the German-speaking Sudetenland of western Czechoslovakia, which the relay organizers had marked on their maps as part of the Reich, ethnic Germans were supportive, but the torch needed a police escort when passing through Slavic-speaking territory. In the final stages of the relay, as the torch approached Berlin on the morning of 1 August, the runners became exclusively blond-haired and blue-eyed Aryans.

Riefenstahl picked up the torch-relay six hours later, as it made its way past the frenzied crowds on Unter Den Linden, on the way to the Olympic stadium, accompanied by a phalanx of Nazi runners and big black Mercedes saloons. However, along the way, the flame had paused at the Lustgarten, where the Hitler Youth and SS had manoeuvred almost 70,000 members into the square while the IOC had lunch with Hitler. Before its final arrival at the Olympic stadium, Hitler, the IOC and the rest of the dignitaries made their way to the *Reichssportfeld* and the opening ceremony. Again, it is Riefenstahl who has defined the moment, capturing the immensity and the grandeur of the setting, the collective focus on Hitler himself – part grandee, part deity – and the vociferous, partisan, excitable nature of the crowd. The parade of nations, in particular, gives a sense of the febrile political atmosphere. The Austrian team's mass 'Heil Hitler' salute evokes an ecstatic response from the crowd, so too the French team's Olympic salute, which appears, to the uninitiated, indistinguishable from that of the Nazi Party.

Past opening ceremonies had closed with artillery salutes, choral singing and the release of doves, but, in *Olympia*'s version of the event, nothing could match the grandeur of Berlin. Riefenstahl makes the canons thunderous, the chorus almost celestial, while thousands of doves completely fill the vast skies above. The sequence closes with the arrival of the final torch-bearer, shot as small, frail and alone against the backdrop of the stadium's gigantic crowd. To a rising crescendo of orchestral rapture and crowd cheers, he surmounts a series of monumental staircases before lighting a great billowing flame in the Olympic cauldron.

The main racial drama of the Berlin Olympics, at the time and in its retelling, was, of course, the victory of Jesse Owens, the black American sprinter and long jumper who won four gold medals and beat the best of the Germans in unequivocal style.[1] However, there were also quiet victories for the Jewish athletes who braved the games. Jewish Hungarians alone won six gold medals, including Ibolya Csák in the high jump, two members of the water-polo team, Karoly Karpati in freestyle wrestling, and the fencers Ilona Schacherer-Elek and Endre Kabos. There were also medals for two Austrian Jews, Ellen Preis and

Robert Fein, as well as the American and Canadian basketball players, Samuel Balter and Irving Maretzky. Yet the Jewish presence at Berlin went unnoticed in the local press, which mainly concerned itself with the endless parade of German medallists. Easily the most successful nation at the games, the Germans won thirty-three gold medals, and a total of eighty-nine, across most of the sports, including athletics, boxing, canoeing, gymnastics, rowing, sailing, shooting and weightlifting. Captain Konrad von Wangenheim was amongst the most popular. After breaking his collarbone in the individual equestrian eventing competition, he still needed to finish the show-jumping course to ensure that Germany could win the overall team medal. He began his round with his arm in a sling, but was still able to give Hitler the Nazi salute. He then promptly fell at the first fence and his horse, Kurfürst, fell on top of him. Both were able to get up and complete the course to tumultuous applause. *Der Angriff*, Goebbels' own pet Berlin paper, and normally in a state of apoplectic anger, found it 'truly difficult to endure so much joy.'2

America's black athletes were treated courteously by Olympic officials, and were the subject of some adulation on the streets of Berlin. When *Der Angriff* complained that US triumphs were based on the use of 'black American auxiliaries', they were sharply reprimanded by the Ministry of Propaganda. Yet, despite the intemperate tone of the paper, *Der Angriff* was right: America's strong showing at the games rested on the remarkable achievements of a dozen African-American athletes. Alongside Owens' three individual golds and a team gold in the relay, there were victories for Archie Williams in the 400 metres, John Woodruff in the 800 metres and Cornelius Johnson in the high jump, as well as a slew of silver and bronze medals in track, field and boxing. The mainstream press in the North celebrated unproblematic American victories, the black press cheered the advance of 'the race' and spread the myth that Hitler had snubbed Owens by refusing to shake his hand. In the South, the sports pages merely recorded the results, if they mentioned them at all. Most tellingly, no paper south of the Mason–Dixon line published a photograph of Owens. Goebbels, in the privacy of his diary, described these victories as 'a disgrace. The white race ought to be ashamed', but he added that it was little wonder, coming, as the athletes did, from 'a country without *Kultur*.' An official in the German Foreign Office reflected that, 'if Germany had had the bad sportsmanship to enter deer or another species of fleet-footed animal, it would have taken the honours from America in the track events.' White Americans were no less wedded to the African-as-animal/subhuman/primitive model of African-American athletic excellence. Dean Cromwell, assistant coach of the US track team, argued, 'the negro excels in the events he does because he is closer to the primates than the white man.'[3]

While the conflicts and contradictions of the great powers were on show at Berlin, there was still some space for the sporting politics of new and nascent nationalisms. The Estonian Kristjan Palusalu won the heavyweight gold medals in freestyle and Greco-Roman wrestling. On his return home, between a third and half of the population of Tallin, the capital of the recently independent Baltic republic, turned out to greet him. The newspaper, *Uus Eesti*, wrote, 'The view on the streets of Tallin gave a beautiful recognition of how strong the feeling of unity among our people is.'[4] He and Estonia's other Olympians were sent on a government-funded, nationwide railway tour. Speeches were given in stations, local bands and orchestras played, and the athletes were showered with gifts, cake and flowers. The rye harvest, the peak moment of agricultural activity in the country, was interrupted for the show. Two Koreans, Sohn Kee-chung and Nam Sung-yong, gold and bronze medallists respectively in the marathon, bowed their heads in 'silent shame and outrage' as the Japanese flag was raised. The two, both born under Japanese imperial rule on the Korean peninsula, had been forced to compete as Kitei Son and Shoryu Nan, romanized versions of the Japanese pronunciation of their Korean names. At home, some newspapers published their pictures with the Japanese flag erased, and saw their editors imprisoned.[5] The British Indians, competing separately from the motherland, still did so beneath the Union Jack. However, in the dressing room, before every match, the hockey team's assistant manager, Pankaj Gupta, secretly produced a Congress tricolour, which the team saluted before entering the field of play.

During the opening week of the games, Hitler hosted a glittering dinner for the diplomatic elite at the Reich Chancellery, but, with just 200 guests, it was easily eclipsed by the parties held in the entertainments arms-race amongst his senior minions. The 'champagne flowed like water' for the 600 guests at the estate of Joachim von Ribbentrop, Hitler's roving diplomatic plenipotentiary. Göring took everyone to the opera and then back to his Berlin palace, where an amusement park had been erected alongside a kitsch eighteenth-century Germanic village complete with its own bakery and inn, and a cast of thousands. World War One flying ace Ernst Udet performed aerial stunts overhead, while disgraced American Olympian Eleanor Holm – excluded from the US team by Avery Brundage for getting drunk on champagne cocktails with the press corps on the steamship that brought them across the Atlantic – was reported to have been swimming naked in the pool. British diplomat Chips Channon recalled, 'roundabouts, cafes with beer and champagne, peasants dancing, vast women carrying pretzels, a ship as a beer house, crowds of gay laughing people, a mixture of luna park and the White Horse Inn.'[6] On the penultimate day of the games, Goebbels held his Sommerfest on Peacock Island – a nature reserve in the middle of the Wannsee. Göring's bash had been gauche but fun; this was gargantuan and uneasy. The army had been called in to build a pontoon bridge from the mainland to the island and served as a guard of oar-bearing honour along it. Girls dressed as Renaissance pages supplied food to 2,700 guests, followed by a firework display of such length and cacophony that the American ambassador, William Dodd, thought it, 'shooting of a kind that suggested war.' The teenage American swimmer Iris Cummings saw it for what it was: 'a power show.'

The whole thing had been a power show, but not entirely on the Nazis' terms. The IOC and the pressure of the boycott campaigns had forced the regime to curb its worst public excesses and accept the limited cosmopolitanism and internationalism of the Olympic movement. Under a measure of global scrutiny, albeit one that rarely went much beyond the most bland of tourist observations, a modicum of the old Berlin was able to emerge. Boxer Max Schmeling thought that 'Berlin regained its uniquely cosmopolitan atmosphere.' Teddy Stauffer, the big bandleader and Germany's King of Swing – a deviant and decadent musical form, according to the regime – played to sell-out crowds. For a short moment, books, banned since 1933, like the novels of Thomas Mann and Stefan Zweig, reappeared in the bookshops. The Gestapo were told to turn a blind eye to foreign homosexuals, and for just a couple of weeks the most virulent and public forms of racism went underground.

It was a small price for the regime to pay, for it got much of what

The Baron. Pierre Fredy, Baron de Coubertin, 1863–1937.

The first International Olympic Committee. From left to right: standing – Gebhardt, Guth-Jarkovský, Kemeney, Balck; seated – Coubertin, Vikelas, Butovsky.

**Making History:
Athens 1896.**

Above. The Martial Art of
the European Aristocracy:
Fencing at the Zappeion.

Left. 'A display of
manly virtues'.
Three of Denmark's
Olympian gentlemen.
From left to right:
Schmidt (track),
Nielsen (fencing) and
Jensen (weightlifting
and shooting).

Human Zoos and Freak Shows, St Louis, 1904. An Ainu man competing at the St Louis Anthropology Days.

Imperial Circus, London 1908. Italy's marathon runner Dorando Pietri falls for the third time in the stadium and is illegally helped to his feet.

A challenge from below,
the Worker's Olympics:
Vienna 1931, Antwerp 1937.

Left. Working-class super heroes.

Below. 'Proletarians of the world,
unite through sport!'

It's Showtime! Los Angeles 1932.

Above. Sun, Sea, Sand and Sport. The Olympics done the LA way.

Below. Antiquity comes to Hollywood. A concrete coliseum for the twentieth century.

The Olympic Family, Garmisch-Partenkirchen, 1936. From left to right: Rudolf Hess, Henri de Baillet-Latour and Adolf Hitler at the opening ceremony of the 1936 Winter games.

Not just Hitler's Games, Berlin 1936. The Indian Hockey Team. They would go on to thrash Nazi Germany 8–1 in the final.

Coming on Strong, Amsterdam 1928, London 1948.

Above. Lina Radke wins the only women's 800m at the games before the 1960s.

Below. Fanny Blankers-Koen wins the 200m.

From Ephebes to Abstraction. Olympic posters, 1912 to 1964.

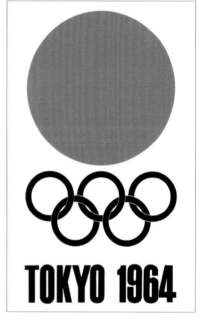

it wanted. Germany's place in the international community was normalized. Hitler, who had been presented as a dictator and tyrant, was shown to have immense domestic popular support. Goebbels himself thought, 'This Olympiad is a really big breakthrough. Fantastic press here and abroad . . . The foreign press is quite wild with enthusiasm.'[7] On matters of organization, scale, efficiency and grandeur, the global press were as one: Berlin had topped everything that had come before it. But there were plenty of complaints and criticisms too. The French found their hosts' nationalist hysteria and regimentation hard to stomach; one account of events at the velodrome described the home crowd as 'blind, chauvinistic and wild.' The *Herald Tribune* was less strident, but still commented that, 'there was a definite absence of warmth of feeling . . . The Olympics were a festival of Germanism.'[8]

The closing ceremony was held at night. Fantastical illuminations created a dome of light above the stadium. The Olympic flame was extinguished. The scoreboard carried the message, 'The Last Shot is Fired.' Three days after the closing ceremony, Captain Wolfgang Fürstner, the officer in charge of the Olympic village, discovered he was to lose his commission as he was now, under the Nuremburg Laws, deemed a Jew. He shot himself in the head. In the weeks following the games, military service for German youth, introduced earlier in the year in breach of the Treaty of Versailles, was doubled in length. The Nazi party decamped to Nuremberg for their eighth congress, an unrestrained torchlit festival celebrating the remilitarization of the Rhineland. The Condor Legion, soon to be joined by the pentathlon gold medallist Gotthard Handrick, started dropping bombs near Madrid – the Luftwaffe's contribution to the fascist cause in the Spanish Civil War. And, for the everyday party members, it was, as the cheerful rhyme of the time went, '*Wenn die Olympiade vorbei, schlagen wir die Juden zu Brei*' – 'When the Olympics are over, we will beat the Jews to a pulp'. It was open season again.

SEVEN

In 1868, the Meiji Restoration toppled the feudal shogunate that had governed Japan for over three centuries and restored the rule of the imperial house. The emperor then served as a figurehead for the new alliance of modernizers determined to emulate and catch up with the Western powers. Foreign expertise and technology were imported; American and European models of business and education were minutely examined, adapted and introduced. Modern sport had not figured on the reformers' shopping lists, but it came anyway.[1] In the last quarter of the nineteenth century, French officers introduced gymnastics, equestrian sports and fencing at the Toyama Military School, while British businessmen brought cricket to Kobe and Yokohama. Football came first to the Japanese navy, via Major Archibald Douglas. Rowing and track-and-field events were popularized by Frederick Strange, an English teacher working at one of Tokyo's prestigious high schools. Rugby was taken up in Tokyo's elite universities, as was baseball, but while the former remained the game of a narrow stratum of the wealthy, the latter diffused across Japanese society with remarkable speed. Despite this flood of foreign imports, Japan's indigenous tradition of the martial arts was strong enough to survive, and was codified and preserved as judo, kendo, and sumo wrestling.

Poised, in their own minds, between East and West, the administrators who founded the Japanese Physical Education Association in 1893 thought sport and physical education had ceased to be merely a pastime or a recreation, but had acquired the same kinds of moral, political and imperial connotations that it had in the West: 'we the Japanese people . . . have the immense responsibility of reconciling oriental and occidental civilizations and . . . have a great destiny to fulfil in the future as the leader of the oriental countries and the most advanced among them . . . this destiny depends largely on the physical condition of the Japanese people.'[2] They were certainly fit enough to deliver a crushing blow to the Tsar's navy in the short 1905 Russo-Japanese War. Japan, barely a presence in international councils before this, could no longer be ignored.

Absent, as were all Asian nations, from the first three Olympic Games, Japan received its first invitation in 1906 and a second in 1908, though both were declined for lack of resources and organization. In 1909, Kanō Jigorō, the educational reformer and inventor of judo, was invited to join the IOC, and, through him, the invitation to the 1912 Stockholm games was accepted. Only two Japanese athletes made the journey, and both performed poorly, confirming reformers' fears about the gap between Japan and the West. Sprinter Mishima Yahiko matched his personal best but finished last in the heats of the 100 metres. Marathon runner Kanakuri Shizo passed out in the middle of the race. Antwerp 1920 went slightly better. The Japanese Olympic Committee managed to send fifteen athletes, Shizo actually finished the marathon this time and Kumasi Kazuya won two silver medals in the men's tennis. They didn't budget terribly well, however, and had to rely on the charity of industrial conglomerates Mitsui and Mitsubishi to pay the return tickets for the team, stranded in Belgium.

Galvanized by shame, but also by the lure of international sporting triumph, the Japanese government began to financially support Olympic teams. Twenty-eight athletes went to Paris in 1924, and, on departure, received the national flag from Prince Chichibu, and thus the considerable honour of the imperial house's approval. Underwritten by increasingly large subsidies, 42 athletes competed in Amsterdam in 1928, then 131 at Los Angeles in 1932 and 180 in Berlin, where Japanese athletes, swimmers and divers were not merely competing but winning gold medals, and, in the case of men's swimming, dominating the opposition. NHK, the state broadcaster, was so eager for Olympic news from the 1932 games that its reporters watched Olympic events live and then recreated and broadcast them from borrowed Los Angeles studios. From Berlin, where radio facilities were eminently superior, NHK broadcast live, twice daily, for the duration of the Olympics.

The correlation between international prestige and Olympic achievement, now established in Japan, made the idea of a Japanese Olympics first plausible, then desirable and, finally, an essential element of foreign policy. In the mid-1920s, the Tokyo Prefecture first began to discuss the idea of an Olympic bid as a way of stimulating the city's recovery from the devastating 1923 earthquake. In 1930, the new Mayor of Tokyo, Nagata Hidejiro, now supported by the Japanese Olympic Committee, announced a bid for the 1940 games, designed to coincide with what senior bureaucrats had deduced to be the 2,600th anniversary of the foundation of the Japanese nation and people. Admittedly, these calculations were based on ancient oral legends only set down in 720 CE as the *Nihon Shoki*, but this was hardly the point. It was, as far as patriots were concerned, an auspicious moment to be celebrating the rising sporting and military prowess of imperial Japan, and the perfect notion around which to build support for a Japanese Olympics in an increasingly nationalist culture. The need for international engagement became all the more urgent in 1931, when the Japanese army, at its own initiative, invaded and occupied Manchuria and established an imperial colony, crowned by a puppet state, in this vast northern corner of China. Unable to have the occupation sanctioned by the League of Nations, Japan left the organization in 1933. Reporting back to the foreign office from the Los Angeles games, Japan's consul, Satô Hayato, declared that, 'This Olympic Games has been very beneficial in erasing anti-Japanese sentiment.' Alternatively, for the more liberal and cosmopolitan wing of Japanese society, this kind of impact meant that the games could be 'an opportunity for a national people's diplomacy', making peaceful inter-societal connections when the inter-state realm was so bellicose.[3] However, Consul Satô spoke for many in the imperial bureaucracy, armed forces and ultra-nationalist circles, arguing that, 'The best way to get the Americans to understand the real Japan is to defeat America and show them the true strength of the Japanese. Rational discourse is completely useless. Americans probably first understood the true strength of the Japanese when the Rising Sun flag was raised . . . during the Olympic Games.'

Thus, the Japanese bid for the 1940 games, officially launched in 1932 and up against Rome and Helsinki, was the first to be a truly state-supported campaign and a matter of pressing public policy. The Tokyo Prefecture put up $100,000, a huge amount then, to fund the campaign. Cabinet ministers and diplomats were recruited. Ambassadors were encouraged to lobby foreign politicians outside of the IOC who might have influence. The decisive move was to send the Japanese IOC delegate, Sugimura Yôtarô, to plead with Mussolini to withdraw Rome's bid, the main challenger for the 1940 games. In the you-scratch-my-back kind of deal that has become the norm in international sports politics, Mussolini announced with unusual candour, 'We will waive our claim for 1940 in favour of Japan if Japan will support Italy's effort to get the XIIIth Olympiad for Rome in 1944.'

Helsinki remained the only plausible challenger, and, in this battle, President Baillet-Latour proved Japan's key ally and an unlikely evangelist for spreading the Olympics beyond Europe and North America. Despite ticking off the Japanese for their deal with the Italians and insisting that they stop lobbying outsiders, Baillet-Latour was a supporter. He effectively arranged for the Japanese to invite him to Tokyo, where he was duly impressed, and offered them key technical and political advice on how to make their candidature a success. A late bid from London, led by the British Olympic Association, was headed off by discreet pressure applied at high diplomatic level. The plan was quietly withdrawn before the IOC's Berlin congress sat down to make their choice. The final vote went Tokyo thirty-seven, Helsinki twenty-six.

Japan had won the 1940 Olympics, but what it would mean and what place they would occupy in Japanese foreign policy was contested from the start. On the one hand, amongst the Japanese members of the IOC and the more liberal members of the bid committee, there remained the hope that the games would be a cosmopolitan festival. Prince Tokugawa Iyesato stated that, 'It is my firm belief that the mission of this Olympic Festival will be to unfold in a marvellous panorama of sports a harmonious blending of the entire world culture.'[4] Others, like Count Sayo, saw it as an opportunity to demonstrate Japan's growing imperial might, to stake a place on the world's sports fields as well as its battlefields. Finally, there were those who believed that Japan's sanctified ethnic uniqueness made the Olympics, at best, an inappropriate event through which to celebrate the foundation of the nation – a dilemma typified by the issue of the emperor's voice. In 1928, during a ceremony to commemorate Hirohito's ascension, his voice was inadvertently broadcast to the nation by NHK radio. It was an act so blasphemous that, on future occasions, the chief executive of the state telecommunications bureau would personally turn off the radio station's microphones during the emperor's rare public speeches. While Mussolini and Hitler made full use of the power of amplification, the power of Japan's emperor was enhanced by silence. Kono Ichiro, one of the more virulently nationalist MPs of the Seiyūkai party, was troubled by the implications of Olympic protocol. Speaking in parliament, he argued, 'Based on this regulation, Prime Minister Adolf Hitler opened the Berlin Olympics. And thus, for Japan, the Emperor would have to play this role. As a Manifest Deity in the realm of the "sacred inviolable" . . . isn't it impossible for the Emperor to stand and make the opening remarks?'[5]

The idea of a torch relay proved even more problematic. Carl Diem, eager that his invention should become an Olympic tradition, was campaigning for a torch relay at the 1940 games almost as soon as they were awarded to Tokyo. With the encouragement of the IOC president, Baillet-Latour, he proposed a 10,000-kilometre route from Olympia to Tokyo that mixed runners, riders and boats, and traced a good section of the ancient silk routes from Asia to Europe. More prosaically, the Japanese organizers wanted to send a warship to Greece, sail for home, and then conduct a short national torch-relay to Tokyo. Count Yoshi, a Japanese member of the IOC, countered with a more modest route via Aden, Bombay and Singapore, less reliant on routes across mainland China, with whom Japan would soon be at war. The Miyazaki Prefecture, located on Japan's southernmost island, campaigned hard for a route that would link the city of Hyūga – where the offspring of the Japanese sun goddess first descended to earth – to Tokyo, home of their descendant, the current emperor. They received considerable support from the nationalist press and the army – the same constituency that welcomed Japan's invasion of China in July 1937. By 1938, with the war in China in full swing, the newspaper *Akhai*, surely half joking, leaked the idea that the organizers were contemplating flying the Olympic flame in kamikaze planes from Olympia to Japan. In public, the organizing committee was reduced to saying, 'We will do our best to hold a flame relay from Athens, but if it is not possible, we are currently considering a Japanese national flame relay.'[6] Yet in March 1938, in total disregard of the realities of geopolitics in East Asia, the IOC awarded Sapporo the 1940 winter games.

All of these debates were abruptly terminated in mid-1938. Now embroiled in a massive military adventure in China, and in full knowledge that war with the United States and the British Empire was inevitable, the now overwhelmingly military government passed the National Mobilization Act. Amongst many measures, the government secured firm control over sporting institutions and began to remodel the curriculum in favour of Japanese martial arts, downgrading Western sports and elevating the place of drill and basic military training in schools. Three months later, with little fanfare, the Japanese pleaded the need for 'the spiritual and material mobilization of Japan', and relinquished the 1940 games.

After the 1924 Paris games, Coubertin never attended another Olympics. He was wheeled out by the Nazis in 1936, his recorded voice was used at the opening ceremony and his approving statement, 'The imposing success of the Berlin Games has served the Olympic ideal magnificently', was widely quoted. The Nazis reciprocated, nominating him the next year for the Nobel Peace Prize. But time had not been kind to the baron. Widowed, cleaned out by disastrous investments and now broke, he wrote to his old friend, Dr Francis Messerli: 'These adverse circumstances have created an agonizing situation. The loss of my personal fortune threatens my life-long effort at enlightening pedagogical progress.' Paying the rent was hard too. The following year, having long been reportedly melancholic in spirit, Coubertin died of a heart attack. He was living alone, close to destitute, in an apartment in Geneva, kept afloat by subventions via Carl Diem from the German government. He was the last to bear his family's noble title. Buried in Laussane, in sight of today's IOC offices, his heart was removed from his corpse and buried at Olympia. As the decade drew to a close the sense of an ending must have been palpable among senior Olympians.

If the realities of the emerging global war had finally hit home for the Tokyo Olympics, the IOC and the increasingly active German sports officials managed to evade them. The IOC accorded Olympic honours to the Nazis' popular leisure corps, Kraft durch Freude, and gave a diploma to Leni Riefenstahl for *Olympia*. The Germans reciprocated, opening a new Olympic institute in Berlin. Despite the obvious horrors of Kristallnacht and the now seemingly inevitable fate of Germany's Jews, the IOC was ready to award the 1940 Winter Olympics to Garmisch-Partenkirchen for a second time, and with no mention, this time, from the president, of any need to respect Olympic rules. When the war finally came and the prospect of any games had collapsed, Reichssportführer von Tschammer sent Carl Diem to occupied Brussels and the office of Count Baillet-Latour with a plan to 'rejuvenate' the IOC with German appointees: the first stage of a planned and wider Nazi takeover of international sporting organizations. The count's response was to settle into immovable inactivity, refusing to call the IOC congress at which this kind of coup could be conducted. By the time the IOC met again, in Lausanne, in 1946, Baillet-Latour and von Tschammer would be dead, two of perhaps the fifty million who perished in the global conflict.

5

SMALL WAS BEAUTIFUL: THE LOST WORLDS OF THE POST-WAR OLYMPICS

LONDON 1948 • HELSINKI 1952 • MELBOURNE 1956
ST MORITZ 1948 • OSLO 1952 • CORTINA D'AMPEZZO 1956

A rather plump lady, partly veiled and wearing what appeared to be a flowing white nightdress, was able to get on to the track, complete half a circle of it, and actually ascend the rostrum and begin a speech with something like, 'Peace' . . . But lack of breath, because of her girth and exertion, and the timely action of one senior Finnish official who did not know she was part of the official ceremony stopped her at this point. She was removed by the police, who later announced that she was a mentally deranged German girl who had come to address 'Humanity'.

Peter Wilson, recalling the opening ceremony
of the 1952 Helsinki Olympics

ONE

One wonders what would have happened to her today? Tasered by secret-service agents posing as stewards? Immolated by a laser beam fired from space, or one of the network of security drones hovering above the stadium? Then charged and tried for terrorist offences? In the collective memory of the immediate post-war games, they are remembered as small and charming, even Edenic – the Olympics, before they were sullied by economic and political imperatives and subject to hyper-militarized security. In some ways, they were Edenic, but, as with Wilson's own memories, the collective's can be most unreliable too. AKA 'The Man They Can't Gag' in his sports column in the *Daily Mirror*, Wilson was amongst the leading figures of his generation of sports writers, bringing a new level of hyperbole to the art; he certainly knew how to tell a good yarn.[1] Writing nearly three decades after the event, we can forgive him a little artistic licence, and, given his preference for a long liquid lunch, I imagine even his initial recollections were a little hazy, but even so he is way off. The few photographs and snippets of film that were taken of Barbara Rotbraut-Pleyer at the opening ceremony of the 1952 Olympic Games do not suggest a women who was plump, out of breath or deranged. Rather, they depict a calm and determined young peace activist trying to make a political intervention. The official report of the games was less florid than Wilson, and rather more gentle: 'Just as the atmosphere in the stadium was at its most hushed and solemn and the archbishop was preparing to read his Latin prayer, an unexpected intermezzo occurred. Dropping over the barrier in front of stand C, a young woman ran along the track and gained the rostrum. There, however, her performance ended without further disturbing the programme.'[2]

A student at the University of Tübingen, she was, the report noted, a 'peace apostle', and her intention was to use the games as a platform for making the case for global peace and disarmament.

Given that the United States conducted massive atomic tests just months either side of the games, and that Chinese and American soldiers would exchange fire in Korea throughout the Olympics, it was hardly an act of derangement to go to the world's most visible celebration of pacifism and internationalism and say to the world, 'Enough!' The Finnish, without any of Wilson's mocking, remember her fondly as the 'Peace Angel' and the Helsinki games as 'the last real Olympics': a golden age of the games, unencumbered by the problems of systematic doping, political boycotts and spiralling costs.[3]

The two other Summer Olympics of the immediate post-war era have also acquired monikers of nostalgia. London 1948 is invariably referred to as the 'Austerity Games', a term redolent of the straitened economic circumstances under which it was held, but also a phrase that carries a sense of simplicity and purity, an Olympics stripped back to just the sport. Melbourne 1956, held at a peak moment of conflict in the Cold War, was swiftly remembered as the 'Friendly Games'.[4] Against a backdrop of the Suez Crisis and the Soviet invasion of Hungary, the games were exalted for rising above these events and offering a globally powerful image of a united, rather than a divided, humanity – the last Olympics to do so before the Cold War came to dominate the narratives of subsequent games. These roseate collective memories have some real basis in the history of the games. That they were staged at all after the firestorm of the Second World War, and that they could still find takers across the world for the notion that a sporting spectacular might be a meaningful, practical and moral response to the madness of international politics, were considerable achievements; all three games attracted more athletes from more nations than Berlin or any prior games. For the most part, they were run by genuine gentlemen internationalist Olympians, and were, by and large, free of bombastic nationalism. In fact, despite everything, the simple pacific cosmopolitanism of the games was real and tangible. The Czech runner Emil Zátopek thought it 'a liberation of the spirit to be there in London. After all those dark days of the war, the bombing and the killing and the starvation, the revival of the Olympics was as if the sun had come out. Suddenly, there were no more frontiers, no more barriers. Just the people meeting together.'[5]

The post-war games were certainly a lot cheaper than Berlin. London 1948, even allowing for inflation, was run on a budget of no more than £3 million, and its biggest infrastructural investment was building a pedestrian walkway less than half a mile long. The organizing committee was ready to provide Olympic visitors with soap, but asked them to bring their own towels. Sporting equipment, down to the last basketball and clipboard, was punctiliously recorded and sold off after the games. When swimming officials submitted a receipt for a meeting held over lunch at Claridge's, they received a furious reprimand from the organizing committee: 'The staff at Wembley are working on an austerity basis and with the utmost economy.'[6] Helsinki had built a new stadium before the war in anticipation of holding the games in 1944. For 1952, given that they had just finished paying massive war reparations to the Soviet Union, the Finns merely repaired the bomb damage to the field and emptied the swimming complex of the fish and vegetable stalls that had used it during the war. The city's infrastructure received an upgrade that now seems Lilliputian: the airport acquired a tiny international terminal, a small Olympic pavilion was added to the passenger port, the main roads were resurfaced and the first, and the then only mini-golf course and only set of traffic lights in the country were installed. Most cherished of all these small legacies was the Linnanmäki amusement park and its gentle wooden roller coaster, built close to the Olympic stadium. Melbourne built itself a new and adventurous modernist aquatic complex, but for the rest it just spruced up the best of its Victorian and Edwardian heritage – like the Royal Exhibition Hall and St Kilda Town Hall.

Perhaps, though, what set these games in nostalgic aspic was television, or rather its absence. These were the last games not to be shown live, at least in part, to a global audience, albeit one heavily concentrated in the United States and western Europe. They were free of the narrative and commercial pressures that television would bring, and they were, of course, free of the money it would generate. They were invisible to the world and remain more inaccessible to scrutiny than their televised successors.

The BBC paid £1,000 for the rights to cover the 1948 games, and mounted its most ambitious outside-broadcast programme ever: over seventy hours of live coverage was transmitted, over seven and a half hours in one day, a feat only exceeded by American coverage of their interminable presidential conventions. Richard Dimbleby and Wynford Vaughan-Thomas, the BBC's most senior broadcasters and key voices at the corporation during the war, fronted the show, but the audience, even with a late flurry of TV purchases before the games, was in front of just 90,000 televisions, overwhelmingly in the south of the country and London; at around £50 a go, a black and white television would cost an average manual worker two months' wages. Television had barely arrived in Finland at all by 1952 and there was no domestic coverage of any kind, nor was the offer from American broadcasters to cover at least some of the games taken up by the organizers. For the moment, the cinema newsreel remained the most important source of visual news, and both the London and the Melbourne organizing committees commissioned official films, shot in glorious quivering Technicolor. Melbourne, if anything, was a step backwards. Despite considerable interest from American and other foreign broadcasters and newsreel companies, the Melbourne organizing committee managed to alienate both constituencies and ended up selling the TV rights just to domestic broadcasters, and then only a few days before the opening ceremony. In a desperate effort to reach beyond the 5,000 homes that had television in Australia, the broadcasters and Ampol Petroleum created TV theatres in their gas stations, and community halls acquired sets. All very cosy, but, as one US correspondent remarked during the games, 'Australia has become the "dark continent" to millions of sports-minded Americans.'[7]

Presiding over this, and intent on preserving the Olympic Games in the image of the now departed Coubertin, were the IOC presidents of the era: the Swede Sigfrid Edström, from 1942 to 1952, and his American successor, Avery Brundage, who held the post for two decades, from 1952 to 1972.[8] The two men met at the 1912 Stockholm games, where Edström was an athletics official and Brundage was a competitor in the pentathlon and decathlon. They had in common a long and successful career in business, conservative politics and anti-Semitism. Edström, appointed to the IOC in 1920, was also the president of the International Amateur Athletics Federation (IAAF), and headed off the challenge of the Women's Olympics by incorporating women's athletics into the IAAF and the games on his own very narrow terms. He had also been instrumental in excluding Paavo Nurmi from the 1932 games for his contravention of the amateur statutes. Brundage won his spurs as the head of the American Olympic Committee after defeating the anti-Nazi Berlin boycott campaign, and by banning the swimmer, Eleanor Holm, for being her own woman and drinking champagne on the transatlantic crossing to the 1936 games. Both remained adamant in their commitment to the notions that the Olympics should remain the preserve of amateurs, that their own narrow conceptions of sport as a social and cultural practice were the self-evident norm, while everyone else's were narrowly ideological, and that sport in the service of internationalism could somehow remain separable from both nationalism and international conflicts.

The milieu in which they emerged and the organization over which they presided – the IOC itself – had been unbendingly white, male and of privileged European descent. Between 1907 and the outbreak of the First World War, forty men were appointed to the IOC, thirty-seven of them from Europe or North America.[9] Along the way, the IOC acquired four princes, a duke and a marquis, six counts and two barons. Its military wing was also reinforced with the arrival of two generals, a commandant and a colonel. The interwar era was little different, when fifty Europeans, seven North Americans and five men from Australia and New Zealand were appointed to the IOC. Latin America did better, with sixteen members. Across the world, aristocratic title remained a very effective route to membership (hello to Japan's Prince Tokugawa Iesato and Iran's Prince Samad Khan), but increasingly one could make the grade by virtue of immense wealth, high political standing, direct involvement in the politics of physical education and either staging the games or establishing new national Olympic committees. Amongst the dozen or so Asian representatives that joined the IOC between the wars, we find the leading Turkish advocate of physical education, as well as the national football and volleyball pioneer Selim Siri Taracan, and the Indian professor G. D. Sondhi, founder of the Asian games. The first Chinese member of the IOC, appointed in 1922, was the Yale-educated diplomat Dr C. T. Wang, joined in 1939 by the then nationalist minister of finance, and reputed to be the richest man in the country, Dr H. H. Kung, though perhaps not as rich as IOC member Sir Dorabji Tata, the Bombay industrialist who personally funded the Indian delegation to the 1924 Olympics. Africa was represented by just two delegates: an Egyptian, who was actually an ethnic Greek from Alexandria, called Angelo Bolanaki, who would then move himself and his IOC affiliation to Greece, and the South African Sydney Farra, who was a white Englishman, scion of a Johannesburg gold-mining house. As late as 1959, IOC member Otto Mayer, when recommending the Kenyan Reginald Stanley Alexander for membership of the committee, could write, 'My idea is he would be a very good member for us. He is young, very Olympic minded; he is British (not a coloured man!), and I wonder if it would not be a good idea to have once a member in that section of the world, that means Africa?'[10] Given the opportunity to redress the balance after the war, when a whole raft of new members joined the IOC, the geographical distribution of members barely changed at all, while known collaborators and fascist sympathizers – like the Frenchman the Marquis Melchior de Polignac, and the Italian General Vaccaro – were welcomed back. In Reginald Honey, the IOC found a shameless and persistent defender of apartheid South Africa.

However, two processes of change were at work that would in time not only transform the composition of the IOC, but also undermine its ideological underpinning. The dismantling of European empires began with Indian independence in 1947 and gathered pace through the 1950s. Avery Brundage fended off the first attempts by the Norwegians and the Soviet Union to expand the IOC's membership and to exclude South Africa. However, in the 1960s and 1970s, an influx of new members, and a recognition of the post-colonial inequalities and injustices within the Olympic movement, would explode in sustained and very visible conflicts over apartheid and American civil rights. The decision, in 1951, by the leadership of the Soviet Union not only to join the Olympic movement, but to make the Olympic Games the central sporting front in the wider cultural Cold War, forced the IOC to, in effect, cede sovereignty to states and accept the government-appointed representatives of the communist and post-colonial world on the IOC. It also meant the beginning of the end of amateurism. Edström, Brundage and the organizers of the post-war games sought to temper this dynamic by insisting on the innocence and amity of the Olympics, and, where they could, imposing their own Olympian solutions on the German, Korean and Chinese questions, but it was an unequal battle. In the 1960s, aided and abetted by television, the sporting dimensions of these two global conflicts would make the Olympic movement's gentlemanly amateurism and apolitical internationalism untenable.

TWO

It says something for the insouciance and gumption of the late imperial British aristocracy that, just two months after the Americans had dropped the atomic bomb on Japan and the Second World War had come to an end, Lord Burghley should get himself to Stockholm to make the case to IOC president Sigfrid Edström that London should host the 1948 Olympic Games. Born David Cecil, he died the 6th Marquess of Exeter, and went through the entire range of Olympian gentleman gears along the way. A gold medallist in the 400-metre hurdles at the 1928 Amsterdam games, he effortlessly moved on to membership of the IOC, a place on its executive committee, and became president of the Amateur Athletics Association; at the same time, he served for thirteen years as a Conservative MP, before being appointed governor of Bermuda in 1943. He was joined in winning and organizing the games by a cast drawn from the sporting patricians and enthusiasts that still ran British sport: Lord Aberdare, a real and lawn tennis amateur champion, Conservative politician and voluble advocate of popular physical education for the nation; Sir Noel Curtis-Bennett, a senior Treasury civil servant, founder of the National Playing Fields Association and a man of such maniacal sporting and bureaucratic zeal that, at one point, he held official posts in over sixty sporting organizations and would die of a stroke while addressing the West Ham Boys and Amateur Boxing Club in 1950; Stanley Rous, the punctilious secretary of the Football Association, who, in 1947, would lead England and the home countries back into world football by re-joining FIFA; as well as past gentlemen Olympic champions, like the runner Harold Abrahams and the rower Jack Beresford.

In the opening sequence of the official film of the 1948 games, a tiny figure clasping the Olympic torch runs across a ridge, somewhere in southern England. On the grassy hilltop, a huge V-shaped copse has been fashioned. The clipped tones of the film tell us, 'V for victory. Victory, not in war, not in wealth, not in tyranny, but in sportsmanship and in peace.'[1] London 1948 was imagined as a warm-hearted internationalist sporting riposte to the nationalist bombast of Berlin 1936 and the tragedy of the Second World War, a return to normality, and one with London and Britain at its centre.

As late as 1946, when London won the postal vote to host the 1948 games, one might have been able to maintain this illusion. Ernest Bevin, the otherwise clear-eyed foreign secretary, predicted that 'in two years' time we should have got into our stride again', but by mid-1947 it was obvious this was not going to be the case. Britain had abandoned the Greek civil war and the front-line fight against communism to the Americans. India and Pakistan had celebrated independence, Burma and Ceylon would soon follow. Two years after the war, rationing was as fearsome as ever, the most obvious bomb damage had been cleared from most city centres but there remained a nationwide housing shortage of crisis proportions. Everything had been made considerably worse by the harshest winter in a generation.

Lord Burghley and his friends may have brimmed with bonhomie and good intentions, but in post-war Britain, nothing moved and nothing happened without the man from the ministry. Burghley found Labour prime minister Clement Attlee, a huge cricket fan, was broadly supportive of the project, and he appointed Philip Noel-Baker as minister for the Olympics. Noel-Baker was an Edwardian Quaker polymath. An academic and Olympian before the First World War, and a conscientious objector during it, he was active in the formation of the League of Nations and won a silver medal in the 1,500 metres at the 1920 Antwerp Olympics. A Labour MP since the late 1920s, he was instrumental in guiding the government's political support for the games and convinced many that the foreign exchange and tourism income that the Olympics would bring would be of considerable help to the country's perilous balance of payments. Unlike some of his Whitehall colleagues, he also considered the games 'a very big political and moral event in the life of the world', and pointed to the success of the 1945 Dynamo Moscow football tour of Britain as an example of the new sports diplomacy.[2] In the run-up to the games, the government was unable to countenance German or Japanese participation, but it was enthusiastic that the Soviet Union should attend. Attlee's radio broadcast welcoming competitors to London, almost certainly scripted by Noel-Baker, was twenty-four-carat Olympian idealism: 'A common love of sport creates a bond of friendship between men and women separated by distance and by lack of a common language. It over-steps all frontiers.'[3]

However, the most pressing argument in government circles concerned impressions. In contrast to the ruling orthodoxy of the interwar Foreign Office – that sport was an irrelevance in determining national standing, and a dangerous form of demagogy at that – it was now accepted that keeping up appearances at international sporting events really did matter. In a memorandum to the Cabinet, Noel-Baker underlined this: 'If the games are to be held in this country, it is essential to our national prestige that they should be a success.'[4] By late 1947, the games became part of a wider Foreign Office mission: 'Our task now, in certain countries, is rather to combat the impression that Britain is in decline.' Money was found to cover the games' renovation and refit costs. The recently nationalized British Rail agreed to halve fares for competitors and officials. London Transport made them free. The Ministry of Supply found spare station wagons and buses for the organizers, who ran their whole transport operation out of a church hall in Wembley. The Ministry of Food decreed that Olympic athletes would receive the Category-A rations, normally reserved for those in occupations – like miners and dockers – that demanded very physical labour. The Olympic torch was designed by the fuel-research unit of the Department of Scientific and Industrial Research. The armed forces, still consuming an unprecedented fraction of the peacetime labour force and government expenditure, were mobilized. The Army and Navy department store provided offices for the organizing committee. The army itself hosted the equestrian events in Aldershot, and seemed to be involved in the stewarding of almost everything. The Royal Navy laid out and policed the sailing course in Torbay; the battleship HMS *George V* and the aircraft carrier HMS *Victorious* provided the backdrop to the competition. The new Firefly-class dinghies were built with the same technology – hot moulding of layers of birch plywood – that had been used in wartime aircraft production, and were built by recycling decommissioned RAF gliders. German prisoners of war, still held in the UK, did most of the labouring on the new pedestrian walkway from the Tube station to the Empire Stadium – the Olympic, later Wembley Way. There was never any question of constructing an

Olympic village when RAF Uxbridge and West Drayton were available and wooden huts in Richmond Park, originally erected to house new army recruits, could be spruced up in a jiffy. They were given a lick of paint and, along with a miscellany of nurses' homes, grammar schools and barracks, were all supplied by the Ministry of Works with the domestic infrastructure of wartime hostels: '34,000 sheets, 13,000 small chairs, 36,000 pieces of crockery and 4,000 wardrobes.' The *Surrey Comet* approved: 'It looks comfortable and yet bears the stamp of austerity.'[5]

The perennial problem of an Olympic stadium was solved by Sir Arthur Elvin, the owner and manager of Wembley Stadium Ltd. Built in 1923 for the 1924 British Empire Games and Exhibition, the stadium went into receivership soon afterwards and was picked up for a song by Elvin. It had been making good money for him ever since, hosting the FA Cup, regular greyhound racing and speedway. Convinced that the games would be good business, he raised the capital to refurbish not only the stadium, but also the Empire Pool, which had to be transformed from a skating rink into an aquatic complex. In a seventeen-day miracle of organization, the entire field was relayed for the games, new seats and a makeshift scoreboard erected, and a platform built for the Olympic cauldron. As with Imre Kiralfy, director of the Franco-British Imperial Exhibition and builder of the White City Olympic stadium in 1908, Elvin was responsible for more than just construction, and provided a whole host of crucial work on design, ticketing and planning. Like Kiralfy, his efficiency, patriotism and indispensability did not, in the absence of real social standing, deem him important enough to sit on the games' organizing committee.

The rest of the facilities were equally make-do-and-mend. The pool, despite everything, retained a crack caused by an exploding German landmine and had to be continuously topped up during the Olympics. Herne Hill Velodrome got a tiny new wooden stand and a temporary booth with twelve telephones. The ageing Earl's Court was wheeled out once again for weightlifting and wrestling; Finchley Lido, normally a site of neighbourhood picnicking and recreational paddling, hosted the water polo. Haringey Arena, deep in working-class north London, put on the basketball, to often small and always uncomprehending local crowds. Hockey certainly went downmarket, making use of the Guinness and Lyon's Corner House company athletics grounds in the western Metrolands of Park Royal and Sudbury, and the sports fields of Chiswick Polytechnic, ringed by mock-Tudor, semi-detached suburban streets. The post-production office of the official film turned derelict air-raid shelters into dark rooms and editing suites.

Official enthusiasm for the games was not always reflective of the public mood. The *Evening Standard*, a leading voice amongst sceptics, stated that, 'The average range of British enthusiasm for the Games stretches from lukewarm to dislike. It is not too late for invitations to be politely withdrawn.'[6] Certainly, in the early summer of 1948, ticket sales for the games remained sluggish, and the sporting nation's attention was firmly focused on the Test series against Australia. The cricket had been the leading story on all the sports pages since the end of the football season. Don Bradman – the greatest batsman of the era – was on his last tour to England, and around 10 per cent of the adult population was, at any one time, tuning in to the live commentary on the BBC. Although, with help from some unusually good August weather, crowds at the games were healthy and given widespread coverage in the written press, as well as on radio and the fledgling domestic TV service, they remained at one remove from the mainstays of sporting passion in the country – cricket, football, boxing, horse racing and rugby league – and their working-class constituencies and professional athletes.

Here, in the world of British amateur sport, an older order remained intact, while professionals, commercialism and popular tastes were kept at bay. The British Olympic Committee and many of its sporting federations implemented the most draconian amateur regulations, refusing even to allow broken-time payments for athletes with salaried employment, or the admission of swimming coaches. Angela Thirkell, in her 1948 novel, *Love Among the Ruins*, typified the upper-class cynicism of the day: 'it seems very silly to have Olympic Games here. To begin with we shall be the only real amateurs, and to go on with, our teams will be perfectly undernourished. Still, if that's what the government wants.'[7] It was an arrangement that ensured the team drew heavily on patrician amateur athletes, and subjected its less privileged stars to either penury or the impossible double bind of full-time work and training; this contrast was typified by the gold-medal winning rowers in the coxless pairs: Dickie Burnell – Eton, Oxford and the London Rifles – whose work as a rowing correspondent for *The Times* did not deem him a professional, and Bert Bushnell, a shipbuilder's apprentice at fourteen, who was not even allowed to join his father's shipbuilding firm lest he contravene the amateur regulations of the Henley Regatta. The relationship between the two, though successful, was incredibly antagonistic. George Wheedon, the nation's star gymnast, had been unable to afford either bus fares or gym fees before the war, and had taught himself in his backyard, doing handstands on flower pots and building his own bars.

The royal family received the IOC and key dignitaries at a grand lunch at Buckingham Palace before throwing a party for 300 athletes. The *News of the World* was bowled over by this kind of gracious populism: 'In a most democratic manner their Majesties conversed amicably with each guest.' But, for George Wheedon, 'It was nothing special really. We shook hands with some royalty. There was some tea and a few buns, but no champagne.'[8] It was this kind of two-tier, upstairs-downstairs thinking that saw the British women's team equipped with additional clothing coupons and sent to Bourne and Hollingsworth, the traditional outfitter for domestic staff in upper-class households, to buy their official kit. Fencer Mary Glen-Haig thought it, 'The sort of thing you might buy for your cook.' While the regulation of athletes' behaviour in the Olympic villages was as austere as their furnishings, better-off competitors could, like the whole Swedish team, decamp to hotel accommodation. For the almost invariably wealthy yachtsmen in Torbay, on the south coast, the local organizers reported that, 'The number of parties that everyone wanted to hold was embarrassing.' In fact, the nightlife was so good that both *Tatler* and *Bystander* were reporting on the presence of the Crown Prince of Norway and the Olympic parties thrown aboard HMS *Anson* and at the Royal Commodore Club.[9]

Both press and public had made Sydney Wooderson the obvious choice from amongst Britain's athletes to light the Olympic flame. This short, bespectacled solicitor was the nation's leading middle-distance runner, holder of the mile world record, and nicknamed 'The Mighty Atom'. However, as Commander Bill Collins, the man in charge of the torch relay, recalled, 'such was the then organizing committee's obsession with a handsome final runner to light the Olympic flame that even the then Queen remarked to me "Of course we couldn't have had poor little Sydney".' Instead, they got the reassuring good looks of privilege in the shape of John Marks, the hitherto anonymous president of the Cambridge University Athletics Club.[10]

The opening ceremony of the games was officially remembered for its splendid pageantry and effortless aplomb. In fact, it was all a little more chaotic and threadbare. Roger Bannister, the middle-distance runner, recalled a last-minute dash through the crowd with a Union Jack to save the team's blushes before they entered the parade of nations without one. The stadium itself was spotless but shabby; the teams' wooden nameplates and Boy-Scout guides made it feel more of a gymkhana than a global spectacular. But that it was happening at all, and in such glorious sunshine, after almost a decade of war and grey austerity, was extraordinary. The *Guardian* reported: 'One found the cynicism dissipating. The scene had a light-ness and delicacy that one had never witnessed before in England. Not a dark garment was to be seen. The stands were like a gigantic hanging garden of mixed stock whose colours were pastel blue and pink. Not a man wore his coat and many knotted their handkerchiefs around their heads. Even the drab concrete of the stadium walls was mellowed by sunshine.'[11]

Lord Burghley, speaking from what was, in effect, a rickety box of corrugated iron hung with thin white cloth, declared, 'At the end of the worldwide struggle in 1945, many institutions and associa-tions were found to have withered and only the strongest had survived. How, many wondered, had the great Olympic Movement prospered?'

Not only had the Olympic movement survived, but, in 1948, it was able to attract a record 4,104 athletes, from a record fifty-nine territories. Amongst the newcomers were India and Pakistan, com-peting for the first time separately as independent nations. Burma and Ceylon joined them. Amongst the remaining British colonies, there were debuts from British Guiana (now Guyana), Jamaica, Sing-apore and Trinidad and Tobago, whose teams reflected something of the complex ethnic mix of these territories. Ceylon was represented by a hurdler, Duncan White, a member of the tiny Burgher ethnic group of mixed Eurasian descent, and winner of a silver medal in the 440-metre hurdles, Singapore by the Englishman and high jumper Lloyd Varberg. Jamaica's gold and silver medallists, Arthur Wint (400 metres) and Herb McKenley (800 metres), as well as Trinidad's silver medallist, Rodney Wilkes (weightlifting), were of African heritage. The two new Latin Americans were Venezuela and Puerto Rico, whose Juan Evangelista Venegas won the nation's first medal, a bronze in the bantamweight boxing. West Asia, liberated from French and British imperial control, and East Asia, relieved of the Japanese and American empires, provided six new Olympic nations: Iran, Iraq, Lebanon, Syria, South Korea and the Philippines.* The popularity of these exotic visitors, and the welcome mix they brought, left BBC commentator, Raymond Glendenning, claiming that 'these games have been the nearest approach to a working League of Nations the world has ever seen.' Meantime, back in the real world, the first weekend of the games was paralleled by a series of 'race riots' in Liverpool. On the Saturday, while an African American, Harrison Dillard, was winning the 100 metres for the USA, a white mob had attacked Liverpool's popular Anglo-Indian restaurant and its predominantly black clientele. On the Sunday and Bank Holiday Monday, even bigger and more volatile crowds made a beeline for black sailors' hostels and the cafes and lodging houses frequented by Liverpool's black population.[12]

Since the addition of a small programme of women's athletics at the 1928 Olympics, when female athletes made up nearly 10 per cent of the competitors, almost nothing had changed. In fact, women made up a smaller percentage of the athletes in London than they had in Los Angeles in 1932 and Berlin in 1936.[13] The wartime gains of women in the labour market in North America and Britain, and in the public realm in continental Europe, where they finally achieved universal suffrage – France, in 1947, and Italy, in 1948, for example – had yet to translate into gains in the sporting world. In 1948, women would be admitted to the new Olympic sport of canoeing and, in 1952, to equestrian sports, but it would take until 1976 for women's events to make up even a quarter of the Olympic programme and a fifth of athletes. In this context, the achievements of

* An interesting footnote on the complexity of ethnicity and citizenship was Jafar Salmasi, who was an Azeri athlete teaching in Baghdad. He discovered weightlifting during a visit to Tehran and, encouraged by the government to compete in a national weightlifting tournament, he won, and found himself representing Iran at the 1948 games, winning a bronze medal. He then returned to Iraq, where he lived until Saddam Hussein came to power, after which he emigrated. He died in Tehran.

the American high jumper, Alice Coachman, and the Dutch sprinter, Fanny Blankers-Koen, are all the more remarkable.

Born in Jim-Crow Georgia, in 1923, Coachman had to overcome the prejudices of both gender and race. Her father thought that 'girls should be dainty and sit on the porch and drink tea and not do sports.' All through her athletic career, she had to use segregated sporting facilities. On her return home from London, where she won the gold medal, Count Basie threw a welcome-home party, the Trumans invited her to the White House and Coca-Cola made her the first African American to endorse the drink, but, when invited to a civic reception in her hometown of Albany, the audience was segregated and the mayor didn't shake her hand.

Fanny Blankers-Koen was born a farmer's daughter in Baarn, in the Dutch province of Utrecht, and excelled from an early age in athletics. A junior member of the Dutch team at the 1936 Berlin games, she was coming into her peak – breaking six different world records – in the early 1940s, but, with the Netherlands under Nazi occupation, organized athletics disappeared. At the end of the war, she give birth to her second child and returned, despite much criticism, to a light training schedule: 'I got very many bad letters, people writing that I must stay home with my children and that I should not be allowed to run on a track with – how do you say? – short trousers.' Thirty years of age by the time of the 1948 games, 'one newspaperman wrote that I was too old to run, that I should stay at home and take care of my children. When I got to London, I pointed my finger at him and I said, "I show you".' And so she did, winning gold medals in the 100 metres, the 110-metre hurdles, the 200 metres and then the final leg in the 4 × 100-metre relay, where, starting behind the Australian, Joyce King, she turned in a blistering final leg to take the tape first.[14]

Sigfrid Edström, IOC president, had closed the games with the words, 'The Olympic games cannot enforce peace . . . but it gives the opportunity to the youth of the world to find out that all men on earth are brothers.' The *Observer*'s leader was proud but wary: 'with none of the nationalistic ostentation which travestied the Olympic spirit in Berlin . . . we can feel modest pride that the London Games have been one of the most successful . . . may we not claim to be leading contenders for the honourable title, Enemies of Nonsense?'[15] In the weeks afterwards, an exchange of letters in *The Economist* condensed two views of this legacy. The cynics and the realists remained unconvinced of the power of the Olympian spirit: 'It is idle to pretend that such successful gatherings can do much to induce a better spirit of international amity. As a result of bitter experience, the Western world has now learned that it is international politics that decide policy, and that the athletes who link arms in one year may be shouldering arms against each other in the next. It is certain that the echo of the crowd at Wembley will have been heard but dimly in the Kremlin.'[16]

But in an impassioned response, Bill Collins, the organizer of the torch relay, thought something else had been at work: 'The Olympic flame was interpreted by all who saw it, or read about it, or were told about it, as a symbol of a brighter future for which all the peoples of the world are yearning . . . politicians are the people who have the greatest say in the world today . . . but they are not necessarily fitted in interpreting to the world the desires of the people that they represent.'[17]

Our nostalgia for the London games is not for a time when the Olympics could actually achieve its cosmopolitan aims, but for one in which its advocates truly believed it might.

THREE

The echo of the Wembley crowd was heard rather more loudly in the Kremlin than anyone might have imagined. Russia, as the Tsarist empire, had last competed in the 1912 Olympics. Since then, no Russian or Soviet national Olympic committee had been formed or invited. In 1920 and 1924, the country was convulsed by the civil war and its aftermath, and no one was playing very much sport of any kind. Under the more stable conditions of the late 1920s and early 1930s, sport found a precarious foothold in Soviet life. Football, in particular, served as a truly popular spectator sport in the big cities, while physical education programmes in the army and schools served to create the new socialist superman. In keeping with the party's foreign doctrine of isolationism and socialism in one country, Soviet sporting contacts were confined to the Red Star workers' Olympiads that it had helped establish, while the IOC's games were condemned, for they were designed to 'deflect workers from the class struggle and train them for new imperialist wars.' In the mid-1930s, international sporting contacts grew and Soviet sports organizations began to petition the leadership to allow them to join their international federations; but a series of defeats by foreign competition made the enterprise appear too risky, and then the devastating consequences of the Great Terror on sporting officials and athletes made international and Olympic participation irrelevant for another decade.[1]

Attitudes inside and outside the Soviet Union seemed to soften in the immediate post-war era. Lord Burghley, chair of the London 1948 games, made a trip to Moscow and suggested that the Soviets might join them. Certainly there was plenty of enthusiasm inside the leading Soviet sports bureaucracies for international competition, but the politburo continued to believe that the benefits of international victory were outweighed by the likely costs of international defeat. As Nikolai Romanov, the chair of the Soviet Sports Committee, recalled, 'To gain permission to go to international tournaments

I had to send a special note to Stalin guaranteeing victory.'[2] However, by 1949, as Stalin's hold on policymaking began to slip, and the party began to recognize the multifaceted nature of the emerging Cold War conflict with the United States, international sports came to be seen as a new battlefield. A 1949 Central Committee resolution stated the party's aims: 'To spread sport to every corner of the land, to raise the level of skill, and, on that basis, to help Soviet athletes win world supremacy in major sports in the immediate future.'[3] In 1951, in anticipation of attending the Helsinki games, the Soviet Union sought both a place on the IOC and recognition of its national Olympic committee.

More progressive members of the IOC, like Lord Burghley and Finland's Erik von Frenckell, were enthusiastic supporters of Soviet participation on authentically Olympian lines; and, for the internationalist claims of the movement to have a scintilla of credibility, even the most reactionary members of the IOC could see that the Olympics without the Soviet Union would be absurd. However, for the staunch anti-communists in the IOC – like its president, Edström; the Dutchman Colonel Scharoo; and the IOC vice-president, Avery Brundage – this presented a number of dilemmas. Hitherto, the IOC's methods of self-recruitment through its informal networks had ensured that the right people joined the club; as Avery Brundage described them, they were 'the same general type and they were soon welded into what has so often been called the "Olympic family".' Sigfrid Edström worried, 'Aside from all of this, who do we know in Russia? The greatest trouble will be to find men we can have present in the IOC. I do not feel inclined to go so far as to admit a communist there.'[4] It wasn't just a matter of having to accept a communist, but one appointed directly by their government to the IOC.

Most difficult of all to accept was the fact that the Soviet sport system was in obvious contravention of the notions of amateurism held dear by the IOC. No one in the leadership of the organization was under any illusion that Soviet athletes, whether in the armed forces or not, were financially supported and able to train full-time. Both sides compromised. The Soviets made minor concessions: stopping the once widespread practice of awarding money prizes to successful sports champions, and making their Olympic application without their usual bellicose demands for international organizations to expel fascist Spain or to make Russian an official language. The

IOC chose to look the other way. The politburo's appointed man, Konstantin Andrianov, was welcomed to the IOC club and Avery Brundage swallowed hard, saying, 'We should accept their [Soviet] declaration and assume that Olympic rules are being followed until we learn to the contrary.'[5]

Reintegrating the Japanese into the Olympic movement proved relatively unproblematic. There was no invitation from the London organizers in 1948, but from 1949 onwards the IOC was encouraging the world's international sports federations to readmit the Japanese in anticipation of their return to the Olympics. In November 1951, Japan signed a peace treaty with the forty-eight nations with which it had been at war. Six months later, the American occupation was officially over and Japan sent sixty-nine athletes to the Helsinki games.

Germany, or rather the Germanies, were another matter. By the time it came to considering German participation in the Olympics, the country had been divided in two, as the Western-occupied zones fused to form the Federal Republic of Germany (FRG) and the Soviet-occupied zone had become the German Democratic Republic (GDR). The IOC continued to consider Germany one country, part of which was a Soviet colonial satellite. So, when the West Germans applied to have their national Olympic committee recognized in 1950, it was assumed to be the singular representative of the German sporting nation and a direct continuation of the German NOC that existed before the war. When the GDR applied for recognition of their own separate national committee, they were encouraged to be part of a united German team at the Helsinki games. Extended discussion followed, but the East Germans were having none of it, and a united German team made up entirely of citizens of the FRG went to Helsinki. The existence of two Korean states, North and South, but just one recognized national Olympic committee, run by the half of the country in the Western sphere of influence, would present the IOC with the same dilemma in the late fifties, when the North Koreans had the political and diplomatic energy to pursue their claim. Faced with the prospect of a joint team, they inevitably declined.

China was another matter. While the IOC was able to impose the fiction of a united Germany at the games, it was unable to do so with China, where both the victorious communists of the People's Republic of China and the defeated nationalists, holed up in their tiny island redoubt of Taiwan, claimed singular sovereignty and authority over the whole nation. In 1948, as the Chinese civil war raged on, the nation still managed to send thirty-one athletes to the London Games – not quite the fifty-four who had travelled to Berlin in 1936, but better than the lone sprinter and flag bearer, Liu Changchun, who had represented the nation in 1932. With the defeat of the nationalists and the declaration of the People's Republic of China by the communists in May 1949, the IOC was presented with a series of dilemmas. The nationalists claimed control over the Chinese national Olympic committee by the expediency of registering a change of office address with the IOC to Taiwan. On this basis, they expected to represent all of China at the 1952 games. However, encouraged by the Soviet Union, the Chinese government planned to send a team to the games too, not initially realizing that they would have to be recognized as a national Olympic committee first. Fierce and often uncompromising exchanges between the IOC and representatives of the two Chinas at a series of meetings on who was allowed to invite whom to the games resulted in a compromise, reached on the eve of the 1952 games. Neither Chinese Olympic committee would be recognized, but both were invited to send athletes in sports where they were recognized by the relevant international federation. The Taiwanese boycotted the games and the PRC's delegation only arrived as the closing ceremony was about to begin.

The Helsinki Olympics had been nearly two decades in the making, their form and meaning shaped by the same forces of war and social change that transformed Finland from the mid-1930s through to the early 1950s. The idea of the 1940 Helsinki Olympics was to celebrate and advertise what would have been over two decades of Finnish national independence, first achieved in 1917 when the Finns decisively broke from Russian control. The bid was led by Erik von Frenckell, a sports-mad Swedish-speaking aristocrat and businessman, who introduced field hockey and football to Finland, sat on the IOC and would eventually run the 1952 games. Beaten by Tokyo in 1936 in the competition to hold the 1940 games, the Finns were promised 1944 instead. When, in 1938, the Japanese, diverted by their titanic invasion of China, returned the games to the IOC, Helsinki picked them up, and by early 1939 had completed its Olympic stadium, with its optimistically modern streamlined white tower, and had begun work on other venues – just in time for the Second World War to begin. The Finns declared themselves neutral, but the Soviet Union invaded anyway, in late 1939. Despite fierce resistance in the Winter War, the Finns were, by spring 1940, forced to surrender and concede territory, and only then did they formally abandon the games. Later that year, a 'national' Olympics was held instead in the new Helsinki stadium, and 30,000 people marked the fallen of the Winter War – amongst them, many of the nation's leading athletes and Olympians. When the Germans invaded the Soviet Union in 1941, the Finns joined in and took their contested territories back, only to lose them all over again to the Red Army in 1944. This time, the peace treaty, signed in 1947, ceded not only land to the Soviet Union, but also significant war reparations and control over Finnish foreign policy, enforcing a 'friendly neutrality' that debarred the country from joining any alliance hostile to the Soviet Union. It was this Finland, a capitalist democracy in the Soviet sphere of influence, that was awarded the 1952 games.

The planning for the Helsinki Olympics reflected two key features of Finnish politics: first, the enduring need for national unity and consensus across party lines; second, the narrow path between East and West that its leaders were required to walk in foreign policy. Certainly, the organizing committees of the games (both in 1940 and 1952), unlike any previous Olympic organization, reflected the entire spectrum of Finnish politics, drawing upon senior members of the left, centre and right parties, future prime ministers and presidents, and supplemented by key figures from the military and the odd gentleman Olympian. The Finns, both Olympic organizers and senior government officials, were enthusiastic supporters of the Soviet Union's decision to join the Olympic movement and attend the Helsinki games. Von Frenckell went out of his way to accommodate them, offering a reorganized torch relay that would send the flame through Soviet territory, and encouraging them to house their team, not in Leningrad or somewhere else across the border, but in Helsinki, at their own separate Olympic village in the newly constructed Technological University of Otaniemi. The Soviets agreed, though they chose to leave the most ideologically suspect – like the Estonian shot-putter, Heino Lipp – at home. The village came equipped with a large portrait of Comrade Stalin, as well as smaller icons of the leaders of the Soviet satellite states – Bulgaria, Czechoslovakia, Hungary, Romania and Poland – whose athletes shared this communist village. The Finns arranged chaperoned 'friendship encounters' with

Western athletes, but were alert enough to the Cold War stakes for the Soviet team that they equipped them with a scoreboard on which to maintain a running tally of the unofficial points and medal competitions between them and the United States. The Soviets returned the favour, wining and dining foreign delegations with conspicuous quantities of steak, caviar and vodka.

Ideologically and linguistically ecumenical, von Frenckell made his welcoming speech at the opening ceremony in four faultlessly spoken languages: Finnish, Swedish, French and English. For the domestic audience, the games really were an alternative to war: 'Finland has the pleasure of providing the battlefield from which the victors and others alike can depart without bitter feelings.' For the Swedish-speaking minority, and with a nod to Finland's worker sports movement, he told them that the games, despite their differences, were an instrument of reconciliation: 'to create externally and internally mutual understanding and trust between linguistic groups and social classes.' Speaking English, now the language of international politics and diplomacy, he offered combat without casualties, competition without anger: 'We welcome this occasion for Finland to form the neutral site where West and East can meet in noble combat, where happy winners will be singled out without bitterness and the desire for revenge on the part of the losers.' Two decades, three wars and tens of thousands of deaths since the Finns first bid for the games, the lighting of the Olympic flame was handed to the athletic exemplars of Finnish endurance, Paavo Nurmi and Hans Kolehmainen, both multiple gold-medal winners and both Olympic marathon champions.

In the overall medals tables, newly inflected with a Cold War dynamic, the USA remained ahead, but not as comfortably as anyone might have imagined. The Americans won forty gold medals compared to the Soviets' twenty-nine, but led just seventy-six against seventy-one when silver and bronze medals were included. The *New York Times*, by its methodology, declared on the final day of the games that the US had won, but then *Pravda* announced the same day that 'the athletes of the Soviet Union have taken first place.' Romanov, head of the Soviet team, convinced the politburo it had been a draw. The Soviets performed particularly strongly in wrestling, gymnastics, weightlifting and athletics, but direct confrontations with the United States were limited. The American press had fun with the 3,000-metre steeplechase, in which Horace Ashenfelter, 'the tall, dark, federal agent', powered past the Soviet world-record holder, 'Comrade Vladimir Kazantsev', at the final water-jump to win the gold medal: the papers mock-chided Ashenfelter as 'the first American spy who had allowed himself to be chased by a Communist', and the headlines read, 'FBI Man Runs Down Russian.'[6] The basketball final between the two, won by the Americans 36–25, roused little more than a grumbling chorus over the Soviets' ultra-defensive play. Perhaps America's greatest triumph was, despite the lack of a local bottling plant, to keep the Coca-Cola flowing; 30,000 cases were imported from the Netherlands, publicly celebrated and available at every Olympic venue.

If the Comintern had wanted to make the case for communism through sport, Hungary was as good, if not a better case than the Soviet Union, winning sixteen gold medals and forty-two overall, and all that with a population of less than ten million. Alternatively, they could point to Czechoslovakia, which provided the singularly most amazing athletic achievement of the games: Emil Zátopek's three gold medals in the 5,000 metres, the 10,000 metres and the marathon. Hungary's success was not entirely surprising, the nation having won ten gold medals at both the 1936 and the 1948 games. Communist Hungary inherited the strong gymnastic and aquatic traditions of bourgeois Budapest, the military's expertise in fencing and added some central state direction. Gold medals in these sports were gilded by the performance of the football team – signed up to the army and concentrated in just two clubs in the capital – who not only won the tournament, but were also beginning to play the innovative, tactically sophisticated game that would bring them global renown as the Magical Magyars. As Ferenc Puskás, the captain, recalled, 'It was during the Olympics that our football first started to flow with real power. It was a prototype of total football; when we attacked, everyone attacked; in defence it was just the same.'

Emil Zátopek was a major in the Czech army, but this self-coached, multilingual autodidact was never really much of a military man. At the 1948 London games, he had won the 10,000 metres and taken the silver in the 5,000 metres, during which his naive tactics and desperate but doomed final sprint had endeared him to the British public. His style, at best, was unorthodox: torso swinging from side to side, head rolling, and a range of grunts and groans emanating from his wheezing frame. At the 1952 games, having won both events, he took on the marathon, racing the distance for the first time. Zátopek, garrulous as ever, introduced himself to the British race favourite, a gruff and unresponsive Jim Peters, before the race. The next time they spoke, both runners were approaching the halfway stage; Zátopek asked Peters whether the pace was too fast and Peters, on the wind up, replied that it wasn't. Zátopek took him at his word and moved up a gear. Peters would soon succumb to cramp, but Zátopek, two minutes out in front, was found chatting to a car load of photographers that drove alongside him.

The Yugoslavian communists had their own points to prove. In 1948, the Yugoslav president, Tito, had broken with Stalin, declaring that the country would pursue an independent national road to socialism, occupying a position equidistant between the two emerging blocs in Europe; this was the kind of autonomy of mind that earned them the undying enmity of Stalin and the CPSU. The two nations were drawn against each other in the opening round of the 1952 Olympic football tournament, a match billed in the press of both countries as a proxy for the deeper ideological conflict between them. With twenty minutes to go, the Soviets were 5–1 down to a rampant Yugoslavia, and facing a trip to Siberia. The Yugoslavian press claimed that the Soviet players were foaming at the mouth, but the scoreboard does not lie: four goals in twenty minutes made it 5–5 and the Soviets had earned a reprieve and a replay. They lost the second game 3–1, and the Soviet press that had hailed the comeback against Tito's fascist clique fell silent. CSKA, the army team who provided the core of the Olympic squad, were quietly disbanded, only reprieved by Stalin's death the following year.

Zátopek's personal haul of gold medals was three times the size of Britain's. With just one gold medal (two silver and eight bronze), it was that nation's worst Olympic performance. Nineteenth in the medal table, it ranked below not only traditional middle-range Olympic powers – like France, Australia and Belgium – but lower than its own minuscule colony, Jamaica. The single British gold medal was won by the equestrian team of Wilfred White, Douglas Stewart and Harry Llewellyn in the show jumping, but the triumph was immediately and almost entirely framed as the work of Captain Harry Llewellyn on Foxhunter.[7] To his credit, Llewellyn always made clear that it had been a team effort, and the final winning round that he rode was a poor one; the best work had been done earlier. None of this mattered to the press or the public. Foxhunter appeared on the front pages, his head set against an aeroplane's tail fin emblazoned with the Union Jack, or in his stall at home, festooned with children and tiny flags. The horse received messages of congratulations from the king and Prime Minister Winston Churchill, and a *Times* editorial declared that, 'Foxhunter must be the most famous animal since Black Beauty . . . show jumping is not learnt overnight and the credit for this glorious performance goes to Colonel Harry Llewellyn and the others who by their loyal and unsparing devotion have made possible a renaissance of British horsemanship.' They also had wealth, privilege and office on their side. Llewellyn was the son of a Welsh coal-mining magnate, Wilfred White came from a landed Cheshire family and Douglas Stewart was a senior career cavalry officer. The mawkish love of the British for animals aside, Llewellyn was really the star. He was tall, dark, charming and very rich. He wore his Windsor hat at a rakish angle, rode in a red jacket and bow tie, and strode around in high leather boots. The aristocracy, seriously impoverished and undermined by the economic and political changes of the previous three decades, still had the kind of cultural élan and social capital that made for mass audiences. For a fraction of that class, sports, show business and celebrity would be their refuge from these new and harsher times.

Thus the greatest legacy of the 1952 games for Britain was the transformation of show jumping, from an elite and virtually unknown sport, into one of the most popular television spectaculars of the decade. Packaged into a one-hour slot, show jumping on the BBC attracted such huge audiences that the Horse of the Year Show was allowed to overrun by an unheard-of sixty minutes. A quiet coda to the renaissance of British horsemanship was the silver medal won by the Danish rider Lis Hartel, in the dressage. Paralysed below the knee by polio, she was the first significantly disabled athlete to compete at the games since George Eyser in 1904 – an American gymnast with a wooden leg.

FOUR

In the opening sequence of the official film of the 1956 Olympics, we fly across the sprawling suburbs of Melbourne, the narrator asking, 'Australia: what is it, exactly? A continent? An island? Almost as large as the United States, it has fewer inhabitants than New York City.' The precise answer to that geographical conundrum never comes, though the film does compare Australia's sheep ranges to the Great Plains. Its depiction of Christmas in the southern hemisphere is California: 'instead of coming down chimneys, Santa rides ashore – on a surf board'; two suburban boys dress a plastic Christmas tree in harsh summer sunlight. Given that Australia, like the United States, is a predominantly British colonial operation built on stolen indigenous lands, the film has a point, but probably not the one intended. Against the backdrop of a busy downtown, the voice asks, 'And Melbourne? Like the previous sites of the Olympic Games, is it an international capital, like London, Los Angeles or Berlin?' The film suggests otherwise. The camera focuses on a large three-dimensional mural, erected above the entrance to Coles department store on Bourke Street. In the foreground, standing in proud relief, is John Batman, the notional founder of Melbourne, who arrived in 1835 and, so it was thought, struck a written deal with representatives of the indigenous Kulin peoples – the Wurundjeri, Boonwurrung and Wathaurong – for possession of the lands around Port Phillip Bay and what became the northern suburbs of the city. Look closely and you can see a small Aboriginal figure crouching to the left of Batman. The voice continues: 'It's just a town, improvised, ad libbed by an English traveller. Ad libbed by John Batman exactly one hundred and twenty years ago. John Batman fought off a thousand kinds of wild animals and built a village. Original name? Dutta Galla. Today . . . Melbourne.'[1]

The mechanized panels of the sign rotate and the fantasy landscape of 1835 is transformed into a bright cartoon of the contemporary city's skyline. In an instant, a century of colonial occupation and tumultuous economic development is erased.

Batman was a land-hungry frontier farmer who had made a living in Van Diemen's Land (now Tasmania) raising livestock and killing Aboriginals at the tail end of the Black Wars – the most extensive acts of resistance to the colonial occupation of Aboriginal land before the natives were defeated and many were forcibly relocated. Dissatisfied by the returns available to him in Tasmania, Batman was amongst many characters seeking to explore the fertile grazing lands around Port Phillip Bay in what would become the state of Victoria. Although Batman did manage to establish his own farm, see the town marked out and its land distributed, alcoholism and syphilis reduced him to pitiful decrepitude and, by 1839, he was dead. The real founder of Melbourne was the British imperial state, in the guise of Governor Bourke of New South Wales, who established the police and civil administration, laid out the city and named it Melbourne after the then British prime minister. The Kulin, whose treaty was sharply abrogated by the government, were subject to the usual terrible ravages of European microbes. Those who survived were forcibly resettled as their land became sheep runs. Above all, Melbourne was a city born of the gold rush of the 1850s, which, together with the wool industry, initiated a population and economic boom that would last until almost the end of the century. By 1890, 'Marvellous Melbourne' claimed to be the second city of the British Empire, with a population half a million strong. Living its own Antipodean belle époque, it boasted the tallest buildings in the southern hemisphere, the most advanced tramways and had sufficient cultural confidence and means to stage its own world fair in 1880.[2]

The puncturing of Melbourne's land, gold and banking booms in the late nineteenth century and the devastating impact of both the First World War and the Great Depression on the extractive industries that ultimately sustained the city, saw its economy and population stagnate. Despite serving as Australia's federal capital until the completion of Canberra in 1927, Melbourne had since come to be seen as increasingly staid and provincial by comparison to Sydney. In the run-up to the games, many in the press fretted that its restrictive drinking laws (nothing after six p.m.), its grim plumbing and mean-spirited hotels would shame it in the eyes of the world – eyes that were, for the most part, supposed to be that of an imaginary

American tourist: cosmopolitan, urbane and probably condescending.

However, another Melbourne was emerging. In the post-war era, the city would begin a second period of explosive growth, this time driven by the new Fordist industries of mass production and consumption – cars, white goods, furniture and retailers – a suburban building frenzy, and waves of migration, first from Europe and, in the 1970s, from Asia – forces that would challenge the dominance of the old Anglo-elites concentrated in banking, law and politics. At this crossroads for the city, the staging of the Olympic Games became an arena in which the cultural contours of the new Melbourne, and in many ways the new Australia, would be fought out.[3]

The key figure amongst conservatives, and the catalyst for the city's bid, was Wilfred Kent Hughes. Scion of upper-class old Melbourne, he went from Oxford to the army and thence to the First World War. He was a hurdler for Australia at the 1920 Antwerp games, before returning to politics as a nationalist party MP and state minister in Victoria. In the interwar period, he was reliably right wing, xenophobic, imperialist and, on occasion – as in his vocal admiration for the early works of Mussolini – a near fascist. He was an advocate for the Empire Youth Movement, Scouting and compulsory national service and physical education in schools – obsessions that coalesced around his management of the Australian team at the 1938 Sydney Empire Games. Captured by the Japanese in Singapore and spending four grim years as a prisoner of war in China, he composed *The Slaves of the Samurai*, a paean to the stern, Spartan ideals he expected of himself and Australia. Together with a group of other POWs – like Edgar Tanner, an Olympic boxer and secretary of the Victoria Olympic Council – he and these conservative Olympians proposed, in 1946, the idea that Melbourne should hold the games. Alone, they had neither the power nor sufficient influence to lead a bid.

This task fell to the modernizers, led by Frank Beaurepaire. Born in working-class Melbourne, he was an amateur swimmer, winning three silver and three bronze medals across three Olympic Games. Awarded a small civic prize for his role in saving a swimmer from a shark attack, he founded Beaurepaire's Olympic Tyres and made a fortune in Melbourne's booming automotive industries. Key supporters from this milieu included the Jewish furniture king Maurice Nathan, hardware retailer and Lord Mayor Sir Harold Luxton, and the rambunctious popular press of Keith Murdoch's *Herald* and *Sun*. They saw the games as an opportunity to refashion Melbourne, to shift its main points of cultural reference away from Britain and reinsert the city into the global economy that had once made it so rich.

The official bid document was bound in the finest merino wool and carried the signatures of hundreds of local sponsors and supporters, most of whom came from the city's new industrial elite, especially automotive dealers, real-estate agents and big retailers. The first campaign, in London, in 1948, under still severe conditions of rationing, saw Beaurepaire sprinkle special consignments of Australian food amongst delegates and influencers. A decision was deferred to a meeting in Rome the following year, and Beaurepaire left no stone unturned. The Pope got a bid book, and a new colour film was made to sell the city to the IOC. With no European cities in the competition, and the Americas vote split amongst six cities from the US, Mexico City, Montreal and Buenos Aries, Melbourne won the final round by a single vote.

Subsequent progress was slow and fractious. The local labour movement was unsupportive, pointing to the enduring post-war housing shortages in the city. A close look at Australia's strict quarantine laws made it clear that the equestrian events would have to be staged elsewhere, and Stockholm was chosen. All through 1953 and 1954, and as late as 1955, IOC president Avery Brundage was making veiled threats that the games could be moved if preparations did not accelerate. The location and funding of the main Olympic stadium were the principal bone of contention. The conservative faction hoped to use and renovate their own riverside Olympic park, but its location would make a huge new building structurally unsound. The Royal Agricultural Showgrounds, surrounded by the city's meat yards, sheep pens, abattoirs and stinking tanneries, was plan B, but the Victoria state government was so alarmed at the cost of redevelopment that it got cold feet; a similar fate befell the even more expensive redevelopment plans for Princes Park, in the suburb of Carlton. It required the intervention of Prime Minister Robert Menzies in a bruising three-day head-banging summit, and the injection of public money, to force all to accept a redeveloped Melbourne Cricket Ground as the venue, and a deal was made that the costs of the games would be split amongst federal, state and city governments, while the public-housing budget would fund Heidelberg Park serving first as an athletes' village and then as a social-housing estate.

Modernist Melbourne's offer to the world was Richard Beck's official poster.[4] Beck, born and trained in Britain, had cut his modernist teeth as part of Frank Pick's celebrated school of designers working for London Transport in the interwar era. Beck arrived in Australia on the eve of the Second World War, and brought with him the new graphic grammar of photomontage and juxtaposition, disembodied text and imagery. The Olympic poster centres on an unfolding concertina of white quadrangles, a constructivist greeting card bearing the Olympic rings and Melbourne's coat of arms. It floats in a serene, dreamy ocean of blue; the design's only concession to the games' classical pretensions, the substitution of a sans-serif font for slim roman capitals.

Uncontroversial as it might appear now, Beck's work was the first Olympic poster not to feature the human form.[5] In 1896, although the press sent sketch artists, there was no poster. In 1900 and 1904, there were posters, but the games were typographically subsumed by their hosts – the world fairs – and visually located by the Eiffel Tower and the exposition's fairgrounds. The 1908 poster, produced by the Franco-British Imperial Exhibition, at last featured an athlete, but he was hardly Hercules. The light blue trim of his kit was more redolent of an Oxbridge blue than an ephebe: his relaxed posture suggests someone ready for a drinks party, not the *stadion*. With a shield in his hand advertising the games' location in the exhibition's Great Stadium, he appears more of an upper-crust sandwich-board man than a sprinting hero. Stylistically, it was Stockholm 1912 that set the coordinates for the Olympic poster over the next forty years. A blond man, exquisitely muscled and very naked, swirls the Swedish flag around him, while the thinnest of orange ribbons miraculously preserves his modesty. Behind him, we glimpse another half-dozen naked men swirling flags: the Union Jack, the Stars and Stripes, the Italian, Portuguese, Norwegian and Japanese amongst them. The games of Antwerp, Paris, Amsterdam, Los Angeles and Helsinki repeated this format, depicting a variety of male athletes in various states of undress, with references to the actual location of the games reduced to the thin watercolour of Antwerp's medieval centre, or a city's coat of arms, or nothing at all. There was no such reticence in 1936. For Berlin, a giant Aryan-Athenian champion looms over the stark silhouettes of the *quadriga* – the four-horse chariot – atop the Brandenburg Gate. The poster for London 1948 is surely an under-stated and democratic riposte to this visual bombast. It depicts a rather quaint and camp *discobolus,* small, in front of the Houses of Parliament, with fonts drawn from the municipal socialist graphic lexicon of the London Underground.

The moderns had three further points of purchase over the sta-ging of the games: the arts festival, the swimming complex and public art. Finally, the lamentable history of the Olympic arts compe-tition was terminated.[6] Held at the virtual insistence of Baron de Coubertin between 1920 and 1952, they had, on occasion, attracted noted artists and writers to their judging panels, but the record of entries hovered between mediocre and hopeless. Nowhere had they been able to effect a real or significant dialogue between the often mutually contemptuous worlds of sport and the high arts. The Mel-bourne Olympic Arts Festival hardly effected a reconciliation between the two. Much of it was hidden away from the main sporting venues, concentrated at the University of Melbourne, the Royal Melbourne Technical College and the city's main library. However, an orchestral performance in the swimming hall, commissions for Leonard French's superb mural, *Symmetry of Sport*, at the Beaurepaire swimming com-plex at the university (used for Olympic training but not competition), and Arthur Boyd's ceramic sculpture, set outside the Olympic stadium, indicated a tentative rapprochement.

The main Olympic swimming complex – the first to be sited entirely indoors – was the only facility newly built entirely for the games, and proved a striking statement of the internationally orien-tated modernism of the new Melbourne. A glass-and-steel irregular lozenge, its V-shaped roof trusses created vast curtain walls of glass that bathed the area in natural light. It was built alongside a small group of contemporaneous and adventurous commissions in the city, like the sleek ICI House – an Antipodean Seagram Building – and Sidney Myer's Music Bowl, whose undulating metal roof, suspended by steel cabling, would be the inspiration for the ultra-modern struc-tures of the Munich 1972 Olympic park. However, perhaps the best of this popular and accessible Australian modernism can be found in the street decorations commissioned for the games. Richard Beck contributed his Olympic colour-coded 'spinmobiles'; there were metal cuts-outs of dancing women, copies of Aboriginal rock-art suspended across downtown boulevards, and a giant neon Olympic torch was hung high in the air above a major crossroads.[7]

It was hardly a revolution, but it was playful and accessible, and, set against the aesthetic of Australia's conservative Olympians, it was Dada. Watching the opening ceremony of the 1956 games, you would have had to pinch yourself to remember that you were not in London in 1948. The MCG, though triple-tiered in places, offered the same unadorned ring of corrugated-iron roof and wooden seating that Wembley had. The show opened and closed with 'God Save the Queen' and the 'Hallelujah Chorus', played by imperial marching bands. Prince Philip, as the representative of the British crown and the head of state, appeared in full naval uniform, just as his father-in-law, the late King George VI, had done in 1948, when he opened the games. The crowd was led in prayer by an Anglican archbishop in canonical dress, and the official programme cast the city as an Anglo-Eden: 'The streets of modern suburban houses of functional design and fabric, with here and there an American-style supermarket or drive-in theatre or bank, combine generally in an ideally English roses-and-lavender setting of home and garden.'[8]

The official film echoed this with its fabulously narrow portrayal of the sporting nation. Shirley Strickland was a middle-class athletic mum from the nice side of town; Chilla Portert was a sheep-sheering high jumper; and the first person in the stadium for the games would be a lady from one of the suburban bowls clubs that formed the backbone of sport in Melbourne. As invisible as the city's indigenous people – whose boomerang, the film informs us, although 'once a deadly weapon . . . is now just a game taught to the tourists' – were the games, often professional, of working-class and migrant Australia: cricket, football, rugby league and, above all, Australian-rules football, the single most popular sport in the city. Given such flagrant disingenuousness, we should all be thankful to Barry Larkin and a group of Sydney University students who, when the torch relay reached Sydney, staged the first great Olympic prank. In protest at the indisputably Nazi origins of the spectacle, they crafted a fake torch, burning a pair of kerosene-soaked national-service underpants. Larkin ran the torch to Sydney town hall where, ahead of the official runner, he was able to pass it to Pat Hills, the Mayor of Sydney, and subsequently disappear.

Out in the real world, things were less tranquil. The Israeli invasion of Egypt and the coordinated Anglo-French occupation of the Suez Canal, just a fortnight before the opening ceremony, saw the Egyptians withdraw from the games and the Iraqis and the Lebanese follow suit. A week later, the Hungarian uprising and the attempt to implement a more humane communism was terminated by the Soviet army, triggering withdrawals by Spain, Switzerland and the Netherlands, the Dutch sending the money saved to charities supporting the beleaguered Hungarians. At the Heidelberg Park Olympic village, the Israelis and remaining Arab nations were discreetly separated, so too the Soviets and the Hungarians, especially since the Soviet Olympic Committee had only just been persuaded to abandon their plans for isolation aboard a floating boat-hotel in the harbour. Even then, they were insisting on separate meal and training times from everyone else. The Australian team, previously housed with the rest of Asia, was shifted back to the English-speaking zone. Earlier in the year, one of China's IOC members, Shou Ti-tung, had called for the Taiwanese Olympic Committee to be expelled, a demand flatly rejected by President Brundage. Two weeks before the games, the PRC did what it had been planning to do all along and officially withdrew in protest at the nationalist renegade's presence. Two years later, they would leave the Olympic movement and Chinese sport would descend into the mayhem and isolationism of the Great Leap Forward and the Cultural Revolution.

Avery Brundage's response to this was, at new heights of disingenuousness, to reiterate, 'We are dead against any country using the games for political purposes, right or wrong. The Olympics are competitions between individuals and not nations.'[9] This from the man who had orchestrated the inclusion of a united German team at the 1952 games, led and exclusively staffed by West Germans. Political intervention was, it seems, permissible for the right people with the right kind of politics. In 1955, the Soviet Union had recognized the GDR as an independent sovereign state rather than an occupied territory. Encouraged and emboldened by their allies, the East Germans made a renewed application to the IOC to register their national Olympic committee. Maintaining the position established in 1952 that there was, whatever the rest of the world might be thinking, one German state and therefore only one German Olympic team, the IOC conceded the recognition of an East German NOC on the condition that it join that team. Representatives of both German NOCs discussed practicalities and agreed that they would march under a German tricolour with white Olympic rings, and that, in lieu of a national anthem that could be agreed upon, official occasions would be marked by Beethoven's 'Ode to Joy'. A West German sports journalist suggested that 'There was no all-German team at all. The "two teams" arrived and departed separately and the relationship between officials of the two NOCs at the Games was more than strained. There was no question of a "team" in the sense of sporting cohesion and human camaraderie. But IOC President Avery Brundage believed in the illusion of having achieved something politics had not: German re-unification. It was a nice depiction, yet a mirage.'[10]

Australia had its then most successful Olympics, winning thirteen gold medals, every champion made an unproblematically regular feller or girl next door. Shirley Strickland was actually a part-time lecturer in physics and maths, but was depicted in the official film and the local press as a manicured suburban housewife, tending to her kids, her lawn and her roses, who just happened to be the reigning Olympic hurdles champion. She won her event, but was, if anything, supplanted as the nation's golden girl by the young sprinter Betty Cuthbert, who won three gold medals, in the 100 metres, 200 metres and the 100-metre relay. Australian Olympic swimming had always been strong, a tradition driven by the same alchemy of climate, swimming pools and vibrant beach and surf cultures that had made California such a successful aquatic-sports zone. In 1956, the team made the most of home advantage. Murray Rose and Jon Hendricks won five gold medals between them. But the nation warmed most to Dawn Fraser, the teenage sensation from working-class Sydney, who made her Olympic debut winning two golds, including the first of her three successive Olympic triumphs in the 100-metre freestyle.

The symbolic conflicts of the Cold War – above all, the head-to-head contest between the US and the USSR in just their second Summer Olympic Games – were still just a subtext, a subterranean narrative. Even though the USSR unambiguously topped the medal table, in the absence of television or newsreel coverage, this kind of story, and the missile-gap, medal-gap hysteria it could evoke, awaited the mass American television audience that would not be ready to watch the Olympics until Rome 1960. Rather, it was the conflict behind the Iron Curtain that surfaced at Melbourne. Australia's small Hungarian migrant community rallied to their team. Five hundred of them met the members of the team arriving at the city's airport, carrying Hungarian flags with the hammer and sickle cut out. They waved their flags and roared as the light middleweight boxer, László Papp, beat the Puerto Rican José Torres to win his third gold medal, but it was in the water-polo competition that they were most voluble.[11]

The Hungarian and Soviet teams had shared a boat from Europe, and fighting had begun on board as the course of the uprising became clear. The teams met in the quarter-finals of the water-polo tournament, and nearly 5,000 Australian Hungarians came along to support their team, many holding handmade signs encouraging defection: 'Stay in Australia'. The Hungarians had always intended to wind up their opponents, and, in the second minute, they got Pyotr Mchvenieradze sent to the sin bin. Early in the second half, with the Hungarians leading 2–0, 'Boris Markarov delivered a hay-maker punch to the eye of Hungary's Antol Belvari.' All hell broke loose. The pool was engulfed in fighting above and below the water. In the final minute of the game, a Russian hit Ervin Zádor so hard that he split his brow, which bled profusely into the water. The crowd came roaring out of the stands and forced the police to intervene. Hungary held on to win 4–0, and Zádor later made clear what had been at stake: 'We felt we were playing not just for ourselves, but our whole country.' Mikos Martin, one of the five members of the team who stayed in Australia after the game, said of the Soviets, 'They play their sports just as they conduct their lives – with brutality and disregard for fair play.'[12]

These clashes aside, Melbourne had been free of the nationalist spite and pomp, but no one was calling it the friendly games. Then, with just a week to go, a Chinese-Australian teenager, John Ian Wing, wrote anonymously to Kent Hughes, the chair of the organizing committee, with an idea to improve the closing ceremony, to make it a little less formal. Given the martial and absurdly anglocentric demeanour that characterized much of the opening ceremony, one wouldn't have given Wing's appeal much chance of success. He wrote,

> The march I have in mind is different than the one during the Opening Ceremony and will make these games even greater, during the march there will only be 1 NATION. War, politics and nationality will be all forgotten, what more could anyone want,

if the whole world could be made as one nation. Well, you can do it in a small way . . . no team is to keep together and there should be no more than 2 team mates together, they must be spread out evenly, THEY MUST NOT MARCH but walk freely and wave to the public . . . It will show the whole world how friendly Australia is.[13]

To Kent Hughes' eternal credit, he took the idea on and persuaded the dry, curmudgeonly Brundage and sceptics on his own committee that it would work. The official report of the games was simply ecstatic: 'A prophetic image of a new future for mankind – the athletes of the world not now sharply divided but . . . marching as one in a hotchpotch of sheer humanity, a fiesta of friendship.'[14]

It wasn't quite like that, and it wasn't quite as Wing had imagined it. The athletes were all mixed up, and they did their best not to march, but, still arranged five abreast and unable to break ranks, you can see that many found it hard to saunter or to find any gear outside of the parade ground. As to 'a hotchpotch of sheer humanity', the Chinese were absent, and the peoples of Africa, if no one else, would have demurred. Their representation was reduced to an all-white South African team, the American returnees of Liberia, the colonial subjects of Nigeria and Kenya, and just independent Ethiopia. Fiesta is perhaps stretching the point, too. The modernists' wider cultural and political ambitions would take another twenty or thirty years to develop and finally vanquish the straight-laced imperial Victoriana of the city. As Sir Harold Luxton said of the failure to liberalize the city's drinking laws for the games, 'I love Melbourne. I've lived here all my life, but it is still deadly dull.'[15] More to the point, outside of the stadium and the people crowded around Australia's paltry 5,000 television sets, no one could see them. At the games to come, television would make the world one, and the Olympics would try to tell it that war, politics and nationality could be forgotten. The parades would be more carefree, a more diverse humanity would be present, but the message would prove even harder to sustain.

6

THE IMAGE IS STILL THERE: SPECTACLE VERSUS ANTI-SPECTACLE AT THE GAMES

ROME 1960 • TOKYO 1964 • MEXICO CITY 1968 • MUNICH 1972

SQUAW VALLEY 1960 • INNSBRUCK 1964 • GRENOBLE 1968

SAPPORO 1972

The games were a beautiful spectacle from every perspective: colours of peace, flags, strength, youth and the fascinating test of the limit of man's strength. They were a spectacle so beautiful that even the impenetrable old Romans, these body-armoured tortoises, these lizards on the wall encrusted by time, ended up taking an interest.

Carlo Levi

The image is still there. It keeps getting wider. If you look at the images of the last century, there's nothing much like it out there. And 'the man' wasn't the one that kept this thing afloat.

John Carlos

ONE

It must have taken something special to get the Roman lizards to look up. Rome surely had seen it all, but then it had never seen anything of the extraordinary scale, complexity and intensity that the Olympics was becoming.[1] Beginning with Rome 1960, each of the next four summer games served as the centrepiece of its host nation's announcement of domestic transformation and international standing. First Italy, then Japan, then West Germany used the Olympics to mark the end of their post-war status as pariahs, as well as serving as the crowning moment of a long period of extraordinary industrial growth and prosperity. Mexico, long considered a poor and marginal state, made the leap into the ranks of industrialized nations by joining the Organisation for Economic Cooperation and Development (OECD) and hosting the Olympic Games in 1968. The intersection of such high-level symbolic ambition with the arrival of global television audiences made the expansion of the Olympics inventible. Eighty-three nations and 5,300 athletes were present at the Rome games; 121 nations took over 7,300 competitors to Munich. To the existing seventeen Olympic sports, the IOC added judo, volleyball, handball and archery. However, the arithmetic growth of the sporting core of the games was met by an exponential growth in the cost of staging them. Even allowing for inflation, the bills at the end of the post-war games were all less than $5 million. Rome 1960, the accounts of which are opaque at best, spent $30 million – though, given the scale of the public works associated with it, this is probably a considerable underestimate. Either way, Tokyo 1964 changed everything. A titanic wave of poured concrete and infrastructural spending, centred in different ways on the games, cost $2.8 billion. Rome had cleaned up its ancient monuments, widened its roads, completed its fascist sports stadia and built a handful of new arenas, but this was a Lilliputian effort compared to Tokyo's ambitions. In Japan, the Olympics was seen as a key element of a national economic strategy to double GDP per head in a decade, and an urban strategy that would utterly transform Tokyo, whose government was planning for a city of over fifteen million people. The games initiated the complete rebuilding of the city's sewage system, the construction of 100 kilometres of urban superhighways, many of them raised high above Tokyo's surface streets, two new subway lines beneath them, a refurbished port and airport, a hyper-modern monorail to take arrivals to the city's four new five-star hotels, and the jewel in the crown – the Shinkansen or 'bullet train', as it is known in the West – the world's fastest passenger train, linking Tokyo and Osaka. Mexico City and Munich couldn't quite compete with this, but each cost something in the region of half a billion dollars and boasted the largest and most architecturally imposing of Olympic villages. Rome's accommodation was made up 1,350 apartments in low-rise blocks; Mexico City's village had 5,000 separate units in buildings up to ten storeys high. Munich created an entire neighbourhood, itself just a part of the huge Olympic park that transformed a vast war-damaged site at the heart of the city.

Rome didn't have to try too hard when it came to cultural resonance, meaningful symbols, known brands and icons, but the next three Olympiads were all consciously and meticulously designed and garlanded with increasingly ambitious and expensive cultural festivals. Tokyo's visuals, designed by Yusaku Kamekura, included the stark but unmissable red-sun poster and the extensive use of the now ubiquitous Olympic sports pictograms; these were first used in 1936 and 1948, but were now part of a comprehensive set of icons and signage that aspired to be accessible to anyone.[2] Mexico's organizing committee awarded the design job to the young American, Lance Wyman, and the message was, 'the sleeping man with the sombrero did not properly represent Mexico.' Wyman responded with a stupendous series of designs that combined the eye-boggling black-and-white patterns of the indigenous Huichol people of Mexico's Pacific coast with Bridget Riley style op art, and the intense pulsating colours of Warholian pop art.[3] For Munich 1972, Otl Aicher, the designer leading the revival of the Bauhaus in the federal republic and linked to the small white-rose resistance movement to Hitler, was the guarantor that the games' design work would be comprehensive, unified, practical and understated. Aicher was very clear about the political importance of the aesthetics of the Munich games: 'Trust cannot be gained through words, but instead only through visual proof and the winning of sympathy. It is not about explaining that this Germany is different, but showing it.'[4] The palette of colours was cool and calm, rejecting the scarlets and gold of Olympic Berlin. Fonts were clean and simple, the sans-serif Univers eradicating every last shred of Gothic tracery. The president of the organizing committee, Willi Daume, treated himself to commissioning twenty-eight high-art posters from contemporary stars like David Hockney and Josef Albers. A vast international programme of music was arranged, with separate strands devoted to classical, contemporary, avant-garde, jazz and folk. The full programme boasted 'fifty-seven operas, seven operettas, three musicals, ten ballets, thirty plays, forty-two orchestral concerts, eight choral concerts, twenty-four chamber and solo concerts, twenty-two orchestras, fifty-six conductors, seventy soloists, and six exhibitions.'[5]

Even with urban stage-sets and cultural spectaculars on this kind of scale, the actual physical audiences for the games numbered in the low millions. The numbers of foreign visitors, always hugely overestimated in advance by organizing committees, remained just a drop in the ocean. What allowed these grander Olympic Games to reach an appropriately large audience was television. Coverage across all media rose. Rome accommodated 2,200 accredited journalists; Munich doubled this to over 4,500 and was so eager to please and ensure good coverage that everyone received their own subsidized room in the Olympic village, equipped with the then unheard-of luxuries of a phone and a colour television. NHK, the Japanese state broadcaster, built the first, and now ubiquitous, Olympic broadcast centre for the 1964 games.

Television, in particular, demanded new facilities and imposed new costs, but it also brought in income. In 1960, the organizing committee of the Rome games managed to sell their television rights to the European broadcasting consortium, Eurovision, and Japan's NHK for small change, and to America's CBS for serious money – a then mind-boggling $394,000.[6] Through a series of relay stations, twelve European countries were able to watch almost one hundred hours of the games live. America and Japan relied upon daily transoceanic flights to bring edited highlights home for prime-time transmission. For the Tokyo games, these began to be replaced by live satellite broadcasting. Still experimental in 1964, it allowed

American viewers to watch most of the Mexico games live, direct and in colour. Even so, in 1960, in grainy black and white, CBS were scoring a ratings share of 36 per cent for the Rome games and advertising revenues big enough to catalyse three decades of fearsome competition amongst the US networks for Olympic television. Tokyo raked in $1.6 million, Mexico City, $10 million and Munich, $18 million. Yet this was just the slow ascent of a curve that would see Moscow 1980 command $88 million in television rights, while, four years later, Los Angeles would receive $287 million. In a self-propelling upward spiral, the games accelerated the purchase of televisions – the number of Japanese TV licences rose from two to sixteen million in the three years before the Tokyo Olympics; West Germany almost doubled its purchase of colour sets in the months leading up to the Munich games – which then generated unprecedented viewing figures. In Japan, 98 per cent of the country watched some of the Tokyo games, with more than 90 per cent watching the opening ceremony and almost three quarters watching a lot. *Ariel*, the BBC's in-house journal, reported with breathless enthusiasm that their late-night live transmissions from Mexico were watched by seventeen million people and, in an era when everything decent in Britain closed before the witching hour, 'Ten million viewers were still watching the Olympics on BBC at midnight and three and a half million kept watching until 1.30 a.m.'[7] It wasn't just in the richest nations that people were watching. From just twenty-one countries who saw the Rome games in 1960, ninety-eight were watching in 1972, testament to both the complete diffusion of television in western Europe and North America and its lightning spread to the urban and the wealthy in Latin America and Asia. Unlike previous years, they would be able to watch each and every final of the games, which, at the behest of American television companies, were finally scheduled in discrete and non-overlapping time slots. It would be just the first of many changes in the programme and form of Olympic events to accommodate the needs of television. The triumph of the medium had important consequences for film, especially newsreels, which were a significant part of the coverage of the Rome games, especially in those countries without a domestic television system; they were all but finished by the early 1970s. It was also the end for the Olympic movie. Although they have continued to be commissioned and produced, Kon Ichikawa's *Tokyo Olympiad* and the multi-director *Visions of Eight* commissioned for the 1972 games remain the last Olympic feature films of any aesthetic significance. The former, in particular, humane and playful, is the genre's best riposte to the superhumans of Riefenstahl's *Olympia*.[8]

Sitting precariously atop this wave of economic and technological change was the IOC, and at the top of the IOC there still sat President Avery Brundage, a man whose countenance seemed ever more vexed and irascible as the 1960s wore on. As late as 1956, he thought the Olympics might be able to disassociate itself from the television age: 'the IOC has managed without television for sixty years, and believe me we are going to manage for another sixty.' It didn't turn out that way. After handing power to negotiate television contracts to organizing committees, TV income began to rise very sharply and, given that the IOC received only a tiny cut of the money, Brundage began to regret his stance: 'The International Olympic Committee has always kept itself free from financial entanglements, so free, in fact, that it has never had enough money to do the useful work it could be doing.'[9] By the mid-1960s, he was joined at the table by the most commercially astute amongst the leaders of the international sports federations and the ever-penurious national Olympic committees. It would take another twenty years for the IOC to regain control over the sale of Olympic TV rights and another ten to take control of the broadcast product itself.[10]

Brundage and the IOC were equally at sea with the sex and drugs and rock 'n' roll dimension of the 1960s. The rising tide of doping and pharmaceutical use in elite sport claimed its first Olympic victim at the Rome games: the Danish cyclist, Knud Jensen, who collapsed during his race under the influence of Roniacol, a vasodilator, and later died in hospital. The fraught issue of gender identities at the games was also addressed, and, in 1968, at both the Grenoble winter games and Mexico City summer games, gender and drug testing were introduced for the first time. As for rock 'n' roll, the Olympics did manage to keep its distance from the most threatening musical innovations of the age, still privileging military bands, orchestral and choral performances and national anthems, but even here there was change, as electronic music graced the opening ceremonies for the first time and jazz festivals accompanied the Mexico City and the Munich games.[11]

Three other issues continued to shake the old Olympic order: the

IOC's Canute-like efforts to reverse the tide of commercialism and professionalism in elite sport; the sporting politics of decolonization; and the enduring presence of Cold War politics in the Olympic movement. The IOC's unbendingly rigid stance on the payment of athletes, even broken-time monies to compensate for time away from work, was made a complete mockery by its de facto acceptance of the Soviet model of elite sport. Having allowed the Soviet Union, its allies and their praetorian guards of full-time state-funded sports people into the Olympic movement, the IOC's ever more hysterical and ineffective policing of athletes from elsewhere appeared hypocritical and ultimately forlorn. Armin Hary, the West German sprinter, was flagrant in his display of both Adidas and Puma shoes at the 1960 games, Alpine skiers were embossed with manufacturers' logos, and the accumulating riches of the new generation of endorsement-heavy professional stars in golf and tennis made it transparently clear to other athletes what they were missing. By 1968, Adidas was cutting a separate deal with the organizing committee of the Mexico City games and setting up its own giveaway shoe shop inside the Olympic village.[12]

As the numbers at the games make clear, the dismantling of European empires in Africa, the Caribbean and Asia created dozens of new nations, who went to the Olympics for the first time. Amongst the many challenges that this demographic shift brought to the IOC was the issue of apartheid and the exclusion of South Africa.[13] Indeed, this became the key unifying cause amongst post-colonial nations, and led to extensive boycotts and exposed the deeply entrenched Eurocentrism and racism of the IOC's old guard. From the late 1950s, the Soviets and the Scandinavians had been agitating for the IOC to look South African apartheid in the eye and ban the country from the movement. Joined by many newly independent African states in the early 1960s, the IOC was forced by this alliance to ask the South Africans for a declaration of non-racial principles. None was forthcoming, and South Africa was excluded from the Tokyo games. A rearguard action by apartheid's apologists saw the IOC mount a fact-finding mission to the country in 1967, which found, to no one's surprise, that everything was just fine in South Africa and that they should be invited to the Mexico City games. The IOC, a body with just one black African member out of seventy-one, agreed. Brundage, aware that the Mexicans would be incensed and fearful of the boycotts that would inevitably follow, accepted the vote, but didn't issue an invitation – a prelude to South Africa's actual expulsion in 1970.

Even more radically, Sukarno's Indonesia, backed by Chinese money, sponsored an alternative Olympic movement: the fabulously named GANEFO – the Games of the New Emerging Forces. In 1962, Indonesia hosted the Asian Games and, pressured by the Asian Games Federation, the Indonesian Olympic Committee agreed to invite nations with whom it did not have diplomatic relations – Israel, Taiwan and North Korea. On the eve of the games, under counter-pressure from the Chinese and the Arab nations, the Indonesians refused to issue the Israelis and Taiwanese with visas. The IOC's response was to suspend Indonesia from the Olympic movement. Anticipating and planning for the move, President Sukarno announced that Indonesia would host GANEFO – the sporting wing of the non-aligned movement that had first been gathered by Indonesia's nationalists at the Bandung Conference in 1955: 'They are said to have sports without politics in the Olympic Games . . . When they excluded Communist China was that not politics? When they are not friendly to the UAR is that not politics? Now let's frankly say sports has something to do with politics. Indonesia proposes to mix sports with politics . . . let us now establish the games of the new emerging forces . . . against the old established forces.'[14]

Despite the IOC issuing threats of Olympic exclusion to any par-ticipants in the games, fifty-one nations sent 2,700 athletes to Jakarta in 1963. It was, logos aside, a carbon copy of the old school, with flags and anthems, oaths and heralds, speeches, torches and flames. Athletically, it was less of a match, as few competitors were potential Olympians; the Soviets, for example, sent a very second-rank delegation of athletes, many of whom were trade-union or youth-movement athletes. Nonetheless, it was thought a consider-able domestic success. A second games was planned for Cairo in 1967, but it was an ultimately much-reduced affair – just seventeen countries attended, all but Guinea from Asia – and was staged in Phnom Penh, in Cambodia, instead. It served as a useful foreign-policy tool for Prince Sihanouk in his struggle with the United States over their support for his domestic opponents, the Khmer Serei, but it was hardly a demonstration of change in the new international order. Had the Chinese, now increasingly focused on the course of the Cultural Revolution, still been interested in GANEFO, they would not have found Indonesia a willing partner. By then, Sukarno had been overthrown and his successor, General Suharto, had secured his rule by way of a nationwide communist purge that would leave many hundreds of thousands of victims.

The basic dynamics of the Cold War continued to be played out at the games. The USA–USSR conflict centred, at the highest level, on the overall medals table. The status of the two Germanys, already normalized in international relations, was confirmed at the games when, in 1968, the West and East German teams competed separately. China's descent into the chaos of the Cultural Revolution and its absence, in effect, from international politics was also duplicated. Each side in the Cold War sparred with the IOC over visas for athletes, nations' nameplates, politically biased judging, threats of defections and actual departures. On occasion, the two main adversaries would actually meet head-to-head, as in the spectacular and politically charged conclusion to the men's 1972 basketball final. However, it was the microscopic movements of a single athlete, amplified a billion times by television, that provided the sharpest commentary on the Cold War. The Czech gymnast Vera Čáslavská, silver medallist in the high beam, turned her head down and away during the playing of the Soviet national anthem in protest over the invasion of her homeland that preceded the Mexico 1968 games, an action that would cost Čáslavská her career.

In creating a stage and a spectacle, now wired to the global television audience, the Olympic movement and its hosts had offered an extraordinary combination of ritual, festival and event, one capable of generating complex state messages and elite projects and communicating them to billions. But in so doing, it opened these channels to others. John Carlos, speaking of his own counter-spectacle, was right. The singular most viewed and revered image of the games in this era was his black-power salute with Tommie Smith during the medal ceremony of the 200 metres at the Mexico City Olympics. That image is still with us. And, like he said, it's not because the man wanted it so. While the unprecedented media coverage of the games in the television era made the Smith and Carlos tableau of hope and resistance possible, it also created the perfect conditions for another defining picture of our time: the man in the balaclava on the concrete balcony of the Israeli team's flat in the Munich Olympic village.

Recalling his attempts to negotiate the release of the kidnapped Israeli athletes and coaches, Walther Tröger, mayor of the Munich Olympic village, paraphrased Issa, leader of the Black September terrorists: Issa couldn't release the hostages, but he did want to thank the Germans who, 'had produced an excellent Olympic Games . . . it offered the Palestinians a showcase where they could bring their grievance to the millions watching on television around the world.'[15]

TWO

Having awarded the 1908 games to Rome, Coubertin hoped that, after a disastrous interlude in 'utilitarian America', the Olympics was about to don a 'sumptuous toga of interwoven art and thought.' Italy at the end of the belle époque might have managed art and thought, but there was precious little sport. Indeed, the late industrialization of Italy had by then produced a very weak sporting civil society. The still-rural aristocracy were enthusiastic about fencing, riding and shooting animals, but little else. The nation's later obsessions with cycling and motorsports could be detected in the first grand road races – both two- and four-wheeled – but their heyday awaited the emergence of a real Italian manufacturing sector. Football and gymnastics aside, few sports had established themselves in the nation's cities. Physical education was almost entirely absent from the school system. Fierce fighting between sports organizations in the northern cities and the capital, and the, at best, lukewarm support of Prime Minister Giolitti, 'a figure difficult to imagine partaking of any form of rapid personal locomotion', saw the games ultimately handed to London.[1] By contrast, Giulio Andreotti, the president of the 1960 Rome Olympics organizing committee, then Christian Democrat minister of defence and on his way to becoming the singularly most important, connected and influential politician in post-war Italy, embraced every cliché of modern Olympism with gusto. In his welcoming address to the games, he imagined that Rome might become the 'sporting capital' of the world, and thought that the Olympic toga would 'appear in Rome in even greater splendour than would have been the case in distant 1908.'[2]

Certainly, by 1960, Italian sporting culture had been transformed.[3] In a variety of ways, Rome did its best to find historical precedents and suggest a national athletic heritage that could account for such splendour. The torch relay began in Sicily, mythologically considered to be the source of the River Alpheus, on whose banks the sanctuary of Olympia had been built. It followed a route that deliberately took in the Greek archaeological legacy in southern Italy, and much was made of the fact that the cauldron was lit by Giancarlo Peris, a Greek-Italian athlete. The gymnastics were held within the remains of the Baths of Caracalla, the wrestling at the Basilica of Maxentius, while the marathon finished under the floodlit Arch of Constantine. Alongside Olympic events, visitors could watch *calcio* – the rough ball-game of Renaissance Florence – reconstructed in Piazza di Siena, or the medieval Umbrian archery contest, the *palio dei balestrieri*.

However, on the matter of the most important era in the development of Italian sport – fascism – the official programme and discourse was remarkably reticent. In fact, it was only under Mussolini that sport became a central element of government policy – at home, as an instrument of national development; abroad, as a demonstration of the new vigour of the Italian empire. Stylistically, Il Duce favoured the hyper-masculinity of boxing, the warrior aura of the equestrian and fencer, and the technical testosterone of motor racing, and these all prospered in the interwar era, but the regime also embraced cycling, athletics and school sports, and reordered football (and all the other sporting organizations) along strictly national and party-controlled lines. With significant state support, Italy was second in the medals table at the 1932 Los Angeles games and third at Berlin. Emboldened by the success of the 1934 football World Cup, hosted by Italy and won by the national team, the regime vigorously bid for the 1940 Olympic Games, before giving way to their new Japanese allies in return for the implicit promise of the 1944 games. In anticipation of those games, the regime completed the complex of sports facilities and stadiums on the north edge of Rome, known as the Foro Mussolini. It was decorated accordingly. Alongside the main athletic stadium, the Stadio dei Marmi, was a warm-up track and sculptural garden of fascist bodily fantasies, ringed by sixty marble athletic figures. As one sardonic American visitor, Eleanor Clarke, wrote, 'Their muscles anatomically impossible, jaws out Duce-fashion, genitals in line with the virility policy . . . gaze either belligerent or loftily dedicated beneath collie-dog brows, hands the size of fur-muffs and tending to hang to the knees.'[4] On the southern edge of the city, the government began to build EUR – Esposizione Universale di Roma. Planned as the site of both a world fair and the Olympic Games, it was imagined as a model fascist city, Vittorio Cini, the senior politician in charge of the project, describing its look as 'the definitive style of the age, that of the 20th year of the fascist era.' Incomplete by the time the war began, EUR was abandoned, and only given new life by the plans for the 1960 games. Indeed, a completed EUR and a refurbished Foro Mussolini were the twin poles of the Rome Olympics. Yet the official programme merely described their architecture as a form of 'vigorous classicism'.

Historical amnesia was an important component of the whole business model of the Rome games. The tight-knit group of politicians and administrators on the committee quietly allocated architectural commissions and building contracts to a small circle of known insiders, especially big northern construction companies and the leading architectural lights of fascism. Marcello Piacentini, the key creator of Mussolini's favoured neoclassicism, was, like the EUR complex he created, rehabilitated and re-employed. Enrico Del Debbio, designer of the Foro Mussolini, added an open-air swimming complex to the now renamed Foro Italia. Active collaborators and supporters of the regime, like Luigi Moretti and Adalberto Libera, were asked to design the Olympic village at Campo Priolo, a huge collection of informal housing built by some of the hundreds of thousands of poor and homeless migrants to the city. Needless to say, the new apartments were passed on to government employees rather than the displaced. The Vatican was not forgotten. Once theologically and ideologically opposed to organized sport, the Church had come round to its usefulness, though it remained deeply suspicious of female athleticism in any form. They were certainly capable of looking the other way on the question of gambling. Totocalcio, the national football pools system established in the 1950s and hugely popular amongst the urban poor, provided the vast majority of the funds for running the games and building and renovating sports facilities. Pope John XXIII was on hand to bless the competitors in a great Mass staged outside St Peter's. In return, the Church was one of the biggest winners from the massive increase in property values in Rome, especially land abutting the upgraded Via Olimpico. Known as the 'Golden Road', it linked the two main Olympic sites in the north and south of central Rome, opening up the western side of the city to new development. However, in the work of Luigi Nervi, responsible for both the Palazzo and the Palazzetto dello Sport, another side of Italy 1960 found concrete expression.

Nervi had trained as an engineer, and devoted much of the 1930s and 1940s to refining the manufacture and use of architectural reinforced concrete. Emblematic of the high-tech, high-design approach of the leading edge of Italian industry, Nervi's two sport palaces – the smaller, a ribbed dome; the larger, a glass and concrete flying saucer – shed every last trace of the fascist past. Bright, airy and human scaled, the fabulous abstract geometric patterns of their roofs were both functional and beautiful, a combination that was making Italy a leading producer and exporter of fridges, televisions, washing machines, typewriters and cars. This, in turn, underwrote the fastest economic growth that the country had ever experienced and initiated its greatest internal migration, as over ten million people, overwhelmingly from the poor agricultural south, upped sticks and headed north to Rome and the industrial dynamos, like Milan and Turin.

Economic change was beginning to generate political change too. The long rule of the Christian Democrats, unambiguously in control since 1948, was beginning to fray as the Communist Party gained in popularity and their own support shrank. In early 1960, an attempt to bolster their position by shifting right and allying themselves with the neo-fascists of the MSI – in both Rome and at a national level – saw anti-fascist riots and demonstrations all over Italy, including in Rome, and eventually the fall of Fernando Tambroni's government and his replacement as prime minister by the more centrist Amintore Fanfini. This opened the way for at least a partial resolution of the most controversial aspect of the fascist inheritance at the Rome games. The Via dell'Impero, which ran from Mussolini's personal obelisk to the main Olympic stadium, was paved with Roman-style mosaics featuring fascist sporting and military triumphs. A petition organized by the Roman left had failed to move the Christian Democrat city council, and saw the communists take the matter to parliament. Pressure applied there, at a national level, forced the Christian Democrats into at least the appearance of change. The Roman authorities effaced just two sections – one that displayed the fascist oath of allegiance, the other a condemnation of the League of Nations' sanctions, imposed after Italy's invasion of Ethiopia – and then added three new sections that celebrated important moments in the formation of the post-war republic: the fall of fascism in July 1943, the referendum establishing the Italian Republic in June 1946, and 1 January 1948, when it acquired a constitution.

The games themselves were to offer more nuanced markers of the new nation. Third in the overall medal table behind the Cold War super powers, Italy could hardly believe its luck. *Corriere della Sera* was talking about sporting triumphs, but it had more than an echo of the nation's astonishment at its own economic transformation: 'It's too good, and too unreal, you have to struggle to be convinced that it is true, that this is not a mirage.' Most celebrated of all was the gold medal in the 200 metres, won by Livio Berruti, a Turinese university student who flipped through his chemistry notes between his semi-final and final, and wore shades when he ran. Antithetical in almost every way to the fascist superman, Berruti celebrated a very different kind of Italian masculinity: 'He wears glasses, even when he runs, and his gestures have the refined delicacy of the intellectual. Those hand gestures suggest that the internal power that makes a champion is really no different from that which prepares an artist or a great man of culture.'[5] Victories in the cycling and the water polo, mainstays of rural and small-town Italy, were celebrated. Working-class Italy had their own sporting champion and cultural autodidact: the boxer, Giovani 'Nino' Benvenuti, who was the son of a fisherman and let it be known that he read Hemingway, owned a Picasso, studied Voltaire and prepared for fights by relaxing to Beethoven violin concertos. In his welterweight final, he floored the Russian, Yuri Radonyak, in the first round, and won a decisive points victory to total delirium from a very rough-and-ready crowd at the Palazzo dello Sport. One witness recalled 'Italian spectators . . . burning newspapers to make torches under the magnificent dome', and saw not only Benvenuti win, but later thought that 'the stadium would be set alight when heavyweight Franco De Piccoli took only one minute and thirty seconds to knock out the portly Russian.' The right had their own tribune too: Captain Raimondo D'Inzeo, the gold medallist in the show jumping, and a leading figure in the local Carabinieri's mounted and violent assaults on anti-fascist protestors earlier that year in Rome.

In total, Italy won thirteen golds at the Rome games and thirty-six medals in all, but just two of those, and both bronzes at that, were won by women: Giuseppina Leone in the 100 metres and the women's fencing team.[6] Given the minuscule participation rate (less than 1 per cent of Italian women were actively playing sport), this was hardly surprising, but it is remarkable that, as late as 1960, both the Catholic Church and the ruling Christian Democrats should have been so uncomfortable, even antagonistic, towards women's sport. During the games, the Vatican forbade the clergy to attend or watch women's events. The communist press reported that, when girls put on sporting kit, 'they are teased by the local boys [and] reproached by the priest in public during the Mass.' The Christian Democrats thought female athleticism the first step towards dictatorship. In an extraordinary editorial in the magazine *Traguardo*, the party argued, 'it begins, in times of peace, with collective outdoor exercises of gymnastics, in T-shirts and shorts. It ends in time of war with lady despots in uniform, who, after the inevitable undoing . . . are hunted down, shorn, imprisoned, killed.' Yet, despite the warning, Italy's press remained captivated by the female presence at the games, giving extensive coverage to the many celebrities who attended – like Elizabeth Taylor and Princess Grace of Monaco – as well as the *olimpidaine*, a corps of bilingual young women, hailing from the very elite of Roman society, smartly dressed and extensively briefed, who served as interrupters during the games.

The flip side of such buttoned-up sexuality was both a large sex industry in Rome – which, despite repeated 'clean-up efforts', remained stubbornly in place before, during and after the games – and an even greater torrent of erotic excitement at the prospect of thousands of 'exotic' women athletes coming to Rome. In keeping with previous games, they were housed in their own segregated village, commanded by the seventy-four-year-old Colonel Giuseppe Fabre, the only man with permission to work there on a full-time basis. It was christened by the Italian press 'the harem of the five circles', thought 'an enormous seraglio' and described as a gigantic chastity belt – an image that cranked up the city's lascivious sexual energy another notch. Some observers made their distaste for the female athletic body clear: 'A trip around the Olympic Village demonstrates how sport brings something masculine, virile, to the delicate organism of the woman. Some swimmers have short, stumpy legs, muscular like those of Hercules.' Another found it all thoroughly 'unnatural': 'In women who run . . . there is frequently something displeasing, forced. They give the impression that the energy impassioned in the nervous system doesn't find the membranes, muscles, bones, suited to receive it.' Innumerable articles lamented that the women athletes had little time to attend to make-up and dress, that they tended unfortunately towards short and shorn hair, and that the toll taken by chlorine on the skin of women swimmers was intolerable. Even the Communist Party found the combination of physicality and femininity too hard to compute. In a long profile of the discus thrower, Paola Paternoster, *Vie Nuove* wrote, 'The champion appeared to us much more woman than athlete', and felt compelled to call in a medical expert to anatomically assess her. Thankfully, medical science gave her the all-clear: 'she has a perfect and harmoniously developed physique.' There were many more who found the village and its occupants the objects of intense desire: 'Among the thousand woman athletes who are guests in Rome, say the well informed, and especially among the Americans, the English, the Russians, the Poles, the Swedish, the Canadians and the Australians, there are some authentic beauties. Phrases like these are tossed around: "optimally calibrated", "refreshing, like a glass of water", "beautiful teeth that bite an apple a day".'[7]

Hardly surprising, then, that, throughout the games, crowds of voyeurs gathered on the flyover section of Corso di Francia that bisected the Olympic village, and trained their binoculars on the women's quarters. Athletes were reduced to taping paper over their windows. Still locked in a profoundly conservative culture, women athletes only really made sense in the Italian press when they managed to find 'time for love, they always find time and they manage unfailingly to get engaged, and get married, even if it's only ten minutes before the Olympic finals.' Paternoster planned to wed immediately after the games. Leone closed her career with the thought that 'the time of competition by now is over . . . now it is time to think about being a good mamma.'

Wilma Rudolph was already a good mama, giving birth to her first daughter at the age of seventeen, just two years before she won three gold medals at the Rome games.[8] Surely no Olympic champion has overcome so many multiple layers of injustice and misfortune, and appeared to do it with such untroubled grace. Born prematurely in 1940, Rudolph was the twentieth of twenty-two children, an African-American baby in the Deep South of the United States. As a child, she was sickly, suffering terrible bouts of double pneumonia and scarlet fever. Polio put her in leg irons between the ages of four and nine, and awkward orthopaedic shoes for another two years after that, and yet, by 1956, at the age of just sixteen, she was a bronze medallist in the 4 x 100-metre relay at the Melbourne games. Italy fell in love with her; everyone fell in love with her; but she kept her distance and her poise. Cassius Clay – then the 'Louisville Lip'; later to become Muhammad Ali, and America's light-heavyweight hope in the boxing – tried and failed to ask her out. A buzzing, if then barely known, presence in the Olympic village, he was dubbed 'Uncle Sam's unofficial goodwill ambassador' by the American press and praised for his 'solid Americanism'. Like so many of his generation, he was still a step away from the political radicalization they would undergo. When asked by an Italian reporter, 'With the intolerance in your country, you must have a lot of problems?' he shot back, 'Oh yeah, we've got some problems, but get this straight – it's still the best country in the world.'

Cold War skirmishing had intensified earlier in the year when an American U2 spy-plane had been shot down over the Soviet Union; its pilot was put on trial for espionage just before the games. Khrushchev had walked out of key East–West negotiations over the future of Germany and Berlin; Eisenhower threw his own hissy fit and cancelled a trip to Moscow. The Olympics, by now, was an established front in the battle. Khrushchev sent a letter, read out to the whole Soviet team in Rome, and its contents were printed as front-page news in *Izvestia* and *Pravda*. The Soviet press suggested that, not only were their own team energized by the usual terrible ragbag of official communist salutations, but the whole world was riveted. One Soviet paper asked an Italian athlete in the village, 'Have you heard about Khrushchev's letter?' to which he is said to have replied, 'Yes, all sportsmen know about it.'

The Taiwanese, who, at the IOC's insistence, were no longer able to claim themselves the representatives of all of mainland China, marched in the opening ceremony under the name Formosa, but also carried a small but very visible sign saying, 'UNDER PROTEST'. As in Melbourne, Germany appeared as a united team, but, beyond the formalities of the opening ceremony, the internal divisions were wider than ever. The GDR was able to claim its first Olympic gold medals when Ingrid Krämer won the women's platform and springboard diving competitions, and their press made sure everyone would know: 'They wanted to pretend to the Romans and all their guests that this woman came from the Adenauer state. But people there know that Ingrid comes from Dresden and was raised in the German Democratic Republic.'⁹

The young American sprinter Dave Sime, who would go on to win the silver medal in the 100 metres, was approached by the CIA to help them in their efforts to get the Soviet long jumper Igor Ter-Ovanesyan to defect during the games. Ter-Ovanesyan declined the advances, but the games would remain a small theatre of espionage and operations over the next decade. Soviet, Eastern European and Cuban teams would all be accompanied by a variety of minders and spooks, keeping an eye on athletes with suspicious political and social outlooks. Even so, athletes kept leaving: Ute Gaehler, an East German on the all-German luge team, at Innsbruck in 1964; András Törő, a Hungarian canoeist, at Tokyo 1964; and the Romanian rower, Walter Lambertus, his countryman, the canoeist, Ivan Charalambij, and the Soviet diver, Sergei Nemtsanov, in 1976.

The West might have looked more attractive to some, but there was no doubt who were the sporting champions of the Rome games. The Soviet Union won 43 gold medals to America's 34, and 103 medals in total to the US's 71. Americans, then still dismissive of sports like gymnastics and wrestling, made the case that their dominance in track and field was still intact, but the *New York Times* was sombre in its assessment: 'The world is stirring, not only politically. It is stirring athletically, too. Nations that weren't in existence at the time of the Melbourne Games four years ago competed here with distinction. The US scares not a soul any more. Once the Americans dominated the show. They don't any more, nor are they likely to do so again.'¹⁰

In fact there were just three nations, absent from Melbourne, that were present in Rome – Morocco, Sudan and Tunisia – but as the break up of Europe's colonial empires gathered pace, so the number of Olympic nations grew. In 1964 sixteen new nations made their debut, all but four of them from Africa, and in the case of Northern Rhodesia/Zambia, one that turned independent during the games itself. In 1968 fourteen first timers appeared, like Barbados, Belize, El Salvador, Honduras and Nicaragua, from the Caribbean and Central America, as well as Kuwait and the US Virgin Islands. In 1972 there were another twelve, including some of the most diplomatically reticent states on the planet: Albania, North Korea, and Saudi Arabia. In Rome they would find their first tribunes: Clement Ike Qatery won a silver in the boxing for Ghana; the weightlifter Tan Howe Liang won Singapore's first medal; Abdoulaye Seye, the Senegalese sprinter, won a bronze medal in French colours, but his country had turned independent just two months beforehand. Pakistan, in a long overdue celebration of national independence, finally toppled the Indians in the field hockey to take their first gold medal, but nothing came close to the symbolic resonance of Abebe Bikila's victory in the marathon.[11]

Bikila served as a member of the Ethiopian Imperial Guard to Emperor Haile Selassie, a man driven into exile by the Italians when they invaded Ethiopia in 1936. He arrived in Rome an unknown, and despite having recorded quite exceptional marathon times he was disregarded by the press. For the maximum of theatrical impact, the marathon was staged at night and lit by thousands of hand-held torches. Key monuments on the route, like the Coliseum and the Circus Maximus, were illuminated by floodlights. Unwittingly, Bikila added his own touch to the set. He had trained in new shoes but found that they blistered his feet and decided to run the race barefoot. When the race leaders entered Rome for the final time at Porto San Sebastiano, Bikila kicked and pulled away, passing the Alum Obelix, a fourth-century Ethiopian royal burial marker that had been looted from the country by Mussolini's army in 1937. When he crossed the line, alone, beneath the Arch of Constantine, he became the first black African Olympic champion.

The closing ceremony was a splendid parade, and the firework show was the best and biggest yet. On the hillsides near the stadium, huge crowds gathered to take a peek, and in the fierce heat and aridity of a Roman summer, sparks from their torches and the display set the ground alight. Ten people were killed in the stampedes. A week later, when the rains finally arrived, the Stadio Olimpico's drainage system was unable to cope, and the Olympic arena became a lake.

THREE

Yoshinori Sakai, born near Hiroshima on 6 August 1945 – the day Enola Gay dropped the bomb – lit the Olympic cauldron. Japan, beaten, devastated, humiliated and occupied, was back. Framed and constrained by the internationalism and pacifism of the Olympic Games, the nation's flag, anthem and emperor were allowed out in public. Instead of a twenty-one-gun salute, Japan released 12,000 brightly coloured balloons. Jet fighters from the JDF passed overhead and left a trail of five coloured Olympic smoke rings. Watched by over 90 per cent of the public on television, the Tokyo games remain the single greatest act of collective reimagining in Japan's post-war history. Even the left-leaning *Asahi Shimbun* could feel comfortable with this level of nationalism: 'We were previously obsessed by the strange illusion that it was desirable to lose our national character and become internationalists. We thought that those who discarded our national flag and anthem were liberated internationalists . . . The two-week-long Olympic Games cultivated the Japanese consciousness among the people.'[1]

But what kind of consciousness? After the shattering defeat of the Second World War and the long, transformative American occupation, the idea of Japan as either a unique and superior civilization or a rising imperial power – the chief ideological propositions of the abandoned 1940 Tokyo Olympics – existed only at the very margins of Japanese politics. Instead, in 1964, the nation was expressed through the extraordinary, explosive transformation of Japan's economy. In less than a generation, Japan had been remade, experiencing almost a decade of double-digit growth that turned it from a rural into an urban society, and saw its industrial giants, in sector after sector, conquer the world's export markets. Rates of economic growth and levels of GDP per capita became the central aim and valediction of domestic politics, and the Tokyo Olympics became both an instrument and symbol of these goals.[2]

Tokyo, laid waste by intensive firebombing in 1945, had been rebuilt in a fashion, but there was a desperate shortage of housing and functioning infrastructure, made worse by the millions of rural migrants that flooded into its booming factories, squatter camps and shack cities, where yakuza gangs, drinking dens and the narcotics business thrived. Even in the early 1960s, one observer thought much of Tokyo 'an ugly sprawl of old wooden houses, scabrous shanties, cheaply constructed stucco buildings and *danchi* – crowded, cramped Soviet-style apartment blocks thrown up to accommodate the postwar influx of people from the rural areas.'³ The population headed towards ten million in a wave of urban sprawl that began to enclose and then engulf a great ring of previously separate towns and prefectures, making the city the largest urban area in the world. It is no coincidence that the bidding team that won the games for Tokyo in 1959 was led by the construction minister, Ichiro Kono, who, along with Tokyo's mayor, Ryotaro Azuma, thought the transformation and modernization of the city the keystone of the nation's economic development. Running the games themselves was another matter; with so much national pride staked on their outcome and interpretation, no one could be prevailed upon to take on the task. With less than two years to go and the absolute insistence of the government, the senior corporate executive Daigoro Yasukawa reluctantly took the job.

Despite the massive scale of its post-war urban growth, Tokyo still relied on a sanitary infrastructure created in the nineteenth century. Flush toilets were very rare; most of the city relied on the daily removal of waste, sucked from beneath buildings by vacuum trucks. Its two metro lines were full to bursting, as were the roads, now filling with the simply gargantuan level of cars rolling off Japan's new production lines. Thus, in addition to the billions of yen spent on the Shinkansen to Osaka, Tokyo acquired an entirely new sewage system, 21 kilometres of monorail from its new international airport to downtown, 40 kilometres of new subway lines, more than doubling the old capacity, and 100 kilometres of new highways – raised roads with two- and three-storey spiral interchanges. The city descended into a hellish miasma of demolition and construction.

It was an overwhelming assault on the senses. The reek of setting cement was everywhere; pollution from the automobiles that clogged the streets and industrial smoke from factories on the city's periphery was so severe that Tokyoites wore face masks, while traffic policemen carried small oxygen cylinders during their shifts. Sidewalk cafes were enclosed by large plastic screens to protect customers from the pervasive smoke and soot, while first-aid stations were strategically located for citizens overcome by the toxic air.[4] In Ginza, the neon heart of Tokyo, a massive sign broadcast the daily atmospheric sulphur-dioxide reading. On the exterior of the giant Nishi Ginza shopping complex, a billboard proudly recorded the level of noise pollution and the threat of phonic damage.

The games were staged in thirty venues, many sited in adjacent prefectures, like Chiba and Saitama. Athletes were housed in one main Olympic village in central Tokyo and four sub Olympic villages. All were joined by a vast network of designated Olympic roads and routes, establishing, in effect, the contours of the new mega-city: the greater Tokyo metropolitan region. Some venues had been built for the 1958 Asian Games and gave an indication of what was to come. The Meiji Olympic Park national stadium – once the proposed site for the 1940 games and its imperial symbolic agenda, later a marshalling yard for raw wartime recruits – was now newly built and recast as the crucible of reconciliation, regional and international cooperation. The Tokyo Metropolitan Gymnasium – a flat, black flying saucer – gave a hint of the cool minimalist modernity of the new sports venues. In keeping with the scale of the whole effort, Tokyo built three new Olympic sites of poured concrete and abstract shapes: the Komazawa sports park and its gymnasium, stadium and control tower, the Yoyogi sports complex and, most impressive of all, Tange Kenzo's national gymnasium, a steel tent formed from the complex undulations of its huge shell-shaped suspension roof.[5] Breathless, *The Times* concluded, 'The arenas have approached new heights of architectural imagination and efficiency. In the press room journalists look blankly over their typewriters at each other. They still feel stunned as they try to pay tribute.'

All this came at a cost that was not merely financial. The systems of subcontracting and on-site security used during the construction of Olympic Tokyo entrenched the role of the city's yakuza in the building industry. Safety standards were so low and so unobserved that there were more than 100 deaths and 2,000 injuries on Olympic-related projects. Land speculation was rife, and the tightly wound connections between politicians, state agencies and large corporations made graft and bribery an inevitable part of the process. The bribes paid to secure bullet-train contracts, which, in turn, led to the resignation of the president of Japanese National Railways, were just the tip of the iceberg. Along the way, hundreds of families were forcibly relocated from Olympic sites, often to shoddy peripheral housing developments.

Inexplicably, the city decided to tear up its tram tracks to make more room for cars. On the eve of the games, as the final building rubble was buried and landscaped, Tokyo swept some citizens away too. Yakuza, whose unmistakable burly street presence was an embarrassment to the organizers, were asked to take a holiday out of town. The beggars and vagrants who made their homes in Ueno Park were swept aside. Stray cats and dogs, numbering in the hundreds of thousands, were systematically exterminated. Taxi drivers were implored to go easy on the horn, drunks were asked not to piss in the gutter and yellow flags were left out at major intersections to help timid tourists cross the chaotic roads.

Tokyo 1964 was cast in concrete, but it was mapped and measured, collated and recorded with electronics. *The Times* considered them the 'Science-fiction Olympics'. Indicative of the rising power and sophistication of Japan's electronics industry, Omega, the Swiss watchmaker and the official Olympic timekeeper since 1932, was displaced by local competitor, Seiko. The company manufactured and donated over 1,300 different Olympic timing devices, from digital stopwatches to huge stadium-sized public clocks. Their subsidiary, Epson, made crystal chronometers and printing timers, nurturing the new technologies that would make it a leading force in laser printers and calculators. Computers were used for the first time to maintain athletes' profiles, collate their performances and distribute this information to the press. The swimming events, hitherto judged by eye, were now started using a starting pistol, turns were checked by touch-sensitive pads, and specially designed cameras could record underwater photo finishes. Timing was now calibrated to one one-hundredth of a second. The opening ceremony featured the games' first use of electronic music; composed by Toshiro Mayuzumi, the piece combined recordings of Japanese temple bells with ambient synthesized sounds played on IBM computers.

With 36 gold medals, the American national anthem was heard more often than any other at Tokyo 1964, but, to a number of observers, particularly in the National Olympic Stadium, it was a very truncated version of 'The Star-Spangled Banner' being played: 'The band got as far as ". . . so gallantly streaming . . ." and then stopped. At first, I thought there was something wrong . . . but no, this was the new official Olympic version.' Robert Whiting reported that Uan Rasey, the lead trumpeter with the MGM studio orchestra, as well as Bob Crosby and the Bobcats, when present at the stadium, finished the job: 'Stationing himself just below the torch . . . he would gallantly pick up on the downbeat side of "O gal-lant-ly streaming" and blare out "and the rockets' red glare . . ." and on to the end.'[6] Bob Hayes, the African-American sprinter, transfixed the crowd, running the first sub-ten-second 100 metres at the games – albeit wind assisted – and took the USA from fifth to first on the final leg of the 4 x 100-metre relay. Joe Frazier bludgeoned his way to the heavyweight boxing gold, accumulating two knockouts, two retirements and a broken finger along the way. Hayes, already a recipient of thousands of dollars and nine new suits from Adidas to wear their sneakers, would go on to be a professional NFL player. Frazier would make millions as the heavyweight champion of the world. First Lieutenant Billy Mills, an unknown to most correspondents, came from nowhere to win the 10,000 metres. The first Native American to win a medal since Jim Thorpe in 1912, his route out of desperate poverty and the loss of his parents was his athletic talent and the other mainstays of American social mobility and athletic prowess: the college scholarship and the military. The Soviet Union may not have had the NFL or the kind of college athletic programmes that the US could boast, but it really didn't need to; its own armed forces provided an almost identical role to the Americans' in supporting 'amateur' elite athletes. Amongst the Soviet gold medallists, the Red Army celebrated the victory of officers like the rower Vyacheslav Ivanov, the boxer Stanislav Stepashkin, and the fencer Grigory Kriss.

Like Prince Constantine, the crown prince of Greece who had won the gold medal in the dragon-class sailing at Rome in 1960, William Northam was Avery Brundage's type of amateur Olympian. A very rich and successful Australian businessman, he took up competitive sailing at the age of forty-six. By the early 1960s, then in his mid-fifties, he graduated to crewing on America's Cup boats. Despite being on the board of major Australian corporations, his schedule was relaxed enough, and his pockets deep enough, that, in 1963, he was able to commission his own 5.5-metre Olympic racing yacht, and then, with his crew, Peter O'Donnell and James Sargeant, thirty years his junior, win Australia's first sailing gold at the Tokyo games. In a pertinent commentary on Britain's still moribund, suffocating class system, three golds were won by impeccably middle-class athletes: Ann Packer (800 metres), Lynn Davies and Mary Rand (both long jump). All three returned to an MBE bestowed by the queen. Ken Matthews also won a gold medal, in the 20-kilometre walk, but he returned to the job offer of running a sports shop in Wrexham. His sin was to be an electrician's mate at a power station, where he trained on the coal-moving conveyor belt. His workmates covered most of the costs of sending him and his wife to the Tokyo games. A public outcry over a decade later saw him receive his own gong.

Don Schollander, the blond American swimmer, won four gold medals, broke three world records and set Japanese hearts alight. Unable to leave the Olympic village without being mobbed, he was inundated with commercial and romantic offers. The US Olympic Committee put aside an entire room to store the 500 baskets of presents, letters and telegrams sent to him. The director of the USOC commented that, 'This is the greatest expression of goodwill for an individual I have ever seen in my life. He is so young, strong and appealing. Japan has just decided he is something of a god in a land where worship is a complex religion.' To this day, Schollander's name and address are used in Japanese textbooks teaching students how to write a letter in English. Ranatunga Karunananda, a 10,000-metre runner from Sri Lanka, was equally lauded. He finished four laps behind the winner, Billy Mills, and was at first jeered in the stadium. His persistence turned the crowd, which cheered him home. An instant media sensation, cast as the embodiment of the Olympic spirit, he was granted an audience with the emperor, while one Japanese housewife wrote, 'I saw you on TV running all alone, and I could not keep back my tears.' Defeat was not always this sweet. The Japanese marathon runner, Kokichi Tsuburaya, entered the national stadium in second place but, reduced almost to a walk, he was passed in the final hundred metres by the sprinting Briton, Basil Heatly. Afterwards, Tsuburaya said, 'I committed an inexcusable blunder in front of the Japanese people. I have to make amends by running and hearing the Hinomaru in the next Olympics.' It took three years of training with persistent back problems for him to realize that his plan was impossible to achieve. In January 1968, he wrote a suicide note apologizing to almost everyone in his life and slit his wrists.[7]

These, in the end, were minor scenes for the hosts. Two sports defined the Japanese experience of the games: judo and volleyball. Both were new to the Olympics – the first sports to be added to the schedule since before the Second World War. Volleyball, invented by William Morgan of the YMCA in the last decade of the nineteenth century as a less strenuous alternative to basketball, spread rapidly through the organization's network of gyms in the Far East, including Japan, where the game's social constituency and meanings moved beyond its original and rather narrow Waspish environments. Judo, though widely diffused by the early 1960s, remained incontrovertibly Japanese.

The sport was codified by Kanō Jigorō. Born in 1860, he was a key figure in the educational establishment of the Meiji Restoration. Intimately acquainted with the West, he was both a traditionalist and a modernizer. He also liked to spar and fight old-style. From the age of seventeen, he attended the leading ju-jitsu schools in Tokyo and systematically collated the fragmented fighting systems that had survived from the Tokugawa era and the rule of the samurai. However, the crude and often violent teaching methods fell short of the spiritual and aesthetic dimensions that Kanō believed a modernized Japanese martial art should possess. In 1882, he founded his own school that taught judo – 'the gentle way' – representing the practice as a journey of moral and social progress. Excising brute force and lethal techniques from its repertoire, judo was a form of fighting that sought to turn an opponent's strengths into weakness, using minimum force for maximum results, favouring technique and style over size and power. It was an outlook that chimed with the ethos of Meiji Japan, a rising power in a world of giants.[8]

By 1900, judo was on the curriculum of the army, navy and police academies. A decade later, it was introduced into the nation's secondary schools and remained, as Kanō had intended, a discipline rather than a competitive sport or a crude adjunct to nationalist ideology. Judo's inclusion in the 1964 games, the first sport on the Olympic programme to be codified outside of Europe and North America, was secured by a vociferous coalition of the Japanese Judo Federation and a broad swathe of members of the Japanese diet, arguing that, 'Judo will at this time enter the limelight as our country's traditional sport, weaving into the games a great special colour.' Parliament authorized the building of the Nippon Budokan, a 15,000-seat temple for all the modernized and codified Japanese sports: judo, sumo, archery and kendo. MP Shoriki Matsutaro claimed it would represent a 'great ideal of peace', which was the 'correct spirit of Japan's national sport.' Fellow member, Matsumae Shigeyoshi, expanded on judo's new role as a tool of internationalist diplomacy: 'Japan's martial arts as world sports . . . must use the opportunity of the coming Tokyo Games to advance to a new track of history for the purpose of advancing international friendship.' The Budokan, built on the site of the long-gone and revered Edo Castle, on land close to the imperial palace, attempted to reflect these historical roots and contemporary redirections. Its fabulous curved roof was lifted from traditional wooden Japanese temples, but it was constructed from precast concrete ribs and sat on vast reinforced concrete buttresses. It was entered through the seventeenth-century Tayasu-mon Gate, but it was also designed with television coverage in mind.

Here, above all, Japan expected victories, and in the opening three contests – light, middle and heavyweight – they duly arrived. However, it was the fourth contest – the open-weight division – that mattered most of all, for, in Kanō's conception of judo, mere body mass should never prevail over technique. In the final bout, Japan's champion, Akio Kaminaga, faced the gigantic Dutchman, Anton Geesink. Parliament was closed for the afternoon; companies put televisions on factory floors so that workers would not skip their shifts; the newspapers were full of verse composed by their readers in praise of Kaminaga. They were all to be disappointed. In an imperious display, Geesink ground his opponent down before trapping him in an unbreakable hold. Kaminaga's calves 'hit the mat again and again, like a fish struggling for its life. Finally the referee called time. Geesink had won.' First there was silence, then there was sobbing as the crowd absorbed the fact that Japanese manhood, in competition with the West, but on its own chosen territory, had been found wanting. Then, as a few Dutch fans sought to rush the stage and congratulate the champion, Geesink raised his hand to stop them and made his formal bow to Kaminaga. The audience rose, applauded and never forgot this act of grace.[9]

In the wake of this disappointment, the pressure on the Japanese women's volleyball team, already immense, was racked up even higher.[10] On the following day, in the hours before the final against the Soviet Union, the streets of every city began to clear as a vast TV audience – nearly 90 per cent of the nation – gathered to watch them. The gender of the leading sectors of the Japanese economic miracle had been male – steel, cars, shipbuilding and electronics – but there was another side to these transformations. Alongside the production-line workers and the salarymen, the Japanese economic miracle was powered by the young women rural migrants who left their families to work in the nation's urban textile industries, and it was from precisely this milieu that the Japanese volleyball team had emerged. Initially the product of paternalism, and then an aid to recruitment and a form of advertising, Japanese textile firms offered volleyball facilities to their female workers. By the 1950s, the entire industry, now booming, was sustaining work teams in a national competition. The core members of the 1964 team were drawn from the Nichibo textile company in Osaka. Their coach, Hirobumi Daimatsu, known in the press as the 'ogre' or the 'demon', had been a platoon commander in the Japanese imperial army and brought military levels of intensity, work and drill to his coaching regimes. The squad was working an 8 a.m. to 4 p.m. shift, before heading for a training session that ran till midnight, with just a twenty-five-minute break. In 1962, the team won the world championship, beating a Soviet team that was considerably taller and more experienced. Now renamed the 'Witches of the East' in the press, Daimatsu upped the team's work rate in anticipation of the 1964 games. Once again, they faced the Soviet Union in the final, and once again, they won, sparking a national celebration that channelled the sheer hard work and unbreakable solidarity of both industrial reconstruction and the team it had nurtured. The Japanese team would go on to win the next two Olympic silvers and a gold in Montreal, but, like the textile companies that had sustained it, that was the end of an era. The long-term decline of the industry, unceasingly undercut from abroad and automated at home, took women's volleyball in Japan down with it.

Ceremonially and organizationally, the games had been conducted without a hitch, but, at the closing ceremony, the compressed energy and ecstasy of the athletes broke loose, charging and dancing wildly through the stadiums, the newly independent Zambians with a hand-painted sign. John Underwood of *Sports Illustrated* was sharp eyed:

> A maverick group of nine New Zealand athletes had a second thought. Grinning preposterously, they broke ranks and began loping around the track in one last ceremonious romp, pausing in their progress to dance impromptu jigs and to sing sudden songs. In front of the imperial box, they repeated their comic opera for Emperor Hirohito himself, bowing from the waist in an exaggerated series of jerks. Distance runner Bill Baillie threw the Emperor a record-breaking kiss. Remarkably, nobody hurried to intervene. The Emperor smiled in spite of himself, and doffed his Western hat.[11]

The Olympics might be powerful enough to change the inflexible etiquette of Japan's royal house, but there were limits. Thirty Olympic gold medals at Tokyo for the Soviet Union, nearly a hundred medals in all, could not save Comrade Nikita Khrushchev. In the middle of the first week of the games, after months of scheming, he accepted the inevitable and took 'voluntary retirement', ceding power and control of the Communist Party of the USSR to its mutinous first secretary, Leonid Brezhnev. And the message of post-atomic peace, of pacific internationalism? On Friday, 16 October, halfway through the games, the People's Republic of China exploded its first atomic bomb.

FOUR

Pedro Ramírez Vázquez, chair of the organizing committee of the Mexico City games and the nation's leading architect, was as brusque a modernist in his outlook as were the aesthetics of his buildings. 'People already know all about the folkloric Mexico, the scenic Mexico and its ancient origins . . . yet no one knows the high levels of efficiency and technical expertise that Mexico has achieved. This is the Mexico that we wish to demonstrate through the medium of the Olympics.'[1] There was some thought and money given to the actual sporting challenge, with most of the nation's Olympic athletes sequestered in intensive training camps for most of the year prior to the games. Mexico's three gold medals from a haul of nine was easily its best ever performance, but Ramírez Vázquez was dismissive of such athletic nationalism. After Mexico's dismal performance at the 1948 Olympics, one official had lamented, 'Mexicans are not athletes, they are poets,' and little in the mindset of the nation had changed.[2] The man in charge of the world's greatest sporting festival, Ramírez Vázquez, argued, 'Of the least importance are the Olympic competitions; the records fade away, but the image of a country does not.' In particular, Ramírez Vázquez and the rest of the Mexican political elite wanted to banish the old stereotypes of languor, inefficiency and corruption – Mexico as the land of slumber and *mañana* – a concatenation of tropes that came together in the foreign press' assumption that Mexico could neither afford the games nor knew how to stage them.

They had some grist for their mill. The building programme for the games was finished perilously late. Just a month before the opening ceremony, the basketball and volleyball venues had no floors, the swimming pools were untiled and there was no furniture in the press centres, but, by mid-October, the infrastructure was complete and the organization held up throughout the games. The worst that could be said was that some were inconvenienced by wet paint in their living quarters, unfired bricks lining their dressing rooms, and the puddle in the corner of the media centre where the roof would not stop leaking.

In this regard, Mexico '68 did demonstrate the country's organizational capacity, but, modern as Mexico might be, there was no way that it could compete with the modernity expressed by Tokyo's gigantic building programme.[3] On a budget of less than a tenth of its predecessor, the committee built only a few new sports arenas, relied on cruelly low wages to keep their costs down, merely rented the Olympic village from a state developer rather than shouldering the costs itself, and looked to cultural and symbolic tools to make their point.

At the heart of this strategy was the Olympics Cultural Festival, which ran for nine months before the games began, staged over 1,500 events and drew on almost the entirety of the nation's intellectuals, writers and artists, as well as inviting contributors from all over the world. It was, if nothing else, cosmopolitan and eclectic. Events began with a schmaltzy Vegas-style light show at Mexico City's Aztec pyramids, with the booming voices of Charlton Heston and Vincent Price narrating the official history of the nation for American tourists. Duke Ellington and Dave Brubeck got the gig; folk ballet from Mexico and indigenous dance from across Africa were showcased; there were exhibitions of American space technology, international colloquia of poets, and a city-wide festival of children's paintings.

This, amongst other things, made Mexico '68 truly the first Olympics in colour. Live television pictures gave it a chromatic intensity only available before in feature films, but the city itself was a visual riot. The signage and pictograms for the different sports were stunning: olive green for rowing, lime green for hockey, purple for cycling, scarlet for basketball. The Route of Friendship – a six-lane superhighway that curved around the south of the city from the Olympic stadium to the village – was studded by eighteen gigantic modernist abstract sculptures that had been specially commissioned for the games, including Jacques Moeschal's *Solar Disk*, a giant steel circle in jade; Herbert Bayer's *Articulated Wall*, a jagged lemon-yellow helix, almost thirty metres high; and Joop Beljon's collection of a giant's chess pieces in wild pink, purple and tangerine.[4] Venues were marked out by massive clusters of multicoloured balloons, a thick white line was painted on the centre of every Olympic route, while the city's squares, gardens and boulevards were planted with hundreds of thousands of flowers, shrubs and trees. The pavements and public spaces around the Olympic and Azteca stadiums were 'awash with magenta and orange waves'. Coloured paint was also a way of concealing the city's numerous shanty towns and chaotic informal markets. Many residents in poor areas were handed paint by officials and told to get to work, 'shocking pink, purple and yellow – temporarily hiding the misery.' It was a similar mistrust, and even shame, of the country's urban poor that animated the national education campaign fronted by Cantinflas, the star of Mexican comic cinema in the 1940s and 1950s. Then, he was the tribune of the new urban working classes. Fresh from the countryside, green but not as foolish as he looked, the old Cantinflas was also capable of wit and wisdom, pricking the pomposity of the powerful. But in 1968, reprising his old character, Officer 777, he too had been co-opted by the PRI (Partido Revolucionario Institucional – the nation's long established single ruling party), and he served up cinema shorts in which he scolded the perceived public threats to Mexico's modern games: mendacious taxi drivers, dissolute football hooligans, foreign hippies, lazy Indian housemaids who were careless with the trash, and lowly traffic officers soliciting bribes.[5]

Amongst the many special and unique elements claimed for the games, Ramírez Vázquez was particularly eager to note that, for the first time, the Olympic cauldron would be lit by a woman: the Mexican hurdler, Norma Enriqueta Basilio. However, the symbolic gains of this move, as a challenge to the prevailing notions of Mexican machismo and a public sphere almost entirely bereft of women, were limited. Predictably, there was not a single woman in a senior position on either the bid team or the management team of the games themselves. As with Rome, the core of the volunteers, translators and assistants at the games were young women of upper-middle-class origins, and, with a special Mexican ethnic twist, they were overwhelmingly light-skinned rather than with an obvious indigenous heritage. The *edecanes*, as they were known, were dressed in minidresses and skirts emblazoned with Wyman's pop-art MEXICO68 logo. Consciously designed to appeal to the male international press corps, contemporary Mexican femininity was reduced to 'pretty girls in psychedelic miniskirts.'

Mexico's relationship to the games' message of peace was even more contorted. The organizers celebrated Mexico's 'independent position with respect to the world's major powers': a member of neither global cold-war alliance; neighbourly to both America and Cuba; a Latin nation, at home in the OECD, but emotionally and politically sympathetic with the new nations of the decolonizing global south. This multipolar Mexico was perfectly suited to the task of international translator, peacemaker and bridge builder. The leading daily newspaper, *Excélsior*, was in raptures over 'the spirit of Mexico, which aspires to the elevation, balance and harmony of humankind.' All across the city, on billboards, banners and posters, on radio and television, the slogan, 'Everything is possible in peace', was repeated ad nauseum. The organizing committee even commissioned a documentary feature film, *La Paz*, to explore the biological and anthropological sources of fraternity and peace. Most ubiquitous of all was the white silhouette of the dove of peace, drawn with the simple elegance of a Matisse cut-out. It was everywhere: reproduced on giant transparent plastic sheeting, hung on lamp posts in every neighbourhood and painted on the sides of buses. Had one looked closely enough during the games, one would have been sure to have seen one or two of them spattered with red paint, or perhaps even blood – the former, an act of protest; the latter, a consequence of repression. Everything was indeed possible in peace, even the notion that the 'real' opening ceremony of an Olympic Games dedicated to harmony, in a city bedecked in the symbols of peace, could turn out to be a massacre, and that, at the most filmed and televised Olympics yet, no camera would be there to see it.

Mexico had been ruled by the PRI in various guises for over half a century. Although there was the formal choreography of electoral politics, the party had never ceded a majority or a major office of state to anyone else. Its control of the media, nationalized industries and all bureaucracies gave it immense powers of patronage and information control, allowing it to marginalize or incorporate any opposition. When this didn't work, there were other options. In 1940, a wave of strikes and labour militancy was cut short when troops opened fire and killed eleven workers. In 1952, protests outside the presidential palace were met by gunfire, killing 200 people. Railway workers and junior doctors were vilified, undermined and imprisoned, where necessary, in the early 1960s. In 1968, the PRI faced a different kind of opponent: the young, urban and educated students of its rapidly expanding universities and technical colleges, radicalized by the tumult of ideas and events spinning across the industrialized world – above all, the example of Berlin and Paris.[6] The Olympics was meant to be a call to the youth of the world, but this wasn't quite what the organizers had in mind.

The first demonstrations caught everyone by surprise. Three months before the Olympics, in July 1968, students from a number of schools marched to mark the tenth anniversary of the Cuban Revolution. A street fight between two of the rival schools on the march was completely transformed by the sudden intervention of the riot police. Attacking both sides, they forced all the students back into their colleges, and then pursued them onto the grounds of their schools and universities, killing four people and, at one point, blowing up an eighteenth-century portico with a bazooka.

Inflamed by the scale and violence of the repression, and now supported by the university authorities (aghast at the state's intrusion on their autonomy) and many of their families, Mexico City's students took to the streets in a rolling programme of strikes, demonstrations and rallies, many of them violently policed. What began as a mere celebration of Castro, turned into a movement calling for the recognition of human rights and due process in the law, challenging and undermining the PRI's claim to have managed the transition to a modern democratic Mexico.

It was hardly surprising, under such pressure-cooker conditions, that student leaders should begin to think more widely about the pathologies of Mexican modernization. The first report of an Olympic dimension to the protests came in late July, as students marched under that banner, 'No Quermos Olympiades.' While careful to state that they had no plans to disrupt the games themselves, the movement found the government's Olympic iconography and disingenuous slogans irresistible material for satire. Posters mimicking the official logo read, 'Mexico: Gold medal for Repression'. Riffing on the regime's dull but ever-present strapline, '1968: Year of the Olympics', students sprayed, '1968: Year of Repression', or, 'We don't want the Olympics, we want a revolution' on walls and official signage.

By early September, the almost daily marches and violent conflicts had begun to subside. The students, now exhausted, were returning to their classes. However, President Díaz Ordaz, who had imported a whole new suite of riot gear from the United States, decided, after much prevarication, to terminate this prolonged threat to the Olympics, now less than six weeks away. In mid-September, the riot police stormed UNAM, the national university, just a stone's throw from the Olympic stadium, and expelled the student leadership from the premises. A fortnight of fighting cowed much of the student movement, so that, on 2 October, a crowd of just 10,000 gathered in Plaza de las Tres Culturas, a square in the new housing development of Tlatelolco. A planned march to a nearby university campus had been cancelled. It was just a rally. In the official version of what happened, armed students fired on the police. In actual fact, the security forces had already surrounded and sealed the square, helicopters hovered above and the white-gloved Olimpia Battalion – a special detail responsible for security during the games – fired on the crowd from the surrounding balconies for about an hour. The death toll remains uncertain, perhaps 250, but this tells us nothing of the gigantic violence exacted upon the thousands of students rounded up, confined, imprisoned and tortured over the coming weeks.

The PRI media machine went into total lockdown and denial. Only a handful of foreign journalists were present, and they, like the *Guardian*'s sports correspondent, John Rodda, spent most of their time in Tlatelolco, face down in a pool of cold water, on hard concrete floors, being prodded by soldiers' bayonets. When asked about the event, Avery Brundage replied, 'I was at the ballet last night.'[7] There was no question that the games would go on.

If the student movement and the Tlatelolco massacre wired the Mexico Olympics into the mainstream mood of rebellion in the industrialized world, the games also channelled the emerging challenge to gender roles and identities, and the increasing prevalence of powerful pharmaceuticals – recreational and otherwise – in society and in sport. Late to recognize these tectonic shifts, the IOC spent the 1960s struggling to keep up, and only in 1968 did it introduce both gender and drug testing at the games, and both have proved deeply controversial. The IOC and the world of athletics had to face the complexity of gender identities when, in the late 1930s, two athletes who had competed at the various Women's Olympics of the interwar era – the Czech Zdeňka Koubková, and the British shot-putter Mary Weston – underwent gender reassignment surgery and changed their

names to Zdeněk Koubek and Mark Weston.[8] It also emerged that
Dora Ratjen, who had competed for Germany in the high jump at the
1936 games, was biologically male, but brought up as a female by
his family. The notion of gender-testing athletes became more pressing in the early 1960s, as Cold War suspicion fell on 'masculine'
women athletes from the Soviet Union.

Gender testing was introduced by the IAAF at the 1966 European
Championships; using chromosomal analysis of buccal cheek cells,
the first athlete to fail a test was Ewa Kłobukowska, a bronze medallist in the women's 100-metre sprint at the 1964 Olympics in Tokyo.
She was found to have the rare genetic condition of mosaicism, her
cells possessing a mixture of male XY and female XX chromosomes.
She was then banned from competing in any future games of either
gender. The same year, the IOC banned Erika Schinegger, the 1966
women's world champion in downhill skiing, when it was shown that
she had internal male sex organs. Kłobukowska and Schinegger were
not, of course, the first intersex athletes. Stanisława Walasiewicz was
born in Poland in 1911, but brought up as Stella Walsh in the United
States. In 1932, competing as a Polish athlete at the Los Angeles
games, she won a gold medal in the women's 100 metres. In 1980,
married, divorced and long retired, she was killed by gunshot wounds
in a robbery. The post-mortem revealed that she had partially developed male genitalia and a chromosomal disorder that gave her
both male and female genetic elements.

The use of drugs in sport had been a much more open affair.[9]
In the early twentieth century, athletes and coaches made use of stim-
ulants like strychnine, alcohol, caffeine, amphetamines, kola nuts
and oxygen. They were openly used in professional cycling, boxing
and walking, but plenty of amateur runners and rowers liked to dip
into the medicine chest too. The IOC was first officially alarmed by
the issue of 'doping' in the late 1930s, but, characteristically, only in
so far as it threatened the amateur ethos.[10] The impact of doping on
the health of athletes was not the problem, as they saw it. Having
stated their opposition to the notion of doping, the IOC then did
nothing, but the matter would not go away. At the 1952 Oslo games,
three speed skaters consumed so much amphetamine sulphate that
they were violently ill, while the amazing performances of Soviet
weightlifters at the Helsinki summer games, later that year, alerted
the US coach, Bob Hoffman, to the use and potential of testosterone

for building muscle. His suspicions were confirmed by a Soviet colleague, and he then experimented with testosterone use for US weightlifters, before embracing Dianabol – the first commercially produced anabolic steroid – and evangelizing about its powers amongst the athletic fraternity. The death of the Danish cyclist Knud Jensen at the 1960 Rome games was, despite his use of a vasodilator, and according to careful analysis of the medical records, caused by heatstroke and a coma that followed his falling off his bike and cracking his skull, not amphetamines.[11] However, this amphetamines story was the widely held belief at the time, sustained by the minor moral panic in the press that accompanied the tragedy, and it forced the IOC to act.

The IOC's doping committee, first established in 1962, spent five torrid years creating a global drugs regime in sport, but failed to properly demarcate its own responsibilities and those of sports federations and Olympic hosts, as well as to make sense of the accumulating medical and scientific research on the subject – a task that was quite beyond the grasp of many members of the IOC. In Mexico, just a single competitor failed the test: the Swedish modern pentathlete, Hans-Gunnar Liljenwall, for drinking too much alcohol. In 1972, with considerably more money and sophisticated technology available, seven athletes had problems, but many of these cases demonstrated the still dubious nature of the testing regime. In the case of some performance-enhancing drugs, the regime seemed simply ridiculous, as it did for the Mongolian judoka, Bakaava Buidaa, who exceeded the permissible caffeine level. There were also problems of logistics and efficiency. Miguel Coll, a Puerto Rico basketball player, failed a test for amphetamine use, but the result took so long to come back from the lab that his team – who would normally have been suspended – were able to complete the tournament. There was also the issue of the still wildly divergent regulations and attitudes of the IOC and the world sports federations. Two cyclists – the Dutchman Aad van den Hoek and the Spaniard Jaime Huélam – were stripped of their bronze medals for taking Coramine, a drug allowed by the ICU but not by the IOC. Also in 1972, the American teenage swimmer, Rick DeMont, was stripped of his gold medal in the 400-metre freestyle after ephedrine was found in his urine – almost certainly from his asthma medicines, an eventuality that the anti-doping regime had not anticipated. Yet it could also accommodate the widespread use of tranquillizers, especially in the shooting events of the modern pentathlon. In 1972, many national Olympic committees called on the sport's governing body, UIPMB, to ban their use, which initially it did. However, trials suggested tranquillizer use in the sport was so pervasive that the UIPMB withdrew its own ban and ended testing altogether. Above all, because there was no test for anabolic steroids, the vast majority of drug taking went unnoticed. Speaking to a US congressional inquiry the following year, an athlete, Harold Connolly, made clear what everyone knew: 'The overwhelming majority of the international track-and-field athletes I have known would take anything and do anything short of killing themselves to improve their athletic performance.' Ken Patera, the weightlifter, was brazen. Rueing his defeat by the Soviet Olympic champion, Vasily Alexeyev, he said, 'Last year the only difference between me and him was that I couldn't afford his drug bill. Now I can . . . we'll see which are better – his steroids or mine.'[12]

If it wasn't the drugs, something else was working. In the men's athletics, every event from the 1,500 metres down, and every field event saw the world or Olympic record broken. In the women's events, every distance but the 400 metres and over half the field events went the same way. All competitors were aided by the thin, rarefied air of Mexico City, allowing them to sprint faster, and hang in the air or fly for longer, though long-distance runners and walkers were held back by its low oxygen content. In some events, new equipment and techniques improved performances. Dick Fosbury revolutionized the high jump with his unique backwards-jumping style, while the arrival of foam mats (at last) and fibreglass poles pushed pole vaulting to new heights. The use of anabolic steroids certainly made a difference. Margarita Gummel, the East German shot-putter, was amongst the first to receive state-administered steroids, and won the gold medal in Mexico. However, in the case of Bob Beamon, the American long jumper, some other magic – statistical and athletic – was at work. On his very first attempt, Beamon leapt 8.9 metres, shattering the previous world record by an unprecedented 55 centimetres. It took nearly half an hour for the distance to be verified, for it was beyond the range of the newly installed mechanical measuring equipment and required the use of an old-fashioned tape measure. He had destroyed the field, ended the competition and set a record that would last for forty-four years with a performance at the very outer statistical limits of his or any athlete's range. When Beamon was finally told the official result, he collapsed on the track in what the doctors called a 'cataplectic seizure'. Yet neither this, nor his small protest at the medal ceremony – his sweats hitched up to reveal his black socks and shoeless feet – were the defining images of 1968. All have been eclipsed by the salute.[13]

In 1963, the comedian Dick Gregory, writing in *Ebony*, America's most successful black lifestyle magazine, had called for an international boycott of the 1964 Tokyo games: 'it is time for American Negro athletes to join the civil rights fight – a fight that is far from won.' Martin Luther King had made his 'I Have a Dream' speech in Washington, Kennedy had been assassinated and black America needed every kind of help it could get to turn the momentum of the civil-rights movement into real change and real legislation. African-American athletes, then amongst the most public figures in the community, did not heed the call in 1964, but Gregory had lit an ember and, after four more years of bitter conflict and rising hopes and expectations, it caught fire.

In 1967, the sprinter Tommie Smith was asked by a reporter at the Tokyo University Games whether there might be a boycott of the Mexico City games. In the febrile, super-racialized atmosphere of the times, Smith's offhand remark – 'Yes, this is true. Some black athletes have been discussing the possibility of boycotting the games to protest racial injustice in America'[14] – triggered a cascade of rumour, claim and counter-claim that such a boycott might really take off.

What turned all the talk into action was the arrival of Harry Edwards. Edwards was a student athlete who had turned down the NFL for a postgrad degree at Cornell in sociology, and had gone back to teach at San Jose State University in California, where Tommie Smith and John Carlos were studying. He took his politics and his methods from Dr King, his aesthetics from the Black Panthers, and had the charisma, the acuity and sometimes the fire of Malcolm X. Edwards came to local and then national prominence when, in 1965, he led a campaign to improve the housing conditions of black athletes at San Jose, who, due to an unspoken colour bar, could not rent accommodation near their own campus and who received no support or help from the university.

The campaign centred on the college's prestigious American-football game with the University of Texas, El Paso. Edwards proposed disrupting the game. The local Hell's Angels promised to show up and ensure that he didn't. Then the Black Panthers weighed in, claiming that they would stop the Angels. Ronald Reagan, governor of California, tried to trump them all by announcing that he would send in the National Guard. Edwards and the dean, conscious of how the whole thing was spiralling out of control, cut a deal and cancelled the game. Edwards, now nationally known and connected, took up the idea that Smith had ignited, networked around the African-American athletic community and, on Thanksgiving Day 1967, launched the Olympic Project for Human Rights (OPHR), setting out an agenda of change that challenged the endemic racism of the Olympic movement, US society and its sporting institutions. African-American athletes remained second-class citizens in much of the country, were systematically excluded from many private sports clubs and were subject to the usual derogatory stereotyping that limited their career options and blocked their progression into coaching and administration. The founding statement of the OPHR stated that, 'We must no longer allow this country to use . . . a few "Negroes" to point out to the world how much progress she has made in solving her racial problems when the oppression of Afro-Americans is greater than it ever was. We must no longer allow the Sports World to pat itself on the back as a citadel of racial justice when the racial injustices of the sports industry are infamously legendary.'[15]

Above all, he proposed a boycott of the 1968 Olympics. In truth, there was never a majority in favour of this amongst the African-American athletes likely to make the US team, but the threat made headlines and kept up the political tension all the way to August 1968, when Edwards finally called it off. Along the way, their campaign was stoked by the IOC's unbelievable proposal, later rescinded, to invite South Africa to the Mexico games, the country having been given the ethical all-clear by apartheid sympathizers in the IOC. The OPHR changed the conversation about race and sport forever in the United States, while Edwards and many of the athletes involved in supporting the campaign endured the attention of the FBI, break-ins to their apartments, hate mail including fake airline tickets to send them back to Africa, and death threats in the post.

Schooled in this environment, Tommie Smith, the world record-breaking winner of the 200 metres at the Mexico games, and John Carlos, who came third, had just twenty minutes to prepare themselves for the final act of this story. Between them, they had a pair of black leather gloves from Smith's wife, a black scarf and some beads; each had a pair of cheap black dress socks. Peter Norman, the Australian silver medallist, knew that something was up and asked to join them. He pinned an OPHR button on his chest. Both Americans stood shoeless on the podium. As 'The Star-Spangled Banner' began, Smith lowered his gaze and lifted his gloved hand straight above his head, Carlos set his at a slight angle; both made a fist. Smith, in an interview with ABC's Howard Cosell the day after, would say this of the moment: 'The right glove that I wore on my right hand signified the power within black America. The left glove my teammate John Carlos wore on his left hand made an arc with my right hand and his left hand to signify black unity. The scarf that was worn around my neck signified blackness. John Carlos and me wore socks, black socks, without shoes to also signify our poverty.'[16]

Initial press coverage, though widespread, was not front-page news in America. Once Avery Brundage, now incandescent at the 'political violation' of the games, ordered the US delegation to expel Smith and Carlos – which they did – it was the only news. Smith, Carlos and Norman were all punished by their sporting federations and subjected to decades of exclusion before their rehabilitation at the end of the twentieth century, but the IOC and its allies had lost control of the spectacle and its meaning. At the closing ceremony, each team was only allowed seven members at the parade, in an attempt to prevent the dangerous exuberance exhibited at the 1964 Tokyo games. In the end, the athletes were unable to contain themselves; they broke ranks and poured out of the stands and onto the track, leaving the white-jacketed Mexican security guards adrift in a whirl of dancing humanity.

FIVE

St Moritz, Swiss host of the 1948 Winter Olympics, may have been physically unaffected by the war, but it had hardly prospered; resources were so strained that the organizers were unable to offer athletes dressing rooms at their venues, so they changed in their hotels and hostels. The terrible toll taken on the rest of Europe, and its indebtedness to the United States, were on show, with Norwegian skiers forced to borrow equipment from the Americans, and the Italians famously hammered 31–1 by the US in the early rounds of the ice hockey. The Oslo games of 1952 bore the marks of the nation's physical and political reconstruction. Before the war, Norwegian sport had been sharply divided between the bourgeois and the workers' sports movements. The experience of occupation and the Nazi-backed Quisling regime, which attempted to take complete control of the nation's sporting institutions, sealed a previously unlikely alliance between these two wings of Norwegian sport. Drawing on considerable state and municipal funds, the city built new skating arenas, transport links to distant mountain ski sites and the winter games' first Olympic village that would, unlike its predecessors, actually be converted into social housing.[1]

Small was still beautiful and exclusive. In the immediate postwar era, there were thirty or fewer nations competing at the winter games, the vast majority of them European, and most of the rest were at least partially industrialized nations (America, Canada, Australasia, Argentina, Chile and Japan). Throughout the 1960s, the numbers would steadily increase, though, given climate, topography, sporting history and scarce resources, very few of the newly decolonized nations of the global south, present at the summer games, were able to compete. Even then, their representatives came by the most unorthodox of routes. India's only winter Olympian, Jeremy Bujakowski, was a skier of Polish descent, whose parents had settled in Kolkata when he was young. Two Filipino skiers, Juan Cipriano and

Ben Nanasca, adopted by New Zealanders and brought up in the mountains of Andorra, skied at the 1972 games. Luge and biathlon were added to the programme, new women's events were created, and the number of athletes increased from just 669 in St Moritz in 1948, to almost double this at Grenoble in 1968. The size of the international press corps increased even faster. Almost absent in 1948, Grenoble accredited over 1,500 journalists. Television coverage, like at the summer games, went from nothing to the live global transmissions in colour that beamed out of Sapporo in 1972.

Squaw Valley aside, the Winter Olympics shifted from small resorts to major centres of population, necessitating the dispersal of many Olympic sites to appropriate mountain locations, and thus increasing the demand for new transport and communication links, and separate Olympic villages. The costs of staging the games rose in an even more exponential fashion. Although quite what precisely was included in the balance sheets of the games varied from one organizing committee to the next, the trend was clear. The cost of Squaw Valley, in 1960, was $20 million. Innsbruck, four years later, doubled it to $40 million. The bill for Grenoble, in 1968, came in at $240 million, and Sapporo, in 1972, given the odd project or two, was a cool $1 billion in the making. Costly as a new ski jump or luge run can be, something other than the Olympic programme itself was driving these games.[2]

Squaw Valley was driven by the ego, real-estate dreams and irrepressible chutzpah of Alexander Cushing. A blue-blooded east-coast commercial lawyer who liked to ski, he first visited Squaw Valley in northern California in 1947, when it was just a big concave bowl at the foot of three fabulous mountain peaks. Convinced of its potential as a high-end winter sports resort, he borrowed some Rockefeller money and set up shop. In 1956, Cushing heard that Reno in Nevada was looking to be the US Olympic Committee candidate for the 1960 games, and thought – as a publicity stunt, if nothing else – Squaw Valley should bid too. Charismatic and gregarious, he sported English tweeds on the ski runs, wore a red bandana over a thatch of red hair and had enough charm to tempt Gene Kelly, Sophia Loren and Bing Crosby to his 'proto' resort. He also wined and dined the members of first the US Olympic Committee and then the IOC with such aplomb that they were able to convince themselves that a location with just one ski chair, two tow ropes and a fifty-person lodge could host the games. Shameless, for he was an aggressive developer and serial transgressor of environmental and planning laws, he argued that Squaw Valley would be a return to a 'pure' winter games, untainted by commercialism or giganticism. He also convinced the governor of California, its state legislators and eventually the governor of Nevada and the federal government itself to put up the money. Walt Disney was brought in to dress the stage with huge 'snow' sculptures made of plaster, which the company claimed looked more like snow than snow. A Disney-orchestrated chorus of 2,500 and a 1,200-piece band were drowned out by the blizzard that accompanied the opening ceremony, but the TV cameras loved the arrival of the Olympic torch by ski. By this time, Cushing had been edged out of the organizing committee by more powerful figures in Californian politics, but he got two free seats for the opening ceremony and made a fortune from the land values and tourism generated by such a generous tax-payer subsidy.

Innsbruck, by contrast, was always a state-led project. Post-war Austria, tainted by its incorporation into the Third Reich, had focused on economic reconstruction and finding its place in the cross-currents of post-war guilt and Cold War politics. One of the few places in which the nation could imagine itself was through skiing, an immensely popular recreation, a rare site of Austrian victories and one of the nation's leading industries. Second in the world only to Germany in the production of skiing equipment, Austria was the world's leading exporter. The games, and the new facilities and roads that accompanied them, were designed to boost the nation's profile, ski-equipment companies and its rapidly growing winter-tourism sector.

While national pride and the health of the winter-sports industries were important to both Grenoble and Sapporo, these interests were eclipsed by much grander economic designs. The technocrats of both France and Japan used the winter games as an instrument of regional development policy, seeking to use the now massive investments required to build dispersed sites, road and rail networks and upgraded housing to boost economic growth in hitherto peripheral and poor regions. Twenty per cent of the cost of the Grenoble games was the roads alone. Its main Olympic village, by far the largest yet at a winter games, became part of a hugely enlarged university. President Charles de Gaulle and Prime Minister Georges Pompidou were ever-present fixtures at these monuments to French *dirigisme*. Sapporo, the main city of the most northerly of Japan's islands, Hokkaido, spent just 5 per cent of its budget on sporting facilities: the rest went on 200 kilometres of new road, a tram system and not one but two new airports.

As an Arctic flank of the global cold war, the winter games were a stage for paranoia, conflict and manipulation. The discovery that the East German women's luge team in Grenoble was, against the rules, heating its sled runners before racing, provided the Western press with ineffable evidence of the communist bloc's mendacity. Bias and misperception was evenly spread, as statistical analysis of the judges' marks in Olympic skating competitions demonstrates. Everyone favoured their own athletes, of course, but the Soviets and their Warsaw Pact allies marked the Americans down, and the Americans, in turn, with their NATO allies, reciprocated.

Most fissile of all the winter sports was ice hockey. In part, this was a consequence of squabbling, like the disagreement over scoring systems that saw the Canadians refuse to attend the 1964 Olympic medal ceremony, and, in part, a consequence of wider diplomatic policies, like the decision of Canada, Sweden and the USA to boycott the 1957 ice-hockey world championships, held in Moscow just months after the Soviet invasion of Hungary. The sport was one of the places in which the Soviet menace, and its capacity to catch up with and surpass the West, took tangible form – as the Red Machine. Prior to the Second World War, Olympic ice hockey – indeed, ice hockey in general – was a virtual Canadian monopoly. However, from 1956, the Soviet Union, drawing on its huge cadre of professional military players, became the dominant power, winning the gold medal in Cortina and then six out of eight golds between 1960 and 1988. Canada would win nothing, and, unable to circumvent the IOC's still strict amateur rulings, they would refuse to send a team to the Sapporo games at all. Their defining Cold War moment in the sport would come, instead, in the specially arranged summit series of eight games, played between their best professionals and the Soviets in 1972.[3]

The 1960 games saw a rare moment of public détente in Olympic ice hockey. During the final break of the USA–Czechoslovakia game, the Soviet captain, Nikolai Sologubov, purportedly sneaked into the Americans' changing room and offered the team oxygen to help them beat the Czechs. That the Soviets should be happy to conspire against their Warsaw Pact allies was testament to the deep and growing tensions between them, expressed on the ice-hockey rink. In 1947, in Czechoslovakia, the game had become associated with the last days of the fragile post-war democracy, during which the national team were crowned world champions in the first post-war tournament, held in Prague. A year later, the Czech Communist Party, with the support of the Red Army, were in power; everyone else was being marginalized or imprisoned. The invasion of 1968, which crushed the Prague Spring, turned antipathy into loathing and wrath. During the 1969 world championships, two Czech victories over the Soviets saw people pour onto the streets of Prague, the second time accompanied by attacks on Soviet military barracks and the gutting of Aeroflot's city-centre office. A Czech response to the tyrannical violence of the crackdown that followed the Soviet invasion could also be seen at the 1972 Sapporo Olympics. Recalling the Czechoslovakia–USSR game, an American ice-hockey player, Mark Howe, said, 'to this day, I've never seen a hockey game more brutal than that. The Czech goalie must have broken five sticks over Russian players.' At 5–2 down in the final third, a Czech defenceman, in possession in the Soviet zone, chose to fire at their bench rather than the goal. He didn't hit anyone and they lost the game.

Since its inception, the Winter Olympics had skated close to the worlds of professionalism and commerce. Chamonix, St Moritz and Lake Placid were all hosts whose politicians and hoteliers sought to make long-term financial gains from staging the Olympics, boosting their appeal as high-end resorts. Figure skating and the best figure-skaters had an enduring appeal on the commercial circuit of ice-dance extravaganzas, circus shows and, eventually, the movies. Given this commercial milieu, and the immense costs associated with serious training in winter sports, the International Skiing Federation (FSI) was always sympathetic to athletes acquiring commercial sponsorships or other sources of income. They clashed sharply with the IOC in 1936 at the Garmisch-Partenkirchen games, after the IOC ruled that ski instructors were, in effect, professionals and thus excluded from the Olympics.

Not surprisingly, Avery Brundage, high priest of amateurism, had developed the most intense loathing for the winter games, which he dismissively referred to as the 'frostbite follies'. At a meeting of the

IOC executive in 1960, he asked the committee to pull back from its commitment to Innsbruck in 1964, with a view to abandoning the winter games altogether, but he was rebuffed. In the meantime, he made it his personal mission to pursue athletes from outside the Soviet bloc who broke the rules. The West German figure-skaters Marika Kilius and Hans Jürgen Bäumler had won silver medals at both the 1960 and 1964 Winter Olympics. Shortly before the Innsbruck games, they had also signed a contract with America's itinerant skating extravaganza, *Holiday on Ice*. Later that year, they were retrospectively disqualified by the IOC. They were hugely popular with the West German public, and the request, by Willi Daume, the head of the German national Olympic committee, that they return their medals was considered a national scandal.

Skating and show business were bad enough, but, by the late 1970s, skiing was also a big business – one in which the leading athletes were openly endorsing products and equally obviously being paid. Matters came to a head before the 1968 games. The FSI and the IOC agreed that, irrespective of what happened in other competitions, the manufacturers' logos would be removed from skiing equipment. Companies and athletes argued that it was impossible to reconstruct equipment at such short notice. The IOC responded with a plan to confiscate everyone's skis at the end of each race, before they got to the television cameras.

Yet the IOC was never going to be able to control a sport that could boast stars of the public appeal and commercial potential of the Frenchman Jean-Claude Killy and the Austrian Karl Schranz, both national heroes and well paid for the honour. Both brought a new level of technical brilliance, hair-raising speed and high-risk calculation to Alpine skiing; Killy was the more cerebral of the duo; Schranz was famed for his relentless search for rule-based and technical edges. Among the most memorable duels was the slalom at the Grenoble games. Killy held the lead, skiing through a pea-soup fog so bad that a third of the field was disqualified. They included Schranz, who had managed to convince officials that he should be allowed a second run and duly took the lead, only to be scratched from the event.

By the time the 1972 Winter Olympics came around, Killy had retired and Schranz, at the third time of asking, was ready to finally win an Olympic gold.[4] However, Avery Brundage was still around too, and as he got older, he got madder and angrier. In Grenoble, in 1968, in a fit of pique, he had refused to participate in the Alpine skiing medal ceremony. On the eve of the Sapporo games, he muttered darkly of his blacklist of forty athletes. Schranz was quoted in the press, asking of the IOC how they can 'understand the real-life situation of top racers, when these officials have never been poor?' Brundage was refreshingly honest when asked why Schranz was then singled out: 'he was the most blatant and the most verbose we could find.' Though he might have added that the TV companies who had paid for rights to the games would never have tolerated the complete removal of Alpine skiers that would have followed, had the IOC been consistent rather than vindictive. Just days before the skiing was due to start, the IOC voted 28–14 to expel Schranz. The Austrian press, near hysterical with rage, called for the rest of the national team to walk out of the games. Schranz returned home alone, but the crowds, at least 100,000 strong, lined the streets from the airport to greet him, and burnt effigies of Brundage. In his farewell address to the IOC, Brundage hoped that 'the Winter Olympics receives a decent burial in Denver.' In his retirement, he grew more bitter and less reticent, arguing that 'this poisonous cancer must be removed without delay.'[5] He almost got what he asked for. The 1976 winter games had been awarded to Denver. Alert to the spiralling costs of staging them and the increasingly harsh environmental impact of the winter-sports industry, a group called Citizens for Colorado's Future put a question on both the state and the city electoral ballots, asking whether Denver should stage the games. On a 93.8 per cent turnout, 60 per cent said no. They were the first electorate to do so, and they would not be the last.

SIX

The 1972 Munich games were not short of spectacular sporting moments. The exuberantly moustachioed Mark Spitz won seven gold medals, broke seven world records and became the world's greatest swimmer. Olga Korbut, the Soviet gymnast, lost the overall gold medal but won the asymmetric bars and a global audience for her intensely televisual elfin charm. West Germany's poster girl, Heide Rosendahl – youthful, lanky and always with her John Lennon glasses – lost the pentathlon by a whisker, but took the gold for the hosts in the long jump. In perhaps the cold war contest par excellence, the USA–USSR men's basketball final saw a narrow US lead turned into a Soviet victory in the final seconds, as timekeeping and refereeing arguments raged. The Americans did not return to pick up their silver medal. All have been eclipsed by the Palestinian Black September movement's attack on the Israeli athletes and coaches in the Olympic village, the day-long, globally televised siege of their apartment complex that followed, and the subsequent firefight at Fürstenfeldbruck airport, which, in total, left eleven Israelis, five of the eight Palestinian terrorists and a German police officer dead.[1] These events have not only supplanted the sporting dimension of the Munich Olympics, but, to a great extent, have eradicated from popular memory the complex meanings and messages that the organizing committee and the wider West German political and cultural elites sought to fashion at the games.

The bid was staged and won in the dying days of Chancellor Ludwig Erhard's last government – a fitting finale for the architect of Germany's social market and economic miracle. The games were then shaped and planned under his successor, Kurt Georg Kiesinger, a Christian Democrat at the head of a grand coalition, increasingly dominated by the rising Social Democrats and their charismatic leader, the then foreign minister, Willy Brandt. The Olympics were brought to fruition and held under Brandt, the first SDP chancellor since the Weimar Republic. In tone and foreign-policy implications, the games received the decisive imprimatur of the Social Democrats and their new Ostpolitik – above all, the agreement that East Germany would not only be represented as a separate team, but accorded all of the formal markers of statehood – its own flag and national anthem, for example – in strict contravention of the Federal Republic's refusal to recognize the GDR. If West Germany was looking for a marker of progress, and a story about its own transformation, it had arrived.

Although the federal government would shoulder most of the costs of the Olympics, the key actors were the two men at the heart of the organizing committee: Willi Daume and Hans-Jochen Vogel. Daume, a member of the Olympic handball team in 1936, was a moderately rich Dortmund businessman in the iron and steel industry, and a devoted Olympian in the mould of Carl Diem, his sometime mentor. He joined the Nazi party in 1937 and served out the war at a Belgian branch of his firm: a plant making tank parts for the army. After the war, he became the most powerful individual in German sport, hoovering up the presidencies of the Deutscher Sportbund, the West German national Olympic committee and, in 1956, a seat on the IOC itself. Hans-Jochen Vogel was the SPD mayor of Munich. Born into the solid middle-classes of Catholic Bavaria, he was thirteen at the outbreak of war and served as a child soldier, an experience that decisively radicalized him. By 1960, and at the age of just thirty-four, he was mayor of Munich, riding a wave of youthful rebellion and energy that had made the city, West Berlin aside, the centre of the nation's emerging countercultures. A powerful, if unique, double act, Daume was the frontman with the kind of old-world flummery that worked on the IOC and Avery Brundage, and Vogel was the organizer and planner. Yet there was also a remarkable coincidence of world view between them. As Chris Young and Kay Schiller put it, these were 'two men from moderately conservative backgrounds motivated by moderately progressive convictions.' Here, in the middle ground of West German politics, an Olympic alliance was built around the aims of returning a transformed, restrained and democratic Germany to the international community, and of atoning for the bombastic sins of Berlin with a games that tried to emphasize the universalism and playfulness of sport, rather than its capacity for marking ethnic divisions and training soldier-citizens.

In the run-up to the games, two complex political and cultural issues preoccupied the organizers. The first was a matter of history. What was the relationship of the Munich games to the Berlin games of 1936, and what, therefore, was the relationship between Nazi and contemporary Germany? In a show of solidarity with the beleaguered city of West Berlin, the Munich organizers held two committee meetings there, but that was as close as anyone wanted to get. It was noticeable that the colour scheme devised for the 1972 games included most hues but for the scarlet and gold that were the chromatic signature of 1936. In direct contrast to the great Teutonic bell that welcomed the world to the Berlin games, Munich opted for an electronic glockenspiel, and traded martial and marching music for easy-listening favourites and Burt Bacharach arrangements, and even cheeky musical commentaries of teams in the parade of nations – the Hungarians were serenaded with 'My Gypsy Rose Lee', an obscure, indeed bizarre musical connection linking the eponymous American stripper of the 1940s with the nation's Raomai peoples. Carl Diem, the chief organizer and designer of the Berlin games and the high priest of the German Olympic imagination, who remained close to Daume until his death in 1962, was commemorated in hundreds of place names in Germany, but it was inconceivable that even a single street in the new Olympic village could be named after him.

Yet, when it came to the staging of Diem's main Olympic legacy – the torch relay – the organizers suffered from a kind of selective amnesia. On the one hand, it was perfectly all right that Krupps should manufacture the torch for 1972, just as they had in 1936 (and this despite the fact that the company was the key armaments producer of the Nazi war effort). On the other hand, the idea that the relay should go via Dachau, the Nazis' original concentration camp, located just north of Munich, was not all right at all.

The second question was a matter of the present. Given that the Olympics was still thought, in some sense, 'a call to the youth of the world', the great wave of popular cultural change that had swept through West German youth, made all the stormier by the hesitancy and disingenuousness of the older generation's response to their own past, had to be addressed. Reflecting on the transformation of both global and West German youth culture in the 1960s, Willi Daume commented that, 'The youth of the world no longer has any understanding for the sort of celebration that revolves around gun salutes, the parading of flags, military marching and pseudo-sacred elements.'[2]

What had begun as part of the wider currents of generational change, educational expansion, affluence and alienation, took political form in West Germany in 1967 as the student-led APO – the extra-parliamentary opposition – and, following the attempted assassination of student leader, Rudi Dutschke, in 1968, they turned riotous.

In a genuine effort to embrace the times, and to find some common generational ground, the Munich organizers looked for symbolic and cultural dimensions to the games beyond the militarism of the twenty-one-gun salute and the phoney philhellenism of the past. Perhaps the clearest expression of this was the Spielstrasse – the street of games – originally conceived as a huge programme of interactive and spontaneous artistic performances all across the Olympic park: a programme that would counter consumerism with active participation, and staged ritual with spontaneous happenings. Extraordinarily, given the laxity of the security services in some areas of the games, it was this threat to Olympic order that provoked the sharpest response from the police. The head of security, Manfred Schreiber, was appalled, claiming that events would be 'hijacked by the public'. As a condition of the Spielstrasse's staging, the police refused permission for a small hill covered with wind-assisted sculpture and giant mobiles, insisted that beer sales here, and here alone, should be banned, and actively intervened in the selection of artists, opposing many on ideological grounds. The idea, floated by a local promoter, that a giant rock concert featuring Led Zeppelin and Frank Zappa might be held alongside the games sent Schreiber into a state of apoplexy. He predicted a deluge of drug taking, hinted at the possibility of epidemics and decried the prospect of this 'unsightly image'. In the end, the Spielstrasse was restricted to five small zones around the new lake in the Olympic park, offering clowning, mime, pantomime and theatre. There were free jazz quartets, the German conceptual artist Timm Ulrichs running a daily Olympic marathon to nowhere on a giant hamster wheel and huge immersive installations that enlivened each of the five senses.

It was phenomenally popular, attracting 1.2 million visitors, more than twice the number that attended all the other cultural events at the games. It also offered a tiny window for critical reflection, as invited international theatre troupes riffed on the meaning of past games, casting the 1912 Stockholm Olympics in a colonial light and tying Mexico '68 to the brutal massacre that preceded it. However, Schreiber had the last word when he took the attack on the Israeli team as an opportunity to close the *Spielstrasse* down entirely.[3]

For all the complexities and ambiguities of hosting an Israeli team at a West German Olympics, the games had begun with considerable promise. Official and unofficial ceremonies, including the Israeli team, were conducted at Dachau. The fencer Dan Alon later recalled, 'Taking part in the opening ceremony, only thirty-six years after Berlin, was one of the most beautiful moments in my life. We were in heaven.'[4]

The Black September group acquired its moniker and its rationale after the Jordanian state violently expelled the PLO from the country in September 1970, forcing them to regroup in the refugee camps of Beirut in Lebanon. Officially completely separate from the PLO, the group was informally coordinated by a senior member of the hierarchy. Precisely how the attack was conceived and why it was ordered is unclear, but it was just one of many such hijacks, sieges and killings orchestrated by a variety of Palestinian groups in this era. On the night of 4 September, most of the Israeli team went to see *Fiddler on the Roof* in central Munich. In a restaurant close by, the eight members of the Palestinian cell received their last briefing, and just after four a.m. they entered the lightly secured Olympic village, made for the Israeli team's quarters and took eleven hostages, two of whom were killed in the initial struggle.

During the ensuing day-long siege, the Palestinians issued a range of demands, including the release of hundreds of Palestinians from Israeli prisons, and a flight to the Middle East, before releasing their hostages. The Israelis, as always, had no intention of releasing anyone. Television cameras covered everything from innumerable angles and vantage points, including the hapless attempt by armed but inexperienced volunteer police officers to sneak up on the apartments over the roofs of the village. The Palestinians were, of course, watching all of this live on East German news. With the afternoon session of the games cancelled, the crowds around the village perimeter fence swelled into the tens of thousands. A series of deadlines were allowed to pass; the West German foreign minister, Hans Dietrich Genscher, and the mayor of the Olympic village, Walther Tröger, negotiated fruitlessly in the apartment, in person, before the terrorists changed tack and requested just transport to the airport with their hostages, and a flight to Egypt.

The West German police waiting for them at Fürstenfeldbruck airport were ill equipped, poorly positioned, incorrectly informed about the threat they faced, badly trained and, in some cases, reluctant to shoot to kill. They opened fire, and, in the ensuing firefight, the nine Israeli athletes, five of the eight gunmen and a German police officer were killed. The following day, a short memorial service was held in the Olympic stadium and the games went on. The IOC still thought it inappropriate to commemorate the fortieth anniversary of the massacre at the 2012 games.

7

THINGS FALL APART: BANKRUPTCY, BOYCOTTS AND THE END OF AMATEURISM

MONTREAL 1976 • MOSCOW 1980 • LOS ANGELES 1984 • SEOUL 1988

INNSBRUCK 1976 • LAKE PLACID 1980 • SARAJEVO 1984 • CALGARY 1988

No one, I believe, needs less convincing than myself that politics are 'in' sport and have always been. Everything in our lives is governed by political decisions. We have varying degrees of freedom, but that freedom is obtained by political decision. What we in sport and the Olympic movement need is the interest and support of politicians, not their interference.

Lord Killanin

ONE

It was hardly *The Prince* or *The Federalist Papers*, but by comparison to the doggerel that hitherto passed for political theory at the IOC, Lord Killanin was a philosopher king. He was an Anglo-Irish aristocrat with the kind of credentials – Eton, Cambridge, the Sorbonne, a British army officer on D-Day – that made him a shoo-in at the IOC, and by the mid-1960s, as befitted a man of impeccable good manners and immense affability, he was the organization's *chef de protocol*. Though he was eminently clubbable, there was always something idiosyncratic about the man. He had covered the Sino-Japanese war for the *Daily Mail*; amongst many other movies, he'd helped produce John Ford's *The Quiet Man*; and, above all, he loved the horse races. In 1971, a year before he won the election to replace Avery Brundage as the president of the IOC, he had joined the club that really mattered: the Irish Turf Club. John Rodda remembered him as 'the Pickwickian figure with the white hair, half moon glasses and pipe', and that, if there was 'a touch of pomposity to go with the presidential position . . . his impishness was never far away . . . He liked . . . to finish the days at the annual IOC sessions having a jar with the journalists.'[1]

Not merely more convivial than the sharp, narcissistic and increasingly bitter Brundage, Killanin maintained some semblance of a connection with the reality of sporting and political change in the twentieth century. Brundage had sent himself and the IOC into impossible contortions, attempting to maintain the always preposterous fictions of the Coubertin era: that the Olympic movement was above politics and beholden to no one but itself; that the amateur ideal of the nineteenth century was still ethically sound and institutionally practical as a way of organizing high-performance sport; and that the IOC could remain blithely unconcerned with the economics of televising and staging the games, delegating almost all of this to organizing committees. On all of the issues, Killanin's eight years as

IOC president would, without finally resolving any of them, mark a decisive break with the past and pave the way for the more fundamental, if pathological, reforms of his successor, Juan Antonio Samaranch.

Killanin, to his credit, had been railing against the absurdity of the IOC's position on amateurism for decades. The state professionalism of the Soviet bloc had long made a mockery of the amateur status required for Olympic athletes. In the wider world, the steady professionalization and commercialization of sports – from skiing to golf, from tennis to basketball – could not be ignored. Killanin, unable and, at this stage, still unwilling to depart entirely from the old order, looked for practical compromises, allowing increasing leeway for athletes to be paid for training and for time away from 'work'. Perhaps more importantly, where Brundage had actively sought a fight, Killanin chose to look the other way as athletes finally began to find ways of earning a living from their talents.

Rather than worrying about how other people earned their living, Killanin worried about how the IOC was going to stay afloat. Avery Brundage's decision to leave television rights sales in the hands of Olympic organizing committees left the IOC unable to influence negotiations or get its hands on much of this rapidly increasing revenue stream. With reserves of just $4 million, a minuscule and over-burdened corps of full-time staff, and the commercially alert sports federations of the world calling for more of a slice of the pie for themselves, Killanin took TV and its promise seriously. The IOC actually acquired a television committee for the first time, re-established itself as a partner in the sale of Olympic rights, and managed to acquire a larger share of the proceeds, as well as finally reacquiring trademark control over its Olympic logos – above all, the rings.[2]

The fruits of these changes would be realized under Samaranch, but, for now, the movement needed to negotiate the crisis of confidence amongst potential hosts, sparked by the financial disaster that was the 1976 Montreal games. Since at least the early 1960s, when Tokyo broke all Olympic expenditure records, the IOC had been fretting over the rising cost of staging the games and the proclivity of governments for spending considerably more on huge arenas and infrastructure projects. Matters were made worse in the early 1970s, for, long before the Olympic flame was lit in Sapporo or Montreal, it was evident that someone there was going to be left with bills of $1 billion and $2 billion respectively. Consequently, where once there had been four, five or more potential host cities for the games, the contest for 1980 was a duel between Moscow and Los Angeles, and Moscow 1980 only happened because the Soviet leviathan could forcibly command the massive resources required.

By the time it came to the 1984 games, only Los Angeles was actually prepared to bid. Denied government funding by referendum and lottery funding by statute, the Los Angeles organizers invented the neoliberal Olympic model on the cheap: reuse what you already have, sell the TV rights for what they are really worth, and get corporations to brand and pay for everything else. For the first time in half a century, the games made money. No games has managed the same feat since, but the fact that Los Angeles did so broke the spell of Montreal and unleashed and underwrote all manner of unsustainable loss-making Olympic monuments. In fact, the funding model for Seoul 1988 was a closer approximation to the funding of future games. Learning the lessons of Los Angeles, television and sponsorship income would steeply rise, but this would still only pay for the ever more elaborate staging and running of the games. The vast capital costs and prestige projects that would accompany this – in 1988, a virtual remaking of Seoul – would be paid for from the public purse.

However, for any of this to make any sense or to be worth anything, the nations of the world needed to show up. Having established itself as the pre-eminent festival and spectacular expression of a collective humanity – the Munich games had attracted a record 122 nations – the Olympics needed humanity to play. Only 88 nations were present at Montreal, 81 at Moscow, and, though 140 were present at Los Angeles, the games were framed by the Soviet bloc's boycott. It was just a dozen countries, but they provided a huge slice of the world's leading athletes, and, in a bipolar Cold War world, an obviously incomplete, fractured humanity was on display. Thus, much of Lord Killanin's presidency was consumed by the politics of both who could come to the games (and under what names and flags), and who wouldn't come and why.

The Montreal games proved particularly demanding on Killanin's time, with two complex issues to be dealt with: the status of the two

Chinas, and the struggle against South African apartheid. It says something for the intransigent anti-communist instincts of the IOC that it tried to maintain the fiction that Taiwan and the People's Republic of China were somehow equivalent entities in the world of intentional affairs for longer than even the US state department. In 1971, Taiwan was replaced at the United Nations by the PRC, but clung on to its place in the Olympic movement, where it was still known as the Republic of China. This was unproblematic while the People's Republic was embroiled with its own affairs; however, by the early 1970s, the government was beginning the process of re-joining the international sporting community. The IOC, still bound to the world of the 1950s, thought that they would be able to accommodate both Chinas at the Montreal games in 1976, albeit with the usual arguments about names and flags. However, the Canadian government had decisively opted for a one-China policy that acknowledged the PRC as the sole international representative of the Chinese. Taiwan would be permitted to compete, but only under a name that did not include 'China'. The Taiwanese huffed and puffed, the IOC fulminated, but there was no room for compromise here and the Taiwanese would not attend. They would only return to Olympic competition in 1984, and then as Chinese Taipei. In 1979, the IOC finally caught up with geopolitical reality and recognized the PRC as the singular Chinese representative to the Olympic movement.

Killanin might have been forgiven for thinking that the issue of South Africa had been resolved, at least as far as the Olympics was concerned, by its suspension from the movement in 1970 and its absence from the games since 1964. However, in the wider world of sport, the isolation of South Africa remained a very live issue. In rugby and cricket especially, official, semi-official and rebel tours of various kinds were organized through the 1970s. They were seen as considerable political victories in Pretoria and evoked enormous opposition amongst African governments and anti-apartheid campaigners in Europe and Australasia. The All Blacks' 1976 rugby-union tour of South Africa led many African states to call for the isolation of New Zealand in international sport, a case made more urgent by the outbreak of enormous riots in Soweto in June 1976, and the phenomenally brutal policing that quelled them. With at least 350 dead on the streets of South Africa, thirty-three African nations called for the IOC to exclude New Zealand from the Montreal Olympics, and, getting no luck there, boycotted the games.*

Nobody was planning to boycott the Moscow games of 1980 until, on 27 December 1979, the Soviet Union sent its troops across the border into Afghanistan in support of their clients, the beleaguered Afghan communist government, fighting the multiple Islamist militias of the mujahideen. A week later, American president, Jimmy Carter, was addressing the nation and making it clear that, amongst a variety of sanctions, the US would, other things being equal, have to boycott the Moscow games. The 1980 winter games, held that February in Lake Placid, New York, took on an even stronger Cold War hue than usual. The gods of scheduling smiled kindly on all the Cold War warriors, and the penultimate game of the final round of the men's ice hockey pitched the much-favoured Soviet Red Machine against the usual bunch of US college students. Hardly part-timers, the majority of the American squad would go on from their college scholarships to play in the NHL, but, in the build-up to the game, they were cast as carefree gentlemen amateurs in contrast to their robotic opponents: 'The grim air of [Soviet] professionalism was in severe contrast to a US team playful and outgoing throughout its practice, a team that has endured all manner of inconveniences for months for just this chance.' Jim Craig, the US goalkeeper, put the mood of much of the nation more bluntly: 'I might have to fight in a war against these guys . . . But now I'm playing hockey. I hate them. I don't hate the hockey players specifically, but I hate what they stand for.'[3]

The game stood at 3–2 to the Soviet Union at the beginning of the third and final period, but in an extraordinary ten minutes of play, the Americans scored twice to make it 4–3 to them. Ten minutes of ferocious Soviet assaults and desperate American defence culminated with commentator Al Michaels' famous call, 'Do you believe in miracles? YES!' Coach Herb Brooks, speaking to President Carter after the game, declared it 'a great win for everybody in sport and the

---

* The politics of these sporting contacts would mainly be fought out between the nations of the Commonwealth, who signed the Gleneagles Agreement in 1977. Despite this, there were South African rugby tours to New Zealand in 1977 and 1981, and to the UK in 1979; these were accompanied by massive protests and acts of civil disobedience by the anti-apartheid movement.

American people in general . . . It just proves our life is the proper way to continue.' Final confirmation of the American way came when they beat Finland 4–2 and sealed the gold medal. The team and the crowd sang 'God Bless America', but, even in the American press, there was a sense of disquiet, with some arguing that the 'Miracle on Ice' 'duplicated, in miniature, many of the emotions and motivations that have fed the fires of every war in history. It was an athletic contest of the highest order. And it was, in the deepest sense, contrary to the Olympic spirit. If these are the last Olympics, no one need ask why.'[4]

NBC, who had paid out $87 million for the rights to cover the Moscow games, staved off a decision long enough that they could collect on the considerable insurance policy they had taken out to cover some of their costs in the event of just such a disaster. Then they took a $40 million hit and did what the American administration was pressing them to do: cancelled their coverage. The government even forbade the use of the US flag at the closing ceremony in Moscow, where Los Angeles was due to take up the Olympic baton.* Under American pressure, but often with significant domestic support, West Germany, Japan, South Korea and another sixty-two nations, drawn from amongst the US' strongest allies and most dependent clients in Latin America, Africa and Asia, joined the boycott. Many western European nations attended, but either passed on the opening ceremony – like the French – or sent just their *chef de mission* to march under an Olympic flag – like the British.

Given the dynamics of the Cold War in the 1980s, one might have imagined, as did much of the American press, that the Soviet Union had long been planning to boycott the 1984 Los Angeles games, in a tit-for-tat, following the boycott of Moscow 1980. However, within the Soviet political and sporting entities, it was long decided that the best revenge was to excel at the games, beating the Americans on American soil, and thus huge financial resources were poured into Olympic preparations. Of course, as part of the game, the two superpowers argued over visas, Aeroflot's access to US airports and the rules of engagement for a Soviet ship docking in Los Angeles

---

* Ever the opportunist, Peter Uebberoth, the LA games' chief executive, got a city flag to the Soviets.

harbour, but these were all serious indications of the Soviets' intention to participate.

The death of the party chairman, Yuri Andropov, in early 1984, and his replacement by Konstantin Chernenko saw an enthusiast for participation replaced with a sceptic, but far more important in changing the course of Soviet thinking were the unlikely consequences of the shooting down of a South Korean civilian airliner in Soviet airspace, in September 1983, killing 269 people. While the event was decried around the world, a group of conservative activists in southern California were sufficiently energized to get the state legislature to call for a Soviet ban, and to create the Ban the Soviets Coalition, dedicated to preventing their participation and encouraging Soviet athletes to defect, if they did. While the local organizers in Los Angeles considered them a distraction, at best, the conversation inside the politburo was sufficiently ill informed and paranoid to think them a real threat. The Soviets decided to withdraw,[5] taking another dozen nations with them, but they could not force the increasingly errant regime of Nicolae Ceauşescu in Romania to join them. Assiduously courted by both the state department and the LA organizers, the Romanians agreed to attend, with a large team paid for by LA '84 and the IOC.

Finally, almost everybody showed up to Seoul 1988; everyone, that is, except the North Koreans. Later to the Olympic Games than their southern counterparts, the North had made their Olympic debut at the Innsbruck winter games in 1964, and had seen participation as a useful foreign-policy tool. Rather than proposing a boycott of Seoul, the regime thought they might share the games, and spent four years alternately suggesting to the South Koreans and the IOC that it would be a fabulous achievement for peace if it could happen, and that there just might be some military accidents if it didn't. The IOC actually offered them the chance to host the football, table tennis and archery, but, by the time the North Koreans had abandoned their maximalist positions, Soviet and Chinese support for them and their boycott had evaporated, and the North Koreans departed from the Olympics to remain increasingly isolated and aloof.[6]

TWO

Responding to his Olympic critics, the mayor of Montreal, Jean Drapeau, replied, 'Two thousand five hundred years ago, Pericles too was criticized for building the Acropolis instead of warships.'[1] Whether the Montreal Olympic park can really rank with the Acropolis, only time will tell, but the claim itself is an unambiguous indicator of the hauteur and ambition of the mayor. The scale of Olympic urban renewal in Tokyo and Munich was so great that the mayors of both cities – Hidejiro Nagata and Hans-Jochen Vogel – were central actors in the staging of the games, but they were bit-part players by comparison to the Napoleonic Drapeau. The instigator and leader of the Montreal bid, Drapeau's office controlled almost every aspect of the games, until, under immense political and financial pressure, he was forced to cede some control to the Quebec provincial government and the actual organizing committee of the Montreal Olympics. When a few opposition councillors dared to challenge the obliteration of the Montreal golf course to make way for the Olympic velodrome, Drapeau tartly informed them that he did not play golf and that it was not an Olympic sport. It was a style born of his unassailable control of the city and his relentless focus on staging urban spectaculars that would put Montreal on the map. Drapeau was a relatively conservative French Canadian nationalist, wedded to a distinct francophone and Quebecois identity, but certainly no friend of separatism. His political constituencies were the francophone small-business people and land owners of Montreal, where a restricted property-owning-based franchise made them unusually powerful electorally, and a select group of the Anglo elite who were big in real estate and development. Convinced that Montreal's future lay in tourism, services, sport and leisure, Drapeau planned to build his way to the future, and began by applying for a major-league baseball franchise, scheming to get a stadium and courting the United Nations to relocate and come north. His first and greatest coup was to win and then stage the last truly successful world fair – Expo 1967.[2] Fifty million people went to see the usual collection of pavilions and gewgaws on a series of artificial islands made from all the rubble excavated to build the city's new metro system, testament to the wave of brutalist redevelopment Drapeau was unleashing across the city. In an interesting premonition of the Olympics, the Expo generated acres of positive global press coverage, cost twice as much as was anticipated and left a considerable debt that Drapeau, with some aplomb, managed to hand on to someone else. It was also an important moment in the development of the new francophone Quebecois nationalism.

Expo '67 and the Montreal Olympics, although primarily staged as instruments of urban policy, became increasingly entwined with the 'quiet revolution' sweeping all Quebec in the 1960s and early 1970s, serving as examples of what a new and much more independently minded society could do. Much to the irritation of the mayor, the president of France, Charles de Gaulle, after a visit to the Expo, was so moved by the renaissance of francophone Canada that he made a speech at Montreal's city hall, declaring, *'Vive Montréal! Vive le Québec! Vive le Québec Libre!'* Until then, Quebec had been ruled by conservative rural francophones and a small Montreal-based Anglo elite that insisted on the use of English as the language of all business. The province's education and health-care systems were dominated by a reactionary Catholic Church; its school-leaving age was just fourteen, literacy was low and 3 per cent of adult women were nuns. But, under the newly elected Quebec Liberal Party, the provincial government made itself a national development agency, secularized the welfare state and invested in French-language education. In time, many of the generation nurtured under these conditions would reject the Liberal Party and they increasingly supported the cause of Quebecois nationalism and even independence. Consequently, the federal government, under Pierre Trudeau, when asked to support the Montreal bid, preferred to get behind the Vancouver bid for the 1976 winter games in an attempt to win the votes of anglophones and the west of the country. The Quebec government and its Prime Minister, Robert Bourassa, might have been more amenable partners, but Drapeau never informed them of his plans, nor did he want to relinquish control to them.

Thus, with neither government backing nor financial guarantees from anyone, the mayor travelled the world, personally met most of the IOC and, in May 1970, with an entirely straight face, pitched to them the promise of a 'modest self-financing games'. The IOC swallowed it, and Drapeau began as he meant to go on. The following day, he had 800 pounds of Quebecois delicacies flown across the Atlantic to the IOC congress in Amsterdam for a celebration banquet.

Once Montreal had won the games, the stakes and costs of security were considerably raised when, just a few months after the award, members of the radical separatist Front de Libération du Québec kidnapped the British consul and a Quebec provincial government Cabinet minister, who was later murdered. A state of emergency was, in effect, declared, federal troops poured into Montreal and thousands of suspects were detained, though ultimately very few were charged or convicted. In this febrile atmosphere, the francophone but deeply conservative Drapeau was a vital ally of both Trudeau and Bourassa. Despite their antipathy to the mayor and his Olympic mission, in 1973, the federal government agreed to fund the security cost of the games, while the Quebec government finally accepted ultimate financial responsibility for the show.

Once preparations began in earnest, issues of design and protocol became embroiled in the usual political controversies.[3] The plan for the torch relay would see the Olympic flame transmitted from Greece to Ottawa via a satellite, in the form of an electronic pulse. Montreal, of course, objected, but, with the federal government seeking to sell the same satellite to Greece, and to show off Canadian telecommunications technology, there was no moving from the capital. The torch's progress from Ottawa to Montreal proved an equally fraught issue, with the organizers choosing a route that ran almost entirely within Ontario, rather than through Quebec, and which only crossed over the St Lawrence River turning into Montreal at the very last moment. Even then, the torch entered the city though the rich anglophone suburbs. The official posters were a battleground, with the local versions being dominated by francophone artists and the federally funded ones deliberately Canadian in their imagery and text. Canada's First Nations remained marginal and voiceless, their place in Canadian history still scripted for them by the colonizers. The choreographers of the opening ceremony had 250 white Canadian dancers teach indigenous Canadians a version of their own ritual moves; they were dressed in the theme-park uniform of fringed jackets and buckskins, and formed five interlocking rings, within which they erected colour-coordinated Olympic tepees.

Most controversially of all, two days before the games were due to begin, Mayor Drapeau ordered the removal of the centrepiece of the cultural festival accompanying the games.[4] It was a shameless act of state censorship, dressed up in utterly bogus claims about public safety. *Corridart* was a series of over sixty installations, exhibitions and pop-up performance spaces that ran for six kilometres along Sherbrooke Street, from the Olympic park to old downtown. Created and curated by the new generation of critical and experimental artists produced by the Quiet Revolution, it featured stage-set houses for theatrical performances, trees turned into athletes dressed in knitted shorts and numbered vests, rock-and-boulder mazes and dozens of scaffolding pyramids displaying pictures of the street's architectural heritage, lost to commercial development. Some of the more odious of the new developments were pointed out by the index fingers of huge red Mickey Mouse hands. One landlord, a close ally of Drapeau, wrote to the press: 'We regret the finger pointing at our building, which many of our tenants and prospective customers take as offensive.' One imagines that Drapeau was equally displeased by Michael Balsam's *Telethon*, which consisted of a public loudspeaker that broadcast a voice listing the cost of the games on a permanent loop. Drapeau's forces, equipped with bulldozers, trucks and a police escort, dismantled and impounded the entire show, and then his legal department fought a decade-long rearguard action through the courts against artists who wanted their work back.

For an Olympic Games that became a byword for financial disaster, the Montreal current account was surprisingly healthy. Total income was $430 million; over half of that came from the Olympic lottery, the rest from a combination of commemorative coin and stamp issues, robust ticket sales at the games and a substantial TV deal with the US network ABC. Montreal also made use of a number of sponsorship deals, licensing agreements and gifts in kind, and its use of existing sports facilities was, in some ways, exemplary. The total running costs of the games were a mere $223 million. When issues of funding were first discussed, Drapeau had argued that, 'The Montreal Games can no more have a deficit than a man can have a baby', but, by 1975, he was depicted in cartoons calling him the city's best-known gynaecologist. The cost of building the 'modest self-financing games' – nearly all of it for the Olympic park – was once vaguely imagined at less than $150 million, but, by 1976, it was already $1.2 billion, and once interest payments on the debt had been factored in, was going to turn into a $2-billion bill.

How did that rack up? Graft, incompetence and vainglory played a part, all made much worse by the insanely late start to preparations. The mayor gave the contract for Montreal's Olympic village – two huge striated concrete pyramids – to known political allies and insiders, without the inconvenience of any competitive tendering process or financing plan. Initially priced at $22 million, their cost was revised up to $43 million and, just three weeks before the games began, came in at $80 million. The use of foreign architects, ignorant of the local geology, meant that the foundations of the velodrome were so inadequate that $7-million worth of concrete had to be poured into the ground before they could start. Eight million dollars was found for a single monumental water-fountain. All this paled into insignificance when measured against the costs of 'the Big O' – aka 'the Big Owe' – the main Olympic stadium, designed by the French architect Roger Taillibert. Again, this commission was the uncontested choice of the mayor, who looked to Taillibert to concoct a building that would indelibly brand Montreal. What he got was a gigantic 80,000-seat concrete stadium with a retractable roof, and an implausible vast swoosh of a tower at one end. Even before it was finished, Drapeau felt he had got what he wanted, describing it as, 'the best monument in North America from the architectural point of view . . . comparable to the monuments of antiquity elsewhere on other continents', but it came with very considerable costs, not least the lives of twelve workers, who died during its construction.

The plans for the stadium, obsessively micromanaged by Drapeau, were only finalized in late 1974, less than two years before the games began. The design was fabulously complex, requiring new materials, one-off machinery and experimental construction techniques. Costs were driven sky high by all of these elements, but were then sent into orbit by the combination of strikes, wild inflation in global steel prices, and price gouging by suppliers, not least of which was Taillibert's own fee, which came in at $45 million – almost twice what the entire architecture profession in Quebec earned in 1974.

In 1975, increasingly alarmed by the escalating costs of the project and its ever more impossible completion date, the Quebec provincial government stepped in, relieved the mayor's office of control, abandoned the tower and the retractable roof, and just about got the thing finished for the opening ceremony. As Jack Ludwig observed on the night, it really was only 'just about': 'temporary ramps and walks . . . wooden flooring that boinged under body-weight. A strong fresh smell of epoxy, the bonding materials used to join the blocks, charged the air with an effluvium of newness. Poorly met joints had been hurriedly filled and packed and sprayed and painted.'[5]

Once the show started, it didn't matter. Bruce Kidd, a Canadian athlete and writer, recalled, 'in such moments you completely forego the knowledge that an entire continent felt it had to depart from these Games, that the island of Montreal was an armed camp, or that the whole celebration cost about ten times what it should have. I know I did. For two weeks all the contradictions seemed to stand still.'[6] Despite the fact that Canada failed to win a gold medal at its own games, the first host to be in this invidious position, the festive mood in Montreal did not appear to diminish. And despite the fact that this monument to municipal imagineering was a sporting triumph for the Soviet Union and its global allies, the huge television audiences that the games were bringing in stayed high. Communist countries occupied seven of the top ten medallists' slots: the Soviet Union, out in front with 49 golds and 125 medals, was joined in second place by East Germany – a nation of just seventeen million people – with 40 golds out of a total of 90 medals. Untroubled by an effective test for anabolic steroids and other commonly government-administered pharmaceuticals, and benefiting from a now long period of state-sponsored elite sport, especially their focus on female athletes, this was a high point for the communist mode of sports production. The GDR's Kornelia Ender won four gold medals in the pool, her team won eleven of the thirteen on offer and East Germany's women were equally dominant in athletics and rowing. The Romanian gymnast, Nadia Comăneci, scored seven perfect tens and won three gold medals in a redefinition of excellence that the electronic scoreboards could not display correctly. Cuba recorded its best Olympic performance yet: six gold medals, including the impossibly leggy Alberto Juantorena, the first and only man to win gold in the 400 metres and 800 metres. For Cold War warriors in the West, there was only the consolation of the Soviet modern pentathlete Boris

Onischenko being disqualified from the competition for cheating in the fencing.

When the party was over, there was still the matter of the $2-billion bill. The federal government took a slice; the bulk of it fell to the Quebec government, who covered the tab with an unpopular tobacco tax. Montreal and Drapeau came away with just $200 million to pay; looking on the bright side, the shortage of cash saved the city from some of the mayor's more fanciful visions, including an insanely destructive inner-city motorway. Bourassa's Quebec Liberal Party proved to be the political fall guys. Tarnished by the Olympic debt, they were hustled out of office by a newly enthused and confident Parti Québécois. Drapeau, despite stinging criticism in the post-games official reports, remained untouchable. In 1978, he could still pull in 61 per cent of the vote in Montreal, and stayed in office until 1986. The tower, described as a 'monument to illusion', was finally completed in 1987, after another $150 million had been blown on it. Montreal cleared the final debts in 2006. The roof never worked, and the baseball team Drapeau craved – the Expos – came and left. The velodrome is now a glorified greenhouse, and the finest physical legacy of the games is the cheap, unshowy Complexe sportif Claude-Robillard, a major centre for high-performance sport in Canada, named after the city's first planning officer, the only person in the municipal machine known to stand up to the mayor.

THREE

Orgcom, the ominously named organizing committee of the Moscow Olympics, was a creature of its times. Created in the interstices of the sprawling late-Soviet state, it was overseen by an executive bureau, run by a presidium, led by socialist heroes, staffed by a hundred vice-presidents and written into the Five-Year Plan. It reported directly to the central committee and thence to the politburo, and had the kind of clout capable of summoning twenty-six separate state agencies to a single, enormous meeting room.

The socialist heroes, recipients of the Order of Lenin, were the two men who ran the games, Ignatii Novikov and Vitali Smirnov. Novikov was of the old school, managing a lead factory before ascending to the Ministry of Electrical Power and the central committee itself. Smirnov, like much of the new nomenklatura, was an uber-bureaucrat, who, in the interlinking worlds of the IOC, Soviet sport and the Soviet state, collected more committee seats, chairs and vice-presidencies than anyone else – a skill that would see him survive and prosper after the fall of communism. In his opening address to Orgcom's presidium, Novikov made clear what was at stake: 'For the first time in all their history, the Olympic Games will be staged in a socialist state – in the capital of our mother country – Moscow.' He then laid out the colossal task facing them: 'This grand-scale political event must be prepared and carried out at the highest political level', and called on them to 'transform Moscow into an exemplary communist city.'[1]

What appears, on the other side of the fall of communism, as an impossibly antiquated lumbering machine, was, for the Soviet Union of the 1970s, the system at its best. Given significant resources by the state, and with enough political capital and connections to overcome many of the usual bottlenecks and informal vetoes that characterized much of Soviet economic life, it was able to build and stage the games in an organized and timely fashion. Orgcom also attracted and promoted the younger, better educated, more cosmopolitan and ambitious members of the nomenklatura, who were drawn to its modernizing agenda and, in this still very closed society, the promise of direct involvement with the outside world. Despite its unfamiliarity with the world of TV rights contracts, sponsorship, advertising, licensing, logos and trademarks, Orgcom proved reasonably adept at forging deals and getting its cut, not least in the agreement with Adidas to supply all of the organizers' uniform needs, gratis.

Yet, despite its superpower status, the Soviets found these encounters remarkably fraught. On the one hand, the games would be 'a showcase for scientific and engineering achievements.' On the other hand, the presence of the world's press, especially the Western press, and the expectation that they would be judging the Soviet Union by their own standards, was a central and perennial concern. In the minutes of a difficult discussion about the lack of suitable hotel rooms in Moscow, Novikov exploded: 'we will have seven thousand five hundred journalists, and if even one of them does not have an international phone line, it will be a world-wide scandal.'

Even if there was a phone line, would it work? The Soviet-designed computer system, ACS-Olympiad, which would collate and distribute all of the sports data and event results, was considered inferior to American and German alternatives; so too the broadcast technology for colour television, though both, in the end, functioned perfectly adequately. Importing the new fibreglass vaulting poles pioneered in America was also considered, but again, for reasons of national pride, rejected. The second-best option was taken: buying them in from East Germany. More prosaically, Orgcom fretted over whether Soviet cash-registers could actually process more than two sales in a row, and whether tourists would cope with the laborious system for foreign exchange: 'Here you have to fill out a form, then stand in line for two hours and then three hours later receive the money.'[2]

Occasionally, Orgcom's records reveal some of the more serious and structural problems of the Soviet system. In the absence of the kind of coercion deployed under Stalin, getting sufficient skilled workers to Moscow to build the Olympic venues, and keeping them there, given the often appalling wages and conditions on offer, forced bureaucrats to consider the use of market mechanisms and incentives. A real shortage of capital to build the new venues saw the leadership endorse the hitherto unacceptable notion of a national sports lottery. Corruption and embezzlement, though not a feature of the games themselves, were endemic at the lower levels of Soviet institutions. In an anonymous letter to the presidium, members of the Soviet national cycling squad complained about their lack of equipment, food, pay and facilities, and noted bitterly that any prize money they won was diverted into 'the pockets of certain people, who use it to buy cars, dachas and apartments, and to maintain a dissolute lifestyle.' This was certainly not the preserve of privileged sports bureaucrats alone. By the late 1970s, Soviet society was becoming steadily more dissolute as vodka and heroin consumption rose, the consequences of which were visible enough for the security services to promise Orgcom that they would 'Cleanse Moscow of chronic alcoholics and drug addicts.'[3]

Thus, on first glance, the Moscow that staged the games was indeed 'the exemplary communist city.' At the centre of everything was the Central Lenin Stadium Complex, the still-roofless national stadium. CSKA, the sporting club of the Red Army, put on the wrestling and fencing. Dynamo, the club of the KGB, hosted the handball, gymnastics and volleyball competitions. Even the trade unions got a look in, being awarded their very own Bitsa equestrian venue. The Soviet tradition of brutalist, if plentiful, public housing received ample expression at the Olympic village, which featured eighteen sixteen-storey concrete towers, dropped into a featureless landscape.

While the Soviet system had proved itself poor at supplying mass consumption, catering to the needs of small elites was a much stronger suit. Enormous care and attention was lavished on the protocol and material comforts necessary for visits from the IOC and the international sports federations, with official guidelines on how to wine and dine the global athletic bureaucracy, separate itineraries for their wives, and a list of recommended presents to be left in their hotel rooms. The drug-testing regime at the games was a case study in the IOC's naivety and the Soviets' capacity for duplicity. The IOC accepted the assurances from the organizers that the laboratories and procedures established for the games were up to scratch, and when not a single athlete failed a single drugs test (over 8,000 of them), they revelled in the 'purest' games in history. Manfred Donike, a West German doctor on the IOC medical commission, conducted some tests of his own on the Moscow urine samples (using a new technique that he had been developing for measuring testosterone levels), and concluded that 20 per cent of them, including sixteen gold medallists, should have failed.[4]

Finally, there was plenty of state-funded high culture, staged in grand people's palaces – circus, ballet, orchestras and folk dance – all of which and more was thrown at the opening ceremony. Eight masters of Soviet sport, in royal-blue suits, goose-stepped the Olympic flag to its pole. Two cosmonauts in the Salyut-6 space station beamed comradely salutations to the big screen of the stadium. Moscow's best trick was the section of the stadium where performers held coloured cards above their heads to make, not only intricate pictures, but complex animations and, for the cauldron lighting, a path above their heads for the final torch carrier.* Socialism's response to Mickey Mouse was the official Olympic mascot, Misha – a slightly ragged brown teddy bear with a huge Olympic-ring belt-buckle on his belly – who, in contrast to the rictus grin of his American cousin, bore a slightly forlorn and glazed demeanour. That said, Misha looked a lot more lively than the politburo. Out of the eighteen full members of the twenty-fifth politburo of the CPSU, fourteen had been born before the revolution. Two had already died in office. Brezhnev, who falteringly declared the games open while nervously consulting his cue cards, was eaten up by emphysema, leukaemia, gout and sleeping pills; he had less than two years to live, and looked like it.

George Plimpton, one of the very few American journalists to report from Moscow, despaired.[5] Indeed, Plimpton's reports for *Time* and *Harper's* remain some of the very few unofficial and observant accounts of the games. Wry, sly and droll, he captured the Cold War paranoia and gossip mongering of visitors, ate truly unspeakable food, went bowling with the locals in Gorky Park, conducted single-word dialogues with taxi drivers – '"Beria" (thumbs down). "Olga Korbut" (thumbs up)' – enjoyed the theatrical trickery of Lenin's mausoleum with Nigerian boxers, and found the whole show strangely unpolitical:

---

* It was the same graphic aesthetic at work in the otherwise utterly execrable official movie, *Oh Sport! You are Peace*, which told the Hellenic part of the Olympic story through a fabulous series of cut-outs and cartoons.

In fact the whole Soviet political presence seems absent from the games. In a city awash with flags, the only Soviet banners I have seen fly from atop the Great Kremlin Palace and off the stern of the *vaporetti* that ply the Moscow River. The official box at Lenin Stadium, roofed, and with a long row of red covered seats, has been empty since the opening ceremonies. That's one thing the Soviet Hierarchy does not do – give its tickets away to secretaries and friends.

The hammer and sickle was an infrequent icon, often giving way to the less charged emblem of the Red Star – a feature of all of the official artwork. What they saw was an endless parade of triumphs for the motherland and for the USSR's socialist brothers and sisters. In the absence of the United States and some of its allies, the already pre-eminent position of the communist bloc in Olympic sports was greatly magnified. Between them, the Soviet Union and East Germany won more than half of all the medals at the games, and in some sports they were even more dominant. In the weightlifting and wrestling, particularly fertile ground for the use of steroids, the Soviets were comprehensive victors, shattering world records. East Germany's women swimmers were as untouchable as they had been in Montreal. John Rodda, for the *Guardian*, wrote, 'the water seemed to turn a deep blue, the East German shade, every time there was a women's event in the pool.'

Soviet and East German athletes were, of course, very good, very talented and very well prepared, but even the best can need a helping hand. In the men's diving final, Aleksandr Portnov was, he claimed, disturbed by applause from the adjacent swimming hall as he attempted a two-and-a-half backward somersault. It ended in an inelegant belly flop and an immediate protest. Awarded a second dive, he performed perfectly and won the gold medal. The Soviets were sufficiently ruffled by everyone else's subsequent protests that the medal ceremony was held back for two days. The Mexican press accused the Soviets of 'systematically robbing' their man, Carlos Girón, of the title, reporting that the Soviet embassy in Mexico City had been deluged by insulting telephone calls and telegrams. The men's triple jump proved equally controversial, with the Brazilian, João de Oliveira, and the Australian, Ian Campbell, called foul on nine of their twelve jumps.[6] On Campbell's fourth jump, he broke the

Olympic record with a distance that would have easily won the competition, but was ruled foul on the most arcane and opaque rule concerning his trailing leg in the skip phase. Oliveira appeared gracious after the event, shaking all the officials' hands, but, sitting in the stands, George Plimpton's neighbour read it differently: 'Don't they realize the Brazilian is being ironic? He's knocking them. He's showing everyone how awful he thinks the judging has been.' Oliveira would lose a leg in a car crash soon afterwards, before drinking himself to death. Campbell abandoned the sport.*

Women's gymnastics was an irony-free zone. In the individual floor-exercise competition, the head judge, the Romanian Mili Simionescu, initially refused to post the scores awarded to Nadia Comăneci, scores which would have put her in silver-medal position, behind Yelena Davydova of the USSR, an outcome she, and much of the gymnastic world, found difficult to accept. The Romanian press came as close as they dared to accusing the Soviets of cheating: 'they grossly violated sports ethics and the Olympic spirit in full view of the world.' Socialist brotherly love was equally in evidence at the very bad-tempered football final between East Germany and Czechoslovakia, which saw four players sent off. The men's pole vault pitched the Soviet favourite, Konstantin Volkov, against the Pole, Władysław Kozakiewicz. When Kozakiewicz secured his gold medal, clearing 5.2 metres, there were loud jeers, and when, a few minutes later, he went on to smash the world record, the Soviet crowd booed him viciously. Turning to the crowd, he bent his arm at the elbow, in what is now known in Polish as 'Kozakiewicz's gesture', and elsewhere as 'Fuck you!' The Soviet ambassador to Warsaw called for him to be stripped of his medal, but, in the context, that autumn, of the formation of the free trade union Solidarity, and its profound challenge to local communist rule, the Polish government insisted that the gesture was the result of an involuntary muscle spasm, and the Polish public voted him sportsman of the year.

It is hard to know quite how the Soviet public read events.

---

* In an intriguing subplot to the competition, the Soviet gold and silver medallists took to the rostrum in Mizuno trainers rather than the Adidas kit with which they had been supplied. This was the outcome of a deal bartered by Lord Killanin with the Japanese company, who had sponsored the torch relay only to find many of the runners wearing Adidas trainers.

Certainly there was considerable enthusiasm for the spectacle, with nearly four million tickets sold to the locals and enormous levels of television coverage. On 28 July, the audience was enjoying gold medals for Sergei Sukhoruchenkov in the cycling road race and Viktor Rashchupkin in the discus. However, away from the television cameras, but just a few kilometres north of the Olympic stadium, the largest spontaneously generated crowd of the Brezhnev era, around 30,000 people, was gathering. They were there for the funeral of Vladimir Vysotsky, a singer-songwriter, unpublished and unrecorded by the official Soviet music agencies, who had built a nationwide following at innumerable informal gigs and through eagerly sought-after samizdat cassettes. He played minor-chord melancholy folk and sang in a gravelly, alcohol-ravaged rasp that drew on the slang of the Gulag and expressed the weary madness of the Soviet system, its intractable lethargy and weight, and the impossibility of making moral choices in its shadow. Never openly critical of the system, he expressed more sharply than any other voice the melancholy, drab stasis of the late Soviet Union; even Brezhnev used to listen to the tapes. Nothing was said in the official press, but still the crowds braved the mounted police to walk with his coffin to the graveyard and say goodbye.

It was goodbye, too, at the closing ceremony, just four days later. The massed bands of the Soviet military marched, giant matryoshka dolls tottered and the crowd wept to Lev Leshchenko, the Red Army crooner's saccharine 'Farewell Moscow'. A giant, inflatable Misha, clutching a thin bunch of helium balloons, was led into the stadium, waving goodbye, before being let loose and floating uncertainly up into the night sky. One observer, then just seven years old, later commented, 'Every Soviet kid at that moment broke into tears. For people like me, this Mishka flying away, it's like a symbol of the end of the Soviet Union.'[7]

FOUR

'We came together in a "national crusade to make America great again," and to make "a new beginning." Well, now it's all coming together. With our beloved nation at peace, we are in the midst of a springtime of hope for America. Greatness lies ahead of us. Holding the Olympic Games here in the United States began defining the promise of this season.'[1] These are the words of Ronald Reagan, making his acceptance speech as incumbent and presidential candidate at the 1984 Republican convention. The Olympic spectacle had been hitched to all manner of ideologies – fascism, communism and all the varieties of nationalism – but in Reagan's America it would serve the cause of neoliberalism too. Reagan and his first administration had already set in train the economic, political and cultural changes that would transform America, and in turn the world. Wrapped in the language of an unabashed Cold War American nationalism, they had begun to dismantle the institutions and ideas of New Deal America, and allowed unemployment to soar as they slashed state spending on welfare and splurged on the military. They had deregulated the banking, finance and telecommunications sectors, while trade unions, already on the slide, were pulverized by legal reforms; and all the time, the beguiling mixture of domestic economic homilies and the rhetoric of self-help and individualism that passed for an economic philosophy was made into the ruling common sense of the era. The president's speeches were peppered with references to the games. Speaking to workers at Westinghouse, then shedding jobs by the thousand, he told them, 'Might we consider taking our cue from our Olympic athletes? Rather than discourage risktaking and punish success, rather than raise taxes, let's go for growth, and let's go for the gold.'[2] Addressing Congress on the need for spending cuts, he said, 'next year's games will show the world what Americans without government subsidy can accomplish.' Peter Ueberroth, the chair of the Los Angeles organizing committee and no less an ideological cheerleader than the president, was sure that the games would exemplify 'the spirit of can-do can-work can-accomplish. You can do these things without being on the government dole.'[3]

The bid, led by Mayor Tom Bradley, was an adamantly low-cost offer, with neither the federal government, the Californian state government nor even the city of Los Angeles actually prepared to put up hard cash or financial guarantees, and as lotteries were still illegal in California, this option was closed too. It was therefore always going to be a games funded and organized almost entirely by the private sector, and in Peter Ueberroth they'd acquired someone with the skills to make that happen and an evangelical zeal for the task. A student athlete who tried out for the US water-polo team in 1956, he made his mark building from scratch America's second largest travel agency, First Travel Corporation. David Wolper, a Hollywood producer on the organizing committee, recommended him, saying, 'That is the cheapest son of a bitch I know, but he will know how to operate this thing.'[4]

There were three essential elements to the business plan: to keep costs very low by building as little new infrastructure as possible; to get the kind of money out of the TV networks that the rating figures should really command; and to go for quality, not quantity, when it came to sponsorship deals. When the books were finally closed, LAOOC returned not the $15 million that Ueberroth had initially thought possible, but a $225 million surplus.

Four things that southern California was not short of – big roads, swish universities, country clubs and conference centres – were all put to Olympic use. The palm-fringed oceanside roads of Santa Monica were perfect for the marathon, the Artesia freeway for time-trial cycling. USC and UCLA dorms were turned into Olympic villages, while their campuses hosted the swimming and the basketball. CSU Fullerton staged the handball; Pepperdine University in Malibu got water polo. The eventing went to the Fairbanks Ranch country club in luscious Rancho Santa Fe, the Anaheim Center got wrestling, and fencing and volleyball went to the convention hall in Long Beach. The Coliseum, which had staged the 1932 games, was upgraded with the newest and most gigantic TV screens and electronic scoreboards, but was otherwise treated like a movie set, not a monument to posterity. A new swimming complex and a velodrome were unavoidable expenses, but, in some of the earliest examples of selling stadium-naming rights, McDonald's paid for the former, and Southland, owner of 7-Eleven, for the latter. The organizers didn't even have to find the money for new changing rooms or maintenance costs: these fell on the universities that would inherit the buildings. USC got the swimming pool, while the velodrome went to California State University Dominguez Hills, in the southern industrial suburb of Carson. College president, Dr Gerth, anxious to get a slice of the money that was heading for the west side of town, got in touch with Ueberroth: 'We had a good conversation and at the end, [Uberroth] asked, "How would you like to have the Olympic Velodrome?" I said, "We'll take it. What is it?"'[5]

It was clear Ueberroth and his team meant business when, in 1979, they told potential bidders for the games' TV rights to deposit $500,000 in their bank account. The five who made the final cut had to come up with another $250,000. They all got their money back, but in the meantime the organizers lived off the interest. ABC came in with the then astronomical bid of $225 million, greater than all of the past Olympics TV-rights fees combined, and more than twice what Moscow had been able to manage. Unlike past committees, they also played hardball with the European and Asian networks, squeezing another $40 million out of them. Seven million tickets were sold in advance, bringing in $140 million in ticket sales, but what took the games into serious profit was corporate sponsorship. Munich and Montreal had dabbled with the form, and the organizers of the 1980 winter games in Lake Placid went into overdrive, recruiting 380 sponsors, but as Ueberroth wryly noted, that added up to 'A lifetime's supply of chapsticks and yoghurt and less than ten million dollars.' Building on the model developed by FIFA for the 1982 and 1986 World Cups, Ueberroth restricted the number of sponsorships, limiting each product area to just one company, ensuring exclusivity, and made $4 million the minimum price for getting on board. Anheuser-Busch, Coca-Cola, Mars and IBM, and another two dozen major corporations fell over themselves to do so. Where competition in a product category was fierce, like 'official soft beverage', the price of entry rose. Coke had to pay $12 million to play. Another forty-three companies were licensed to sell 'official' Olympic products, and 532 official suppliers were mercilessly milked for cut-price or free goods and services, like official florists, Conroy's, responsible for the bird-of-paradise tropical Olympic bouquets handed to every medallist. All told, another $130 million rolled in. The stadiums and venues remained mercifully free of the most obvious corporate logos, but the screens and billboards of the world were overwhelmed. Coke, on top of their sponsorship costs, spent another $30 million on advertising, most of it backing Team USA and, however implausibly, connecting the consumption of soda with patriotic sporting success. Anheuser-Busch, in their ubiquitous commercial, 'Heartland', had two taciturn, plaid-shirted Midwestern farmers quietly watch the Olympic-torch relay pass through their endless prairie fields, nodding and clapping approvingly. McDonald's, having already paid for a new swimming pool, spent another $32 million on promotions, most tellingly, their 'The US wins, you win' campaign, in which customers received a scratch card embossed with one Olympic event. If America won the gold in that event, the card could then be redeemed for a Big Mac; a silver meant regular fries, and a bronze got you a small soft drink. Patterns of causation are complex, but it is more than mere symbolism that the sharpest uptick at the beginning of America's obesity epidemic should coincide with this unsavoury alliance of fast-food corporations, raucous nationalism and high-performance sport.[6]

Ueberroth, like any good corporate executive, looked for new revenue streams too, and the Olympic torch relay looked ripe for commercialization. AT&T paid the cost of the whole event, and at one point there were plans to sell the relay, stage by stage, at $3,000 a shot, to individual citizens and corporate sponsors – a policy later changed to $3,000 donations to a charity of one's choice. The Greeks, especially their national Olympic committee, were critical – until Ueberroth reminded them how much money they were making out of the Olympic Flame Hotel and the souvenir shops at Olympia. The relay was televised and the president had been watching. In his radio address to the nation on the eve of the games, Reagan was rhapsodic: 'Everywhere the torch went people came out of their homes and poured into the streets to cheer and wave the flag and urge the runners on. This outpouring reflected, I think, the new patriotism that has swept our land. Crowds spontaneously began singing "America the Beautiful" or "The Battle Hymn of the Republic".'[7] No wonder that Reagan was the first American president to actually attend and open an American Olympics. When, a few days later, he got to the

Coliseum for the opening ceremony, he would not be disappointed; the new patriotism had made it all the way to Los Angeles.

The design of the ceremony had originally been put out to the Disney corporation, but when the best they could come up with was a glorified parade of cartoon characters with bugles and banners, Ueberroth fired them. Under David Wolper – whose back catalogue included *Roots*, *The Thorn Birds* and *Willy Wonka and the Chocolate Factory* – the brief for the opening ceremony was to put on something with emotional charge that cost less than the $10 million the highly priced tickets for the show would bring in. He toyed with a car-based parade, wondered if waterfalls could cascade down the steps of the Coliseum or whether a giant globe could be made to inflate in the centre of the arena, but settled for a Broadway extravaganza in the sun. 'The Music of America' was built around the 1,000-piece McDonald's All-American Olympic Marching Band and a 1,200-person chorus, all volunteers. This was hokum on a grand scale, their fabulous formation marching in chocolate-box soldier uniforms to the songbook of US college sports, culminating in the creation of a huge outline of America. 'The Pioneer Spirit' was a rose-tinted hootenanny of country dancing and westward expansion, minus the genocide. 'Dixieland Jamboree' was a predictably sanitized run-through of the New Orleans jazz and gospel story, though graced by Etta James' pumpin' version of 'When the Saints Go Marching In'. But the organizers saved the best for 'Urban Rhapsody'. In this sequence, an ensemble of eighty-four grand pianos, the players of which were all dressed in identical powder-blue tuxedos, banged their way through Gershwin's *Rhapsody in Blue* and a host of Broadway musical favourites. Reagan departed from the IOC's official opening script with his more folksy, 'Celebrating the twenty-third Olympiad of the modern era, I declare open the Olympic Games of Los Angeles!' Ed Moses, the 400-metre hurdler, was so laid-back that, while taking the athlete's oath, he completely blanked on the third line and took three or four nervous attempts to get back on script.

In a deliberate riposte to the popular card-holding montages of the Moscow games, the entire audience in the Coliseum held up squares that made the brightly coloured flags of every participating nation. America's own struggles with race and the Olympics were the subtext of the final legs of the torch relay, run by Jesse Owens' grand-daughter, Gina Hemphill, and Rafer Johnson, gold medallist in the decathlon at the 1960 Rome games. Perching at the top of a precarious aluminium ladder, Johnson was the first black athlete to light an Olympic cauldron. By the time Vicki McClure, an unknown local grocery checker, had led a rendition of the Diana Ross hold-hands-with-your-neighbour classic, 'Reach Out and Touch (Somebody's Hand)' there wasn't a dry eye in the house. Secretary of State George Shultz is reported to have turned to a bystander and said, 'Eat your heart out, Chernenko.'[8]

Whether the general secretary of the Communist Party of the USSR was watching was another matter. The Soviets had declined to take a TV feed – though, as the ABC commentary team never tired of saying, there were multitudes of Russians heading for the Estonian city of Tallinn, where clandestine Finnish TV signals could be picked up. Had he done so, he would have seen a turkey shoot. The United States cleared up, taking eighty-three gold medals, more than one third of the total, and occupying considerably more of the TV broadcast time. Frank Deford, in *Sports Illustrated* magazine, worried: 'God only knows what the 2.5 billion people around the globe who are watching the games will think of a vain America, so bountiful and strong, with every advantage, including the home court, revelling in the role of Goliath, gracelessly trumpeting its own good fortune while rudely dismissing its guests.'[9] ABC looked at the ratings and the advertising revenues and carried on regardless. They also noted that the female part of the Olympic audience was growing and would soon be the majority and key advertising demographic. LA '84 obliged: with women athletes finally topping 20 per cent of the field, Los Angeles was the most feminine games yet. Synchronized swimming and rhythmic gymnastics, both women-only Olympic sports, made their debuts. A women's marathon was run for the first time and Morocco's 400-metre hurdler, Nawal El Moutawakel, became the first female Olympic champion from a Muslim nation.

The Soviets may not have been watching, but, for the first time, the Chinese were. Finally returned to the Olympic Games, and with live television feeds at home, the PRC saw its team win an unprecedented fifteen gold medals, considered to be an 'historic breakthrough' and 'an encouraging great jump in China's national revival.'[10] The public at home could also be incredibly harsh. The high jumper, Zhu Jianhua, was expected to win in Los Angeles. When he didn't, the windows of his house in Shanghai were broken and his family assaulted.

So, too, the American public when it came to Carl Lewis, who, despite the crude protestations of Daley Thompson, the British winner of the decathlon, was the athlete of the games. Indeed, as Andrew Anthony argued, 'in 1999 he was voted athlete of the century by, among others, a Unesco panel, the International Olympic Committee and *Sports Illustrated*. And it would be fair to say that the athlete of the 20th century would not find too much competition from previous centuries. So let's make that of all time.'[11] Lewis was making the first of his four appearances at the Olympic Games, and matched Jesse Owens' 1936 Berlin performance, winning four gold medals in the 100 metres, 200 metres, 4 x 100-metre relay and the long jump. He would go on to win nine Olympic golds and thirteen world championships, and would remain unbeaten in the long jump for a decade. Yet the Los Angeles crowd and much of mainstream America remained uncomfortable with their greatest ever athlete. After posting two extraordinary distances in the 1984 Olympic long jump, Lewis felt a sharp twinge and, given that he still had two events to go, decided to sit out the next four jumps and see if his opponents could better him. They couldn't, but the crowd responded with vicious boos of disappointment and affront. He had global fame, an avid sense service of the commercial and extraordinary looks, and although he made a lot of money, it was not nearly as much as it should have been. Promised endorsements with Coke and Nike vaporized around the same time that the press was flooded with rumours and accusations that – Lord forbid – he might be gay. Whatever he liked to do in his spare time, Main Street found it hard to comprehend that the fastest man in the world could sport a faded flat-top like Grace Jones, shimmer in his Lycra bodysuits and trade trainers for stilettos in the Pirelli calendar. Prior to the games, there were undercurrents of concern. Los Angeles had, for a decade, been haemorrhaging manufacturing jobs, abandoning industrial plants, demolishing factories and creating great wastelands of urban decay. It was often smog-bound, perpetually on the verge of gridlock and, in the early 1980s, gripped by a crack-cocaine epidemic and the armed violence of its gangs and police department. What the visitor and the television viewer saw was rather different:

A hot-pink star crowned a Technicolor totem pole, dripping with banners and bunting in teal and turquoise, laced with panels of tangerine and fluorescent peach. Towering against the blue sky on a yellow ziggurat made of scaffolding, this vibrant monument stood above candy-striped colonnades, surrounded by a sea of pyramid-roofed gazebos, all glinting in the Californian sun. Saturated with a supercharged rainbow and screaming with psychedelic joy.[12]

They were the brilliant creations of the designer Deborah Sussman, who, along with the architectural practice Jerde, created the colour palette, graphic language and pop-up building blocks of what they called 'festive federalism' – the design language used to dress every Olympic venue and space in the city.[13] In contrast to the red, white and blue that garlanded the city in 1932, Sussman's colour palette drew on the great waves of migration that had swept into Los Angeles in the 1970s: a riot of Pacific-rim tropicana and Latino urbanism; hot pinks, chrome yellow, magenta, vermilion and aqua. Sprayed like confetti across the city, there were canopies, flags and hangings on chain-link fences, pasteboard triumphal arches, huge cardboard stars, great towers formed from shipping tubes and ziggurats of jewel-coloured present boxes. They were tatty a fortnight after the games had finished, and taken down soon after. Their main legacy was a decade-long outbreak of crepe hangings and camp in the nation's most miserable shopping malls. The legacy of the Los Angeles Olympics as a whole was a little more robust. Demonstrating that the games could be run at a profit dispelled some of the toxicity that Montreal had brought to the games and helped ensure that the bidders came back. The sponsorship model was so good that it was taken over by the IOC itself, cutting local organizers out of the main deals. However, its cut-price capital costs have proved unrepeatable. Economics aside, the most discernible impact of the LA games was its reshaping of the closing ceremony, now incomplete without an array of the host's leading pop celebrities and musicians, but graced for the first time, in 1984, by a real star. Michael Jackson was the obvious choice, but his relationship to Pepsi made him a non-starter at an Olympic Games that Coke had invested in so heavily. Fortunately, there was another and a better alternative: the undisputed star of smooth and smooch, Mr Lionel Richie. Unlike later singers,

Richie performed live, oozing class in his blue-sequinned jacket and tight white slacks. A stadium-sized neon-lit dance floor pulsated around him as he thanked the crowd and sang an Olympic-length version of 'All Night Long'. He then ascended on a shimmering gold Olympic podium, while more than 400 break-dancers took to the floor. A calypso paean to non-stop decaffeinated hedonism, Richie's performance of the song reads not like the end of the party, but the invitation to the next few decades of America's debt-fuelled consumption binge. Lionel's main refrain was 'Party, karamu, fiesta, forever', but it is worth hearing the hint of an imperative and an injunction in his sign off, 'Feel good! Feel good!' The vast majority of the games' profit was, as promised, ploughed into youth sports programmes through the LA '84 foundation. Peter Ueberroth would be back. He was appointed head of Rebuild Los Angeles after the 1992 LA riots, trying and failing to pick up the pieces of this fractured city, which, in the face of the titanic economic forces unleashed in the Reagan years, no amount of 'can-do' could heal.

FIVE

South Korea, perilously constituted as half of the peninsula at the end of the Second World War, and facing an organized and aggressive communist North Korea, was an eager Olympian, sending their first team to the 1948 London games and thereby securing the country's only allotted Olympic slot for more than two decades. The Korean War that broke out the following year, and which would rage for four more, left an already conflict-ravaged country in ruins. The 1950s, under strongman Syngman Rhee, were hardly conducive to the development of elite sport, nor was there much political capital to be made from increasing popular participation.

The rise to power in 1960 of army general Park Chung Hee signalled a sea change in South Korea. The already authoritarian state was refashioned as a vast national development agency, orchestrating the country's miraculous and unbelievably speedy industrialization. Two decades later, South Korea, from being amongst the poorest countries in the world, was approaching European standards of living, and was winning export markets in sector after sector. Not mere technocrats, Park and his regime always sought to frame the headlong rush for growth in the language of national development, and it was here that sport found its place in the new order; the healthy nation required healthy bodies. National pride and position would be aided by international sporting prowess. As with so many things in post-war South Korea, an entire sector of life was built from scratch, and, in the late 1970s, the regime began to consider a bid for the Olympic Games as a way of cementing their progress.[1]

In 1979, Park was assassinated by his own head of security. Resistance to the subsequent military coup led by Generals Chun Doo Hwan and Roh Tae Woo was fiercest in the city of Kwangju, where students and workers were attacked by army units in a week-long battle that left, according to official figures, 300 dead, and, according to the opposition, more than 2,000. President Chun consolidated his rule with a wave of arrests, a crackdown on the press, and the harassment of oppositional leaders and organizations, but he was well aware that South Korea – now industrialized, urbanized and increasingly educated – could not be ruled by force of arms alone. The idea of a Seoul Olympic bid was revived and, in 1981, in the West German spa town of Baden-Baden, the IOC awarded the city the 1988 games. Interestingly, it appears that the IOC's decision was significantly shaped by the terrible lapses of protocol made by their competitors, Nagoya, who made sidelong criticisms of an opposing bid and admitted that a tiny anti-Olympic movement was at work in their city. Slaughter on the streets of Kwangju and the deplorable state of human rights in South Korea were, by contrast, deemed irrelevant.[2]

The importance of the games to the Korean junta can be seen by the scale of the preparations. Roh Tae Woo, number two in the hierarchy, was put in charge and simultaneously made the country's first minister of sport. Taking Tokyo 1964 as its model, the government allocated almost $4 billion for the construction of a vast Olympic park, an upgrade of the nation's telecommunications systems, an overhaul of Seoul's transport infrastructure and the 'beautification' of the host city. The Han River, hideously polluted by the nation's breakneck industrialization, was cleaned and transformed, the great webs of visible electrical cabling that had hurriedly supplied the city in the 1950s and 60s were hidden and hundreds of thousands of trees and flowers were planted in the city's verges and squares. Drawing on the great network of state and parastatal organizations at their command, from city mayors to head teachers to youth groups, the government's Central Council for Pan-National Olympic Promotion mobilized almost 60,000 volunteers to assist in the running of the games, while the government promised lifetime pensions for future Olympic medallists and helped establish professional baseball and football leagues. From the pronouncements of the regime, and the smooth running of the Asian Games, held as an Olympic dry run in 1986, everything appeared to be on track.

However, the forces that had produced the 1980 protests had not gone away, indeed they now encompassed the new middle classes of the big cities, and they began pressing the regime to introduce direct elections for the presidency in 1987 as a prelude to a fuller democratization. In the spring of 1987, President Chun attempted to close down the debate by announcing that all constitutional issues were to be postponed until after the Olympics, and that his successor would be their organizer, Roh Tae Woo. Seoul exploded as trade unions, university students, church congregations and white-collar workers poured into the streets. The regime responded with a steadily intensifying barrage of batons and tear gas until, on 9 June, the student protester, Lee Han Yeol, was hospitalized by a tear-gas grenade embedded in his cracked skull (his funeral, held in July, would attract 1.6 million mourners). The following day, a quarter of a million people, by far the largest protest so far, took to the streets of two dozen cities. A week later, the National Rally for the Banishment of Tear Gas Grenades saw 1.5 million protest, while parts of the newly emboldened press began to report on foreign reactions to the conflict and the real possibility that Seoul might lose the games.

Inside the junta, the hard and soft liners battled it out, the former arguing for a full military mobilization, the latter for compromise. Precisely what tipped the argument in favour of the latter remains unclear. However, it is unquestionable that the fate of the Seoul Olympics was an important factor in Roh's thinking and the internal victory of the reformers. Present in Seoul in the midst of the fighting, on a long-arranged trip, IOC president Samaranch spoke to Roh and others. Ever the soul of discretion, he revealed little of his conversations, but, on 29 June, Roh Tae Woo told the nation that, 'At a time when the Olympics are around the corner, all of us should be responsible for preventing the national disgrace of being mocked and derided by the international community because of a division on the national consensus.'[3] Consequently, the government would accept almost all of the opposition's demands – including free and direct presidential elections, the protection of civil liberties and a widespread political amnesty – and asked that the nation join them in a shared programme of national renewal. 'It will be the consistent hope of not only myself but also of you, the people, that we should carry out successfully . . . the continuous economic development, the peaceful transition of government, and the 1988 Seoul Olympics which will be a golden opportunity for national prosperity, thereby placing the country on the road towards becoming an advanced country.' It was enough to calm the protests, keep the games and then, given a fatal division between the leading figures in the opposition, allow Roh Tae

Woo to swap his fatigues for a business suit and to win the presidential election in December.[4]

Much of the politics of South Korea's transition had been conducted on television – the global broadcasts of the street fighting and the national addresses of Chun and Roh – so too the games they produced.[5] Anxious to keep public assembly to a minimum, the Seoul games featured few decorated public spaces or gatherings beyond the tightly secured venues, but they had much of the population glued to their new televisions: nearly 90 per cent switched on to some of the games and more than half watched a great deal. Some of the key events, especially athletics finals, were broadcast at the most unusual times, often early in the morning, but this was prime time in the United States. NBC had paid a record $300 million for the TV rights, and they were not about to let Seoul's thirteen-hour time difference from the east coast of the United States get between them and the advertising revenues they expected.[6] In any case, South Korea's victories – their twelve gold medals easily the nation's best Olympic performance – came elsewhere: in martial sports, like wrestling, boxing and judo, and in table tennis and archery, which were indicators of the changing geography of Olympic sports and the rising influence of East Asia.

Archery, which had returned to the Olympics in 1972, had been an American sporting fiefdom sustained by a simply gigantic level of popular participation. In the late 1950s, *Sports Illustrated* estimated that there were four million archers in the USA. South Korea is now the world's strongest archery nation, and the shift began at Seoul. Products of the new state-funded elite-sport programmes in the country, South Korea's archers have won the majority of Olympic archery medals since.* By the time the nation's top archers, Park Sung-Hyun and Park Kyung-Mo, announced their marriage in 2008, the sport was making headlines on the front pages of everything from the serious broadsheets to the celebrity photo magazines.

Apocryphally, table tennis had the most imperial of origins. Searching for after-dinner entertainment, British officers in India in the late nineteenth century carved a champagne cork into a ball and

---

* A brief revival for US archery in the shape of Olympian slacker Justin Huish, gold medallist at Atlanta in 1996, fizzled out after he was busted for possession of marijuana.

batted it back and forth across their dinner table with the lids of cigar boxes. Taken back home, it turned into a minor upper-class craze, known informally as 'whiff-whaff' or 'flim-flam'. The game began to assume its modern form in 1901, when Jacques of London first manufactured hollow celluloid balls with reliable bounce and spin, and relaunched it under the trademark Ping Pong. The codification of the game as a competitive sport was led by the eccentric English aristocrat Ivor Montagu, who founded the International Table Tennis Federation (ITTF). Cheap, simple, easy to learn and fabulously compulsive, a staple of youth clubs and barracks rooms everywhere, it reached across Europe, the Americas and, above all, into Asia – a fact underlined by Japan's Hiroji Satoh's world championship victory in 1952, using, for the first time, foam-backed bats, whose speed and potential for spin transformed the game. The immense popularity of the sport in Asia came to global attention in the 1970s when, in the era of Ping-Pong diplomacy, the formal rapprochement between the American and Chinese governments was oiled by table-tennis competitions.[7] Thus, on the grounds of global popularity, table tennis would have been included in the games long before Seoul, but, as Ivor Montagu found his own ITTF world championships perfectly satisfactory, thank you very much, there was no approach to the IOC until after his retirement in the 1970s. South Korea won two golds at the Seoul games. Since then, aside from the Swede Jan Ove Waldner, in Barcelona in 1992, and South Korea's Ryu Seung Min, in 2004, China has won every table-tennis gold medal at the games.

While Asia's presence at the Olympics had significantly grown by 1988, it remained the case that only one Olympic sport – judo – had been codified outside the West. In 1988, taekwondo, Korea's own modernized martial art, was introduced to the global television audience, first as a mass performance at the opening ceremony, then as a demonstration sport and subsequently as a full Olympic sport. It has roots over a millennium old in the three kingdoms of medieval Korea, which developed a variety of fighting systems, most notably, *taekkyeon*, which was popularized across the peninsula by an itinerant group of Buddhist and Confucian warriors – the Hwarang or 'Flowering of Manhood'. United as a single peaceful kingdom in 936, and averse to engagement with the outside world, Korea ceased to have much use for the martial arts until the country was invaded and colonized by the Japanese in the early twentieth century. As part of its wider drive to eradicate Korean culture and identity, the Japanese banned *taekkyeon*, an act which underwrote its Korean nationalist credentials and created a network of clandestine practitioners dedicated to its survival. The practice was given a significant boost by one its greatest devotees, General Choi Hong Hi. Imprisoned by the Japanese during the Second World War, he spent this time melding aspects of karate with *taekkyeon*; during the Korean War, he ran the 'Fist Division', a crack regiment that practised his remodelled martial art. A spectacular demonstration to President Syngman Rhee in 1952 ensured that it became compulsory across the South Korean armed services and, in 1955, under some government duress, all of the nation's martial-arts schools were required to merge their practices into a single unified fighting style – taekwondo. On the sport's full Olympic debut, South Korea shared the medals with China, Cuba, Australia and Greece. In this respect, taekwondo was an early emissary in what became known as the K-wave, the flowering of South Korea's culture industries and their successful export of TV series, electro pop and fantasy video games to Asia and beyond.[8]

If the Seoul games marked the beginning of a new, more democratic and open era in South Korean life, it also marked the end of an Olympic era: this was the final games to be held under an IOC charter that still distinguished between amateurs and professionals. The villains of the piece now were neither sham amateurs nor hidden professionals but the pharmaceutically enhanced. Two Bulgarian weightlifters were stripped of their gold medals after failing doping tests, after which the entire team withdrew from the competition. That was news in south-east Europe, but when the Canadian, Ben Johnson, winner of the men's 100 metres, tested positive for steroids, it was the only news. Seoul was lucky, then, to have one last real Olympic hero. Lawrence Lemieux, a Canadian sailor, was running second in his Finn-class race on an open-sea course shared with the finals of the 470 two-person boats. Sailing in remarkably strong winds and high waves, he had lost the lead, unable to see an eight-foot-high buoy obscured by the swell. Still poised to make a challenge for the gold, he saw that a Singaporean 470 had capsized, leaving one crew-member grasping the hull but bleeding profusely, and the other dangerously adrift. Lemieux sailed towards them, flipped one into his boat and, against the wind, held it steady against the up-turned 470. Relieved by the South Korean navy, he returned to the race, and still finished twenty-first of thirty-two.

8

BOOM! THE GLOBALIZATION OF THE OLYMPICS AFTER THE COLD WAR

BARCELONA 1992 • ATLANTA 1996 • SYDNEY 2000

ALBERTVILLE 1992 • LILLEHAMMER 1994 • NAGANO 1998

SALT LAKE CITY 2002

We look upon the IOC as God. Their wish is our command.

Chen Xitong, Chairman of the Beijing 2000 bid commission

The Olympic Games are organised by individuals. They are not angels and saints. If you want angels and saints, go organise the Olympic Games in heaven, not on earth.

Jean-Claude Ganga, IOC Member

ONE

When the IOC reviewed the bids to host the 1984 summer games, there was a shortlist of one. Tehran, then subject to the first great wave of demonstrations that would go on to destroy the Pahlavi monarchy, pulled out, leaving only Los Angeles, which was not in a deferential mood. The games would go to California and they would be done the LA way, with the IOC entirely cut out of television and sponsorship deals. Hardly the stuff of divine power. By the time Barcelona was awarded the 1992 games, the number of applicant cities had crept up to five. The 1996 games went to Atlanta, who beat off five other competitors, and by the time the mayors of the world's cities had absorbed the erroneous lessons of Los Angeles and Barcelona – that the games really could turn a profit, and turn a city from a backwater to a global icon – there was a flood of wannabes: eight candidates fought over the games in 2000, and eleven in 2004. The games had become so desirable that the IOC, in whose gift they lay, was able to take on the garb of the divine amongst its many suppliants. It would later transpire, however, as Jean-Claude Ganga made clear after he, along with five other divinities, was expelled from the IOC on charges of corruption, that the gods had feet of clay and that the IOC dwells on this earth not in heaven.[1]

These were the games awarded and conducted under the presidency of Juan Antonio Samaranch. Elected to the post in 1981, he served until his retirement in 2001 and utterly transformed the IOC and its games.[2] Born in 1920, in Barcelona, to a family of textile industrialists, Samaranch managed to sit out much of the Spanish Civil War, before re-emerging under Franco's dictatorship as a banker, enthusiastic amateur boxer and roller-hockey fanatic. Almost entirely bereft of a public persona, virtually inaudible as a public speaker and seemingly disinterested in ideas and intellectual pursuits, Samaranch, like many of his generation of global sports administrators, excelled in the acquisition and accumulation of contacts, influence and official positions in the interlacing worlds of politics, business, diplomacy and sport. In the 1950s, he found himself in charge, first, of Spanish roller hockey, and then of the sport's international federation. Unable to win a seat on Barcelona's city council, he was appointed provincial deputy for the city by the ruling party. Organizing the 1957 Mediterranean Games gave him his entree into the Spanish Olympic Committee and, from thence, as chair of the committee, to the Olympic Games in Rome and Tokyo, where he caught the eye of Avery Brundage – a man always on the lookout for the competent but compliant. By 1966, he was on the IOC and then, with Brundage's approval, ascended in the 1970s to the executive board and a vice-presidency. By this time, Franco was dead, Spain was democratizing and his domestic political career was over, but alternative options were available, and Samaranch made his own seamless transition to the new order by being appointed Spain's ambassador to the Soviet Union during its preparations and staging of the games in 1980 – a networking opportunity behind the iron curtain he did not pass up.

His predecessor as president of the IOC, the avuncular Lord Killanin, had run a very loose operation. He continued to live and work from his homes in Britain and Ireland, and was an occasional visitor to Lausanne, where much of the day-to-day and indeed strategic work of the organization was orchestrated by the formidable Madame Monique Berlioux, who had served as the IOC director, and in effect the chief executive of the whole organization, since 1971. Avery Brundage had paid all his own bills, shelling out up to $100,000 a year of his own money on Olympic business, and increasingly treated the organization as his personal fiefdom. Killanin's more modest financial position saw him insist that the IOC cover his expenses, while his attitude to the IOC was infinitely more collegial and less bound by Brundage's religious veneration of what he understood as Coubertin's Olympism. In short, Brundage declared and insisted, Killanin consulted and negotiated.[3]

All this was to change. Samaranch, firmly installed in his suite at the delightful Lausanne Palace, was the first IOC president since Coubertin to make the city his home, to treat the post of president as a full-time occupation and to ensure that it was well remunerated. Within three years of arriving, he forced the resignation of Monique Berlioux. She was not directly replaced, and, just in case any other competitor should arise, her job was broken up into a swathe of new and less powerful posts. Brundage had thought the IOC like a cross between an authoritarian cult and his own Chicago corporation. Killanin had treated it like the old-fashioned gentlemen's club it was. Samaranch knew that it was also a political institution, and, as in Franco's Spain, political authority had to be concentrated, bureaucratized and engrained from the top. He ensured his control over the organization by devoting considerable time and energy to IOC appointments, later acquiring the power to directly install his own nominees without reference to anyone else. The wearisome problem of age and term limits, which would have prevented him running beyond his first three terms, were graciously lifted by the IOC, enabling him to stay on until 2001.

Master in his own house, Samaranch deepened his political power through his membership of a wider network of sports administrators and businesses, predominantly but not exclusively Latin in their origins, who had come to dominate much of world sport in the 1980s and 1990s.His close associates, allies and partners included João Havelange, the Brazilian president of FIFA who was instrumental in his successful election as IOC president; [4] Mario Vázquez Raña, the billionaire Mexican businessman and president of the Association of National Olympic Committees; the Italian president of the IAAF, Primo Nebiolo; and Horst Dassler, head of Adidas – then the world's largest and most commercially aggressive sportswear company – and the most important individual in nurturing the new nexus of global sports administrators, TV networks and multinational corporations.

It was Dassler, Havelange and a PR man, Patrick Nally, who forged the template for the commercialization of global sporting spectaculars, beginning with FIFA and the World Cup. In this new political economy, FIFA was able to massively increase the value of its sponsorships by restricting their number, allowing only one company in any given product category and offering them only to multinationals. Thus, a small number of sponsors whose needs were closely catered to – prepared advertising space, protection from ambush marketeers, the best seats in the house – delivered a huge rise in income. Television rights were to be vigorously sold by an independent marketing agency – in this case, the infamous ISL – in return for a guaranteed and very large sum of money. These deals were paralleled by the hidden circuits of exchange. In this world, the allocation of TV rights by the FIFA executive (and, later, regional and national officials) would be tied to large payments by broadcasters and marketers to sports administrators' offshore bank accounts, or those of their relatives, fronts and cronies, in a lava flow of cash that only finally stopped in 2001 when hubris and disastrous over-expansion saw the company go bankrupt; a similar culture of decision-making could be seen at work in the allocation of hosting rights. In addition, much of the money returning to FIFA would be passed to national and regional football associations, proving a sensationally useful form of political patronage for the organization and its president. All of this was made possible by the *omertà* that existed amongst senior officials, the collusion of sponsors and broadcasters, the opaqueness of Swiss law as it applied to international organizations and the abject failure of the press, police and legal authorities to investigate and prosecute the organization until very recently.

It was in these realms of commercialization and governance that Samaranch's era saw the biggest shifts. First, Killanin's tentative attempts to modernize the IOC's amateurism were deemed both insufficient and impractical. Testament to Samaranch's deep pragmatism and subterranean political manoeuvring, the amateurism clause on the Olympic charter, which had caused so much discord and conflict, disappeared without any rearguard action or even much of a goodbye. The Olympic movement's embrace of commercial sport did not, of course, stop here. Under Killanin and Brundage, the IOC had lost control over the Olympics' trademarks, sponsorship programme and TV-rights sales, and, as a consequence, saw very little of the then rapidly rising new revenue streams. Samaranch, bit by bit, clawed back control and money for the IOC, using much of it to sustain his rule, channelling it to international sports federations, the national Olympic committees that organized Olympic teams (NOCs) and the Olympic solidarity budget that supported developing nations and their athletes. For small sports federations with limited income, and many NOCs, this was their only reliable financial support, bringing Samaranch innumerable allies and clients.[5]

The colossus of the sports–industrial complex was inevitably coming the games' way. Whoever had become IOC president would have been making these kinds of moves. The unique contribution of Samaranch – or, to give him some of his many official titles, the Marquis of Samaranch, Knight Grand Cross of the Italian Republic, holder of the Polish Order of Merit and the Russian Order of Honour – to the movement's mutant growth was his devotion to its global status. Protocol under Samaranch meant that he was accorded the rank of a head of state, was accommodated and transported accordingly, and referred to as 'His Excellency'. An international visit to any sporting occasion, and in this task he was assiduous, would always be combined with papal, royal, presidential and prime ministerial audiences.

Perhaps the greatest asset of all was his mastery of vacuity. In press conferences, he was impossible to pin down, showing brilliant verbal sleight by only answering unasked questions, diplomatically diverting attention and politely obstructing and obfuscating any critical barb. At times, he could reach stunning levels of deliberate amnesia, simply ignoring questions posed to him during IOC sessions, or dismissing volumes of well-documented criticism over evictions and displacements at Olympic venues with a roll of his eyes and an early break for lunch. Above all, he had the old-school tact and selective myopia that allowed him to ignore the problems of systematic doping in sport and the increasingly venal behaviour of other members of the club. Anyone searching his speeches for any sense of what the purpose of it all was, beyond the most anodyne of platitudes – peace and friendship, amity and harmony – will be doing so in vain. The only remarks of Samaranch's that trouble the historical record are his ubiquitous comments at that end of an Olympiad, that they had, except for the case of Atlanta, been 'the best games ever'. Quite what made them the best remained to be seen. What was certain was that, on Samaranch's watch, and in the midst of the Olympic boom he had nurtured, they were the biggest ever.

One measure of the Olympic boom was the torch relay.[6] When the Germans staged the first, in 1936, its twelve-day journey through seven countries, borne by over three thousand runners, was considered an extraordinary and extravagant gesture. London 1948, austere in every way, staged a relay of almost the same distance, but with half the number of athletes. It is a measure of the games' exponential growth that the Barcelona relay of 1992, by no means the grandest of the era, lasted six weeks, went to every continent and, at 60,000 kilometres, was almost twenty times longer than its predecessors. Atlanta really made its assets sweat, holding a Coca-Cola-sponsored cavalcade over ninety-two days, exclusively in the United

States, live on TV, and sending the torch and advertising rates into orbit aboard the space shuttle *Columbia*. After a relatively moderate Sydney relay, confined to Australia and a tour of Oceania's micro islands, Athens and Beijing went global. The Greeks sent their torch on a seventy-eight-day odyssey, 78,000 kilometres long; the Chinese sent theirs away for 129 days, carried over 130,000 kilometres by 21,800 runners.

Controlling the size and cost of the torch relay has been the least of the problems that the IOC has inherited from this era. Measured by the number of national Olympic committees present at the games, the globalization of the Olympics appeared to peak in Munich in 1972, when 123 countries sent teams – the culmination of a decade and a half of European decolonization and national independence in the global south. The boycotts that affected the games after this meant that it was not until 1992 that the total was exceeded. The 169 teams that attended Barcelona were swollen by the break-up of the Soviet Union and Yugoslavia, and the emergence of new micro-nations in Oceania, the Gulf and the Caribbean. By London 2012, the figure had grown to 204.

More countries were coming to play more sports in more ways. The number of Olympic sports was fixed at twenty-one from 1972 to 1984. In every subsequent games, there were additional new sports, new events in old sports and, across the board, the creation of women's events where there had been few or none. From around 200 gold medals awarded in the 1980s, the number topped 300 in the twenty-first century. The end of the IOC's notion of amateurism opened the door to tennis, whose global circuit of stars brought glamour and ratings. Baseball and softball offered the same prospect, but America's MLB refused to allow its best players to depart in what was still mid-season. The new economic geography of the post-Cold War world, and its turn to the Pacific Rim, saw the addition of badminton, table tennis and taekwondo: all sports with a global presence, but particularly strong in East and South-East Asia. From the other side of the Pacific Ocean, three Californian codified sports joined the games: beach volleyball, first played on the beaches of Los Angeles in the 1930s; triathlon, invented in San Diego in the mid-1970s; and mountain biking, first tried out in Marin County, north of San Francisco, in the early 1980s.

Thus, the previous record of 7,800 athletes at Munich 1972

was smashed by the 9,330 in Barcelona, twenty years later, and peaked at just under 11,000 at Beijing in 2008. The IOC did manage to curb the number of officials and judges at the games. They had outnumbered athletes in 1992, but were squeezed down to a mere 8,000 at London 2012. Coaches and administrators aside, every other category of accredited persons at the games grew rapidly. Thirty-five thousand volunteers worked for Barcelona in 1992, doubling to 70,000 at Beijing in 2008. The accreditation of a seemingly enormous media corps of 13,000 in 1992 was dwarfed by the 21,000 that got a press pass at Athens and the 25,000 at London; and that is to say nothing of the increasingly large unaccredited media presence at the games.

The Olympics was already an expensive show by the early 1990s. The running costs of the summer games have steadily risen, from around a billion dollars in Barcelona, to the two to three billon it cost to stage Beijing and London. At the same time, the organizers' share of IOC global sponsorship monies and broadcast rights, as well as rising income from local sponsorship, lotteries and event ticket sales, broadly balanced this, allowing various organizing committees to claim a small surplus or profit. Barcelona sold 3.8 million tickets, Atlanta and Sydney more than seven million apiece. The $636 million that Barcelona's TV rights brought in had almost doubled in value by 2004, when Athens commanded $1.5 billion, and quadrupled by 2012, when the world's broadcasters came up with $2.6 billion to cover the London games.

However, the murky and often totally opaque nature of Olympic accounting, and the removal of most capital costs from these figures, renders the claims of profitability absurd. Preparing for the 1992 games cost the Spanish state, Catalonia and the city of Barcelona around $5 billion. Atlanta, which had long promised to be an entirely private-sector affair, was in actual fact massively subsidized by the US federal government and the Georgia state government, which covered not only security costs but a plethora of infrastructure projects. Sydney, which spent heavily on land reclamation, train lines and its new Olympic stadium, faced a bill of around $3 billion, and then Athens took matters to a new level, with its costs spiralling to $16 billion. The question remains: why? Why did it get to the point that Greece, an already insolvent country of just ten million people, would stage an Olympic Games that cost as much as the prior five or six put together? And why, for the seventeen days it lasted, might it even have appeared to be a good idea?

Some sources of growth were beyond the control of the IOC. The geography of the post-Cold War world, the pattern of state formation, and thus the number of teams, was, even for the gods of the IOC, outside their remit. The increasing size of the media industry could hardly be laid at its door. The rising cost of the Olympic security bill, already high in the 1990s, was sent stratospheric after 9/11. The IOC's extravagant personal tastes, and the grotesque culture of luxury and entitlement that it nurtured, shaped the expectations of both international sports federations and bid committees who, to an increasing extent, opted for expensive iconic architecture and unnecessarily over-engineered venues, and suffered from all the pathologies of murky tendering: price gouging, graft and gigantic cost overruns. But it remained the case that the Olympics proved uniquely and phenomenally popular with the global television audience, and that made it phenomenally popular with corporate sponsors and urban elites, who wanted to put their cityscapes and brands in front of billions.

Global TV-viewing figures are notoriously unreliable and come in a variety of forms.[7] For much of this era, the IOC preferred to quote average programme audience data, which included those who had watched at least three minutes of an event, and usually gave the peak figure, or they simply quoted the reach of their broadcasts, which was an estimate of the numbers of people it might be viewed by, given how many broadcasters in how many countries were showing it to how many people. Research suggests that these figures are often considerable overstatements, though they increasingly understate the numbers who consume the games online or through a mobile device. Whatever the actual figures, the direction of travel is clear. Barcelona was broadcast to 160 countries, Atlanta to 216 and Sydney to 220, almost the entire planet. The cumulative viewing hours of the Seoul games was 10.4 billion, rising to 19.6 billion for Atlanta and 34 billion for Athens. The average Japanese TV-viewer was watching more than thirty hours of the Olympics, while the games were occupying 20 per cent of global prime-time television for the seventeen days they were on. All of this coverage was multiplied many times over by the sponsors. For example, in 1996, in Atlanta, Coca-Cola paid $40 million up front to be the official soft drink of the games, put the same into buying land and building a Coca-Cola amusement park and Olympic museum, paid for the entire torch relay, and then spent $1.3 billion on a global marketing budget entirely keyed to the games.[8]

The highest viewing figures of all were recorded by the Olympic opening ceremonies, which, given their rising cost, scale and complexity, makes them one of the best metrics of the Olympic boom.[9] Barcelona changed the whole feel of the opening ceremony by the simple expedient of holding it at night, transforming the occasion from a big country fair into a real theatrical spectacular. For the first time, temporary flooring was introduced, hiding the turf and athletics track that had made even the grandest occasions feel like something close to a school sports day. It eschewed the marching bands, under-rehearsed school children and Broadway choreography of past ceremonies in favour of avant-garde dance, post-modern circus, visual arts and experimental theatre. Novelty and made-for-television drama shaped the lighting of the Olympic cauldron. Barcelona had the Paralympian archer Antonio Rebello fire a flaming arrow into a vertical plume of gas; Lillehammer brought the flame to the stadium by ski jumper; Atlanta's use of a fragile Muhammad Ali was second to none in the pathos and celebrity stakes; Sydney sent the ritual flame through water and into the sky, while the Greeks – Europe's most enthusiastic smokers – seemed to ignite the dipping head of a huge, luminous cigarette lighter. Barcelona told some kind of story about the Mediterranean, Catalonia, Spain and Europe. Sydney showcased the informality of the larrikin, the mate culture of the golden era, with its outback cowboys making horseback Olympic rings and a gigantic banner of welcome dropped from the stadium roof that read, 'G'day', and then paired this with impenetrable but beautifully costumed accounts of the continent's bizarre ecology, Aboriginal history and new multicultural migrations. Athens, in the most demented rewriting of history yet, sent a parade of historical tableaux on wheels around the stadium, that went from the Minoans, to the Athenians, to the Byzantine Empire, and then jumped 1,500 years of inconvenient tutelage to the Franks and Ottomans, before ending on the Greek War of Independence, the 1896 games and Maria Callas. There then followed a special light show that was impossible to comprehend, but apparently depicted Hellenic science and philosophy as the sole historical fount of contemporary reason and technological advance. If this was the end of history, it was not, as Francis Fukuyama had speculated, a realm of bland agreement and ideological consensus, but a cacophony that signalled the end of coherence, plausibility and verifiable argument, a world in which false consciousness was replaced by the fragmentation of consciousness, pulverized by the photons of the Olympic spectacular.

TWO

In earlier eras, when ideology still counted for something, the IOC and its games had faced critics and competitors who attempted to stage their own alternative sporting spectaculars. The workers' sports movement had put on their own people's Olympics. The emerging powers of the decolonized world tried with the GANEFO games. Protestant fundamentalists had opposed the Amsterdam 1928 games on moral grounds. In the decade after the Cold War, however, neither old-school muscular socialism, nor third-way anti-imperialism had any ideological purchase on global sport. The struggle over women's inclusion in Olympic sport, and the terms of their admittance, continued to be played out at the games and within the IOC and other sports bureaucracies, but there was no external challenger or obvious sporting social movement to connect to. However, the new critics argued that the global sporting spectacular, in alliance with over-blown urbanism and city branding, was a pernicious and reactionary force. A coalition of environmentalists and anti-tax groups had stopped the 1976 Denver winter games in its tracks. Thus, the most powerful opposition to the Olympic movement came from those who challenged the very idea that sport, certainly in the form of the tele-vised spectacular, was of any real social value at all, and the Olympic bids from Amsterdam, Toronto and Berlin were opposed, for the first time, by systematically anti-Olympic movements which were power-ful enough to derail their ambitions.

Amsterdam, bidding for the 1992 games in the mid-1980s, set the tone.[1] Here, a coalition of left and environmentally inclined local councillors and the extensive squatting movement in the city operated under the umbrella 'Nolympics'. As one of the main homes of modern situationism and public happenings, the city's counter-culture was peculiarly alert to the power and importance of spectacle, super sensitive to the state's control of land, housing and development, and schooled in all kinds of militant action and comic provocation. Their alternative bid campaign proved to be one of the sharpest and funniest ever. The campaign video featured a nightmare tour through the city's traffic jams, examined the appalling rate of bike thefts and muggings, and featured an Olympic torch used to light spliffs and bombs alike.[2] When the circus came to town, every member of the IOC was sent a bag of marijuana and a letter signed by Mayor van Thijn: 'After the South African diamonds, we're sending you something with which you can clear your mind. The Dutch Olympic Committee would like to acquaint you with one of the products of Amsterdam. We hope in this manner to exert a positive influence on your decision. Our national product can be obtained in 500 legal sales outlets.' A gathering of officials from the world's international sports federations, waiting for a canal-boat tour, were pelted with tomatoes and eggs by one hundred activists before the riot police charged them all. When the IOC convened in Lausanne for the deciding vote, the protesters joined them, surrounding their deluxe shuttle buses and letting off an Olympic-torch smoke-bomb at precisely the moment that the committee gathered for its traditional photograph.

Toronto's anti-Olympic movement was rather more sober, but no less effective.[3] Calling itself the 'Bread Not Circuses' coalition, it was led by a cluster of individuals and organizations dealing with homelessness, poverty and social housing in the city. They compiled a devastating 'anti-bid' book, reminding readers that this was a city where 100,000 people were using food banks and 20,000 were homeless – a number that was rising – and so, consequently, it simply could not afford the games. In a unique encounter, testament to the quality of Canadian democracy, Bread Not Circuses was actually allowed to meet with visiting members of the IOC evaluation committee and to air their concerns. Openness in these matters, while praiseworthy, was a disastrous political tactic. The IOC, then and since, has shown itself very averse to these kinds of organized protest, and ever more hysterically insistent that bid cities, their citizens and their press, present North Korean levels of collective enthusiasm and ideological unity. When Toronto was unceremoniously eliminated from the competition, ultimately won by Atlanta, the committee president – plumbing mogul and former Olympic yachtsman, Paul Henderson – angrily laid the blame on the protestors' shoulders. Back home, anti-games activists celebrated in the city's portlands, once intended as the site of Toronto's Olympic stadium, but now declared an 'Olympic-free zone'.

Berlin's bid for the 2000 summer games was first conceived of before the fall of the Wall, as an exercise in Ostpolitik, but the actual reunification of the city and its new status as Germany's capital gave the organizers real hope that they might be in the running.[4] The city's many alternative cultures and communities, nurtured in its years of isolation, had other ideas. The IOC congress, held in Berlin in 1991, required the protection of 1,500 police officers, and forty-one arrests were made during three days of citywide protest, orchestrated by the AOK (Anti-Olympic Committee). A demonstration on bikes, involving more than 600 cyclists, was broken up by truncheon-wielding police. The following year, the Carl Diem plaque was stolen from Berlin's Olympic stadium and this memorial to the chief organizer of the 1936 games was held to ransom. Olympic flags that were put up around the city were persistently taken down. In an open letter sent to all members of the IOC, the AOK warned them that they needed to look up from their 'one-sided conversation with venal politicians, sports officials and the construction mafia.' Another voice had now entered the debate.

> This letter announces another Berlin: the Berlin of protest and resistance to imperialism, capitalism and the 2000 Olympics; the anarchists, dropouts, punks, gays and lesbians, the alternatives, the stone throwers, the fire eaters, the grafters, the poor, the drunkards and the madmen.[5]

Over the next twelve months, Berlin was hit by scattergun Olympic protests of many kinds. Companies and banks associated with the bid were attacked with firebombs. Expensive cars were sprayed with anti-Olympic graffiti. In a second open letter to Samaranch, the AOK darkly warned, 'We will ensure that the Berlin Games are a nightmare for you and your sponsors.' When the IOC made a final visit, in spring 1993, 10,000 people took to the streets, forcing the authorities to mobilize 4,500 police and to cordon off large areas of the city. In the late summer, East Berlin's cable television suddenly disappeared; its vandalized junction boxes were found plastered with anti-games stickers. The games went to Sydney.

It is over two decades now since the Barcelona games opened and, even there, the paint is peeling; the city, though enriched, has been counting the costs of the overdevelopment of its tourism industry and the long-term gentrification of much of the beachfront, both processes initiated by the games. Atlanta looks like the sugar-frosted land-grab it always was. The never-ending war on drugs in high-performance sport has seen many medallists of the era retrospectively stripped of their medals, and, in Athens, the new ruins of the new Olympia are the boom's most telling legacy.

THREE

Barcelona was truly kaleidoscopic. With a record 169 countries attending the games and almost a third of them winning some kind of medal, the games offered an abundance of powerful national symbols and narratives. The parade of nations was a guide to the new geography of the post-Cold War world. A real united Germany attended, not the ersatz joint team of the Brundage years. The Soviet Union, dissolved in 1991, yielded up the newly independent Baltic states of Estonia, Latvia and Lithuania, who sent national teams for the first time since 1936. The remainder of the USSR hung on in the ghostly form of the short-lived CIS or Commonwealth of Independent States, an arrangement of such ambiguity and fragility that its athletes competed merely as the Unified Team and marched under the neutrality of the Olympic flag. Yugoslavia, broken by civil war and succession, had by now lost Croatia, Bosnia and Slovenia, all of whom competed independently, leaving just Serbia and Montenegro as the rump.

On the twentieth anniversary of the Munich massacre, Yael Arad became the first Israeli to win an Olympic medal. 'Maybe we now say, if it is possible, that we have avenged this murder,' she said, after winning a silver in the judo. 'I think we owe it to the families and to the people of Israel.'[1] It would take another four years, and a terrorist attack on the Atlanta games, for the IOC – in the shape of Samaranch's closing address – to publicly mention the massacre.

Indonesians lined the streets of Jakarta in their millions to welcome home their first Olympic gold medallists – the badminton stars, Susi Susanti and Alan Kusuma. In the last decades of Dutch imperial rule, the game acquired popularity amongst the educated Javanese and Chinese of Jakarta, who were attracted to a sport that seemed more Asian than European, and certainly not Dutch. After independence, it had been deemed the national sport by Indonesia's government, and they paid for Susanti and Kusuma to tour the capital's streets in an open-topped limousine to which a giant shuttle-cock had been attached.

For the British, there was pathos in defeat. In the 400-metre semi-final, Derek Redmond pulled up short as he tore through a hamstring. His father leapt from the stands and onto the track, then helped his son over the line; the crowd gave them a standing ovation. China celebrated the ice-cool bravery and gymnastic brilliance of youth. Fu Mingxia, just thirteen, but in a fast-track state training college since the age of nine, became the youngest Olympic gold medallist of all time, flying from the vertiginous height of the 10-metre diving board, a cipher of the ruthless pursuit of development that the country's economic and sporting ministries had imbibed, and the great leap in the dark that these changes represented. South Africa, then locked into the constitutional talks that would bring an end to apartheid, returned to the Olympics for the first time since 1960. There were just eight black athletes out of over ninety, testament to the exclusionary nature of most sports in the country, but it was Nelson Mandela, not F. W. de Klerk, who attended the opening ceremony and who, as ever, set a tone of pragmatic reconciliation: 'I would have liked it to be a reflection of our population . . . but there has to be a starting point.'[2] A wider reconciliation with the once toxic apartheid state was signalled in the women's 10,000 metres. The white South African, Elana Meyer, duelled for much of the race with the Ethiopian Derartu Tulu, before Tulu broke away to become the first black African woman to win an Olympic gold medal. The two then ran a victory lap to enormous acclaim, cloaked in their national flags, hand in hand.

Yet, for all this, the athletes were overshadowed. As George Vecsey argued in the New York Times, 'The athletes never had a chance. No matter how well they jumped and ran and rowed, they could never dominate these Summer Games. The city won the Games. The people of Catalonia won the Games. Always, there were the fantastic spires of Sagrada Familia shimmering in the background, or the fountains of Montjuïc, or the towers of Tibidabo in the distance.'[3] Barcelona had staged a globally televised, grand and operatic games, in which it made itself the leading character. What, just a decade earlier, had been a post-industrial backwater, a Mediterranean rustbelt port, was reinvented for the rest of the world as a cultural centre, an architectural jewel, a leading tourist destination

The Empire Strikes Back, Rome 1960. The Ethiopian Abebe Bikila wins the marathon beneath the Arch of Constantine.

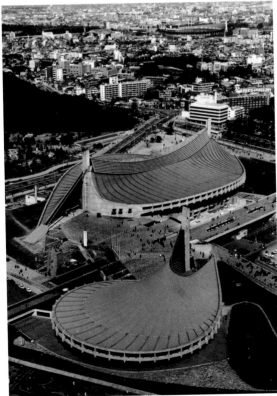

The Science Fiction Olympics, Tokyo 1964. Tange Kenzo's Yoyogi National Gymnasium.

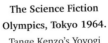

The Image Remains, Mexico 1968.

Left. Tommie Smith (centre) and John Carlos give the black power salute supported by Australian Peter Norman.

Above. Bob Beamon jumps 8.9 m and off the scale.

Spectacle vs Anti-Spectacle, Munich 1972, Los Angeles 1984.

Above. Armed police, live on German television, drop onto the roof above the apartments where the Israeli Olympic team are being held hostage.

Below. Lionel Richie takes fiesta to the closing ceremony.

Perfection, Montreal 1976. Rumanian teenager Nadia Comăneci on the beam
– the first ever performance to be awarded a perfect score of 10.

For Love of Brand and Country, Barcelona 1992.

Above. The Dream Team, (*left to right*) Larry Bird, Scottie Pippin, Michael Jordan, Clyde Drexler, Karl Malone, receive their gold medals.

Below. The view from the Montjuic Aquatics Complex.

Welcome Home, Athens 2004.

Above. The Hellinikon Olympic canoe and kayak centre, ten years after the games.

Below. The Olympic Swimming Complex remains unused to this day.

The Anti-Olympics, Vancouver 2010 and Rio 2016.

Above. A man protests near the newly opened Olympic tent village in downtown Vancouver.

Below. Another family home in Villa Autodromo is demolished, under guard, to make way for the Olympic Park.

and an exemplar of modern high-density urbanism. Five specially constructed camera towers allowed global broadcasters twenty-four/seven access to beautifully framed shots of the city's skyline.[4] The aquatics complex looked out from Montjuïc across the entire cityscape. The Olympic village sat at the centre of a gleaming redeveloped docklands, in touching distance of pristine urban beaches. With an eye to the middle-brow millions of the Western world, the organizers commissioned the pop-operatic 'Barcelona' from Queen's frontman, Freddie Mercury, and Spanish diva, Montserrat Caballé. Mercury was dead by the time the games came around, but they played the song anyway at the start of the opening ceremony, the perfect soundtrack for a shameless tourist travelogue of the city. The same target market was being wooed at the closing ceremony with Andrew Lloyd Webber's Hispanic kitsch 'Amigos Para Siempre', sung by Sarah Brightman and José Carreras.

It worked. In the years since the games, Barcelona has become one of the world's leading tourist and conferencing destinations, experiencing visitor growth so large that the city is now beginning to take measures to discourage any more. Its reputation amongst architects, planners and Olympic bid committees rose even faster. In 1999, RIBA awarded its Gold Medal prizes to the entire city. No subsequent Olympics bid book was complete without reference to the Barcelona model and its promise of urban transformation.

However, while Vescey's take on the games, and the city's subsequent plaudits all ring true, they are only part of the story. Contrary to the ruling wisdom, Barcelona, rather than creating a model of Olympic urbanism that others could follow, was actually the product of an almost unique set of circumstances that may well be unrepeatable. Vecsey and the global audience may have been focusing on the city, but, in Spain itself, things looked very different. Beneath a very thin veneer of internationally orientated imagery, Barcelona 1992 was actually a burning crucible of Spanish cultural and political conflict.[5]

In some ways, it is obvious Barcelona had to be a one-off. It really was an undiscovered jewel. How many other cities could claim an artistic heritage that included Miro, Picasso and Gaudi? But Barcelona's uniqueness was also political. Contrary to almost every other Olympic urban intervention, Barcelona's grew from a very long-term programme of urban development. The games was a crowning achievement, not a catalyst. Barcelona's development was also distinguished by a model of urbanism that privileged public space over private space, and public transport over private transport. It eschewed showy architecture, preferring fabulous restorations, paid attention to the micro details of streets and squares, shade and shrubbery, and prioritized liveability over profitability.[6] Both aspects of the Barcelona model were secured by the Catalan Socialist mayors, Narcís Serra and Pasqual Maragall, who ran the city for two decades from the late 1970s.

Equally rarely, the Barcelona games were funded and staged at a moment when all three levels of government, despite being run by different parties, had good reason to cooperate.[7] For the city of Barcelona, the games were the logical conclusion of its development programme and concentrated effort to shift the city from an industrial to a service- and tourist-led economy. The Spanish socialist government of Prime Minister Felipe González saw the games as one of a series of grand projects designed to fix the image of the new Spain – modern, democratic, high tech – in the global eye. Nineteen ninety-two had been designated by Madrid as 'The Year of Spain', and would also see Seville host the World Expo, and the country's first high-speed train routes open. Finally, the Catalan government, known as the Generalitat and run by Jordi Pujol and the conservative nationalists of Convergència i Unió, looked to the Olympics as a way of projecting Catalonia outside of Spain and testing its place inside the new Spain.

Such a range of support was just as well, because Barcelona did not come cheap. In fact, it was probably the most expensive games since Tokyo 1964. Depending on what one counted, the complete renovation of Barcelona's airport, docklands and beaches, sewage networks and metro systems, ring roads, main plaza and green spaces cost the best part of $5 billion. Actual Olympic sporting facilities were just a fraction of this, with the organizers making good use of buildings left over from the 1929 world fair, like the Palau de la Metallúrgia; the facilities of the city's big sports clubs, FC Barcelona and Espanyol; new venues built long in advance of the games, like the velodrome; and allowed just the odd flourish, like Santiago Calatrava's communications tower outside the Montjuïc Olympic stadium.

Support was not, however, universal. The Spanish state and the games organizers rightly anticipated attacks on the Olympics from three directions: ETA, the armed wing of Basque separatists; Terra Lliure, an armed Marxist-nationalist cell in Catalonia; and the left-wing GRAPO (Grupos de Resistencia Antifascista Primero de Octubre). The latter two mounted a series of operations in the late 1980s and early 1990s against Olympic targets, like banks sponsoring the games, but were subject to major round-ups and arrests before the games began. ETA, under sustained pressure from the Spanish security services, attempted to disrupt the electricity supply for the opening ceremony, an action thwarted by the police and blacked out by the press. Ultimately, the biggest threat to the games came from much more mainstream Catalan nationalism. In 1989, in a taste of things to come, the crowd booed both King Juan Carlos and the Spanish team at the re-inauguration of the Olympic stadium in Montjuïc. In late 1991 and early 1992, a loose coalition of groups concerned with the Catalan dimension to the Barcelona games began to make their voices heard.* Over an increasingly volatile few months, the demands came thick and fast. At the most radical end of the spectrum, there were calls for a separate Catalan team to be recognized by the IOC and included in the games as the hosts. Across the board, there was an insistence that key national symbols – the flag, or *senyera*, the anthem, 'Els Segadors', the national dance, the *sardana*, and the Catalan language itself – should not only be included in the ceremonial aspects of the games, but accorded the correct status, especially by comparison to Spain itself. At the same time, there were calls for a boycott of the games, huge demonstrations at Olympic venues and threats to flood the stadiums with militants and banners.

In early June, the games' organizers, Mayor Maragall and Jordi Pujol, declared a Paz Olimpica – an agreement on most of the key ceremonial demands of the nationalists, backed by the historic

---

* They included: the Catalan Olympic Committee (COC), which had been calling for the independent participation of a Catalan team at the Barcelona and future Olympic Games; Òmnium Cultural, the leading Catalan language organization; a more radical newcomer in the field, La Crida a la Solidaritat; Accio Olímpica, a Catalan youth cultural group backed by the moderate nationalists in the Convergència i Unió party; and Esquerra Republicana de Catalunya (ERC), a party at the more radical separatist end of Catalan nationalism, then with significant representation in the Catalan Parliament.

announcement that national television would for the first time broadcast the games in Catalan as well as Spanish.

Significant as these announcements had been, the Paz Olimpica failed to satisfy the more radical nationalists, who, true to their word, took their protests to the ceremony held to welcome the arrival of the Olympic flame from Olympia. The torch was to land on a beach by the ancient ruins of Empúries, a small Catalan town founded by ancient Greek colonists in the sixth century BCE. In actual fact, it would take at least another millennium and a half for Catalonia to emerge in any form, but no matter. When the flame was finally handed over, a militant rushed the stage and draped a 'Freedom for Catalonia' banner around the plinth on which it rested. Spanish TV edited the incident out of its coverage, but the banner remained there for the rest of the ceremony and appeared on the front pages of the nation's newspapers. When Javier Solana, the socialist minister of education in the national government, rose and spoke in Spanish, he was drowned out by booing.

Over the next nine days, as the torch relay wound its way around Catalonia, it was preceded by a caravan of leafleters, flag wavers and protestors. In the nationalist stronghold of Banyoles – venue of the Olympic rowing – 400 police were stationed there for the duration of the relay. In Montserrat, both the bishop and Mayor Maragall were drowned out by *independencia* chants. With the departure of the torch to the rest of Spain, there was a lowering of the rhetorical temperature, and the Paz Olimpica held. The nationalists, recognizing that actually disrupting the Olympics might prove very counterproductive, pulled back and publicly agreed not to actively intervene in the games themselves. The conflict over identity moved on to the balconies of the city's innumerable apartments. The Olympic torch returned to a city simply festooned with flags. The overwhelming presence was the *senyera*. Sometimes it hung alone; sometimes it was amended with more radical separatist slogans; often it was accompanied by the flag of the city of Barcelona itself. Representing the city's many internal migrants, it could have been seen flying alongside the flag of another Spanish region. In a minority of cases, one might have seen it with a Spanish flag, though few dared to fly this alone.

If the displays of flags on Barcelona's balconies were a rough plebiscite on the political identities of its citizens, the ceremonial dimensions to the games themselves were a guide to the complex conflicts and alliances of Spanish politics. The Basques, Catalans and others were being offered an accord guaranteeing their cultural and linguistic status and entrenching the devolution of powers to regional assemblies in the constitution. Thus, Catalonia was not permitted its own team, or accorded any special place in the parade of nations or within the Spanish team itself, but, for those who knew what they were listening to, the opening ceremony began on an unmistakably Catalan note; Carlos Santos' Olympic fanfare was played on the reedy *tenora*, an instrument usually heard accompanying Catalonia's national dance, the *sardana*. In the opening minutes of the ceremony, the Catalan flag and the Catalan anthem were accorded the same status as their Spanish counterparts. At the closing ceremony, on every Olympic venue and all public buildings within the city, the *senyera* flew alongside the flags of Spain, Barcelona, the European Union and the IOC. Inside the venues, despite an official ban, nationalist militants organized to display flags and banners, where possible, in direct view of the cameras. For the duration of the games, Catalan, alongside Spanish, English and French, was an official Olympic language, given pre-eminence in what became interminably long stadium announcements and text-heavy signage. When King Juan Carlos stood to declare the games open, he began in Catalan: 'Benvinguts tots a Barcelona – welcome, everyone, to Barcelona'. The rest of his speech was lost to the wild applause of the crowd. The delicate political balancing act was completed by foregrounding less divisive regional identities that all sides could accept, like Barcelona as a Mediterranean and, above all, a European city.

For on the issue of the European Community alone, Spain's rival forces could agree. Centrists of left and right saw it as an essential stabilizing force in Spain's transition to democracy, the Basques and Catalans looked to it as a political umbrella under which their small nations might one day shelter, while the poor and peripheral regions of Castilian Spain eyed its agricultural subsidies and structural funds. Europe looked to the Barcelona Olympics for its own purposes, the Commission budgeting for $16 million worth of Olympic-associated advertis-ing and promotional work. European Commission president Jacques Delors was accorded the status of a head of state by the Olympic protocol committee, and Beethoven's 'Ode to Joy', now established as the European anthem, was sung in Catalan, Spanish and German. At the climax of the parade of nations, the athletes were surrounded by twelve enormous human pyramids, known in Catalan as *castles de xiquets*, each representing one of the then dozen members of the European Union. The crowd turned on the blue or gold torches, left on their seats, to make a stadium-wide European flag, echoing the blue and gold star fireworks that closed the ceremony.

All very well for the high brow, but this was the Spain of *Hola!* – home of the most fawning form of celebrity journalism yet invented. In this regard, the games turned out to be one long and fantastically successful photo shoot for King Juan Carlos and the royal family. Despite the fearsome republican currents in Catalonia, and his status as Franco's designated successor as head of state, his role in foiling the 1981 right-wing coup and his steadfast commitment to democratization had endeared him to much of the public. With his unprecedented, electric use of Catalan in the opening ceremony, the king became the kind of national symbol that all but the most incorrigible separatists could stomach. The rest of the royal family gave able support. Princess Elena obligingly cried when her brother, Prince Felipe, carried the national flag at the head of the Spanish team. The king's overt, ecstatic public celebration of Fermín Cacho's unlikely victory in the men's 1,500 metres ensured his demotic credentials. There were more celebrations as Spain won an unprecedented thirteen golds out of a total of twenty-two medals, and on every occasion the champions would take their bows wrapped in both the Spanish flag and the flag of their home region. Most significantly of all, athletes who had expressed strong Catalan identities before the games, like the outspoken Barcelona midfielder, Pep Guardiola, and Eli Maragall of the Spanish women's hockey team, celebrated their golds draped in the Spanish and Catalan flags. Spain's victory in the men's football tournament, beating Poland 3–2 with a final-minute winner, was all the more amazing for being staged in Barcelona's Camp Nou. Under Franco, the stadium had been the single most important gathering place in which Catalans could express resistance to the suppression of the language and culture, and the crude authoritarianism of his regime. Now Spanish flags were flown in the stands and Spanish chants rang out.

One set of athletes in Barcelona stamped themselves and their brand on the games with an extravagant theatricality every bit as compelling as the city's urban drama: the Dream Team.[8] Often unremarked upon, Barcelona was the first games played under Samaranch's revised Olympic charter that no longer distinguished between amateurs and professionals. With the door now open and the NBA eager to globalize the game by showcasing the very best, the 1992 US men's national basketball team, to use its official title, was the first to draw on the stars of the NBA rather than the best of the college kids. That it was the best basketball team in the world, the most talented ever, and that it was going to win the gold medal were never in question: it was the manner of the triumph, and the unprecedented media fever it was able to generate, that truly marked it out. Dream Team it may have been, but it was composed of the leading individual stars that had been at the heart of the NBA's rise from marginality in the 1960s and 1970s to mainstream entertainment in the 1980s and 1990s, with the kind of revenue stream to match. Larry Bird and Magic Johnson, the team captain, were the white/black, Boston/Los Angeles, Celtics/Lakers match-up that had defined the league in the 1980s, and they were joined by the cream of the crop from the 1990s – above all, Michael Jordan, already established as the game's greatest player and most fearsome commercial asset. This was the America of 'shock and awe', the single superpower with the technology and resources to take on anyone in any combination and win.[9] As Charles Barkley said before the team's first match, 'I don't know much about Angola, but I know they're in trouble.' This was the America of triumphant capitalism, whose hyper-commercial sports machine, long excluded from the games, would now demonstrate its effortless superiority above all to the vanquished forces of socialism in the form of state-supported basketball. This was the America of galactic stardom, of individuals who, through the alchemy of advertising and branding, were turned into superhumans, heroes and villains. The Dream Team offered more stories, more photo opportunities and more angles than any other Olympic circus: the Johnson–Jordan struggle for generational supremacy; the quiet fuming of Clyde Drexler; Charles Barkley, the ugly American on the field and the pussy cat amongst the people on Las Ramblas; and, of course, the love of brand and their loyalty to sponsors. The team received their gold medals in official Reebok kit, but Michael Jordan, son of Nike, took to the rostrum with an American flag pinned across its logo.

FOUR

For the people of Atlanta, the XXVIth Olympiad stands over the future like the cloud-capped peak of Mount Olympus. It is a dream to be grasped, a thought to be scaled, a moment to be embraced. As a dream, it has drawn the city together in a bond of desire far greater than anything before.[1]

There had been disingenuous Olympic visions before, the cosmopolitan promise of sport had been pressed into the service of narrow-minded ideologies and nationalisms, but if their rhetoric had been metaphorically and ethically empty, they lacked no shortage of content. Atlanta trumped them all in its utter vacuity. In the official mythology of the games, Billy Payne, a well-connected Atlantan lawyer, lay sleepless in his bed, glowing with communitarian ecstasy; he had just concluded a successful fundraising campaign to buy an organ for his church in suburban Dunwoody. Rising from his bed, he told his wife, 'We need to find another cause to build this experience again,' and that cause was bringing the Olympic Games to Atlanta.[2] Billy's gang of high-end lawyers, marketers, corporate executives and professional party-throwers went on the road with their dream and the biggest hospitality budget of any bid committee yet. They certainly knew how to do largesse. As Sinan Erdem, an IOC member from Turkey, recalled of his trip to the city, 'We went to our rooms and there was luggage when we got there. And it was mine!'[3] They also knew how to play politics. The one thing that anyone outside of the United States might know about Atlanta, and that might work in their favour, was that it had served as the base for Martin Luther King and the civil-rights struggle. Thus, their key recruit to the bid was Atlanta's ex-mayor, Andrew Young. As a lieutenant of Martin Luther King at the height of the civil-rights struggle, and as the Carter administration's ambassador to the UN, he had the kind of kudos and networks that brought a lot of African and developing-world votes Atlanta's way. As to what would be achieved, which dream would be realized, Young couldn't quite nail it down; indeed, he seemed to subcontract the issue to the almighty: 'Could it be that Atlanta could play a special role in the plan of God?'[4]

Despite this kind of backing, the city was never the favourite to land the 1996 centennial games. Athens, host in 1896, was the obvious symbolic choice, but many on the IOC could see that its urban and sporting infrastructure was never going to be ready in time. Toronto, fatally weakened by the scale and arguments of its anti-Olympic movement, fell out of the penultimate round of voting, and its voters, already inclined to North America, gave their votes to Atlanta over Athens.

Largesse and luck aside, Joel Babbit, once Atlanta's chief of marketing, asked, 'How did we get the Olympics?' and answered himself: 'Confidence and salesmanship. After all, it's not like we had great architecture and the Mediterranean.'[5] A more cynical though clear-eyed observer thought that the bid committee did this by coming up with 'The biggest lie they could possibly think of, and ran around the world telling everybody about it until it became true.'[6]

To be fair, Payne and his Olympian boosters ran with two very questionable ideas. First, that Atlanta was a global city, internationally connected and ready to put on the spectacular. In fact, much of Atlanta's infrastructure – its freeways, trains and sewers – were woefully inadequate when set against the gigantic growth of the city. Atlanta's global footprint hinged on having a busy international airport hub and being the headquarters to the world's most global brand, the pioneer of multinational corporate operations, Coca-Cola, and the new player in television and global news, Ted Turner's CNN. In themselves, these were not inconsequential assets, but, in almost every other way, Atlanta remained a deeply provincial second-tier city. That, in a sense, was the core of their second dubious proposition: that Atlanta was the capital of the new South. In this version of the story, Atlanta was not only economically and demographically the most dynamic city in the most dynamic region in the United States, but it was also the fulfilment of its most famous son's dream, an exemplar of the racial equality and entrenched civil rights envisaged by Martin Luther King before his assassination in 1968. But, scratch the surface of this Atlanta, and its notion of Southernness was little more than good manners, hospitality and hot cornbread. Take a look at the geographical and economic realities of the new Atlanta and weep.

Atlanta was certainly not Birmingham, Alabama, but it was hardly a city of racial harmony.[7] The integration of public housing and schooling, accompanied by so much rancour and violence in much of the South, was achieved relatively peacefully in Atlanta, if only because anything else was deemed too disruptive to the business of making money. In this, at least, Atlanta lived up to its self-perception as 'the city too busy to hate'. However, these changes were accompanied by a profound economic and geographical reconfiguration of the city that made segregation a de facto rather than a de jure reality. Two decades of rapid economic growth had been almost entirely concentrated in Atlanta's suburbs and satellite cities. The persisting demographic differences between city and suburbs were made sharper by white flight and the concentration of the poor and the homeless, overwhelmingly African Americans, in the city of Atlanta itself, where the poverty rate was touching 60 per cent and the homicide rate was the second highest in the nation. Here, the route of interstate 85 and other major roads was designed to separate predominantly black and predominantly white neighbourhoods, a reality confirmed by the practice of giving the same avenue a different name, depending on which ethnic zone it was passing through. Public housing was very precisely located in existing black neighbourhoods, especially in the south of the city. The white north-east, by contrast, remained a project-free zone. While the civil-rights movement and the demographic shifts helped create a black democratic majority at city hall, politicians' leverage was limited, and their tax base progressively moved out to the suburbs. The redevelopment that did occur in the 1970s and 1980s, led by the longstanding commercial and property elites of the city, was overwhelmingly showpiece and fortress architecture. Atlanta built itself an off-the-shelf signature skyline of postmodern pedimented skyscrapers, soaring atria and high walls of impenetrable mirrored glass. On the ground, what could be held was secured by combined whole-block developments and sealed shopping complexes that turned their face to the street, serviced by underground car parks and air-conditioned walkways. Between them lay the shack cities, scrapyards, parking lots and no-go areas, the fragmenting neigbourhoods in terminal decline and the enclaves of public housing, left to physically and spiritually rot.

The geography of poverty and exclusion was tangible physical evidence of how little had changed since the civil-rights movement, and three symbolic conflicts at the Atlanta games reinforced this impression. First was the choice of Stone Mountain Park to host the tennis, archery and cycling, a place venerated by many as the site of the Ku Klux Klan's second incarnation in 1915, and offering perfect views of the park's dominant feature, a gigantic carved bas-relief of Confederate president Jefferson Davis and Generals Robert E. Lee and Thomas J. 'Stonewall' Jackson. More contentious was the presence of the Georgia state flag, which was expected to hang at every Olympic venue. Up until 1956, it had featured the original Confederate stars and bars design, but, in a deliberate riposte to the rising tides of the civil-rights movement, the legislature had changed it to incorporate the battle flag of the Confederacy – the blue-starred saltire of Dixie. The local chapter of the NAACP were vociferous in arguing that honouring the Confederacy and its army was hardly suitable for the cosmopolitan festival of a united humanity. Moves to change the flag gathered support amongst business leaders; the state governor, Zell Miller, wanted to remove the cross, and protest surrounded the flag's use at the Atlanta Super Bowl in 1994, but the voting public remained against, and the flag flew throughout the games.[8] Perhaps the most telling event of all was the fate of the two art festivals staged alongside the games. 'Rings: Five Passions in World Art' was put on at the High Museum of Art in the centre of the city, notable only for the paucity of its collection and its unadventurous tastes, shipping in Rodin's *The Kiss*, Mattisse's *The Dancer* and an El Greco from the Prado in Madrid. On the south side of town, in an area that almost no Olympic visitor would have wandered into, was 'Souls Grown Deep', a path-breaking display of over 500 works of vernacular or outsider African-American art. Originally scheduled for the High, it was effectively banished to City Hall East on the campus of Emory University, disconnected from the Olympic transport network and made virtually invisible in the organizers' PR.[9]

It was in this intellectual and cultural vacuum that the newly established organizing committee, Atlanta city council and the city's Chamber of Commerce sat down to flesh out Billy's dream, or at least agree on the games' slogan. A huge and expensive search came up with alternatives so unbelievably anodyne – 'Atlanta: A Great Place to Live and Work' and 'Atlanta: A City of Immense Pride' – that they actually canvassed opinion on some of the wilder haikus that the general public had sent in: 'Atlanta: An Island in a Sea of Rednecks' and 'Atlanta and the World. Yes!' Five years after they began, the best the organizers could do was, 'Atlanta: Come Celebrate Our Dream', and no one was any closer to knowing what that dream was.

Atlanta's mascot proved equally depthless. 'Whatizit' debuted at the closing ceremony of the 1992 Barcelona games.[10] Unlike any prior Olympic mascot, it was neither human nor animal, and bore not the slightest reference to Atlanta or the South, but was a demented blue, anthropomorphized foam earplug – the kind of meaningless cipher routinely created by the hyper-commercial graphic studios of American advertising and animation. Sent back to the drawing board, Whatizit was told to work out and lose some pounds. Thinner, more athletic and with longer limbs, it got the cosmetic treatment too, acquiring a nose and losing the lightning-bolt eyebrows and its scary bottom row of teeth, before being relaunched on the world as 'Izzy'. Matt Groening, creator of *The Simpsons*, thought it 'a bad marriage of the Pillsbury Doughboy and the ugliest California Raisin.' *Time* was blunter, describing it as 'A sperm in sneakers.' There was no shortage of Izzy kitsch in the games' merchandizing zones, but curiously there were insufficient life-size suits to see him promenade much at the venues.

Payne and his friends had promised an Olympic Games funded entirely by the private sector: a modernized version of Los Angeles 1984, but with turbocharged levels of sponsorship and television money. As with all neoliberal fantasies, the project actually rested on the massive and multifaceted involvement of every level of the American state, the short-circuiting of institutions of democratic control, the use of force, where necessary, and all on terms unambiguously favourable to a tiny slice of private and already-powerful interests. The press might have lampooned the games' marketing, but on the central questions of finance and development, they were entirely supine. The only challenge to the organizers came from a small part of organized labour, who demonstrated over the committee's insistence on non-union construction sites, and activists in the social-housing sector, who published alternative guides to Atlanta, written by an anti-Olympic mascot called Spoilsport. Neither got much of a hearing in the press or on the committees. By contrast, the construction industry, which was very well represented on the various bodies involved with the games, was heard. Atlanta '96 was built by day-labourers, barely making the minimum wage, most of them recent Hispanic arrivals, many of them illegal; margins remained good, wages low, working conditions poor and local unions weak.

Poor Atlantans didn't see much of the more than half a billion dollars of public money that was spent on the games by the state of Georgia, the federal government and the city of Atlanta and the various suburban counties that staged events. Neither the $250 million found for an upgrade of the international airport, nor the $112 million of public money allocated to higher education that the Board of Regents in charge of the Georgia state university system were prevailed upon to spend building the Olympic village was likely to benefit them. The city's World Congress Centre, owned by the state of Georgia, was given a very expensive makeover. Millions were found to improve the facilities at the very upscale Gainesville Country Club, where the rowing competitions were to be held. By contrast, the adjoining city of Newton, which lay on the other side of the interstate freeway and was overwhelmingly African American, received nothing.

The city of Atlanta itself had by now been almost entirely cut out of the picture. With the Atlanta organizers committed by law to spending, as the colloquialism went, 'nothing outside the fence', Olympic monies were entirely corralled in the venues and official spaces alone. So much for trickle-down economics. The city's tiny Olympic development agency, CODA, was so short of cash to support renewal and rehousing in the low-income neighbourhoods of central Atlanta that it invited American Express to become the city's credit card, a ploy to extract $2 million from the games' official credit-card sponsors, Visa. The search for funds was so desperate that the mayor seriously contemplated launching a mile-long balloon into geostationary orbit over the city to serve as a vast Olympic billboard. In the final reckoning, CODA's biggest project, paid for by the federal government, was the $12 million spent on smartening up the street-scapes of the Martin Luther King historic site, a few miles east of the main Olympic sites, but, for the duration of the games, effectively in another world.

Atlanta was not the first Olympic city to declare war on its homeless citizens or to try to hide its shack cities. Tramps and rough sleepers had been part of the mix expelled from downtown Berlin, Tokyo and Moscow, along with gangsters, drug addicts and prostitutes. Mexico City had told its poor to paint their shacks in blocks of psychedelic colour. Seoul, on a grander scale than anyone hitherto, had combined Olympic preparations with a gigantic state-led assault on temporary and low-income housing in the inner city. Atlanta did both. Soon after the city had won the bid, Atlanta's soup kitchens started reporting regular and inexplicable drop-offs in client numbers, eventually realizing that they always immediately preceded IOC visits to the city. Some homeless people were locked up, some were scared off, and some were put on the bus. A partnership between the police, city hall and an NGO called Project Homeward Bound supplied homeless Atlantans with one-way bus tickets to anywhere else in the country they could plausibly claim a bed or find family members. Complaints to city hall flooded in from municipalities across the South where this human flotsam washed up. Simultaneously, a raft of the most punitive and specific homeless ordinances was issued by the city government. It became a criminal offence to urinate in public, camp in the city centre and panhandle. Not content with preventing them pissing, sleeping and begging, it also became an offence for the homeless to recline in a public place, to be in a car park without a car, and to loiter anywhere. At one point, the council contemplated criminalizing the removal of an object from a trash can, but settled for outlawing blocking a sidewalk, being in an abandoned building and spitting. Equipped with this kind of legislative armoury, Atlanta's police repeatedly swept downtown, mass producing arrest-and-charge dockets already stamped, 'African American. Male. Homeless.' Towards the end of the process, when the organizers actually descended to street-level themselves, they were amazed and alarmed to discover that the depopulated spaces of downtown were a desert, deliberately engineered to lack shade, entirely bereft of water fountains. A local tycoon donated nearly $2 million to install both for the games on a purely temporary basis. Between 1990 and 1996, 30,000 people were evicted or removed from the Olympic Ring, the small zone around downtown where most of the games facilities were to be concentrated.

The Olympic stadium itself, just south of downtown, was a $209 million gift to Ted Turner's Atlanta Braves. The Olympic organizing committee furnished the tycoon and his franchise with total control over the stadium, its naming rights, concessions and sky boxes. The city threw in 10,000 parking spaces, carved out of what was left of the Summerhill neighbourhood. They also paid for the conversion of the elliptical Olympic stadium into a characteristic baseball horse-shoe, and covered the demolition of the old Fulton County stadium that the Braves had previously occupied. It was a deal so brazen that even the disinterested watchdogs of MAOGA, the Metropolitan Atlanta Olympic Games Authority, had a problem. In the only serious organized opposition to the games to come from anywhere near mainstream Atlanta, Martin Luther King III, son of the civil-rights leader, led black political communities in a challenge to Olympic organizers, and squeezed some small concessions from them: cutting back on the city's largesse to the Braves, appointing more minorities to the organizing committee's workforce and quietly abandoning plans to showcase golf as an Olympic demonstration sport at the notoriously all-white Augusta club, home of the US Masters.

A different fate awaited three public-housing projects right at the heart of the Olympic Ring. Techwood, the oldest social housing in the United States, and the Clark Howell and East Lake Meadows homes were strategically positioned between Coca-Cola's head-quarters, the Georgia Dome and Georgia Tech University, and the organizers earmarked much of the land for the Olympic village. All three estates, while poor and riddled by long-term neglect from city hall, remained viable communities, with low turnover and high occupancy rates, but while they and a few allies in the social-housing movement made the case for renovation and restoration, the Olympic committee and the Atlanta Housing Authority ran rings around them. The AHA, in particular, was instrumental in ratcheting up the pressure on tenants, mixing financial inducements and offers of public housing at some considerable distance with the stick of zealous measures to punish infractions and late rents, to push people out. Here, as with developments around the other Olympic venues, redevelopment included just a handful of town houses, almost none of them within the financial reach of the neighbourhoods displaced. In the final reckoning, less than 7 per cent of public-housing tenants in the Olympic Ring were rehoused there.

All of this still left Techwood Park. It was a few dozen blocks at the very heart of the Olympic Ring, referred to as the 'pit' or the 'void' by the reptilian real-estate business, who for years had been looking at ways of removing it. Techwood Park was actually a hive of activity. It housed dozens of small businesses and yard-based operations. It also contained 10 per cent of Atlanta's homeless shelters. Although clearly run down, it was, by the city's standards, in good shape, with over 85 per cent of its building stock in a reasonable order of repair; but scrap yards and doss houses are not the stuff that dreams or high property-values are made of. Billy Payne, in another concocted moment of philanthropic reverie, is credited with the idea that Techwood should be bulldozed and rebuilt as the Centennial Olympic Park; funded by philanthropy, it would serve as the physical hub of the games themselves and then be passed on as a legacy of precious green space to the city. Once again, the city of Atlanta was bypassed. Payne checked in with Governor Miller and Coca-Cola chairman Robert Goizueta, who gave their blessing. Avoiding all the city's planning and zoning agencies, the state of Georgia gave its own World Congress Centre, adjacent to Techwood Park, the power to condemn buildings and buy up the land. Coca-Cola stepped up and bought a piece of the action, earmarking it for a permanent corporate theme park. The $50 million required to make the Centennial Olympic Park happen was to come from the city's main philanthropic body, the Woodruff Foundation, the Atlanta Chamber of Commerce and the public, who, at thirty-five dollars a pop, were invited to buy two million commemorative bricks to be used in its construction. Just in case anyone was under the illusion that the space would function like a traditional public park, the games' security chief put them right. There would be no financial charge to get in, but 'we will establish conditions of admission'. A fence was to be erected on its perimeter to 'control the crowds and keep out the riff-raff'. Takers for a place in urban philanthropic history were thin on the ground, and Home Depot struggled to sell even a fraction of the bricks. The solution was to sell the space itself. Centennial Park was parcelled out in multimillion-dollar bundles to the AT&T Olympic Global Village, Swatch's enormous Swatchtower, General Motors' City of Motion, McDonald's and, largest of all, the Coca-Cola Amusement Park.

During the games, the park handled up to 70,000 people at a time, hundreds of thousands over a whole day. An entire parallel real-estate market emerged for camera positions on buildings that afforded an aerial view of the place. George Vecsey in the *New York*

Times thought it just tawdry: 'Centennial Park seemed to be a jumble of metal and stone, plastic and neon, an old pecan tree and a few patches of grass, chain-link fence and tarps on the edges, tents and signs bearing the names of corporate sponsors . . . Stuckey's. That's what it reminds me of, the old chain of stores that sprung up alongside the highways, where you could get gas, buy a hot dog and candy plus stock up on concrete lawn statues and souvenir mugs and gaudy T-shirts.'[11]

But this is to underestimate Centennial Park in both its complexity and its pathologies. No mere afterthought or pop-up, it had been a strategic act of occupation, erasing Techwood Park and its population while securing the land values of its neighbours. Always imagined as a simulacrum of the public park and public space, it emerged in its Olympic guise as a garish collage of theme park, commercial exhibition and state agricultural fair. There was a memorial statue of Baron de Coubertin, an acre of air-conditioned official Olympic gift shopping, six acres for the sponsors' village, laser shows from General Motors, where the Olympic centenary was paired with a hundred years of the automobile, Olympic history the Coke way in the Coke Olympic museum and, most popular of all, the dancing Olympic-ring water-fountain show, a straight take on the aesthetics of the Vegas strip. It was, as one Atlantan critic stated, 'A realm in which the boundaries between advertisement, entertainment and education have been permanently effaced by a more profound pecuniary truth.'[12]

Then, early in the morning on 27 July, three ugly pipe-bombs exploded, planted just hours earlier by a home-grown libertarian terrorist, Eric Rudolph, a man with a track record of attacks on abortion clinics and a lesbian nightclub. One woman died when a nail penetrated her skull, a Turkish cameraman had a heart attack and 111 others were wounded, but the show went on. Three days later, Centennial Park marked the tragedy, thanked the sponsors and reopened for business.

Beyond the park, the size and number of advertising hoardings in the city, already the highest per capita in the US, grew. New city ordinances allowed downtown skyscrapers to be transformed into vertical advertisements. Local licences for product sales and concession spaces were multiplied, particularly as the committee had overestimated the price it could command for other forms of sponsorship. Consequently, the city's main shopping streets and the

pedestrianized routes into the Olympic venues were simply overflowing with concession stalls of every conceivable kind.

Once the games began, Atlanta's already fragile transport system
began to melt. Rejecting the idea of any serious investment in the
city metro system (despite the availability of 90 per cent federal
funding), the organizers and the state government preferred to invest
in management speak, a computer-controlled traffic system that
didn't work and 3,000 buses, donated from the rest of the country,
to do the job. With over 10 per cent of the drivers in the Olympic
fleets coming from out of town, one might have expected the organizers to pay special attention to their knowledge of local routes and
crystal-clear signage, but here was precisely the kind of place where
the pin-sharp business people of Atlanta liked to make smart savings.
Not surprisingly, every day brought stories of transport disasters:
buses, athletes and journalists that had taken the wrong turn, gone
to the wrong venue or, most disastrously for the Georgian judoka,
David Khakhaleishvili, gone round in circles. Khakhaleishvili was
disqualified from defending the title he had won in 1992 because he
was late for a weigh-in held just one mile from the Olympic village.
IBM's much trumpeted 'Info 96' information and record system persistently broke down, with events and times being reported so late
that it acquired the nickname 'Info 97'.

More than ever, it was almost impossible, despite its ubiquity on
screens of every kind, to concentrate on the sport, to really see the
extraordinary athletic performances that were going on. Tony Kornheiser was just one of many correspondents, domestic and foreign,
who signed off by hardly mentioning them: 'When I close my eyes
and picture Atlanta, I see a giant Miller Lite can or a giant Bud
can . . . And I'll hear the familiar strains of "Macarena" wafting from
the beer gardens . . . And I'll reflect on . . . the crush of people in
Centennial Park waiting in line in the heat for hours to get into
"The Super Store"'.[13] In the end, a single athlete, if only for fleeting moments, banished the visual and ethical chaos of the Atlanta
games. Erica Good called it right: 'To paraphrase Popeye, we are
what we are. Terrorists, we've got 'em. Chrome-plated pickup trucks
filled with cheerleaders, those too. Bad coffee – plenty of it. Commercialism that threatens to overwhelm any remaining vestige of
sportsmanship? Yup . . . and Michael Johnson.'[14]

Michael Johnson was the hyper-rational, hyper-commercial,

ramrod-straight king of US athletics. He became the first man to win gold in both the 200 metres and the 400 metres, and set new world records in both. In fact, in the 200 metres, he smashed the world record with his unorthodox but brilliant upright stance, short stride and pumping-piston arm action, and, through it all, his TV-friendly, shining gold Nike sneakers tore up the track. Yet, even then, there was a relentless perfectionism about Johnson. At the very top of the world, he was curiously unsatisfied: 'I always knew that I could run faster than I ran. I spent my entire career trying to run a flawless race – which is rare for anyone. I ran out of career time before I achieved my perfect race.' Reviewing his amazing 200-metre final, Johnson dryly noted that his fourth step was a stumble and that he slowed in the final metres.

In the lead-up to the closing ceremony, local radio called for the crowd to chant 'Best ever! Best ever!' prior to President Samaranch's closing speech, the accolade he had accorded the previous two games. Maybe they should have done, for he merely proclaimed the games 'exceptional' – a snub that was both pointed and economical. That it came from a man under whose rule the Olympics had been most systematically aligned with the forces of commercialism gave it about the same moral weight as Billy's dream.

FIVE

Sydney beat Beijing in the competition to host the 2000 games by just two votes. As would become clear later, this was predominantly a function of some very judicious gift giving, from a very well-funded vote-buying budget, but in the immediate aftermath of the IOC vote, Sydney was praised for its vote-winning vision. The city had sold itself and the country as a sporting cornucopia of sun-kissed swimmers and runners, of easy outdoor athleticism, with a special emotional relationship to the Olympic movement. Melbourne 1956 and the great Australian Olympic teams of the 1960s were flooded with sepia tint. In fact, Australian Olympic sport went into a precipitous decline after Melbourne, reaching its nadir at the 1976 Montreal games, when the country won just five medals – entirely outstripped by the state-sponsored athletes of the communist bloc and, indeed, much of the West too. The Australia bidding for the games in 2000 was not the casual amateur sporting paradise of 1956, but an altogether more professional, hard-nosed operation. Since the creation of the Australian Institute for Sport in 1981, successive governments, in pursuit of global sporting prowess, had poured money and technology into elite sporting programmes, and created a national talent identification system that looked at almost a quarter of the nation's schoolchildren.

Sydney also, in sharp contrast to its main competitor, Beijing, sold itself as clean and green. Having decided to build the new Olympic park on toxically contaminated land in the west of the city, and alert to the environmental claims of the successful Lillehammer bid for the Winter Olympics, a green approach to the games appealed to both the city's public and the IOC. The fact that Beijing's air pollution was self-evidently so awful made it all the better. Beijing also worried some, though not many, of the IOC's members because of its human-rights record. Sydney played on these fears too, offering itself as an 'unproblematic democracy', and giving the IOC a chance to stage an Olympic Games in support of reconciliation in Australia between its white majority and its indigenous minority.[1]

Melbourne 1956 might have looked like the golden age to white Australia, but, for post-war European migrants and its indigenous peoples, it was an age of marginalization and institutionalized racism. In the forty years since, Australia had managed to integrate its Greeks and Slavs, but Aboriginal Australia remained sharply separate and discontented. This fact was underlined by the 50,000 who protested on the day of Australia's bicentenary in 1988, arguing that the beginning of a genocide and land grab was nothing to celebrate, and the presentation of the Barunga Statement to Labour prime minister Bob Hawke – a document drawn up on bark by Aboriginal leaders, calling for a complete historic settlement of the issues of land, language and human rights.[2] In 1991, the federal government of Hawke's successor, Paul Keating, created the Council for Aboriginal Reconciliation, established and charged with drawing up a programme of legal reform and social change that would be completed in 2000 – the hundredth anniversary of the Australian federation and the year of the Sydney games. Keating's government went on to pass the 1993 Native Title Act and, in 1995, established the Royal Commission, Bringing Them Home, or, to give its full title, the Report of the National Inquiry into the Separation of Aboriginal and Torres Strait Islander Children from Their Families, the definitive statement of the appalling practice of separating children and their families, which, in its own words, amounted to a 'genocide'.

Aboriginal Australia divided over the relationship of reconciliation to the Olympics. More moderate opinion viewed the games as an opportunity for Australian and Aboriginal identities to be displayed as equals. Easily the most famous Aboriginal Olympian, 400-metre runner Cathy Freeman, had done just that when celebrating her gold medal at the 1994 Victoria Commonwealth games, running a victory lap draped in both the Australian and the Aboriginal flags. More radical groups continued to argue for protest and chafed at the organizers' efforts to incorporate their culture, like the Sydney bid's use of indigenous artists and musicians for the final push at the IOC's Monaco congress.

However, the whole tenor of the debate changed when Keating's Labour government fell, in 1996, to John Howard's Liberal Party, who, while never repudiating the process of reconciliation, at best never really had their heart in it. Radical Aboriginal opposition to the Sydney games was incensed by Howard's refusal to apologize for the stolen generation, and called for a boycott of the games. More moderate forces were opposed, in a position well argued by Freeman: 'Calls for an Aboriginal boycott of the Olympics frustrate me. There is no point to it . . . There is more to gain by Cathy Freeman being on the world stage representing the Aboriginal people than not being there.'[3] The majority pointed to the positive connotations of having the boomerang on the Olympic torch and a relay that began from the sacred Aboriginal site, Uluru.

If the politics of reconciliation made some kind of anti-Olympic protest at Sydney inevitable, there was no shortage of other groups who organized in the run-up to the games.[4] Amongst the most visible protests came from Rentwatchers, a campaign group keeping an eye on the baleful impact of Olympic development on the Sydney rental-property market, as well as Olympic-related evictions. They staged mock medal ceremonies in 1998 and 1999 in the central business district: landlords won the bronze for 'opportunism and greed', silver went to real-estate agents for 'ingenuity and greed' and gold to the developers for 'world-record profits in these hard times.' Drawing ideas and inspiration from the increasingly boisterous anti-globalization movement in Australia, the Anti-Olympic Alliance (AOA) brought all of these campaigns together in early 2000 – from the Red Cross to Reclaim the Streets, from Critical Mass to the Salvation Army (networked by the new *Indymedia* websites), the first time action had been organized and advertised on the internet. When the IOC coordination team made a visit to Sydney in February 2000, they were met by protesters anonymized in gorilla skins and orange boiler suits. In May, the city government and organizing committee had to rely on a significant military mobilization – 'three Black Hawk helicopters, two police launches, fifteen mounted police officers and one hundred and fifty SWAT team police'[5] – to clear 150 protestors (many of them children) from Bondi Beach, where they planned to erect a huge beach-volleyball stadium. Through it all, the Olympic minister and the head of the organizing committee, Michael Knight, lambasted protesters as unAustralian, whingers and ragbags. These phrases were endlessly repeated in the brilliant television satire, *The Games*, which ran alongside the final two years of the Olympic preparations. It was a role ably continued by Channel 7's

nightly Olympics comedy show, *The Dream*, and their unofficial curmudgeonly mascot, 'Fatso – the fat-arsed wombat', whose immense
popularity made the dire official mascot redundant.

Yet, as one observer sharply noted,

> Come September many erstwhile hardened-objectors became
> converts. They rang talk back radio to repent. They had seen
> the light. They were happy to queue for hours to buy tickets
> to obscure sporting spectacles like synchronized swimming or
> Greco Roman wrestling. A madness gripped them . . . On the
> balmy evening before the opening ceremony hundreds of thou-
> sands crowded the city streets eager and spirited. Strangers
> talked openly to each other. Those who were caught in crowds
> expressed no rancour. There was an atmosphere of benign,
> cheerful tolerance of any inconvenience brought on by the
> Olympics.[6]

On the opening day of the games, just 500 people marched from
the Aboriginal tent-city to John Howard's house, stopping the traffic
but very little else. Demonstrations in support of Aboriginal rights,
planned for the airport, failed to materialize. Once the sport started,
protest was even more muted, fragmented and poorly attended.
Marches in the centre of the city and demonstrations at sponsors'
offices were attended by dozens rather than thousands. The AOC
concentrated what little fire it had on the live sites and 'public' Olympic spaces in the city, challenging the restrictive by-laws that had
been passed on political action. Activists handed out leaflets reading,
'DANGER! You have just been handed an illegal LEAFLET containing
unAustralian sentiments, from an Olympics criminal.' The opening
ceremony and the sporting spectacular swept them away, its most
potent moment, the lighting of the Olympic cauldron. The crowd
roared its approval when Cathy Freeman's name was announced.[7]
Responses to Freeman's torch-lighting varied. In barely disguised
expressions of racist distaste, the letters pages of some papers
described how Freeman's performance had, at best, left one reader
'feeling flat'; at worst, another reader called it an 'embaressment'
and an 'absolute disgrace'. But mainstream op-eds brimmed over
with self-congratulation. The *Age* gushed, 'We always knew Cathy
Freeman could walk on water. Who better than this popular young

Aboriginal women to express, to all Australians, the hopes for reconciliation?'

It was hard for the Australians to take notice of anyone else. The Thai police officer, Lieutenant Colonel Wijan Ponlid, won a gold in the flyweight boxing and returned to a new house, twenty million baht and a job promotion and was paraded at the front of a procession of forty-nine elephants through the city of Bangkok, but was invisible in Sydney. Cameroon beat Spain after a penalty shoot-out in the men's Olympic football final at the Olympic stadium. No one cared in the Olympic city, but the whole of Africa celebrated the continent's second global football trophy. At four a.m., the streets of Yaoundé were full of dancing crowds. Even the parade of Australian gold medallists, from cyclists to shooters, from the women's water-polo team to the equestrian eventers, struggled for significance. There really was only one competitor who mattered. The headlines had appropriated her, 'Our Cathy', and claimed she would run 'The race of our lives'. According to Kim Beazley, leader of the federal opposition, Freeman was running the '400 metres of national reconciliation.' By this point, there was very little opposition on the track or as a narrative. Her main competitor, the brilliant French sprinter Marie-José Pérec, had cracked under the pressure and fled the country soon after arriving. In a cauldron of noise, Freeman dominated the final, seeming to smash through the finishing line before crumpling to the ground, where she remained for over a minute. Freeman had kept her side of the bargain. It remained for white Australia to keep its. For the world audience, the closing ceremony offered up the politically mute Australian stars with global reach: pop diva Kylie Minogue, golf leviathan Greg Norman, comedian Paul 'Crocodile Dundee' Hogan and supermodel Elle Macpherson. But, for the locals who could read the signs, it was the musicians who were the real stars. Darren Hayes, one half of the pop duo Savage Garden, performed in a T-shirt bearing the Aboriginal flag. Yothu Yindi, kings of Aboriginal rock, played 'Treaty' – their classic statement of indigenous resistance. Australian alt-rock royalty, Midnight Oil, wearing T-shirts emblazoned with the word 'Sorry!', chose to play their reconciliation-themed single, 'Beds Are Burning', apparently the favourite of the still unapologetic Prime Minister John Howard, sitting in the audience.

SIX

The Lake Placid Winter Olympics of 1980 had lasted just twelve days, featured only thirty-nine actual gold-medal events and attracted a mere 1,000 athletes from pretty much the thirty or so national Olympic committees (two thirds of whom were European) that had been attending the games for the previous decade or two. But, by the time the games got to Salt Lake City in 2002, the show lasted seventeen days, ensuring two weekends of prime-time television, and featured 2,400 athletes, from seventy-eight nations, competing for nearly eighty gold medals.[1] Curling had been added to the roster; short-track skating had arrived; women's events had been added in biathlon, ice hockey and bobsleigh; and mogul skiing and snowboarding, the first of what would become an avalanche of new extreme or freestyle winter sports, made their debuts. Accredited journalists at the games tripled in number, TV personnel multiplied more than ten times over and, underwriting everything, the value of its television rights went through the roof: Lake Placid had commanded just $21 million in 1980 Calgary, in 1988, had pushed it up to $325 million and Salt Lake City pulled in $737 million. The growth of income from corporate sponsorship matched this. Throw in the exponential growth of volunteers, security personnel and members of the 'Olympic family', including sponsors and their friends, and, by 2002, the total number of accredited people at the winter games was almost 90,000. Not surprisingly, the bill for just putting on the show, let alone building the roads, ski lifts and other paraphernalia that resorts required, went the same way: $168 million for Lake Placid, $700 million for Albertville, in 1992, and Salt Lake City cost a cool $1.2 billion.

As with the summer games, the boom of the Winter Olympics was driven not only by the internal logics of globalization, television, commercialized sport and advertising, but also by the increasingly ambitious local economic and political projects it had been hitched to. Sarajevo 1984 was a small exercise in Yugoslav nationalism, though the bitter struggles amongst the state's constituent republics in the run-up to the games, over prestige and finance, foreshadowed the terrible break-up to come.[2] Calgary 1988 was a forlorn attempt to prove that this prairie city was more than Mounties, rodeos and the oil industry.[3] Albertville and Lillehammer were significantly more ambitious, tying the games to major programmes of regional economic development and the global branding of both cities, and, in Lillehammer's case, of Norway too, and both received a large tranche of public money.[4] Prior to the games, Albertville was a small French Alpine town that nobody outside the Savoie region had heard of. It sat at the centre of five small winter resorts, none of which alone could stage an Olympic Games, but networked together they might. Having ensured Barcelona beat Paris to the 1992 games, Samaranch soothed his francophone allies by directing a lot of support Albertville's way. The French state ordered one hundred acres of protected forest to be cut down and put a billion dollars into what it and the organizers called 'The Planet of the French Olympics'. It was a planet that, for the duration of the games, closed each day with the electro-pop symphonies of Jean-Michel Jarre and high-tech laser light shows, and included a stupendous new mountain-road network, five Olympic villages, five skating rinks, and innumerable gondolas and ski lifts. The French Alpine tourist industry got what it wanted and the games acquired its first great white elephant: the bobsleigh run at La Plagne, built on old mine-works so shaky it was sinking from the very start, and exposed to so much sunlight that freezing the track was almost impossible.

Lillehammer, then a tiny inland Norwegian town of just 23,000, was struggling to keep those few residents it had, as Norway's oil boom drew people to the coast. The games were a local and then a national-level project, designed to channel a gigantic programme of state-funded investment into winter sports and tourist facilities. However, by contrast to the elephantine urbanism of French *étatisme*, Norwegian social democracy trod more carefully. With Prime Minister Gro Harlem Brundtland, the noted environmentalist, in power, there was, at Lillehammer, an unprecedented commitment to thinking through the environmental implications of the games. Facilities were located with a rare sensitivity. The bobsleigh run was designed to hug the contours of the mountain, allowing all of its ancillary cooling pipes and supports to be hidden; the ski-jump run was effectively invisible. Ice hockey was held in the largest indoor space ever created within a mountain – another showcase for Norway's exceptional engineering industry. Trees were protected from contractors, who faced stiff fines should they be damaged. Energy use and savings were exemplary. As one of the world's most significant donors of foreign aid, the Norwegians used the Lillehammer games to establish the first Olympic humanitarian aid programme and to highlight the plight of Sarajevo – host to the games in 1984, but then besieged and broken in the gruesome Bosnian civil war.

Nagano was the brainchild of the then richest man in Japan, Yoshiaki Tsutsumi, who, amongst other things, owned a number of hotels in the hitherto unknown mountain resort, which, although just a hundred miles from Tokyo, was hard to reach and under-resourced.[5] Nineteen billion dollars later, it had a bullet train to Tokyo, new mountain expressways, an entirely refitted telecommunications system and winter-sports facilities in profusion. It was an almost perfect microcosm of the wider infrastructural binge that the Japanese government was unleashing in an effort to lift the country out of its post-bubble trough, and it was characterized by the same hidden networks of favours, rigged bids, and tenders specially designed to exclude foreign competition. The short boost this brought to Nagano's economy soon disappeared, and even Tsutsumi himself would prove vulnerable, as the value of his property portfolio crumpled in the early twenty-first century.[6]

The boom finally exploded in late 1998, when KTVX, Salt Lake City, reported that the local organizing committee of the 2002 games had been paying for Sonia Essomba to attend the American University in Washington.[7] Sonia was the daughter of the Cameroonian member of the IOC, the late Rene Essomba, and, as it turned out, she was just one of thirteen beneficiaries of similar scholarships dispensed by the games organizers. Then Intermountain Healthcare revealed that the organizers had spent $28,000 on treating hepatitis and performing knee and cosmetic surgery on 'individuals connected to the IOC.' None of this would have been much of a surprise to anyone who had moved in IOC circles. Anyone familiar, for example, with the final days of the bidding war for the 1992 summer games, when the Brisbane bid committee flew in AU$300,000 worth of fresh seafood, care of Rupert Murdoch, for its campaign receptions in

East Berlin, would be inured to the IOC's tolerance for ostentatious overconsumption. Nor would it have come as a shock to readers of Vyv Simson and Andrew Jennings' *The Lords of the Rings*: published in 1992, the book laid out in great detail the entire power structure of global sport, as well as the dubious practice that had become commonplace especially amongst members during Olympic bid competitions.[8]

That there was so much surprise is testament to the opacity of the IOC under Samaranch, its adamant insouciance in not seeing what was in front of its eyes and the free pass effectively given to global sports organizations by politicians, broadcasters, sponsors and the press on matters of governance and legality. In the wake of their failed bids, Toronto, Manchester and Amsterdam had all reported back to the IOC on obvious instances of malpractice: IOC committee members soliciting money for votes, changing first-class to economy tickets and pocketing the difference, combining visits to a bid city with vacation-length stopovers, in opulent circumstances, on the way there and back. In 1991, the IOC had attempted to block these manoeuvres, and set a ceiling of $200 on the value of any gifts that members could accept, but they were whistling in the wind. The IOC's now pathological culture of gift-giving was uncontrollable. Standards and expectations were set at the top of organizations, and President Samaranch gave a fearless lead. He never accepted presents himself, passing them on to the IOC museum, but, as Kim Warren, a member of the Salt Lake City bid committee, recalled, 'He had to fly in on a private jet. He had to stay in the presidential suite – it had to be the finest room in the city. There was a particular type of NordicTrak [sic] he works out on, so we had to get that piece of equipment. We had to have limousines for him – Lincoln Town Cars weren't good enough.'[9]

Alongside the feeding frenzy of revelations, accusations and denials that flooded the global press, no less than six investigations were mounted into the Salt Lake City bid: the risible efforts of the organizers' own ethics commission; the US Olympic Committee's investigation, headed by Senator George Mitchell; the FBI and the Department of Justice got in on the act, weighing up the case for criminal prosecutions; a subcommittee of the House of Representatives fulminated; and the IOC's own contribution was the Pound

Commission, led by the Canadian lawyer and rising star of the committee, Dick Pound.

What became transparently clear from all of this work, and the many admissions and revelations that emerged from other bid committees, was that Salt Lake City was just the latest example of almost two decades of steadily rising graft. How Atlanta spent its 'official' $7.3 million hospitality budget is still shrouded in mystery, since Fulton County Court, Georgia, determined that its records were not subject to the Open Records Act. Whatever they did spend, and on whom, they knew how to do it the right way; for the party that preceded Atlanta winning the US Olympic Committee's endorsement as a bid city, 'The Atlantans rented a townhouse, had butlers in tuxedos greet guests and serve champagne, and arranged for 10 strolling violinists to work the room playing "Georgia on My Mind."'[10] They really didn't miss a beat. Their opponents, Melbourne, invited Hae-Jung Kim – a South Korean pianist whose father, Un-yong Kim, just happened to be a member of the IOC – to play with the Melbourne Symphony Orchestra. Atlanta trumped them. Come the games, Hae-Jung Kim was a soloist at the city's Olympic Arts Festival and played two concerts with the Utah Symphony Orchestra.[11] In the race for the 1998 Olympics, Nagano upped the stakes with a 'hospitality budget' of $25 million, a specially chartered private train to take Samaranch from Tokyo airport to the city, and a personal donation of $1 million from Yoshiaki Tsutsumi to the president's pet project, the IOC Museum in Lausanne (local industrialists coughed up another $19 million). Quite how the rest of the money was spent remains unclear. When, in the wake of the Salt Lake scandal, the Nagano committee was asked for its accounts, it transpired that the ninety relevant boxes had been burnt as part of the tidy-up.[12]

Sydney's pitch to the IOC was wholesome: the first truly green summer games in the southern hemisphere's most sporty nation, promising a grand symbolic reconciliation of white and Aboriginal Australia. However, the committee had made other plans. Brisbane and Melbourne's bid campaigns had been outgunned; Sydney raised its vote-buying budget to AU$28 million. Gough Whitlam, the former prime minister and one of the leading figures in the sporting boycott of apartheid South Africa, was sent to Africa to win support. Australian IOC member, Peter Coles, was dispatched to Paris for a four-month sojourn with the central purpose of wining, dining and drumming up support amongst the committee colleagues who were passing through. Huge Aboriginal paintings were donated to the IOC's museum. The daughter of Sepp Blatter, the president of FIFA (and IOC member), got herself a job in Australia, as did the son-in-law of Romanian IOC time-server, Alexandru Siperco. Agents with connections to the IOC, promising votes and discretion, were engaged. In the final days of the campaign, in Monte Carlo, at the IOC's 1993 congress, John Coates, president of the bid committee, recalled the strategy: 'We decided that as we had to do it, we would be the best whores you could find between Rome and Marseilles.'[13] A last-minute donation of AU$50,000 was offered to the Kenyan and Ugandan national Olympic committees, and gifts were showered on their IOC members, Charles Mukora and General Frances Nyangweso. Sydney won the final round of the election by two votes.

Salt Lake City, which had lost the fight for the 1998 winter games to Nagano, was taking note – literally, as members of the Sydney bid team passed on many of their dossiers on IOC members' peccadilloes to Salt Lake City while enjoying remarkably frequent and convivial stays in the city. This really was small beer, though; House Republican Fred Upton, on reviewing the bid committee's papers, described 'Pages and pages of Cabbage Patch dolls, shopping sprees, carburetor kits, brake pads, jewelry, children's clothes and shoes, golf clubs, Spode china, computer parts.'[14] There were shotguns at $1,500 a go, credit cards issued to IOC members when they came to town, and trips to the Super Bowl; and then, of course, there was the extensive payment of tuition fees, medical bills and the jobs for family friends that had started the ball rolling.

Two members of the IOC resigned before the Pound Commission could get to them: the Finn, Pirjo Haggman, whose husband had acquired suspicious posts in Toronto and Salt Lake City during those city's bids, and the Libyan, Bashir Mohamed Attarbulsi, who fell on his sword too when it became clear that Salt Lake had paid his son's tuition fees at the city's Brigham Young University. Of the six members of the IOC that were expelled, Paul Wallwork, the permanent secretary of Samoa's Ministry of Sport, was the cheapest. His wife got a $30,000 loan that she actually paid back. The Chilean, Sergio Santander, asked for $10,000 in support of his mayoral election campaign in Santiago, while Abdel Gadir, a former minister of sport in Sudan, made do with just $25,000. The Malian, Lamine Keita, and the Ecuadorian, Augustin Arroyo, were more expensive, with Salt Lake covering around $100,000 worth of university tuition fees for their children, and, in the case of Arroyo's daughter, sorting out a job at the Utah Department of Economic Development and on the organizing committee itself. But topping them all was Jean-Claude Ganga, a diplomat from the Republic of Congo, known amongst the Salt Lake bid team as 'the human vacuum cleaner'. His travel expenses alone were $115,000. Tom Welch, the then head of the bid committee, went into business with him, creating Claudet Investments, a vehicle for speculation in Salt Lake City's housing bubble. It transpired that the medical bills were for Ganga's hepatitis, his wife's cosmetic treatments and his mother-in-law's knee. Salt Lake estimated his vote cost around a quarter of a million dollars. Even President Samaranch had to take notice.

Samaranch's response to the greatest crisis of legitimacy faced by the Olympic movement was unusually bold, creating the IOC 2000 Reform Commission.[15] Its members were half drawn from the IOC and half from outside, including the UN general secretary, Boutros Boutros-Ghali, the former US secretary of state, Henry Kissinger, NBC Sports chairman Dick Ebersol, and the former Norwegian foreign minister, Thomas Stoltenberg. Its fifty recommendations were all accepted by the IOC, though subsequently a good few have not been acted upon. The composition of the IOC itself was partially transformed; a core of seventy self-selected members were to be complemented by fifteen representatives of Olympic athletes, fifteen presidents of the international sports federations and fifteen members drawn from the national Olympics committees. Individuals would serve an eight-year term under a seventy-year age limit. Future presidents would be allowed a single additional four-year term. Although they would retain the final say over the election of host cities, visits by IOC members were banned; the new bidding process, though less prone to compromising individual members of the IOC, shifted even more power and influence to the insiders of the executive committee and the president's office. The power of the international sports federations (whose presidents were still able to visit host cities on official business), which remained amongst the most unreformed and unaccountable institutions on the planet, was also significantly increased. Whatever its structural shortcomings, the reform package was enough to stem the vertiginous collapse of the IOC's legitimacy. Indeed, the reforms went further than those proposed by its critics.

The subsequent rehabilitation of the organization was secured by Samaranch's preferred successor, the Belgian Olympic yachtsman and orthopaedic surgeon, Jacques Rogge. In this, at least, Samaranch made a contribution to the reform of the grotesque IOC culture he had helped nurture; Rogge's main opponent was the South Korean, Kim Un-yong, who was at the time reported to be canvassing voters with the promise of massively increased IOC expenses, and who would later be tried and convicted at home on a wide range of bribery charges. Rogge, meanwhile, described himself as 'a sober, decent, maybe boring, efficient guy', which was true, except for the 'maybe'. Dick Pound, who also ran in the presidential election, was only slightly unfair when he exclaimed, 'Rogge speaks five languages – and says stuff-all in all of them.' He was never the man to reinvigorate or reinvent the Olympic ideal, or to articulate a new social mission for sport, but – in the absence of vision – decency and efficiency in the governance of the IOC, both of which he possessed in abundance, were verging on the revolutionary.

The Salt Lake City Olympic organizers culled their senior management rather more briskly, appointing a new chief executive: Mitt Romney. An LDS (Church of the Latter Day Saints) insider, he had made a fortune as a venture capitalist and had been a Mormon bishop and stake president of the Church in Massachusetts. He tried to persuade the press corps that these were not the 'Mormon games' and, contrary to expectations, served champagne at his media conferences, but he also appointed further members of the LDS to a senior-management team already Mormon heavy.[16] He then persuaded the LDS to offer up more land and volunteers for the games and turned Temple Square – a block in downtown Salt Lake – into the Olympic medals plaza, ensuring that every ceremony gave the world a good view of the Mormon temple and the LDS main office. The Church, which had tried to remain in the background during the games preparations, took them as an opportunity to try to persuade the rest of America that the LDS was not a modern cult or a heretical Christian sect, but just part of America's broader religious diversity.

If Midwestern civic boosterism, the winter-sports tourist industry and the LDS on a quiet makeover made for strange cultural bedfellows at the Salt Lake City Olympics, the meaning of some of its sporting events was equally discordant. Snowboarding, for example, stood at one remove from the high-performance ethic of the Olympic spectacle, and for Utah, at any rate, swam dangerously close to all kinds of counter-cultural currents. Brad Steward, one of the US snowboard team, speaking after the sport's debut at the 1998 Nagano Olympics, said:

> Do you believe what started on these icy little hills and back-country zones and places on the side of the road; these illegal, dysfunctional, unwanted sections of the mountain that snow-boarders took over and turned into parks, and pipes and lifestyles . . . Do you believe we made it here? . . . I think it was that same kind of feeling that scientists working on the atomic bomb had. They'd achieved this remarkable scientific accomplishment and then it was: Oh my God, what wrath have we brought?[17]

Hardly the Manhattan Project, but it was certainly a clash of cultures. Freestyle skiing, in its many forms, emerged in the United States in the 1950s and early 1960s. Ski ballet and flipping and jumping – the basis of freestyle skiing – were the products of émigré Europeans, like the Norwegian Olympic medallist Stein Eriksen, experimenting on American slopes.[18] Mogul skiing, through and over bumps and small hills, was the product of the western United States, in an off-piste backwoods scene that, very early on, was associated with radical attitudes, anti-Vietnam War sentiments and not a little marijuana between runs. Sherman Poppen's patented Snurfer – a primitive snowboard, steered by a rope – was released in 1966, sold over three quarters of a million units and initiated the boom.[19]

In common with BMX biking, snowboarding's early culture privileged recreation over records, and play over performance, but the Olympics offered these sports sensational coverage and status, and they, in return, offered the games a touch of the anti-establishment magic and youthful television-viewers then flocking to ESPN's Winter X-Games. The skateboard industry and fraternity have so far resisted this trade, but freestyle winter sports have made the crossover. The ensuing contrasts were brilliantly illustrated by the first snowboard gold-medal winner, Canada's Ross Rebagliati, who was tested positive for marijuana and stripped of his medal before it was decided that, as THC was then not a banned substance and had no performance-enhancing effects, he could have it back. Rebagliati has recently gone into the medical marijuana business with a branded product, Ross's Gold.

Figure skating has proved considerably more controversial.[20] The 1994 Lillehammer games was dominated – in the press, if not on the ice – by the feud between the American stars, Tonya Harding and Nancy Kerrigan. Harding had conspired with her ex-husband, who attacked Kerrigan in the run-up to the games, injuring her with a hammer. Kerrigan finished second, in the end, while Harding, clearly distressed, flunked her final performance to come in eighth, a satisfactory denouement to the soap opera it became, pitching willowy, middle-class Kerrigan against the blue-collar tough-girl Harding.[21] The pairs competition in Salt Lake City was inflamed by the biggest judging scandal in the sport ever. The Russians, Yelena Berezhnaya and Anton Sikharulidze, won the gold over the Canadian pair, Jamie Salé and David Pelletier, despite a manifestly inferior, error-strewn performance and the howls of a disbelieving crowd. Close examination of the voting revealed that the French judge, Marie-Reine Le Gougne, had been pressured to mark the votes up in a deal between the head of French skating, Didier Gailhaguet, the Russian authorities and an Uzbek gangster called Alimzhan Tokhtakhounov, acting as the go-between. Over the coming weeks, she would issue retractions and contradictory statements before being banned from the sport for three years by the International Skating Union; despite this the ISU did not see fit to conduct a serious examination of the scandal. The situation was only resolved when the IOC and the international skating federation awarded the Canadians a second gold.[22]

Of course, none of this would have happened if the people who ran figure skating had spent a fraction of the energy they devoted to policing athletes' sexuality on policing judges.[23] The costumes of Katarina Witt, the great East German champion, had been deemed so provocative at the 1984 and 1988 games that an entire convoluted 'Katarina Rule' was written into the sports handbook, detailing exactly what could and couldn't be covered. Women have only recently been allowed to compete in trousers, same-sex couples could not compete together, and all the expectations in judging their artistic performance are rooted in an aesthetic of feathers, sequins and monstrous make-up. Men, by contrast, are increasingly marked on difficulty and athleticism, a shift in scoring that has made quadruple jumps the guarantor of both unimpeachable heterosexuality and medal-winning scores. This, in what is, quite obviously, the campest Olympic event, springs from the biggest denial of all: that there are no homo-sexual men in the sport. US figure-skating judge Jon Jackson, writing in 2006, claimed that, 'at least seven of the 14 male Olympic figure skating medallists from the past 20 years are known in certain circles to be interested in other men. In fact, in at least five countries the entire men's singles figure skating team is made up of gay men.'[24] Yet, of course, in all this time, only one skater has come out at the peak of his fame – the Briton John Curry: the 1976 Olympic cham-pion. Johnny Weir, the Canadian champion, only went public on his sexuality after he retired from Olympic competition, after Vancouver 2010, where he had been ridiculed by commentators on French-language television for his 'effete' demeanour. By contrast, the two Brians – who battled it out in Calgary, in 1988 – were more coy. Silver medallist, Brian Orser, was outed by a boyfriend a decade later, while Brian Boitano only came out when appointed by Presi-dent Obama to the Sochi 2014 delegation – a deliberate riposte to Russia's recently passed homophobic laws. Many in the West were appalled that the winter games should be held there, yet, in figure skating, at any rate, they remain a bastion of entrenched and casual homophobia everywhere.

SEVEN

Welcoming visitors to the sparkling Athens Olympic complex, one volunteer was heard crying to the crowd, 'Enjoy yourselves. When will we ever see days like this again?'[1] After the most chaotic, last-minute Olympic construction schedule ever, the Athens games were happening, and it was a miracle. The novelist Petros Markaris suggested the mood had changed in June when, against all known form, the Greek national football team won the European football championships, beating the hosts, Portugal, in the final with a mixture of eye-watering opportunism and defensive defiance: 'Who said that miracles could not happen twice in the same summer? Miracles are part of the Greek survival system: if everything else goes wrong, there is still a miracle waiting for us as a last resort.'[2]

Greece had been riding its luck and banking on a miracle for over a decade. Since the mid-1990s, the country had been recording unprecedented levels of economic growth and even more precocious levels of consumption. Driven by the global financial boom, and allowed access to global capital markets through the most miraculous act of all – getting inside the Eurozone – Greek borrowing, both public and private, rose to record levels. Atop this frenzied mountain of debt, Greek politics and the Greek state remained unreformed. It was a minuscule welfare state, riddled with corruption, where access to services, jobs and pensions came as a form of political patronage, precariously sustained on a microscopic fiscal base that allowed the rich and middle-class professionals to avoid tax altogether. With both PASOK, the governing social democrats since 1981, and the opposition, New Democracy, in thrall to these networks of support, there was no pressure for reform – indeed, all the pressure was to extend the good times indefinitely on the never-never. And, sitting atop it all, drawing on the manic energies, insatiable appetites and inflated self-importance that the boom nurtured, was the games.

The economics of Athens 2004 remain opaque enough that, more than a decade later, the president of both the bid and the organizing committees, Gianna Angelopoulos-Daskalaki, the first woman to hold either position at any games, and now at a Greek economic think tank, is still actively researching the question of where all the money went.[3] Best estimates are that an initial budget of $4 billion mutated into a $16 billion bonanza, making Athens, at the time, the most expensive games – and, per capita, still the most expensive. Compared to the $300 billion of total public debt accumulated by the Greek state before the financial crisis of 2008, let alone the debts of Greek financial institutions, this was just a few percentage points, but the manner of its spending is as good a window as any on the pathological dynamics of the Greek boom.

The unevenness of Greek economic development in the 1970s and 1980s saw ever more people leave the often destitute countryside and small towns and head for Athens. The boom of the 1990s redoubled these flows. The city's population swelled to the point that its road and rail networks became hopelessly inadequate, its traffic jams legendary. The bus fleets that took up the slack were old and heavily polluting, making the often appalling air quality of the city even worse. The simply incredible archaeological heritage that remained in the heart of the metropolis was being eaten away by acrid yellow smog. Given the political and administrative miasma that had passed for urban development in Athens up to this point, it was hardly surprising that the Athenian, and thus the national, political elites saw the games as the opportunity to build in seven years what should have been done over the previous quarter of a century. Thus, the Athens Olympics began with a bill for a new international airport, a new urban road network, metro systems and tramways, telecoms infrastructure and a total makeover of the city's precious archaeological zones.[4]

This, however, was not enough. With regard to the main Olympic stadium, the organizers insisted on 'an architectural landmark of international recognition.' The Spanish architect Santiago Calatrava was commissioned to completely remodel an existing facility with enormous tubular steel arcs, onto which two fabulous leaf-shaped roofs of laminated glass were attached. It was beautiful, eye-catching and exquisitely complicated and expensive. Two major clusters of venues were built south of the city, centred on state-owned brownfield sites at Faliro Bay and Elliniko. The former, cut off from the

Aegean by a strip of coastal highway, had become a wasteland, and dangerously prone to flooding. It was completely remodelled: an entire racecourse was moved and three new stadiums, including one just for beach volleyball, were added. Useless to contractors and suppliers, not a single temporary or pop-up venue was created. The sports that, but for basketball, absolutely nobody played in Greece were parked at the vast Hellinikon Olympic Complex, south of central Athens, on the site of an old airport. The hangars were converted into fencing and handball halls, and specialist stadiums were raised for baseball, field hockey and slalom canoeing. With many other local constituencies and clients to satisfy, the organizers spread out the goodies. There was a new building at the University of Piraeus that hosted weightlifting; the Goudi Complex featured brand new facilities for badminton and modern pentathlon. Despite claiming to be running the greenest games ever, the Athens organizers planned to build a rowing complex on what they described as degraded wetlands, but what archaeologists considered the site of the Battle of Marathon, and ecologists and the European Commission classed as a rare and precious ecological gem. Having deliberately left the site off the Europe Union's list of protected areas, the organizers were forced to scale back their grandiose plans when Greece's small environmental NGOs won a rare victory in court.

To be fair to Athens, the original budget hadn't banked on 9/11. In the febrile conditions of the War on Terror, and with the occupation of Iraq, Athens had to sign thirty-eight security agreements with twenty-three countries. After the Al-Qaeda-aligned Madrid metro bombings in early 2004, they asked for NATO's assistance in conducting air and sea patrols, and in protecting against nuclear, chemical and biological attack. In 2002, Salt Lake City required the deployment of around 4,000 soldiers; Athens declared a no-fly zone over Olympic venues and other sites, and called up 10,000 as part of a total security force numbering 70,000. Together with NATO, they provided twenty-four-hour aerial and open-sea surveillance, continuous external patrols by the coastguard and a blimp mounted with ultra-sensitive sensors, while the government installed a permanent system of submarine seabed detectors, high-resolution cameras and radiation detection devices on the country's borders, not to mention around 1,400 CCTV cameras in all the Olympic venues. All told, the organizers found themselves spending €1.2 billion on security, six times more than was spent on Sydney 2000.[5]

If security was a truly unexpected source of inflation, the costs of doing business in the Greek public sector surely should have been anticipated. Costa Bakouris, at one point the most senior executive amongst the Athens organizers, said he had to step down because 'he refused to accept that all bids – whether they were for major infrastructure projects or for the carpeting of the Olympic village – should be roughly three times as high as they were in Sydney.'[6] Others, of course, were able to accept these prices. However, more expensive than even the unusually high costs of graft-driven transactions in the Greek public sector were the consequences of lateness. For almost three years after winning the games, the organizers and government did nothing, distracted by internal fighting and the imperative of getting in the Eurozone. The torrid progress of the construction programme, when it did finally start, provided the foreign press with an endless array of headlines, comedy and barbs. Greeks themselves joked that Chinese visitors in Athens would look at their preparations and say, 'We will have everything ready in Beijing by 2006.' To which the locals replied, 'So will we.' The roof of the main stadium, painstakingly constructed on site, was moved into position on the very day the IOC set as a make-or-break moment for the venue's use. Just a week before the opening ceremony, the dress rehearsal was accompanied by the ear-shattering noise of circular saws and jack hammers. On the eve of the games, the *Guardian* noted, 'At the whitewater kayaking venue there were reports that flagpoles have yet to be put up. The seats at the road cycling venue were just being installed and at the main Olympic stadium the fountains were only turned on yesterday.'[7]

Reputational issues aside, the real cost of this was financial. Facing impossible deadlines and the tight labour market of the boom years, contractors brought in thousands upon thousands of Albanians, who worked round the clock, seven days a week, on three continuous shifts; hundreds of floodlights were deployed to make night work possible, and the price of specialist materials and wages climbed and climbed. After the games, the shoddy standards of building, the poor use of materials and the incomplete finishing that came with all of this would become obvious. But, on 12 August 2004, all of that could be put to one side, a mere detail compared to the miraculous realization that the games would actually happen and that Athens looked extraordinary. The gods did offer the Greeks and their guests a chance to reflect, a momentary puncturing of the great bubble of hubris that would envelop the entire Olympic spectacle. On the day before the games began, Ekaterini Thanou – Greece's 100-metre silver medallist at Sydney and the best prospect for a domestic gold medal in athletics – and her partner, the sprinter Konstantinos Kenteris, appeared at the accident and emergency rooms of an Athenian hospital after crashing on their motorbike. They had also, it soon transpired, missed their third drug test of the season that afternoon – a transgression that would almost certainly have resulted in their suspension from the games, and a good deal of further drug testing. It was, of course, an inept charade. Demonized and excluded at the time, the two were later exonerated of criminal charges in the Greek courts, the pair's unfortunate coach required to take the fall for their erratic behaviour.

As the first summer games to be held since the establishment of WADA (the World Anti-Doping Agency), the 2004 Olympics featured the most sophisticated pharmaceutical and administrative armoury yet. Athens caught a lot of people out. Greek weightlifter Leonidas Sampanis was found to have double the level of permitted testosterone in his body when he won his bronze medal. He was one of just thirteen weightlifters with similar chemistry. Irina Korzhanenko, the Russian shot-putter, was found to have been on steroids while competing at the ancient site of Olympia itself. The Irish equestrian Cian O'Connor lost his gold medal in show jumping after his horse, Waterford Crystal, tested positive for anti-depressants, while the German rider Ludger Beerbaum and his colleagues were stripped of their team gold medal, as Beerbaum's horse, Goldfever, appeared to have been taking betamethasone – an entirely useless, but nonetheless prohibited substance. In total, thirty-seven athletes tested positive, two of whom were horses, and fifteen of whom were subsequently stripped of their medals, some as late as 2012, after protracted legal conflicts.

By then, no one knew or cared about any of this. Ian Sinclair found the consensus amongst Athenians in 2010 was that 'it had been a monumental, epoch-defining opening ceremony . . . Everybody had the DVD of the firework night, it was still selling. Nobody remembered what happened after that.'[8] Greece began to wake from its Olympic reveries in December 2004, when the European Commission issued its first formal warning to the country, having found that the government had falsified national budget deficit data in the run-up to joining the Eurozone, illegitimately moving gigantic swathes of debt off the public books. The official report of the games, which appeared soon after, tentatively suggested that the bill had now doubled from $4.5 billion to $9 billion.

Both were a long way off the mark. By the time the global financial crisis had forced the Greek government into bailout negotiations and to bare its books to the world, Greek public debt was close to $300 billion, and the cost of the games was estimated at $16 billion. In a rare reversal of German–Greek power relations, the telecommunications giant, Siemens, was subject to a huge corruption investigation, launched by the Greek government, into how the company acquired contracts for supplying Hellenic Telephone and the Athens Olympics with key electronic security systems. Siemens was forced to write off some debts and invest a few hundred million in Greece, a drop in the ocean against the repayments to German banks flowing in the other direction.

Athens is not the only games to have left a legacy of white elephants, of inappropriately sized and located stadiums, expensive maintenance bills and shoddy construction. Moreover, not everything was a complete disaster. The new museums, the pedestrianized spaces around the key Hellenic ruins, the metro and the airport all gave the city something close to the kind of infrastructure it really needed, albeit at madly inflated prices. Staging the Paralympic Games was a major boost to making Athens' public buildings and transport at least partially wheelchair accessible, and, it may be desperately unimaginative, but the international broadcast centre made a successful transition to the upscale Golden Mall. Quadrennial reviews in the international press, gloating over the depth of Greece's fall and the scale of its folly, forget that at least half of the venues have seen some kind of anaemic post-Olympic sporting use.[9] AEK Athens, for example, the city's third football team, occupy the main Olympic stadium; Olympiakos, the leading basketball team, play in Faliro Bay.

But there is no hiding the unique scale of the disaster, the neglect and the waste. In 2011, one visitor found the official entrance to the main Olympic complex in Maroussi 'stripped of all assets including copper piping, electricity points and marble tiles.' The security guards reasoned, 'I don't know why we're here now . . . Thieves took everything of value, I guess we're just here to stop the squatters moving in.'[10] Inside the complex, AEK Athens attracted crowds of less than 20,000 to a stadium built for four times that; in 2014, a violent pitch invasion by the club's fans saw it punished and relegated to even lowlier depths. The complex was also intended to serve as a permanent base for Greece's elite track-and-field competitors, to be generously funded by the Hellenic Olympic Committee. By 2010, this money had all but disappeared, leaving athletes and their coaches unpaid for months. The stadium roof persistently leaked, while, inside the building, the heating was only allowed on for an hour a day. Having sent 150 athletes to Beijing in 2008, the Greeks could afford to send just twenty-three to London in 2012. Under conditions of extreme austerity in the years since, matters have not improved: 'Girdered tunnels mimicking cypress avenues lead nowhere. The structures in the park are monumental but somehow anorexic: a futurist city that was never completed. It's an island between motorway and railway, surrounded by decommissioned dark glass boxes, failed corporate entities, unpopular estates, scrap metal dumps, breakers' yards, slogan-sprayed mosaic walls with laurel wreath symbols. The death of the grand project is the history painting of our time.'[11]

The Olympic village had fared even worse. Sited on land at some distance from any kind of infrastructure, employment or transport, it had just one thing going for it: the land was state owned and cheap. Built for 10,000 guests at its peak, the village was always intended to become low-cost social housing, and, after the games, a lottery was held for the chance to buy or rent, at sub market rates, in what planners anticipated would be a thriving, mixed community. In fact, 90 per cent of the apartments were allocated to households suffering serious poverty and/or major health and disability issues. By 2015, the rate of unemployment, amongst the few of working age, was 60 per cent. Faced with absurdly high property taxes, the estate's thirty-two shops dwindled to just four. Promises of new schools and nurseries were broken, leaving residents' children to be educated in Portakabins. The swimming pools enjoyed by the athletes for just a few weeks in 2004 were never filled again.[12]

The fate of the Olympic press village was rather different. Planned as a 6,000-person apartment complex to be opened for the foreign press in 2004 and then transformed into social housing, it was actually opened in 2005 as 'The Mall', announcing itself as the largest shopping complex in south-eastern Europe. This little Olympic miracle required a specially arranged change in the law, allowing Lamda – a construction firm owned by Greece's richest man, Spiro Latsis – to build a much-reduced village somewhere else and an enormous mall on the site instead. Despite a series of rulings in the Council of State and the Supreme Court that have found the building contravenes environmental laws, the mall was built and operated as the largest illegal structure in the country, if not Europe, until the law was changed again in 2011 to retrospectively make it legal. Needless to say, none of the side deals that were done, including reimbursing the local authority or funding the construction of a public park, were concluded.[13]

These were the best of the assets. Like the nationalized banks that tried to ring-fence their most toxic debts in a 'bad bank', the organizers passed on the hardest-to-sell facilities to Hellenic Olympic Properties. Only one of those buildings, the Badminton Hall, had a truly successful conversion and post-Olympic life, reopening in 2007 as the Badminton Theatre. A number of the venues, along with their huge maintenance and running costs, were simply handed on. Athens' police force was given the shooting range, the Greek Rowing Federation got the Schinias Centre, and their equestrian equivalents, the Marcopoulo riding venue. The latter has limped on, but it has proved impossible to find reasonable use for a 280-horse dressage facility in a country where the sport is microscopically small. The rowing complex held one world championship, in 2008, but is steadily giving way to weeds and stray dogs. The University of Piraeus never used its new gymnasium, due to the complete collapse of Greek college sporting budgets, and eventually turned it into mundane office space. The grandiose and essentially baseless plans for the Faliro Complex included converting facilities into an open-air theatre, conference centre, opera house, archaeological park and a military and naval museum. What actually happened was that the Olympiakos basketball team used the bigger of two Peace and Friendship stadiums, while the smaller survived on a thin diet of heavy-metal concerts and visits from Holiday on Ice. The beach-volleyball stadium became overgrown, and the pedestrian walkways that sought to return this part of Athens to the sea fragmented and broke. It wasn't quite what the boosters had in mind, but Ian Sinclair found an authentic, if melancholy, urbanism here:

> The overpasses and underpasses, the stilted highways and giant hoardings, the irrigation ditches and empty canals, the mesh fences and graffiti-splashed junction boxes form an edgy parkland where anything could happen. Permitted paths vanish into dunes of landfill, into neurotic traffic, into rail tracks and tramways . . . The Olympic Park, that corrupted legacy, is like mid-period Fellini: kite flyers, moody urbanists in long coats, white cars parked in unlikely places, a glitter of sea you can never quite reach.[14]

The Galatsi Olympic Complex, which had hosted table tennis and rhythmic gymnastics, seemed certain to be turned into another mall. In 2006, a lease was signed with a Portuguese developer, money was invested and work on the site began, only for the project to entirely disappear in the labyrinthine world of Greek planning bureaucracy.[15] Under pressure from foreign creditors and their own increasingly desperate politicians, the Galatsi Complex was packaged up with other Olympic sites in a privatization sell-off. There have been no takers for Galatsi or for the Hellinikon Complex.

Some Athenians are comfortable with their decline: 'The Games are just empty buildings; we have no use for them. But they have become monuments, so we can handle them and live with them. We are used to living among ruins. They are just ruins, they were never anything else.'[16] For those whose ruins were not merely metaphorical, they once again took on the sheen of the miraculous. In late 2015, faced with unprecedented levels of migration from Syria and West Asia, the Greek government considered siting refugee camps on these still unsold Olympic venues.[17]

9

GOING SOUTH: THE OLYMPICS IN THE NEW WORLD ORDER

ATHENS 2004 • BEIJING 2008 • LONDON 2012 • RIO 2016

TORINO 2006 • VANCOUVER 2010 • SOCHI 2014

We can afford to do the Olympics. We're Britain. We're not some Third World country.[1]

Tony Blair

We need to cheer up. We need to understand and feel that we are capable of pulling off major, large-scale projects and do so on schedule and with good quality.[2]

Vladimir Putin

ONE

Quite who or what is the Third World in the twenty-first century is a moot point, but Tony Blair's assumption that only the very richest zones of the global north could afford to stage the games is simply not true. There have been successive Winter Olympics in Torino and Vancouver, but, alongside London, they are the exceptions in an era that has seen a decisive shift in the geography of not just the Olympics, but all global mega-events and world sporting championships, towards the rising powers of the global south. As the summer games head to Rio in 2016, three Olympics of the last decade – Beijing 2008, Sochi 2014 and Rio de Janeiro 2016 – will have been held in one of the core giants of this global transformation – the BRIC nations of Brazil, Russia, India and China. India may not have staged the games itself, but, alongside its central place in global cricket, it has hosted a maniacal Commonwealth Games in Delhi and joined the Formula-1 circus. The World Cup, the games' only serious competitor as a global spectacular, went to South Africa in 2010, Brazil in 2014 and is heading for Russia in 2018 and Qatar in 2022. This is a result of four things. First, that after a decade or two of breakneck industrialization and booming commodity prices, many parts of the global south are able to afford mega-events. Second, the lure of new and opening sports-markets has made sponsors and governing bodies keen to send their brands and events there. Third, the idea that the games could serve as a marker of national economic development and global connectedness – established in the 1960s at Tokyo and Mexico City – gained considerable ground in an era of unprecedented industrial development in the global south. Finally, the predominantly authoritarian governments of the region have found it much easier to work the established networks of corruption in the allocation of hosting rights by many sporting federations, while facing little or no criticism at home.

One consequence of this new pattern of hosting has been that the already rising costs of staging the games took a sharp turn upwards on a curve that was already looking worryingly exponential. Vancouver and London, at the cheaper end of the scale, cost $10 billion and $16 billion dollars apiece. But when the new powers of the new world order chose the games to mark their global rise and remake their cities, nothing short of the gargantuan would be possible. It looked as if Beijing had set a new and surely unbreakable record, spending $40 billion, but the bill for the pharaonic enterprise that was the Sochi winter games, in 2014, was $51 billion, making it the most expensive Olympic Games ever held, more than all of the previous Winter Olympics combined.

This giddy boom in the cost of the games has occurred under the IOC presidency of Jacques Rogge, a man whose most demotic gesture was the hitherto implausible notion that the president of the IOC should actually stay a night in the Olympic village. He delivered exactly the kind of careful, unimaginative leadership that he had promised, redeeming the IOC's standing without ever completely effacing the air of the old boys' club that hung over it. He quietly implemented the bulk of the Agenda 2000 reforms that emerged in response to the Salt Lake City bidding scandal, focused hard on keeping sponsors and media companies happy and improved the institution's own financial health, building up nearly a billion dollars' worth of reserves in the process. There were anaemic attempts to trim the size of the games and cap the total number of official accreditations. Baseball and softball were edged out of the games – predominantly because MLB would not release its stars mid-season, and because its standards on steroids and drug testing remained worryingly lax – and wrestling was ejected at one point, only to be reinstated. Yet, golf, a sport hardly in need of more global coverage, and rugby union were added to the summer games, while the winter games acquired innumerable and exotic forms of freestyle skiing and snowboarding.

At the same time, it became increasingly obvious, even to the IOC, that the routine economic arguments and cost–benefit analyses peddled by worldwide magistracy of management consultants in an effort to justify hosting the games could not be made to stack up. Every single piece of reasoned research on the subject demonstrates that the net economic gains of hosting the games, in terms of investment, growth, employment, wages and tourism, range between the minuscule and the negative.[3] Thus, the Olympic movement came to rely rhetorically on other benefits of hosting the games: in particular, the environmental improvements that came with hosting the Olympics, and the sporting and social legacies that the games could leave behind. Neither case has been made compellingly. Athens was a particularly disingenuous and disastrous games, environmentally speaking. Judged by its own claims, environmental NGOs found almost every single target had been abandoned or missed. Beijing remains one of the most polluted places on earth. Rio, which intended to use the games as a way of turbocharging investment in the city's woefully inadequate sewage systems, abandoned the project altogether.

The legacy left by the games' new sports facilities has also proved problematic. Athens was the worst offender, leaving a whole herd of white elephants across the cityscape. Beijing's venues for kayaking, beach volleyball, BMX biking and baseball remain entirely unused. London has, in effect, given its Olympic stadium to a Premier League football club, while Sochi's Olympic stadium – used only for the opening and closing ceremonies – is now, and at great expense, being refitted as a football stadium for a handful of games at the 2018 World Cup, in a city with no football team of any significance. However, even under the most enlightened and foresighted planning regime, it is a chimera to think that building world-class facilities for high-performance sport, in isolated Olympic parks, is the most cost-effective way of raising levels of popular participation in sport and exercise.

The wider social and urban legacy of the Olympics has proved even more dismal, for the kind of redevelopment unleashed by the games has produced a depressingly familiar litany of problems. Forced relocation, especially of the poor and marginal, was a huge issue in Seoul in 1988 and at Atlanta in 1996, but took on a new order of magnitude when over a million people were affected by the preparations for Beijing 2008. Promises of social housing as a legacy of the Olympic village in Vancouver and London were downgraded to the point of extinction, while much of the urban space produced around Olympic projects has proved to be lifeless gated communities, sealed off from their urban surroundings. Whether Rogge's IOC noticed any of this or not, prospective hosts and the public had, with the consequence that serious Olympic bids were becoming thin on the ground. The competitions for the 2020 summer games and the 2022 winter games were the least competitive.[4]

This, however, was not Rogge's problem. After serving for twelve years, he stepped down in 2013 and was replaced by a German, Thomas Bach. An Olympic gold medallist in fencing in 1976, Bach worked as a lawyer before, like Sepp Blatter, earning his sports-governance chops at Adidas and at the German national sports federation. Already blessed by the hand of Samaranch, who ensured his arrival on the IOC and subsequent election as vice-president, Bach was quietly anointed by Rogge as his successor. And if this was not enough, Bach could also claim the firm friendship and campaigning support of Sheikh Ahmad al-Sabah, the Kuwaiti aristocrat, member of the IOC, president of the Association of National Olympic Committees (in control of $400 million worth of IOC largesse for global sporting federations) and a self-confessed kingpin in the worlds of Asian and global sports politics.[5] He began his time in office armed with an agenda for minor change – paring down the size of the games, squeezing down budgets and making marginal shifts in the organization's governance – and conducted a whirlwind tour of potential hosts for the 2024 and 2026 games, trying to drum up support for what appeared to be an increasingly costly and politically treacherous task. What might have been an era of tougher scrutiny of the IOC has, so far, been almost acclamatory. It takes quite something for the IOC to look like the better end of sports governance, but the world governing bodies of football and athletics have managed to make it appear that way – the former, by virtue of the massive and systemic crisis of corruption at FIFA and its regional confederations; the latter, due to the equally shattering levels of corruption and collusion between the IAAF and the Russian sporting authorities in covering up athletes' doping.

As yet, no amount of corruption in global sports bodies or Olympic construction programmes, and no amount of systematic doping and cheating can keep the global public away from the games. The world continues to watch the Olympics in increasing numbers. The coverage achieved by earlier technologies of print, radio and even satellite television have been dwarfed by an avalanche of change: mobile telephony, cable television and the internet and social media have combined to raise the size of the audience and engagement of the world with the Olympics to unprecedented levels. London

2012 claimed that at least half of the humans on the planet – 3.6 billion people – watched at least a minute of the games. Broadcast to almost 200 countries, it could claim a global prime-time audience of 200 million, and substantially more for key events and moments.

But conventional TV viewing was now hugely supplemented by the use of on-demand streaming services available on the websites of official broadcasters; estimates suggest over 8.5 billion page views and more than 1.5 billion videos viewed, and this is to say nothing of the Olympic imagery consumed on mobile devices and shared on social media. Sochi 2014 demonstrated that, alongside this vast migration to cyberspace, the Olympic spectacular remained the king of mainstream viewing too. In the US, despite the unfriendly time difference, the games proved the most successful for NBC ever, allowing it to rule prime time every night for seventeen days, out-scoring the other three main networks combined and attracting a new and younger demographic.

The games continue to offer spellbinding moments of individual human brilliance and collective cosmopolitan awe, from the super-human swimming of Michael Phelps to the unprecedented speed of Usain Bolt. But just as the power of the spectacle grows, so the capacity of any one power or voice to shape its meaning diminishes. The authoritarian conditions of China and Russia meant that there was little organized protest against their recent games at home, but both faced a more inquisitive global audience, a more demanding press and an alliance of global social movements seeking to counter their Olympic narratives. Where domestic conditions allow, variants of the anti-Olympic movements first sighted in the 1980s and 1990s have re-emerged – small in Torino and London, but a real presence at Vancouver 2010 and in the preparations for Rio 2016. But, so far, the efforts of this array – international NGOs, diaspora communities, social justice and welfare campaigners, indigenous activists, anarchists and environmentalists – have yet to conjure an anti-spectacle on a scale or in a form that can begin to compete with the spectacle that the Olympic Games has now become.

As ever, an important indicator of the growing scale of the games, as both a financial commitment and a pervasive global spectacle, is the cost of its opening ceremonies and the importance conferred upon them.[6] Indeed, it can be argued that these spectaculars mark the biggest innovation in the aesthetics of the Olympics since Riefenstahl's *Olympia*. Her great achievement was to transform the material of the Berlin opening ceremony into a film so powerful, and so widely viewed, that it extinguished any other memory or version of the moment – a task made infinitely easier by the absence of television. In a world of instant digital global broadcasting, the organizers of contemporary opening ceremonies have not had the luxury of months of editing, reshooting and post-production time that Riefenstahl enjoyed, nor could they assume the kind of art-house audience she had in mind. Today's impresarios have had to make the opening ceremony a movie on the spot, and not just any old movie, but a super popular blockbuster that, like its Hollywood equivalent, must simultaneously try to appeal to domestic and international audiences.

All that costs money. Torino and Vancouver, who spent around $20 million and $30 million on their opening ceremonies respectively, were not in that blockbuster league. They relied upon an older school of Olympic theatre, relatively low-tech and therefore cheap: they drew heavily on musical theatre, TV spectaculars and circus traditions for their look and choreography. Thus, the Torino ceremony was directed by Ric Birch, a producer whose credits included the Los Angeles 1984 and Barcelona 1992 openers, and who was schooled in rock videos, while Sydney and Vancouver were the work of David Atkins, who began his career with the hit musical *Hot Shoe Shuffle*. By contrast, Beijing initially outsourced their ceremony to Mr Blockbuster himself, Steven Spielberg, only for him to back out, protesting the Chinese involvement in Darfur and its associated abuses of human rights. He was replaced by the leading Chinese filmmaker of his generation, Zhang Yimou, whose *Red Sorghum* and *Raise the Red Lantern* had documented fragments of China's past in opulent colours. London 2012 was directed by Danny Boyle, whose credits included *Trainspotting* and the Oscar-winning *Slumdog Millionaire*, and was scripted by the TV and film screenwriter, Frank Cottrell Boyce. Sochi was put in the 'safe hands' of Konstantin Ernst, a major TV and film executive with a penchant for modern patriotic blockbusters like *Anna Karenina* and *Leningrad*. Rio, given Brazil's immense economic difficulties, chose to commission a low-budget affair commensurate with the poverty of the creative but desperately underfunded domestic film industry, and have handed the job to three of the most important talents in Brazilian cinema: Fernando

Meirelles, director of the acclaimed *City of God*, and Daniela Thomas and Andrucha Waddington, the team that made the brilliant Sao Paulo coming-of-age movie, *Linha de Passe*. The others have been working with Hollywood-sized budgets, estimated to be $45 million for London, at least $100 million for Sochi and $150 million for Beijing. Of course, Hollywood has to pay for its extras and its sets; by contrast, the Olympic stadium has already been accounted for, and the tens of thousands of volunteers that make up the gigantic casts of these affairs come free. Seen in this light, they really are comparable financially and aesthetically to the movies released alongside them. Beijing's opening ceremony cost the equivalent of that year's James Bond film, *Quantum of Solace*, or the superhero action movies, like *Iron Man* and *The Dark Knight*. Sochi came in at about the same price as the historical biopic *Lincoln*, and Ridley Scott's high-tech biblical flick, *Exodus: Gods and Kings*.

With this kind of money at stake, and access to the very latest in digital enhancement, Olympic organizers have been taking no chances. Lip syncing by key performers, first seen at Sydney 2000, became more prevalent, most notably in Beijing during the song apparently sung by Lin Miaoke, who, it later emerged, was miming for the pitch-perfect but insufficiently photogenic Yang Peiyi. Technical disasters, like Sydney's problems with lighting the Olympic cauldron, were avoided by the expediency of filming another version first. When one of Sochi's gigantic floating snowflakes failed to transform itself into an Olympic ring, domestic television cut away to footage of one they made earlier.[7] For the firework finale in Beijing, which saw a brilliantly coordinated display of pyrotechnic footprints stamping their way across the city, Chinese state television broadcast footage that was entirely computer manufactured. Alongside the techniques of the film industry, the Olympic opening ceremony has increasingly drawn on the world of pop. Since Lionel Richie closed the Los Angeles Olympics in 1984, every games has featured the host's most successful and most globally accessible pop acts. Previously the mainstay of the closing ceremony – like Al Green and the Staples Singers at Atlanta, or Kylie Minogue at Sydney – they became the stars of the opening show in the twenty-first century. Beijing featured pop luminaries like Liu Huan, Karen Mok, Han Hong and Sun Nan, as well as the PRC's celebrated classical pianist, Lang Lang. London, which made the nation's pop culture heritage a central element of the show, gave live spots to Paul McCartney and Ray Davies, and the Arctic Monkeys featured almost the entire high canon of British pop and rock as backing tracks: The Who's 'My Generation', 'Satisfaction' from the Stones, 'She Loves You' from the Beatles, Bowie's 'Starman', Queens's 'Bohemian Rhapsody' – even 'Pretty Vacant' by the Sex Pistols. While all of this represents an admirable recognition of popular tastes in the hitherto unspeakably stuffy atmosphere of Olympic ritual, the combination of blockbuster movie and stadium mega-concert has often proved a bizarre medium through which to tell history – and that, for all the Olympian flummery, is what states and Olympic organizers have been paying up for.

In China and Russia, history is a matter of high state policy, a constant reference in framing the legitimacy of the regime. The Chinese, in particular, are still in full airbrush mode, systematically removing any reference in school books and on the internet to the great disasters and tragedies of the PRC – the Great Leap Forward of the late 1950s and its accompanying famines, the convulsions and gulags of the Cultural Revolution and the violent suppression of the Tiananmen Square democracy movement. The Russian state, unable to manage quite such high levels of surveillance, has nonetheless, under Putin, had the school history syllabus rewritten, refocusing attention on the state builders of the past, gliding over the terror of the 1930s. In a minor key, politicians and educationalists have squabbled over the content of the British school history syllabus too, primarily over the balance of British and world history, conventional constitutional and monarchal narratives against more popular cultural histories. All three nations' contemporary historical predilections and narratives were on show in their opening ceremonies.

All three had their lacunae. As David Remnick put it, of Sochi: 'What did you expect, the Purges?' Beijing glided from the foundation of the PRC to the contemporary, without a glance at the disasters and famines of the Great Leap Forward or the chaos of the Cultural Revolution. Sochi passed on the purges, the Non-aggression Pact with the Nazis and Chernobyl. London gave a wide berth to its rich history of rioting and the violence of imperial conquest and rule. Beijing's gargantuan depictions of its great pre-modern technological innovations – gunpowder, printing, the compass – served to remind the world that, from a Chinese point of view – one that stretches back over 5,000 years – the global balance of technological and military power in the nineteenth and twentieth centuries is an aberration. For most of recorded history, the Middle Kingdom has been the centre of the world and, if the Chinese-conquest-of-space sequence that closed the show is to be read metaphorically, it is going to be so again. Sochi couldn't manage quite such a triumphant narrative of resurgent great-power status, but it bent the facts as best it could with its high-tech Cyrillic alphabet of Russian cultural greats and its bombastic floating tableaux of ballet dancers and Cossacks.

London, by contrast, demonstrated the extent to which the British have responded to their post-imperial decline, by writing the imperial chapter of their history out altogether. In its place was a surreal comedy of historical misremembrance: the clearance of the countryside as a children's TV show, the industrial revolution rendered in the tones of *Oliver!* the musical, and a society bound, since 1945, by its love of socialized medicine, children's literature and the litany of the post-Beatles pop-rock canon. That contemporary elites should wish to tell such stories, in such ways and on such scale, is not really surprising. That they should do so as the overture to the global pinnacle of the now highly commercialized world of high-performance sport remains extraordinary.

TWO

Making his New Year's address to the nation in 2002, the then general secretary of the Chinese Communist Party, later to become the nation's president, Jiang Zemin, said that 'Gaining membership of the World Trade Organization, winning the right to stage the 2008 Olympics, and hosting world leaders at a major summit in Shanghai signal a good opening chapter for China's development in the new century.' China could even look forward to its first appearance at the World Cup finals.[1]

Thus, for the Chinese, the hosting of the games was always seen and understood as part of an epochal shift in the nation's relationship with the outside world, a process of change that paralleled the economic reforms that had ignited the largest and fastest industrial revolution in history. With the personal approval of Deng Xiaoping, China had first bid for the 2000 games, when its strong candidature was pipped by Sydney in the final round of voting. Although it would later transpire that Sydney's key votes had been bought, the Beijing bid had been undermined by the long and loud criticism, coming from international human-rights NGOs, the American media and the House of Representatives, on human-rights issues: both the past transgression of the 1989 Tiananmen Square massacre and the country's enduring control of dissent and opposition.

China returned to the bidding fray in the late 1990s, looking to host the 2008 games, and, as annual growth headed to dizzying double-digit heights, the country appeared to be on a roll. Hong Kong was returned to the PRC by the British in 1997, so too Macao, from the Portuguese, in 1999 – the same year the PRC celebrated its half century. Promising a green Olympics to counter its terrible record on environmental degradation, and a people's Olympics to counter its authoritarian aura, Beijing won the vote in 2001 at a canter. For the optimists on the IOC, and much of the Western diplomatic community, the games were understood as both reward and test for China's re-engagement with the international order after decades of isolation or direct opposition, one that would lead to the opening and democratization of China domestically, and, it was hoped, encourage China to bind itself to the liberal order of international institutions and laws erected by the global north in the preceding half century.

The Chinese themselves had other ideas. First and foremost, the games were a demonstration of China's reacquired prosperity, strength and orderliness. Second, their conception of the global order remained at odds with the fuzzy cosmopolitanism of international human-rights regimes. China started from the principle that sovereignty and autonomy were the preconditions of entry into the international order, rather than subservience to international law. Moreover, while cooperation, collaboration and mutual understanding were admirable, this should not extend to interference or ethical comment on the politics of other nations, especially China.

However, the meaning of the Beijing games was not confined to China's place in the global order, but was an unambiguous statement of the immense economic change that it had undergone. There was never any question that the scale and physical grandeur of the games was going to outdo anything that had come before, and the government backed up that intention with a budget of $40 billion. What do you get for that kind of money? By way of comparison, and as testament to the greatest wave of infrastructure building ever seen in world history, the Beijing games could have bought you the Three Gorges Dam (the world's largest, costing $28 billion and, not unlike the Olympics, displacing over a million people); then add the Tibet–Qinghai line, a 1,000-kilometre mountain-ridge railway, binding Tibet to mainland China, for $3.5 billion; the world's largest collection of nuclear reactors, at Qinshan, a snip at $2.2 billion; and, for good measure, throw in Lingang New City, where $4.5 billion gets you a brand-new town of a million people, and still with $1.8 billion in change.

While some venues were located outside the capital – like the equestrian events in Hong Kong and the sailing venue in Qingdao – the focus was overwhelmingly on Beijing. Standing in a long tradition of imperial architectural statements, the post-reform CCP looked to make its mark on the city. Mao had begun his reign with the transformation and enlargement of Tiananmen Square; later, he would add a touch of Soviet monumentalism, while the most significant legacy of the era was the heavy industrial plants concentrated in republican Beijing. In the immediate post-Mao era, small clusters of dreary towers had been built, but there was little, architecturally, to signal that this was the capital of a country that was self-evidently about to become the largest economy in the world.[2]

In its Olympic incarnation, Beijing's transformation was so vast and so furious that the city government was issuing new maps every three months. Construction counted for nearly a fifth of a booming urban economy, growing, at its peak, at a stratospheric 17 per cent a year. In the seven years between winning the bid and hosting the games, Beijing completed an international airport terminal that was the world's largest (if only for a few months, before it was eclipsed by Dubai), added 50,000 hotel rooms, spent $3.6 billion alone on a network of fibre-optic cables and completely renewed the city's main sewage system, laying 400 miles of piping. The metro, extensive in the 1990s, added eight subway lines and innumerable other surface links, and that is to say nothing of the thirty-one Olympic venues themselves. For almost a decade, a thick, immovable pall of construction dust, exhaust fumes and factory smoke hung over the city. Already surrounded by three beltways, Beijing's monstrous fourth ring-road was completed, and the immense circuits of the fifth and sixth were added. All are now full of traffic. Beijing's complete mutation into the Inferno of hyper-industrialization awaits only the building of the much-vaunted seventh ring.

The appalling state of Beijing's atmosphere was highlighted in April 2006 when the city hosted an important national environmental conference only to be struck by a dust storm, blowing in from the Gobi Desert, which combined with the already gritty city air to shut the place down. The authorities, to be fair, have thrown the book at the problem, closing coal-fired power stations, raising environmental standards for vehicle and factory emissions, shifting heavy industry out of the city and taxing cars and building public transport at an epic rate, but the scale of Beijing's growth has simply defied every effort to decisively improve air quality.

Beneath this fug of particulates, diesel fumes and acid rain, the city's rebuilding required the relocation of, according to the Geneva-based housing NGO, COHRE, 1.5 million of its citizens.[3] The Chinese foreign ministry countered by saying it was just 6,000 households, all of whom had been generously compensated and resettled. The reality is certainly closer to COHRE's numbers than the official count. Moreover, the 'relocation' process in China was characterized by the absence of the rule of law, little due process and sometimes no warning of eviction, massive asymmetries of power between developers and citizens, and only in the rarest of circumstances reasonable compensation. The city's 'nail houses' – single properties, still occupied, on otherwise cleared development zones, whose owners were holding out – became small symbols of defiance to this process, like the Qing-era bakery that held out in the Qianmen area, one of the city's oldest neighbourhoods to be razed to provide shopping space sufficiently opulent for Olympic Beijing.[4] While many of the blocks cleared for the games held little of architectural distinction, the massive destruction of the city's hutongs – its oldest functioning residential neighbourhoods, characterized by high density and poor sanitation, but immensely festive and intense street life – was a considerable loss.

The city that has emerged from this is a distinctly more fragmented one, with strange clusters of development popping up like mushrooms in a desolate landscape of highways, slip roads, vast sculpted verges, and the dead spaces between them. Much of this is mediocre, at best, but one cannot accuse Olympian Beijing of a lack of architectural ambition – it had just been concentrated. The city chose to bejewel this vast, frenetic reworking with four extraordinary buildings. The National Theatre is a giant titanium-and-glass ellipsoid, set in a huge square pool of water. The CCTV building is a pair of sleek, black, angled skyscrapers that join and twist in an improbable Möbius curve. The Olympic stadium, now almost always called the Bird's Nest, is half a billion pounds' worth of arena, around which a great web of interlacing steel provides a curtain and the roof. Alongside, sits the Water Cube, a luminous blue box of thin metal girders and high-tech stretched translucent plastic, creating walls of beautifully lit asymmetrical bubbles.

All were designed by foreign architects, and, though each has gone to strenuous lengths to incorporate architectural and symbolic references to Chinese thought, cosmology and tradition, they all appear to have landed in Beijing from elsewhere. The fact that all four are so fabulously and cinematically modern and are set in their own aseptic spaces, set back from the surrounding world, makes them appear all the more like recently grounded alien space craft. Stupendous performers on television, the sports facilities, in particular, have proved expensive to maintain and sadly underused. Unquestionable monuments to the scale of China's ambitions and contemporary means, they tell us almost nothing about the contents of its heart and the texture of its dreams.

If the character of modern China was only obscurely inscribed in its Olympic architecture, perhaps something more tangible can be discerned from the way it conducted Olympic business and handled Olympic politics. The Chinese state and its subaltern industries and allies proved supremely competent in planning and implementing immense infrastructure projects, and when compared to other members of the BRIC group – India, Russia and Brazil – did it with considerably less corruption. The vexed question of intellectual property rights in Chinese commercial law and business practice, notorious for its rip-offs, fakes, corporate espionage and hapless systems of patent law, copyright and trademarking, proved sufficiently robust when the state chose to enforce the law to keep Olympic fakery and ambush marketing under control. That said, its architectural practice and subcontractors proved ruthless competitors, deftly undercutting their more glamorous international competition and snatching contracts from under their noses. Politically, the CCP was in its element, keeping total and absolute control domestically over the course of the games, the message of the media and the conduct of the public itself, backing huge campaigns in Beijing to discourage spitting, and encourage queuing and smiling. The foreign media were then welcomed and, for a short window, the tight regulations governing visas, transport and journalistic conduct in the PRC were loosened.

Despite these efforts, the Beijing Olympics proved internationally vulnerable in two areas in particular: the PRC's relationship with the Sudanese government, and its long-standing occupation of Tibet, opposed both at home and in the global Tibetan diaspora.[5] With respect to Sudan, China had been a long-standing supporter of Khartoum, offering and delivering aid, arms and infrastructure projects since the 1970s. Hardly disinterested, the Chinese conducted $3.9 billion worth of trade with Sudan, invested $15 billion in its oil industry and owned 40 per cent of the national petroleum company. However, by the mid-2000s, Sudan had become, in Western circles, a 'pariah state', convulsed by a civil war in Darfur. In this western region of the country, the Sudanese Liberation Movement, broadly representing the non-Arab population, was fighting a determinedly pro-Arab government. Khartoum responded aggressively, discreetly supporting the notorious Janjaweed militia primarily responsible for the violent ethnic cleansing of non-Arabs from many parts of Darfur and the widespread abuse of human rights. A coalition of human-rights activists, Hollywood celebrities and athletes successfully labelled Beijing the 'Darfur Olympics' or 'Genocide Olympics' in the American media, charging the Chinese with failing to pressure their Sudanese clients, selling them weapons and vetoing UN resolutions that condemned the government in Khartoum and supported the SLM. Thus, the US Olympic Committee chose as its flag bearer the 1,500-metre runner Lopez Lomong, a Sudanese refugee and active supporter of the Darfur campaign. The Chinese were hurt, and in some ways found it all incomprehensible. Seen from the perspective of a Chinese model of international relations, they had done all that could be expected: enjoining their Sudanese friends to enter peace talks, but remaining publicly neutral on questions of sovereignty in another nation. As for oil, the US had little problem supporting equally unpleasant regimes all over the world, and, in any case, the Russian and Malaysians were just as deep into Sudanese oil as the Chinese were.

The question of Tibet was harder to shrug off. In early 2008, rioting broke out in the regional capital, Lhasa, and spread across the country.[6] Events began when Chinese police broke up a peaceful Tibetan independence rally, but, in so doing, they managed to spark the great pyre of resentment that had built up during the long occupation, made considerably more flammable in recent years by the massive influx of Han Chinese settlers into Tibet, and the enduring marginalization, economically, politically and culturally, of the indigenous peoples. The riots were overwhelmingly directed at the property and persons of the Han Chinese and other minorities. The subsequent Chinese security operation, although portrayed by the Tibetans as brutal, appears to have been relatively controlled; that said, killings by both rioters and the police ran into the hundreds.

Thus, alongside a whole host of campaigns concerned with China – from international journalists protesting reporting restrictions to Amnesty International concerned with human rights – the Free Tibet

movement was the most prominent in the politics of Beijing's gigantic, five-continent Olympic torch relay, held just a few months later.[7]
Liu Qi, the head of Beijing's organizing committee, had his speech
disrupted in Olympia. In Athens, when the Greeks officially handed
over the flame to the Beijing games, demonstrators shouted 'Free
Tibet', unfurled banners and caused enough trouble for a dozen or
so to be detained by the police.

Things got altogether more serious as the torch made its way
through Britain, France and the USA. In London, torch carriers were
jostled, and, at one point, forced to make a tactical retreat onto a
bus. The vigorous response of the assembled troupe of Chinese security goons was accurately described as thuggish. In Paris, despite
shortening the route and cancelling a number of public events, 3,000
police were required on the relay, with numerous attempts by pro-
Tibetan demonstrators to put the flame out with fire extinguishers (a
number of them successful). The relay disappeared into a warehouse,
in San Francisco, as pro-Chinese government and pro-Tibet demonstrators clashed in AT&T Park. Argentina, by comparison, was a
breeze, as the antis held an alternative torch march through the city,
and Tanzania and Oman were trouble free. However, the torch relay's
brief stop in South Asia occasioned such an outbreak of worry and
paranoia about anti-Chinese and pro-Tibetan demonstrations that,
in Pakistan, the relay was held behind closed doors, in an empty
stadium, while the Indian police treated the tiny run through New
Delhi as a maxim-security event. The presence of members of the
Chinese diaspora and pro-government supporters at demonstrations
in Europe and America was redoubled in Asia, where, in Indonesia,
Australia and Japan, they came to outnumber protestors. In Hong
Kong, where a few brave pro-democracy activists appeared on the
route, they were engulfed and overwhelmed.

Dissent in Beijing during the games, despite the thoughtful provision of official protest spaces by the authorities, was absent. The
stage was entirely left to the CCP, the IOC and its corporate sponsors.
The faultless immensity of the opening ceremony made it very clear
to even the most inattentive TV viewer that China was big, back
and meant business. The huge state elite-sports programme, in overdrive since the first Beijing Olympic bid in the early 1990s, delivered
the top spot: one hundred medals and fifty-one golds, especially
strong in shooting, weightlifting, boxing, fencing, gymnastics, judo

and diving.[8] An indicator of the intensity of the programmes these athletes had been through was how young some of them were, and how often they seemed to marry within their sport.

Beyond any one nation's achievements, Beijing did see truly extraordinary feats of human performance. Five world records were broken in athletic events – a remarkable haul, given that only seven records had been set at the previous four games combined – and twenty-five of thirty-four in the swimming events. Both sports also produced a single exceptional athlete who held the world's attention: the American swimmer Michael Phelps, and the Jamaican sprinter Usain Bolt.

Phelps won eight gold medals in Beijing, eclipsing Mark Spitz's previous record of seven, achieved at Munich in 1972. Swimmers have been making steady progress in breaking world records over the last forty years, but have been aided by important technological developments: the availability of bigger deep pools, with fewer waves and less turbulence drag, and improvements in swimming kits. Beijing was notable for its remarkably deep waters, and the use of new polyurethane body suits rather than textile-based kit, the impact of which on streamlining was so large that, in 2009, FINA (the sports governing body) banned their use. Even so, Phelps brought a work ethic (in part, a response to his ADHD) and an anatomy uniquely suited to swimming. Standing six feet four inches high, he has the wingspan and torso of a considerably taller man, making him especially buoyant and powerful, relative to his height, weight and drag. His hands and feet, although not off the scale, are very large and fabulously good at shifting water. Finally, his capacity to recover from athletic exertion, especially his very low rate of lactic-acid production, gives him an edge over other swimmers, nearly all of whom will be swimming multiple times a day during competition.[9]

Usain Bolt, already a world-record holder, but barely known beyond the elite athletic circuit, took the world's breath away at Beijing. First, he won the 100 metres in a record 9.69 seconds, and then he smashed Michael Johnson's 200-metre record, set in Atlanta twelve years earlier. The set was completed with a world-record-breaking win for the Jamaican men in the 100-metre relay. Bolt would repeat these achievements at 2012, winning three golds as part of Jamaica's comprehensive domination of sprinting, their athletes winning eleven of the eighteen medals available, while Shelly-Ann Fraser-Pryce won the women's 100 metres at both games.

Bolt's brilliance is, like Phelps', partly a matter of individual bio-physics. Sprinters achieve maximum speeds by taking fewer, longer strides than their competitors, and Bolt, an unusually tall six feet five inches for a champion, takes a mere forty-one in a 100-metre race, the norm being closer to forty-five. Normally, his size would be a major disadvantage in the opening 10 metres of a race, where short, powerful steps are essential to building momentum, but Bolt has managed to find the technique to minimize his problem.

However, as the broader progress of Jamaican sprinters suggests, something bigger is at work.[10] It is an astonishing fact that an island of just two million people should achieve such dominance, especially in a sport where the barriers to participation are low and the potential athlete pool is enormous. The same questions apply to the world of music, where the island and its diaspora have proved an implausibly fertile source of ideas, innovations and great tunes. One commentator noted, of Jamaican music, that 'creatively it just seems to take place at a higher amperage. It may be an island effect. Isolation does seem to breed these intensities sometimes.'[11] This is certainly true of secondary-school athletics in Jamaica, which attracts a remarkable level of fervour. Champs, the annual inter-school competition, is a week-long affair and just the tip of a whole mountain of athletic activity centred on high schools, which aggressively compete to recruit the best athletes, and actively coach and nurture them. Beyond high school, the leading athletes can enter a network of coaches, academies and sponsorships (many created by former athletes) that give them the chance of turning professional. Just in case they need reminding of the economic escape-route that the sport offers, Usain Bolt's mansion sits in the blue hills above the national stadium where Champs takes place.

Phelps was shy, and relatively uncommunicative. Bolt was not. Indeed, his charisma and appeal is simply incomparable to any Olympic athlete. One has to go back as far as Olga Korbut, in 1972, to find an Olympian with the televisual stardust, tangible humanity and global appeal of Usain Bolt. Funky, funny, even wise, indisputably his own man and comfortable in his own skin, Bolt announced his athletic brilliance and deep humanity in the final microseconds of the Beijing 100 metres, slowing down to celebrate as he realized that his opponents had been burnt and vanquished. His charming treatment of volunteers and helpers and his fabulously choreographed post-race celebrations, from the archer (poised to fire an arrow skywards from an imaginary bow) to the dance-hall moves he puts on with such uncluttered aplomb, have brought him admiration, riches and love. Yet, in a remarkable X-ray of what little is left of the soul of contemporary Olympism, IOC president Jacques Rogge chose to criticize Bolt's Beijing celebrations as disrespectful and suggested that his self-appellation of 'legend' at the London games was unwarranted.

The latter is surely absurd pique. To suggest that only longevity ensures legendary status is to be completely blind to the scale of Bolt's performance (in a sport that does not usually favour longevity). As to the celebrations, Rogge's reaction seems a measure of Olympism's deracination, the severance of high-performance sport from the warmth and joy and spontaneity that human beings are capable of. As Max Weber put it: 'Spiritualists without soul. Hedonists without heart. This nullity imagines itself the apex of civilisation.'[12]

THREE

The London 2012 games, although held under the premiership of David Cameron at the head of the Conservative-dominated coalition government, were, in their conception, tone and form, the bequest of New Labour and its long thirteen years in office. That they altered so little under Labour's successors is a measure of the wafer-thin cultural and political distance between them as much as the depth of Labour's imprimatur.[1]

Two earlier projects had shaped the thinking of the nation's political and sporting elites about the London Olympics. First, the multiple if unsuccessful bids by Manchester and its Labour city council to stage the games, and its subsequent hosting of the 2002 Commonwealth Games, legitimized the whole notion of sports- and event-driven regeneration. Second, there was the Millennium Project, which the first New Labour administration inherited from its predecessors. Its dismal flagship was a huge and expensive tent of an arena, designed by Richard Rogers, sited on the once deeply toxic wasteland on the Greenwich peninsula in south-east London and intended to cast a wistful look back to the festival of Britain in 1951, while saying something defining about the country's future. With control over its exhibits handed over to corporate sponsors, it was, needless to say, an entirely unsuccessful endeavour, but the need for British projects remained. Indeed, given the steady rise of Welsh and Scottish nationalism and the drift of support away from the Labour Party in what were once its strongholds, the need to find British projects was all the more urgent.

The key figure in initiating the London bid was the minister of culture and London MP, Tessa Jowell, who could see that a London games opened up regeneration possibilities much greater than Manchester, and a version of Britishness more compelling than the millennium fiasco.[2] She found a powerful ally in the Labour Mayor of London, Ken Livingstone, who, though sceptical, was ready to support

the bid in return for promises of economic and social development
and investment in east London. Tony Blair gave his approval, not on
the basis of any considered review of the development case, it seems,
but as a response to Jowell's provocations that he lacked the leadership and vision and sense of adventure for the task. The bid, then
priced at a laughably low £2.3 billion, centred on the redevelopment
of a strip of the Lea Valley, in east London, near Stratford. A vast and
toxic brownfield site would be cleaned and converted into a green
Olympic park, bound to a whole array of transport networks connecting this once marginal part of the city right to the centre. More
ambitiously, and sensing the IOC's unease with the opulent boosterism and white elephants of recent games, London 2012 promised
legacies – a sustainable city, a healthier and more active nation, a
better life for the disabled. To this they added the trump card of
Sebastian Coe, recently ennobled and retired from frontline Conservative party politics. An Olympic champion and consummate insider,
he could be brusque with the press, but had the kind of oleaginous
charm that made him the perfect figurehead for the bid. A final flourish in Singapore, in 2005, saw Tony and Cherie Blair work the room
and Sebastian Coe make his pitch alongside thirty kids from London's
super-diverse East End, and, to the amazement and chagrin of the
favourites, Paris, the 2012 games were awarded to London.

The day after the bid had been won, London awoke to the news
that four suicide bombers had blown themselves up in the capital,
three on the Tube and one on a bus. The 7/7 bombings killed fifty-
two members of the public, as well as the four British jihadis, and
injured more than 700 people. Thus, the heightened securitization of
the Olympic Games, already well advanced at Athens and Beijing,
took another step upwards. It wasn't quite Beijing, which had spent
$6.5 billion on security and installed 300,000 CCTV cameras, but
London still spent $2 billion and planned to deploy over 50,000
police officers, military personnel and private security guards, as well
as hosting upwards of 1,000 members of America's security forces.[3]
Already fabulously well equipped with CCTV cameras, London
experimented with the most advanced face-recognition technologies
on public transport and in public space, while it devised plans to
hermetically seal the private spaces of Olympic venues – a strategy
given tangible expression by the eleven-mile blue security fence
that encircled the entire Olympic park. It was an unintended but

pin-sharp irony that the games' mascots – Wenlock and Mandeville – should so obviously resemble anthropomorphized CCTV cameras; but then there were toy police officers with cameras for faces on sale in the Olympic concession stores.

The vast majority of the workforce was to be supplied by the private-security behemoth, G4S, who had won a £284-million contract to provide 13,700 guards; but, just a fortnight before the games were due to begin, they had recruited only 4,000 and trained even fewer. The contract was cancelled and the army was asked to step in. The hapless administration, cavalier attitude to the public realm, of which the games were just one example, and mean minimum-wage policy of G4S were all characteristic of one of the most unsavoury sectors of the British economy, but most telling of all was the shamelessness of chief executive, Nick Buckles, who had the temerity to demand that the company still receive its £55 million management fee.[4]

The redevelopment of the Lea Valley and the building of the new Stratford took its cue from the London Docklands. Steered by the Thatcher governments of the early 1980s, the recipe began by creating an unaccountable development quango, the LDDC (London Dockland Development Commission), slavishly receptive to business needs, then giving it all the planning controls normally wielded by elected local councils and adding gigantic public subsidies to build the transport infrastructure required to make the land valuable, and to keep afloat whatever developers it had got into bed with as they went through the wild gyrations of speculative property booms. All of which resulted in Canary Wharf. The Olympic version of this model, in which the Olympic Delivery Authority was the key planner-developer, delivered on time, if nowhere near the original and unfeasibly low bid budgets. They and the organizing committee, like much of the British state, handed out an enormous amount of work – something in the region of half a billion pounds' worth – as well as authority, and consequently policy direction, to private consultants, especially in the fields of accountancy and project management.[5] The final reckoning was a bill of just under £9 billion – nearly four times the costs proposed in the bid documents in 2005.

Extraordinarily, the final plan for Stratford allocated a huge swathe of land between the new transport interchange and the Olympic park to mall developers, Westfield, ensuring that almost every person attending the games would have to run the gamut of its predictably dull, garish chain stores. Inside the park, much of the architecture was functional, if undistinguished, modernism – Zaha Hadid's undulating aquatics complex the only nod to iconic architecture and immense budget overruns. Yet, for all the furious public-relations that accompanied the games, the profusion of legacies, post-games uses and Olympic win-wins, nudges and synergies, the meaning of the games remained curiously undefined.

This deficiency was underlined by the popularity and acid satire of the cult BBC sitcom *2012*, celebrated for both its brilliant parallel of the organizers' dilemmas and its almost unbearable accuracy in reproducing the meaningless gabble of the games PR machine. As Iain Sinclair tartly remarked, it appeared to depict, 'The long march towards a theme park without a theme.'[6] It was a sentiment confirmed by the installation of Anish Kapoor's sponsored sculpture, the *ArcelorMittal Orbit*, 'a 377-foot tower . . . which looks like a roller coaster that has been put in a trash compactor.'[7] Ugly, inappropriate and vacuous, this corporate gewgaw offered long queues for a ride to the top and a view of the park. It has proved so popular that it is being repurposed as a glorified helter-skelter.[8]

For the domestic audience, at any rate, it was, in the end, a games about Britishness, albeit one, from its settings, that was skewed to the aristocratic, the monarchical and the home counties – the equestrian events in Greenwich Park; the rowing at Dorneywood, home of Eton's boat club; beach volleyball at Horse Guards Parade; tennis at the All England Club in Wimbledon; and archery at Lords, the home of cricket. But, for that to become self-evident, it required the cultural pyrotechnics of the opening ceremony to shatter the carapace of defensive cynicism and indifference that much of the public had affected. Secure in the knowledge that it could put on a great show, Britain now awaited the gold medal that would open the patriotic floodgates.

They came in a deluge. Cyclist Bradley Wiggins' time-trial gold and Helen Glover and Heather Stanning's victory in the rowing were just the first of twenty-nine gold medals and sixty-five medals in all, a blizzard of Union Jacks that peaked on 'Super Saturday' when three golds earlier in the day were crowned by three more in the Olympic stadium: Jessica Ennis in the heptathlon, Mo Farah in the 10,000 metres and Greg Rutherford in the long jump. Though later denied and clarified, a senior BBC executive sent a memo in the midst of the games, saying of the Director General, 'Mark Thompson is increasingly unhappy that we are focusing far too much on Team GB's performance to the exclusion of all else.'[9] Compared to the written press, the BBC was positively restrained. Dominic Sandbrook, writing in the *Daily Mail*, can stand proxy, albeit at the more florid end of the scale, for much of the commentary from both left and right: 'Even for people who detest sport, the past two weeks have been a patriotic extravaganza, with few parallels in our recent history . . . A particular joy has been the rekindling of Britishness itself – which, we are so often told, is in danger of dying out. Indeed, if Alex Salmond and his Scottish Nationalists had had their way, there would have been no British team at these Olympics at all.'[10]

Yet for all of the unvarnished and uncontrived patriotism in the air, it was a complex, variegated and not always comfortable Britain that was on show. The men's football tournament was emblematic of the complexity of identity and sporting representation in the post-devolution isles.[11] Formed long before either the IOC or FIFA came into existence, the football associations of the United Kingdom cover the four constituent home countries – England, Scotland, Wales and Northern Ireland – and continue to do so, by virtue of a series of deals agreed with the world governing body. No such deal has been made with the IOC, which continued to insist that there would be a British team at 2012 or none at all. While both Gordon Brown's Labour government and the English FA were enthusiastic supporters of the idea, the Celtic football associations and many fans were dismayed at the prospect. First, because they feared it would set a precedent that FIFA's considerable anti-British constituency would seek to make permanent, thus extinguishing them. Second, because in post-devolution Britain, the idea of yielding hard-won sporting identity and independence was unacceptable. The Scottish Football Association made it clear to its players that, though they would be permitted to join such an enterprise, it would be considered an act of betrayal. Given the antipathy of both the Celtic FAs and most of the usual supporters of the four nations, the British football team played to full houses, of, for the most part, crowds normally absent from such places, with a management and squad that was, but for a couple of Welshmen, entirely English.

By comparison to the sporting nation usually on show, dominated by men's professional football, rugby and cricket, London 2012 was unquestionably more gender-balanced.[12] Women's sport was highlighted by the presence, for the very first time, of Saudi Arabian women athletes, while the Tunisian runner Habiba Ghribni won the country's first female gold medal. British women performed exceptionally, the nation lauding well-known athletes, like Jessica Ennis and the cyclist Victoria Pendleton, but also new stars and gold medallists, like the boxer Nicola Adams, the tae kwon do champion Jade Jones and the cyclist Laura Trott. That said, glaring inequalities and double standards remained: both the Australian and the Japanese football federations sent their men to the games first class and their women's team economy class. A British weightlifter, Zoe Smith, was the subject of unpleasant attacks on social media, as trolls found her frame insufficiently feminine for their liking, while the brilliant performances of the African-American gymnast Gabby Douglas were obscured by media sniping over her hair.

The British team was a pretty good avatar of the nation's ethnic diversity, though, as in football and other sports, athletes of Afro-Caribbean and mixed heritage were more present that those of South Asian descent. However, none of their achievements spoke to the moment like Mo Farah's double gold-medal triumph in the 5,000 metres and 10,000 metres. Born in Mogadishu, Somalia, he arrived in Britain at the age of eight, a refugee from the country's brutal civil war. A practising Muslim and an East-End boy, he lifted the roof off the Olympic stadium in the final victorious laps of the 10,000-metre final, igniting an orgy of British cosmopolitan self-congratulation. The poet Michael Rosen tweeted that Nick Griffin – leader of the racist British National Party – just choked on his dinner, but once again Dominic Sandbrook was amongst the most ebullient about new Olympic Britons: 'What better symbol could there be of a united, inclusive country in the post-imperial age? What better advert for British identity: confident and colour-blind? What better answer to those who insist that Britishness is dead, and multi-culturalism is the future? And what better rebuke to the narrow-minded nationalists who want to break up our country and reduce it to a handful of petty fragments?'[13]

Twenty-first century Britain has certainly become a more diverse society and, in places, a more feminized nation, but its enduring inequalities of class have not only remained but, if anything, under conditions of sharply rising economic inequality, become even more apparent. Of all the many institutions in Britain that reproduce and entrench class inequalities, the public-school system is amongst the most important. Educating just 7 per cent of the age cohort, these selective fee-paying 'charities' bag almost half of all places at Oxford and Cambridge universities (themselves equally powerful engines of class reproduction), and supply 35 per cent of MPs, 54 per cent of senior journalists and 70 per cent of the judiciary.[14]

The world of Olympic sport is no different. Research by the Sutton Trust on Team GB at Beijing found that one third of athletes, 37 per cent of medallists and half of the gold-medal winners were educated in fee-paying public schools. The performance at London 2012 was almost identical, and although the state sector could boast sport protégés of the calibre of Jessica Ennis, Bradley Wiggins and Victoria Pendleton, schools with just 7 per cent of the nation's teenagers supplied Ben Ainslie, Chris Hoy, 50 per cent of all the rowers and sailors and every last member of the equestrian team. A corollary of this kind of talent pool was that Team GB was disproportionally represented by athletes from the south-east of England, where wealth and private schools are concentrated, though there remain some delightful regional idiosyncrasies – such as the whole shooting squad hailing from the rural south-west of England.

Politicians and columnists, eager to read the runes of victory, sought to interpret the games on their own terms. On the right, the MEP Daniel Hannan wrote, 'families are much better than government agencies as providers of education, inspiration, healthcare, social security and discipline'.[15] Boris Johnson, Conservative Mayor of London, claimed, 'Kids in this country are seeing that there is a direct correlation between effort and achievement, and the more you put in, the more you get out. That is a wonderful, Conservative lesson about life.'[16] Quite what Hannan thought would have happened had not government agencies built and staged the games as well as supporting elite UK sport is unknown. On the left, the *Guardian* sought to claim road racing and Bradley Wiggins for a contemporary progressive agenda: democratic, accessible, both individual and communal. Looking more closely at the super-rational, high-tech obsessives that made the British cycling team the leading force in the world, Will Hutton argued that 'British sport embraced a new framework of sustained public investment and organised purpose, developing a new ecosystem to support individual sports with superb coaching at its heart. No stone was left unturned to achieve competitive excellence. The lesson is simple. We could do the same for economy and society, rejecting the principles that have made us economic also-rans and which the coalition has put at the centre of its economic policy.'[17]

The London Paralympic Games revealed deep paradoxes in the life of Britain's disabled citizens. On the one hand, on the most basic of measures – tickets actually sold for the games – London embraced them like no other host. Athens sold 850,000 tickets, Sydney sold 1.2 million, Beijing sold 1.8 million, but had to give away the same number to fill the city's venues.[18] London pretty much sold out. Two and a half million tickets, and not just for the Olympic stadium and the aquatics centre, but for wheelchair fencing, sitting volleyball, blind football and *boccia*, a cross between petanque and bowls developed for athletes with cerebral palsy, but now extended to motor-neurone disabilities of all kinds. More than that, once there, the crowds were not only large, but raucous, engaged and joyous. On the other hand, the technology company Atos, an official sponsor of the Paralympic Games, was widely reviled for its treatment of disabled and mentally ill people in its work as the main contractor delivering the government's punitive Work Capacity Assessments – tests for disabled benefits claimants.[19]

Historically speaking, it is fitting that the Paralympics should finally truly go mainstream in Britain, which, since the Second World War, has been the hub of the disability sports movement, though, like so many things, its catalytic force was a foreign refugee.[20] Fleeing the Nazis, the Jewish-German neurosurgeon Ludwig Guttman arrived in Britain in 1939, taking up a post at Stoke Mandeville hospital in Buckinghamshire. Responsible for the treatment of paraplegia, common amongst war veterans, he thought it was the 'most depressing and neglected subject in all medicine', and pioneered an alternative and much more active, humane and rounded regime of rehabilitation. In this light, sport was seen as both a physiological treatment and a way of reintroducing the pleasure of the body to the broken. In 1948, alongside the London Olympics, two archery teams from Stoke Mandeville and another hospital, the Star and Garter, in Richmond, competed in what observers hoped might become 'the disabled men and women's equivalent of the Olympic games.' After building international connections with like-minded groups, the International Stoke Mandeville Games Committee (ISMGC) was launched in 1959 and began to hold four-yearly games. Although the IOC awarded Guttman its highest honours, and the Paralympic Games was held in the aftermath of the 1960 Rome and 1964 Tokyo Olympics, the two remained institutionally and culturally separate. It was only in Seoul, in 1988, and Barcelona, in 1992, that the two were practically integrated, a move sealed in 1996, with the creation of today's International Paralympic Committee, which has run the games (summer and winter) ever since, in parallel with the IOC.

These changes, while enormously welcome in raising the standing of Paralympic sport, and important contributors to improving building and infrastructure access for disabled people in host cities, have nurtured an increasingly perplexing sporting culture. On the one hand, mainstream Paralympic sport has sought to portray itself and its athletes as just that – athletes – and asks broadcasters and the public to collude in that notion. Thus, we have the excruciating situation where, during a swimming race involving athletes with perhaps just one or two limbs, the commentary team feels unable to even explain mechanically how their disability affects their mode of propulsion. Yet, at the same time, the whole circus trades on the relentless narratives favoured for disabled people: triumph over tragedy, individual will power as the key to personal success, and empowerment in an unequal, inaccessible world. Certainly, London 2012 broke new ground with its depiction, especially in Channel 4's TV coverage, of the disabled as superhumans, androids with special powers, something close to Marvel's mutant heroes, the X-Men, and the use of disabled comics and presenters.[21]

The golden glow of the games, a Britain 'at ease with itself', as Boris Johnson hopefully suggested, did not last long. Within days of the Paralympic closing ceremony, and the inevitable return of football to the centre of the country's sporting attention, a whole series of unattractive comparisons was drawn, in which football became a repository of all the most demonized aspects of working-class Britain.[22] Won on the promise of legacy, the bequest of the London games has, so far, fallen a long way short of its promise. The sporting legacy is particularly unhealthy. In 2015, Sport England, the government body charged with getting the country active, reported that, even on its pitifully unambitious measure – the percentage of the population taking part in sport once a week – Britain had become less active since the games, with the 2012 figure of 15.9 million (36 per cent of the population) falling to the 2015 figure of 15.5 million (33 per cent).[23]

However, as research on the impact of Sydney 2000 and the 2002 Commonwealth Games in Manchester had already demonstrated, spending on high-end infrastructure and a televised spectacular simply cannot shift the seemingly inexorable slide in most affluent countries towards sedentary lifestyles and an epidemic of obesity. In the few societies that have bucked the trend – Finland, for high levels of activity, and Japan, for low levels of obesity – the key factors have been low levels of social inequality and, in the case of Finland, long-term investment in micro projects, like cycle lanes and pedestrianization. Not only did the London Olympics fail to deliver any of this, but the Conservative coalition savagely cut the funding that was available to school sport, and dismembered a developing sports-schools network that had been delivering an enhanced programme of cooperation. Local government funding was pared back to the bone, with the inevitable consequence that playing fields, leisure centres and youth services declined or closed, amongst them the Don Valley Stadium in Sheffield, where Jessica Ennis first trained. Above all, the era of Conservative austerity benefit cuts, low wages and high rents has ensured that there are more poor people, and more people with tight budgets in Britain, for whom expenditure on sport and leisure is amongst the first things to be jettisoned.[24]

The real winners of the Olympic Games have been West Ham United and their already wealthy owners, David Gold and David Sullivan, who will be moving into the £429 million Olympic stadium, which the public is paying a further £160 million to convert into something more to their liking. With 54,000 seats and a plethora of banqueting opportunity built into the stadium, West Ham will be paying a peppercorn rent. If Britain had wanted a tangible example and a potent symbol of the way in which its economy has been rigged and restructured for the benefit of the very wealthy, then this was legacy indeed.[25]

FOUR

The kinds of anarchic, provocative anti-Olympic movements prominent in some candidate cities in the 1980s and 1990s, and a minor
presence at Sydney 2000, were absent from both Athens and Beijing
– drowned by cynicism in the former, corralled by fear of the Chinese
state in the latter. London saw more street protest over the passage
of the Beijing torch relay than over the redevelopment of Stratford;
the energies of the disaffected and the marginal were all burnt out
by the looting, glorified as riots, that tore across London the summer
before the games. Where there was protest, the politics and meanings
of the games were primarily contested in the international media and
on the internet, rather than in the host city itself. Vancouver 2010
proved the exception, generating the most multifaceted and vociferous anti-Olympic protests of the twenty-first century – not just on the
airwaves, but on the ground.[1]

At first glance, Vancouver, famed for its easy-going liveability,
might appear an odd stronghold of such sentiments. The city council
had actually secured public approval for the games in a plebiscite in
2003, albeit one in which only a quarter of voters bothered to show,
and the 'yes' campaign had 140 times more funding than the 'no'
campaign. The organizers, hypersensitive to linguistic and symbolic
issues, appeared to bend over backwards to include francophone and
indigenous Canada. The Olympic torch relay was scheduled to make
300 stops on First Nations lands, the organizers based their lamentable mascots on a First Nations cartoon bestiary of mythic creatures,
made considerable funds available for indigenous cultural events,
and other government monies were funnelled to tribes who signed
up to be 'hosts' alongside VANOC (Vancouver Organizing Committee). Despite this, over a third of British Colombia's Indian peoples
refused to participate, and, at the more radical end of the scale, there
was a considerable level of protest centring on the enduring issue
of First Nations' sovereignty, for the land in the mountains around

Whistler, where much of the games would actually happen, was indisputably the ancient territory of the Coastal Saltish people and, as far as they and Canadian law were concerned, their claim was still unresolved.

In 1763, the British established formal legal precedent on these matters with the issue of a Royal Proclamation stating that only the Crown could obtain indigenous lands in Britain's Canadian colonies, and only by treaty. The government of British Columbia, which only joined the Canadian Federation in 1871, had signed very few treaties with the locals, leaving the vast majority of indigenous claims unresolved. Considerable efforts were made legally and politically to extinguish native title in the early and mid-twentieth century, but in a series of landmark judgements won in British Columbia in the 1970s, the still unresolved claims of First Nations were upheld.

Since then, the ownership, regulation and use of land in British Colombia has been the lightning conductor for a whole host of other issues, like the poverty, inequality and marginalization endured by Canada's Indians. The plan to build the Sea-to-Sky highway from Vancouver to the mountain venues in Whistler, through Eagleridge Bluffs – a sacred indigenous site – attracted considerable protest from First Nations activists, who were joined, on this occasion, by the more militant end of the environmental movement in the region, concerned at the destruction of forests and biodiversity, under the slogan, 'No Olympics on Stolen Native Land.' During a demonstration in May 2006, a First Nations elder, Harriet Nahanee, and the veteran environmentalist Betty Krawczyk were arrested and jailed pending trial; both were in their seventies. Nine months later, protestors stormed the stage during a countdown-to-the-games event in downtown Vancouver, demanding their release. A month later, Nahanee contracted pneumonia and died in prison. Activists responded by stealing the gargantuan Olympic flag that had been flying from City Hall, and appeared on social media in traditional dress as the native warrior society, with the flag as their booty.

The vexed question of who is the sovereign power at an Olympic Games was further highlighted by the issue of women's ski jumping. As far back as 1991, the IOC had decreed that all new Olympic sports must be open to both genders. The ruling did not, however, apply to the events that were present at the original summer and winter games; thus, ski jumping, hitherto entirely masculine, was given a bye. In the run-up to Vancouver, the leading women ski jumpers, then regular competitors on the world circuit, took the local organizing committee, VANOC, to court, claiming gender discrimination. The Canadian judge ruled that the failure to have a women's ski-jumping competition was a breach of the Canadian constitution and its gender-equality legislation, but that, given that the Canadian organizers had conceded sovereign control over the matter to the IOC, there was nothing that could be done by a Canadian court. The IOC, thus insulated by its almost unique jurisprudential status, tried to defuse the matter, claiming that their decision had been made on a 'strictly technical basis', noting insufficient numbers of top-class athletes and participating nations. The same logic would also have excluded the equally narrow world of male ski-jumping, and it was not a factor when it came to including the obscure and even more narrowly played practice of ski-cross. Whatever the legal niceties, it remained the case that ski jumping was a bastion of the most antiquated and unexamined sexist prejudice. As late as 2005, the FSI president, Gian-Franco Kapser, argued, in an echo of the discredited medicine of the 1920s that had erroneously deemed women's participation in endurance and contact sports injurious to health, that ski jumping 'seems not appropriate for ladies from a medical point of view.'[2]

In the absence of women ski-jumpers at the games themselves, double standards were firmly applied to Canada's women's ice-hockey team. Jon Montgomery was wildly celebrated for glugging on a large pitcher of beer given to him by a member of the crowd while walking towards the podium to collect his gold medal in the skeleton, commentators claiming that this was when 'the party really started.' However, when the women's ice-hockey team was secretly filmed at a post-final party on the rink, toking on cigars and drinking beer, the complete opposite of everything that happens in the genteel world of male ice-hockey, they were roundly condemned for their disrespect of the games.[3]

Rule fifty-one of the Olympic charter, setting out the basis on which an Olympic Games should be run, states that 'No kind of demonstration or political, religious or racial propaganda is permitted in any Olympic sites, venues or other areas.' Vancouver went one better, passing a local by-law that prohibited banners and posters that 'did not celebrate' the Olympic Games, though those that would 'enhance the festive atmosphere' were permissible. In 2009, Jesse Corcoran exhibited a small graffiti piece outside of the Crying Room Gallery, consisting of five interlacing circular faces – four grimacing, one smiley. The work was removed by the authorities, disingenuously claiming that they did so under an old anti-graffiti statute and not the Olympic celebration rule, but they were eventually forced by the courts to reinstall the piece, by which time the city was pockmarked by anti-Olympic slogans.

In any case, the Vancouver Integrated Security Unit, which combined twenty different intelligence and security agencies, surely had bigger fish to fry? With a budget of over a billion dollars, British Columbia's police force took the opportunity to buy a lot of new Kevlar, semi-automatic weapons became the new norm for policing demonstrations in the city, and an innocuous sounding medium-range acoustic device was acquired – actually a military-grade sonic weapon for use at demonstrations. The Canadian Border Service Agency relentlessly policed downtown for undocumented illegals and demanded residents prove their citizenship; 1,000 CCTV cameras were erected across the city, while the local police chief, Jamie Graham, boasted to the press that every anti-Olympic protest group was being infiltrated.

Of course, there is nothing like the siren cry of a low-flying police helicopter in urban space to bring out the anarchists and the confrontational, and, together with human rights, environmental and First Nations activists, Vancouver's preparations stoked the nascent anti-Olympic movement. What, however, gave the protests wider traction and a foothold in the city was the public's disenchantment with the spiralling costs of the event – rising from $1 billion to $8 billion – the loss of any of the promised social housing at the post-games Olympic village and, under conditions of fiscal austerity, the diversion of public money to keep bankrupt developers afloat. Housing NGOs, campaigners for the homeless and some residents were mobilized by the aggressive gentrification in the city centre, linked to the games. Downtown Eastside, an eight- by fifteen-block zone that was the poorest in the nation outside of native Canadian settlements, but close to the new Olympic waterside developments, was the main target, subject to the city council's fabulously disingenuous Project Civil Society and the Assistance Not Shelter Act – the former, a programme for policing the homeless and warding off the marginal; the latter, a legal instrument that could force rough sleepers into hostels.[4] Clustered around networks like the No Games 2010 Coalition and 2010 GamesWatch, this eclectic group of activists descended on a parking lot in the Eastside, owned by the notorious developer Concord Pacific. The site had the additional merits of being a clearly visible landmark in an official 'Olympic Corridor ' and was earmarked for a development of high-priced condominiums.

More than a year before Occupy Wall Street would claim Zucotti Park, the Olympic tent village the protesters established would be the symbol and practical centre of resistance to the games. Native elders tended sacred fires; music, protest and political workshops were held; Christian justice groups, peaceniks and the local Power of Women residents' group fed and organized a considerable crowd, swollen by an influx of university students, thoughtfully given the games off class by their schools. In conscious emulation of the tactics and language of the 2001 anti-G7, anti-globalization protest in Seattle, just across the border, the small Heart Attack March – 'clogging the arteries of capitalism' – made its way to the business district. A lot of corporate plate glass got smashed, the police were hot to try out some of their new toys, but a more vital oppositional energy could be found in the VIVO Media Arts Centre, where demonstrators, bloggers, filmmakers and artists gathered for daily screening of protest actions and live performances. The Vancouver movement, uniquely, could claim its own short-lived pirate radio, staffed by poet-activists. Of course, you had to be looking out for them. America watched Americans. Late-night comedian Stephen Colbert, who was personally funding the US short-track skate-team, got more coverage than the whole protest moment combined. Once Alexandre Bilodeau had finally won Canada's first Olympic gold medal as host, at moguls freestyle skiing, a more comfortable beer-swilling Canadian patriotism kicked in, peaking when, with the men's ice-hockey final tied 2–2, Canada–USA, Sidney Crosby, the new hope of the national game, scored the golden goal. Fuckin' A!

Apocryphally, the idea of the Sochi 2014 games was hatched amongst a skiing party in Austria, who wondered why it was that Russia, despite fabulous mountains, could not boast a ski resort of the calibre of Alpine Europe. It was a skiing party that just happened to include the Austrian chancellor, Wolfgang Schüssel, president of the Russian Republic, Vladimir Putin, and his close associate, the fabulously rich businessman Vladimir Potanin, owner of a small and then inaccessible ski resort in the mountains east of Sochi, called Krasnaya Polyana.[5]

Putin, as in so many things, has inherited a core belief of the Soviet political elites: that prowess in international sport is an important demonstration at home and abroad of the power and even the grandeur of the state. These are precisely the metrics that have shaped his entire reign: the reassertion of the power of the Russian state at home over recalcitrant oligarchs, troublesome democrats and opposition parties, and restive republics; and the establishment of Russia's place as a major player in international affairs and master of its own sphere of influence. Funded for over a decade by the gigantic fiscal bonanza of a booming world economy, sky-high commodity prices and a great lake of hydrocarbons and minerals, Putin's governments have achieved all this by building a giant military security complex, imprisoning oligarchs who don't share nicely, fixing elections and reducing parliament to a talking shop, ruthlessly harassing opponents and nosy journalists and taking almost complete control of newspapers and television. In the absence of any really significant shift in living standards and life chances for the majority of the population, evidenced by the still catastrophic decline in male life expectancy and the widespread problems of drug abuse, poverty and mental illness, Putin has offered the Russian public vitriolic popular nationalism, a vicious, almost medieval homophobia that has effectively aligned him with Christian evangelicals, like Billy Graham, television to rot the soul, and the occasional circus. All of these instruments of rule would be found at work at Sochi 2014, which itself was just part of a wider commitment by the regime to host and sponsor international sport, which includes Gazprom's sponsorship of the World Cup and UEFA Champion's League, hosting the World Athletics Championships in 2013 and securing the World Cup in 2018.

Putin personally attended and worked the room at the IOC congress in 2007 that awarded the 2014 games to Sochi, a small resort city on the east coast of the Black Sea, where Russia abuts the Caucuses. To many, it seemed an odd choice. Under both the Romanovs and the communists, Sochi was a holiday destination: a rare corner of Russia blessed with sub-tropical weather, warm water and palm trees. Great for frozen Muscovites, but hardly the stuff out of which a winter-sports spectacular is born. There were mountains and Vlad-imir Potanin's tiny resort, but connecting this region to Sochi would require an epic feat of engineering.

Infrastructural and meteorological issues aside, Sochi was hardly ticking the risk-free box. In 2008, the long-brewing conflict between Georgia and Russia turned to open warfare after President Putin openly supported the breakaway Georgian republics of South Ossetia and Abkhazia – which lies directly to the east of Sochi. Across the nearby and turbulent Russian republics of North Ossetia, Ingushetia, Dagestan and Chechnya the already active Islamic insurgency saw Sochi as a new point of attack. The leading Chechen Islamist, Doku Umarov, described it as, 'Satanic dancing on the bones of your ances-tors', and, in 2013, a group of militants bombed the ski lift at Mount Elberus, 150 miles south-west of Sochi, and opened fire on a car, killing three tourists. The Circassians weren't happy either. Once the occupants of the area around Sochi, they were crushed by the Tsar's army in 1864 and expelled from the region. From a population of perhaps 1.5 million in the mid-nineteenth century, there were cur-rently less than 25,000 ethnic Circassians in Sochi. The siting of skiing and snowboarding venues on Red Hill, the site of the decisive and, for the Circassians, terminal battle of the war with Russia, sparked a global campaign against the games amongst the diaspora.[6]

Putin's personal relationship to the region is instructive. He has two dachas in the region, the latest and most opulent in the remote area of Lunnaya Polyana, deep in the Sochi national park – a Unesco designated world-heritage site. Here, Putin has built himself two monstrous chalets with their own helipad, power station and per-sonal ski lifts onto the local slopes, an installation that Unesco has recorded as a meteorological station. Thus, occupation of the terri-tory was not enough. It needs to be built on: as the president himself said, 'We need to understand and feel that we are capable of pulling off large-scale projects.'[7] Seen from this perspective, the Sochi games were an act of fortification, a statement of grandeur and an import-ant mechanism of economic redistribution.

Sochi was always going to be expensive, given the complete absence of any sporting infrastructure, but in the detailed research compiled by the Russian NGO Fund for the Fight Against Corruption, Sochi's Olympic projects were, on average, 42 per cent more expen-sive than the best equivalents elsewhere.[8] Taking out the 'Russian surcharge' for a moment, the $51 billion bill looks more like $30 billion – still expensive, but, given the scale of the project and the enormous engineering challenges of the rail and road route from the city to the mountains, a less implausible total. All of the money, one way or another, came from the Russian public sector. The majority was direct funding by federal, city and local governments; investments were also made by government-owned companies, like Russian Railways and Gazprom, which have found themselves diversifying from transport and hydrocarbons into the winter tourism business; and additionally extensive state-backed loans were made to obscure public–private partnerships. The 'Russian surcharge' is, of course, the many-layered, engrained system of kickbacks and off-book payments that any construction project in the country must negotiate. Given the closeness of many of the key figures dispersing these monies to President Putin, the Sochi games proved a remarkably good instrument for recycling Russian oil and mineral wealth to a small circle of allies. Alexey Miller and Vladimir Yakunin, the chief executives of Gazprom and Russian Railways, both began their careers alongside Putin, working in the St Petersburg city administration of the 1990s. The next tier of allies and oligarchs would also need their share. Russian Railways allocated the vast majority of its construction work to Transyuzhstroy, a company founded by Yakunin's vice-president at Russian Railways, with his wife on the board of its majority stakeholders, and SK Most, owned by Gennady Timchenko, another Putin ally from the old days.

There were limits as to how much could be raked off. Akhmed Bilalov, vice-president of the organizing committee, had the uncomfortable experience of trying to explain to President Putin how the cost of the ski-jumping venue had quadrupled to $256 million. The next day, he fled the country. Finally, at the level of the construction sites themselves, Russian conglomerates and their partners found themselves beholden to the local networks of organized crime, many of which date back to the Soviet era. Needless to say, despite extensive reporting on these issues, and multiple shootings amongst the criminal gangs, no cases have been investigated, let alone come to court.

Given the grandeur of the organizers' ambitions, the fact that there were a mere 2,000 forced relocations during the preparations for Sochi is testament to how small the city was, rather than how sensitive or merciful the planners were. Consequently, there were nowhere near enough local workers to serve such a pharaonic project, and tens of thousands of migrants, predominately from central Asia, were imported. Conditions, even by Russian standards, were poor. Aside from the inevitably low wages, long hours and poor safety conditions, many workers were cheated of their salaries, lived in grim conditions and had their passports confiscated by unscrupulous contractors. Combining this workforce with impossible last-minute schedules, and budgets suddenly cut to the bone by the multiple layers of graft required to get anything done, made for some very poorly assembled facilities, gleefully lampooned on social media by American and European journalists.[9] Water, Wi-Fi and heating were often absent, and one German photographer reported arriving to find workers and stray dogs wandering through his hotel suite.

By contrast, there were no half measures for Putin's Ring of Steel – now the sixth Olympic ring, perhaps – a multilayered system of military control and surveillance surrounding Sochi in ever more impregnable concentric circles. It was estimated to have cost $2 billion and deployed at least 70,000 security personnel.[10] This might have been enough to keep the Islamists out, but the sharpest attacks against the regime were made in the global media, where the regime's attitude to homosexuality, and its recent laws prohibiting 'Gay Propaganda', attracted the most opprobrium.

In fact, this was just the legislative and public face of a great wave of virulent homophobia in Russia. Russian responses to Western probing were, on occasion, laughable. The mayor of Sochi, Anatoly Pakhomov, told the BBC that, in a city of half a million people, there were no gay people at all, and as to visitors, 'We just say that it is your business, it's your life. But it's not accepted here in the Caucasus where we live. We do not have them in our city.'[11] When the president was pressed on how foreign members of the LGBT community would feel coming to Sochi, Putin told them that they could 'feel calm and at ease,' but with the kicker that they should, 'Just leave kids alone, please.' Putin's insistence on conflating homosexuality and paedophilia might have appeared an 'odious canard' in New York, but it went down just fine in Russia, as did the games themselves.

Russia topped the medal table with thirteen golds and thirty-three of all kinds, and they got them any way they could. Victor Ahn,

the South Korean short-track skater, was just one of a number of
athletes who had recently acquired Russian citizenship, and who
went on to win medals for the motherland – in Ahn's case, three
individual golds and a relay victory too. Figure skater Adelina Sotnikova managed to beat the South Korean Kim Yuna to the gold
medal, despite Kim's lead in the compulsory round and her flawless
performance in the free skate, compared to Sotnikova's own more
technically demanding, but error-prone performance.[12]

On the ground, one observer thought that Olympic Sochi 'seemed
like an extravaganza anywhere: buttoned up, locked down, corporate and best followed on television.'[13] Punk provocateurs Pussy Riot
made an appearance in the second week of the games. Walking on
to a city street twenty miles from the Olympic park, they began to
play, 'Putin Will Teach You to Love the Motherland', and were set
upon by Cossacks with horsewhips; as David Remnick put it, 'In a
pure expression of Putinism, a Cossack smashed Pussy Riot's guitar.'
Domestic Putinism, that is. For the foreign dimension, one needed to
wait a little. Just four days after the games and the IOC's Olympic
truce had come to an end, pro-Russian militias began occupying
government buildings in Sebastopol, a prelude to Crimea's secession
from the Ukraine and its embrace of Russia, while the Russian Parliament gave the president authority to support Russian speakers
mobilizing in the eastern Ukraine.

FIVE

In 2009, at the IOC congress in Copenhagen, Rio de Janeiro, unusually, chose the nation's central-bank president, Henrique Meirelles, rather than a former Olympian or leading politician, to give the keynote address to the committee, due later in the day to vote on the hosting rights for the 2016 games. Meirelles, aware that many of the IOC were concerned as to whether Brazil was ready to host and pay for a games, was able to argue that the country was enjoying its most sustained period of high growth, high employment and low inflation, while the recent discovery of vast reserves of oil would cushion any slowdown in the economy.[1] Suitably mollified, and driven above all by the widely held notion that it was, in an era of economic transformation in the global south, time to award the games to South America, the IOC voted, ahead of Chicago, Madrid and Tokyo, to give the games to Rio.

Just seven years later, the IOC, the global financial community and the Brazilians themselves were wondering what any of them had been thinking. The Brazilian economy has proved remarkably fragile. Despite weathering the initial storm of the 2008 world financial crisis, the subsequent global slowdown and the collapse of commodity prices have seen the country enter its steepest and longest recession, the value of the currency has halved on international markets and income from oil has collapsed; and all at a time when the always utterly fictive bid budget was turning into a final bill approaching $20 billion.

The IOC's concerns were made considerably worse by the events of June 2013. While hosting the Confederations Cup – an extended warm-up and dress rehearsal for the football World Cup that was to come the following year – small-scale protests over public transport fare rises in the major cities met with horrifying levels of police violence, snowballed and then mutated into a massive outpouring of citizen protest over the lamentable state of Brazil's infrastructure, schools and health care, and the appalling waste and corruption that characterized Brazilian public life, exemplified by the preparations for both the World Cup and the Olympic Games.[2]

Political concessions and promises of health and education spending from President Dilma Rousseff (never delivered on), and the imposition, in effect, of a militarized state of emergency at the World Cup, ensured there was, beyond a tiny activist core, no repeat of these protests in 2014. The IOC, reasonably enough, was rattled, and, in April 2014, after taking an unusually detailed look at what was actually happening on the ground, declared Rio's preparations 'worse than Athens', which, of course, made them 'the worst ever.'[3]

The economic crisis aside, this was a depressingly predictable turn of events. Had the IOC taken a look at what had happened at the Pan American Games, staged in Rio in 2007, rather than listening to the economic illiteracy of its central bank, or swooning over the usual tourist-brochure photography of the city, they might have thought otherwise. Those games came in at over six times their original budget. All of the socially minded environmental and transport plans meant to accompany the games were scrapped and none of the new venues had any kind of public use or access after the games. In any case, they were overwhelmingly concentrated, along with the athletes' village, in the new upscale suburb of Barra da Tijuca. The village, intended as a real-estate bonanza, was built so badly that it proved a financial and housing catastrophe: unfinished, in places unliveable, and very unsellable. Most telling of all, while the Brazilian authorities sealed off the event in the usual hermetic bubble of police lines and cameras, other wings of the security services fought a fierce month-long battle with the drug gangs of the Complexo do Alemão, a hilltop favela just a few miles from the games, that left over forty dead and an entire neighbourhood confined to their houses.

Rio's preparations for the Olympics have been conducted in a similar vein. Barra da Tijuca is again the main zone of development, with a second run at an Olympic village bonanza. Simultaneously, the city police have attempted, by force of arms, to pacify the favelas and poor suburbs where the writ has not run. At considerable human and financial cost, drug gangs and organized criminals have been displaced or marginalized from some neighbourhoods, there have been tiny pockets of infrastructure spending, but, for the most part, the violence and viciousness of the police make their rule little different from that of their foes, perhaps even worse.

The one key difference between 2007 and 2016 is that, this time around, at least some of the guilty parties are being brought to justice, for the world of Brazilian sport became engulfed in the Petrobras scandal that was cutting a swathe through the nation's elites. Initiated in late 2014 as Operation Car Wash, federal police used the testimony of a whistleblowing senior executive from the state-owned oil leviathan, Petrobras, to lead to a vast network of bribery, money laundering and embezzlement in the allocation of Petrobras contracts and, indeed, public-sector work of all kinds. Over the next eighteen months, as the case came together, accusations of corruption were levelled and pursued against over one hundred leading politicians, particularly in the ruling Workers' Party, Petrobras executives and some of the richest and most powerful businessmen in the country.

Brazil's sports administrators, initially in parallel, were in almost as much trouble. In May 2015, the US attorney general and the Swiss government announced they were conducting an extensive investigation into corruption in global football, and together they arrested fourteen football and media executives, many of them at FIFA's favourite hotel in Zurich. The FBI was primarily concerned with kickbacks earnt in the USA, or paid via US banks, from the sale of media rights by officials of CONCACAF (the Confederation of North, Central American and Caribbean Football) and CONMEBOL (the South American Football Confederation), many of whom also had executive positions at FIFA. The Swiss were investigating the voting on the hosting of the 2018 and 2022 World Cups, as well as other dubious transactions involving FIFA officials. Together, these two investigations, still ongoing, have revealed what has long been transparent to all but the most blinkered: that the upper reaches of the world of football governance were systematically corrupt, selling TV rights and hosting rights for substantial kickbacks.

Brazilians, inevitably, featured heavily on the list of those resigning before they were deposed (FIFA honorary life president, João Havelange, ex-head of Brazilian football, and FIFA vice-president, Ricardo Teixeira), and those arrested, charged and extradited to the United States – most notably, José Maria Marin, the man who organized Brazil's 2014 World Cup. Brazil's own corruption investigators charged the leader of the nation's volleyball federation with wide-ranging illegalities in 2015, while Carlos Nuzman, the man who had previously run Brazilian volleyball before moving on to be head of both the Rio 2016 organizing committee and the Brazilian national Olympic committee, was accused of the most serious malpractice during his campaign to hold onto the presidency of the BOC. It is an extraordinary coincidence that, in 2011, the only person who had ever challenged him for the post – Eric Maleson, president of the country's Lilliputian winter-sports federation – should, on the eve of the election, be charged with fraud, disqualified from the competition on minor procedural grounds and have his offices raided by his opponent's factotums.[4]

In early 2016, the investigations surrounding Petrobras took on an Olympic dimension. Luís Adams, the attorney general, announced that he was examining the relationships between Eduardo Cunha, then speaker of the lower house of parliament, and the Olympic work undertaken by the nation's biggest construction companies – in particular, the $475,000 he had received from the company, OAS, which had won the contract to build Rio's BMX, canoeing and mountain-bike venues, as well as much of the work on its rapid bus lanes. Given that the chief executives of four of the five companies that won the overwhelming majority of Olympic contracts were, at this point, languishing in jail, awaiting trial, or were already imprisoned on similar corruption charges, there will no doubt be more of this to come. Hundreds of thousands of Brazilians took to the streets, calling for President Dilma's impeachment, a request the opposition in the Brazilian Congress actively pursued.[5]

In May 2016 the lower house, half of whose members face criminal charges of one kind or another, voted to impeach Dilma, an act embellished by Rio politician and former army parachutist Jair Bolsonaro, who compared the moment to the military coup of 1964 and as Perry Anderson notes, 'dedicated his ballot to Colonel Carlos Brilhante Ustra, torturer-in-chief of the dictatorship that followed.' The vote was confirmed by the equally compromised Senate, which elevated Vice-President Michel Temer to the Presidency. With the federal government, whatever its complexion, consumed by its own problems, and the organizing committee, led by Nuzman, barely able to deal with the operational budget, let alone the construction programme, the Rio games have increasingly became the project of

Mayor Eduardo Paes and his presidential ambitions. Here, at least, the Rio games have acquired a modicum of focus and organizational competence. The perilous state of the Brazilian economy has forced sharp cutbacks in the staging and organizational budget of the games, the scale of VIP dining has taken a hit and volunteers are now being asked to pay for accommodation. Nonetheless, the venues in the Olympic park, the facilities in the Olympic village and the many temporary constructions in the Deodoro zone are finished or on plausible schedules. The once immense transportation plans have been scaled back to two key projects: the rapid-transit bus routes, and the metro extension to the Olympic park. Even by Brazilian standards, the metro is looking very last minute, and will probably require an astronomical injection of federal money to be done on time. The BRT will be finished, though at considerable cost, and with many forced removals of families whose homes used to hug the old autoroutes. But this is really beside the point, for the problem is that such vast resources have been poured into the transport needs of Barra da Tijuca, while the huge swathes of people in the Zona Norte, the people most dependent on public transport, enduring long and expensive bus rides to work in the centre, have once again been neglected.

Perhaps it is better to be neglected by the Brazilian state? Some of the 600 families who used to live in Vila Autódromo might think so.[6] A stable and relatively prosperous favela, fabulously positioned for access to the rest of the city, it is an informal settlement, started in 1967 by fishermen and construction workers near Jacarepagua Lagoon, where an old racing track once stood, and where plans for the Olympic park required their removal. Despite considerable resistance to the government entreaties to move, by early 2015, only forty families remained, driven by a combination of stubborn resistance and a nerve that allowed some of them, just for once, to actually get the market or above the market rate for their properties, rather than the usual dismal or token payments that developers hand out. As late as April 2015, the last hold-outs were protesting their case, blocking the morning rush-hour traffic, creating three-hour tailbacks into the city.

Focused as the mayor might be, and notorious as Brazil is for coming up with the goods at the very last minute, there is one Olympic deadline that has already been abandoned. The bid's excessive and frankly disingenuous plans to completely refit Rio's notoriously awful sewage and water systems, as well as to clean all of the city's polluted watercourses, beaches and bays, will not happen. A grim, if expected, outcome for Rio's poor, who continue to live with the most minimal of sanitary arrangements, and a potentially disastrous decision for the games themselves. The IOC, the world's sailing authorities and the Brazilian organizers continue to insist that, on standard bacterial measures, the waters of Guanabara Bay (sailing), the Rodrigo de Freitas Lagoon (rowing and canoeing) and Copacabana beach (triathlon) are within acceptable limits and perfectly safe for competitors. This, despite the fact that 50 per cent of the sewage reaching these areas is completely untreated. Whatever the monitoring equipment says, sailors in these Olympic waters have recently encountered 'mattresses, cars, washing machines, tables, televisions, couches and chairs as well as dead dogs, horses and cats.'[7] The Brazilian Olympian Lars Grael reported finding four human corpses over the last couple of years of sailing on the bay, while a colleague, Thomas Low-Beer, lost a championship race after sailing straight into a sofa. Research commissioned by the Associated Press, measuring virus levels in the water, found concentrations of sewage-related pathogens 1.7 million times higher than the safe permissible level used in southern California, and not just near the shore, but deep out to sea. Reports from the Croatian and Austrian sailing camps held in the bay in summer 2015 described outbreaks of serious gastroenterological illness. Some athletes are proposing to come early and sail often in the hope that, like much of Rio's population, they will eventually acquire some immunity. Others are hoping that antibiotic mouthwash might do the trick. Rio's government was still claiming that a last-minute sewage-pipe programme was going to make all the difference; meantime, it invested in the preposterously named eco-boats and barriers, which are actually tugs that fish out shopping carts and carrion, and mobile buoys and booms that will try to keep the filth and the foam from the TV cameras.[8]

By contrast, progress on the Porto Maravilha has been rather more advanced.[9] Considered in all promotional literature to be a central Olympic project, this huge redevelopment of the city's historic dock district is actually only home to the media village and a small technical-operations centre. Not much, but enough for the programme

to acquire the urgency of Olympic projects and a gigantic public–
private partnership, in which the city government has handed over
the planning and governance of the city's largest ever development
to a consortium of three private construction companies (all, needless
to say, embroiled in the Petrobras scandal). Its centrepiece is the
extraordinary Museu do Amanhã (Museum of Tomorrow). Designed
by Santiago Calatrava and described as an 'other-worldly edifice that
looks like a cross between a solar-powered dinosaur and a giant
air-conditioning unit', it is dedicated to issues of sustainability, climate
change, energy use and urban living, and encourages its visitors to
contemplate the complex choices involved in securing a sustainable
future.[10]

It is hard to imagine that staging the Olympic Games for $20
billion is part of the solution. One wonders whether the museum will
also ask its visitors to think about what the cost of security will be in
a sustainable future. The demonstrations that engulfed the Confederations Cup in 2013 were triggered by brutal police responses to
protests over bus-fare rises in São Paolo. This time around, the
authorities have put their prices up in January rather than June, and
the protest that followed in São Paolo, 3,000 strong, was met by tear
gas, stun grenades and water cannon. They have yet to resume. It
seems unlikely that the nation, now utterly exhausted by the struggle
for the presidency and the impeachment of Dilma, will return to the
streets for the games. Yet Rio looks set to spend somewhere around
$2 billion on security, deploying 85,000 personnel – more even than
Sochi – for just seventeen days of urban peace. This, in the country
of the future, is the Olympics of tomorrow.

Conclusion

To change or be changed? That is the question.

Thomas Bach, IOC President

It is a dilemma that the International Olympics Committee, despite its enduring conservatism, has navigated with some aplomb. Indeed, the political flexibility of its leadership has often proved vital in maintaining the organization's pre-eminent position in global sport. Coubertin made his peace with the world fairs and the inevitable nationalism of international sport. Baillet-Latour's IOC nipped the Women's Olympics in the bud and signed on with both Hollywood and the Third Reich. Brundage swallowed his anti-communism and let the Soviet Union into the IOC, ensuring the pre-eminent status of the games in global sport and dooming the defence of amateurism. Samaranch delivered the coup de grace and, against the grain of almost a century of Olympian disdain for money, made a series of decisive alliances with professional sport and the global cultural industries, which secured the IOC's economic independence and the games' global reach. Thomas Bach, their successor, faces a moment of change too; but the challenge to Bach's IOC is not from an alternative model of sport, disgruntled nation states and athletes, or excluded minorities; the problem is the Olympics itself.

In the twenty-first century, the games, already expensive and increasingly bound to the grandest of urban-development projects, were given a shot of fiscal and architectural steroids by the soaring ambitions of, amongst other things, the Greek and Brazilian booms, China's return to great-power status and Russia's determination to let us know it never lost it. The already soaring costs of Olympic security in the 1990s were sharply increased by the fallout of 9/11 and the increasing preference of the IOC and the organizers to wall and defend aseptic Olympic spaces in the host cities scrubbed clean of the homeless, protestors and guerrilla marketeers. Jacques Rogge's presidency, primarily concerned with re-establishing the reputation and probity of the IOC after the Salt Lake City scandal, and tending to the needs of sponsors, was remarkable for its almost compete indifference to the financial and social consequences of the urban giganticism that it had let loose and then nurtured. Indeed, despite the already overcrowded sporting schedule, Rogge oversaw the addition of golf and rugby sevens to the summer games, and a swathe of new extreme and alternative sports to the winter games.

The citizens of potential host cities in North America and Europe were less sanguine about the escalating costs and dubious benefits of hosting the games, and their scepticism has made an Olympic bid an increasingly hard political act to manage. Consequently, the 2018 winter games produced a field of just three candidates, as did the competition for the 2020 summer games. Alarm bells finally rang at the IOC when local referenda scuppered potential bids for the 2022 winter games from St Moritz/Davos, Krakow and Munich. The war in Ukraine terminated Lviv's plans, and the Swedish government pulled the plug on a bid from Stockholm.[1] Finally, Oslo, where even the IOC's polling showed a 50–36 majority against hosting the games, withdrew after the Norwegian government announced it would not fund the event. The IOC was left with the unenviable choice of Beijing, where there were no mountains, and all the same controversies that accompanied Beijing 2008, or Almaty, in Kazakhstan, where there was no shortage of mountains and snow, but little else, except for an even more unattractive and intransigently authoritarian regime in charge.

It was to this problem, in particular, that Thomas Bach was speaking when, in December 2014, at an extraordinary IOC congress in Monaco, he launched his own proposals for regime change at the IOC – Agenda 2020 – and asked whether the IOC would be able to change itself before change was forced upon it. Much of the report was concerned with making it cheaper and easier to bid for the games and to stage them, favouring refurbishment over new builds, and reimagining the relationship between the IOC and its hosts as something closer to a partnership than the hard-nosed franchise operation it had become. However, in both his speech and in the report itself, there was a recognition that something bigger was at stake. 'We need to change because sport is too important in society to ignore the rest of society. We are not an island.' Hardly a sociological revelation, but, for the president of the IOC, an institution devoted to securing its own economic, political and moral autonomy from all other social actors and asserting its sovereignty over many, it was an oblique recognition that the public standing of global sport and its institutions was heading for junk-bond status. What Bach was alluding to, but chose not to articulate, was that there is, in the world of global sport, at the centre of which sits the IOC, a series of profound and interconnected crises at work. Crises that are too big for society to ignore, or for sport to be able to resolve itself, and which, as a consequence, are eating away what little is left of the IOC's and the sporting world's moral authority.

The IOC's own problems with the giganticism of the games and the widespread cultures of corruption that colonized the bidding process to host them, are not confined to the Olympics. Spiralling costs, declining tangible benefits, white-elephant stadiums built under dangerous and sometimes repressive working conditions, with significant resources lost to corruption and rake-offs in the construction industry, have all been a feature of the South African, Brazilian and Russian World Cups, though none has triggered the kind of infrastructural binge that has accompanied the Olympics. The Qatar 2022 World Cup, however, is about to out-build everybody with projected expenditures in the region of $200 billion. Similarly, the vote buying that came to characterize Olympic bids before Salt Lake City has become widespread. The allocation of the football World Cup, in particular, appears to have been endemically corrupt, though the final say awaits the investigation of the Swiss and American legal authorities. The probity of the bidding process for the World Athletics Championship has also come into question, particularly the award of the 2021 championship to Eugene, Oregon – home of Nike – without any kind of bidding process at all.[2] Ominously for the IOC, which hitherto has believed its new bidding procedures were corruption free, the French authorities investigating corruption in global athletics have opened a file on the contests to host the 2016 and 2020 summer games.[3]

Equally, the IOC's own crisis of governance and legitimacy, which followed the Salt Lake City scandal, was just the first of more than a decade's worth of governance scandals in global sport. The Mexican president of the FIVB (and member of the IOC), Rubén Acosta, ran the sport for over a decade, amassing a huge fortune from personal commissions on the sale of global volleyball's TV rights.[4] Global football has gone into meltdown. Investigations launched by the FBI into money laundering and kickbacks on the sale of the TV rights on North and South American football tournaments have led to the high-profile arrests of senior executives in media companies, national and regional football associations and members of FIFA's executive committee. At the same time, FIFA's own ethics committee has banned its recent president (and IOC member), Sepp Blatter, and general secretary, Jérôme Valcke, from any involvement in football.

The IOC might have been forgiven for thinking that the creation of WADA (World Anti-Doping Authority) would have relieved it of a problem that had been plaguing the games and the wider world of sport since the 1930s. While the IOC has certainly ceded control over the issue to WADA, the first decade of the organization's existence has mainly served to demonstrate the endemic scale of the problem, clarify the institutionalized forms of doping in high-level sport, expose the active collusion of many in senior positions within sporting bureaucracies with doping and bring all of organized sport into disrepute. Old friends of the medicine chest, like wrestling, weightlifting and swimming, continued to see athletes disqualified and scandals erupt, but cycling has taken most of the headlines.[5] A series of criminal and journalistic investigations in France, Spain and the USA demonstrated that almost every team and every rider on the road-racing circuit in the 1990s and early 2000s was culpable, up to and above all Lance Armstrong, Olympic bronze medallist and seven-times winner of the Tour de France.[6] Whatever ground had been recovered by WADA's work and the cathartic revelations of past misdemeanours was entirely ceded by the exposure, in 2015, of Russia's systematic, state-backed doping policy in athletics and other sports. A policy made all the more insidious and successful by the active collusion of senior figures at the IAAF itself, and the relative ease with which WADA could be circumvented.

Doping is certainly not burnishing the moral authority of sport, moreover it continues to threaten the health and well-being of athletes, but, as the enduring popularity of major-league baseball and European road racing testifies, the sporting public is remarkably tolerant of its impact on sporting competition. Lance Armstrong may have been juiced to the eyeballs, but at least he and all other cyclists in a similar pharmacological state were trying to win – and, good as the juice was, there were no guarantees. Attitudes to match-fixing, which, for the most part, still turns on the much easier task of trying to lose, are very different, for, at this point, all uncertainty and narrative authenticity is drained from the spectacle. Reduced to a bad pantomime, the joke is on us. Again, match fixing has a long and dishonourable history: Manchester United and Liverpool players fixed a match between themselves in 1915, while the 1919 baseball World Series in the United States was thrown by members of the Chicago White Sox. Under their peculiar round-robin systems of qualification, gamesmanship in badminton and fencing often creates situations where athletes will, in effect, gift a game to opponents from the same country to ensure their qualification. Sports that involve judging have long proved susceptible to financial and political manipulation, as the Olympics' own experience with skating and gymnastics testifies. In Italian and Brazilian football, an end-of-season exchange of points to prevent relegation is virtually the norm. Problematic as these forms of fixing are, they pale into insignificance against the wave of organized criminal match-fixing facilitated by the emergence of the global offshore gambling industry and new forms of spread-and-spot betting, driven by the seemingly insatiable taste for sports gambling in the highly unregulated markets of India and East Asia.[7] In just the last decade, there have been innumerable fixing scandals: Pakistani test cricketers were paid to bowl specific no balls; players in football games at every level, from the bottom of the Bosnian second division to the UEFA champions league and Olympic qualifiers, have missed goals and saves. In South Korea, match fixing has been uncovered in volleyball and basketball and shown to be endemic in Japanese sumo.[8] Responding to a flurry of scandals in the game, international tennis' own watchdog, the Tennis Integrity Unit, has amassed evidence of match fixing against sixteen of the top fifty men's players.[9]

When, in the early 1990s, the IOC finally removed the definition of amateurism from its charter, the ghost of the gentlemen athletes of the belle époque, and Coubertin's vision of the games as a 'display of manly virtues' – by the right kind of man, for the moral education of everyone else – were laid to rest. While this was a precondition of the Olympics actually embodying its universalist and inclusive aspirations, and, as part of a wider set of changes, it helped tip the gender balance of athletes and events at the Olympics towards fifty–fifty, it has come at a price. Most obviously, it has meant that the singular most important component of the now hybrid model of Olympic sport is hard-nosed commercialism and high-performance professionalism. While this has been very good business for the IOC, it is not the material out of which a transcendental social mission and purpose for sport is likely to be forged. Coubertin and his immediate successors could still convince themselves and others that their games were humanist spiritual and religious rites, and a legitimate platform on which to display the moral and physical superiority of Europe's male ruling classes and officer corps. This will no longer wash. Thus, the IOC, in an attempt to reinvent its social and moral mission, has aligned itself with the new discourses of global politics – universal human rights, mass participation in sport and environmental sustainability. Other global sports organizations, equally bereft of a contemporary moral compass, have gone down the same path. The crisis here lies, not in their choice of moral argument or cause, but in the systematic failure of these organizations and their mega-events to deliver on their own values and promises.

The claim of the IOC, and indeed many international sports bodies and their commercial supporters, that their spectacular product is the catalyst for raising participation in sport and exercise, and thus a powerful tool in the complex policy-mix required to encourage healthier lifestyles, is poorly supported. Amongst certain communities, where sport has become a well-established and plausible route out of poverty, the commercial spectacular continues to dazzle and engage. Jamaican's sprinting victories, Central American boxing champions, African footballers' success in Europe and that of Dominican players in major-league baseball, all continue to help encourage the next generation of sporting hopefuls. However, across most affluent nations, despite more sport of all kinds on more screens than ever, all staged at an increasingly intense visual and rhetorical pitch, there has been no corresponding increase in participation in organized sport; indeed, in many nations, there is a perceptible decline. The narcissism of these societies has been sufficiently powerful to drive the better off to the gym, but it seems that no amount of gold-medal performances or world records can counter the consequences of sedentary lifestyles and the industrialized food sector.

The immediate future of the Olympics has been secured by East Asia. Tokyo will host the summer games in 2020, the winter games will be held in South Korea, in Pyeongchang, in 2018, and in Beijing in 2022, but there is little on offer here to suggest any new directions in the games. While none of these games will approach the scale or the costs of Beijing 2008 or Sochi 2014, they are hardly austere in design. Pyeongchang's budget is $10 billion and rising, and the Tokyo games is expected to cost in the region of $20 billion. Beijing is claiming it will cost as little as $4 billion to stage the winter games, but, with a projected bullet train from the capital to the new winter-sports resorts alone costed at around $4 billion, this seems a quixotic figure at best. Yet, despite all the resources lavished on them, these games seem remarkably anodyne in their conception. For both South Korea and China, the hosting of the summer games in 1988 and 2008 respectively served as an announcement of their newly acquired status as leading industrial and economic powers. Hosting the winter games, in both cases for the first time, appears to announce their transformation into post-industrial economies, with a substantial middle class with money and leisure time, and a highly developed winter-sports and tourism industry.[10] Beijing 2008's motto was that of a rising hegemon: 'One World. One Dream.' Beijing 2022 is the promise of après-ski cocktails and hot tubs: 'Joyful rendezvous on snow and ice.' President Xi Jinping, no less, has promised that China will raise the participation rate in winter sports from less than 2 per cent of the country to over 22 per cent, but quite where the 300 million new winter-sports enthusiasts are to come from, beyond relatively small numbers of wealthy recreational skiers (and how they are to get to any snow or ice) is less clear. Equally dismal is the winter games' contribution to Olympic sustainability. Preparations for Pyeongchang have involved cutting down tens of thousands of trees on the slopes of Mount Gariwang, including many rare and ancient specimens. The loss of this relatively undisturbed forest environment is considered 'an ecological disaster' by local NGOs. Plans for the new ski-runs and facilities in Beijing, or rather in the Xiao-haituo Mountains, seventy miles north of Beijing, require large tranches of the Songshan National Nature Reserve, an area particularly rich in rare bird life. In both cases, national laws regulating building in national parks have been overridden by Olympic exigencies.[11]

Tokyo 2020 appears a more ambitious project, drawing inspiration from the 1964 games, which not merely announced the re-entry of Japan into the world order, but heralded its emergence as an industrial and technological power and served as an important catalyst in the rebuilding of Tokyo itself. Thus, the 2020 bid cast the games as an opportunity to reinvent Tokyo as the city of the future, and, in so doing, to help drag the city and the country out of the prolonged deflationary gloom that has enveloped Japan since the 1990s. So far, most energy and attention has been focused on the building of a new Olympic stadium in the Meiji Park. The initial commission was won by Zaha Hadid's monstrously ugly design. Reasonably likened to a gigantic bike helmet, it towered over the sacred park space and was, at 252 billion yen (£1.6 billion), set to be the most expensive stadium ever built. A massive and scathing campaign of protest over the scale and look of the building saw the plans scrapped and, after a new round of submissions, the commission was awarded to a more restrained and conventional design by a Japanese architect, Kengo Kuma, that will still cost over a billion dollars. As to the future, Tokyo 2020 looks set to be a showcase for gadgetry: self-driving cars that ferry athletes to and from the Olympic village; power-assisted limbs and robotic suits making exercise and sport accessible to an increasingly elderly population; another generation of yet higher-resolution cameras and screens, faster mobile phones and the next wave of intelligent translation machines for visitors. The Japanese microelectronics industry is no doubt excited, but, if this is the best that the Olympics can inspire, then it needs to get out of the futures business.

Will Agenda 2020 prove enough change to keep the IOC ahead of the game, to tackle the multiple intersecting crises of governance, legitimacy and purpose that afflict contemporary sport? In the realm of bidder and hosting, its main preoccupation, the signs are not positive. Certainly there was not enough there for the people of Hamburg and Boston, who decisively rejected proposed bids by their city governments. The IOC has ended up with four candidate cities – Los Angeles, Rome, Paris and Budapest – though it is hard to believe that Hungary, now the epicentre of some of the most viscous nativism, nationalism and anti-migrant politics in Europe, is a serious candidate. The document proposes minor advances in transparency, but nowhere is it able to address the fundamental democratic and accountability deficits of an entity that is, in effect, an international organization – connecting and regulating the global and international sport space on behalf of the global system of states – the equivalent of the World Bank or the WTO, but is legally constituted as an NGO under Swiss law, which makes it accountable to no one, a situation made even worse by its pattern of self-recruitment. No amount of strategic partnerships with the United Nations, sponsors, sports federations and other NGOs will fill that gap; nor will the creation of an Olympic television channel and a micro-cultural programme create the circuits of communication and engagement that could connect the organization to the global public.

Thus, the tragedy of Agenda 2020 is not that it is inadequate to the task of reforming global sport in general, and the IOC in particular; these are not simple problems or ones that the IOC is going to solve alone. Rather, the tragedy of Agenda 2020 is that, beneath the contorted language of corporate change – repositioning, benchmarking, leadership – Bach and his minions are operating under the illusion that they are still part of a social movement – a force for value-driven action and goals, shielded from and antithetical to the demands of economic and politics. 'Progress for us means strengthening sport in society by virtue of our values'. But who is 'us'? There is the IOC and then there are stakeholders: the national political and economic coalitions that constitute organizing committees, the sporting-goods industry, the world's sporting media, transnational corporate sponsors, national and international sporting bureaucracies, none of whom look like or act like a social movement. There are Olympians and Olympic officials, but there is no Olympic public and there are no Olympian activists. The change has already been wrought on the IOC, for there are just the whirring wheels of a small but immensely connected and powerful bureaucracy.

Reflecting on how, if at all, the bureaucratization of the modern world could be reversed, Max Weber asked how the institutions we have created might be made to heed imperatives other than their own, or the siren calls of political power and material interests. 'No one knows who will live in this cage in the future, or whether at the end of this tremendous development entirely new prophets will arise, or there will be a great rebirth of old ideas and ideals.' There are no new Olympian prophets on the horizon, nor any sign that the core of Coubertin's ideals will ever be anything other than set dressing again. Under these circumstances, Weber imagined the future of bureaucracy as 'mechanised petrification embellished with a sort of convulsive self-importance'. There can hardly be a better commentary on the state of the IOC. In the absence of something altogether more radical than Agenda 2020, the same may become true of their games, too.

Coda 2017: After the Party

There were many extraordinary performances at the Rio games. Usain Bolt, Mo Farah and Simone Biles of course, but really nothing quite topped Thomas Bach's sensational debut as IOC president at his first Summer Olympics. At a breakfast meeting held the day after the closing ceremony, he took the gold medal for disingenuousness, saying, 'These were marvellous Olympic Games in the *cidade maravilhosa*. The Olympic Games Rio 2016 have shown the best of the *cariocas* and Brazilians to the world.' Really? Let us put aside for the moment the idea that the games were already a disaster before they began. Let us ignore the notion that preparations for the games exemplified the very worst of Brazilian clientelistic politics, its widespread corruption and its voracious politicians and property developers. Let us pass over the fact that most of the infrastructure that was built benefited the already wealthy at the cost of tens of thousands of forced relocations. Let us pretend that the bankruptcy of Rio state and its public services on the eve of the games had nothing to do with the show.

If we were just to take the games as we saw them then the most abiding memory of the Rio Olympics was surely the acres of seats – cool Atlantic blue, tropical yellow, rainforest green – all empty, and no amount of bluster from the organizers about how many tickets they had sold or given away could disguise them. While a few sports and a few sessions approached full houses, many – like much of the rugby sevens, handball and weightlifting – were desperate and forlorn. Even the crowds for free events like the road racing and triathlon were underwhelming. The last-minute giveaway of tickets, nominally to schools, failed entirely to plug the holes left by ticket prices that excluded the majority of the city. Poor transport and slow security made a small contribution but the empty stands were testament to the indifference of the wealthy minority to much of the programme and the shameful waste of generous allocations to the sponsors and the 'Olympic family'; a tableau made all the more unpleasant by the arrest of the Irish IOC member Pat Hickey on charges of shameless ticket reselling.[1]

A large crowd was no guarantee of an Olympian atmosphere. The booing meted out to President Michel Temer at the opening ceremony was crude, but a great improvement on the inane clowning of the crowd during the taking of the Olympic oaths at the opening ceremony. Both were preferable to the treatment given to French pole vaulter Renaud Lavillenie, who was viciously booed by the crowd during the competition he lost to the Brazilian Thiago Braz da Silva, and then again during the medal ceremony.[2] As the head of Globo TV is reported to have said, 'Brazilians don't like sport, they like winning.'

Successful as the Olympics were in confining our attention to the main show, the backstage stories that did emerge were illuminating. It is a shame that the Olympic broadcast consortium did not train its cameras on the IOC's buffets and its counting room, where per diems of between $450 and $900 were handed out to every IOC member. It would have made a great double bill alongside the volunteers working without being fed and the cleaners doing fifteen-hour shifts but banned from the public areas of the Olympic village.[3] The same could be said for much of the rest of the city. Beyond the Olympic bubbles, there was a pervasive sense – even in mainstream sports coverage – that Rio was hosting a party to which the vast majority were not invited; a point made with stark clarity by the photographs of residents of the city's favelas watching the fireworks of an opening ceremony – and one that depicted a cartoon version of their neighbourhoods – for which tickets would cost many weeks' wages.

That Thomas Bach could offer such oleaginous praise to his hosts in the face of all this was a triumph indeed. However, such feats of ideological and political flexibility pale compared to the indecent haste in which Bach and the IOC have moved on from Rio, leaving an unparalleled post-games disaster. Indeed Bach had the cheek to claim, looking over his shoulder, that the Olympics financial model had passed its very own 'stress test'. That is not how it looks from the *cidade maravilhosa* in its post-Olympic pomp.

Rio state remains $31 billion in debt with absolutely no sign of any new revenue streams to ease the pain. The city has been wracked by strikes and protest from teachers, the police and public-sector workers whose pay has not gone up while inflation rages, if it is paid at all. Rio's previous state governor, Sérgio Cabral, is under arrest and facing a variety of charges of corruption. The mayor, Eduardo Paes, has had his assets frozen by a Rio judge investigating payments he received in connection with the construction of the Olympic golf course. As for the transport legacy, the Metro is running at a fraction of capacity, with only 80,000 journeys a day as against the quixotic target of 300,000. Its routes remain geographically useless to all but the wealthy, the price of its tickets out of most people's reach. The rapid bus network, Rio's nod to the needs of its poorer citizens, is in actual fact focused on servicing the wealthy areas around the Olympic park, while the key routes that would have benefited the working class of the Zona Norte were cancelled.[4]

The VTL light rail system now connects the new port development with the central bus terminal and Santos Dumont, the city's small domestic airport. This is great news for tourists but hardly anyone else. Other lines that would be more useful to local residents have also been cancelled. Consequently the system is bringing in very little income but, given the nature of the public–private partnership which built it, the bankrupt city government has guaranteed two and a half decades of profits to the private developers. Meantime the unseen legacy of these projects is the enormous damage done to the streetscapes, pavements and the public squares of many neighbourhoods, which have seen businesses and shops close as footfall and traffic have declined. Simultaneously twenty-eight conventional north–south bus routes, vital for many commuters, have been cut in two by the new works. The refusal of any of the public transport services to recognize each other's cards and fares or apply Rio city discounts – in the quite reasonable belief that the government will never reimburse them – has made the situation almost impossible.[5]

The fate of the cable car built in Providência against the express wishes of local residents can stand proxy for much of the favela's Olympic experience. Never more than a tourist gewgaw, its construction required the destruction of much of Plaza America Brum, the only patch of public space in the neighbourhood. The cable no longer works and there is, under current financial concessions, no expectation that it will ever do so again.[6] The fate of the Police Pacification Units and the favela pacification programme they were entrusted with is not dissimilar. Never popular, later despised, the vast security operation before and during the games kept a kind of peace – though one studded by the everyday homicides and violent attacks that characterize the city. Even that is no longer available as the crime rate has risen, police strikes have become common and prison rioting has brought the whole security apparatus to breaking point. For all that, those still in the favelas are the lucky ones. The majority of those citizens who were relocated to make way for Olympic venues and infrastructure under the government's Ma Casa Ma Vida programme ended up in the most appalling peripheral estates, thrown up where land was at its very cheapest and transport links absent or impossibly distant. Developers left undistinguished barrack-like blocks of flats with poor or non-existent connections to energy and sewage systems. They have all become subject to the rule of gangs, while many residents have been subject to intimidation and threats from banks, as they struggle with impossible mortgages and, if they are connected, exorbitant utility bills.[7]

The Maracana at least has retained its enduring capacity to reflect, even to lead the city's social climate. It became, just months after the games, a ruin. With no plan developed for its regular use and continuing squabbles over who was responsible for its maintenance, no one paid for the electricity. Eaten by worms, the pitch became unplayable, not that any games had been arranged. Then the power was cut off and it turned brown. The rest of the complex was steadily looted, thieves taking televisions, copper wire and seats.[8] The Olympic park at least maintained the security detail but as it was effectively moth-balled at the end of the Paralympics it came at the cost of making it entirely inaccessible to the public. Not a single facility had found a new owner or plausible reuse plan.

The Olympic village, with an occupancy rate of around 10 per cent, has not proved the real-estate bonanza envisaged by its builders. Indeed things are so bad that the new mayor of Rio, Marcello Crivella, has been trying to persuade banks to offer low-interest mortgages to state employees who buy there. The Deodoro Olympic zone and its facilities, which were supposed to become a public park, have been closed by Rio city council and the operating company that maintained it has been fired.[9] The golf course where a round costs $74 – more than a week's minimum wage – is struggling and may close. For all this, Carlos Nuzman, president of the Rio organizing committee, and Mayor Eduardo Paes were awarded the IOC's gold Olympic Order.

No one should be surprised by the capacity of the IOC for myopia or its perverse insistence on honouring the guilty. At its Rio congress there was, amongst much talk of renewing the IOC's membership and executive committee, still plenty of love for old boys like the Cameroonian president of the Confederation of African Football Issa Hayatou and Mounir Sabet, who amongst the sinecures he had accumulated was head of Egypt's national Olympic committee. Both had exceeded the IOC's seventy-year age limit for normal members; they were deemed worthy of honorary membership, which allowed them to continue on the committee and retain their perks.

Hayatou is no doubt getting his reward for sheer endurance, with twenty-eight years at the head of African football, and as a member of its executive committee at the top of FIFA too. Alongside innumerable accusations of corruption it remains incontrovertible that ISL, FIFA's notorious and now defunct media-rights agency, paid millions to Hayatou through overseas bank accounts. His position, and that of other executives, was only preserved by the fact that there was, at the time of the payments, no legal definition of corruption in international organizations in Switzerland. This, as another generation of football executives and media companies have learnt to their cost, is no longer the case. The American and Swiss legal authorities swooped on the organization in connection with kickbacks for media deals and the hosting of the 2018 and 2022 World Cups, but Hayatou emerged unscathed. After Sepp Blatter's resignation, he assumed the throne as interim president of FIFA itself. His stony-faced claim at the time that neither he nor the organization was corrupt would have been a match for Bach's Rio triumphs.

General Mounir Sabet, although no doubt a military officer, businessman and sports administrator in his own right, is best understood as the brother of Suzanne Mubarak, and thus the brother-in-law of the late Egyptian president Hosni Mubarak. Once at the centre of the old regime, Sabet served as a co-director of innumerable offshore companies alongside his sister and Mubarak's other corporate front men. The 'Panama Papers' have revealed, amongst other things, his directorship of a Paris-based arms-dealing company. If it wasn't his contribution to the Olympic values of peace and pacifism that won him honorary membership perhaps it was his record on transparency. Certainly his record of suspected corruption and money laundering was serious enough for both the Swiss and Canadian authorities to freeze his bank accounts and assets.

The IOC is not an organization that learns from history, but even the IOC must have felt a glimmer of déjà vu as in late 2016 they watched events in South Korea unfold. In a remarkable parallel to the course of Rio 2016, the hosts of the PyeongChang 2018 Winter Olympics struggled with a budget that had ballooned from $3 billion to over $12 billion before being engulfed in a tumultuous national corruption scandal reaching all the way up to the presidential office (the nation's first women incumbent in both cases), occasioning huge public protest, impeachment proceedings in the South Korean legislature and finally ignominious retirement. President Park Geun-hye, who had hoped to crown her five-year term in office by opening the games in February 2018, sits in limbo while the constitutional court considers her impeachment. Her erstwhile friend and fixer Choi Yoon-sun is under arrest and on trial. Both are accused of pressuring Korean corporations to make considerable donations to a series of foundations and allied organizations tied to the president in return for political favours.

The PyeongChang organizing committee and various oversight committees in regional and national government have gone to great lengths to tell the world that none of their Olympic tenders are 'contaminated' by corruption. However, Choi's daughter Jang Shi-ho – once a dressage competitor – is known to have established a sports NGO that possessed a remarkable capacity for winning government funding and support. Samsung saw fit to give the operation $6 million. It also benefited from a decision to make one of the 2018 Olympic skating rinks a permanent rather than temporary structure, which would then be taken over by the same NGO. Moreover in early 2017, police raided the offices of four Korean companies involved in the building of the high-speed railway line to Gangneung – home of the Olympic skating venues – which they believed to have secretly collaborated to ensure that all four got a share of the £3.7 billion project.[10] Despite all this Choi Kwang-shik, a former minister of sport, was able to convince himself that, 'The Winter Olympics will let us show that we have reached the level of an advanced nation.' No doubt this now includes extensive networks of hidden and unaccountable exchanges of money and power.[11]

As yet things remain more prosaic in Japan and China, where money and smog are the main problems. Tokyo 2020 has become embroiled in protracted and bitter internal conflicts over a budget that was heading towards $30 billion. In late 2016 the new governor of metropolitan Tokyo, Yuriko Koike, whose administration was due to shoulder much of the cost, lashed the organizing committee for its extravagance and the absence of something as basic as a chief financial officer, and insisted on a upper budget limit of a mere $17 billion.[12] The new mayor of Beijing, Cai Qi, has money to spend, but as the $40 billion lavished on Beijing 2008 demonstrates, there may not be enough money in all of China to fix Beijing's air pollution. Promising, once again, the 'greenest games ever', the city actually experienced a sharp decline in its already appalling air quality after the 2008 Olympics. A short-lived period of improvement that peaked for the games themselves went sharply into reverse, leaving the city's twenty million citizens regularly engulfed in poisonous smogs. If the air above the games does not burnish the IOC's environmental credentials, the artificial snow on the slopes of Zhangjiakou, home of the skiing events, will. Here, in one of China's most arid zones, reservoirs built for drinking water will be diverted to the half-pipes and hairpin turns of the alpine runs.[13]

The IOC may remain oblivious to the enduring and ineradicable pathology of its model, but the rest of the world is not.[14] In the contest to host the 2024 Summer Olympics, Boston and Hamburg had already bailed out before the Rio Games. Rome and Budapest have followed suit. Speaking to the press in September 2016 the recently elected mayor of Rome, Virginia Raggi, said, 'The Olympics are a dream that turn into a nightmare. I don't have all the facts about Rio, but we have the image in our eyes of the citizens of Rio.' Having campaigned as part of the Five Star Movement on an explicit promise to cancel the show, she then led the city council in a vote against the bid and won.[15]

While never the favourite, Budapest's bid had looked more solid, with very strong backing from Prime Minister Viktor Orbán, the Hungarian government and much of the opposition. This perhaps was its Achilles heel, for the prospect of the games provided the perfect foil for grassroots protestors who felt unrepresented by any of the political parties. In just a few weeks in early 2017 the Momentum Movement gathered over a quarter of a million signatures on a petition to force a referendum on the Olympic bid, and with a view to spending the money earmarked for the games on health and education. Knowing that they would inevitably lose such a vote, Orbán and the mayor of Budapest tactically withdrew the bid altogether.[16]

And then there were two, Paris and Los Angeles, neither of which dared to hold a referendum themselves for they too would surely have been lost. With even less interest being displayed in hosting the 2028 games this diminished competition for 2024, and as the world's cities absorbed the reality of Rio's experience, the IOC bought themselves some time, announcing that they would award both Olympiads simultaneously; Los Angeles was happy to go with 2028 and Paris got 2024. What kind of spectacle do they promise? What ideological motifs will they try and hang on these toxic rings? France's President Macron was obsequious: 'Olympic values are our values. They are threatened, called into question by many today, so it's the best moment to defend them.' Mayor of Los Angeles Eric Garcetti said in a similar vein, 'I am confident that the summer games in Los Angeles will exemplify both the Olympic ideal and the American spirit.' Maybe we should just take them at their words and assume they really do think that their politics and those of the IOC are identical; a politics that is impervious to empirical evidence or popular complaint; a politics that operates in secret and trades in fantasy. Perhaps, once again, the Olympic movement has proved lithe and spritely enough to adapt itself to our times.

Notes

Chapter 1, Section One

1. On Soutsos, see D. Young, *The Modern Olympics: A Struggle for Revival*, Johns Hopkins University Press (1996), pp. 1–8.
2. P. de Coubertin, *Olympism*, Comité International Olympique (2000), p. 297.
3. *Scholia in Lucianum*, 41.9.42–46.
4. Ibid.
5. A. Vott et al, 'Sedimentary burial of ancient Olympia (Peloponnese, Greece) by high-energy flood deposits – the Olympia Tsunami Hypothesis', 2nd INQUA-IGCP-567 International Workshop on Active Tectonics, Earthquake Geology, Archaeology and Engineering (2011), Corinth, Greece.
6. C. Habicht, *Pausanias' Guide to Ancient Greece*, University of California Press (1998).
7. Cited in M. Polley, *The British Olympics: Britain's Olympic Heritage 1612–2012*, English Heritage (2013).
8. Cited in P. Radford, 'The Olympic Games in the Long Eighteenth Century', *Journal for Eighteenth-Century Studies*, *35(2)*, (2012), pp. 161–184.
9. D. Flower, *Voltaire's England*, Folio (1950), p. 4.
10. Cited in M. Polley, *The British Olympics: Britain's Olympic Heritage 1612–2012*, English Heritage (2013), p. 19.

Chapter 1, Section Two

1. Originally published as R. Chandler, *Travels in Asia Minor: or an account of a tour made at the expense of the Society of Dilettanti*, J. Booker (1817), p. 294.
2. S. Dyson, *In Pursuit of Ancient Pasts: A History of Classical Archaeology in the Nineteenth and Twentieth Centuries*, Yale University Press (2008).
3. Key sources drawn on for the ancient Games include: M. Finley and H. Picket, *The Olympic Games: The First 1000 Years*, Viking (1976); N. Spivey, *The Ancient Olympics*, Oxford University Press (2005); S. Miller,

Arete: Greek Sports from Ancient Sources, University of California Press (2012); M. Golden, *Sport and Society in Ancient Greece*, Cambridge University Press (1998); N. Crowther, 'Visiting the Olympic Games in Ancient Greece: Travel and Conditions for Athletes and Spectators', *International Journal of the History of Sport*, *18*(4), (2001), pp. 37–52.

4. Pausanias (V, 24, 9).

5. Cited in A. Guttmann, *The Olympics, A History of the Modern Games*, University of Illinois Press (2002), p. 116.

6. Herodotus, *Histories*, 6.103.2.

7. Plutarch, *Themistocles*, 17.2.

Chapter 1, Section Three

1. Cited in A. Arvin-Berod, 'In France, the idea of the Olympic Games crosses the centuries', *Olympic Review* (321), (1994), pp. 339–341.

2. D. Young, *The Modern Olympics: A Struggle for Revival*, Johns Hopkins University Press (1996); J. MacAloon, *This Great Symbol: Pierre de Coubertin and the Origins of the Modern Olympic Games*, Routledge (2013); D. Young, 'Further thoughts on some issues of early Olympic history', *Journal of Olympic History* 6.3 (1998), pp. 29–41.

3. On Much Wenlock and Liverpool, see M. Polley, *The British Olympics: Britain's Olympic Heritage 1612–2012*, English Heritage (2012). See also R. Physick, *Played in Liverpool*, English Heritage (2007).

4. P. Lovesey, *The Official Centenary History of the Amateur Athletic Association*, Guinness Superlatives (1979), cited in Polley (2012), p. 69.

5. The account of the Zappas games and Greek Revivalism, as well as the Athens games in 1896, draws from D. Young, *The Modern Olympics: A Struggle for Revival*, Johns Hopkins University Press (1996); MacAloon (2013); M. Smith, *Olympics in Athens 1896: The Invention of the Modern Olympic Games*, Profile Books (2004); and R. Mandell, *The First Modern Olympics*, University of California Press (1976).

6. *Athena*, 8 November 1859, cited in Young (1996), p. 22.

7. *Ague*, 16 November 1859, cited in ibid.

Chapter 1, Section Four

1. J. MacAloon, *This Great Symbol: Pierre de Coubertin and the Origins of the Modern Olympic Games*, Routledge (2013), p. 26.

2. See the account of this in MacAloon (2013), pp. 27–30.

3. Ibid.

4. Cited in ibid, p. 51.

5. Cited in ibid, p. 54.

6. Cited in ibid, p. 58.

7. R. Mandell, *The First Modern Olympics*, University of California Press (1976).

8. In his book, *This Great Symbol: Pierre de Coubertin and the Origins of the Modern Olympic Games*, Routledge (2013), MacAloon, personally and politically more sympathetic to Coubertin, opts for a form of 'deep and multiple determined wish fulfilment' and argues that Thomas Arnold served as an imago, 'a complicated psychological representation in which an external personage is blended with a set of condensed psychic needs and relations', p. 60.

9. Cited in D. Young, *The Modern Olympics: A Struggle for Revival*, Johns Hopkins University Press (1996), p. 75.

10. Cited in ibid, p. 74.

11. P. de Coubertin, *L'idée olympique* (1908), trans. as *The Olympic Idea: Discourses and Essays*, Karl Hofman (1967).

12. Cited in Young (1996), p. 75.

13. Cited in ibid, p. 78.

Chapter 1, Section Five

1. The role of the aristocratic convention is well dealt with in C. Murphy, *International Organization and Industrial Change: Global Governance Since 1850*, Polity Press (1994).

2. This roster of the emergent global peace moment included the Englishman Hodgson Pratt, who founded the International Arbitration and Peace Association; Ruggero Bonghi, the Italian writer and president of the 1891 Universal Peace Congress in Rome; the then current and future presidents of the International Peace Bureau, the Belgian Henri La Fontaine, and the Danish politician Frederic Bajer, not to mention the organization's director, Ellie Decommum, and committee member Frederic Passy, who, along with the organization and its presidents, was a recipient of the Nobel Peace Prize.

3. K. Moore, 'A neglected imperialist: the promotion of the British empire in the writing of John Astley Cooper', *The International Journal of the History of Sport*, 8(2) (1991), pp. 256–269. D. Gorman, 'Amateurism, Imperialism, Internationalism and the First British Empire Games', *The International Journal of the History of Sport*, 27(4) (2010), pp. 611–634.

4. MacAloon (2013), p. 158.

5. Ibid, p. 160.

Chapter 1, Section Six

1. Cited in P. de Coubertin, *Olympism: Selected Writings*, ed. Norbert Müller, Lausanne: International Olympic Committee (2000), p. 314.
2. Cited in D. Young, *The Modern Olympics: A Struggle for Revival*, Johns Hopkins University Press (1996), p. 98.
3. Coubertain (2000), p. 322.
4. Cited in Young (1996), p. 112.
5. Cited in MacAloon, *This Great Symbol: Pierre de Coubertin and the Origins of the Modern Olympic Games*, Routledge (2013), p. 212.

Chapter 1, Section Seven

1. Cited in D. Young, *The Modern Olympics: A Struggle for Revival*, Johns Hopkins University Press (1996), p. 117.
2. *New York Times*, 29 March 1896, cited in M. Smith, *Olympics in Athens 1896: The Invention of the Modern Olympic Games*, Profile Books (2004), p. 151.
3. Cited in Smith (2004). Haranlambous Anninos was an Athenian writer whose reflections and reports were in the collection originally published as C. Beck, *The Olympic Games BC 776–AD 1896* (2 vols.), Robertson (1896).
4. Cited in Young (1996), p. 146.
5. G. S. Robertson, 'An Englishman at the first modern Olympics, 1896', *Fortnightly Review*, (June 1896), pp. 944–957.
6. Ibid.
7. Cited in Young (1996), p. 161.
8. Cited in Smith (2004), p. 189.
9. Cited in Young (1996), p. 159.
10. Ibid, p. 164.
11. Robertson (1896).

Chapter 2, Section One

1. Simmel, cited in D. Rowe, 'Georg Simmel and the Berlin Trade Exhibition of 1896', *Urban History*, Volume 22, Issue 2 (1995), pp. 216–228. P. de Coubertin, *Olympism: Selected Writings*, ed. Norbert Müller, Lausanne: International Olympic Committee (2000), p. 636.
2. Much of the material on the world's fairs is drawn from the following:

A. Geppert, *Fleeting Cities: Imperial Expositions in Fin-de-Siècle Europe*, Palgrave (2010); P. Greenhalgh, *Ephemeral Vistas: The Expositions Universelles, Great Exhibitions and World's Fairs, 1851–1939*, Manchester University Press (1988); R. Rydell, *All the World's a Fair: Visions of Empire at American International Expositions, 1876–1916*, University of Chicago Press (2013); Z. Celik and L. Kinney, 'Ethnography and Exhibitionism at the Expositions Universelles', *Assemblage*, (1990), pp. 35–59; J. Findling, *Chicago's Great World's Fairs*, Manchester University Press (1994).

3. *Official Catalogue of the Great Exhibition of the Works of Industry*, Spicer (1851), p. 145.

4. Cited in E. Larsen, *The Devil in the White City*, Vintage (2003), p. 311.

5. J. Findling, 'Chicago Loses the 1904 Olympics', *Journal of Olympic History*, *12*(3) (2004).

6. Cited in S. Brownell (ed.), *The 1904 Anthropology Days and Olympic Games: Sport, Race, and American Imperialism*, University of Nebraska Press (2008), p. 48.

7 . Cited in L. Yttergren and L. Bolling (eds.), *The 1912 Stockholm Olympics: Essays on the Competitions, the People, the City*, McFarland (2012), p. 10.

Chapter 2, Section Two

1. Cited in J. E. Findling and K. D. Pelle, *Encyclopedia of the Modern Olympic Movement*, Greenwood (2004), p. 30.

2. Cited in Gaston Meyer, 'Paris 1900', in Lord Killanin and John Rodda (eds.), *The Olympic Games 1984*, Willow (1983).

3. *Concours Internationaux d'Exercises Physiques et de Sports*: Rapports, Imprimerie Nationale (1900), p. 72.

4. *L'Auto-Vélo*, 1900, cited in Findling and Pelle (2004), p. 31.

5. *Official Guide to the Louisiana Purchase Exposition*, Official Guide Company (1904), p. 7.

6. G. Matthews and S. Marshall, *St Louis Olympics, 1904*, Arcadia Publishing (2003); G. Matthews, *America's First Olympics: the St Louis Games of 1904*, University of Missouri Press (2005).

7. P. Kramer, 'Making concessions: race and empire revisited at the Philippine Exposition, St Louis, 1901–1905', *Radical History Review* (73), (1999), pp. 75–114; L. Carlson, 'Giant Patagonians and Hairy Ainu: Anthropology Days at the 1904 St Louis Olympics', *Journal of American Culture 12*(3), (1989), pp. 19–26.

8. See S. Brownell, *The 1904 Anthropology Days and Olympic Games: Sport, Race, and American Imperialism*, University of Nebraska Press (2008).

9. See W. J. McGee, *Official Catalogue of Exhibitions – Department of Anthropology* (1904), p. 88, cited in Brownell, *The 1904 Anthropology*

Days and Olympic Games: Sport, Race, and American Imperialism, University of Nebraska Press (2008), p. 48.

10. 'A Novel Athletic Contest', *World's Fair Bulletin*, 5 September 1904, cited in H. Lenskyj and S. Wagg (eds.), *The Palgrave Handbook of Olympic Studies*, Palgrave (2012), p. 49.

Chapter 2, Section Three

1. 1906 and its politics are covered in K. Lennartz, 'The 2nd International Olympic Games in Athens, 1906', *Journal of Olympic History*, 10, (2002), pp. 3–24; for a first-hand account, see T. Cook, *The Cruise of the Branwen: Being a Short History of the Modern Revival of the Olympic Games, Together with an Account of the Adventures of the English Fencing Team in Athens in MCMVI*, Ballantyne (1908).

2. *Daily News*, 23 May 1908, cited in R. Jenkins, *The First London Olympics: 1908*, Hachette (2008), p. 175.

3. *Evening Standard*, 24 November 1906.

4. *Bystander*, 25 July 1908, cited in Jenkins (2008), p. 160.

5. Ibid, p. 145.

6. Official Report, 1908, p. 137.

7. Cited in Jenkins (2008), p. 142.

8. Ibid, p. 137.

9. *World*, 8 July 1908, cited in ibid, p. 108.

10. Ibid, p. 114.

11. Cited in ibid, pp. 152–153.

12. 'The Olympics at the Franco-British Imperial Exhibition', *Vanity Fair*, 29 July 1908, cited in Jenkins (2008), p. 258.

13. *New York Times*, 25 July 1908.

14. *Daily Mail*, 27 July 1908.

15. Cited in Jenkins (2008), p. 224.

16. *L'Illustrazione Italiana*, 2 August 1908, cited in Jenkins (2008), p. 235.

Chapter 2, Section Four

1. Cited in L. Yttergren and H. Bolling (eds.), *The 1912 Stockholm Olympics: Essays on the Competitions, the People, the City*, McFarland (2012), p. 5.

2. *Dagens Nyheter*, 14 July 1912, cited in ibid, p. 161.

3. *Aftonbladet*, 10 July 1912, cited in ibid, p. 165.

4. *Dagens Nyheter*, 4 July 1912, cited in ibid, p. 163.

5. *Idun*, No. 3, 1912, cited in ibid, p. 162.

6. *Stockholm Tidningen*, 15 July 1912, cited in ibid, p. 166.

7. Cited in ibid, p. 164.
8. *Aftonbladet*, 12 July 1912, cited in ibid, p. 164.
9. Cited in ibid, p. 167.
10. *New York Times*, 7 July 1912, cited in ibid, p. 167.
11. S. Heck, 'Modern Pentathlon and the First World War: When Athletes and Soldiers Met to Practise Martial Manliness', *International Journal of the History of Sport, 28*(3–4), (2011), pp. 410–428; S. Heck, 'A Sport for Everyone? Inclusion and Exclusion in the Organisation of the First Olympic Modern Pentathlon', *The International Journal of the History of Sport, 31*(5), (2014), pp. 526–541.
12. Cited in Heck, 'A Sport for Everyone?' (2014), p. 537.

Chapter 3, Section One

1. Cited in R. Renson, *The Games Reborn: The VIIth Olympiad*, Pandora (1996), p. 29.
2. 'Aileen Riggin Soule: A Wonderful Life In her own words', at http://ishof. org/assets/aileen_riggin.pdf
3. Cited in Renson (1996), pp. 39–40.
4. Cited in ibid, p. 30.
5. *L'Auto*, 3 August 1914.

Chapter 3, Section Two

1. J. Lucas, 'American Preparations for the First Post World War Olympic Games', *Journal of Sport History*, *10*(2), (1983); N. Müller and R. Tuttas, 'The role of the YMCA: especially that of Elwood S. Brown, Secretary of physical education of the YMCA, in the worldwide expansion of the Olympic Movement during de Coubertin's presidency', in K. Wamsley, S. Martyn, G. MacDonald and R. Barney (eds.), *5th International Symposium for Olympic Research, Sydney*, (2000), pp. 127–134; R. Gems, 'Sport, Colonialism, and United States Imperialism', *Journal of Sport History*, *33*(1), (2006); S. Pope, 'An army of athletes: Playing fields, battlefields, and the American military sporting experience, 1890–1920', *The Journal of Military History*, *59*(3), (1995), p. 435.
2. A. Waquet and J. Vincent, 'Wartime rugby and football: Sports elites, French military teams and international meets during the First World War', *International Journal of the History of Sport* 28.3–4, (2011), pp. 372–392; S. Hübner, 'Muscular Christianity and the "Western Civilising Mission": Elwood S. Brown, the YMCA, and the Idea of the Far Eastern Championship Games', *Diplomatic History*, (2013).

3. G. Wythe and J. Hanson, *The Inter-Allied Games, Paris, 22 June to 6 July 1919*, The Inter Allied Games Committee (1919); T. Terret, 'Prologue: Making men, destroying bodies: Sport, masculinity and the Great War experience', *The International Journal of the History of Sport*, 28(3–4), (2011), pp. 323–328.

4. Cited in T. Terret, 'The Military "Olympics" of 1919', *Journal of Olympic History* 14 (2), (2006), p. 28.

5. Wythe and Hanson (1919), p. 37.

6. Cited in Terret (2006) p. 27.

7. Cited in ibid, p. 26.

8. Cited in P. Beck, *Scoring for Britain: International Football and International Politics, 1900–1939*, Routledge (2013), p. 94.

9. Thierry Terret, 'The Albertville Winter Olympics: Unexpected Legacies – Failed Expectations for Regional Economic Development', in J. A. Mangan and Mark Dyreson (eds.), *Olympic Legacies: Intended and Unintended*, Routledge (2010), p. 21.

10. Cited in J. Lucas, 'American Preparations for the First Post World War Olympic Games', *Journal of Sport History*, 10 (2), (1983), pp. 30–44.

Chapter 3, Section Three

1. R. Renson, *The Games Reborn: The VIIth Olympiad*, Pandora (1996), p. 24.

2. Key sources on Antwerp 1920 – alongside the definitive Renson (1996) – are R. Renson and M. Den Hollander, 'Sport and business in the city: the Antwerp Olympic Games of 1920 and the Urban Elite', *Olympika*, 6 (1997), pp. 73–84; M. Llewellyn, ' "Olympic Games are an international farce": the 1920 Antwerp games and the question of Great Britain's participation', *Olympika*, 17, (2008), pp. 101–132.

3. Cited in Renson (1996), p. 33.

4. Cited in ibid, p. 73.

5. Cited in ibid, p. 54.

6. Ibid, p. 74.

7. Cited in ibid, p. 76.

8. See his memoir, J. Langenus, *Voetbal van hier en overal*, Snocek-Ducaju (1943), cited in Renson, (1996), p. 62.

9. Cited in ibid, pp. 86–88.

Chapter 3, Section Four

1. P. de Coubertin, *Olympism: Selected Writings*, ed. Norbert Müller, Lausanne: International Olympic Committee (2000), p. 711.

2. Cited in S. Cahn, *Coming On Strong: Gender and Sexuality in Women's Sport*, University of Illinois Press (2015), p. 32.

3. See ibid, p. 33.

4. F. Carpentier and P. Lefèvre, 'The modern Olympic Movement, women's sport and the social order during the inter-war period', *The International Journal of the History of Sport*, *23*(7), (2006), pp. 1112–1127; T. Terret, 'From Alice Milliat to Marie-Thérèse Eyquem: Revisiting Women's Sport in France (1920s–1960s)', *The International Journal of the History of Sport*, *27*(7), (2010), pp. 1154–1172.

5. In a letter from Baillet-Latour to Godefroy de Blonay, cited in Carpentier and Lefèvre (2006), p. 1122.

6. K. Wamsley and G. Schultz, 'Rogues and Bedfellows: The IOC and the Incorporation of the FSFI', in K. Wamsley, S. G. Martyn, G. H. MacDonald, and R. K. Barney (eds.), *Bridging Three Centuries: Intellectual Crossroads and the Modern Olympic Movement*, International Centre for Olympic Studies (2000), pp. 113–118.

7. Cited in Paauw and Visser, *Model voor de Toekomst: Amsterdam, Olympische Spelen 1928* (*A Model for the Future: Amsterdam, Olympic Games 1928*), De Buitenspelers (2008), p. 194.

Chapter 3, Section Five

1. T. Terret, *Les Paris des Jeux Olympiques de 1924*, Atlantica (2008); T. Terret, *Les Jeux Olympiques de 1924 et les Presses Francophones, Recorde: Revista de História do Esporte*, *1*(1), Français (2008); Comité Olympique, *Les Jeux de la VIII Olympiade, Paris 1924, Rapport Officiel* (1924).

2. C. Culleton, 'Competing Concepts of Culture: Irish Art at the 1924 Paris Olympic Games', *Estudios Irlandeses*, (9), (2014), pp. 24–34.

3. Cited in J. Findling and K. Pelle (eds.), *Encyclopedia of the Modern Olympic Movement*, Greenwood (2004), p. 84.

4. Cited in M. Dyreson, 'Scripting the American Olympic Story-Telling Formula: The 1924 Paris Olympic Games and the American Media', *Olympika*, *5*, (1996), pp. 45–80; M. Llewellyn, 'Chariots of discord: Great Britain, nationalism and the "doomed" 1924 Paris Olympic Games', *Contemporary British History*, *24*(1), (2010), pp. 67–87.

5. T. Terret, C. Ottogalli-Mazzacavallo and J. Saint-Martin, 'The Puliti affair and the 1924 Paris Olympics: Geo-Political issues, National pride and

fencing traditions', *The International Journal of the History of Sport,* *24*(10), (2007), pp. 1281–1301.

6. *Guardian,* 11 July 1924.

7. Cited in T. Mason, *Passion of the People? Football in South America,* Verso (1995), p. 31.

8. Cited in B. Oliver, 'Before Pelé there was Andrade', *Observer,* 24 May 2014.

9. D. Séguillon, 'The origins and consequences of the first World Games for the Deaf: Paris, 1924', *The International Journal of the History of Sport,* *19*(1), (2002), pp. 119–136.

10. Ibid.

Chapter 3, Section Six

1. P. Jørgensen, 'From Balck to Nurmi: the Olympic movement and the Nordic nations', *The International Journal of the History of Sport,* *14*(3), (1997), pp. 69–99; L. Yttergren, 'The Nordic games: visions of a winter Olympics or a national festival', *International Journal of the History of Sport,* *11*(3) (1994), pp. 495–505.

2. Cited in R. Huntford, *Two Planks and a Passion: the Dramatic History of Skiing,* A & C Black (2009), p. 320.

3. P. Arnaud and T. Terret, *Le Rêve Blanc: Olympisme et Sports D'Hiver en France: Chamonix 1924, Grenoble 1968,* Presses Universitaires de Bordeaux (1993).

4. Cited in Huntford (2009), p. 79.

5. J. Hines, *Figure Skating: A History,* University of Illinois Press (2006); M. Adams, 'The manly history of a "girls' sport": Gender, class and the development of nineteenth-century figure skating', *International Journal of the History of Sport,* *24*(7), (2007), pp. 872–893; M. Adams, 'Freezing social relations: Ice, rinks, and the development of figure skating', *Sites of Sport: Space, Place, Experience,* 5, (2004), pp. 7–72; E. Kestnbaum, *Culture on ice: figure skating and cultural meaning,* Wesleyan University Press (2003).

6. On the history of curling, see A. Guttmann, *Sports: The first five millennia,* University of Massachusetts Press (2004), pp. 249–251. See also the useful collection of material at http://curlinghistory.blogspot.co.uk.

Chapter 3, Section Seven

1. N. Valentinov, *Encounters with Lenin,* Oxford University Press (1968), p. 30.

2. Cited in D. Steinberg, 'The workers' sport internationals, 1920–28', *Journal of Contemporary History* 13.2, (1978), pp. 233–251. The other key works on the workers' sports movement drawn upon are: S. Jones, 'The European Workers' Sport Movement and Organized Labour in Britain Between the Wars', *European History Quarterly*, *18*(1), (1988), pp. 3–32; R. Wheeler, 'Organized sport and organized labour: the workers' sports movement', *Journal of Contemporary History*, (1978), pp. 191–210; A. Kruger and J. Riordan (eds.), *The Story of Worker Sport*, Human Kinetics Publishers (1996); J. Tolleneer and E. Box, 'An alternative sport festival: the third Workers' Olympics, Antwerp, 1937', *Stadion* 12/13, (1987), pp. 183–190; J. Wagner, 'Prague's socialist Olympics of 1934', *Canadian Journal of History of Sport*, 23(1), (1992), pp. 1–18.

3. Cited in Kruger and Riordan (1996), pp. 7–8.

4. Cited in ibid, p. 14.

5. Cited in ibid, p. 12.

6. Cited in Steinberg (1978), p. 235.

7. S. Jones, 'Sport, politics and the labour movement: the British workers' sports federation, 1923–1935', *The British Journal of Sports History*, *2*(2), (1985), pp. 154–178; S. Jones, *Sport, Politics and the Working Class: Organised Labour and Sport in Inter-War Britain*, Manchester University Press (1992).

8. N. Rossol, *Performing the Nation in Interwar Germany. Sport, Spectacle and Political Symbolism 1926–1936*, Palgrave (2010).

9. Cited in N. Rossol, 'Performing the Nation: Sports, Spectacles and Aesthetics in Germany 1926–1936', *Central European History*, no. 4, 43, (2010), p. 626.

10. R. Edelman, *Serious Fun: A History of Spectator Sport in the USSR*, Oxford University Press (1993); B. Keys, 'Soviet sport and transnational mass culture in the 1930s', *Journal of Contemporary History*, *38*(3), (2003), pp. 413–434.

11. Cited in R. Krammer, 'Austria: New Times Are With Us', in Kruger and Riordan (1996), p. 91.

Chapter 3, Section Eight

1. The key work on the Amsterdam games is R. Paauw and J. Visser, *Model voor de Toekomst: Amsterdam, Olympische Spelen 1928* (*A Model for the Future: Amsterdam, Olympic Games 1928*), De Buitenspelers (2008). See also P. Mol, 'Sport in Amsterdam, Olympism and other influences: the inter-war years', *International Journal of the History of Sport*, *17*(4), (2000), pp. 141–152.

2. Cited in Paauw and Visser (2008), p. 34.

3. P. Scharroo and J. Wils, *Gebouwen En Terreinen voor Gymnastiek, Spel en Sport, Handleiding voor den Bouw, den Aanleg en de Inrichting*, N.V. Prometheus (1925).
4. Cited in Paauw and Visser (2008), p. 60.
5. Cited in ibid, p. 62.
6. Cited in ibid, p. 114.
7. Cited in ibid, p. 110.
8. Cited in ibid, p. 327.
9. Cited in ibid, p. 201.
10. Cited in ibid, p. 201.
11. Cited in ibid, p. 229.
12. Cited in ibid, p. 11.

Chapter 4, Section One

1. Cited in B. Keys, *Globalizing Sport: National Rivalry and International Community in the 1930s*, Harvard University Press (2013), p. 94.
2. Organising Committee for the Olympic Games in Los Angeles in 1932, *The Games of the Xth Olympiad, Los Angeles 1932: Official Report* (1933), p. 359.
3. Ibid, p. 362.
4. Cited in S. Dinces, 'Padres on Mount Olympus: Los Angeles and the production of the 1932 Olympic mega-event', *Journal of Sport History*, *32*(2), (2005), p. 137.
5. C. McWilliams, *Southern California: An Island on the Land*, Gibbs Smith (1946), p. 157.
6. J. Slater, 'Changing partners: The relationship between the mass media and the Olympic Games', in *Fourth International Symposium for Olympic Research*, University of Western Ontario (1998), pp. 49–69.
7. Cited in M. Dyreson, 'Marketing national identity: The Olympic Games of 1932 and American culture', *Olympiaka: The International Journal of Olympic Studies*, vol. IV, 1995, pp. 23–48.
8. Press coverage and much besides is well covered in R. Mandell, *The Nazi Olympics*, University of Illinois Press (1971); A. Krüger and W. Murray (eds.), *The Nazi Olympics: Sport, Politics, and Appeasement in the 1930s*, University of Illinois Press (2003); A. Krüger and A. Auguts, 'The ministry of popular enlightenment and propaganda and the Nazi Olympics of 1936', in *Proceedings of the Fourth International Symposium for Olympic Research*, University of Western Ontario (1998).
9. L. McKernan, 'Rituals and Records: the Films of the 1924 and 1928 Olympic Games', *European Review*, *19*(04), (2011), pp. 563–577.
10. D. Denby, 'The seat of power', *New Yorker*, 7 June 2010.

11. S. Bach, *Leni: The Life and Work of Leni Riefenstahl*, Vintage (2008); G. McFee and A. Tomlinson, 'Riefenstahl's Olympia: ideology and aesthetics in the shaping of the Aryan athletic body', *International Journal of the History of Sport*, *16*(2), (1999), pp. 86–106.

Chapter 4, Section Two

1. R. Barney, 'A Research Note on the Origins of the Olympic Victory Podium', in *Global and Cultural Critique: Problematizing the Olympic Games: Fourth International Symposium for Olympic Research*, (1998), pp. 219–25.
2. On the Olympic Village, see, J. White, ' "The Los Angeles Way of Doing Things": The Olympic Village and the Practice of Boosterism in 1932', *Olympika 11*, (2002), pp. 79–116; M. Dyreson and M. Llewellyn, 'Los Angeles is the Olympic city: Legacies of the 1932 and 1984 Olympic games', *International Journal of the History of Sport*, *25*(14), (2008), pp. 1991–2018.
3. Cited in White (2002), p. 96.
4. Cited in Dyreson (1995), p. 38.
5. On the other side of Los Angeles, see M. Davis, *City of Quartz: Excavating the Future in Los Angeles*, Verso (2006).
6. On the development of the torch relay, see K. Lennartz, 'The genesis of legends', *Journal of Olympic History*, *5*(1), (1997), pp. 8–11.

Chapter 4, Section Three

1. Organising Committee for the Olympic Games in Los Angeles in 1932, *The Games of the Xth Olympiad, Los Angeles 1932: Official Report*, (1933), p. 30, cited in Dinces, 'Padres on Mount Olympus: Los Angeles and the production of the 1932 Olympic mega-event', *Journal of Sport History*, *32*(2), (2005) p. 144.
2. Organising Committee for the Olympic Games in Los Angeles in 1932, *The Games of the Xth Olympiad, Los Angeles 1932: Official Report*, (1933), p. 335. Cited in S. Dinces, 'Padres on Mount Olympus: Los Angeles and the production of the 1932 Olympic mega-event', *Journal of Sport History*, *32*(2), (2005), p. 144.
3. Warwick S. Carpenter, 'On to the Olympic Games!,' *Country Life* (62), June–July 1932, p. 74. Cited in Dyreson (1995), p. 25.
4. 'Sports of the Times; The Grand Dame of the Olympics', *New York Times*, 3 July 1984.
5. On Hollywood and the Olympics, amongst other things, see the excellent

M. Dyreson, 'Marketing Weissmuller to the World: Hollywood's Olympics and Federal Schemes for Americanization through Sport', *International Journal of the History of Sport*, 25(2), (2008), pp. 284–306; M. Dyreson, 'The republic of consumption at the Olympic Games: globalization, Americanization, and Californization', *Journal of Global History*, 8(02), (2013), pp. 256–278.

Chapter 4, Section Four

1. W. Baker, 'Muscular marxism and the Chicago counter-Olympics of 1932', *International Journal of the History of Sport*, 9(3), (1992), pp. 397–410.
2. Cited in S. Dinces, 'Padres on Mount Olympus: Los Angeles and the production of the 1932 Olympic mega-event', *Journal of Sport History*, 32(2), (2005), pp. 137–65. Mooney was eventually pardoned after it became obvious in the late 1930s that the whole thing was cooked up.
3. 'STUNT FOR MOONEY JEERED: Finale of Olympiad Marked by Demonstration; Crowd Cheers Arrest of Participants', *Los Angeles Times*, 15 August 1932, cited in Dinces (2005), p. 149.
4. 'Will Rogers Remarks', *Los Angeles Times*, 4 August 1932, cited in Dyreson, (1995) p. 38.
5. Cited in ibid, p. 40.
6. Grantland Rice, 'For Men Only?', *Collier's* (90), 24 September 1932, cited in ibid, p. 37.
7. Cited in ibid, p. 42.
8. 'The World Beating Girl Viking of Texas', *Literary Digest* (114), 27 August 1932, cited in S. Cahn, *Coming on Strong: Gender and Sexuality in Women's Sport*, University of Illinois Press (2015), p. 115.
9. E. Yamamoto, 'Cheers for Japanese Athletes: The 1932 Los Angeles Olympics and the Japanese American Community', *The Pacific Historical Review*, (2000), pp. 399–430; D. Welky, 'Viking girls, mermaids, and little brown men: US journalism and the 1932 Olympics', *Journal of Sport History*, 24, (1997), pp. 24–49.
10. Cited in Yamamoto (2000), p. 32.
11. Cited in B. J. Keys, *Globalizing Sport: National Rivalry and International Community in the 1930s*, Harvard University Press (2013), p. 113.

Chapter 4, Section Five

1. Cited in B. J. Keys, *Globalizing Sport: National Rivalry and International Community in the 1930s*, Harvard University Press (2013), p. 137.
2. On the making and transport of the bell, see M. Meyer, 'Berlin 1936', in

J. Gold and M. Gold (eds.), *Olympic Cities: City Agendas, Planning, and the World's Games, 1896–2016*, Routledge (2010).
3. In a letter from the IOC president to Lewald, dated 3 May 1933, cited in Keys (2013), p. 138.
4. Baillet-Latour, cited in ibid, p. 138; Edström, in a letter to Brundage, 4 December 1933, cited in L. Yttergren, 'Questions of Propriety: J. Sigfrid Edström, Anti-Semitism, and the 1936 Berlin Olympics', *Olympika*, 16 (2007), pp. 77–92.
5. On the boycott movement, see C. Marvin, 'Avery Brundage and American Participation in the 1936 Olympic Games', *Journal of American Studies*, 16(01), (1982), pp. 81–105; M. Gottlieb, 'The American Controversy over the Olympic Games', *American Jewish Historical Quarterly*, (1972), pp. 181–213; A. Kruger, ' "Once the Olympics are through, we'll beat up the Jew": German Jewish Sport 1898–1938 and the Anti-Semitic Discourse', *Journal of Sport History*, 26(2), (1999), pp. 353–375; A. Guttmann, 'The "Nazi Olympics" and the American Boycott Controversy', in P. Arnaud and J. Riordan (eds.), *Sport and International Politics: The Impact of Fascism and Communism on Sport*, Routledge (2003), pp. 31–50.
6. Cited in Keys (2013), p. 118.
7. A. Gounot, 'Barcelona against Berlin. The project of the People's Olympiad in 1936', *Sportwissenschaft*, 37(4), (2007), pp. 419–428; X. Pujadas and C. Santacana, 'The Popular Olympic Games, Barcelona 1936: Olympians and Antifascists', *International Review for the Sociology of Sport*, 27(2), (1992), pp. 139–148.
8. Drawn from a variety of *New York Times* reports, all cited in Keys (2013), p. 150.

Chapter 4, Section Six

1. On Owens, see, D. McRae, *In Black and White: The Untold Story of Joe Louis and Jesse Owens*, Simon and Schuster (2014); C. Young, ' "In Praise of Jesse Owens": Technical Beauty at the Berlin Olympics 1936', *Sport in History*, 28(1), (2008), pp. 83–103; D. Wiggins, 'The 1936 Olympic Games in Berlin: The response of America's black press', *Research Quarterly for Exercise and Sport*, 54(3), (1983), pp. 278–292.
2. Cited in B. J. Keys, *Globalizing Sport: National Rivalry and International Community in the 1930s*, Harvard University Press (2013), p. 153.
3. All the above cited in ibid, p. 155.
4. D. Lell and K. Voolaid, 'Every Nation Has Her Own Olympics: The Estonian Example', in *Proceedings: International Symposium for Olympic Research*, International Centre for Olympic Studies (2008), pp. 547–52.

5. See K. Lennartz, 'Kitei Son and Spiridon Louis: Political Dimensions of the 1936 Marathon in Berlin', *Journal of Olympic History*, *12*(1), (2004), pp. 16–28.

6. Cited in D. Large, *Nazi Games: The Olympics of 1936*, W. W. Norton (2007), p. 219.

7. Cited in Keys (2013), p. 155.

8. Cited in A. Krüger and W. Murray (eds.), *The Nazi Olympics: Sport, Politics, and Appeasement in the 1930s*, University of Illinois Press (2003), p. 63.

Chapter 4, Section Seven

1. For an overview of sport in modern Japan, see A. Guttmann and L. Thompson, *Japanese Sports: A History*, University of Hawaii Press (2001).

2. Cited in S. Collins, 'Special issue: The missing Olympics: the 1940 Tokyo Games, Japan, Asia and the Olympic Movement', *International Journal of the History of Sport*, *24*(8), (2007), p. 962.

3. See Collins (2007); M. Polley, 'Olympic diplomacy: the British government and the projected 1940 Olympic games', *International Journal of the History of Sport*, *9*(2), (1992), pp. 169–187.

4. Cited in Collins (2007), p. 1064.

5. Cited in ibid, p. 1088.

6. Cited in ibid, p. 1081.

Chapter 5, Section One

1. P. Wilson, 'Helsinki: 1952', in J. Rodda (ed.), *The Olympic Games 1984*, Willow (1983).

2. Organising Committee for the Games of the XV Olympiad, *The Official Report of the Organising Committee for the Games of the XV Olympiad, Helsinki 1952* (1953), p. 240.

3. This argument has been most explicitly made in Finland by A. Raevuori, *Viimeiset oikeat olympialaiset: Helsinki 1952 (The Last Real Olympics, Helsinki 1952)*, Ajantus (2002).

4. J. Hughson, 'The Friendly Games – The "Official" IOC Film of the 1956 Melbourne Olympics as Historical Record', *Historical Journal of Film, Radio and Television*, vol. 30, issue 4 (2010).

5. Cited in J. Hampton, *The Austerity Olympics: When the Games Came to London in 1948*, Aurum Press (2012), p. 99.

6. Ibid, p. 32.

7. Cited in G. Davison, 'Welcoming the world: The 1956 Olympic Games and the re-presentation of Melbourne', *The Forgotten Fifties, Australian Historical Studies*, vol. 28, no. 109, pp. 64–76.

8. Key sources on the two presidents include: A. Guttmann, *The Games Must Go On: Avery Brundage and the Olympic Movement*, Columbia University Press (1984); C. Marvin, 'Avery Brundage and American Participation in the 1936 Olympic Games', *Journal of American Studies, 16*(01), (1982), pp. 81–105; L. Yttergren, 'Questions of propriety: J. Sigfrid Edström, anti-Semitism, and the 1936 Berlin Olympics', in *Olympika, 16*, (2007), pp. 77–92; L. Yttergren, 'J. Sigfrid Edström and the Nurmi Affair of 1932: The Struggle of the Amateur Fundamentalists against Professionalism in the Olympic Movement', in *Cultural Imperialism in Action: Critiques in the Global Olympic Trust*, (2006), pp. 111–126.

9. The composition and politics of the IOC is covered in C. Hill, *Olympic Politics*, Manchester University Press (1996); P. Charitas, 'Imperialisms in the Olympics of the Colonization in the Postcolonization: Africa into the International Olympic Committee, 1910–1965', *International Journal of the History of Sport*, (2015), pp. 1–14; P. Charitas and D. Kemo-Keimbou, 'The United States of America and the Francophone African Countries at the International Olympic Committee: Sports Aid, a Barometer of American Imperialism? (1952–1963)', *Journal of Sport History, 40*(1), (2013), pp. 69–91; P. Charitas, 'Anglophone Africa in the Olympic Movement: The Confirmation of a British Wager? (1948–1962)', *African Research & Documentation*, (116), (2011), p. 35.

10. Cited in D. Maraniss, *Rome 1960: The Olympics that Changed the World*, Simon and Schuster (2008), p. 55.

Chapter 5, Section Two

1. The official 1948 film can be viewed at https://www.youtube.com/watch?v=VajWojMkY5I.

2. Cited in P. Beck, 'The British government and the Olympic movement: the 1948 London Olympics', *International Journal of the History of Sport, 25*(5), (2008), pp. 615–647.

3. Ibid.

4. Ibid.

5. Cited in J. Hampton, *The Austerity Olympics: When the Games Came to London in 1948*, Aurum Press (2012), p. 57.

6. Ibid, p. 23.

7. Ibid, p. 24.

8. Ibid, p. 187.

9. Ibid, pp. 275–287.
10. Ibid, Collins cited in *The Times* obituary, 22 December 2006.
11. *Guardian*, 30 July 1948.
12. D. Kynaston, *Austerity Britain, 1945–1951*, Bloomsbury (2008), p. 292.
13. L. Emery, 'Women's participation in the Olympic Games: A historical perspective', *Journal of Physical Education, Recreation & Dance*, 55(5), (1984), pp. 62–72.
14. 'Olympian Ahead of Her Time', *International Herald Tribune*, 2 October 1982.
15. Cited in Hampton (2012), pp. 303–305.
16. *The Economist*, 21 August 1948.
17. *The Economist*, 11 September 1948.

Chapter 5, Section Three

1. Cited in P. D'Agati, *The Cold War and the 1984 Olympic Games: A Soviet–American Surrogate War*, Palgrave (2013), p. 58.
2. N. Romanov memoir, cited in J. Riordan, 'Sport after the Cold War', in S. Wagg and D. Andrews (eds.), *East Plays West: Sport and the Cold War*, Routledge (2007), p. 152.
3. Letter, Brundage to Edström, dated 6 April 1947, cited in J. Parks, 'Verbal gymnastics', in ibid, p. 33.
4. Ibid, p. 34.
5. Brundage to all IOC members (no date; possibly 1952, shortly after he assumed the presidency), cited in J. Riordan, 'The rise and fall of Soviet Olympic champions', *Olympika*, 2, (1993), pp. 25–44.
6. Cited in J. Findling and K. Pelle (eds.), *Encyclopedia of the Modern Olympic Movement*, Greenwood (2004), p. 143.
7. All quotations cited in S. Crawford, 'Foxhunter and Red Rum as national icons: Significant equestrian episodes in post-Second World War British sports history', *Sport in History*, 27(3), (2007), pp. 487–504.

Chapter 5, Section Four

1. The official film can be seen at https://www.youtube.com/watch?v=EDA5BvvtDsM.
2. G. Davison, *The Rise and Fall of Marvellous Melbourne*, Melbourne University Press (1979).
3. G. Davison, 'Welcoming the world: The 1956 Olympic games and the re-presentation of Melbourne', *Australian Historical Studies*, 27(109), (1997), pp. 64–76.

4. J. Hughson, 'An Invitation to "Modern" Melbourne: The Historical Significance of Richard Beck's Olympic Poster Design', *Journal of Design History*, *25*(3), (2012), pp. 268–284.

5. J. Hughson, 'The cultural legacy of Olympic posters', *Sport in Society 13.5*, (2010), pp. 749–759.

6. R. Stanton, *The Forgotten Olympic Art Competitions: The Story of the Olympic Art Competitions of the 20th Century*, Trafford (2000); D. Brown, 'Revisiting the Discourses of art, beauty and sport from the 1906 Consultative Conference for the Arts, Literature and Sport', *Olympiaka 5*, (1996), pp. 1–24.

7. D. Islip, '1956 Olympic Decorations: the final fling', *Fabrications*, *11*(1), (2000), pp. 26–43.

8. *Opening Ceremony: Official Programme Melbourne Olympics 1956*, cited in G. Davison, 'Images of the city', at http://www.emelbourne.net.au/biogs/EM00742b.htm.

9. Cited in M. Killanin and J. Rhodda (eds.), *The Olympic Games 1984*, Collins Willow (1983), p. 148.

10. Cited in N. Lehmann, *Internationale Sportbeziehungen und Sportpolitik der DDR, Teil I* (*International Sports Relations and Sports Politics of the GDR, Part 1*), Lit Verlag (1986), p. 309.

11. Account of the water-polo match at http://www.smithsonianmag.com/people-places/blood-in-the-water-at-the-1956-olympics-1616787/?no-ist= ; R. Rinehart, '"Fists flew and blood flowed": Symbolic Resistance and International Response in Hungarian Water Polo at the Melbourne Olympics, 1956', *Journal of Sport History*, *23*, (1996), pp. 120–139.

12. 'A sweet and bloody victory for Hungary', in *Sports Illustrated*, November 1956.

13. Cited in J. Findling and K. Pelle (eds.), *Encyclopaedia of the Modern Olympic Movement*, Greenwood (2004), p. 152.

14. Ibid, p. 152.

15. Cited in D. Dunstan, 'Sir Harold Luxton', in *Australian Dictionary of Biography*, vol. 10, Melbourne University Press (1986).

Chapter 6, Section One

1. C. Levi, *Fleeting Rome: In Search of La Dolce Vita*, John Wiley (2005); J. Carlos and D. Zirin, *The John Carlos Story: The Sports Moment that Changed the World*, Haymarket Books (2011).

2. J. Traganou, 'Tokyo's 1964 Olympic design as a "realm of [design] memory" ', *Sport in Society*, *14*(4), (2011), pp. 466–481.

3. E. Zolov, 'Showcasing the "Land of Tomorrow": Mexico and the 1968 Olympics', *The Americas*, *61*(2), (2004), pp. 159–188; E. Carey,

'Spectacular Mexico: Design, Propaganda, and the 1968 Olympics', *Hispanic American Historical Review*, *95*(4), (2015), pp. 698–699.

4. K. Schiller and C. Young, *The 1972 Munich Olympics and the Making of Modern Germany*, University of California Press (2010), p. 94.

5. Ibid.

6. M. de Moragas Spa, N. Rivenburgh and J. Larson, *Television in the Olympics*, John Libbey (1995), p. 21.

7. Cited at http://www.vtoldboys.com/mexico68.htm.

8. N. Masumoto and G. MacDonald, '"Tokyo Olympiad": Olympism Interpreted from the Conflict Between Artistic Representation and Documentary Film', *International Journal of Sport and Health Science*, *1*(2), (2003), pp. 188–195; I. McDonald, 'Critiquing the Olympic documentary: Kon Ichikawa's Tokyo Olympiad', *Sport in Society*, *11*(2–3), (2008), pp. 298–310; D. Martinez, 'Politics and the Olympic film documentary: the legacies of Berlin Olympia and Tokyo Olympiad', *Sport in Society*, *12*(6), (2009), pp. 811–821. There may well be a good Olympic movie still to be made, but the stranglehold on the slot acquired by the unbearably dull American director Bud Greenspan has made it, so far, impossible. See L. Roessner, 'Sixteen Days of Glory: A Critical-Cultural Analysis of Bud Greenspan's Official Olympic Documentaries', *Communication, Culture & Critique*, *7*(3), (2014), pp. 338–355.

9. Cited in S. Wenn, 'Lights! Camera! Little Action: Television, Avery Brundage and the 1956 Melbourne Olympics', *Sporting Traditions*, *10*(1), (1993), pp. 38–53; S. Wenn, 'Growing pains: The Olympic movement and television, 1966–1972', in *Newsletter NASSH*, (1995), pp. 70–77.

10. S. Wenn, 'A turning point for IOC television policy: US television rights negotiations and the 1980 Lake Placid and Moscow Olympic festivals', *Journal of Sport History*, *25*, (1998), pp. 87–118.

11. B. García, 'The concept of Olympic cultural programmes: origins, evolution and projection', *Centre d'Estudis Olimpics, University lectures on the Olympics*, (2002), pp. 1–15; N. Aso, 'Sumptuous re-past: The 1964 Tokyo Olympics arts festival', in *Positions: East Asia Cultures Critique*, *10*(1), (2002), pp. 7–38.

12. On Hary, Adidas and the sports goods industry, see the excellent B. Smit, *Pitch Invasion: Adidas, Puma and the Making of Modern Sport*, Penguin (2007); the wider debate over amateurism is covered in M. Llewellyn and J. Gleaves, 'The Rise of the "Shamateur", The International Olympic Committee and the Preservation of the Amateur Ideal', in *Problems, Possibilities, Promising Practices: Critical Dialogues on the Olympic and Paralympic Games*, International Centre for Olympic Studies (2012), p. 23; S. Wagg, 'Tilting at Windmills? Olympic Politics and the Spectre of Amateurism', in *Handbook of Olympic Studies*, Palgrave (2012), pp. 321–37.

13. C. Hill, *Olympic Politics*, Manchester University Press (1996); M. Smith, 'Revisiting South Africa and the Olympic Movement: The Correspondence of Reginald S. Alexander and the International Olympic Committee, 1961–86', *International Journal of the History of Sport*, *23*(7), (2006), pp. 1193–1216; D. MacIntosh, H. Cantelon and L. McDermott, 'The IOC and South Africa: a lesson in transnational relations', *International Review for the Sociology of Sport*, *28*(4), (1993), pp. 373–393.

14. On this extraordinary episode in sports history, see T. Pauker, 'Ganefo I: sports and politics in Djakarta', *Asian Survey*, (1965), pp. 171–185; R. Lutan and F. Hong, 'The politicization of sport: GANEFO – A case study', *Sport in Society*, *8*(3), (2005), pp. 425–439; C. Connolly, 'The Politics of the Games of the New Emerging Forces (GANEFO)', *International Journal of the History of Sport*, *29*(9), (2012), pp. 1311–1324; T. Gitersos, 'The sporting scramble for Africa: GANEFO, the IOC and the 1965 African Games', *Sport in Society*, *14*(5), (2011), pp. 645–659; R. Field, 'Re-Entering the Sporting World: China's Sponsorship of the 1963 Games of the New Emerging Forces (GANEFO)', *International Journal of the History of Sport*, *31*(15), (2014), pp. 1852–1867; I. Adams, 'Pancasila: Sport and the Building of Indonesia – Ambitions and Obstacles', *International Journal of the History of Sport* 19.2–3, (2002), pp. 295–318.

15. Cited in S. Reeve, *One Day in September: The Full Story of the 1972 Munich Olympics Massacre and the Israeli Revenge Operation*, Skyhorse Publishing (2011), p. 51.

Chapter 6, Section Two

1. Cited in R. Bosworth, 'Rome 1960: Making Sporting History', *History Today*, *60*(8), (2010), p. 18.

2. Ibid.

3. S. Martin, *Sport Italia: The Italian Love Affair with Sport*, I. B. Tauris (2011); D. Maraniss, *Rome 1960: The Olympics that Changed the World*, Simon and Schuster (2008); T. Brennan, 'The 1960 Rome Olympics: spaces and spectacle', in *Proceedings: International Symposium for Olympic Research*, International Centre for Olympic Studies (2010).

4. Cited in Bosworth, 'Rome 1960: Making Sporting History', *History Today*, *60*(8), (2010), p. 20.

5. C. Levi, *Fleeting Rome: In Search of La Dolce Vita*, John Wiley (2005), p. 159.

6. N. Zonis, 'City of Women: Sex and Sports at the 1960 Rome Olympic Games', in P. Morris (ed.), *Women in Italy 1945–60: An Interdisciplinary Study*, Palgrave (2006), pp. 77–91.

7. Cited in ibid, pp. 82–83.
8. C. Gissendanner, 'African American women Olympians: The impact of race, gender, and class ideologies, 1932–1968', *Research Quarterly for Exercise and Sport*, *67*(2), (1996), pp. 172–182.
9. Cited in Maraniss (2008), p. 160.
10. Cited in Maraniss (2008), p. 384.
11. T. Judah and R. Girard, *Bikila: Ethiopia's Barefoot Olympian*, Reportage Press (2008); R. Chappell and E. Seifu, 'Sport, culture and politics in Ethiopia', *Culture, Sport, Society*, *3*(1), (2000), pp. 35–47.

Chapter 6, Section Three

1. Cited in S. Wilson, 'Exhibiting a new Japan: the Tokyo Olympics of 1964 and Expo '70 in Osaka'. *Historical Research*, *85*(227), (2012), pp. 159–178.
2. J. Abel, 'Japan's Sporting Diplomacy: The 1964 Tokyo Olympiad', *International History Review*, *34*(2), (2012), pp. 203–220.
3. R. Whiting, 'Olympic construction transformed Tokyo', *Japan Times*, 10 October 2014.
4. Ibid; see also R. Whiting, 'Negative impact of 1964 Olympics profound', *Japan Times*, 24 October 2014.
5. C. Tagsold, 'Modernity, space and national representation at the Tokyo Olympics 1964', *Urban History*, *37*(02), (2010), pp. 289–300.
6. R. Whiting, 'Schollander, Hayes were spectacular at Tokyo Games', *Japan Times*, 17 October 2014.
7. All cited in R. Otomo, 'Narratives, the body and the 1964 Tokyo Olympics', *Asian Studies Review* 31.2, (2007), pp. 117–132.
8. A. Niehaus, '"If you want to cry, cry on the green mats of Kôdôkan": Expressions of Japanese cultural and national identity in the movement to include judo into the Olympic programme', *International Journal of the History of Sport*, *23*(7), (2006), pp. 1173–1192; M. Villamón, D. Brown, J. Espartero and C. Gutiérrez, 'Reflexive Modernization and the Disembedding of Jūdō from 1946 to the 2000 Sydney Olympics', *International Review for the Sociology of Sport*, *39*(2), (2004), pp. 139–156; K. Carr, 'Making way: War, philosophy and sport in Japanese judo', *Journal of Sport History*, *20*(2), (1993), pp. 167–188.
9. I. Buruma, *Inventing Japan: 1853–1964*, Random House (2004).
10. C. Tagsold, 'Remember to get back on your feet quickly: the Japanese women's volleyball team at the 1964 Olympics as a "Realm of Memory"', *Sport in Society*, *14*(4), (2011), pp. 444–453; H. Macnaughtan, 'The Oriental Witches: Women, Volleyball and the 1964 Tokyo Olympics', *Sport*

in History, *34*(1), (2014), pp. 134–156; I. Merklejn, 'Remembering the oriental witches: Sports, gender and shōwa Nostalgia in the NHK narratives of the Tokyo Olympics', *Social Science Japan Journal*, (2013).

11. J. Underwood, 'An Exuberant Finish in Tokyo', *Sports Illustrated*, 2 November 1964.

Chapter 6, Section Four

1. Cited in C. Brewster and K. Brewster, *Representing the Nation: Sport and Spectacle in Post-revolutionary Mexico*, Routledge (2013), p. 71.

2. K. Brewster, 'Patriotic pastimes: the role of sport in post-revolutionary Mexico', *International Journal of the History of Sport*, *22*(2), (2005), pp. 139–157; K. Brewster, 'Reflections on Mexico '68', *Bulletin of Latin American Research*, *29*(s1), (2010), pp. i–vii; K. Brewster and C. Brewster, 'Special Issue: Representing the nation: sport, control, contestation, and the Mexican Olympics', *International Journal of the History of Sport*, *26*(6), (2009), pp. 711–880.

3. A good overview of this can be found in M. Barke, 'Mexico 1968', in J. Gold and M. Gold (eds.), *Olympic Cities: City Agendas, Planning, and the World's Games*, *1896–2016*, Routledge (2010), pp. 233–246.

4. K. Wendl, 'The Route of Friendship: A Cultural/Artistic Event of the Games of the XIX Olympiad in Mexico City – 1968', *Olympika*, *7*, (1998), pp. 113–134; L. Castañeda, 'Choreographing the Metropolis: Networks of Circulation and Power in Olympic Mexico', *Journal of Design History*, (2012), pp. 285–303.

5. K. Brewster, 'Teaching Mexicans How to Behave: Public Education on the Eve of the Olympics', *Bulletin of Latin American Research*, *29*(s1), (2010), pp. 46–62.

6. K. Witherspoon, *Before the Eyes of the World: Mexico and the 1968 Olympic Games*, Northern Illinois University Press (2008); R. Hoffer, *Something in the Air: American Passion and Defiance in the 1968 Mexico City Olympics*, Simon and Schuster (2009); E. Carey, *Plaza of Sacrifices: Gender, Power and Terror in 1968 Mexico*, UNM Press (2005).

7. Cited in Hoffer (2009), p. 116.

8. R. Ritchie, J. Reynard and T. Lewis, 'Intersex and the Olympic games', *Journal of the Royal Society of Medicine*, *101*(8), (2008), pp. 395–399; S. Wiederkehr, ' "We shall never know the exact number of men who have competed in the Olympics posing as women": Sport, gender verification and the Cold War', *International Journal of the History of Sport*, *26*(4), (2009), pp. 556–572.

9. T. Hunt, *Drug Games: The International Olympic Committee and the Politics of Doping, 1960–2008*, University of Texas Press (2011); P. Dimeo,

A History of Drug Use in Sport: 1876–1976: Beyond Good and Evil, Routledge (2008).

10. J. Gleaves and M. Llewellyn, 'Sport, Drugs and Amateurism: Tracing the Real Cultural Origins of Anti-Doping Rules in International Sport', *International Journal of the History of Sport*, *31*(8), (2014), pp. 839–853.

11. V. Møller, 'Knud Enemark Jensen's death during the 1960 Rome Olympics: A search for truth?', *Sport in History*, *25*(3), (2005), pp. 452–471.

12. Cited in http://www.washingtonpost.com/wp-dyn/content/article/2010/08/21/AR2010082102538.html and Hunt (2011), p. 42.

13. H. Edwards, *The Revolt of the Black Athlete*, New York: Free Press (1969); D. Hartmann, *Race, Culture, and the Revolt of the Black Athlete: The 1968 Olympic Protests and Their Aftermath*, University of Chicago Press (2004); T. Smith and D. Steele, *Silent Gesture: The Autobiography of Tommie Smith*, Temple University Press (2008); J. Carlos and D. Zirin, *The John Carlos Story: The Sports Moment that Changed the World*, Haymarket Books (2011).

14. H. Edwards, *The Revolt of the Black Athlete*, New York: Free Press (1969), cited in D. Wiggins and P. Muller, *The Unlevel Playing Field: A Documentary History of the African American*, University of Illinois Press (2005), p. 288.

15. Edwards (1969), p. 190.

16. Cited in Hoffer (2009), p. 177.

Chapter 6, Section Five

1. See S. Kvarv, 'The Labour Movement's Perception of Sports and the Winter Olympics in Oslo in 1952', *International Journal of the History of Sport*, *29*(8), (2012), pp. 1215–1230.

2. Overviews of the winter games include: S. Essex and B. Chalkley, 'The changing infrastructural implications of the winter Olympics, 1924–2002', *Bollettino della Società Geografica Italiana* (2002), pp. 1–14; S. Essex and B. Chalkley, 'Mega sporting events in urban and regional policy: a history of the Winter Olympics', *Planning Perspectives*, *19*(2), (2004), pp. 201–204; S. Essex, 'Driving urban change: the impact of the winter Olympics, 1924–2002', in J. Gold and M. Gold (eds.) *Olympic Cities: City Agendas, Planning, and the World's Games, 1896–2016*, Routledge (2007), pp. 56–79; L. Gerlach (ed.), *The Winter Olympics: From Chamonix to Salt Lake*, University of Utah Press (2004).

3. On ice hockey and the Cold War, see J. Soares, 'Cold War, Hot Ice: International Ice Hockey, 1947–1980', *Journal of Sport History*, *34*(2), (2007), p. 207; P. Conlin, 'The Cold War and Canadian nationalism on ice: federal government involvement in international hockey during the

1960s', *Canadian Journal of History of Sport*, *25*(2), (1994), pp. 50–68;
M. Jokisipila, 'Maple leaf, hammer, and sickle: international ice hockey
during the Cold War', *Sport History Review*, *37*(1), (2006), p. 36;
J. Wilson, '27 remarkable days: the 1972 summit series of ice hockey
between Canada and the Soviet Union', in *Totalitarian Movements and
Political Religions* 5.2 (2004), pp. 271–280.

4. L. Loew, 'Karl Schranz and the International Debate on Amateurism,
Sapporo 1972', *Olympika*, *17*, (2008), pp. 153–168.

5. *New York Times*, 6 February 1973, cited in J. Findling and K. Pelle (eds.),
Encyclopedia of the Modern Olympic Movement, Greenwood (2004),
p. 289.

Chapter 6, Section Six

1. Sources on the Munich games include: K. Schiller and C. Young, *The
1972 Munich Olympics and the Making of Modern Germany*, University
of California Press (2010); D. Large, *Munich 1972: Tragedy, Terror, and
Triumph at the Olympic Games*, Rowman & Littlefield (2012); S. Reeve,
*One Day in September: The Full Story of the 1972 Munich Olympics
Massacre and the Israeli Revenge Operation 'Wrath of God'*, Skyhorse
Publishing (2011); A. Vowinckel, 'Sports, Terrorism and the Media: The
Munich Hostage Crisis of 1972', *Esporte e Sociedade*, *6*, (2007), pp. 1–16;
S. Diffrient, 'Spectator sports and terrorist reports: filming the Munich
Olympics, (re)imagining the Munich Massacre', *Sport in Society*, *11*(2–3),
(2008), pp. 311–329.

2. Cited in Schiller and Young (2010), p. 132.

3. A fabulous thirty-minute film of the performances and installations on the
Spielstrasse can be seen at https://www.youtube.com/watch?v=
PoIFP59U3L4.

4. Cited in Schiller and Young (2010), p. 188.

Chapter 7, Section One

1. J. Rodda, 'Lord Killanin', 27 April 1999, *Guardian*.

2. S. Martyn and S. Wenn, 'Lord Killanin's Path to Olympic Commercialism',
Journal of Olympic History 2 (2008), pp. 40–46.

3. Cited in S. Wagg and D. Andrews (eds.), *East Plays West: Sport and the
Cold War*, Routledge (2007), p. 229.

4. All cited in Mary McDonald, '"Miraculous" Masculinity meets
militarisation: narrating the 1980 USSR–US men's Olympic ice hockey
match and Cold War politics', in ibid, pp. 222–234.

5. R. S. Edelman, 'The Russians Are Not Coming! The Soviet Withdrawal from the Games of the XXIII Olympiad', *International Journal of the History of Sport*, *32*(1), (2015), pp. 9–36.
6. S. Radchenko, 'Sport and Politics on the Korean Peninsula – North Korea and the 1988 Seoul Olympics', https://www.wilsoncenter.org/publication/sport-and-politics-the-korean-peninsula-north-korea-and-the-1988-seoul-olympics#sthash.0DjEStTY.dpuf (2011).

Chapter 7, Section Two

1. Cited in T. Teixeira, 'The XXI Olympiad: Canada's Claim or Montreal's Gain? Political and Social Tensions Surrounding the 1976 Montreal Olympics', in H. Lenskyj and S. Wagg (eds.), *The Palgrave Handbook of Olympic Studies*, Palgrave (2012), pp. 120–133. Other key sources on the Montreal games include J. Ludwig, *Five Ring Circus: The Montreal Olympics*, Doubleday Canada (1976); A. der Maur, *The Billion-Dollar Game: Jean Drapeau and the 1976 Olympics*, James Lorimer (1976); B. Kidd, 'The culture wars of the Montreal Olympics', *International Review for the Sociology of Sport*, *27*(2), (1992), pp. 151–162; D. Latouche, 'Montreal 1976', in J. Gold and M. Gold (eds.), *Olympic Cities: City Agendas, Planning and the World's Games*, Routledge (2012), pp. 247–267.
2. D. Paul, 'World cities as hegemonic projects: the politics of global imagineering in Montreal', *Political Geography*, *23*(5), (2004), pp. 571–596.
3. J. Adese, 'Colluding with the Enemy? Nationalism and Depictions of "Aboriginality" in Canadian Olympic Moments', *American Indian Quarterly*, *36*(4), (2012), pp. 479–502.
4. J. Redfern, 'Interview: Melvin Charney', *Canadian Art*, 15 December 2001.
5. J. Ludwig, *Five Ring Circus: The Montreal Olympics*, Doubleday (1976), pp. 2–3.
6. E. Kidd, 'Future Games', *Ottawa Journal*, 21 August 1976, p. 128.

Chapter 7, Section Three

1. Cited in J. Parks, *Red Sport, Red Tape: The Olympic Games, the Soviet Sports Bureaucracy, and the Cold War, 1952–1980*, Doctoral dissertation, UNC Chapel Hill (2009), p. 274.
2. Ibid., p. 293.
3. Ibid., p. 295.

4. See T. Hunt, *Drug Games: The International Olympic Committee and the Politics of Doping, 1960–2008*, University of Texas Press (2011), p. 66.

5. G. Plimpton, 'Moscow Games', *Harper's*, October 1980, and 'Paper Tourist: A Yank in Moscow', *Time*, 4 August 1980.

6. R. Jackson, 'The forgotten story of Ian Campbell', *Guardian*, 7 August 2013.

7. 'This Moscow man remembers the 1980 Summer Olympics as a beautiful fairy tale', http://www.pri.org/stories/2014-02-07/moscow-man-remembers-1980-summer-olympics-beautiful-fairy-tale.

Chapter 7, Section Four

1. See the transcript in the *New York Times*, 24 August 1984, http://www.nytimes.com/1984/08/24/us/convention-dallas-republicans-transcript-reagan-s-speech-accepting-gop. html?pagewanted=all.

2. Cited in R. Gruneau and R. Neubauer, 'A gold medal for the market: the 1984 Los Angeles Olympics, the Reagan era, and the politics of neoliberalism', in *The Palgrave Handbook of Olympic Studies*, Palgrave (2012), pp. 134–154.

3. Key sources on the Los Angeles games include B. Shaikin, *Sport and Politics: the Olympics and the Los Angeles Games*, Praeger (1988); C. La Rocco, 'Rings of Power: Peter Ueberroth and the 1984 Los Angeles Olympic Games', *Financial History*, 81(10), (2004), pp. 1–13; S. Wenn, 'Peter Ueberroth's Legacy: How the 1984 Los Angeles Olympics Changed the Trajectory of the Olympic Movement', *International Journal of the History of Sport*, 32(1), (2015), pp. 157–171; M. Dyreson and M. Llewellyn, 'Los Angeles is the Olympic city: Legacies of the 1932 and 1984 Olympic games', *International Journal of the History of Sport*, 25(14), (2008), pp. 1991–2018; M. Dyreson, 'Global Television and the Transformation of the Olympics: The 1984 Los Angeles Games', *International Journal of the History of Sport*, 32(1), (2015), pp. 172–184; M. Llewellyn, J. Gleaves and W. Wilson, 'The Historical Legacy of the 1984 Los Angeles Olympic Games', *International Journal of the History of Sport*, 32(1), (2015), pp. 1–8.

4. Cited in K. Reich, *Making It Happen: Peter Ueberroth and the 1984 Olympics*, Capra Press (1986), p. 28.

5. J. Haramon, 'A Look Back: Velodrome Built for 1984 Olympics Brought CSU Dominguez Hills Recognition as Sports and Entertainment Venue', (2009), http://www.csudhnews.com/2009/08/velodrome/.

6. View the McDonald's 1984 Olympic Games commercials at https://www.youtube.com/watch?v=JBnVtUpCV28 and https://www.youtube.com/watch?v=1zaLMWizN4s, and for a discussion of the promotion, see

http://www.nytimes.com/1984/08/10/business/advertising-big-mac-s-olympic-giveaway.html.

7. Ronald Reagan, *Radio Address to the Nation on the Summer Olympic Games*, 28 July 1984, accessible at http://www.reagan.utexas.edu/archives/speeches/1984/72884a.htm/.

8. 'Olympics Open Amid Pomp, Glittery Circumstances', *Washington Post*, 29 July 1984.

9. F. Depford, 'Cheer, Cheer, Cheer For The Home Team', *Sports Illustrated*, 13 August 1984.

10. Cited in Z. Lu and F. Hong, *Sport and Nationalism in China*, Routledge (2013), p. 104.

11. A. Anthony, 'Speed: the Sequel', *Observer*, 30 September 2007. Thompson performed a victory lap at Los Angeles wearing a T-shirt that bore the words, 'Is the world's second greatest athlete gay?' He, like Lewis, has had a tetchy relationship with the general public. See the excellent R. Chalmers, 'The Champion That Time Forgot: why do we find it so hard to love Daley Thompson?', *Independent*, 22 October 2011.

12. O. Wainwright, 'More is more: the gaudy genius of the late Deborah Sussman', *Guardian*, 27 August 2014.

13. See ' "Festive Federalism" at the 1984 Los Angeles Olympics' at http://www.experiencingla.com/2012/07/festive-federalism-at-1984-los-angeles.html, (28 July 2012); D. Walker, 'Los Angeles Olympiad 84', at http://www.bdonline.co.uk/los-angeles-olympiad-84/5040770.article (website registration necessary), (July 1984); R. Rosenblatt, 'Olympics: Why We Play These Games', *Time*, 30 July 1984.

Chapter 7, Section Five

1. On the development of Korean sport, see G. Ok, 'The Political Significance of Sport: An Asian Case Study – Sport, Japanese Colonial Policy and Korean National Resistance, 1910–1945', *International Journal of the History of Sport* 22.4, (2005), pp. 649–670; H. Nam-Gil and J. Mangan, 'Ideology, Politics, Power: Korean Sport-Transformation, 1945–92', *International Journal of the History of Sport*, 19(2–3), (2002), pp. 213–242; Y. Ha, *Korean Sports in the 1980s and the Seoul Olympic Games of 1988*, Doctoral dissertation, Pennsylvania State University (2000); E. Hong, 'Elite sport and nation-building in South Korea: South Korea as the dark horse in global elite sport', *International Journal of the History of Sport*, 28(7), (2011), pp. 977–989.

2. J. Manheim, 'Rites of passage: The 1988 Seoul Olympics as public diplomacy', *Western Political Quarterly*, (1990), pp. 279–295.

3. Cited in J. Larson and H. Park, *Global Television and the Politics of the Seoul Olympics*, Westview Press (1993), p. 161.

4. D. Black and S. Bezanson, 'The Olympic Games, human rights and democratisation: lessons from Seoul and implications for Beijing', *Third World Quarterly*, 25(7), (2004), pp. 1245–1261.

5. B. Bridges, 'The Seoul Olympics: Economic miracle meets the world', *International Journal of the History of Sport*, 25(14), (2008), pp. 1939–1952; E. Koh, 'South Korea and the Asian Games: The first step to the world', *Sport in Society*, 8.3, (2005), pp. 468–478.

6. S. Collins, 'Mediated Modernities and Mythologies in the Opening Ceremonies of 1964 Tokyo, 1988 Seoul and 2008 Beijing Olympic Games', *International Journal of the History of Sport*, 29(16), (2012), pp. 2244–2263.

7. N. Griffin, *Ping-pong Diplomacy: The Secret History Behind the Game that Changed the World*, Simon and Schuster (2014).

8. J. H. Cho and A. Bairner, 'The sociocultural legacy of the 1988 Seoul Olympic Games', *Leisure Studies*, 31(3), (2012), pp. 271–289.

Chapter 8, Section One

1. Chen, quoted in D. Booth and C. Tatz, 'Swimming with the big boys? The politics of Sydney's 2000 Olympic bid', *Sporting traditions* 11.1, (1994), pp. 3–23. Ganga is quoted in J. Calvert, 'How to buy the Olympics', *Observer*, 6 January 2002.

2. On Samaranch and his era, see C. Hill, *Olympic Politics*, Manchester University Press (1996); V. Simpson and A. Jennings, *The Lords of the Rings*, Simon and Schuster (1992); R. Pound, *Inside the Olympics: A Behind-the-Scenes Look at the Politics, the Scandals, and the Glory of the Games*, Wiley (2004).

3. M. Killanin and M. Morris, *My Olympic Years*, Secker & Warburg (1983).

4. On FIFA under Havelange, see D. Yallop, *How They Stole the Game*, Hachette (2011); J. Sugden and A. Tomlinson, *Badfellas: FIFA Family at War*, Mainstream (2003).

5. R. Barney, S. Wenn and S. Martyn, *The International Olympic Committee and the Rise of Olympic Commercialism*, University of Utah Press (2002); A. Tomlinson, 'The commercialization of the Olympics: Cities, corporations and the Olympic commodity', in K. Young and K. Wamsley (eds.), *Global Olympics: Historical and Sociological Studies of the Modern Games*, JAI Press (2005); M. Payne, *Olympic Turnaround: How the Olympic Games Stepped Back from the Brink of Extinction to Become the World's Best Known Brand*, Greenwood (2006).

6. Data is all drawn form the excellent survey, J. L. Chappelet, 'Managing the size of the Olympic Games', *Sport in Society*, *17*(5), (2014), pp. 581–592.

7. For an overview of the relationship between TV and the Olympics, see A. Billings, *Olympic Media: Inside the Biggest Show on Television*, Routledge (2008); M. de Moragas Spa, N. Rivenburgh and J. Larson, *Television in the Olympics*, John Libbey (1995).

8. G. Collins, 'Coke's Hometown Olympics: The Company Tries the Big Blitz on Its Own Turf', *New York Times*, 28 March 1996.

9. A. Tomlinson, 'Olympic spectacle: Opening ceremonies and some paradoxes of globalization', *Media, Culture & Society*, *18*(4), (1996), pp. 583–602; R. Puijk, 'Producing Norwegian culture for domestic and foreign gazes: The Lillehammer Olympic opening ceremony', in A. Klausen (ed.), *Olympic Games as Performance and Public Event: The Case of the XVII Winter Olympic Games in Norway*, *94*, Berghahn Books (1999), pp. 97–136; T. Heinz Housel, 'Australian nationalism and globalization: Narratives of the nation in the 2000 Sydney Olympics' opening ceremony', *Critical Studies in Media Communication*, *24*(5), (2007), pp. 446–461; J. Hogan, 'Staging The Nation: Gendered and Ethnicized Discourses of National Identity in Olympic Opening Ceremonies', *Journal of Sport & Social Issues*, *27*(2), (2003), pp. 100–123; J. Traganou, 'National narratives in the opening and closing ceremonies of the Athens 2004 Olympic Games', *Journal of Sport & Social Issues*, *34*(2), (2010), pp. 236–251; A. Mobley, 'Sharing the dream: The opening ceremonies of Beijing', *Journal of Sport & Social Issues*, *32*(4), (2008), pp. 327–332.

Chapter 8, Section Two

1. Anon, 'The Great Victory of the Household Garbage: The Self-Abuse of Nolympics', available at http://thing.desk.nl/bilwet/Cracking/nolympics.html.

2. 'Lights, Camera . . . Too Much Action', *Los Angeles Times*, 15 October 1986.

3. The Toronto campaign and the anti-Olympics movements in general are well covered in H. Lenskyj, 'When winners are losers: Toronto and Sydney bids for the Summer Olympics', *Journal of Sport & Social Issues*, *20*(4), (1996), pp. 392–410; H. Lenskyj, *Olympic Industry Resistance: Challenging Olympic Power and Propaganda*, SUNY Press (2008).

4. C. Colomb, *Staging the New Berlin: Place Marketing and the Politics of Urban Reinvention Post-1989*, Routledge (2013), pp. 191–200.

5. 'Chronologie – Olympia Bewerbung Berlin 90er Jahre', available at http://autox.nadir.org/archiv/chrono/olymp_chro.html.

Chapter 8, Section Three

1. W. Montalbano, 'Israeli Medals Fail to Erase Munich Horror', *Los Angeles Times*, 8 August 1992.
2. Mandela quoted in J. Jeansome, 'Forgive and Forget, Mandela Urges South Africa', *Los Angeles Times*, 26 July 1992.
3. G. Vecsey, 'Sports of The Times; Heartfelt Adeu, Adeu: Barcelona Won Gold', *New York Times*, 10 August 1992.
4. M. de Moragas Spà, N. Rivenburgh and N. García, 'Television and the construction of identity: Barcelona, Olympic host', in M. de Moragas and M. Botella (eds.), *The Keys to Success: The Social, Sporting, Economic and Communications Impact of Barcelona '92*, Universitat Autonoma de Barcelona (1995), p. 92.
5. The key source on the domestic politics of the Barcelona games is J. Hargreaves, *Freedom for Catalonia? Catalan Nationalism, Spanish Identity and the Barcelona Olympic Games*, Cambridge University Press (2000).
6. T. Marshall (ed.), *Transforming Barcelona: the Renewal of a European Metropolis*, Routledge (2004); F. Monclús, 'The Barcelona model: and an original formula? From "reconstruction" to strategic urban projects (1979–2004)', *Planning Perspectives*, 18(4), (2003), pp. 399–421; M. Balibrea, 'Urbanism, culture and the post-industrial city: Challenging the "Barcelona model" ', *Journal of Spanish Cultural Studies*, 2(2), (2001), pp. 187–210.
7. J. Botella, 'The political games: agents and strategies in the 1992 Barcelona Olympic Games', in M. de Moragas and M. Botella (eds.), *The Keys to Success: The Social, Sporting, Economic and Communications Impact of Barcelona '92*, Universitat Autonoma de Barcelona (1995).
8. On the Dream Team, see M. Ralph, 'Epilogue: It was all a dream (wasn't it?)', *International Journal of the History of Sport*, 24(2), (2007), pp. 311–316; C. Cunningham, 'Basketball Bedlam in Barcelona: The Dream Team, a Reflection of the Globe's "New Order" ', in *Proceedings: International Symposium for Olympic Research*, International Centre for Olympic Studies (2006), pp. 86–99.
9. On the wider globalization and commercialization of the NBA, see W. LaFeber, *Michael Jordan and the New Global Capitalism*, W. W. Norton (2002); D. Andrews, *Michael Jordan, Inc.: Corporate Sport, Media Culture, and Late Modern America*, SUNY Press (2001).

Chapter 8, Section Four

1. The Atlanta Committee for the Olympic Games, *The Official Report of the Centennial Games* (3 vols), Peachtree (1997).

2. Quoted in M. Starr, 'No Payne, No Games', *Newsweek*, 16 July 1995.

3. Quoted in 'Getting Olympics: No Simple Game', *Washington Post*, 21 September 1993.

4. A. Young, *A Way Out of No Way: The Spiritual Memoirs of Andrew Young*, Thomas Nelson (1994), p. 142.

5. Quoted in P. Goldberger, 'Atlanta Is Burning', *New York Times*, 23 June 1996.

6. C. Rutheiser, *Imagineering Atlanta: The politics of place in the city of dreams*, Verso (1996).

7. Key sources on the Atlanta games, especially its urbanism, include C. Rutheiser, *Imagineering Atlanta: The Politics of Place in the City of Dreams*, Verso (1996); C. Rutheiser, 'How Atlanta lost the Olympics', *New Statesman*, 125(19), (1996), pp. 28–29; P. Queensberry, 'The Disposable Olympics Meets the City of Hype', *Southern Changes*, vol. 18, no. 2, (1996), pp. 3–14; C. Rutheiser, 'Assessing the Olympic Legacy', *Southern Changes* vol. 18, no. 2, (1996), pp. 16–19; D. Whitelegg, 'Going for gold: Atlanta's bid for fame', *International Journal of Urban and Regional Research*, 24(4), (2000), pp. 801–817; S. Gustafson, 'Displacement and the Racial State in Olympic Atlanta 1990–1996', *Southeastern Geographer*, 53(2), (2013), pp. 198–213; A. Beaty, *Atlanta's Olympic Legacy*, Centre On Housing Rights and Evictions (2007).

8. Rutheiser, *Imagineering Atlanta* (1996), pp. 242–243.

9. S. Duncan, 'Souls Grown Deep and the Cultural Politics of the Atlanta Olympics', *Radical History Review*, 2007 (98), (2007), pp. 97–118.

10. K. Sack, 'Atlanta and Izzy: No Medals for the Olympic Mascot', *New York Times*, 30 June 1996; R. Sandomir, 'ATLANTA DAY 7: The Mascot Vanishes? Where Is Izzy?' *New York Times*, 26 July 1996; S. Zebulon Baker, 'Whatwuzit?: The 1996 Atlanta Summer Olympics Reconsidered', in *Southern Spaces*, Emory University (2006).

11. G. Vescey, 'Sports of The Times; Atlanta Sends Up The Balloons', *New York Times*, 14 July 1996.

12. Rutheiser, *Imagineering Atlanta* (1996), p. 267.

13. T. Kornheiser, 'The end is just such a deflating experience', *Washington Post*, 5 August 1996.

14. Cited in Alistair Cooke, *Letter From America: Atlanta Olympics 1996*, 9 August 1996, available at http://www.bbc.co.uk/programmes/articles/3r16W7hz2LZcbl8N9CJk4nj/atlanta-olympics-1996-9-august-1996.

Chapter 8, Section Five

1. T. Magdalinski, 'The reinvention of Australia for the Sydney 2000 Olympic games', *International Journal of the History of Sport*, *17*(2–3), (2000), pp. 305–322; R. Cashman, *The Bitter-Sweet Awakening: The Legacy of the Sydney 2000 Olympic Games*, Pan Macmillan (2006); K. Toohey, 'The Sydney Olympics: Striving for legacies – overcoming short-term disappointments and long-term deficiencies', *International Journal of the History of Sport*, *25*(14), (2008), pp. 1953–1971.

2. G. Morgan, 'Aboriginal protest and the Sydney Olympic games', *Olympika*, *12*, (2003), pp. 23–38.

3. On Cathy Freeman, see C. Elder, A. Pratt and C. Ellis, 'Running Race: Reconciliation, Nationalism and the Sydney 2000 Olympic Games', *International Review for the Sociology of Sport*, *41*(2), (2006), pp. 181–200.

4. The anti-Olympics movement at Sydney is well covered in H. Lenskyj, *The Best Olympics Ever? Social Impacts of Sydney 2000*, Suny Press (2012).

5. Ibid, p. 197.

6. G. Morgan, 'Aboriginal protest and the Sydney Olympic games', *Olympika*, *12*, (2003), p. 26.

7. T. Heinz Housel, 'Australian nationalism and globalization: Narratives of the nation in the 2000 Sydney Olympics' opening ceremony', *Critical Studies in Media Communication*, *24*(5), (2007), pp. 446–461.

Chapter 8, Section Six

1. Data is all drawn from the excellent survey J. Chappelet, 'From Lake Placid to Salt Lake City: The Challenging Growth of the Olympic Winter Games Since 1980', *European Journal of Sport Science*, *2*(3), (2002), pp. 1–21.

2. N. Moll, 'An Integrative Symbol for a Divided Country? Commemorating the 1984 Sarajevo Winter Olympics in Bosnia and Herzegovina from the 1992–1995 War until Today', *Politička misao*, *51*(5), (2015), pp. 127–156; J. Walker, 'Olympic ghosts in a former warzone: what the legacy of 1984 means for Sarajevo today', *Visual Studies*, *27*(2), (2012), pp. 174–177.

3. H. Hiller, 'The Urban Transformation of a Landmark Event: The 1988 Calgary Winter Olympics', *Urban Affairs Review*, *26*(1), (1990), pp. 118–137.

4. R. Spilling, 'Mega event as strategy for regional development: The case of the 1994 Lillehammer Winter Olympics', *Entrepreneurship & Regional*

Development, 8(4), (1996), pp. 321–344; T. Terret, 'The Albertville Winter Olympics: Unexpected legacies – failed expectations for regional economic development', *International Journal of the History of Sport*, 25(14), (2008), pp. 1903–1921.

5. S. WuDunn, 'Japan's King of the Mountain; The Man Who Made Nagano Also Owns Part of It', *New York Times*, 6 February 1998.

6. D. Hamilton, 'The Party's Over in Nagano', *Wall Street Journal*, 22 February 1998.

7. B. Mallon, 'The Olympic bribery scandal', *Journal of Olympic History*, 8(2), (2000), pp. 17–27; S. Wenn and S. Martyn, ' "Tough Love": Richard Pound, David D'Alessandro, and the Salt Lake City Olympics Bid Scandal', *Sport in History*, 26 (1), (2006), pp. 64–90; D. Booth, 'Gifts of corruption?: Ambiguities of obligation in the Olympic movement', *Olympika 8*, (1999), pp. 43–68; D. Booth, 'Olympic city bidding: An exegesis of power', *International Review for the Sociology of Sport*, (2011); R. Sullivan, 'How the Olympics were Bought', *Time*, 1 February 1999; J. Calvert, 'How to buy the Olympics', *Observer*, 6 January 2002.

8. Originally published as A. Jennings and V. Simson, *The Lords of the Rings*, Simon and Schuster (1992).

9. Quoted in R. Sullivan, 'How The Olympics Were Bought', *Time*, 1 February 1999.

10. Cited in F. Allen, *Atlanta Rising: The Invention of an International City 1946–1996*, Taylor Trade Publishing (1996), p. 237.

11. See M. Fisher and B. Brubaker, 'Privileged World of IOC's Members Under Scrutiny', *Washington Post*, 23 January 1999.

12. D. Macintyre, 'Japan's Sullied Bid', *Time*, 1 February 1999; M. Jordan and K. Sullivan, 'Nagano Burned Documents Tracing '98 Olympics Bid', *Washington Post*, 21 January 1999.

13. Quoted in D. Booth and C. Tatz, 'Swimming with the big boys? The politics of Sydney's 2000 Olympic bid', *Sporting Traditions* 11.1, (1994), pp. 3–23.

14. Quoted in I. Molotsky, 'Olympics: Corruption Allegations Investigated', *New York Times*, 15 October 1999.

15. R. Pound, *Inside the Olympics: A Behind-the-Scenes Look at the Politics, the Scandals, and the Glory of the Games*, Wiley (2004); J. MacAloon, 'Scandal and governance: inside and outside the IOC 2000 Commission', *Sport in Society*, 14(03), (2011), pp. 292–308.

16. L. Gerlach, 'The "Mormon Games": Religion, Media, Cultural Politics, and the Salt Lake Winter Olympics', *Olympika 11*, (2002), pp. 1–52.

17. Quoted in C. Wiseman, 'People's History of Snowboarding', 9 February 2014, available at http://xgames.espn.go.com/xgames/snowboarding/article/10421440/a-people-history-snowboarding-olympics.

18. Watch Stein Eriksen talking about experimenting with and developing

new jumps and flips at https://www.youtube.com/watch?v=
A6Qwwonh39Y

19. S. Howe, *(Sick): A Cultural History of Snowboarding*, Macmillan (1998).

20. On the historical trajectory of gender, sexuality and skating, see M. Adams, 'From Mixed-Sex Sport to Sport for Girls: The Feminization of Figure Skating', *Sport in History*, *30*(2), (2010), pp. 218–241; M. Adams, *Artistic Impressions: Figure Skating, Masculinity, and the Limits of Sport*, University of Toronto Press (2011).

21. C. Baughman, *Women on Ice: Feminist Essays on the Tonya Harding/Nancy Kerrigan Spectacle*, Psychology Press (1995).

22. A. Kramer and J. Glanz, 'In Russia, Living the High Life; in America, a Wanted Man', *New York Times*, 1 June 2013.

23. M. Adams, 'Freezing social relations: Ice, rinks, and the development of figure skating', *Sites of Sport: Space, Place, Experience* (2004), pp. 57–72; A. Feder, ' "A Radiant Smile from the Lovely Lady": Overdetermined Femininity in Ladies' Figure Skating', *TDR* (1994), pp. 62–78; S. Wise, 'Artistic Impressions: Figure Skating, Masculinity, and the Limits of Sport', *International Journal of the History of Sport*, *29*(10), (2012), pp. 1490–1492.

24. Quoted in A. Jones, 'The Frozen Closet', *Newsweek*, 30 January 2014.

Chapter 8, Section Seven

1. Quoted in N. Malkoutzis, 'How the 2004 Olympics Triggered Greece's Decline', *Bloomberg Business*, 2 August 2012, available at http://www.bloomberg.com/news/articles/2012-08-02/how-the-2004-olympics-triggered-greeces-decline.

2. P. Markaris, 'Gridlocked Greeks still paying for the miracle of Athens', *Guardian*, 21 December 2004.

3. D. Mackay, 'Angelopoulos-Daskalaki commissions study into true cost of Athens 2004', *Inside The Games*, 7 August 2014, available at http://www.insidethegames.biz/articles/1021753/angelopoulos-daskalaki-commissions-study-into-true-cost-of-athens-2004.

4. M. Gold, 'Athens 2004', in J. Gold and M. Gold (eds.), *Olympic Cities: City Agendas, Planning and the World's Games*, Routledge (2012); P. Kissoudi, 'The Athens Olympics: optimistic legacies – post-Olympic assets and the struggle for their realization', *International Journal of the History of Sport*, *25*(14), (2008), pp. 1972–1990; P. Kissoudi, 'Athens' post-Olympic aspirations and the extent of their realization', *International Journal of the History of Sport*, *27*(16–18), (2010), pp. 2780–2797.

5. M. Samatas, 'Security and Surveillance in the Athens 2004 Olympics:

Some Lessons From a Troubled Story', *International Criminal Justice Review*, *17*(3), (2007), pp. 220–238; M. Samatas, 'Surveilling the 2004 Athens Olympics in the aftermath of 9/11: International pressures and domestic implications', *Security Games: Surveillance and Control at Mega Events* (2011), pp. 55–71.

6. Quoted in J. Heyer, ' "We Are Greedy and Asocial": Corruption Continues Virtually Unchecked in Greece', *Spiegel Online*, 16 October 2012, available at http://www.spiegel.de/international/europe/corruption-continues-virtually-unchecked-in-greece-a-861327.html.

7. L. Donegan, 'Athens ready to dispel "last minute" myth', *Guardian*, 13 August 2004.

8. I. Sinclair, 'The Colossus of Maroussi', *London Review of Books*, vol. 32 no. 10, 27 May 2010, pp. 30–33.

9. See, for example, the spirited if overstated defence from M. Nevradakias, 'The True Olympic Legacy of Athens: Refuting the Mythology', *Huffington Post*, 7 August 2012, available at http://www.huffingtonpost.com/michael-nevradakis/mythology-an-olympic-sport_b_1745857.html.

10. F. Govan, 'Greece's Olympic dream has turned into a nightmare for Village residents', *Daily Telegraph*, 23 June 2011.

11. Sinclair (2010), p. 30.

12. J. Van der Made, 'Struggling to survive, Greece's Olympic villagers ponder referendum choice', 5 July 2015, available at http://www.english.rfi.fr/economy/20150705-struggling-survive-greeces-olympic-villagers-face-referendum-choice.

13. N. Kalmouki, 'Illegally Built Athens Mall to be Legalized', *Greek Reporter*, 4 June 2014, available at http://greece.Greekreporter.com/2014/06/04/illegally-built-athens-mall-to-be-legalized/.

14. Sinclair (2010), p. 31.

15. J. Chaffin and K. Hope, 'Decline and fall of Greece's Olympic legacy', *Financial Times*, 30 December 2011.

16. Sinclair (2010), p. 33.

17. K. Gordon, 'In Athens, former Olympic venues now play host to refugees', *Baltimore Sun*, 12 November 2015, available at http://darkroom.baltimoresun.com/2015/11/in-athens-former-olympic-venues-now-play-host-to-refugees/#1.

Chapter 9, Section One

1. M. Gross, 'Jumping Through Hoops', *Vanity Fair*, 9 May 2012.

2. K. Radia, 'Putin: "Can't Feel Weak" in the Face of Terror Threats to Sochi Olympics" ' at http://abcnews.go.com/blogs/politics/2014/01/putin-cant-feel-weak-in-the-face-of-terror-threats-to-sochi-olympics.

3. This case is made in the incomparable A. Zimbalist, *Circus Maximus: The Economic Gamble Behind Hosting the Olympics and the World Cup*, Brookings Institution Press (2015).

4. See J. Pramuk, 'The Winter Olympics problem – nobody wants them', available at http://www.cnbc.com/2015/08/07/the-winter-olympics-problem-nobody-wants-them.html and L. Abend, 'Why Nobody Wants to Host the 2022 Winter Olympics', available at http://time.com/3462070/olympics-winter-2022/.

5. His roster of successful allies and friends, alongside Bach, includes Salman al-Khalifa, who secured the presidency of the Asian Football Confederation, and the organizers of the Buenos Aires Youth Olympics planned for 2018. See O. Gibson, 'Fifa powerbroker Sheikh Ahmad may hold key to Sepp Blatter's successor', *Guardian*, 3 June 2015, available at http://www.theguardian.com/football/2015/jun/03/sheikh-al-sabah-fifa-powerbroker-sepp-blatter.

6. On opening ceremonies in general, see A. Tomlinson, 'Olympic spectacle: Opening ceremonies and some paradoxes of globalization', *Media, Culture & Society*, *18*(4), (1996), pp. 583–602; J. Hogan, 'Staging the Nation: Gendered and Ethnicized Discourses of National Identity in Olympic Opening Ceremonies', *Journal of Sport & Social Issues*, *27*(2), (2003), pp. 100–123.

7. See R. Mendick, 'Sochi opening ceremony glitch: "This is bad, but it does not humiliate us" ', *Telegraph*, 8 February 2014, available at http://www.telegraph.co.uk/news/worldnews/europe/russia/10626384/Sochi-opening-ceremony-glitch-This-is-bad-but-it-does-not-humiliate-us.html.

Chapter 9, Section Two

1. Key sources on Beijing 2008 include M. Price and D. Dayan (eds.), *Owning the Olympics: Narratives of the New China*, University of Michigan Press (2009); S. Brownell, *Beijing's Games: What the Olympics Mean to China*, Rowman & Littlefield (2008); G. Jarvie, D. J. Hwang and M. Brennan, *Sport, Revolution and the Beijing Olympics*, Berg (2008); P. Close, D. Askew and X. Xin, *The Beijing Olympiad: The Political Economy of a Sporting Mega-Event*, Routledge (2006).

2. On the reshaping of Beijing, see C. Marvin, ' "All Under Heaven" – Megaspace in Beijing', in M. E. Price and D. Dayan (eds.), *Owning the Olympics: Narratives of the New China*, Digital Culture Books (2008), pp. 229–259; and Ian G. Cook and Steven Miles, 'Beijing 2008', in J. Gold and M. Gold (eds.), *Olympic Cities: City Agendas, Planning and the World's Games, 1896–2016*, 2nd ed., Routledge (2011).

3. COHRE, *One World, Whose Dream? Housing Rights Violations and the*

Beijing Olympic Games, Centre on Housing Rights and Evictions (2008); A. M. Broudehoux, 'The social and spatial impacts of Olympic image construction: The case of Beijing 2008', in *The Palgrave Handbook of Olympic Studies*, Palgrave (2012), pp. 195–209.

4. J. Yardley, 'Little Building Defies Beijing's Olympic Ambitions', *New York Times*, 9 August 2007, available at http://www.nytimes.com/2007/08/09/world/asia/09china.html?_r=0.

5. A. C. Budabin, 'Genocide Olympics: the campaign to pressure China over the Darfur conflict', *CEU Political Science Journal*, *4*(4), (2009), pp. 520–56; this and other human-rights issues are dealt with in S. Brownell, 'Human rights and the Beijing Olympics: imagined global community and the transnational public sphere', *British Journal of Sociology*, *63*(2), (2012), pp. 306–327.

6. R. Barnett, 'The Tibet Protests of Spring 2008', *China Perspectives*, (3), (2009), p. 6.

7. J. Horne, and G. Whannel, 'The "caged torch procession": celebrities, protesters and the 2008 Olympic torch relay in London, Paris and San Francisco', *Sport in Society*, *13*(5), (2010), pp. 760–770; K. Edney, 'The 2008 Beijing Olympic Torch Relay: Chinese and Western Narratives', *Journal of Current Chinese Affairs – China aktuell*, *37*(2), (2008), pp. 111–125.

8. F. Hong, P. Wu and H. Xiong, 'Beijing ambitions: An analysis of the Chinese elite sports system and its Olympic strategy for the 2008 Olympic Games', *International Journal of the History of Sport*, *22*(4), (2005), pp. 510–529.

9. A. Hadhazy, 'What makes Michael Phelps so good?', *Scientific American*, 18 August 2008, available at http://www.scientificamerican.com/article/what-makes-michael-phelps-so-good/.

10. See the argument outlined in R. Moore, *The Bolt Supremacy: Inside Jamaica's Sprint Factory*, Yellow Jersey (2014).

11. John Jeremiah Sullivan, cited in R. Moore, 'From Usain Bolt to "Donkey Man" – how Jamaica stays so fast', *Guardian*, 19 August 2015, available at http://www.theguardian.com/sport/2015/aug/19/searching-for-the-next-usain-bolt-at-jamaicas-elite-school-for-sprinters.

12. M. Weber, *The Protestant Ethic and the Spirit of Capitalism: and other writings*, Penguin (2002).

Chapter 9, Section Three

1. M. Perryman (ed.), *London 2012: How Was It For Us?* Lawrence & Wishart (2013).

2. M. Gross, 'Jumping through Hoops', *Vanity Fair*, May 2012; M. Lee, *The*

Race for the 2012 Olympics: The Inside Story of How London Won the Bid, Random House (2006).

3. B. Houlihan and R. Giulianotti, 'Politics and the London 2012 Olympics: the (in)security Games', *International Affairs, 88*(4), (2012), pp. 701–717; S. Graham, 'Olympics 2012 security: welcome to lockdown London', *City, 16*(4), (2012), pp. 446–451.

4. See A. Taylor, 'How The Plan To Privatize London's Olympic Security Turned Into A Disaster', *Business Insider,* 18 July 2012; Szu Ping Chan, 'Timeline: how G4S's bungled Olympics security contract unfolded', *Telegraph,* 21 May 2013, available at http://www.telegraph.co.uk/finance/newsbysector/supportservices/10070425/Timeline-how-G4Ss-bungled-Olympics-security-contract-unfolded.html.

5. M. Raco, 'The privatisation of urban development and the London Olympics 2012', *City, 16*(4), (2012), pp. 452–460.

6. I. Sinclair, *Ghost Milk: Calling Time on the Grand Project,* Penguin (2011), p. 12.

7. M. Gross, 'Jumping through Hoops', *Vanity Fair,* May 2012.

8. See D. Hill, 'London's Olympic legacy three years on: is the city really getting what it needed?', *Guardian,* 23 July 2015.

9. J. Halliday, 'Olympics 2012: BBC denies Thompson criticized news coverage of Team GB', *Guardian,* 10 August 2012.

10. D. Sandbrook, 'How glorious, after years of our national identity being denigrated, to see patriotism rekindled', *Daily Mail,* 10 August 2012, available at http://www.dailymail.co.uk/debate/article-2186815/The-rebirth-Britishness-How-glorious-years-national-identity-denigrated-patriotism-rekindled.html.

11. See D. Goldblatt, *The Game of Our Lives: The Meaning and Making of English Football,* Penguin (2014).

12. P. Donnelly and M. K. Donnelly, *The London 2012 Olympics: A gender equality audit,* Toronto: Centre for Sport Policy Studies (2013).

13. Sandbrook (2012).

14. A. Smith, D. Haycock and N. Hulme, 'The class of London 2012: Some sociological reflections on the social backgrounds of Team GB athletes', *Sociological Research Online, 18*(3), (2013), p. 15; see also http://www.suttontrust.com/newsarchive/third-british-olympic-winners-privately-educated/.

15. D. Hannan, 'Multiculturalism? Nonsense. The Olympics are a victory for patriotism and common British values', *Daily Mail,* 10 August 2012.

16. Shiv Malik, 'Boris Johnson spells out the Olympics' moral message to rioters and bankers', *Guardian,* 6 August 2012.

17. W. Hutton, 'Olympics: the key to our success can rebuild Britain's economy', *Guardian,* 11 August 2012, available at http://www.

theguardian.com/commentisfree/2012/aug/12/will-hutton-olympics-economic-recovery.

18. Data drawn from J. L. Chappelet, 'Managing the size of the Olympic Games', *Sport in Society*, *17*(5), (2014), pp. 581–592.

19. See E. Addley, 'Paralympic sponsor Atos hit by protests', *Guardian*, 31 August 2012, available at http://www.theguardian.com/society/2012/aug/31/paralympic-sponsor-atos-hit-protests.

20. Key sources on the history of the Paralympic Games: S. Bailey, *Athlete First: A History of the Paralympic Movement*, John Wiley (2008); J. Gold and M. Gold, 'Access for all: the rise of the Paralympic Games', *Journal of the Royal Society for the Promotion of Health*, *127*(3), (2007), pp. 133–141; D. Legg and R. Steadward, 'The Paralympic Games and 60 years of change (1948–2008): Unification and restructuring from a disability and medical model to sport-based competition', *Sport in Society*, *14*(9), (2011), pp. 1099–1115; K. Gilbert and O. Schantz, *The Paralympic Games: empowerment or side show?* (vol. 1), Meyer & Meyer Verlag (2008).

21. P. D. Howe, 'From Inside the Newsroom: Paralympic Media and the Production of Elite Disability', *International Review for the Sociology of Sport*, *43*(2), (2008), pp. 135–150.

22. G. Wheatcroft, 'From Jessica Ennis to Joey Barton. Could a contrast be more ghastly?' *Guardian*, 16 August 2012.

23. A. Sedghi, 'Olympic legacy failure: sports participation figures', *Guardian*, 5 July 2015, available at http://www.theguardian.com/news/datablog/2015/jul/05/olympic-legacy-failure-sports-participation-figures.

24. D. Conn, 'Olympic legacy failure: sports centres under assault by thousand council cuts', *Guardian*, 15 July 2015; J. Riach and O. Gibson, 'Olympic legacy failure: access to school sport now a postcode lottery', *Observer*, 5 July 2015.

25. 'Taxpayers to foot bills for some services at West Ham's Olympic Stadium', *Guardian*, 9 October 2015.

Chapter 9, Section Four

1. Key sources on the games include J. Boykoff, 'The anti-Olympics', *New Left Review*, *67*, (2011), pp. 41–59; J. Boykoff, 'Space matters: the 2010 Winter Olympics and its discontents', *Human Geography*, *4*(2), (2011), pp. 48–60; J. J. Silver, Z. A. Meletis and P. Vadi, 'Complex context: Aboriginal participation in hosting the Vancouver 2010 Winter Olympic and Paralympic games', *Leisure Studies*, *31*(3), (2012), pp. 291–308; C. M. O'Bonsawin, ' "No Olympics on stolen native land": contesting

Olympic narratives and asserting indigenous rights within the discourse of the 2010 Vancouver Games', *Sport in Society*, *13*(1), (2010), pp. 143–156.

2. A. Travers, 'Women's ski jumping, the 2010 Olympic games, and the deafening silence of sex segregation, whiteness, and wealth', *Journal of Sport & Social Issues*, *35*(2), (2011), pp. 126–145; J. Laurendeau and C. Adams, ' "Jumping like a girl": discursive silences, exclusionary practices and the controversy over women's ski jumping', *Sport in Society*, *13*(3), (2010), pp. 431–447.

3. L. Edwards, C. Jones and C. Weaving, 'Celebration on ice: double standards following the Canadian women's gold medal victory at the 2010 Winter Olympics' *Sport in Society*, *16*(5), (2013), pp. 682–698.

4. J. Kennelly and P. Watt, 'Sanitizing public space in Olympic host cities: The spatial experiences of marginalized youth in 2010 Vancouver and 2012 London', *Sociology*, *45*(5), (2011), pp. 765–781.

5. The planning for and political economy of the games are well dealt with in M. Müller, 'State dirigisme in megaprojects: governing the 2014 Winter Olympics in Sochi', *Environment and Planning A*, *43*(9), (2011), pp. 2091–2108; R. W. Orttung and S. Zhemukhov, 'The 2014 Sochi Olympic mega-project and Russia's political economy', *East European Politics*, *30*(2), (2014), pp. 175–191.

6. These issues are well covered in E. Persson and B. Petersson, 'Political mythmaking and the 2014 Winter Olympics in Sochi: Olympism and the Russian great power myth', *East European Politics*, *30*(2), (2014), pp. 192–209; and B. Petersson, 'Still Embodying the Myth? Russia's Recognition as a Great Power and the Sochi Winter Games', *Problems of Post-Communism*, *61*(1), (2014), pp. 30–40.

7. Cited in D. Remnick, 'Patriot Games', *New Yorker*, 3 March 2014.

8. Fund for the Fight Against Corruption. 2014. Entsiklopediya trat Sochi-2014 (Encyclopedia of Expenditure for Sochi 2014). Moscow: Fund for the Fight Against Corruption.

9. 'Russia: Migrant Olympic Workers Cheated, Exploited At 1-Year Countdown to Winter Games, IOC Intervention Urgently Needed', 6 February 2013, available at https://www.hrw.org/news/2013/02/06/russia-migrant-olympic-workers-cheated-exploited.

10. S. Zhemukhov and R. W. Orttung, 'Munich Syndrome: Russian Security in the 2014 Sochi Olympics', *Problems of Post-Communism*, *61*(1), (2014), pp. 13–29.

11. 'Sochi 2014: No gay people in city, says mayor', BBC, 24 January 2014, available at http://www.bbc.com/news/uk-25675957.

12. J. M. Curry, 'Sochi 2014: 1.5m sign petition calling for inquiry into figure skating gold', *Guardian*, 21 February 2014, available at http://www.

theguardian.com/sport/2014/feb/21/sochi-2014-south-korea-russia-figure-skating-gold-sotnikova-kim-yuna.

13. D. Remnick, 'Patriot Games', *New Yorker*, 3 March 2014.

Chapter 9, Section Five

1. A full transcript of this gagfest is available at http://www.americanrhetoric.com/speeches/henriquemeirellesrio2016olympicspeech.htm.

2. D. Goldblatt, *Futebol Nation: A Footballing History of Brazil*, Penguin (2014).

3. O. Gibson, 'Rio 2016 Olympic preparations damned as "worst ever" by IOC', *Guardian*, 29 April 2014.

4. J. Cruz, 'Rio's fragile Olympic spirit', 10 May 2013, available at http://www.playthegame.org/news/news-articles/2013/rio's-fragile-olympic-spirit/.

5. S. Wade and M. Savarese, 'Brazil attorney general alleges bribes tied to Rio Olympics', 22 December 2015, available at http://bigstory.ap.org/article/a154ff2b597d49c8a8f623164e7ea381/brazil-attorney-general-alleges-bribes-tied-rio-olympics.

6. S. Gregory, 'Meet the Impoverished Brazil Residents Who Won't Move for the Olympics', *Time*, 27 December 2015.

7. J. Clarke, 'Sailing Through the Trash and Sewage of Guanabara Bay', *New Yorker*, 23 August 2015.

8. B. Brookes and J. Barchfiled, 'AP Investigation: Olympic teams to swim, boat in Rio's filth', 30 July 2015, available at http://bigstory.ap.org/article/d92f6af5121f49d982601a657d745e95/ap-investigation-rios-olympic-water-rife-sewage-virus; J. Clarke, 'Sailing Through the Trash and Sewage of Guanabara Bay', *New Yorker*, 23 August 2015; S. Romero and C. Clatey, 'Note to Olympic Sailors: Don't Fall in Rio's Water', *New York Times*, 18 May 2014, available at http://www.nytimes.com/2014/05/19/world/americas/memo-to-olympic-sailors-in-rio-dont-touch-the-water.html.

9. Fernanda Sánchez and Anne-Marie Broudehoux, 'Mega-events and urban regeneration in Rio de Janeiro: planning in a state of emergency', *International Journal of Urban Sustainable Development* 5.2, (2013), pp. 132–153; Anne-Marie Broudehoux, 'Accumulation by multiple dispossessions: The case of Porto Maravilha, Rio de Janeiro', in *The Second ISA Forum of Sociology*, Isaconf (1–4 August 2012); C. Gaffney, 'Gentrifications in pre-Olympic Rio de Janeiro', *Urban Geography*, (2015), pp. 1–22.

10. J. Watts, 'Museum of Tomorrow: a captivating invitation to imagine a sustainable world', *Guardian*, 17 December 2015.

Conclusion

1. See 'Voters deliver resounding no to Munich 2022 Winter Olympics bid', Deutsche Welle, 11 November 2013, available at http://www.dw.com/en/voters-deliver-resounding-no-to-munich-2022-winter-olympics-bid/a-17217461; L. Arbend, 'Why Nobody Wants to Host the 2022 Winter Olympics', *Time*, 3 October 2014.
2. See 'French authorities investigating IAAF's Eugene 2021 World Athletics Championships decision', *Guardian*, 15 December 2015.
3. O. Gibson, 'French police widen corruption investigation to 2016 and 2020 Olympic bids', *Guardian*, 1 March 2016.
4. Acosta's time at the FIVB is well covered in Play the Game's summary, available at http://www.playthegame.org/media/2641683/FAV-FIVB-summary-by-Play-the-Game-Oct2014update.pdf.
5. See, inter alia, A. Krasimirov, 'Eleven Bulgarian weightlifters test positive for steroids', Reuters, 20 March 2015, available at http://www.reuters.com/article/us-doping-bulgaria-weightlifting-idUSKBN0MG2CJ20150320; 'IWF suspends world champion Aleksei Lovchev', Associated Press, 25 December 2015, available at http://bigstory.ap.org/article/8e05d89b2ae3496b9fe1bbacb2202e14/iwf-suspends-world-champion-aleksei-lovchev; M. Pavitt, 'Wrestling medallist among five more doping cases to emerge at Toronto 2015', *Inside the Games*, 20 July 2015, available at http://www.insidethegames.biz/articles/1028838/wrestling-medallist-among-five-more-doping-cases-to-emerge-at-toronto-2015; K. Crouse, 'Shadow of Doping Is Never Far From Pool', *New York Times*, 2 August 2015.
6. See D. Walsh, *From Lance to Landis: Inside the American Doping Controversy at the Tour de France*, Ballantine Books (2007); P. Dimeo, 'Why Lance Armstrong? Historical context and key turning points in the "cleaning up" of professional cycling', *International Journal of the History of Sport*, *31*(8), (2014), pp. 951–968; W. Voet, *Breaking the Chain: Drugs and Cycling – The True Story*, Random House (2011).
7. D. Hill, 'The Insider's Guide to Match-fixing in Football', Anne McDermid (2013); M. R. Haberfeld and D. Sheehan, *Match-fixing in International Sports*, Springer (2014).
8. Japan's sumo scandals', The *Economist*, 10 February 2011; Choe Sung Han, 'South Korea Cracks Down on Match-Fixing Epidemic', *New York Times*, 21 February 2012.

9. S. Cox, 'Tennis match fixing: Evidence of suspected match-fixing revealed', BBC Sport, 18 January 2016, available at http://www.bbc.com/sport/tennis/35319202.

10. C. Beam, 'Beijing's Winter Olympics: Conspicuous Consumption in the Snow', *New Yorker*, 31 July 2015.

11. J. McCurry and E. Howard, 'Olympic organisers destroy "sacred" South Korean forest to create ski run', *Guardian*, 16 September 2015.

Coda 2017: After the Party

1. https://www.theguardian.com/sport/2016/aug/19/oci-investigation-illegal-ticket-sales

2. The crowd booing during the pole vault medal ceremony can be seen here: https://www.youtube.com/watch?v=WY8Q2Jc_G2c

3. https://www.theguardian.com/sport/2016/aug/19/cleaners-at-rios-athletes-village-paid-just-140-an-hour; http://www.independent.co.uk/sport/olympics/rio-2016-thousands-of-olympic-volunteers-quit-over-long-hours-and-lack-of-food-a7194776.html

4. https://sports.vice.com/en_us/article/a-legacy-of-crisis-rio-after-the-olympics; https://www.theguardian.com/world/2016/dec/20/what-is-rio-olympic-legacy-brazil

5. On the VTL http://www.rioonwatch.org/?p=33799

6. On the cable car http://www.rioonwatch.org/?p=34709

7. http://edgeeffects.net/olympic-legacies/

8. http://uk.reuters.com/article/uk-soccer-brazil-maracana-idUKKBN14U2MO

9. http://riotimesonline.com/brazil-news/rio-real-estate/parque-radical-in-rios-deodoro-olympic-sports-complex-closed/

10. http://www.insidethegames.biz/articles/1036652/four-companies-raided-amid-alleged-corruption-involving-pyeongchang-2018-railway-line

11. http://bigstory.ap.org/article/026efc428642422d8d5fe6105f75d59d/political-scandal-overshadows-south-korea-2018-olympic-prep; http://www.insidethegames.biz/articles/1046143/pyeongchang-2018-caught-up-again-in-south-korean-political-scandal; https://www.jacobinmag.com/2017/02/olympics-south-korea-corruption-environment/

12. http://www.playthegame.org/news/news-articles/2017/0265_tokyo-governor-cuts-through-olympic-nostalgia/

13. http://energydesk.greenpeace.org/2015/08/04/beijing-olympics-how-china-will-clean-up-its-air-for-the-global-sporting-event/; http://www.scmp.com/news/china/article/1295644/pollution-free-days-beijing-olympics-now-just-happy-memory

14. Swiss Canton rejects 2026 bid, http://www.insidethegames.biz/

articles/1046967/swiss-canton-votes-against-2026-winter-olympic-bid-in-referendum

15. https://www.theguardian.com/world/2016/oct/11/italy-suspends-rome-2024-olympic-games-bid

16. http://hungarianspectrum.org/2017/02/01/momentums-anti-olympics-drive-is-already-a-success/; http://hungarianspectrum.org/2017/02/24/viktor-orban-avoids-humiliation-at-the-hands-of-the-international-olympic-committee/

Index

Picture Credits

extracts reading groups
competitions books new
discounts extracts extracts
competitions reading groups events
books discounts
new extracts
events books reading groups
extracts new titles reading groups
interviews events
events extracts extracts books
discounts interviews
new books events events
events new interviews new books extracts
discounts extracts discounts
www.panmacmillan.com
extracts events reading groups books
competitions books extracts new